T0241825

Lecture Notes in Artificial Intelligence 784

Subseries of Lecture Notes in Computer Science
Edited by J. G. Carbonell and J. Siekmann

Lecture Notes in Computer Science

Edited by G. Goos and J. Hartmanis

Francesco Bergadano   Luc De Raedt   (Eds.)

Machine Learning: ECML-94

European Conference on Machine Learning
Catania, Italy, April 6-8, 1994
Proceedings

Springer-Verlag

Berlin Heidelberg New York
London Paris Tokyo
Hong Kong Barcelona
Budapest

Series Editors

Jaime G. Carbonell
School of Computer Science, Carnegie Mellon University
Schenley Park, Pittsburgh, PA 15213-3890, USA

Jörg Siekmann
University of Saarland
German Research Center for Artificial Intelligence (DFKI)
Stuhlsatzenhausweg 3, D-66123 Saarbrücken, Germany

Volume Editors

Francesco Bergadano
Dipartimento di Matematica, Università di Catania
Via Andrea Doria, I-95100 Catania, Italy

Luc De Raedt
Department of Computer Science
Celestijnenlaan 200A, B-3001 Heverlee, Belgium

CR Subject Classification (1991): I.2.6, I.2.3-4, I.2.8

ISBN 3-540-57868-4 Springer-Verlag Berlin Heidelberg New York
ISBN 0-387-57868-4 Springer-Verlag New York Berlin Heidelberg

CIP data applied for

Typesetting: Camera ready by author
SPIN: 10132037   45/3140-543210 - Printed on acid-free paper

Foreword

The European Conference on Machine Learning 1994 (ECML-94) continues the tradition of earlier EWSLs (European Working Sessions on Learning) and last year's ECML, which was held in Vienna. The aim of these meetings is to provide a major platform for presenting the latest and most significant results in the area of Machine Learning.

This year, 88 papers were submitted and 19 were accepted for verbal presentation at the conference. These contributions are published as full papers in this volume. In addition, 25 contributions were selected for poster presentation and are published in this volume as extended abstracts. The selection was based on the evaluation of at least three referees for every submitted paper, and was finalized at a Program Committee meeting in Leuven, where all members were invited. This was made possible by the financial support of the European Community, through the ESPRIT Network of Excellence on Machine Learning. The result was the selection of high quality contributions, that continue to place the European Conference on Machine Learning at the highest standards of international events in Artificial Intelligence and Computer Science.

The scientific program includes the presentation of three invited talks. The invited speakers are Michael Kearns (Bell Labs) and Lorenza Saitta (University of Torino). An invited panel on industrial applications is chaired by Yves Kodratoff (Universite Paris-Sud). Invited papers by Lorenza Saitta and Yves Kodratoff are also included in this volume.

We wish to thank all researchers who have submitted a paper, as well as the members of the Program Committee and the referees for the work they have done.

January 1994
Catania
Leuven

Francesco Bergadano
Luc De Raedt

Acknowledgements

ECML-94 is organized under the auspices of the Italian Association for Artificial Intelligence (AI*IA)

The organization of ECML-94 was made possible by the generous contribution of the following Sponsors:

The Commission of the European Communities
The ESPRIT Network of Excellence in Machine Learning
Consiglio Nazionale delle Ricerche
Dipartimento di Matematica, Universita di Catania
Laboratory for Logic Programming and Artificial Intelligence,
        Katholieke Universiteit Leuven
Azienda Autonoma Provinciale per l'Incremento Turistico,
        (AAPIT, Catania)
Banca Popolare Santa Venera

A special thanks goes to people who have helped us in the organization of the conference. Besides the members of the organizing committee, we wish to thank Prof. Alfredo Ferro, who has given useful initial advice and support during the organization. The conference organization agency "La Duca Viaggi" was essential to the success of ECML-94.

Program Chairmen

Francesco Bergadano, University of Catania, (Italy)
Luc De Raedt, Katholieke Universiteit Leuven, (Belgium)

Program Committee

Ivan Bratko (Slovenia)	Katharina Morik (Germany)
Pavel Brazdil (Portugal)	Igor Mozetic (Austria)
Wray Buntine (USA)	Stephen Muggleton (UK)
Floriana Esposito (Italy)	Enric Plaza (Spain)
Jean-Gabriel Ganascia (France)	Lorenza Saitta (Italy)
Igor Kononenko (Slovenia)	Derek Sleeman (UK)
Yves Kodratoff (France)	Paul Vitanyi (The Netherlands)
Nada Lavrac (Slovenia)	Gerhard Widmer (Austria)
Stan Matwin (Canada)	Stefan Wrobel (Germany)

Organizing Committee

H. Ade, V. Cutello, G. Gallo, D. Gunetti, G. Sablon.

List of Referees

Agnar Aamodt
Hilde Ade
Esma Aimeur
Eugenio Alberdi
Andreas Albrecht
Kryztof Apt
Siegfried Bell
Gilles Bisson
Marko Bohanec
Robin Boswell
Marco Botta
Maurice Bruynooghe
Rui Camacho
R.M. Cameron-Jones
Leonardo Carbonara
Claudio Carpineto
Karine Causse
Bojan Cestnik
Peter Clark
Vincent Corruble
Susan Craw
R. Lopez de Mantaras
O. Deste
Saso Dzeroski
Pete Edwards
Werner Emde
Cao Feng
Claudio Ferretti
Bogdan Filipic
Peter Flach

A. Flexer
Johannes Furnkranz
Matjaz Gams
Bernhard Ganter
Roberto Gemello
Robert Germic
Olivier Gey
Attilio Giordana
Lenka Gladavska
Marko Grobelnik
Stephan Grolimund
Daniele Gunetti
Joachim Hertzberg
A.G. Hoffmann
Robert Holte
Klaus Jantke
Aram Karalic
Jorg-Uwe Kietz
Volker Klingspor
Karmen Krivicic
Matjaz Kukar
Guillaume Le Blanc
Gabriele Lolli
Ashesh Mahidadia
Donato Malerba
Abdelhamid Mellouk
Stephane Moscatelli
Majorie Moulet
Isabelle Moulinier
Claire Nedellec

Piergiorgio Odifreddi
Ruediger Oehlmann
David Page
Jan Paredis
Uros Pompe
Bernhard Pfahringer
Ross Quinlan
Geber Ramalho
Anke Rieger
Celine Rouveirol
Gunther Sablon
Claude Sammut
Michele Sebag
Giovanni Semeraro
Edgar Sommer
Ashwin Srinivasan
Irene Stahl
Johan Suykens
Birgit Tausend
L. Torgo
Tanja Urbancic
Wim Van Laer
Stefano Varricchio
Alen Varsek
Maarten van Someren
Gilles Venturini
Steffo Weber
Zijian Zheng
T. Zrimec

Table of Contents

Extended Abstracts

Chapter 1

Invited Papers

Industrial Applications of ML: Illustrations for the KAML Dilemma and the CBR Dream

Y. Kodratoff

LRI, Equipe Inference et Apprentissage,
Univ. Paris-Sud F-91405 Orsay

Abstract. This paper presents several industrial applications of ML in the context of their effort to solve the "KAML problem", i.e., the problem of merging knowledge acquisition and machine learning techniques. Case-based reasoning is a possible alternative to the problem of acquiring highly compiled expert knowledge, but it raises also many new problems that must be solved before really efficient implementations are available.

1 Introduction

There are many sides to the description of what an industrial application is. In a recent paper (Kodratoff, Graner, and Moustakis, 1994) we summarized some of the experience gained during the CEC project MLT in counseling a user on which of the many types of machine learning (ML) to use for his special application. In this presentation, we shall consider two of the main subfields of the ones that need merging for an industrial application, seemingly the richest in generating future research problems: validation of KBS, and merging of ML into a knowledge acquisition (KA) method. The first one is almost untouched by specialists in ML, while the second one led to much work, some of it will be reported in the rest of the paper.

As just said, real-world applications require validation of the programs used. Let us speak briefly of what means validation in our context, and what ML can have to do with it.

It seems that "validation" takes three different meanings in the context of KBS. All different types of knowledge originate from the expert's knowledge which is not directly accessible, thus the KA system helps the expert to gather his knowledge in the KA system knowledge level. In KADS' knowledge level, one finds the models, such as the model of tasks, the model of expertise etc. In the model of expertise, one finds knowledge about the strategies, the tasks, the inference, and the domain. All these kinds of knowledge are usually considered validated because they issue "directly" from the expert. This gives us a first kind of validation, by which an expert reconsiders his own knowledge at the knowledge level, and checks its validity. This is not enough in reality since experts do make mistakes from time to time, and even when they agree on the actions to take, they also often disagree on the reasons (that is, what knowledge to use) why these actions are to be taken. It is always good to compare such validated knowledge to the real world. The knowledge must thus be translated to the symbol level, i.e., a language into which programs can be written, to be checked against real applications. During this process, many mistakes are possible, and we have here need for a second kind of validation, the classical one in software engineering, that the knowledge level (the "specification") matches correctly the symbol level (the "algorithm"). During the verification process, the expert will find misbehaviors of the system, that will request some changes. This is the also known as the classical "trial and error" validation technique. Notice however the complication arising because transformations can be performed either at the symbol, or at the knowledge level.

Validation can make use of ML techniques, for both incompleteness and incorrectness. The knowledge to be considered is threefold: the rules of expertise, a deeper kind of knowledge given by a semantic-net and a set of integrity constraints, and a set of examples. When anomalies are detected, the correction is performed according to sets of positive and negative examples of the concept to revise (Lounis, 1993a, 1993b). Let us underline that very little, besides the cited work of Lounis, has been done in this direction. One can however consider that (Morik et al., 1994) have used MOBAL as a validation system in a medical application. They make use of the deductive abilities of MOBAL in order to find contradictions among the rules learned so far, and then solve by induction these contradictions. MOBAL is not a validation system but it presents so many functionalities that it can be also used in that way, and for this particular medical application, it seems it has been a very efficient way to use it.

During the last year, there have been a good many workshops on industrial applications of ML, and on the merging of ML into a KA method. We will give a few examples of these applications in the following. What must be kept in mind, though, is that all real-real-world applications met very nicely the requirements of the KA + ML workshops, because they had to solve this problem in the first place. All considered what is the essential difference between an academic and an industrial work? The academic chooses the data in a repertory of such available data, while the industrial receives data from his users, often demanding ones. These repertories, at least in ML, tend to contain quite a variety of data of various levels of difficulty, but for all of them, the KA phase has been completed beforehand. Thus, the industrial is not only under pressure of his users, but he has also to count on them to perform the KA phase which is a crucial one as we all know. In the following, I will refer to this problem as to the KAML problem, with this mild joke that we indeed need camels to help us crossing the desert that expands between the fertile plains of industrial applications, and the nice oases of academic research.

As a coarse view, one can say that with respect to KAML, academics have produced one very interesting approach, known as knowledge refinement. On another hand, we personally dug five different ways of integrating ML and KA out of the solutions of the people that tackled real-world applications of ML. This paper is mainly devoted to the description of solutions to the KAML problem, together with the industrial applications that led to these solutions. We shall successively speak of the following: the knowledge refinement approach, how existing ML technique must be adapted to meet real life requirements, what kind of knowledge can be acquired from a human expert in order to obtain good ML results, why KA needs ML to enhance the rate of the acquisition, the problem if finding new representation schemes to meet experts' requirements, how to acquire compiled knowledge, and finally the promises and challenges of the CBR approach.

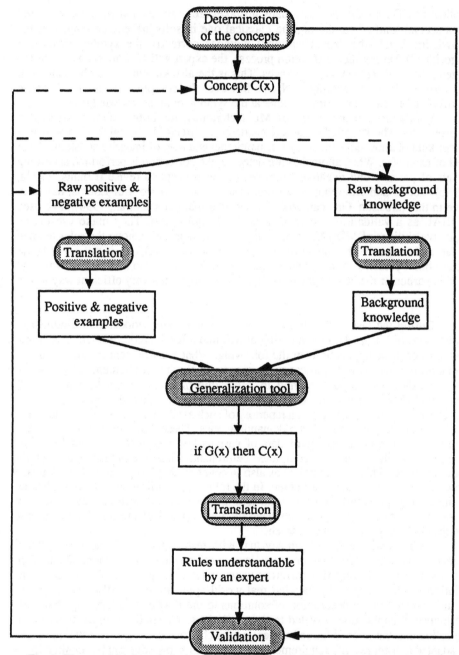

Fig. 1. The acquisition cycle in (Cannat & Vrain, 1988; Kodratoff & Vrain, 1993)

2   Knowledge refinement

We shall not give here any detailed description of the different revision techniques since they received already considerable acknowledgment in the academic community. We shall however give in section 2.3 a brief account of recent research on the topic, and recall some of the earlier work that we did on knowledge refinement roughly around 1985, for an application to air-traffic control, and on DISCIPLE.

2.1 Air traffic control

Our work on air traffic control has been published first in 1988 (Cannat & Vrain, 1988), and more recently under a more detailed form (Kodratoff & Vrain, 1993). Very simply put, we used a refinement cycle which makes explicit the role of the user, as indicated in figure 1 below. It includes the steps necessary to transform the knowledge given by the expert and the learned knowledge. The examples and the knowledge base given by the expert must be translated into a representation adapted to the generalization tool. In order to make the validation step easier, the learned knowledge must be translated back into a representation understandable by the expert. The importance and difficulty of these translation stages are generally underrated by academics, while they are the very condition at which an application can take place. In principle, the main difficulty comes from that humans do not understand easily relations in first order logic, even when their knowledge, being strongly relational, makes non-stop use of it (Kodratoff & Vrain, 1993).

2.2 DISCIPLE

The main idea behind DISCIPLE (Kodratoff & Tecuci 1987a, 1987b), and behind more recent versions, APT (Nédellec, 1992; Nédellec and Causse, 1992) and Neo-DISCIPLE (Tecuci 1993; Tecuci and Duff, 1994) is exactly the one of user-driven revision, with the idea that experts are better at checking solutions than building theories. DISCIPLE thus proposes a solution to a problem that will become a positive example if the user agrees with the solution, and a negative example if he disagrees. He then chooses among possible causes for his agreement or disagreement, and these causes are used to refine logically the existing rules, by adapting (i.e., generalizing or particularizing depending on the cases) the conditions of the rules to the positive and negative examples. This has been used in a bank application in order to help eliciting the knowledge of experts (Nédellec et al., 1994), but it also requests a patient user that accepts to "play" with the system in order to build the initial data base that can be quite extensive.

2.3 Some Recent Results - and Problems

As implicitly said above, applications of ML systems show that the initial domain theory provided by the user and possibly completed by the ML system tends to be incomplete and incorrect. Furthermore, ML systems may add incorrect concept definitions they have learned from incorrect example descriptions or insufficient domain theory. This explains the increasing interest in automatically revising incorrect and incomplete domain theories. Some of the propositional systems are described in (Ginsberg, 1989; Ourston and Mooney, 1990; Craw and Sleeman, 1990; Cain, 1991; Towell, Shavlik, and Noordewier, 1991; Wilkins, 1991), and some of the first order revision systems are found in (Shapiro, 1983; Sammut and Banerji, 1986; Pazzani, 1988; Muggleton and Buntine, 1988; Bergadano and Giordana, 1989; Duval, 1991; Wogulis, 1991; Richards and Mooney, 1991; Rouveirol, 1992; DeRaedt, 1992; Nédellec, 1992; Nédellec and Causse, 1992; Esposito et al., 1993; Morik et al., 1993; Feldman and Nédellec, 1994).

The revision problem can be described as containing two problems, two phases, and two strategies.

The two problems are the completeness problem: given a theory T, and an example E of the concept C, such that T does not recognize the positive example E of C as an example of C, build a theory T' that recognizes E, and the correctness problem: given a theory T and a negative example NE of the concept C, such that T recognizes the negative example E of C as an example of C, build a theory T' such that T' does not recognize NE.

The two phases are the localization of the culprit clause and the refinement itself.

The two strategies are the monotonic and the non-monotonic one. In the monotonic approach, the version space is reduced by eliminating inconsistent hypotheses for ever, while non monotonic algorithms may reconsider pruned hypotheses. One can find several examples of these two strategies in (Nédellec and Rouveirol, 1993)

3   Adapting ML to meet real-life requirements.

In a yet unpublished paper, (Schmalhofer et al., to appear) report a very thorough experience on solving the KAML problem for specific industrial needs. These authors report finding it necessary to adapt both conceptual clustering and explanation-based learning, by integrating expert consultation inside the ML algorithms.

Also typical of this approach is (Esposito, Malerba, and Semeraro, 1993, 1994) which describes an application to document layout recognition in the context of a software environment for office automation distributed by Olivetti. These authors extended a star algorithm (Michalski, 1983) by a flexible matching algorithm, and used a data analysis discriminant system to speed up the star algorithm.

More generally, it seems that a multistrategic approach is needed for many applications that work already quite well by using statistical methods, but that can be still enhanced when some more symbolic treatment is also performed.

3.1   ML Solves KA Problems

Ml can be used to solve KA problems in which the representation of knowledge is so complex that traditional KA becomes unbearable.

Example 1. Fault detection in helicopter blades
This application asked the authors (El Attar and Hamery, 1994) to deal with two different problems. First, detection an repair of faults of an helicopter blade is not only a technical process, but also a kind of judicial one, since the repairing person is responsible in case of an accident. The system must thus also give the best possible "argument" to explain why a given repair is suitable. The data being of a symbolic/numeric nature, the authors had to produce the rules that would combine these two natures in the way the best suited to the existing validation procedures. Secondly, one of the most important features to determine is a set of intervals into which detection and repair of faults takes place. These intervals were not immediately available from the experts, they had to be directly acquired from the examples, in such a way that the results were still understandable by (and agreeable to) the experts.

Example 2. Learning on French justice system
The problem met here is the classical one of the missing values, in its very special version where there are many "don't care" values that are not significant to the solution, as for instance, the values of the attribute "color of the feathers" for a mammal. One usually simply tries to cut the problem in pieces that avoid such kind of problems, but it appears that the existing (French) judicial knowledge is under such a form at present that one has to deal explicitly with this problem. Tree generating procedure cannot deal very well with this kind of problem, this is why (Venturini, 1994) adapted genetic algorithms technique to rule generation.

Example 3. refining rules for a production system (Terano and Muro, 1994).
Once rules have been learned by in a classical way, it is always possible to consider that one can improve them by searching in the space of all possible rules, in the vicinity of the existing rules. Genetic Algorithms are obviously well-adapted to solve this kind of search problem since strong parents are already available.

4 Helping ML by some additional knowledge

4.1 Biasing the ML mechanism with acquired knowledge
It makes explicit which information is essential to decrease the combinatorics of ML, and acquires this knowledge by elicitation.

Example 4. Learning to design VLSI.
Learning the most specific generalization form a set of examples is one of the basic problems of ML since it is of the best ways to reduce the complexity of the set of examples, while keeping their common properties. At the zeroth order, this problem is relatively trivial since it amounts to Michalski's "dropping rule" (Michalski, 1983), together with some of his "climbing hierarchies" rule when the dropping is done cleverly. In first order representations (actually, we speak here of relational representations making use of universally quantified variables), however, this problem becomes quickly very difficult (Kodratoff and Ganascia, 1986) because each subpart of an object can be bound to any other subpart of another object, thus leading to a combinatorial explosion. Some work has been done to deal with this complexity, as by using Bisson's distance measure, for instance (Kodratoff and Bisson, 1992). Application to VLSI design requires a relational representation (Hermann and Beckmann, 1994) since it must represent the bindings of the different parts of the circuit. These authors present an original solution making use of the user's knowledge of what parts can be possibly bound to other parts. This is a knowledge which is well-known by the experts, but which is not acquired classically in KA systems because they perform no learning and do not need this information. In other words, it is very clear here that a new kind of knowledge has to be acquired because of the learning component.

4.2 The ML mechanism is impossible without manually acquired knowledge

ML requirements make it necessary to ask more information, or a new kind of information to the expert.

Example 5. Prediction of cylinder banding
In the printing industry, banding is a nuisance known for long. In his ICML presentation, Bob Evans (Evans and Fisher, 1993) signaled that the usual approach is to understand the causes of banding, and failed. In that sense, usual causal KA has been failing to solve this problem. Driven by the requirements of his induction algorithm, Evans promoted a new approach, a more pragmatic one, by which he proposes to find only conditions at which banding will appear. He reported having many difficulties having the specialists answering his "trivial" questions, until unexpected features appeared in the prediction for banding, and were confirmed by experience.

5 Adapting KA to meet real-life requirements

Example 6. EBL learning of operational rules in the Pilot Assistant
Honeywell has developed a pilot's associate that contains as much as possible of the knowledge relative the military piloting skills. This system contains six interconnected large expert systems. Each of them needs continuous maintenance since the methods for fight and counter-fight are constantly evolving, and maintenance must be done by a varying set of experts. These constraints make it necessary to have a kind of global knowledge repository of easily understandable and maintainable knowledge, from which it will be translated into the language of each expert system. This top knowledge is gathered in a systematic way by means of an EBL component. Domain knowledge is acquired in a classical way, it is then transformed into a standard representation by means of one example, and of a criterion of operationality (Miller and Levi, 1994).
In this very case, one can see than ML became a new way of gathering expert knowledge by merging theoretical knowledge and examples.

Example 7. Road and train traffic control
The problem of transportation engineering makes use of complex mathematical models that limit their practical interest, especially in case of rapid changes. The introduction of a ML component, together with the difficulties due to the domain complexity forced (Arciszewski et al., 1994) to develop an original KA process. In short, one has to make a careful decision on which simplifications to the real-world problem will lead to a model which still realistic and with which one can still work.

6 Develop new representations to allow experts to express their knowledge

Example 8. Improving manufacturing processes (Riddle, Segal, and Etzioni, 1994)
The Boeing company decided to use ML in order to improve some of its manufacturing processes. There are many problems to solve prior to applying the induction mechanism, and they are all more or less of a KA nature. These authors find five problems to address to begin with, and we shall point at two of them here.
Choosing instances: what do we exactly call an example of behavior we are going to learn from? In the case of manufacturing, is an instance a set of alarms with the associated events, the history of a rejection of manufactured part, etc.? This a "pure KA" problem which is no addressed by classical KA, and that must be solved for KAML.
Finding relevant attributes. Thus problem is better known than the former one, and it is indeed addressed by KA techniques. Unfortunately, humans are much better than machines to deal with irrelevant attributes, and application of subsequent ML

techniques request more attention to the problem of irrelevant attributes than it is usual in KA.

Particularly for the first of these problems, one thus notices that new KA methods must be developed in order to represent the information necessary to the ML algorithms.

Example 9. KAML for decision under constraints
We participate in the development of a part of a decision making assistant in which we are in charge of the most "interpretative" part, by which want the plans of the enemy are recognized, and its intentions accordingly interpreted (Barès et al., 1994). The way humans handle this problem is by merging three kinds of different knowledge, general principles of tactics, intelligence information, and the doctrine of both sides. In order to merge these three kinds of information in a retrievable form, we had to develop a special knowledge representation framework, inspired from Schank's XPs (Schank, 1986; Schank and Kass, 1990), in which a special part is devoted to the slow emergence of a plan when some partial information confirms its activation.

7   Use ML to acquire knowledge usually compiled by experts

7.1   Acquiring perceptual chunks

Example 9. Solving geometry problems.
This is a difficult application, if not an industrial one. In many cases, finding an elegant solutions depends on finding the correct "perceptual chunk" that triggers a particularly efficient strategy. This is a problem similar to acquiring search control knowledge as addressed by PRODIGY (Minton et al., 1989). The work of (Suwa and Motoda, 1994) however addresses the particular problem of gathering chunks of a perceptual nature for problem solving in such a way that their preconditions are easy to detect and discriminant. Besides, these chunk may well act as simple hints that drive the solution in the good direction, without reaching the desired goal directly. In general, experts are unable to provide directly such perceptual information. PCLEARN learns them by analyzing success proof trees, and selecting the objects that are recognizable to its recognition rules to build a chunk of them.

7.2   Acquire plan abstractions

In (Schmalhofer and Tschaitschian, 1993; Schmalhofer et al., to appear), the authors describe a methodology (which makes use of a user-controlled conceptual clustering and explanation-based learning, as already noticed) for acquiring production plans in mechanical engineering. The experts obviously are able to provide concrete plans on how to solve a specific problem, but the mentioned system can be viewed as helping them to generate also abstract plans that make their experience easier to apply to new problems.

7.3   Hopes raised by CBR

Guy Boy (1987, 1991) shows with some detail how becoming an expert is transferring causal knowledge to the recognition of situations in which an immediate solution is available. In other words, a beginner solves the problems with deep domain knowledge, while the expert is able to recognize the situations where a solution is available without the need of a complex reasoning. CBR does mimic this attitude, and should be thus explored also as a good way of representing very compiled expert knowledge.

8   CBR solutions and problems

The goal of CBR is efficient reuse of knowledge, NOT the building of causal theories. This statement stresses the difference between classical Data Base (DB) approaches, and this new way to deal with shallower information. It tells to users wanting to build or to express causal theories that they have better to make use of classical DB, not of CBR. The negative side effect of deep causal theories is that it transforms the story of the case so much that the user no longer recognizes the case. On the contrary, CBR has indeed the negative effect that the causal theory is kept implicit throughout the reasoning process, but the positive one that the story of the case is easy to recognize.

In other words, taking into account shallow information has the positive features of being fast and easy to understand for user, and the negative one of failing when a deep model is actually needed. We shall see how more interrogation of the user can gather extra-knowledge which will be used in order to represent deep knowledge, in another way than the classical one.

In practice, as we suppose each reader knows, CBR works by extracting from the base of cases the cases whose description are the nearest to the description of the target, then use the solution of these nearest cases to find a solution for the target. This is very similar to rules by the substitution (description --> condition, solution --> action), but as opposed to rules, there is no explicit causal link between the descriptions and the solutions. For example, a case of an plane accident can well contain the color of the eyes of the pilot, or any other spurious information.

8.1   Knowledge acquisition issues

A first obvious problem is the definition of the knowledge representation of the cases themselves. A case contains all the information necessary to be able to recompose what has been happening in the external world. For aircraft incidents, for example, one could define a case by the information necessary to rerun the incident on a simulator. As one can see, a "case", as opposed to the more traditional knowledge representation systems, is never defined in general, it depends on the application it describes. This relaxation on the constraints will request that some extra knowledge is asked to the domain expert, as we shall see in the following.

The domain expert, as is almost always the case of AI oriented applications, is requested to build an ontology of his application domain: What are the features of the domain, when are they significant, what are the semantics of these features, what are their domain of values, what are the relations among features (i.e., organizing the knowledge of the domain).

In order to define an efficient similarity measure, the knowledge acquisition process must include, besides the "plain" field knowledge, seven types of knowledge, particular to CBR. It is interesting to identify those types in order to avoid bad surprises in applications. They are:

    a - the similarity measure itself,

    b - rules possibly included in the similarity measure. These rules can be of two kinds b1 - domain theory (used for instance to saturate the description of a case)

b2 - rules allowing to compute local similarity measures

c - integrity constraints of the field,

d - domains of significance of the features,

e - contexts in which a given similarity measure is efficient, being understood that in most cases, a similarity measure is efficient when it uses significant features (see d above).

f - transfer functions for translating the solutions of the base into the possible ones of the target.

g - constraints relative to the application of the cases in order to avoid absurd solutions.

We shall give more detail on all these points below, recalling first that the similarity measure is often a simple syntactic measure of the type Hamming measure, as used in Data Analysis. Using such a simple measure is problematic since retrieving a good case is essential to CBR, and since cases contain shallow knowledge: a simple measure will tend to recognize shallow similarities of limited interest. The above special requirements represent the extra knowledge necessary to keep available the story of the case. In other words, they constitute the form deep knowledge takes in CBR: it is a very unusual form, certainly a non-causal one.

8.2 Verification and validation

By its principle, CBR gathers information coming directly from the user, to be used directly by him. It is thus always possible that incorrect information is provided. A controller of some sort is necessary in order to verify the cases. In the context of CBR, validation has several meanings.

a - One must verify the coherency of the information contained in the descriptions of the cases. A pilot may, for instance, inverse in time the sequence of events, all in good faith. When shown a simulation, he will willingly acknowledge his error.

b - One must validate the solution proposed by the expert. Some solutions, considered as satisfactory by a given expert, will be validated also by an expert of "higher level", and used in order to give future advice on how to behave in a similar situation. Some other solutions will be considered as unsatisfactory by the expert of "higher level", and used in order to give future advice on how not to behave in a similar situation.

c - One must validate the whole system, by performing systematic studies of its application to yet "unknown" cases.

8.3 More on the similarity measure

It is used to retrieve cases similar to the target case; it computes the distance between the descriptions of the target case, and the descriptions of the base cases, preferably giving more importance to more significant features.

It may be completed by a rule-based choice: similarity measure is used to select the k nearest cases, and rules choose among them which are the best. This leads to complex similarity measures that are not simply the computation of a distance but also take into account rules and/or integrity constraints in order to optimize the choice.

It may be necessary to define even more complex measures by taking into account the consequences of the proposed solutions (see an example below in section 8.4).

One further point is that a given measure is usually not valid on the whole set of examples, it is necessary to set up sub-domains, or regions, and a similarity measure valid for each region. In satellite diagnostic, ESA contractors developed such a context sensitive similarity measure. Another solution can be performing an initial clustering leading to an organization of the base, giving in turn an initial evaluation of the possible regions. Defining these regions can be also seen as part of the interrogation of the expert. Notice how different from classical requests is knowledge elicitation in the context of CBR.

8.4   Transfer of base solution to target

There at least three ways to transfer the base solution to the target.

- No transfer procedure is necessary because the cases are directly submitted to user.

- A trivial transfer: the solution of the base is applied to the target with no change. This is quite dangerous and can lead to very absurd solutions, like proposing to a ship to "go down" because it has been a good solution for a plane.

- A real transfer which implies the existence of a pattern matching and of a transfer function. When a base case similar to the target case has been retrieved, its solution cannot be usually applied straightforwardly to the target, some transformations must be done in order to adapt the solution to the descriptions of the target. This transformation is obviously obtained as follows.

Compute the set of substitutions unifying the descriptions of the target with those of the base (they are called "replacements" when a constant is replaced by a constant). Apply the substitutions or replacements found in the descriptions to the solution of the base, this gives the solution of the target.

This operation is obviously always necessary in order to avoid trivial mistakes in the target solution. It can be made to comprise some deep knowledge by recording transfer functions associated to some replacements. For instance, suppose that the case base is relative to cars, and that the solution recommends to slow down to some speed in some descriptions. Suppose that the target case is relative to mopeds, then one must replace car by moped in the target solution, and one must also say that such a replacement must be associated to a function linking the changes in speeds of cars to the changes in speeds of mopeds. This function obviously expresses deep knowledge about driving cars and mopeds. It is clear that all these functions compress the information much less than a formal theory of the speeds for each vehicle. It is very useful when such a theory is not known, and when partial knowledge only is available.

In order to transfer a solution to the target, two different kinds of rules can be used. The first kind is of the form

IF   (in descriptions)   A --> B
THEN   (in solution)   A --> B AND C --> D

where the added part C --> D expresses the changes due to the substitution A --> B. For instance, such a rule can be:

IF   (in descriptions)   woman --> man
THEN   (in solution)   woman --> man AND pregnant --> future father

The second kind is relative to the transfer of parameters in functions appearing in the solution. It has the form:

Knowing that the substitutions (x/x', and y/y') occur between base and target,

IF   (in base)   parameter x is in description, and parameter y is in
                            solution and y = f(x)
THEN   (in target)   parameter x' is in description, and parameter y' is in
                            solution then y' = f(x')

This adaptation may happen to lead to absurd conclusion, this is why, one must define conditions on the limits of the changes to bring into a solution when transferring from base to target. For example, suppose that the base contains a slow growth process to happen in conditions X, and the target contains a very rapid growth process to happen in exactly same conditions X, then one can apply a transfer rule of the form

IF   (in descriptions)   slow --> fast
THEN   (in solution)   increase speed of measurements.

Nevertheless, this rule must be restricted by the condition that if the recommended speed becomes higher than what any kind of material can stand then this base case must be ruled out how high the similarity might be.

All these rules are difficult to build, and they are necessary each time causality is not implicitly taken into account in the shallow representation.

8.5 A conclusion on using CBR

It is quite usual to consider that the predictive power of Science comes from the building of causal theory allowing to explain successions of events. This attitude leads to discard many non-causal facts thus looked upon as spurious. In some cases, as for examples bases of air-traffic incidents, this leads to forget circumstances linked to the "story" of the events, as they have been lived by the expert. Retrieval of past cases becomes tedious for the expert. More generally, we would like to point at the new attitude of accepting in some conditions to rely on shallow, non-causal knowledge, either because it is important, or because causal knowledge seems to evade the scientist's efforts. In other words, the link between predictability and causality is no longer deemed compulsory, but simply desirable. Predictability itself is achieved through the recognition of a conjunction of values of shallow features.

CBR involves such a non-causal knowledge acquisition. The price to pay for this attitude is obvious. It may well happen that cases superficially very near to each other are actually very different. There are two solutions to this problem. The most obvious one is to use hybrid systems that stick to a causal model as far as possible, and switch to CBR when failing on a problem (or the reverse: Do CBR, and check if the causal model validates the findings of CBR). One should notice however that this is not suitable when the shallow knowledge is really needed. This is why we would like to explore here the second solution which is to stay in the CBR framework, but to improve it so as to take into account, in a new way, the deep knowledge:

- define domains of significant features in order to know in which context which features should be used to compute the similarity,

- define domains of similarity measures in order to know in which context which similarity measure should be used,

- use classical CBR to select a few cases that might be useful, and select among them those that are really to be used by

- ruling out those that violate known integrity constraints,

- rule out those cases that are not confirmed by given rules that might have another form than integrity constraints

    - checking the consequences of the choice of a case, i.e., select according to the applicability of the cases,
    - refine the application of the case.

To conclude, it will be often the case that CBR is more efficient than a causal model, especially when the formalization of the field is still incomplete. In order to increase its efficiency, it may be necessary to collect supplementary knowledge which is very different from the one normally considered as causal by scientists.

9   Final Conclusion

As a first conclusion, we would like to stress that our experience tells us that ML is not an easy solution for KA, but that the solution of the KAML problem goes through improvement of both KA and ML, thus it still needs much research work. Industrial applications are playing the role of pointer to academic research to problems that are somewhat underestimated nowadays.

We presented here some examples of seven solutions to the problems of integrating ML and KA, there might be more problems and more solutions that we did not meet yet.

Acknowledgments

The ESPRIT contract MLT has been the first to show how many applications of many different kinds can be done of ML. The help of the CEC is thus gratefully acknowledged. This paper is based on the workshops on industrial applications of ML we organized with Pat Langley at EMLC'93 and IMLC'93 , the workshop on KA + ML we organized with George Tecuci and Smadar Kedar at IJCAI'93, and finally on a "Special Interest Group" on CBR taking place at the Human Machine Interactions and Artificial Intelligence in Avionics and Space congress held in Toulouse, Sept. 28-30, 1993. During this last workshop, we received much interesting information from Michele Visciola from ALENIA, Richard Kraft from NASA Ames, François Allard kindly shared his ESA experience, and we had a long discussion on flight incidents and CBR with Jean Claude Wanner in preparation of the group.

References
.

Arciszewski T., Khasnabis S., Khurshidul Hoda S., Ziarko W. "Machine Learning in Transportation Engineering: A Feasibility Study," *Applied Artificial Intelligence*, special issue on applications of ML, 1994.

Barès M., Canamero D., Delannoy J. F., Kodratoff Y. "XPlans: Case-Based Reasoning for Plan Recognition," *Applied Artificial Intelligence*, special issue on applications of ML, 1994.

Bergadano F., Giordana A., "Guiding Induction with Domain Theories", in *Machine Learning III: An Artificial Intelligence Approach*, pp. 475-492, Kodratoff Y. & Michalski R. (eds.), Morgan Kaufmann, 1989.

Boy G. A. *Intelligent Assistant Systems*, Academic Press, London UK, 1991

Boy G. A. "Operator Assistant Systems," *International Journal of Man-Machine Studies* 27, 1987, pp. 541-554.

Cain T., "The DUCTOR: A Theory Revision System for Propositional Domains", in *Proceedings of the 5th International Machine Learning Workshop (IWML-91)*, Evanston, June 1991.

Cannat J. J., Vrain C. "Machine Learning Applied to Air Traffic Control" Colloque *International Homme-Machine et Intelligence Artificielle dans les domaines de l'Aéronautique et de l'Espace*, Toulouse, France, 28-30 September 1988, pp. 265-274.

Craw S., Sleeman D. "Automating the Refinement of Knowledge-Based Systems," *Proc. ECAI90 Conference*, Aiello L (Ed.), pp. 167-172, Pitman, London 1990.

De Raedt L., *Interactive Theory Revision, an inductive logic programming approach*, Academic Press, 1992.

Duval B., "Abduction for Explanation-Based Learning", in *Proceedings of the European Working Session on Learning (Machine Learning, EWSL-91)*, pp. 348-360, Lecture Notes in Artificial Intelligence, Y. Kodratoff (Ed.), Springer Verlag, March 1991.

El Attar M., Hamery X. "An Industrial Expert System Acquired by Machine Learning", *Applied Artificial Intelligence*, special issue on applications of ML, 1994., 1994..

Esposito F., Malerba D., Semeraro G., "Specialization in Incremental Learning: The Negation Operator", in *Proceedings of the AAAI Spring Symposium on Training Issues in Incremental Learning*, Stanford University, March 1993.

Esposito F., Malerba D., Semerano G. "A Multistrategy Learning Approach to Document Recognition," *Applied Artificial Intelligence*, special issue on applications of ML, 1994.

Evans B., Fisher D. "Mitigating Delays in Printing with Interactive Machine Induction," unpublished communication at the IMLC'93 workshop on industrial applications of ML, Amherst, July 1993.

Feldman R., Nédellec C., to appear in IKAW'94, Banff.

Ginsberg A., Theory Revision via prior Operationalization", in *Proceedings of National Conference on Artificial Intelligence*, pp. 590-595, Aug. 1989.

Hermann J., Beckmann R. "LEFT - A System that Learns Rules about VLSI-Design from Structural descriptions", *Applied Artificial Intelligence*, special issue on applications of ML, 1994.

Kodratoff Y., Bisson G. "The Epistemology of Conceptual Clustering: KBG, an Implementation", *J. of Intelligent Information Sys. 1*, 57-84, 1992.1992?

Kodratoff Y., Ganascia, J. G. "Improving the generalization step in learning", in *Machine Learning: An artificial intelligence approach, Vol. 2*, Michalski R. S., Carbonell J. G., Mitchell T. M. (eds.), Morgan Kaufmann , pp. 215-244, 1986

Kodratoff Y., Graner N., Moustakis V. S. "Can Machine Learning Solve my Problem?", *Applied Artificial Intelligence*, special issue on applications of ML, 1994.

Kodratoff Y., Tecuci G. : "DISCIPLE-1 : Interactive Apprentice System in weak theory Fields", *Proc. IJCAI-87*, Milan Aug. 87, pp. 271-273.

Kodratoff Y., Tecuci G. : "What is an Explanation in DISCIPLE," *Proc. Intern. Workshop in ML*, Irvine 1987, pp. 160-166.

Kodratoff Y., Vrain C. "Acquiring First Order Knowledge about Air Traffic Control," *Knowledge Acquisition 5*, pp. 1-36, 1993.

Lounis H. "Integrating Machine-Learning Techniques in Knowledge-Based Systems Verification", ISMIS'93, 15-18 June 1993, Trondheim, Norway. (Proceedings to appear in LNCS, Springer-Verlag, 1994).

Lounis H. "Knowledge-based Systems Verification: A Machine-Learning-Based Approach", 2nd European Symposium On Verification & Validation (EUROVAV'93), 24-26 March 1993, P. de Mallorca, Spain.

Michalski, R. S., "A Theory and Methodology of Inductive Learning," in *Machine Learning: An Artificial Intelligence Approach, Vol. 1*, R. S. Michalski, J. G. Carbonell, T. M. Mitchell (Eds.), Tioga, Palo Alto, CA, pp. 83-134, 1983.

Miller C. A., Levi K. R. "Linked-Learning for Knowledge Acquisition: A Pilot's Associate Case Study", *Knowledge Acquisition*, special issue on merging KA and ML, 1994.

Minton S., Carbonell J. G., Knoblock C. A., Kuokka D. R., Etzioni O., Gil Y. "Explanation-based learning: a problem solving perspective," *Artificial Intelligence 40*, pp. 63-118, 1989.

Morik K., Wrobel S., Kietz J. U., Emde W. *Knowledge Acquisition and Machine Learning - Theory, Methods, and Applications*, Academic Press, 1993.

Morik K., Potamias G., Moustakis V. S. , Charissis G. "Knowledgeable Learning Using MOBAL: A Medical Case Study", *Applied Artificial Intelligence*, special issue on applications of ML, 1994.

Muggleton S., Buntine W. "Machine Invention of First Order Predicates by Inverting Resolution", in *Proceedings of the 5th International Machine Learning Workshop*, pp. 287-292. Morgan Kaufmann, 1988.

Nédellec C. "How to specialize by Theory Refinement", in *Proceedings of the 10th European Conference on Artificial Intelligence* (ECAI-92), Aug. 1992.

Nédellec C., Causse K. "Knowledge Refinement Using Knowledge Acquisition and Machine Learning Methods", *Current Developments in Knowledge Acquisition: EKAW-92*, T. Wetter & al Eds., Springer-Verlag, May 1992.

Nédellec C., Correia J., Ferreira J. L., Costa E. "Machine Learning goes to the bank," *Applied Artificial Intelligence*, special issue on applications of ML, 1994.

Nédellec C. et Rouveirol C., "Hypothesis Selection Biases for Incremental Learning", in Proceedings of the AAAI Spring Symposium on Training Issues in Incremental Learning, Stanford University, March 1993.

Ourston D., Mooney R. J., "Changing the Rules : A Comprehensive Approach to Theory Refinement" in *Proceedings of National Conference on Artificial Intelligence*, pp. 815-820, Aug. 1990.

Pazzani M. J., "Detecting and Correcting Errors of Omission after Explanation-Based Learning", in *Proceedings of the Eleventh International Joint Conference on Artificial Intelligence*, pp. 713-718, Detroit, Aug. 1989.

Richards B. L., Mooney R. J. "First-order Theory Revision," *Proc. 8th Intern. ML Workshop*, pp. 447-451, Evanston IL, 1991.

Riddle P., Segal R., Etzioni O. "Representation Design and Brute-Force Induction in a Boeing Manufacturing Domain," *Applied Artificial Intelligence*, special issue on applications of ML, 1994.

Rouveirol C. "Completeness of inductive procedures", in *Proc. of the 8th International Machine Learning Workshop (IWML-91)*, Morgan Kaufmann, June 1991.

Sammut C. A., Banerji R. B., "Learning Concepts by asking Questions", in *Machine Learning II : An Artificial Intelligence Approach*, pp. 167-192, R. S. Michalski J. G. Carbonell and T. M. Mitchell (Eds.) Morgan Kaufmann, 1986.

Schank R., *Explanation Patterns: Understanding mechanically and creatively*, Lawrence Erlbaum 1986.

Schank R. C., Kass A. "Explanations, Machine Learning, and Creativity," in *Machine Learning: An Artificial Intelligence Approach, Volume III*, Y. Kodratoff and R. S. Michalski (Eds.), Morgan Kaufmann, San Mateo, pp. 31-48, 1990.

Schmalhofer F. Tschaitschian B. "The acquisition of a procedure schema from text and experience", *Proc. 15th An. Conf. of the Cognitive Science Soc.*, Boulder CO, pp. 883-888, June 1993.

Schmalhofer F., Reinartz T., Tschaitschian B. "A Unified Approach to Learning for Complex real World Domains", to appear, a version has been made available during the IJCAI'93 workshop on KA + ML.

Shapiro E. Y. *Algorithmic program debugging*, MIT press, Cambridge, MA, 1983.

Suwa M., Motoda H. "PCLEARN: A Computer Model for Learning perceptual Chunks," *AI Communications*, special issue on applications of ML, 1994.

Tecuci G. "Plausible Justification Trees: A Framework for the Deep and Dynamic Integration of Learning Strategies," *Machine Learning 11*, 1993.

Tecuci G., Duff D. "A Framework for Knowledge Base Refinement through Multistrategy Learning and Knowledge Acquisition," to appear in *Knowledge Acquisition*, 1994.

Terano T., Muro Z. "On-the Fly Knowledge Base Refinement by a Classifier System," Proc. 2nd World Congress on Expert Systems, Lisbon Jan. 1994, and *AI Communications*, special issue on applications of ML, 1994..

Towell G. G., Shavlik J., Noordewier M. O. "Refinement of Approximately Correct Domain Theories by Knowledge-Based Neural Networks," *Proc. Eighth Nat. Conf. on AI*, pp. 861-866, Boston 1990.

Venturini G. "Analyzing French Justice with a Genenetic-Based Inductive Algorithm", *Applied Artificial Intelligence*, special issue on applications of ML, 1994.

Wilkins D. C., Knowledge Base Refinement as Improving an Incorrect and Incomplete Domain theory, in *Machine Learning III: An Artificial Intelligence Approach*, pp. 492-513, Kodratoff Y. & Michalski R. (eds.), Morgan Kaufmann, 1989.

Wogulis J "Revising Relational Domain Theories," *Proc. 8th Inter. Workshop on ML*, Morgan Kaufmann, June 1991.

Knowledge Representation in Machine Learning

Filippo Neri and Lorenza Saitta

Dipartimento di Informatica, Unversità di Torino, Corso Svissera 185, 10149
TORINO (Italy), Email: {neri,saitta}@di.unito.it

Abstract. This paper investigates the influence of knowledge representation languages on the complexity of the learning process. However, the
aim of the paper is not to give a state-of-the-art account of the involved
issues, but to survey the underlying ideas. Then, references will be provided only occasionally and all the specific quantitative results are left
to the presentation. Finally, the paper is intentionally unbalanced, because a larger space is given to those issues that are more novel or less
investigated in the literature.

1 Introduction

A large variety of approaches (e.g., symbolic, connectionist, reinforcement-based,
evolutionary), of methodologies (such as inductive, deductive, abductive, analogical, case-based) and of algorithms are currently available to address the problem
of building learning machines. Even if these approaches have been able to offer
solutions to some interesting real problems, a large scale application of automatic
learning techniques to real life has still to come. A major problem against an
easy scaling up is computational complexity. Given a problem, i.e., the specification of a task (e.g., classification, control), the nature of the target knowledge
(for instance, expressible in propositional or predicate logic) and the description
of the environment in which learning has to take place (availability of examples,
background knowledge or teacher, presence of noise), first an approach has to
be chosen and, then, a method compatible with the approach, eventually implemented in a specific algorithm, has to be selected. Obviously, the task, the
target knowledge and the environment have all a relevant impact on the choice
of suitable approaches and algorithms. The resulting global selection exhibits a
complexity which delimits the maximum size of the solvable problems. However,
the choices are usually not unique and more or less wide room is left for some
kind of optimisation. We are interested here, in particular, in the trade-off between reduction in the complexity of learning and quality of learned knowledge,
due to issues of knowledge representation and reasoning. By complexity, we mean
algorithmic complexity; complexity evaluated as minimum number of training
examples is only handled as a parameter possibly affecting the preceding one.
Problems of algorithm efficiency are not handled here and we will assume that
the selected algorithm is as much optimised as possible. The nature of the target
knowledge affects the amount of computational resources needed in more than
one way. The first one is through its very nature: for instance, hypotheses expressed as first order logic formulf may have to be found in infinite search space;

moreover, some operations on them (e.g., matching), are inherently exponential [11]. Complex hypotheses (for instance, concepts with several modalities) may require an excessive number of training examples. On the other hand, reasoning mechanisms, used to learn, span a wide range of complexity, and not all of them are equally applicable to any type of target knowledge. A typical example, in this respect, is time- dependent knowledge, such as the one needed for describing the behaviour of a dynamical system. Among the several issues that arise in the analysis of the mentioned trade-off and in finding possible equilibrium points , we will concentrate here on the possible relationship between the type of formalism selected for representing the target knowledge and the means for reducing the amount of search for good hypotheses. When the solution of a learning problem (i.e., a body of knowledge) is hidden inside a very large hypothesis space, the probability of finding it or, at least, a good approximation of it, may be very small, requiring thus a large amount of computational resources. We will consider here four ways of coping with this situation.

- To reduce the size of the hypothesis space,
- To focus the search toward a subspace of the hypothesis space,
- To improve of the learning environment,
- To increase the search exploration power.

Each one of the four kinds of approaches may or may not be either applicable or effective, depending on the type of representation chosen for the target knowledge. The goal of this talk is precisely to investigate this dependency. For types of representation we intend a broad partition of representation formalisms, such as symbolic (e.g., rule sets, decision trees, logical formulf), connectionist (set of numerical parameters), bit- strings, exemplars or time-dependent functions.

2 Size Reduction of the Hypothesis Space

A first and obvious way of possibly easing the search for a hypothesis is to limit the size of the hypothesis space itself. This can be done (as usually it is) by imposing constraints on the target knowledge, aimed at limiting the expressive power of the representation language. This kind of restriction may prove effective in obtaining, for instance, polynomial learnability [as in the COLT approach], but, on the other hand, increases the probability of loosing the correct hypothesis, if this one cannot be represented in the reduced language. Still, we might want to obtain an approximate solution and to evaluate how good it is [5, 22].

An important dichotomy, in this respect, is propositional (<attribute- value> pairs descriptions) versus First Order Logic (relational) representation languages. Using a FOL language, many problems, such as, for instance, matching or testing for subsumption, become computationally intractable and even the very notion of generality may acquire more than one meaning [20, 1, 2]. As a consequence, more strict restrictions have to be imposed on the language syntax (e.g., determinate literals) or semantics (e.g., only one-to-one variable-constant unification), in order to keep computational complexity acceptable. It is not surprising, then, that relational target knowledge has not been considered, until recently, in connectionist and evolutionary approaches and that the problem of defining an adequate metrics between structured exemplars or descriptions is still an unsolved problem.

There are at least two possible ways of coping with the problem of language expressiveness: one is constructive learning, i.e., a dynamic definition of the hypothesis language, according to the needs emerging during learning. Constructive induction has been mostly addressed in symbolic approaches, even though some kinds of ANN may be considered as being able to perform it, as well, by dynamically changing their structure and not only their weights. Another way of handling the problem is to use representation languages at different levels of details (a fundamental aspect of the human thought), i.e., to use abstraction. Abstraction has been mainly used in problem solving [19], and only recently the ML community started to pay attention to this mechanism [6, 12, 7]. Notwithstanding the multiple definitions of abstraction, all their proposers agree on the intuitive meaning of abstraction as a mechanism to build up a simpler representation scheme than the one in which the problem at hand has been originally formulated.

Abstraction, dealing with transformations between representation spaces, offers a new perspective to learning, in that it addresses the fundamental dilemmas involving knowledge simplicity, meaningfulness, predictivity and task-dependency. In learning, abstraction has to be distinguished from generalisation (even though some authors have used the two terms as synonyms) and is in no way intended as an alternative mechanism to it; on the contrary, generalisation and abstraction have complementary properties and goals. Generalisation has been, and remains, the basic mechanism for searching hypotheses, whereas abstraction provides a mechanism for representing these hypotheses on a hierarchy of levels. In other words, abstraction is basically an organisational mechanism, which imposes an internal structure to the world, in such a way that a meaning can be easily associated to the component parts of the structure, reducing thus the cognitive effort for handling the world representation. As an example, it is much more difficult to associate the concept of a table to the thousands of pixels in a table picture rather than to a structure composed by some interrelated legs and top.

Then, a useful notion of abstraction in learning is one that preserves both the more-general-than relation and the extensional properties of concepts (i.e., their coverage) across hierarchical levels of representation spaces. This amounts to the fact that any hypothesis, generated inside any representation space (usually through a generalisation/specialisation process), is guaranteed to be extensionally equivalent to the same hypothesis represented in any other more or less abstract space. In other words, generalisation deals with the extensional aspect of concepts, whereas abstraction deals with the intensional one. We can summarise by saying that abstraction has to do with suitably representing hypotheses, generalisation with finding hypotheses. We do not want that uncontrolled generalisation occurs only as a side-effect of knowledge representation changes of the same hypothesis. This point appears even more clearly if we have to translate, from one level to another, also a domain theory, which should be kept semantically equivalent.

A semantic abstraction, preserving concept extension, is somewhat in contrast with most definitions proposed in AI. On the other hand, it is well on the line of the Abstract Data Types theory, used since a long time, for instance, in structured programming, in program specification and analysis and as a basic concept of object-oriented languages. The property of being at constant information is fundamental for this kind of abstraction: in fact, the semantics of a program shall be exactly the same, whatever the level of details used to describe the program may be. On the other hand, the abstract data types theory has a feature which is absent from the abstraction used so far in AI. This last, in fact, has been only concerned with changes in the language predicate set, whereas the first one builds up objects (i.e., the data types), defined in terms of properties and interactions with the external world and other objects; each object has to be addressed as a whole, disregarding its internal structure and actual implementation. The process of building up compound conceptual objects, synthesising groups of elementary pieces of information available in the ground world, and, then, hindering their internal structure in the abstract world, is the central core of the abstraction mechanism in learning. It has been frequently used in pattern recognition, especially in image analysis.

For these reasons, not only new predicates [17], but also new terms as compound objects have to be invented [7]. Building up new data types, representing intermediate concepts useful to describe higher-level ones, is the key both for obtaining meaningful, human-like concept representations and for reducing the combinatorial complexity of the learning process. Results in this sense have already been reported. The introduction of term abstraction is a key difference between the notion of abstraction sketched here and constructive induction, as it is handled, for instance, in ILP [16]. It is possible to quantitatively evaluate the reduction in search and matching obtained by introducing new compound terms both in the hypothesis language and in the (possibly available) domain theory.

Even though abstraction can be usefully applied to propositional languages to compact knowledge bases, its major role emerges in first order languages, exactly because of the strong impact on complexity due to the definition of composite objects. An interesting question is whether abstraction can play a role in connectionist approaches, by associating an individuality to specific subnets, in such a way that they could be used as building blocks to construct larger networks. And, if yes, whether this internal structuration spontaneously emerges as a consequence of increasing the size of the networks. If this would be the case, we could assist to the natural creation of symbols from the subsymbolic representation level for the sake of saving cognitive efforts.

3 Focusing the Search toward Hypothesis Subspaces

A very effective way of focusing the search in a space of hypotheses is to use a-priori knowledge, which limits the search to that subset of hypotheses that can be explained by the theory itself. This line of reasoning, started with the EBL methodology, has led, more recently, to the multistrategy approach, attempting to control complexity by using more sophisticated learning system, including different reasoning mechanisms, with the aim of better exploiting the variety of available a- priori information [13, 14, 4, 21]. Central to this kind of approach is the notion of explanation , connected, in turn, with the nature of the used knowledge and the reasoning mechanism performed to obtain it: inductive, deductive, abductive or analogical. Attempts have been done to characterise the nature of a hypothesis obtained with these methods, trying to clarify, at the same time, the philosophical foundations of learning [13]. In particular, a precise definition of the inductive/abductive nature of a hypothesis has been suggested [2]. This definition tries to capture the intuitive feeling that the only support of an inductive explanation is a supposed similarity between unobserved individuals and observed ones. In other word, an inductive hypothesis allows the validity of properties, observed on a set of individuals, to be extended to unobserved individuals, whereas an abductive one allows unobserved properties to be applied to observed individuals. Hence, the generation of an inductive hypothesis does not need a theory relating each other properties, whereas the generation of an abductive hypothesis does. The distinction between inductive and abductive hypotheses strictly parallels the dichotomy extension vs. intention. In fact, inductive hypotheses are related to (concept) extensions, whereas abductive hypotheses are related to (individual) intensions.

It can also be shown, both theoretically and experimentally, that the use of an abstract causal model of the domain, in connection with abductive reasoning, has the advantage of strongly reducing both the search in the hypothesis space and the required number of examples, keeping at the same time high the probability of finding a good hypothesis. The reason of the potentially limited complexity of abducing first causes, in comparison with a deductive approach, mostly resides in the possibility of making assumptions about the state of the world and in the possibility of using the abstract predicates occurring in the casual model to produce a skeleton of the target knowledge, to which surface details can be added later [23]. Another interesting debate, related to the nature of knowledge and the mechanisms to use it, is that between analogy [26] and case-based reasoning. In fact, the notion of analogy still deserves further clarification.

A-priori knowledge has also been used to help the designer in the definition of an ANN structure, obtaining interesting results toward the integration of symbolic and subsymbolic learning techniques [24].

4 Improvement of the Learning Process

Another way to cope with complexity is to try to exploit at the best the already available sources of information, i.e., to improve the learning process instead of improving the learning algorithm or increasing the number of training examples, This means that we can try to exploit the possible presence of a teacher (human or environmental) and this can be done in at least two ways: developing systems that interact with a human expert, seeking for his/her advise especially during the revision task [15], or to carefully select the order in which information (typically examples) are presented to the system, in order to strictly guide and speed up the hypothesis formation process.

Example ordering has receiving increasing attention [3], in the framework of incremental learning and dependency upon the presentation order of the examples is a matter of controversy. On one hand, order independence could be desirable, because training examples can be chosen more freely, there is no need of backtracking and there is a smaller danger of overfitting. On the other hand, we experience, in human learning, that a suitable presentation order of selected examples can help the learner to quickly focus on the important aspects of the matter, generating thus a robust kernel of knowledge, to which border cases and exceptions can be easily added later. However, performed experiments and theoretical computations (using Gold's paradigm) show that the number of training examples required to attain the same level of performance can be drastically reduced by taking order effects into accounts [18].

The study of order effects are particularly relevant in ANN, in connection with the problem of forgetting.

5 Increase of the Search Exploration Power

If we do not have sufficient a-priori knowledge and help, then we have to rely on search. To this aim, genetic algorithms offer a powerful, domain-independent method: they have been first used in machine learning associated to Holland's classifier model, but have also been exploited in other frameworks, for instance, to train neural nets instead of the classical back propagation algorithm.

Recently, also the symbolic machine learning approach took advantage of genetic algorithms for concept induction in propositional calculus [25]. From these first experiments, genetic algorithms proved to be an appealing alternative to classical search algorithms, because of their exploration power and their suitability to exploit massive parallelism.

Recently, the extension of the genetic search to concept descriptions in First Order Logic [8, 9] greatly extended the potential of this approach. Moreover, it has been possible to extend the method to learn disjunctive concepts, by proposing a new model of evolution under the selection operator. A theoretical study, involving the determination of the system's asymptotic behaviour, has shown that the new model leads to an equilibrium state between the alternative disjuncts, which, hence, will not disappear, if the population is sufficiently large. Realistic bounds for the cardinality of the population have been derived. With the same technique, also the classical model of selection and the one of Goldberg's sharing functions method have been analysed. The results are that in the classical model only the best disjunct will survive, however large the population is. The sharing functions also show a non trivial equilibrium point, but only under given conditions. Moreover, the evaluation of the shared fitness is quadratic with the cardinality of the population, whereas the same evaluation in the new model is only linear. An extensive experimentation confirms the theoretical results. These results are compared with those asymptotically obtainable from symbolic learning algorithms (such as FOIL) and ANN [10]. Comments on the impact of parallelism will also be done.

6   Conclusions

The talk will give a comparison among techniques usable to reduce the computational complexity of the learning process (intended in a broad sense), in connection with their suitability in dependence of the representation formalism used for the target knowledge. Quantitative results are given, where appropriate and possible.

References

1. Buntine W. (1988). Generalized Subsumption and Its Applications to Induction and Redundancy, Artificial Intelligence, 36, 149-176.
2. Console L., Saitta L. (1992). Abduction, Induction and Inverse Resolution, Proc. First Compulog-Net Workshop on Logic Programming in AI (London, UK).
3. Cournejols A. (Ed.). AAAI Spring Symposium on Order Effects in Incremental Learning (Stanford, CA, 1993).
4. De Raedt, L., Bruynooghe, M. (1991): CLINT: A Multistrategy Interactive Concept Learner and Theory Revision System. Proc. First International Workshop on Multistrategy Learning (Harpers Ferry, WV), pp. 175-190.
5. Devroye L. (1988): Automatic Pattern Recognition: A Study of the Probability of Error . IEEE Trans. on Pattern Analysis and Machine Intelligence, 10 : 530-543.
6. Drastal G., Czako G., Raats S. (1989): "Induction in an Abstraction Space", Proc. IJCAI-89, (Detroit, MI), pp. 708-712.
7. Giordana A. & Saitta L. (1990). Abstraction: a General Framework for Learning", Working Notes of the Workshop on Automated Generation of Approximations and Abstractions (Boston, MA, 1990), pp. 245-256.
8. Giordana A., Sale C.(1992). Genetic Algorithms for Learning Relations. Proc. Int. Conf. on MAchine Learning (Aberdeen, UK).
9. Giordana A., Saitta L. (1993). Learning Relations using Genetic Algorithms. In Michalski R. & Tecuci G. (Eds.). Proc. Multistrategy Learning Workshop (Harpers Ferry, VA).
10. Giordana A., Saitta L. (1994). Learning Multimodal Relational Concepts using Genetic Algorithms: A new Theoretical Model and Experimention. Tech. Rep. TR 94-3, Dip. Informatica, Torino.
11. Haussler, D. (1989): Learning Conjunctive Concepts in Structural Domains . Machine Learning, 4 , 7-40.
12. Knoblock C. (1989). Learning Hierarchies of Abstraction Spaces. Proc. 6th Int. Workshop on Machine Learning (Ithaca, NY).

13. Michalski R. (1991): Inferential Learning Theory as a Basis for Multistrategy Task-Adaptive Learning . Proc. First International Workshop on Multistrategy Learning (Harpers Ferry, WV), pp. 3- 18).

14. Michalski R., Tecuci G. (Eds.). Proc. Multistrategy Learning Workshop (Harpers Ferry, VA, 1991, 1993).

15. Morik K. (1987): Acquiring Domain Models . Int. Journal of Man- Machine Studies, 26 , 93-104.

16. Muggleton S. (1991). Inductive Logic Programming, New Generation Computing, 8, 295-318.

17. Muggleton S., Buntine W. (1988). Machine Invention of First-Order Predicates by Inverting Resolution. Proc. 5th Int. Conf. on Machine Learning (Ann Arbor, MI), pp.339-352.

18. Neri F. & Saitta L. (1993). Exploiting Example Selection and Ordering to Speed-Up Learning. In A. Cournejols (Ed.), AAAI Spring Symposium on Order Effects in Incremental Learning (Stanford, CA, 1993).

19. Plaisted D. (1981). Theorem Proving with Abstraction. Artificial Intelligence, 16, 47-108 (1981).

20. Plotkin G. (1970). A Note on Inductive Generalisation. Machine Intelligence, 5, 153-163.

21. Saitta L. (Ed.). Notes of the ML-Net Multistrategy Learning Workshop (Blanes, Spain, 1993).

22. Saitta L., Bergadano F. (1993). Pattern Recognition and Valiant's Learning Framework. IEEE Trans. Pattern Analysis and Machine Intelligence.

23. Saitta L., Botta M. & Neri F. (1993). Multi-Strategy Learning and Theory Revision , Machine Learning. 11 (2/3).

24. Towell G., Shavlik J. (1991):Refining Symbolic Knowledge using Neural Networks , Proc. Workshop on Multi-Strategy Learning (Harpers Ferry, WV), pp. 257-272.

25. Vafaie H., De Jong K. (1991): Improving the Performance of a Rule Induction System using Genetic Algorithms , Proc. Workshop on Multi-Strategy Learning (Harpers Ferry, WV), pp. 305-315.

26. Veloso M., Carbonell J. (1991): Learning by Analogical Replay in PRODIGY: First Results , Proc. EWSL-91 (Porto, Portogallo), pp. 375-390.

Chapter 2

Regular Papers

Inverting Implication with Small Training Sets

David W. Aha[1], Stephane Lapointe[2], Charles X. Ling[3] and Stan Matwin[4]

[1] Naval Center for Applied Research in Artificial Intelligence,
Code 5514, Naval Research Laboratory, Washington, DC 20375 USA
[2] DREV, P.O. Box 8800, Defence Research Establishment Valcartier,
Courcelette, Quebec, G0A 1R0 Canada
[3] Department of Computer Science, University of Western Ontario, London, Canada
[4] Department of Computer Science, University of Ottawa, Ontario Canada

Abstract. We present an algorithm for inducing recursive clauses using inverse implication (rather than inverse resolution) as the underlying generalization method. Our approach applies to a class of logic programs similar to the class of primitive recursive functions. Induction is performed using a small number of positive examples that need not be along the same resolution path. Our algorithm, implemented in a system named CRUSTACEAN, locates matched lists of generating terms that determine the pattern of decomposition exhibited in the (target) recursive clause. Our theoretical analysis defines the class of logic programs for which our approach is complete, described in terms characteristic of other ILP approaches. Our current implementation is considerably faster than previously reported. We present evidence demonstrating that, given randomly selected inputs, increasing the number of positive examples increases accuracy and reduces the number of outputs. We relate our approach to similar recent work on inducing recursive clauses.

1 Introduction

Inducing recursive relational Horn clauses, or logic programs, is important for several reasons. First, recursion is the basic technique in logic programming, where iteration is achieved by recursion. Second, important classes of functions (e.g., primitive recursive functions) are defined recursively. Third, as we have pointed out in an earlier paper (Lapointe, Ling, & Matwin, 1993), constructive learning in the inductive logic programming (ILP) context requires the ability to learn recursive relations.

The shortcomings of existing ILP systems for inducing recursive clauses have been discussed in the recent literature, and are by now well understood (Lapointe & Matwin, 1992; Muggleton, 1992; Idestam-Almquist, 1993). It is generally believed that the θ-subsumption mechanism is the main source of difficulty in inducing recursive clauses in popular ILP systems (e.g., FOIL (Quinlan, 1991) and GOLEM (Muggleton & Feng, 1990)). Several authors have initiated work on ILP systems that are not founded on θ-subsumption. These systems are based on the idea that generalization, necessary for inducing general clauses from specific examples, should be based on *inverse implication* rather than *inverse resolution*.

We have proposed an approach and an implementation that shows how a specific inverse implication technique can induce a class of important recursive functions given very few examples.

In this paper, we extend our earlier work by proving that our method is complete (i.e., with respect to implication) for a specific class of logic programs that is structurally similar to the class of primitive recursive functions. Syntactically, the class of programs that our CRUSTACEAN system can learn has the form

$$p(A_1, \ldots, A_n).$$
$$p(A_1, \ldots, A_n) \leftarrow p(B_1, \ldots, B_n),$$

where A_i and B_i are possibly complex logical terms (e.g., list constructors). This is a good indication of the power, in terms of expressiveness, of the class we have considered since it is well known that the class of primitive recursive functions can be used to represent almost any algebraic function. The class of purely logical relations contains such practically useful logic programs as appending and splitting lists, deleting a given element from a list, reversing lists, and arithmetic functions such as addition and factorial. In addition, our approach requires only a very small number of training examples. Methods based on θ-subsumption typically (e.g., in a classroom environment) require tens of training instances to induce some of the functions mentioned above.

This paper describes CRUSTACEAN, a system that generalizes the inverse implication approach first applied in LOPSTER (Lapointe & Matwin, 1992). CRUSTACEAN relaxes one of the limiting assumptions of LOPSTER, which required that training instances belong to the same chain of recursive calls. By removing this assumption, much less user's knowledge of the recursive relation is required than was required by LOPSTER. In LOPSTER, the user had to know either the base clause of the recursion or the recursive clause (i.e., in order to supply two examples that belong to the same chain of recursive calls). In CRUSTACEAN, the input examples are completely independent. This direction of research is motivated by our goal to develop efficient, practically usable ILP systems that assume no additional knowledge other than the strong hypothesis bias (i.e., the class of logic programs the system can induce). The current version of CRUSTACEAN has been significantly optimized compared to the version first reported in (Aha, Ling, Matwin, & Lapointe, 1993). We describe some of these optimizations in Sect. 3. Section 4 of this paper describes a theoretical characterization of CRUSTACEAN's abilities, Sect. 5 summarizes empirical results, and Sect. 6 relates our contributions to other work on inverse implication. We begin by describing some of the basic concepts underlying our approach in Sect. 2.

2 Basic Concepts

There are three notions, underlying our approach. These notions were first introduced, in a slightly different form, in LOPSTER (Lapointe & Matwin, 1992).

They are useful for building tools that can then be used to hypothesize the recursive concept definition from the structure of terms of $n \geq 2$ examples of that concept. These notions are (1) subterms, (2) embedding terms, and (3) generating terms. We will define them here informally, using an example as an illustration.

Given two terms t_1 and t_2, t_1 is a *subterm* of t_2 iff there exists a third term t_e, called an *embedding term* of t_1, such that substituting t_1 for a variable in t_e (i.e., embedding t_1 in t_e) we obtain a term identical to t_2 up to an additional substitution necessary to produce the specific constants (in general, subterms) in t_1 and t_2. For example, suppose that the two terms are $t_1 = []$ and $t_2 = [c, a] = [c, a|[]]$. Then t_1 is a subterm of t_2, where $t_e = [c, a|\text{Subterm}]$, and substituting $[]$ for the variable *Subterm* in t_e yields t_2 (i.e., the additional substitution in t_1 is vacuous here).

If t_1 is a subterm of t_2 realized by the embedding term t_e, then the *generating term* of t_e (of *depth* n) is a term t^V, such that V occurs exactly once in t^V, and that substituting t^V for V $n-1$ times in t^V produces t_e up to a substitution. Intuitively speaking, the generating term decomposes the embedding term into repeated applications of n identical substitutions. Again, let us consider the above example. The embedding term $[c, a|\text{Subterm}]$ has two generating terms. The first is $t^V = [c, a|V]$. It has a depth of 1 because we can obtain t_e from t^V directly (i.e., there is no need to substitute t^V for V). There is also a generating term at depth 2 for t_e, namely $t^V = [X|V]$. If we substitute t^V for V once, then we obtain $[X|[Y|V]] = [X, Y|V]$.

We can informally describe the mechanics of CRUSTACEAN as follows. It assumes that the target theory consists of one purely recursive clause R and one base clause B. If CRUSTACEAN is given positive examples P_1 and P_2, then P_1 can be proven by resolving B_1 and R repeatedly where B_1 is a specialization of B. Therefore, arguments of B_1 are subterms of P_1. Similarly, arguments in B_2 are subterms of P_2. Therefore, to infer the recursive clause R and the base clause B, CRUSTACEAN computes, for all the training examples, all the subterms. The base clause is then induced from the *least general generalization* (lgg) (Muggleton & Feng, 1990) of these subterms. The resulting embedding terms must contain the same generating term since the same recursive clause R is used in the proofs of the positive examples (i.e., except for those positive examples that are instantiations of the base clause). Therefore, the next step is to find the matching generating terms that form the basis for constructing the recursive clause. The next section describes CRUSTACEAN and an example of its processing in more detail.

3 Description of CRUSTACEAN

CRUSTACEAN is a generalization of Lapointe and Matwin's (1992) LOP-STER system.[5] Both systems are based on inverse implication rather than θ-

---

[5] An earlier version of CRUSTACEAN was described in (Aha, Ling, Matwin, & La-

subsumption. Their main difference is that CRUSTACEAN does not require that the positive instances be on the same inverse resolution path. Effectively, this means that the user does *not* need to know the definition of the target relation a priori.

Table 1. CRUSTACEAN induces a set of recursive relations and filters them according to constraints provided by its inputs

```
Given: P: a set of positive examples
       N: a set of negative examples

CRUSTACEAN(P, N)
  1. Relations ← Induce_relations(P, N)
  2. Output: Filter_relations(Relations, P, N)

Induce_relations(P, N)
  1. S ← Subterms(P)
  2. G ← Generating_terms(S)
  3. C ← Combinations(S, G)
  4. ∀c ∈ C :
    IF Legal_match(c) THEN
      4.1 b ← Base_clause(c)
      4.2 IF Inconsistent(b, N) THEN
          4.2.1 r ← Recursive_clause(c)
          4.2.2 Relations ← Relations ∪ {⟨b, r⟩}
  5. Output: Relations

Filter_relations(Relations, P, N)
  1. Discard all redundant relations
  2. Discard all infinitely recursive relations
  3. Discard all relations that resolve with any n ∈ N
  4. Discard all relations that cannot resolve with all p ∈ P
  5. Output: Remaining relations
```

Table 1 summarizes CRUSTACEAN's control algorithm and I/O behavior. CRUSTACEAN inputs both a set of positive and a set of negative examples of a predicate and outputs singly recursive relations LP=(BC,RC) with base clause BC and recursive clause RC such that

---

pointe, 1993). The current version removes the requirement to constrain the set of constants that may appear in the induced relations, attempts to induce relations from all matching sets of generating lists rather than only those with highest summed depth, requires that their summed depth be at least two, and incorporates several efficiency improvements.

1. LP resolves with each positive example and no negative example and
2. at least one of the positive examples can resolve with RC.

Each argument BC_j ($1 \leq j \leq$ arity(LP)) of BC is the lgg of S_{ij} ($1 \leq i \leq n$), where S_{ij} is a subterm of P_{ij} (i.e., the jth argument of positive example P_i) obtained by recursively applying a structural decomposition operator D_j N_i times. Each argument RC_j in the head of RC is the lgg of the subterms generated by applying D_j to P_{ij}, where each P_i contributes N_i subterms. Each argument C_j of RC's (single) condition comes from applying D_j once to RC_j.

CRUSTACEAN's behavior is illustrated using the last_of example (Table 2) throughout the remainder of this section. In our illustration, pairs of subterms and embedding terms are represented using square bracket notation for lists. "Subterm" is used in the embedding terms to refer to the location of the subterm within the corresponding entire term. For example, the pairing [a,[Subterm]] pairs a subterm "a" with an embedding term "[Subterm]" for the term "[a]". We represent lists as dotted pairs (e.g., "[a,b]" is our shorthand for "pair(a,pair(b,[]))").

CRUSTACEAN calls Induce_relations to induce relations for the given predicate and then calls Filter_relations to discard those that do not pass all of its filters.

The positive examples are last_of(a,[c,a]) and last_of(b,[x,y,b]). Function Induce_relations begins by computing, for each positive example's arguments, its set of subterms and their embedding terms (Step 1). Step 2 then computes their corresponding generating terms. The first example's subterms and embedding terms are shown below on the left. The corresponding generating terms and depths are displayed to their right.

```
[ [a,Subterm] ],              [ [empty,0] ],
[ [[c,a],Subterm],            [ [empty,0],
  [c,      [Subterm,a]],        [pair(1),1],
  [[a],    [c|Subterm]],        [pair(2),1],
  [a,      [c,Subterm]],        [pair(2)/pair(1),1],
  [[],     [c,a|Subterm]] ]     [pair(2),2 & pair(2)/pair(2),1] ]
```

There is one list for each argument of last_of. Since the first argument is a constant, it has only one subterm (i.e., itself). There are five subterms for the second argument (i.e., [c,a]). For example, the third subterm of the second argument is [a]. Its embedding term is [c|Subterm] since the substitution of [a] for *Subterm* in this expression yields the complete second argument [c,a]. Its only generating term is pair(2) at depth 1, meaning that the subterm is accessed by decomposing the argument once using *pair* and selecting its second argument. When we write *none* for a generating term, we mean that it is not defined for that subterm (i.e., no decomposition is required to access the subterm from the complete argument because they are identical). Two generating terms exist for the last subterm of the second argument. One of these yields the subterm via two recursive decompositions of pair(2) while the other does so via a combination of two such decompositions at depth 1 (i.e., the former decomposes the second argument

once per recursive call while the latter decomposes it twice per recursive call).
The same information for the second example is shown below.

```
[ [b,Subterm] ]                    [ [none,0] ]
[ [[x,y,b],Subterm],               [ [none,0],
  [x,        [Subterm,y,b]],         [pair(1),1],
  [[y,b],    [x|Subterm]],           [pair(2),1],
  [y,        [x,Subterm,b]],         [pair(2)/pair(1),1],
  [[b],      [x,y|Subterm]],         [pair(2),2 & pair(2)/pair(2),1],
  [b,        [x,y,[Subterm]]],       [pair(2)/pair(2)/pair(1),1],
  [[],       [x,y,b|Subterm]] ]     [pair(2),3 &
                                       pair(2)/pair(2)/pair(2),1] ]
```

Induce_relation's third step computes, for each example separately, the cross
products of its subterms and its generating terms. Some combinations are discarded since they cannot contribute to the induction of recursive clauses. For example, combinations at different non-zero generating depths are discarded since
they require a different number of decompositions per argument. This yields the
six combinations of subterms (left) and generating terms (right) below for the
first example.

```
[[a,Subterm], [[c,a],Subterm]]          [[none,none],0]
[[a,Subterm], [c,       [Subterm,a]]]   [[none,pair(1)],1]
[[a,Subterm], [[a],     [c|Subterm]]]   [[none,pair(2)],1]
[[a,Subterm], [a,       [c,Subterm]]]   [[none,pair(2)/pair(1)],1]
[[a,Subterm], [[],      [c,a|Subterm]]] [[none,pair(2)],2]
[[a,Subterm], [[],      [c,a|Subterm]]] [[none,pair(2)/pair(2)],1]
```

Although the last two combinations have identical combinations of subterms,
they are paired with different generating terms and depths. The nine combinations for the second example's subterms (left) and generating terms (right) are
shown below.

```
[[b,Subterm],[[x,y,b],Subterm]]         [[none,none],0]
[[b,Subterm],[x,        [Subterm,y,b]]] [[none,pair(1)],1]
[[b,Subterm],[[y],      [x|Subterm]]]   [[none,pair(2)],1]
[[b,Subterm],[[y,b],    [x,Subterm,b]]] [[none,pair(2)/pair(1)],1]
[[b,Subterm],[[b],      [x,y|Subterm]]] [[none,pair(2)],2]
[[b,Subterm],[[b],      [x,y|Subterm]]] [[none,pair(2)/pair(2)],1]
[[b,Subterm],[b,        [x,y,[Subterm]]]] [[none,
                                           pair(2)/pair(2)/pair(1)],1]
[[b,Subterm],[[],       [x,y,b|Subterm]]] [[none,pair(2)],3]
[[b,Subterm],[[],       [x,y,b|Subterm]]] [[none,
                                           pair(2)/pair(2)/pair(2)],1]
```

The cross product of the combinations found for these two positive examples
thus yields 6 × 9 = 54 total combinations, which is output by the call to Combinations in Step 3. Step 4 in Induce_relations tests these 54 combinations. For
each combination, it first attempts to match their generating lists. For example,
the first attempted match involves the following lists.

```
[[a,Subterm],[[c,a],Subterm]]        [[none,none],0]
[[b,Subterm],[[x,y,b],Subterm]]      [[none,none],0]
```

This match is immediately rejected because the summed depths of these lists of generating terms is zero, whereas the summed depths must be at least two to ensure, with high probability, that the induced recursive clause is sufficiently general.[6] If the summed depth is zero, then both examples' combinations of subterms are instantiations of the base clause. For such combinations, the recursive clause cannot be induced (i.e., because the pattern of decompositions performed during recursion cannot be determined). If the summed depths was only one, then one combination of subterms would require exactly one recursive call. Later, we will show how CRUSTACEAN induces the arguments for the head of the recursive clause by computing the lgg's of the examples' arguments prior to decomposition. In this case, the lgg would be computed over only one decomposition per each argument, which would cause them to be overly specific. Thus, CRUSTACEAN requires that the summed depths of a match be at least two.

One of the remaining 53 matches being considered attempts to match the second combinations for each instance:

```
[[a,Subterm],[c,[Subterm,a]]]        [[none,pair(1)],1]
[[b,Subterm],[x,[Subterm,y,b]]]      [[none,pair(1)],1]
```

Here the summed depth is two, which is sufficient. Lists of generating terms match only if the generating terms match for each argument. The *none* generating term matches any term. All other generating terms must match exactly, both in the function used to decompose the term and its selected argument (i.e., the second arguments in both of these lists decompose their arguments using the "pair" function's *first* argument). In this case, the lists match. Step 4.1 then computes the matching lists' base clause from their subterms, which are shown below for this example.

```
First example: (a,c)
Second example: (b,x)
```

A potential base clause is induced from these subterms by computing the least general generalization (Muggleton & Feng, 1990) of each argument. This match thus yields last_of(A,B) as a potential base clause. Step 4.2 discards potential base clauses that resolve with any of the negative examples. For example, this clause is discarded since it resolves with the only negative example (i.e., last_of([x,y],[x])). However, the match between the following subterms and generating terms yields last_of(A,[A]), which does not resolve with any negative example.

```
[[a,Subterm],[[a],[c|Subterm]]]      [[none,pair(2)],1]
[[b,Subterm],[[b],[x,y|Subterm]]]    [[none,pair(2)],2]
```

---

[6] The induced recursive clause may still contain irrelevant constants under some circumstances.

In this case, Induce_relations calls Recursive_clause on this combination to induce a recursive clause. The arguments in the head of the recursive clause are taken from the least general generalization over the arguments from the iterative decompositions of each example. Each example contributes the number of iterations equal to the depth of its list of generating terms. The first iteration is the example itself, while the ith iteration is generated by applying the decomposition specified by the list of matched generating terms $i-1$ times to the example. The iterative decompositions for this match, one from the first example and two from the second example, are shown below.

```
(a,[c,a])
(b,[x,y,b])
(b,[y,b])
```

This last iteration is generated by applying the decomposition [none,pair(2)] to (b,[x,y,b]). The lgg of these iterations yields the arguments (A,[B,C|D]). Thus, the head of the induced recursive clause is last_of(A,[B,C|D]). The recursive call of the induced recursive clause is constructed by applying the decomposition specified by the matched generating terms. This yields last_of(A,[C|D]), and the complete induced relation is shown below.

```
last_of(A,[A]).
last_of(A,[B,C|D]) :- last_of(A,[C|D]).
```

Although the recursive clause shown here differs from the more typical

```
last_of(A,[B|C]) :- last_of(A,C),
```

the induced clause is more accurate; there is no need to invoke the recursive clause when only one element remains in the list and it does not resolve with the base clause.

Note that, if the summed depths of the matched lists of generating terms was one, then only one iteration would be used to induce the recursive clause, which causes it to be overly-specific. Thus, as mentioned earlier, Legal_match (Step 4) requires that the summed depths of the list of generating terms in a match must be at least two.

Only one of the other matched combinations yields a base clause that does not unify with any negative example. That combination is shown below.

```
[[a,Subterm],[[],[c,a|Subterm]]]      [[none,pair(2)],2]
[[b,Subterm],[[],[x,y,b|Subterm]]]    [[none,pair(2)],3]
```

Their lists of generating terms match, their iterations are

```
(a,[c,a])
(a,[a])
(b,[x,y,b])
(b,[y,b])
(b,[b]),
```

and the induced base and recursive clauses are shown below.

```
last_of(A,[]).
last_of(A,[B|C]) :- last_of(A,C).
```

Thus, Induce_relations outputs only two induced relations for last_of.

Filter_relations is then called with these two relations. They differ, so both pass the redundancy filter. They also pass a simple test that detects infinitely recursive relations. They are then tested to see if they resolve with any negative example. The second relation resolves with negative example last_of([x,y],[x]), indicating that it is too general. Thus, it is discarded, leaving only the correct target relation (see also Table 2), which does not resolve with the negative example and does resolve with all of the positive examples.

4 Theoretical Analysis

This section describes a theoretical analysis of CRUSTACEAN. We provide a characterization of the structure of logic programs that it can induce. Furthermore, we show that our algorithm is complete for the family of logic programs that we have defined. That is, it induces all *least general* logic programs of the family that are consistent with the training examples. The hypothesis language of CRUSTACEAN is restricted to a specific class or family of singly-recursive logic programs. The following definition captures this targeted family.

Definition 1. (Definition of SR) SR is defined as the family of singly-recursive logic programs LP=(BC, RC) of the following syntactic form:

$$BC = p(a_1, a_2, ..., a_n).$$
$$RC = p(b_1, b_2, ..., b_n) \leftarrow p(c_1, c_2, ..., c_n).$$

where p is a predicate symbol, a_i, b_i, and c_i are terms, and, for every i $(1 \leq i \leq n)$ either

1. $c_i \neq b_i$, c_i is not a ground term (i.e., it contains at least one variable), and c_i is a subterm of b_i, or
2. $c_i = b_i$.

Furthermore, the first condition above must be satisfied for at least one i $(1 \leq i \leq n)$.

Any logic program LP $\in$ SR consists of a base clause BC and a singly-recursive clause RC. The last part of this definition ensures that at least one argument is decomposed (i.e., simplified) by applications of the recursive clause. This avoids meaningless logic programs that have an infinitely recursive clause such as $p(X) \leftarrow p(X)$. The family SR includes many interesting and non-trivial recursive logic programs.

Example 1.

$$BC_1 = \text{last\_of}(A, [A])$$
$$RC_1 = \text{last\_of}(A, [B, C|D]) \leftarrow \text{last\_of}(A, [C|D])$$

$LP_1 = (BC_1, RC_1)$ belongs to the family SR; the first arguments of the recursive clause satisfy the second condition of Definition 1 and the second arguments satisfy the first condition.

Muggleton's (1992) definition of nth powers and n^{th} roots of a clause will be useful for describing the output of our algorithm. First, we need to define the function L, which contains only linear derivations of Robinson's (1965) function R.

Definition 2. (Resolution closure) Let T be a set of clauses. The function L is recursively defined as

$$L^1(T) = T$$
$$L^n(T) = \{C | C_1 \in L^{n-1}(T), C_2 \in T, C \text{ is the resolvent of } C_1 \text{ and } C_2\}$$

Definition 3. (n^{th} powers and roots of a clause) A clause D is an nth power of a clause C iff D is a clause in $L^n(\{C\})$ except for the renaming of variables. Similarly, C is an nth root of D if and only if D is an nth power of C.

For instance, $p(f(f(X))) \leftarrow p(X)$ is a second power (i.e., the square) of $p(f(X)) \leftarrow p(X)$.

Proposition 4. *(Completeness of CRUSTACEAN for SR) Given a set of positive examples P and a set of negative examples N, CRUSTACEAN will output every logic program LP=(BC,RC) in SR with the following properties.*

1. *LP is complete and consistent with respect to P and N, and there exists a $p \in P$ such that BC θ-subsumes a $n^{th} \geq 1$ power of $\{RC, p\}$.*
2. *LP is a lgg under implication of P, or recursive clause RC is the least general n^{th} root of RC' for a given $n \geq 2$, where LP'=(BC,RC') is a lgg under implication of P.*

We can only provide a sketch for Proposition 4's proof at this time for a simple extension of CRUSTACEAN.[7] Let GT=$\{GT_1, \ldots, GT_n\}$ be an arbitrary list of matched generating terms constructed from examples P with arity n. Let the depth of each $p_i \in P$ be D_i. Each GT_j defines how to decompose each p_{ij} into an arbitrary subterm s_{ij} ($1 \leq j \leq n$). Let BC and RC be the base and recursive clauses constructed from this match. Each argument BC_j is the lgg of subterms s_{ij} for all i. For all $p_i \in P$, RC resolves with each argument p_{ij} to yield

---

[7] The extension is a filter in Filter_relations that removes all outputs θ-subsumed by other outputs. We plan to implement this in the near future.

s_{ij}, requiring $D_i \geq 0$ resolution steps. Therefore, LP=(BC,RC) is complete with respect to P. After construction, a filter ensures that LP cannot resolve with any $n \in N$. Thus, it is also consistent with N. Since at least one $D_i \geq 1$, then BC θ-subsumes the resolvent of RC_{D_i} and p_i, where RC_{D_i} is the D_i^{th} power of RC.

By construction, LP implies every clause in P. Our hypothesized simple extension of CRUSTACEAN adds a filter for removing outputs that θ-subsume other outputs (e.g., LP=(BC,RC), where another output LP'=(BC',RC') exists such that BC θ-subsumes BC' and RC θ-subsumes RC'). Since BC is constructed from the lgg of subterms of P, and RC from the lgg of generating term applications on P, then LP can be an lgg under implication of P. However, GT_j can contain $S \geq 2$ repeating sequences of decomposition operators. CRUSTACEAN outputs every LP=(BC,RC_s), where s is a divisor of S. Fewer repeats correspond to simpler and often more general recursive definitions. Since RC_S is a S/s power of RC_s under substitution θ_s, then each RC_s is a least general S/s root of RC_S, where LP=(BC,RC_S) is a lgg under implication of P. This completes our sketch.

CRUSTACEAN's output consists of all the least general logic programs of SR under implication for all depths of recursive clauses (i.e., the depth of a recursive clause corresponds to the number of times it is used to prove all the positive examples). Since the θ-subsumption notion of generality is only incomplete for self-recursive clauses (i.e., for expressing generality relations between different powers or roots of a clause) (Muggleton, 1992), no output is more general under θ-subsumption than any other output, although one might be more general than another under implication (e.g., as when the first recursive clause is a root of the second).

Example 2. Let $P = \{p(f(f(0,a),b)), \ p(f(f(f(f(0,a),b),a),b))\}$ and let $N = \{p(s(0))\}$. Consider the following logic programs belonging to SR:

$$\begin{aligned}
\mathrm{LP}_1 &: \mathrm{BC}_1 = p(0) \\
&\quad\; \mathrm{RC}_1 = p(f(V,X)) \leftarrow p(V) \\
\mathrm{LP}_2 &: \mathrm{BC}_2 = p(0) \\
&\quad\; \mathrm{RC}_2 = p(f(f(V,a),b)) \leftarrow p(V) \\
\mathrm{LP}_3 &: \mathrm{BC}_3 = p(X) \\
&\quad\; \mathrm{RC}_3 = p(f(V,X)) \leftarrow p(V) \\
\mathrm{LP}_4 &: \mathrm{BC}_4 = p(0) \\
&\quad\; \mathrm{RC}_4 = p(f(f(V,X),b)) \leftarrow p(V)
\end{aligned}$$

LP_2 is output because it is a lgg of P under implication. RC_1 is the least general second root of RC_2 (up to a substitution) and $\mathrm{BC}_1 = \mathrm{BC}_2$. Therefore LP_1 is also output. LP_3 is not output since overly general BC_3 resolves with the negative example. The other outputs are complete and consistent with respect to P and N. However, RC_4 is not a lgg since it is more general than RC_2 and has the same term structure. Furthermore, is not a least general n^{th} root of any other RC' for a given LP'=(BC$_4$,RC'). Therefore, LP$_4$ is not output.

5 Empirical Evaluation

The following two subsections summarize our evaluations of CRUSTACEAN.
Section 5.1 evaluates its performance when the inputs are manually selected,
thus approximating optimal conditions. Section 5.2 instead evaluates its performance when the inputs are randomly selected, which tests CRUSTACEAN's
robustness.

5.1 Evaluation with Manually Selected Inputs

We conducted ten experiments with CRUSTACEAN to investigate its ability
to induce relations when given positive examples not on the same inverse resolution chain.[8] The relations used in the experiments were previously used to test
LOPSTER (Lapointe & Matwin, 1992). However, the positive examples used
here were modified so as to not be on the same inverse resolution path.[9] The
positive examples, negative examples, and target relation for each experiment
are summarized in Table 2. CRUSTACEAN output the correct target relation
for each of the experiments; no other relations were output. Average run-times
were collected from a set of 25 runs on a SUN SPARCstation 10 and are reported
in Table 3. CRUSTACEAN is implemented in Quintus Prolog.

5.2 Evaluation with Randomly Selected Inputs

Although this evaluation demonstrated that CRUSTACEAN performs well
with manually selected inputs, it provided no insight on how CRUSTACEAN
performs under less optimal conditions. Therefore, we evaluated its performance
when the inputs were not manually selected. We hypothesized that as more positive examples were input, CRUSTACEAN's accuracy would increase and its
number of outputs would decrease.

In these experiments, terms whose types are recursive data structures (e.g.,
list, successor) were generated randomly from a uniform distribution on structure
depth in the range $[0, 4]$. All constant terms and list subterms were randomly
generated from a uniform distribution on the 26 lower case letters. Some arguments were generated so that they satisfied relation-dependent constraints when
positive examples were requested. For example, when generating a positive example for the *member* relation, the first argument was selected randomly from
the list's elements.

We examined CRUSTACEAN's performance when it was given two and
three randomly selected positive instances. We varied the number of negative

---

[8] These were also used to test an earlier version of CRUSTACEAN reported by Aha,
Ling, Matwin, and Lapointe (1993). However, this more advanced version does not
constrain what constants are allowed to appear in the induced clauses. It also reduces
the cpu time required to solve these ten problems by approximately 24%.

[9] The experiment with factorial contained positive examples that were on the same
inverse resolution chain, but this was unavoidable due to its definition.

Table 2. Sets of positive (+) and negative (−) examples given as input in the 25 experiments and the relations induced by CRUSTACEAN

+ append([d],[],[d])
+ append([a,b],[c],[a,b,c])
− append([d],[e],[d,e,f])
− append([a],[],[])
append([],A,A).
append([A|B],C,[A|D])
  :- append(B,C,D).
	+ member(3,[1,2,3,4])
	+ member(j,[k,j])
	− member(3,[1,2,5])
	− member(a,[c,d])
	member(A,[A|B]).
	member(A,[B,C|D])
	  :- member(A,[C|D]).

+ delete(c,[a,b,c,d],[a,b,d])
+ delete(1,[2,1],[2])
− delete(d,[d,2],[d])
delete(A,[A|B],B).
delete(A,[B,C|D],[B|E])
  :- delete(A,[C|D],E).
	+ noneIsZero([s(s(0))])
	+ noneIsZero([s(0),s(s(s(0)))])
	− noneIsZero([s(0),0])
	noneIsZero([]).
	noneIsZero([s(A)|B])
	  :- noneIsZero(B).

+ extractNth(s(s(0)),[y,z],z)
+ extractNth(s(s(s(0))),[a,b,c,d],c)
− extractNth(s(s(0)),[x,y],x)
extractNth(s(0),[A|B],A).
extractNth(s(s(A)),[B,C|D],E)
  :- extractNth(s(A),[C|D],E).
	+ plus(s(0),s(0),s(s(0)))
	+ plus(s(s(0)),0,s(s(0)))
	− plus(0,s(0),s(s(0)))
	− plus(s(0),0,0)
	− plus(0,0,s(0))
	plus(0,A,A).
	plus(s(A),B,s(C))
	  :- plus(A,B,C).

+ factorial(s(s(s(0))),
      s(s(s(0)))* (s(s(0))*s(0)))
+ factorial(s(s(0)),s(s(0))*s(0))
− factorial(s(s(s(0)))),
      *(s(s(s(s(0)))),s(s(s(0)))))
fact(s(0),s(0)).
fact(s(s(A)),s(s(A))*B)
  :- fact(s(A),B).
	+ reverse([1,2],
	      append(append([],[2]),[1]))
	+ reverse([x],append([],[x]))
	− reverse([x,y],append([],[x]))
	reverse([],[]).
	reverse([A|B],append(C,[A])) :-
	  :- reverse(B,C).

+ last_of(a,[c,a])
+ last_of(b,[x,y,b])
− last_of([x,y],[x])
last_of(A,[A]).
last_of(A,[B,C|D])
  :- last_of(A,[C|D]).
	+ split([x,y],[x],[y])
	+ split([1,2,3,4],[1,3],[2,4])
	− split([x,y],[x,y],A)
	− split([a],[],[a])
	− split([],[],[a])
	− split([a],[],[])
	split([],[],[]).
	split([A,B|C],[A|D],[B|E]) :-
	  :- split(C,D,E).

Table 3. Average runtimes (25 runs) in cpu seconds and number of combinations of subterms processed for the ten relations (see Table 2)

Name	Cpu Time	#Combinations
append	0.7	981
delete	0.7	1152
extractNth	0.5	765
factorial	0.5	912
last_of	0.1	54
member	0.1	78
noneIsZero	0.1	50
plus	0.1	156
reverse	0.4	720
split	12.3	10948

instances from 0 through 25. Test sets included 100 randomly selected instances Positive and negative instances were generated with equal probability. Selections of all terms and instances were done with replacement. The accuracy of an output relation on a test set is defined as the percentage of correct classifications it provides among those instances. The accuracy of a set of output relations is their average accuracy. The accuracies displayed in Table 4 for each relation are averages across all runs. Runs were repeated ten times for each relation, where each run used a different randomly selected training set for each relation.

Table 4 summarizes the results for each relation when ten negative instances were input. Accuracies increase as more positive instances are input. However, they are not 100% for two reasons. First, the randomly generated positive examples can share structure or constants that yield overly-specific outputs. Second, the randomly generated negative examples do not always resolve with the overly general outputs. Both of these conditions can prevent CRUSTACEAN from outputting the (correct) target relation. Nevertheless, our experiments provide evidence that accuracy increases with the number of positive input examples. Although not shown here, accuracy also increases with the number of negative input examples.

For all but two relations, the number of outputs decreased sharply as the number of positive examples increased because the only lists of generating terms that can match for $n+1$ positive examples must be a subset of those that match for the first n examples.[10] Increasing numbers of negative examples also reduced the number of outputs, in this case because they filtered overly-general outputs.

---

[10] Except when adding additional positive examples satisfies CRUSTACEAN's constraint that the summed depths of a match be at least two. This occurred for *delete* and *split* here.

Table 4. CRUSTACEAN's average accuracies and number of outputs (10 runs) given two or three randomly selected positive examples with ten randomly selected negative examples

Name	2 Positive Inputs		3 Positive Inputs	
	Accuracy	#Outputs	Accuracy	#Outputs
append	63.0%	22.5	73.8%	15.0
delete	61.7%	20.4	71.3%	20.4
extractNth	60.0%	12.0	78.0%	5.0
factorial	78.5%	8.7	88.1%	3.5
last_of	74.4%	2.7	88.4%	1.4
member	65.2%	2.2	76.2%	1.8
noneIsZero	72.9%	7.0	79.3%	6.5
plus	63.5%	9.8	85.5%	5.8
reverse	80.5%	22.0	85.5%	8.9
split	78.3%	15.6	85.7%	22.3

6 Relationship with Previous Work

Since recursive relations are prevalent in logic programs written in PROLOG, recursive clause generalization under implication received extensive studies in the last few years. Lapointe and Matwin (1992) first proposed and implemented an inverse implicator called LOPSTER. When given two positive examples C and D of the same predicate, LOPSTER infers a recursive clause R such that R can be resolved with C and their resolvents *repeatedly* to prove D. That is, $C, R \models D$. This is equivalent to $R \models D \leftarrow C$.

Muggleton (1992) described a theoretically complete (though inefficient) algorithm that essentially computes generalization R from the recursive clause $D \leftarrow C$. However, both systems require the two examples given (C and D) to be on the same resolution chain resolved with R. This means that some a priori knowledge on the target theories must be known. This restriction is removed in our CRUSTACEAN system. It inputs a set of examples that are not necessarily on the same resolution chain. It infers a recursive clause and a base clause such that resolving positive examples with the recursive clause (eventually) yields instances of the base clause.

Idestam-Almquist (1993) proposed *recursive anti-unification* as a method for computing the minimal general generalization under implication (MinGGI) of a set of recursive clauses. There are two major differences between his algorithm and LOPSTER, which is related to CRUSTACEAN. First, LOPSTER generalizes from two examples C and D, which can be regarded as one recursive clause $D \leftarrow C$, while MinGGI generalizes from a set of recursive clauses. The MinGGI of one recursive clause is simply the clause itself. Second, Idestam-Almquist's algorithm induces minimally general recursive clauses. LOPSTER instead induces the *least* general recursive clauses that maximize the number of recursive calls in the resolution proof (i.e., by selecting matched lists of generating terms with maximal depth). This allows it to produce the simplest recursive clauses. This clause is more general than other recursive clauses under self-resolution. For instance, given the two examples

$$p(s(s(s(s(0)))))$$
$$p(s(s(s(s(s(s(0))))))),$$

LOPSTER yields $p(s(X)) \leftarrow p(x)$. On the other hand, given the clauses

$$p(s(s(s(s(0))))) \leftarrow p(0)$$
$$p(s(s(s(s(s(s(0))))))) \leftarrow p(0),$$

MinGGI would output $p(s(s(X))) \leftarrow p(X)$.

Another recent ILP system that is closely related to CRUSTACEAN is Cohen's (1993) FORCE2. Its class of learnable theories is similar to CRUSTACEAN's: one "closed" linearly recursive, ij-determinate clause and one base clause. The techniques used in FORCE2 are also closely related in essence to the ones in CRUSTACEAN in several aspects, except that FORCE2 can be regarded as a model-driven system, while CRUSTACEAN is data-driven. Instead of finding recursive literals (with generating terms) from the structural difference of subterms via sub-unification between given examples as in our systems, FORCE2 enumerates all possible recursive literals. Although FORCE2 has been proven to be a PAC-learning algorithm due to its restrictive representation, the enumeration algorithm would inevitably generate many recursive literals (and clauses) that would not be induced by CRUSTACEAN.

Another difference is that FORCE2 is provided with an oracle that answers the query if a positive example is a specialization of the (unknown) base clause. This oracle is needed because, after FORCE2 hypothesizes the recursive clause, it then hypothesizes other instances of the target predicate to be true by "force-simulating" (i.e., decomposing) given positive examples using the recursive clause repeatedly, until the oracle says the hypothesized instance is a specialization of the base clause. All such instances are collected and generalized to form the base clause via lgg.

CRUSTACEAN does not interact with an oracle. The only constraint it has is that the positive examples can be reduced to specializations of a common but unknown base clause. A large number of subterms of positive examples are explored to find such specializations, as well as the recursive literals for the recursive clause. Therefore, CRUSTACEAN can potentially produce overly-specific or overly-general base clauses, which result in unintended recursive clauses. Most of these unintended clauses can be removed by checking their consistency with the positive and negative examples, and through a few other constraints and heuristics. If our system were given the same oracle as in FORCE2, then its efficiency would be improved greatly.

Another primary difference between CRUSTACEAN and the algorithms proposed by Muggleton, Idestam-Almquist and Cohen is that its class of learnable theories is quite restricted. The recursive clause must be purely rather than linearly recursive, and their are certain restrictions on the terms. We feel that these restrictions, and other heuristics, are justified by CRUSTACEAN's efficiency (i.e., it performed well on the benchmark ILP clauses in Sect. 5). This again reflects our goal of designing efficient and practical ILP systems that assume little or no knowledge on the target theories except the class of such theories.

7 Conclusion

We have described CRUSTACEAN, a system that induces recursive relations from examples using a form of inverse implication. We have detailed the algorithm, as well as an example that illustrates its working. CRUSTACEAN produces purely recursive logic programs, syntactically similar to primitive recursive functions. We have also characterized the class of functions for which CRUSTACEAN is complete; CRUSTACEAN will produce the least general logic programs and their corresponding n^{th} roots (Muggleton, 1992) with respect to the the class of considered logic programs.

We believe that our approach is a practical method for inducing recursive clauses. The class of functions for which it is applicable is larger than it may seem at first glance since, unlike some other systems (e.g., IRES (Rouveirol, Puget 1990)), the literals are unflattened. When selecting the input examples, the user does not need to know the base clause, which is required by LOPSTER, or the recursive clause, which is required by practically all approaches based on θ-subsumption. Only a small number of examples are required. Finally, empirical results indicate that many practical and non-trivial recursive relations (e.g., list reversal, usually taught only in the second year of the Computer Science curriculum) can be learned in under one cpu second.

Future work will includes proving the conjecture expressed in Proposition 4, implementing the extension mentioned in its sketch, and further improving CRUSTACEAN's efficiency. We will also plan to extend CRUSTACEAN so that it can induce a larger class of logical relations (i.e., left-recursive relations) of the form

$$p(\ldots).$$
$$p(\ldots) \leftarrow p(\ldots), q(\ldots).$$

Acknowledgements

Thanks to our reviewers for their useful comments. The authors' email addresses are aha@aic.nrl.navy.mil, lapointe@jupiter.drev.dnd.ca, ling@csd.uwo.ca, and stan@csi.uottawa.ca respectively.

References

Aha, D. W., Ling, C. X., Matwin, S., & Lapointe, S. (1993). Learning singly-recursive relations from small datasets. In *Proceedings of the IJCAI-93 Workshop on Inductive Logic Programming.* Chambery, France: Unpublished.

Cohen, W. (1993). Pac-learning a restricted class of recursive logic programs. In *Proceedings of the Third International Workshop on Inductive Logic Programming* (pp. 73–86). Bled, Slovenia: J. Stefan Institute.

De Raedt, L. (1992). *Interactive theory revision: An inductive logic programming approach.* London: Academic Press.

Idestam-Almquist, P. (1993). Recursive anti-unification. In *Proceedings of the Third International Workshop on Inductive Logic Programming* (pp. 241–254). Bled, Slovenia: J. Stefan Institute.

Lapointe, S., Ling, X. C., & Matwin, S. (1993). Constructive inductive logic programming. In *Proceedings of the Thirteenth International Joint Conference on Artificial Intelligence.* Chambery, France: Morgan Kaufmann.

Lapointe, S., & Matwin, S. (1992). Sub-unification: A tool for efficient induction of recursive programs. In *Proceedings of the Ninth International Conference on Machine Learning* (pp. 273–281). Aberdeen, Scotland: Morgan Kaufmann.

Ling, X. C. (1991). Inductive learning from good examples. In *Proceedings of the Twelvth International Conference on Artificial Intelligence* (pp. 751–756). Sydney, Australia: Morgan Kaufmann.

Muggleton, S. (1992). Inverting implication. In *Proceedings of the First European Workshop on Inductive Logic Programming.* Vienna, Austria: Unpublished.

Muggleton, S., & Buntine, W. (1988). Machine invention of first order predicates by inverting resolution. In *Proceedings of the Fifth International Conference on Machine Learning* (pp. 339–352). Ann Arbor, MI: Morgan Kaufmann.

Muggleton, S., & Feng, C. (1990). Efficient induction of logic programs. *Proceedings of the First International Workshop on Algorithmic Learning Theory* (pp. 368–381). Tokyo, Japan: Japanese Society for Artificial Intelligence.

Quinlan, J. R. (1991). Determinate literals in inductive logic programming. In *Proceedings of the Twelvth International Joint Conference on Artificial Intelligence* (pp. 746–750). Sydney, Australia: Morgan Kaufmann.

Robinson, J. A. (1965). A machine-oriented logic based on the resolution principle. *Journal of the Association for Computing Machinery, 12*, 23–41.

Rouveirol, C., & Puget, J. F. (1990). Beyond inversion of resolution. In *Proceedings of the Seventh International Conference on Machine Learning* (pp. 122–130). Austin, TX: Morgan Kaufmann.

A Context Similarity Measure

Yoram Biberman

Department of Mathematics and Computer Science
Ben-Gurion University of the Negev
P.O.B. 653, 84105 Beer-Sheva, Israel
e-mail: yoramb@cs.bgu.ac.il

Abstract. This paper concentrates upon similarity between objects described by vectors of nominal features. It proposes non-metric measures for evaluating the similarity between: (a) two identical values in a feature, (b) two different values in a feature, (c) two objects. The paper suggests that similarity is dependent upon the context: It is influenced by the given set of objects, and the concept under discussion. The proposed Context-Similarity measure was tested, and the paper presents comparisons with other measures. The comparisons suggest that compared to other measures, the Context-Similarity suites best for *natural concepts*.

1 Introduction

The notion of similarity is fundamental in many areas of cognition and computer science. The most frequent approach to similarity is to interpret it as a closeness in a spatial sense. According to this approach, objects are represented as points in a geometrical space; similarity between objects is inversely related to the distance between the objects, where the distance is measured by some metric function.

Many similarity measures exist in the literature (cf. [6] for a short survey of different measures), yet most of them are truly suited for continuous or ordered variables, but not for nominal (symbolic, unordered) ones. The most frequently used similarity measure for nominal domains is the City-Block one. The City-Block measure evaluates the similarity between every two identical values in a feature as equals to one, and the similarity between every two different values as equals zero. The similarity between two objects is the sum of the similarities of their features.

This paper concentrates upon similarity in the context of learning. ExeMplar-Based LEarning Models (EMBLEMs) suggest that concepts are learned by memorizing examples; the main information the learner needs to store in his/its memory is the classified examples the teachers supply; no general information in the form of rules is induced; the learner classifies new examples by comparing them to stored exemplars. EMBLEMs are represented in machine learning by Aha Kibler and Albert's *Instance-Based Learning (IBL)* [2], Stanfill and Waltz's *Memory-Based Reasoning* [11], Salzberg's *Generalized Exemplar Theory* [9], *Protos* of Porter et al. [7], and others. These models are based upon similarity between objects, yet, as described above, for nominal domain variables some of them use the naive City-Block or modifications of it as their similarity measure. Aha Kibler and Albert write: "we have not yet experimented with sophisticated definitions for defining similarity for symbolic-valued attributes." ([2], p. 62)

Following Tversky [12], this paper suggests that similarity is not a fixed property, but is dependent upon the context, that is, *the given set of examples*, and *the concept under discussion*. For example, if we present subjects the countries: USSR, China, Germany, Austria, they would tend to say that USSR is most similar to China, but if we replace Austria by Taiwan most subject would indicate that USSR is most similar to Germany. This finding evidences that the similarity between a pair of examples is dependent upon other examples that are presented, i.e., upon the context. Similarly, the similarity between USSR and Cuba is perceived as large when the concept under discussion is political system, but as small when the relevant concept is geographical area. Thus the similarity between two objects is not fixed for all contexts, but changes. Tversky notes that "judgments [of] similarity depend on context and frame of reference that, in turn, are determined by the nature of the task and the set of objects under consideration." ([12], p. 340)

The next section presents my motivation and intuition. Sections 3 and 4 present functions for evaluating similarity between: (a) two primitive values in a feature (e.g. the colors red and green), (b) two examples (e.g. an apple and an orange). Section 5 presents experiments with the the proposed Context-Similarity measure, and suggests that among the measures that were tried Stanfill and Waltz's Value Difference Metric (VDM) [11] performs best on domains that contain many irrelevant features, while the Context-Similarity performs best with *natural concepts*; Sect. 5.1 explains which concept are considered *natural*. Briefly stated, natural concepts can not be defined by necessary and sufficient conditions, are structured, may change with time and context, and generally have no sharp boundaries.

2 Motivation

The City-Block measure evaluates two different values in a nominal scale feature as contributing zero to the overall similarity between their examples. In many cases this evaluation is inaccurate as even in nominal domains humans differentiate between different degrees of similarity (e.g. the color red is more similar to orange than to blue, the material paper is more similar to textile than to metal, the faculty computer science is more similar to mathematics than to literature). Medin and Schaffer [5] suggest that the similarity between every pair of nominal values should be represented by a unique parameter. They do not specify how this parameter would be set. Protos [7], an EBL system, implements an elaborated similarity measure for nominal variables; in Protos this is achieved using the assistance of an expert that supplies the necessary domain theory (e.g. the colors red and green are equivalent for the purpose of classifying apples). Here I would like to propose a few principles that may guide one in an effort to evaluate the similarity between two different nominal values. The aim is to evaluate this similarity in a more subtle manner than assuming it is zero, without relying on the assumption that this knowledge is supplied by an external source.

Metric similarity measures assume that the contribution of two equal values to the perceived similarity between their examples is equal for all values. I also question this assumption: Think of two people who are anarchists versus two people that hold main-stream political views; or think of two left handed people as opposed to two right handed people. I suggest that two examples that share an exceptional value (property) in some feature are perceived as more similar one another than two examples that share a common value. In other words, there is a 'pop-out' effect to a unique value which causes the examples to be perceived as similar to each other, and stand in contrast to the rest of the examples. Tversky [12] demonstrated this idea by saying that we perceive two identical twins as more similar to each other than two identical cars; the reason to this phenomenon is that there are only two identical twins 'of a certain model', but many identical cars of a certain model.

A third property of many of the existing measures is that their similarity evaluation is not affected by the concept under discussion. This assumption is also inaccurate in many cases; for example a concept like 'apples' contains both green and red members; thus red and green should be considered similar for the task of classifying apples; but cucumbers are always green, therefore if one needs to classify cucumbers she should consider red and green as dissimilar; another example that demonstrates this idea involved the 'items' USA and USSR; these two countries were similar with respect to the concept 'the Great Powers' but not with respect to 'communist countries'. I, therefore, suggest that when a system needs to evaluate the similarity between two objects it should do so with respect to a certain concept.

Finally, following Medin and Schaffer [5], Hintzman [4] and Porter et al. [7] it is proposed that the similarity between two objects is determined *by an interaction* of the different components. This assumption is in contrast to independent cue models, like the City-Block one, which assume that the overall similarity is a function of the independent components that are summed.

These considerations lead me to propose a set of non-metric functions for evaluating similarity between examples described by nominal attributes, in the context of a categorization task.

3 Similarity of Features

This section proposes a similarity measure between two values in a feature. The next section utilizes this measure, and presents a measure of similarity between objects.

The features similarity measure considers two cases: whether the two values to be compared are equal or not.

Denote the similarity function between two values by s_{val}; this function is composed of s_{eq} which computes the similarity between two equal values, and

s_{dif} that handles the case where the values are different; finally S_{ex} denotes the examples similarity measure.

3.1 Elements with Equal Values

In contrast to the minimality axiom of the metric approach, I suggest that the similarity between two identical elements is not necessarily equal for all values (this implies that the triangle inequality also does not hold). The similarity between two examples that share a same value v in a feature is perceived as larger if v is less frequent in the population.

Denote by P the set of all examples supplied by the teachers, by $|P|$ the size of P, and by $|v|$ the number of examples with a value v. The contribution of two equal values $v_{1f} = v_{2f}$ in a feature f to the similarity between the examples that contain them, E_1 and E_2, is negatively correlated with their frequency in P. Therefore it is defined to be: $s_{eq}(v_{1f}, v_{2f}) = \frac{|P|-|v_{1f}|}{|P|}$.

Yet, the similarity between the two values might be an artifact that contributes nothing to the categorization task, or might be irrelevant for the concepts that should be learned; but then the the occurrence rate of the value in the different concepts would be more or less equal (e.g., if being in favor of the Israeli-Palestinian agreement is meaningless for the categorization of members of the Israeli parliament into the different parties then the proportion of supporters of this agreement in the different parties would be more or less equal). In other words, the variance of the value's occurrence rate in the different concepts would be small. Denote this variance by $var(v, CS)$. We , therefore, conclude that for the task of categorization, the contribution of two equal elements to the similarity between their examples, should be defined as:

$$s_{eq}(v_{1f}, v_{2f}) = \frac{|P| - |v_{1f}|}{|P|} \cdot var(v_{1f}, CS) .$$

3.2 Elements with Non-Equal Values

The above expression evaluates the contribution of two equal values to the similarity between their examples. For a pair of non-equal values I suggest the following considerations:

- **Similarity between different values:** If two objects (e.g. an orange and a lemon) belong to the same concept, and share equal values in many features (e.g. texture, kind-of-peeling, juicyness, season-in-which-eaten), then we tend to perceive them as generally similar, and conclude, that in particular in those features where they have different values (e.g. oranges' color is orange while lemons are yellow) the values are similar with respect to the concept under discussion. In other words, the similarity between two different values v and u in a feature f with respect to a concept C, is positively influenced by pairs of examples that belong to C, contain the values v and u in f, and share equal values in many other features. In a dual manner:

– **Difference between different values:** If two objects (e.g. an apple and a tomato) belong to different concepts (e.g., one is a fruit while the other is a vegetable), and share equal values in many features (e.g., texture, kind-of-peeling, juicyness, taste), then these features make them relatively similar; in order to explain why they belong to contrasting concepts we tend to assume that v and u are relatively different, and they, at least partially, cause to the split between concepts. In other words, the similarity between two different values v and u in a feature f, with respect to a concept C, is negatively influenced by pairs of examples E_1, E_2, where E_1 belongs to C, E_2 does not belong to C, E_1 has the value v (or u) in f, E_2 has the value u (or v) in f, and E_1, E_2 share many other properties.

An implementation of the above principles is as follows: Let E^v and E^u be two examples that share equal values $v_1, ..., v_m$ in a subset of their features, but have different values v and u in some feature. The effect of this pair over the perceived similarity between v and u can be expressed as $effect(E^v, E^u, v, u) = \sum_{i=1}^{m} s_{eq}(v_i, v_i)/n$, (where n is the total number of features used to describe each example). If both E^v, E^u belong to a same concept C then this effect is positive over $s_{dif}(v, u, C)$; if, on the other hand, E^v belongs to C, while E^u belongs to $C^{'}$ (or vice versa) then their effect over $s_{dif}(v, u, C)$ is negative. $s_{dif}(v, u, C)$ is calculated by averaging over all pairs of examples that contain v, u, and at least one of them belong to C. Formally expressed:

$$s_{dif}(v, u, C) = \frac{\sum_{E_v \in S^v, E_v \in C, E_u \in S^u, E_u \in C} effect(E_v, E_u, v, u)}{n_1} -$$

$$\frac{\sum_{E_v \in S^v, E_v \notin C, E_u \in S^u, E_u \in C} effect(E_v, E_u, v, u)}{n_2} -$$

$$\frac{\sum_{E_v \in S^v, E_v \in C, E_u \in S^u, E_u \notin C} effect(E_v, E_u, v, u)}{n_3}$$

where S^v denotes the set of examples that have a value v, n_1, n_2, n_3 denote the number of examples that enter into each of the three summations.

3.3 Elements with Missing Values

In many real life domains some feature values are missing from certain examples. In these cases the similarity measure should estimate the similarity between a missing value and present one, or between two missing values.

Different estimations can be made in such cases. Aha et al. [1] choose a 'cautious' approach: If either values of a pair is missing, then it is assumed that the two values are maximally different from each other. The Context-Similarity proposes a more optimistic estimation, namely the similarity between a value v and a missing value (with respect to a concept C) is estimated as the average similarity of v to every other value (with respect to C), weighted by the relative frequency of this value (e.g., if in some feature there are three different values v, u and w; such that $s_{dif}(v, u, C) = 1$, $s_{dif}(v, w, C) = 0$, and there are twice many examples that have u than w; under these assumptions, the similarity between v and a missing value with respect to the concept C equals 0.66). The similarity between two missing values is evaluated along the same line as the average similarity between every pair of values with respect to C.

Formally expressed: Let $v, v_1, ..., v_m$ be the set of values in some feature, $s_{dif}(v, v_1, C), ..., s_{dif}(v, v_m, C)$ the similarity between v and each v_i ($i = 1, ..., m$) with respect to some concept C; $| v |$ denotes the number of examples that have the value v. The similarity between v and a missing value $-$ is defined to be:

$$s_{dif}(v, -, C) = \frac{\sum_{i=1}^{m} s_{dif}(v, v_1, C) \mid v_i \mid}{\mid v_1 \mid + ... + \mid v_m \mid}$$

4 Similarity of Examples

The previous section described the contribution of two values in a feature to the perceived similarity between their examples; denote this similarity by $s_{val}(v_1, v_2)$.

The similarity between two examples $E_1 = (v_{11}, ..., v_{1m})$, and $E_2 = (v_{21}, ..., v_{2m})$ is defined to be:

$$S_{ex}(E_1, E_2) = \left(\sum_{i=1}^{m} s_{val}(v_{1i}, v_{2i})/m \right)^r$$

where r is an odd natural number, larger than one.

The only point of interest in this definition is the condition over r. A larger value of r will yield larger interactions between the values of the different features, as it would produce larger terms, i.e., terms that are composed of more factors. An odd r is necessary in order to preserve the sign of the sum (that might be negative). This consideration was proposed by Medin and Schaffer [5] in their context model, and by Hintzman [4] in his MINERVA 2—learning from examples model.

Raising the sum by a power larger than one has another property: If a classifier that needs to classify an example E sums the similarity of E to a subset of the different concepts then raising the sum of the features similarity by a power greater than one 'amplifies' the similarity of more similar examples, and cuts down the similarity of less similar items, thus creating a preference to a set that contains few items very similar to E over a set that has more members that are less similar to E. For example, assume that the sums of the features similarities of E to two members of a concept C_1 are 0.5 and 0, while these sums to two members of C_2 are 0.25 and 0.25. If the sum of the feature similarities is not raised by a power, then E is equally similar to the two concepts; if, on the other hand, the sum of the features similarity is raised by a power greater than one, then E is found to be more similar to C_1 than to C_2. In the experiments described bellow the value of r is irrelevant.

5 Experimental Results and Discussion

The presented similarity measure was tested on a variety of examples. The next subsection presents the domains that were used in the experiments. Section

5.2 presents two experiments that compare between the Context-Similarity and four other similarity measures: The City-Block measure, Stanfill and Waltz's [11] Weighted Feature Metric (WFM) and Value Difference Metric (VDM), and Tversky's Contrast similarity measure [12].

5.1 The Examples that were Used in the Experiments

This section overviews the domains that were used in the experiments, and their main properties. This overview would later enable us to draw preliminary conclusions regarding the question "which similarity measure is best suited for which class of concepts?". I suggest that this kind of research is no less important than proposing a new similarity measure, as no measure would be best for all domains, therefore it would be desired if we could match between the possible measures and the different domains.

The examples that were used were obtained from the repository of machine learning databases cited in the University of California, Irvine (UCI). Figure 1 presents a statistic overview of the examples.

Anderson and Matessa write: "It is informative to engage in horse races between learning algorithms. Different algorithms will work optimally given different data sets, and it should be our first task to understand the characteristics of the domains to which the algorithms are adapted" ([3], p. 293). Psychologists and philosophers distinguish between *natural concepts* versus *logical* ones. The idea is that logical concepts can be defined by a set of necessary and sufficient conditions, have sharp boundaries, and are unstructured—all members of a concept belong to the concept and represent it equally (prime numbers, grandmothers are examples of logical concepts). Natural concepts, on the other hand, can not be defined by a set of rules, have no sharp boundaries, and are structured—some members represent their concepts better that others. Most concepts humans use in everyday life are natural (e.g. furniture, vehicles). Three of the databases that are used in the following experiments are good examples of domains that contain natural concepts: (a) The 'Zoo' domain contains different kinds of animals. (b) The 'LED display' example can be described as an 'artificial natural concept': It is artificial on the one hand, as it is produced by a computer program, but it has many characteristics of natural concepts on the other hand; it also resembles the kind of concepts psychologists use in their laboratory experiments that aim to investigate human categorization in natural domains. (c) 'Hayes-Roth and Hayes-Roth (1977)' is an example of a database that was borrowed from such experiments. The characterization of other concepts with respect to the 'logical' versus 'natural' property is less obvious.

In some databases, the number of attributes used to describe each example is large. Two of these databases (#5 and #6) describe different diseases, and their attributes were proposed by experts in these fields. One can wonder about their dimensionality, and whether an expert, when diagnosing a patient, considers this number of variables. The answer is 'no'; some of the attributes are irrelevant for some of the diseases, and are not used by a human expert. The complete set is needed in order to cover all the possible categories, but every

The domains that were used in the experiments

Domain #	Domain	Number of examples	Number of predicting attributes	Number of values in attribute	Number of concepts	Frequency of most frequent concept (%)	Missing values
1	1984 U.S. Congressional voting	435	16	2	2	61	y
2	LED display	500	7	2	10	10	n
3	LED display + 17 irrelevant attributes	500	24	2	10	10	n
4	Tic-Tac-Toe endgame	958	9	3	2	65	n
5	Standardized audiology	226	69	2	24	48	y
6	Lung cancer data	32	56	3	3	41	y
7	E. coli promoter gene sequences (DNA)	106	57	4	2	50	n
8	Primate splice-junction gene sequences (DNA)	1200	60	4	3	50	n
9	Zoo	101	16	2	7	41	n
10	Hayes-Roth & Hayes-Roth (1977)	160	4	4	3	41	n

Fig. 1. A statistic overview of the examples.

single example would contain many values that practically imply that this attribute or this symptom is missing, and is not needed for the classification of the patient. From the examples presented by Porter et al. [7] it seems that only about a dozen attributes are actually used by a human expert to diagnose each patient. Databases #7 and #8 are taken from molecular biology. Each example in them describes a sequence of nucleotides in the DNA. The learning algorithm relates to each nucleotide as an attribute. Some of the nucleotides sequences (i.e., the examples) are responsible for a certain biochemistry activity (e.g., the production of protein). The task of the algorithm is to identify whether a specific sequence (i.e., a certain example) initiates this activity, and thus belongs to the desired concept, or not. It is known that some of the nucleotides in each sequence, (e.g., some of the attributes in the example) are the ones that evidence whether the sequence initiates the activity or not (e.g., whether the example belongs to the target concept or not), but in different examples different nucleotides are the ones that determine the behavior of the sequence, in other words, in different examples different attributes evidence on membership of the desired concept. Therefore one needs a large set of attributes though for each example only a subset of them actually determines the type of the example. We may conclude that in some domains a large number of attributes is needed, though in each examples some of the attributes might be irrelevant

Some of the domains contain missing values. Missing attribute values degrade the performance of a learning algorithm; yet some algorithms (e.g., ID3) are more susceptible to missing attributes than others, or make certain assumptions on the distribution or prevalence of the missing values. Quinlan, calls the percent of the missing values 'the ignorance level'. He writes: "in practice, an ignorance level of even 10% is unlikely" ([8], p. 99). Naturally, Quinlan's decision trees perform poorly on databases that contain many missing values. EMBLEMs are generally less susceptible to missing values than decision trees, thus we can expect that the performance of an EMBLEM would degrade less than the performance of a decision tree based algorithm when the database contains missing attributes.

5.2 A Comparison with Other Similarity Measures

A similarity measure as described above is only a tool that can be used by a learning algorithm, and composes a central component in any EMBLEM. In this section the similarity measure is relatively isolated from other possible components of a learning algorithm in order to evaluate it on its own.

A Nearest Neighbour Classifier. The most simple examination of the Context-Similarity in a learning task would probably be to incorporate it in a nearest-neighbour classifier, and compare the performance of this classifier with those of one that uses another measure. Such a comparison was made with four other measures. All the comparisons were performed in the same manner: Each classifier received 70% of the examples as a training set, and was tested on the remaining 30% of the examples. [1] [2] . All the classifiers were tested on the same training set and test set. For each classifier and each domain fifty runs were executed. Figure 2 depicts the results of this experiment.

If we examine the figure we notice that in eight out of the ten domains the Context-Similarity performs better than the City-Block one. In some of these domains the difference is greater than in others. Whether the difference is meaningful or not is probably task dependent. As the City-Block measure is cheaper to compute, in each implementation it should be considered whether it is worth using the more expensive Context-Similarity measure or not.

A comparison between the Context-Similarity and the Contrast-Similarity shows that in almost all databases the former performs better. Shanon describes the Contrast-Similarity as "the one that defines the state of the art in the field [of cognitive similarity measures]" ([10], p. 308). If one accepts Shanon's statement then the above finding may seem surprising: How does it happen that a computational model performs better than a cognitive one? I may try to suggest few possible answers to this question, (the different answers do not necessarily exclude each other):

---

[1] Exceptions are the Audiology database and the Hayes-Roth and Hayes-Roth database. In these two databases the examples are divided into standard training set and test set, therefore, a single run was performed with each of them

[2] If a test item was most similar to n training set examples, i.e., its similarity to all of the n examples was equal, m out of them from the correct concept, and $n - m$ from wrong ones, then its classification level was taken to be m/n

Average classification rates

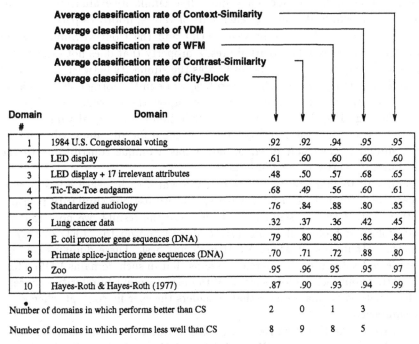

Domain #	Domain					
1	1984 U.S. Congressional voting	.92	.92	.94	.95	.95
2	LED display	.61	.60	.60	.60	.60
3	LED display + 17 irrelevant attributes	.48	.50	.57	.68	.65
4	Tic-Tac-Toe endgame	.68	.49	.56	.60	.61
5	Standardized audiology	.76	.84	.88	.80	.85
6	Lung cancer data	.32	.37	.36	.42	.45
7	E. coli promoter gene sequences (DNA)	.79	.80	.80	.86	.84
8	Primate splice-junction gene sequences (DNA)	.70	.71	.72	.88	.80
9	Zoo	.95	.96	95	.95	.97
10	Hayes-Roth & Hayes-Roth (1977)	.87	.90	.93	.94	.99

Number of domains in which performs better than CS   2   0   1   3

Number of domains in which performs less well than CS   8   9   8   5

Fig. 2. The classification rates of five different nearest neighbour classifiers, on a set of ten domains. Each classifier is based on a different similarity measure. For each classifier a comparison with the Context-Similarity based algorithm is also presented: in how many domains this classifier performs better (less well) than the Context-Similarity based one

- The Contrast-Similarity models human similarity scaling well, but humans do not represent objects by vectors of a fixed size. Actually, when Tversky proposed his model one of his main arguments was that people represent objects by *sets of features*; different objects are represented by different sets (and not by a fixed set, as is usually done in machine learning).

- The contrast model describes objects by sets of qualitative features. These features might be either identical or different, but there are no graded degrees of similarity between features.

Stanfill and Waltz, in their MBRtalk system [11], proposed two new similarity measures: the *Weighted Feature Metric (WFM)*, and the *Value Differences Metric (VDM)*.

As can be seen in Fig. 2 the Context-Similarity performs better than WFM in eight out of the ten domains, and better than VDM in five of them. The difference between WFM and VDM is that the latter evaluates separately the similarity between every pair of values (thus allowing v to have different distance from u than from w), while the former assume that the similarity of a value to all other values is equal (i.e., the distance of v from u is equal to its distance from w). We may, therefore, conclude that a more 'fine' similarity evaluation, one that assigns a unique similarity value to each pair of values, improves performance.

The three main differences between VDM and the Context-Similarity are that the former gives weights to attributes, a property that does not exist in the latter; on the other hand, the latter evaluates the similarity between any pair of values *with respect to each concept separately*, while in the former the similarity between any pair of values is not dependent upon the concept to which the examples belong. Thirdly, in VDM the contribution of two equal values to the similarity between the objects they describe is equal for all values, while in the Context-Similarity each pair of equal values has a unique contribution to the overall similarity between their objects.

It is difficult to characterize the domains in which each measure is superior, or to generalize from these results when should we use one similarity measure or another. Yet, if we try, tentatively, to analyze the results, we note that on the two molecular biology domains (#7 and #8) and on the 'LED display + 17 irrelevant attributes' database VDM performs best. These domains contain *many* irrelevant attributes. It, therefore, seems that in such domains VDM's feature weighting approach is more successful than the Context-Similarity's concept dependent method (i.e., a method that considers the specific concept when evaluating similarity).

Now, turn to the following items: the 'zoo' database, which composes 'classic' natural concepts, and the 'Hayes-Roth and Hayes-Roth' example, that is intended to be an artificial natural concept. On these databases the Context-Similarity performs best. These results hints that the Context-Similarity suites better than other measures for natural concepts. This conclusion is not definite as for example in the 'LED display' domain, which is essentially similar to the 'Hayes-Roth and Hayes-Roth' example, the Context-Similarity does not perform better than the other measures.

Figures 3 and 4 compares between a Context-Similarity based nearest neighbour classifier and two others (VDM and City-Block) on two different domains ('1984 U.S. Congressional voting' and 'E. Coli promoter gene sequences (DNA)'). the figures present the classification rates of each classifier as a function of the size of the training set. The two main findings that are presented in these figures are: (a) The accuracy of both classifiers improve gradually as the size of the training set grows. (b) Generally, if one classifier performs better than another, it does so for all sizes of training sets and test sets; in other words, in most domains it is not the case that while for certain sizes of training sets one classifier performs better, for other sizes another classifier is more accurate.

Overall Similarity. The experiment reported above involved a nearest neighbour classifier. The performance of this classifier is affected by the similarity of a test item E to a single example in each concept—the example that is most similar to E; the similarity of E to other members of each concept does not affect the prediction of the classifier. The experiment demonstrates a common

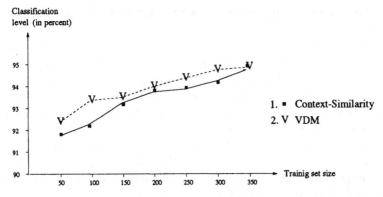

Fig. 3. The classification rates of a Context-Similarity based nearest neighbour classifier versus a VDM based nearest neighbour classifier on the domain '1984 U.S. Congressional voting'. The x axis denotes the size of the training set, the y axis denotes the classification rate of each classifier.

usage of a similarity measure in learning tasks, yet it examines only one aspect of the similarity measure.

In order to examine another aspects of a similarity measure I propose another experiment: A common assumption in clustering and concept learning is that members of a same concept are relatively similar to each other, while members of contrasting concepts are relatively dissimilar. The extent that this assumption is valid varies across domains; some domains satisfy it well, as each of their concepts is centered in a definable region that is well separated from regions occupied by other concepts; other domains satisfy this assumption more loosely either as their concepts are composed of more than a single cohesive and distinct cluster, or as the separability of the concepts is less sharp. Yet, to some extent, this assumption holds, especially if, using some clustering method, we divide

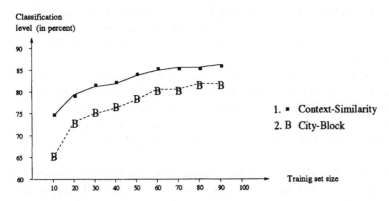

Fig. 4. The classification rates of a Context-Similarity based nearest neighbour classifier versus a City-Block based nearest neighbour classifier on the domain 'E. Coli promoter gene sequences (DNA)'.

each concept to a set of sub-concepts in a way that aims to create cohesive and distinct categories.

If we accept this 'intra concept similarity versus inter concept dissimilarity' assumption, then we would prefer a similarity measure that reflects this property best. Therefore, this could be another criterion for evaluating a similarity measure. To quantify the extent that a similarity measure expresses this property of a set of concepts, I propose a measure that divides the average similarity between pairs of examples that belong to a same concept, by the average similarity between pairs of examples that belong to contrasting concepts. A larger value of this measure is preferred, as it evidences that the average similarity within a concept is large, while the average similarity between concepts is small. The wb measure could therefore be defined as:

$$wb ::= \frac{\frac{1}{n} \sum_C \sum_{E_i, E_j \in C} sim(E_i, E_j)}{\frac{1}{m} \sum_{C_i} \sum_{C_j \neq C_i} \sum_{E_k \in C_i, E_l \in C_j} sim(E_k, E_l)}$$

where C, C_i, etc. denote concepts, E_i etc. denote examples, $sim(E_i, E_j)$ etc. denote the similarity between E_i and E_j as evaluated by the similarity measure that is examined, n and m denote the number of elements that are summed in the two summations.

This measure does not take into account the variance of the similarity scores of the examined similarity measure. One may argue that if two similarity measures score the same grade in wb, yet one of them produces more homogeneous evaluations then the other, then the first is preferred. Therefore to account for the variance of the scores each similarity measure produces, the numerator and denominator of the above wb measure are divided by the standard deviation of the similarity scores of the within/between pairs respectively.

The five similarity measures that are used in the experiments were examined using the wb measure on the ten domains that were presented before. Figure 5 presents the results of this experiment. As expected, the wb scores of most measures in most domains is larger than one, which evidence that, as expected, the evaluated intra concept similarity is larger than the inter concept similarity. This result is in accordance with the 'intra concept similarity versus inter concept dissimilarity' assumption, and thus strengthen our confidence in the assumption and the proposed experiment.

If we calculate the average wb scores for each similarity measure on the ten domains, we obtain the following results: Contrast Similarity—1.18, City Block—1.32, WFM—1.46, VDM—1.63, Context Similarity—1.67. This oredering of the measures resembles the ordering from the previous experiment. Thus, again, we see that the Context-Similarity performs best, though only slightly better than VDM.

The results reported above were obtained on the original domains. As was mentioned earlier, some of the domains that are used are not composed of concepts that comprise a single distinct cluster. In a similar experiment the original domains were first subject to a clustering program (a variant of the k-means method). This version of the experiment was composed of two phases: In the

The ratio: within concept similarity to between concept similarity

		City-Block	WFM	VDM	Contrast-Similarity	Context-Similarity
1	1984 U.S. Congressional voting	1.73	1.82	2.20	1.79	2.76
2	LED display	1.99	1.84	1.84	1.61	2.20
3	LED display + 17 irrelevant attributes	1.21	1.15	1.41	1.16	1.80
4	Tic-Tac-Toe endgame	1.02	1.06	1.12	1.00	1.05
5	Standardized audiology	1.12	1.46	1.51	0.69	1.28
6	Lung cancer data	1.24	0.93	0.95	0.97	1.29
7	E. coli promoter gene sequences (DNA)	0.86	1.40	1.33	0.93	0.70
8	Primate splice-junction gene sequences (DNA)	0.96	1.26	1.25	0.96	0.83
9	Zoo	1.98	2.53	3.07	1.66	3.88
10	Hayes-Roth & Hayes-Roth (1977)	1.17	1.21	1.62	1.10	0.93

Each item in this table presents the following measure for some similarity measure in a certain domain:

$$\frac{\text{Average similarity of pairs of items that belong to the same concept}}{\text{Standard deviation of the similarity scores of items the belong to the same concept}}$$

$$\frac{\text{Average similarity of pairs of items that belong to contrasting concepts}}{\text{Standard deviation of the similarity scores of items the belong to contrasting concepts}}$$

Fig. 5.

first phase the clustering program was executed on each domain; the program divided each concept into a set of homogeneous and distinct sub-concepts each having a unique label. The output of the clustering program served as the input to a second phase that was identical to the original experiment (as described in the preceding section). The results of this experiment were even more in favor of the Context-Similarity: Its score on the wb measure was improved from 1.67 to 2.12, and the gap between it and VDM grew from 0.04 to 0.52.

As aforesaid, the difference between this experiment and the previous one is that while in the former the results are dependent on the similarity of a probe item to a single example in each concept, in the latter all the possible pairs enter into the calculated measure. Though the two experiments differ in some aspects they both evaluate the same similarity measures using the same domains. We may raise the question what is the correspondence between the results of the two experiments? To answer this question I calculated the Pearson correlation between the average accuracy of the five classifiers in each domain, and the average wb ratios of the corresponding similarity measures on these domains. The Pearson correlation equals 0.46. The fact that the correlation is positive confirms the intuition that there is, or there should be, a correspondence between the two aspects that are examined. The finding that the correlation is not very large may be interpreted as an evidence that the two experiments do not examine the same property.

6 Conclusions

This paper presented a context similarity measure, and compared it with other measures. Not surprisingly, in some cases the Context-Similarity measure performs better than other measures, while in other examples it was less accurate. As a conclusion of this paper I would like to suggest that future research should try to either combine the different measures, or characterize more thoroughly which similarity measure is best suited for which class of concepts.

Acknowledgements

I am grateful to Eliezer L. Lozinskii for helpful comments on draft of this paper. I also want to thank Murphy, P. M., & Aha, D. W. who are in charge of the *UCI Repository of machine learning databases* [Machine-readable data repository], Irvine, CA: University of California, Department of Information and Computer Science. and to professor Jergen at Baylor College of Medicine, who created the audiology database.

References

1. D. W. Aha and D. Kibler. Noise-telerant instance-based learning algorithm. In *Proc. of the 11'th Int. Joint Conf. on AI*, pages 794–799. Morgan Kaufmann, 1989.
2. D. W. Aha, D. Kibler, and M. K. Albert. Instance-based learning algorithms. *Machine Learning*, 6:37–66, 1991.
3. J. R. Anderson and M. Matessa. Explorations of an incremental, Bayesian algorithm for categorization. *Machine Learning*, 9:275–308, 1992.
4. D. L. Hintzman. "schema abstraction" in a multiple trace memory model. *Psychological Review*, 93:411–428, 1986.
5. D. L. Medin and M. M. Schaffer. Context theory of classification learning. *Psychological Review*, 85:207–238, 1978.
6. R. S. Michalski, R. E. Stepp, and E. Diday. A recent advance in data analysis: Clustering objects into classes characterized by conjunctive concepts. In L. N. Kanal and A. Rosenfeld, editors, *Progress in Pattern Recognition (Volume 1)*, pages 33–56. North-Holland, New York, 1981.
7. B. W. Porter, R. Bareiss, and R. C. Holte. Concept learning and heuristic classification in weak-theory domains. *Artificial Intelligence*, 45:229–263, 1990.
8. J. R. Quinlan. Induction of decision trees. *Machine Learning*, 1(1):81–106, 1986.
9. S. Salzberg. A nearest hyperrectangle learning method. *Machine Learning*, 6:251–276, 1991.
10. B. Shanon. On the similarity of features. *New ideas in psychology*, 8:307–321, 1988.
11. C. Stanfill and D. Waltz. Toward memory-based reasoning. *Communications of the ACM*, 29:1213–1228, 1986.
12. A. Tversky. Features of similarity. *Psychological review*, 84:327–352, 1977.

Incremental Learning of Control Knowledge for Nonlinear Problem Solving

Daniel Borrajo[1] and Manuela Veloso[2]

[1] Carnegie Mellon University, School of Computer Science, Pittsburgh, USA,
on leave from Universidad Politécnica de Madrid, Facultad de Informática,
Departamento de Inteligencia Artificial, Madrid, Spain
[2] Carnegie Mellon University, Department of Computer Science,
Pittsburgh, PA 15213, USA

Abstract. In this paper we advocate a learning method where a deductive and an inductive strategies are combined to efficiently learn control knowledge. The approach consists of initially bounding the explanation to a predetermined set of problem solving features. Since there is no proof that the set is sufficient to capture the correct and complete explanation for the decisions, the control rules acquired are then refined, if and when applied incorrectly to new examples. The method is especially significant as it applies directly to nonlinear problem solving, where the search space is complete. We present HAMLET, a system where we implemented this learning method, within the context of the PRODIGY architecture. HAMLET learns control rules for individual decisions corresponding to new learning opportunities offered by the nonlinear problem solver that go beyond the linear one. These opportunities involve, among other issues, completeness, quality of plans, and opportunistic decision making. Finally, we show empirical results illustrating HAMLET's learning performance.

1 Introduction

Problem solving uses generalized operators describing the available actions in a task domain, to search for a solution to a problem by selecting, instantiating, and chaining appropriate operators. Control knowledge can be added to the planning procedure to guide the search improving the planning performance. It has been the focus of attention of several researchers, present authors included, to learn control knowledge, i.e., automate the acquisition process of these guiding heuristics.

One approach to learning control knowledge from a problem solving trace consists of generating explanations for the individual decisions made during the search process. These explanations become control strategies that are used in future situations to prune the search space [16]. There is also work done on doing the generation of control rules without problem solving episodes, by statically looking at the domain description [8]. However, these strong deductive approaches invest a substantial explanation effort to produce correct control strategies from a single problem solving trace. Alternatively, inductive approaches acquire correct learned knowledge by observing a large set of examples [20, 26].

In this paper, we present HAMLET,[3] a system that learns control knowledge incremental and inductively. HAMLET uses an initial deductive phase, where it generates a bounded explanation of the problem solving episode. Upon experiencing each new problem solving episode, HAMLET refines its control knowledge incrementally acquiring increasingly correct control knowledge.

The paper is organized in nine sections. Section 2 overviews the complete architecture of HAMLET, and PRODIGY as the substrate problem solver. Section 3, 4 and 5 discuss the three learning phases, namely the generation of the bounded explanation from the problem solving search tree, the generalization of the rules by induction, and the refinement strategy driven by encountered negative examples. Section 6 presents an example that illustrates the execution of the learning algorithm on a problem from a logistics transportation domain. Section 7 shows empirical results from different domains. Section 8 compares our approach with previous related work. Finally section 9 draws conclusions.

2 Overview of the Architecture

HAMLET learns effectively control knowledge from a problem solving experience. This work is developed within the nonlinear problem solver [22, 5] of the PRODIGY architecture [6]. In this section we provide a description of PRODIGY's nonlinear planner and we also present HAMLET's architectural components.

2.1 The Substrate Problem Solver

The nonlinear problem solver in PRODIGY follows a means-ends analysis backward chaining search procedure reasoning about multiple goals and multiple alternative operators relevant to the goals. Figure 1 sketches the problem solver's algorithm. The inputs to the procedure are the set of operators specifying the task knowledge and a problem specified in terms of an initial configuration of the world and a set of goals to be achieved.

The planning reasoning cycle, as shown in Figure 1, involves several decision points, namely: the *goal* to select from the set of pending goals and subgoals (steps 2-4); the *operator* to choose to achieve a particular goal; the *bindings* to choose in order to instantiate the chosen operator (step 4 combines the operator and bindings selection); *apply* an operator whose preconditions are satisfied (step 5) or continue *subgoaling* on a still unachieved goal (step 3-4). Dynamic goal selection from the set of pending goals enables the planner to interleave plans, exploiting common subgoals and addressing issues of resource contention. Search control knowledge may be applied at all the above decision points: which relevant operator to select from the possible available ones, which goal or subgoal to address next, whether to reduce a new subgoal or to apply a previously selected operator whose preconditions are satisfied, or what objects in the state to use as bindings of the typed variables in the operators. Decisions at all these

---

[3] "HAMLET" stands for *H*euristics *A*cquisition *M*ethod by *L*earning from s*E*arch *T*rees.

---

1. Check if the goal statement is true in the current state, or there is a reason to suspend the current search path. If yes, then either return the final plan or backtrack.
2. Compute the *set* of *pending goals* $\mathcal{G}$, and the set of *applicable operators* $\mathcal{A}$.
3. Choose a goal G from $\mathcal{G}$ or select an operator A from $\mathcal{A}$ that is directly applicable.
4. If G has been chosen, then
   - *expand goal* G, i.e., get the set $\mathcal{O}$ of *relevant instantiated operators* for the goal G,
   - choose an operator O from $\mathcal{O}$,
   - go to step 1.
5. If an operator A has been selected as directly applicable, then
   - *apply* A,
   - go to step 1.

Fig. 1. A skeleton of PRODIGY's nonlinear problem solving algorithm.

choices are taken based on user-given or learned control knowledge to guide the search and convert it into an intelligent commitment search strategy [22]. Control knowledge guides the search process and helps to prune the exponential search space. Previous work in the linear planner of PRODIGY uses explanation-based learning techniques [16] to extract from a problem solving trace the explanation chain responsible for a success or failure and compile search control rules therefrom. Similar efforts within the linear planner of PRODIGY were done to learn control rules from partially evaluating the domain theory [8, 19].

The paper presents instead our on-going work in learning individual control rules for the nonlinear problem solver of PRODIGY [4]. We have identified several challenging problems in extending directly the previous explanation-based algorithms developed for the linear planner to the nonlinear one, since in nonlinear planning we face learning opportunities, including issues of plan quality, and opportunistic decision making. Our work applies directly to nonlinear problem solving which trivially encompasses linear problem solving. In our nonlinear problem solving framework, HAMLET learns control rules for individual decisions compiling the conditions under which the rules are to be transferred to individual decision steps in other problems. Alternative learning approaches in nonlinear planning include learning complete generalized plans as in [12], or developing a case-based learning method that provides cases as a form of global strategic knowledge [24], as discussed in the related work section.

2.2 HAMLET's Components

HAMLET has three main modules: the Bounded-Explanation learner, the Inducer and the Refiner. The Bounded-Explanation module learns control rules from the search tree. These rules are either over-specific or over-general, so they should be refined. The Induction module solves the problem of over-specificity by making them more general from more positive examples. The Refinement module attacks the over-generality by finding situations in which the learned rules were used wrongly. HAMLET gradually learns and refines so that, at the end, it converges to a concise set of correct control rules.

Figure 2 shows HAMLET's modules connected to PRODIGY. Figure 3 presents the procedure schematically, where ST and ST' are search trees, L is the set of control rules, L' is the set of new control rules learned by the Bounded Explanation module, and L" is the set learned induced from L' and L. We explain in detail each one of HAMLET's components in the next sections.

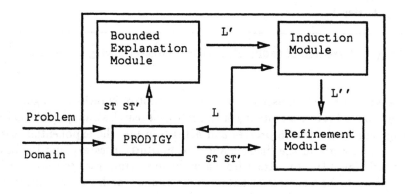

Fig. 2. HAMLET's high level architecture.

Let L refer to the set of learned control rules.
Let ST refer to a search tree.
Let P be a problem to be solved.
Initially L is empty.
For all P in training problems
    ST = Result of solving P without any rules.
    ST' = Result of solving P with current set of rules L.
    L' = Bounded-Explanation(ST, ST')
    L"= Induce(L,L')
    If needs-refinement-p(ST, ST')
    Then L=Refine(ST, ST',L")

Fig. 3. A high level description of HAMLET's learning algorithm.

3 Bounded Explanation

In this initial phase, HAMLET learns control rules directly by loosely explaining the problem solving search tree. The algorithm relies on three main parts: labeling and credit assignment on the search tree; the actual generation of the control rules; and the generalization of the control rules.

3.1 Labeling the Search Tree and Credit Assignment

When solving a problem, the problem solver generates a search tree. The domain theory implicitly defines a subgoaling structure that links goals with the operators that achieve those goals. In a linear planner, the search tree reproduces exactly this structure, since interleaving of goals and subgoals at different search spaces is not allowed. However, in nonlinear problem solving, there is a variety of different interleaved ways to traverse the subgoaling structure which are captured in the search tree. This leads to a very large search space so that there is no tractable way to generate a correct explanation for the decisions made from a unique problem solving experience.

The labeling algorithm of HAMLET traverses the search tree top-down to label first the leaf nodes. It assigns three kinds of labels to the leaf nodes: *success*, if it was a solution path; *failure*, if it was a failed path; and *unknown*, if the planner did not expand the node. After labeling the leaf nodes, it backs up the values up to the root of the search tree. Figure 4 summarizes this labeling strategy. The credit assignment is done at the same time as the labeling, and it consists of identifying the decisions for which learning will occur.

At each decision choice to be learned, HAMLET has access to information on the problem state and meta-level planning state, which is explicitly maintained in the search tree structure. Examples of meta-level knowledge at each node, available to the learning procedures, include the goals that had not been achieved, the goal the planner is working on, and in general the alternatives known to have failed or succeeded. This information is used by the generation module to create the pre- and post-conditions of the control rules.

The parameter *eagerp* controls the situations from which control rules are generated. If *eagerp* is *true*, HAMLET will learn a select rule,[4] whenever a node has a success child. If *eagerp* is *false*, HAMLET follows a conservative learning mode. A rule is then learned only if all of its children are labeled success or failure and there is at least one child labeled failure. These two different modes correspond to different levels of learning eagerness.

The parameter *optimal-learning-p* allows to learn only from the best solution found,[5] where we can incorporate different quality criteria. If *optimal-learning-p* is *true*, HAMLET delays learning until it traverses the complete tree and finds

---

[4] A select rule, when applied, selects an alternative and rejects all others for which there is not a select control rule.

[5] We consider currently best as shortest solution and less number of nodes. We will extend this criterium according to the results of [18].

```
procedure LABEL (node eagerp)
  for all successors of node do
    LABEL (successor eagerp)
  case of
    null(successors):
      case of
        solution-path: label node as success.
        failed-path: label node as failure.
        untried: label node as unknown.
    there is at least one unknown successor:
      if eagerp AND there are success children
        then if optimal-learning-p
              then store the "best" successor
              else LEARN the "best" successor
             label node as success
        else label node as unknown.
    there are only success and failure:
      if optimal-learning-p
        then store the "best" successor
        else LEARN the "best" successor
      label node as success.
    there are only failures
      label node as failure.
    there are only successes
      label node as success.
```

Fig. 4. A skeleton of the labeling and credit assignment algorithm

the best solution. In that case, after labeling, it descends only through the best solution path, learning from every decision according to the selected level of eagerness.

This algorithm builds upon some early previous work on learning and problem solving, including [14, 17]. We extend these pioneering methods in several dimensions, as discussed in section 8.

3.2 Generation of Control Rules

HAMLET proceeds to generate each control rule by acquiring its corresponding pre- and postconditions. The preconditions of the control rule need to establish the relevant conditions under which the decision was made and also define the situations under which the rule can be re-applied. The appropriate set of features that we consider in our bounded explanation technique has evolved from previous work of the first author [3]. Although there is no guarantee that this set of features is a sufficient set, there have been a number of iterations in the design of the set, to generate our confidence on it. Furthermore the empirical experiments confirm that the set is appropriate and the induction and refinement phases increase its application efficiency.

HAMLET learns four kinds of control rules: select a goal from the set of pending goals, select an operator to achieve a goal, select bindings for the chosen operators, and decide whether to apply an operator when its preconditions are met in the current state of the search, or continue subgoaling selecting a goal from the set of unachieved goals. Each rule corresponds to a generalized target concept. The target concepts are each one of the possible decisions to be made attached to some of the preconditions required to make them. For instance, for an operator decision, a target concept might be *select operator <op> to achieve the goal <goal>*. The number of target concepts of a given domain is $O + P + 2O \sum_{i=1}^{O} p(O_i)$, where O is the total number of operator schemas in the domain, P is the number of predicates of the domain, and $p(O_i)$ is the number of postconditions of the operator O_i.[6] HAMLET generates a set of rules for each target concept, each one with a conjunctive set of preconditions. This representation can be viewed as the disjunction of conjunctive rules, as we can learn several rules for the same target concept. This is equivalent, therefore, to learning a DNF description of the target concept.

Each kind of control rule has a template for describing its preconditions. The templates share a set of common features for all kinds of control rules, but each one has certain local features. Examples of common features, which become meta-predicates of the control language, are:

- True-in-state <assertion>: tests whether the <assertion> is true in the current state of the search for the solution.
- Other-goals <list of goals>: test whether any of the goals in the <list of goals> is a pending goal in the current node of the search tree.
- Prior-goal <goal>: tests whether <goal> is the first goal of the conceptual path of the node the planner is in.

Similarly, examples of the other features are:

- Current-goal <goal>: tests whether the <goal> is the one that the planner is trying to achieve.
- Candidate-applicable-op <operator>: tests whether the <operator> is applicable in the current state.

The preconditions of the control rules are created using the information on the state and the meta-level state linked to the corresponding decision node in the search tree. The postconditions are the decisions to be made, such as (*select operator unstack*), or (select goal (on <x> <y>)).[7] See section 6 for an

---

[6] This number is the sum of the number of target concepts for each kind of learned control rule. For instance, the *select operator* kind of control rule has two variables: the operator, and a goal that can be achieved by that operator. Therefore, in this case, the number of target concepts for that kind is $O \sum_{i=1}^{O} p(O_i)$.

[7] Variables are represented in brackets.

example of a learned control rule. After the rule has been created, it is parameterized, imposing the condition that two variables cannot be bound to the same
value. After the induction phase, the rule is checked against the possible negative
examples of the target concept. At the beginning, the set of negative examples for
each target concept is empty. Section 5 explains the refinement module including how to identify negative examples. Section 6 shows an illustrative example
of the learning process.

Figure 5 shows an example of a learned control rule in the blocksworld domain [10] learned after PRODIGY solves the Sussman's anomaly [21]. The control
rule allows the problem solver to select the goal of holding a block, *block1*, over
the goal of having another block, *block3*, on top of *block1*, given that there are
three blocks on the table, and the goal of holding *block1* was created as a subgoal
of the goal of having *block1* on top of another block, *block2*. This control rule
allows PRODIGY later to solve similar nonlinear problems more efficiently than
before the rule is learned.

```
(control-rule SELECT-ON-1
 (if ((candidate-goal (HOLDING <BLOCK1>))
      (prior-goal (ON <BLOCK1> <BLOCK2>))
      (true-in-state (ON-TABLE <BLOCK1>))
      (true-in-state (ON-TABLE <BLOCK2>))
      (true-in-state (ON-TABLE <BLOCK3>))
      (other-goals ((ON <BLOCK3> <BLOCK1>)))))
 (then SELECT GOALS (HOLDING <BLOCK1>)))
```

Fig. 5. Rule learned in the blocksworld for selecting the goal *holding* over the goal *on*
for interfering block configurations.

4 Inductive Generalization

The rules generated by the bounded explanation method may be over-specific,
as also analyzed in [9]. Particularly, the rules may be over-specific in the aspects
explained below. The more over-specific the rules are the lower the transfer to
other problems.[8] We follow up the deductive phase with a generalization algorithm that inductively modifies the rules based on new examples, reducing the
set of preconditions. The rules may become over-general but their transfer potential increases. We have devised ways of inducing over the following aspects of the
learned knowledge, that practically cover all the features in the preconditions.

- *State:* Most of the rules are over-specific because they keep many irrelevant
  features from the state.

---

[8] Note that in order to apply a control rule, we require that the rule totally matches
a decision making situation, i.e., all the preconditions need to be satisfied.

- *Subgoaling structure:* By relaxing the subgoaling links, for example as captured by the *prior-goal* meta-predicate, since the same goal can be generated as a subgoal of many different goals (see section 3).
- *Interacting goals:* Identifying the correct subset of the set of pending goals that affect a particular decision extending the learning scope also to quality decisions.
- *Type hierarchy:* The generalization level to which the variables in the control rules belong considering the ontological type hierarchy that is available in the nonlinear version of PRODIGY.
- *Operator types:* Further learning from an operator hierarchy to enlarge the scope of the generalization procedure.

The inductive component of HAMLET currently considers the following inductive operators relative to one or more of the above aspects:

- *Preserve main preconditions:* HAMLET is able to remove "unimportant" preconditions that are found not to affect the validity of the control rule. It keeps the *main preconditions*, i.e., the preconditions that have variables directly related to the learned decision.
- *Delete rules that subsume others:* A rule subsumes another rule of the same target concept if there is a substitution that makes its preconditions a superset of the other.
- *Intersection of preconditions:* From two rules, R_1 and R_2 of the same target concept, create a new rule with preconditions the intersection of the preconditions of R_1 and R_2 (when the intersection is not empty).
- *Refinement of subgoaling dependencies:* If there are two rules, R_1 and R_2 sharing some preconditions, but their prior goals are different, they are merged into a new rule that tests for the presence of any of the prior goals of the two rules.
- *Refinement of goal dependencies:* Similar to the previous one, but, in this case, it refers to the meta predicate *other-goals*.
- *Relaxing the subgoaling dependency:* If there is no evidence that the prior goal is needed, it gets deleted until needed.
- *Find common superclass:* When two rules can be unified by two variables that belong to subclasses of a common class (except for the root class), this operator generalizes the variables to the common class. We implemented previously a variation of this technique applied to the parameterization procedure of a single rule [2].

HAMLET tries to find an intersection of two rules using all these operators. If it finds a correct intersection that does not cover any previous negative example, a new rule is created, and the two previous ones are deleted. However HAMLET can backtrack to that learning point, and try an alternative way of intersecting the rules. This should not be considered as *plain* backtracking. When HAMLET "backtracks" to that point, it accumulated more information than when the alternative was generated, since it has found a new negative example, and it can now do better generalizations. The inductive phase significantly improves the transfer potential of the rules as it generalizes their application conditions. The inductive operators are triggered by positive examples, but also take into account the negative examples found so far as we describe in the next section.

5 Refinement

After the two previous learning phases, HAMLET may have produced over-general rules in special situations (due to the inductive operators, e.g., intersection). An over-general rule is beneficial for our inductive learning strategy as it may provide negative examples of its application. There are two main issues to be addressed: how to detect a negative example, and how to refine the learned knowledge according to it (making the rule more specific).

A negative example for HAMLET *is a situation in which a control rule was applied, and the resulting decision led to either a failure (instead of the expected success), or a worse solution than the best one for that decision.*

Once identified a negative example for a certain rule, the negative example is processed against all the current rules for the same target concept. Figure 6 shortly describes the procedures used for the refinement.

In a nutshell, the refinement module will try to relax the effect of the inductive operators by adding the tests removed in the inductive steps. The goal is to find a larger set of literals that covers the positive examples, but not the negative examples. It first checks the type of the control rule. The types are deduced, induced, and refined. Deduced are the rules generated by the Bounded-Explanation module. Induced are the ones that were generated by inducing from two rules. Refined are the ones generated by refining an existing rule, because it covered negative examples. The procedure *add-new-preconds* (not shown) does the following: for each precondition of the whole rule, having in mind even the ones that were not main preconditions, adds that precondition to the preconditions, and tests whether it covers the negative examples or not. If not, then returns the new preconditions. The procedure *find-new-intersection* (not shown) searches for other bindings of the variables of the rules from where it generated the rule, so that the new bindings substituted on the preconditions of one of those rules do not cover the negative examples.

One of the key things of any inductive method is to capture the right features in the learned description of a concept. In respect to this issue, the current version of HAMLET gets rid of irrelevant features if it learns positive examples of a target concept that do not have those features in common, or it finds negative examples of the target concept where those features are also present. In those cases, the eager inductive and refinement modules will remove these features. To speed up the convergence of the learning, we are currently introducing more informed elaborated ways of removing and adding features from the description of the target concept, such as information gain measures, similarly to [20]. These

```
procedure refine-rule (rule)
  if covers-negative-examples-p(rule)
    then
      if type(rule)=deduced
        then refine-deduced-rule(rule)
        else for all rule1 in rules(target-concept(rule))
                refine-induced-rule(rule1)
      else if deletedp(rule)
              then undelete-rule(rule)

procedure refine-deduced-rule (rule)
  preconditions=add-new-preconds(rule)
  if preconditions
    then create-rule(preconditions,postconditions(rule))
  delete-rule(rule)

procedure refine-induced-rule (rule)
  rule1=originating-rule1(rule)
  rule2=originating-rule2(rule)
  preconditions=find-new-intersection(rule1,rule2)
  if preconditions
    then create-rule(preconditions,postconditions(rule))
    else refine-rule(rule1)
          refine-rule(rule2)
  delete-rule(rule)
```

Fig. 6. High level description of the algorithm for the refinement of control rules.

methods have been tested on an analysis of a complete set of examples, and we are now exploring extending them to our incremental learning procedures.

The hill climbing performance of our global learning algorithm will approach the ultimately correct control knowledge by converging gradually closer from both over-specific and over-general rule sets. Our learning algorithm reasons about and converges from points in the generalization space as it is prohibitively costly to maintain both the specific and general sets as in the version space method [17].

6 Illustrative Example

We show now an example of the learning method applied to a logistics domain where we illustrate the phases of the generation of the control rules and their inductive refinement.[9] In this domain, packages are to be moved among different cities. Packages are carried within the same city in trucks and across cities in

---

[9] This domain was first introduced in [23].

airplanes. At each city, there are several locations, e.g. post offices and airports. This transportation domain represents a considerable scale up in length of the solution, size of the search space, and other difficult learning issues, such as non-linearity, un-optimality of solutions, and a large number of planning alternatives.

Consider the following problem solving situation illustrated in Figure 7. There are two cities, *city1* and *city2*, with one post-office each, respectively *post-office1* and *post-office2*, and with one airport each, namely *airport1* and *airport2*. Initially, at *post-office1*, there are two objects, *object1* and *object3*, and two trucks, *truck1* and *truck3*. At *airport1* there is an airplane, *airplane1*, and another object, *object2*. At *city2*, there is only one truck, *truck2*, at the city airport, *airport2*. There are two goals: *object1* must be at *post-office2*, and *airplane1* at *airport2*. This problem is interesting because both the object and the airplane need to be moved to a different city. HAMLET will learn, among other things, that the object should be loaded into the airplane (or any other needed carrier) before the airplane moves.

The optimal solution to this problem is the following sequence of steps:

- *(load-truck object1 truck1 post-office1)*,
- *(drive-truck truck1 post-office1 airport1)*,
- *(unload-truck object1 truck1 airport1)*,
- *(load-airplane object1 airplane1 airport1)*,
- *(fly-airplane airplane1 airport1 airport2)*,
- *(unload-airplane object1 airplane1 airport2)*,
- *(load-truck object1 truck2 airport2)*,
- *(drive-truck truck2 airport2 post-office2)*,
- *(unload-truck object1 truck2 post-office2)*.

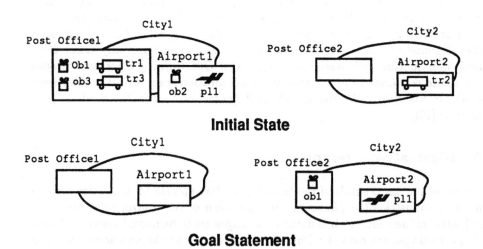

Fig. 7. An illustrative example - initial state and goal statement

Notice that although in this example, the optimal plan corresponds to this unique linearization, in general the learning procedure can reason about a partially-ordered dependency network of the plan steps.

HAMLET labels and assigns credit to decisions made in the search tree generated by PRODIGY. The rule in Figure 8 is learned at one of the decisions made, namely when PRODIGY finds that it should delay moving the carriers until the object is loaded.[10] The rule says that the planner should plan first to achieve *(inside-truck object1 truck1)* before moving the carriers, including *truck1* and *airplane1*. This is a very effective control rule, since if the problem solver works first on any of the other two goals, it will arrive to an un-optimal solution, where carriers would have to do trips not needed.

```
(control-rule SELECT-INSIDE-TRUCK-1
  (if ((target-goal (INSIDE-TRUCK <OBJECT1> <TRUCK1>))
       (prior-goal (AT-OBJ <OBJECT1> <POST-OFFICE2>)) **
       (true-in-state (AT-TRUCK <TRUCK1> <POST-OFFICE1>))
       (true-in-state (AT-TRUCK <TRUCK2> <AIRPORT2>))
       (true-in-state (AT-TRUCK <TRUCK3> <POST-OFFICE1>)) *
       (true-in-state (AT-AIRPLANE <AIRPLANE1> <AIRPORT1>))
       (true-in-state (AT-OBJ <OBJECT1> <POST-OFFICE1>))
       (true-in-state (AT-OBJ <OBJECT2> <AIRPORT1>))
       (true-in-state (AT-OBJ <OBJECT3> <POST-OFFICE1>))*
       (true-in-state (SAME-CITY <AIRPORT1> <POST-OFFICE1>))
       (true-in-state (SAME-CITY <AIRPORT2> <POST-OFFICE2>))
       (other-goals ((AT-TRUCK <TRUCK1> <AIRPORT1>)
                     (AT-AIRPLANE <AIRPLANE1> <AIRPORT2>)))))
    (then SELECT GOALS (INSIDE-TRUCK <OBJECT1> <TRUCK1>)))
```

Fig. 8. Rule learned by HAMLET after applying the Bounded-Explanation.

This example, though simple,[11] shows a learning opportunity that is needed in order to deal with new problems effectively and with quality. This learning possibility is not encountered by a linear problem solver who handles multiple goals independently. It would also not be compiled as a local choice by other learning methods applied to nonlinear planning [12, 23].

The preconditions are the initial bounded explanation of the problem solving decision. This rule is over-specific, since, among other things, it records the positions of other trucks available and another object present at the post office, which turn out to be irrelevant features for this instantiated target concept. The operator *Preserve Main Preconditions* removes the preconditions that we marked with

---

[10] For simplicity we use the same names for the instances in the problem and the variables in the rule. Note however that the names in the rules refer to general variables.

[11] In our extensive empirical tests we ran problems of much greater complexity. Section 7 shows the results of some of these tests.

a star (*) in the description above. Note that there are still irrelevant features kept, such as *truck2* and *object2*, because they are at a location directly related to the goals rejected in the decision, namely *airport2*. The operator *Relaxing the Subgoaling Dependency* removes the precondition on the prior-goal that we marked with a double star (**).

Now suppose that we encounter a new problem where the goal is the same but there are no additional trucks or objects, and there is an additional airplane. Figure 9 shows a rule that HAMLET would learn in this case, after applying the same operators as before.

```
(control-rule SELECT-INSIDE-TRUCK-2
 (if ((target-goal (INSIDE-TRUCK <OBJECT1> <TRUCK1>))
      (true-in-state (AT-TRUCK <TRUCK1> <POST-OFFICE1>))
      (true-in-state (AT-AIRPLANE <AIRPLANE1> <AIRPORT1>))
      (true-in-state (AT-AIRPLANE <AIRPLANE2> <AIRPORT1>))*
      (true-in-state (AT-OBJ <OBJECT1> <POST-OFFICE1>))
      (true-in-state (SAME-CITY <AIRPORT1> <POST-OFFICE1>))
      (other-goals ((AT-TRUCK <TRUCK1> <AIRPORT1>)))))
 (then SELECT GOALS (INSIDE-TRUCK <OBJECT1> <TRUCK1>)))
```

Fig. 9. Rule learned by HAMLET in a second problem. It will help HAMLET generalize the rule in Figure 8.

The inductive method combines these rules with the operator *Intersection of Preconditions*, as they refer to the same decision. It also merges the goals in the *other-goals* meta-predicate. HAMLET generates a new rule, which consists of the intersection of the rules, being, therefore, more general than the initial two rules. Figure 10 shows the resulting rule.

```
(control-rule SELECT-INSIDE-TRUCK-3
 (if ((target-goal (INSIDE-TRUCK <OBJECT1> <TRUCK1>))
      (true-in-state (AT-TRUCK <TRUCK1> <POST-OFFICE1>))
      (true-in-state (AT-AIRPLANE <AIRPLANE1> <AIRPORT1>))
      (true-in-state (AT-OBJ <OBJECT1> <POST-OFFICE1>))
      (true-in-state (SAME-CITY <AIRPORT1> <POST-OFFICE1>))
      (other-goals ((AT-TRUCK <TRUCK1> <AIRPORT1>)
                    (AT-AIRPLANE <AIRPLANE1> <AIRPORT2>)))))
 (then SELECT GOALS (INSIDE-TRUCK <OBJECT1> <TRUCK2>)))
```

Fig. 10. Rule induced from the rules in Figures 8 and 9.

The induced rule is "almost" fully correct and it becomes "completely" correct after a couple of more training situations. Irrelevant features are removed with more positive examples, while important features are captured by the refinement with negative examples. HAMLET proceeds in this hill-climbing way searching the hypotheses space converging to the set of correct rules.[12] It induces and generalizes upon experiencing positive examples and it refines the learned control rules, when negative examples are found.

7 Empirical Results

We have been performing extensive empirical experiments in several domains. We report here results from the logistics transportation domain [23] and the blocksworld domain (where we experience nonlinear learning situations, similar to the Sussman's anomaly [21]). The results illustrate our main claims about the effectiveness of the combined deductive and inductive methods. The nonlinear version of PRODIGY we are using has embedded several domain-independent search heuristics [1]. Therefore, the substrate problem solver has some underlying "intelligence" that makes it difficult for a learning mechanism to outperform it by large. However, as we will show, HAMLET is able to perform considerably better.

In the blocksworld, we used a set of 100 problems randomly generated from which HAMLET learns the control rules. It learned 14 control rules. These rules were applied to a test set of 200 randomly generated problems. We varied the time bound given to PRODIGY to solve the problems from 100 to 300 seconds obtaining similar results for the different time bounds. Figure 11 shows the results obtained with 100 seconds of time bound. The unsolved problems are accounted for in the running time by a term equal to the running time bound.

In the logistics domain, we performed a training phase of 350 problems, 300 one-goal problems and 50 two-goal problems. We used the resulting learned 22 control rules in testing with three test sets of different complexity in terms of initial state and number of goals. We again varied the time bounds, from 150 to 300 seconds, obtaining similar results to the ones shown in Figure 11 for a time of bound of 150 seconds.

Domain	Number of Problems per Test Set	Unsolved problems		Running time (sec)		Nodes explored	
		without rules	with rules	without rules	with rules	without rules	with rules
Blocksworld	200	43	19	5402	2872	34065	9513
Logistics	300	57	25	9890	5615	13443	7798

Fig. 11. Table that reflects the performance of HAMLET in two different domains: blocksworld and a logistics transportation domain.

---

[12] Since it is an incremental inductive system, the performance of HAMLET depends on the order of the examples given.

The main conclusion from the table is that the number of unsolved problems drops from 21.5% to 9.5% in the blocksworld, and from 19% to 8.3% in the logistics. This corresponds to a considerable increase in the solvability horizon of the problem solver when using the rules. Also, since the matcher for the control rules is not using any optimum retrieving and organization algorithm [7], the time spent matching the rules represents the usual utility problem. The results shown in the table are especially relevant as the use of the learned set of rules outperformed the base-level problem solver even with the rudimentary matcher.

8 Related Work

There are several dimensions along which we can compare this work with previous approaches, including the representation, the granularity, the correctness of the control knowledge, and the essence of the substrate problem solving algorithm.

With respect to the representation, control guidance to prune the problem solving search space has been introduced as additional preconditions of the operators of the domain in simple one-goal planning situations, such as in [14, 17]. In our framework, control knowledge is explicitly distinct from the set of operators describing the domain knowledge because it introduces knowledge about the various problem solving decisions, such as selecting which goal/subgoal to address next, which operator to apply, what bindings to select for the operator or where to backtrack in case of failure. This clear division between the declarative domain knowledge, i.e., the operators, and the more procedural control knowledge simplifies both the initial specification of a domain and the automated acquisition, i.e., the learning of the control knowledge.

Learned control knowledge can be local or global. Local control knowledge is used on each decision of a problem solver, while global knowledge guides the problem solver strategy as a whole. [23] develops a case-based learning method for PRODIGY that consists of storing individual complete problems solved to guide the planner when solving similar new problems. The guiding similar plans provide global control knowledge in the sense that they consist of a chain of decisions. Other examples of learning global knowledge although with different granularities are [10, 11, 12, 13, 25]. These systems learn macro-operators or complete generalized plans HAMLET, however, learns local control rules that apply independently to individual decision steps with greater potential for transfer. We are already studying the integration of the two kinds of strategic knowledge, since we believe they have complementary benefits to the problem solver.

Previous work has usually learned control knowledge on simple problem solvers such as linear planners with no more than one goal [8, 14, 15, 16, 17, 19, 26]. In this kind of problem solver the underlying complexity of interleaving goals at different levels of the search does not exist, so the learning methods lack these learning opportunities. Other new learning opportunities not present in linear problem solving, consist of opportunistic operator choices driven by other planning goals. In our case, the nonlinear planner introduces this factor of complexity and the learning task becomes more challenging, due to having to find the right language for describing the hypotheses among other things. Also, the kinds of domains/problems we use are more complex than the previously studied ones, except in [23]. There is no immediately clear way to directly compare our results to other systems that learn local control rules, because none applies to nonlinear problem solving.

Another difference can be found in the way positive and negative instances are presented to the system. Systems like [15, 20, 26] are one-step learning algorithms in that they work on all examples at one time. However, HAMLET learns incrementally the control knowledge.

Usually, rules produced by learning methods are worse than the ones produced by the experts. However, learning methods produce those control rules much faster than the experts, since the acquisition of control knowledge is much harder than the acquisition of domain knowledge. We believe that one could get better results if one could present the learned rules to the expert and he or she could refine them to make them more accurate. Then, the issue of clarity of the rules is a major point and HAMLET's rules are very easy to read and require very little effort to debug or refine.

9 Conclusions

The approach we have presented addresses a new speedup learning strategy to efficiently acquire control knowledge for improving the performance of a nonlinear problem solver. We proposed a solution where we combine a bounded deductive explanation method with an inductive technique. In this case, the tradeoff between the accuracy of the learned control knowledge, and the learning effort required is addressed by bounding the learning step with a fixed set of tests that have been manually adapted from the experience of the authors. Upon experiencing new problem solving episodes, HAMLET refines its control knowledge incrementally acquiring increasingly correct control knowledge. Therefore, HAMLET combines analytical-based learning, using the problem solving search tree, and induction-based learning, refining and generalizing the control rules from examples. We showed empirical results that demonstrate the improvement that this learning strategy provides to PRODIGY's nonlinear problem.

Acknowledgements

We greatly appreciate the help from Juan Pedro Caraça-Valente in previous steps of the research, and insightful comments from Jaime Carbonell, Alicia Pérez, and the anonymous reviewers.

This work was sponsored for the first author by a grant of the Ministerio de Educación y Ciencia and the project CO44-91 from Comunidad de Madrid.

For the second author, this research was sponsored by the Wright Laboratory, Aeronautical Systems Center, Air Force Materiel Command, USAF, and the Advanced Research Projects Agency (ARPA) under grant number F33615-93-1-1330. The views and conclusions contained in this document are those of the authors and should not be interpreted as necessarily representing the official policies or endorsements, either expressed or implied, of Wright Laboratory or the U. S. Government. The U. S. Government is authorized to reproduce and distribute reprints for Government purposes notwithstanding any copyright notation thereon. This manuscript is submitted for publication with the understanding that the U. S. Government is authorized to reproduce and distribute reprints for Governmental purposes.

References

1. Jim Blythe and Manuela M. Veloso. An analysis of search techniques for a totally-ordered nonlinear planner. In *Proceedings of the First International Conference on AI Planning Systems*, College Park, MD, June 1992.

2. Daniel Borrajo, Juan P. Caraça-Valente, and José Luis Morant. Learning heuristics in planning. In *Sixth International Conference on Systems Research, Informatics and Cybernetics*, Baden-Baden, Germany, 1992.

3. Daniel Borrajo, Juan P. Caraça-Valente, and Juan Pazos. A knowledge compilation model for learning heuristics. In *Proceedings of the Workshop on Knowledge Compilation of the 9th International Conference on Machine Learning*, Scotland, 1992.

4. Daniel Borrajo and Manuela Veloso. Bounded explanation and inductive refinement for acquiring control knowledge. In *Proceedings of the Third International Workshop on Knowledge Compilation and Speedup Learning*, pages 21–27, Amherst, MA, June 1993.

5. Jaime G. Carbonell, and the PRODIGY Research Group. PRODIGY4.0: The manual and tutorial. Technical Report CMU-CS-92-150, School of Computer Science, Carnegie Mellon University, June 1992.

6. Jaime G. Carbonell, Craig A. Knoblock, and Steven Minton. Prodigy: An integrated architecture for planning and learning. In K. VanLehn, editor, *Architectures for Intelligence*. Erlbaum, Hillsdale, NJ, 1990. Also Technical Report CMU-CS-89-189.

7. Robert B. Doorenbos and Manuela M. Veloso. Knowledge organization and the utility problem. In *Proceedings of the Third International Workshop on Knowledge Compilation and Speedup Learning*, pages 28–34, Amherst, MA, June 1993.

8. Oren Etzioni. *A Structural Theory of Explanation-Based Learning*. PhD thesis, School of Computer Science, Carnegie Mellon University, 1990. Available as technical report CMU-CS-90-185.

9. Oren Etzioni and Steven Minton. Why EBL produces overly-specific knowledge: A critique of the prodigy approaches. In *Proceedings of the Ninth International Conference on Machine Learning*, pages 137–143, 1992.

10. Richard E. Fikes and Nils J. Nilsson. Strips: A new approach to the application of theorem proving to problem solving. *Artificial Intelligence*, 2:189–208, 1971.

11. G. A. Iba. A heuristic approach to the discovery of macro-operators. *Machine Learning*, 3(4):285–317, 1989.

12. Subbarao Kambhampati and Smadar Kedar. Explanation based generalization of partially ordered plans. In *Proceedings of AAAI-91*, pages 679–685, 1991.

13. Richard E. Korf. Macro-operators: A weak method for learning. *Artificial Intelligence*, 26:35–77, 1985.

14. Pat Langley. Learning effective search heuristics. In *Proceedings of IJCAI-83*, pages 419–421, 1983.

15. C. Leckie and I. Zukerman. Learning search control rules for planning: An inductive approach. In *Proceedings of Machine Learning Workshop*, 1991.

16. Steven Minton. *Learning Effective Search Control Knowledge: An Explanation-Based Approach*. PhD thesis, Computer Science Department, Carnegie Mellon University, 1988. Available as technical report CMU-CS-88-133.

17. Tom M. Mitchell, Paul E. Utgoff, and R. B. Banerji. Learning by experimentation: Acquiring and refining problem-solving heuristics. In R. S. Michalski, J. G. Carbonell, and T. M. Mitchell, editors, *Machine Learning, An Artificial Intelligence Approach*, pages 163–190. Tioga Press, Palo Alto, CA, 1983.

18. M. Alicia Pérez and Jaime G. Carbonell. Automated acquisition of control knowledge to improve the quality of plans. Technical Report CMU-CS-93-142, School of Computer Science, Carnegie Mellon University, April 1993.

19. M. Alicia Pérez and Oren Etzioni. DYNAMIC: A new role for training problems in EBL. In D. Sleeman and P. Edwards, editors, *Proceedings of the Ninth International Conference on Machine Learning*. Morgan Kaufmann, San Mateo, CA, 1992.

20. J. Ross Quinlan. Learning logical definitions from relations. *Machine Learning*, 5:239–266, 1990.

21. Gerald J. Sussman. *A Computer Model of Skill Acquisition*. American Elsevier, New York, 1975. Also available as technical report AI-TR-297, Artificial Intelligence Laboratory, MIT, 1975.

22. Manuela M. Veloso. Nonlinear problem solving using intelligent casual-commitment. Technical Report CMU-CS-89-210, School of Computer Science, Carnegie Mellon University, 1989.

23. Manuela M. Veloso. *Learning by Analogical Reasoning in General Problem Solving*. PhD thesis, School of Computer Science, Carnegie Mellon University, Pittsburgh, PA, August 1992. Available as technical report CMU-CS-92-174.

24. Manuela M. Veloso and Jaime G. Carbonell. Derivational analogy in PRODIGY: Automating case acquisition, storage, and utilization. *Machine Learning*, 10:249–278, 1993.

25. Hua Yang and Douglas Fisher. Similarity-based retrieval and partial reuse of macro-operators. Technical Report CS-92-13, Department of Computer Science, Vanderbilt University, 1992.

26. J. Zelle and R. Mooney. Combining FOIL and EBG to speed-up logic programs. In *Proceedings of IJCAI-93*, 1993.

tried out. Those algorithms that do not match the data can be excluded, and so, a great deal of computing effort effort can be saved.

In order to achieve this aim, we need to determine which dataset features are relevant. After that, various instances of learning tasks can be examined with the aim of formulating a 'theory' concerning the applicability of different machine learning and statistical algorithms. The process of constructing such a theory can be considered as a kind of *meta-level learning*. The knowledge concerning as to which algorithm is applicable can be summarized in the form of rules of the form: If the given dataset has characteristics C1..Cn, then classification algorithm A is (may be) applicable.

Each rule can in addition be qualified using certain statistical measures, such as estimates of correctness. For reasons explained later we prefer to use estimates of how informative each rule is. Rules concerning applicability of algorithms can be constructed manually, or with the help of some (semi-)automatic method. In this paper we are concerned with the application of machine learning methods to this problem.

Previous work on comparative studies has usually considered only a few algorithms (e.g. neural networks and decision trees) and these were done usually on few datasets only (a comprehensive review of previous work appears in D.Michie, et al. (1994)). As the number of tests was generally limited, few people have attempted to automate the formulation of a theory concerning the applicability of different algorithms. One exception was the work of Aha (1992) who represented this knowledge using rule schemata. One example of such a rule schema is:

> If (# training instances < 737)   AND
>   (# prototypes per class > 5.5) AND
>   (# relevant attributes > 8.5)
> Then IB1 >> C4

where IB1 >> C4 means that algorithm IB1 is predicted to have significantly higher accuracies than algorithm C4. Our approach differs from Aha's in that we are not concerned with just a comparison between two algorithms, but rather a group of algorithms. This task is more challenging than a set of pairwise comparisons. Also, out rules are suitably quantified and so our recommendations are more refined.

There is, however, an alternative solution to the problem of how we can go about selecting a suitable classification algorithm. Instead of attempting to *predict* which classification algorithm would perform well, we can try out all different algorithms and examine the outcome. This approach has been adopted by Shaffer (1993) who compared three different classification algorithms - C4.5, C4.5rules and back propagation. The algorithms were evaluated on five different datasets using cross-validation (CV). The objective of the method is to consider each dataset in turn, and in each case select that algorithm that appears to give the highest success rate. In this context CV could be considered as another (more complex) classification algorithm. The experimental results have shown that CV is superior to any of the individual algorithms. This method has, of course, the disadvantage that it requires a lot of processing time before the final answer can be given. For some classification algorithms the learning times may be of the order of hours, particularly if we use large industrial datasets (such as the ones used in StatLog). Besides, we have to have all classification algorithms available and the expertise to use them. Our approach avoids these difficulties.

Characterizing the Applicability of Classification Algorithms Using Meta-Level Learning

Pavel Brazdil [1]
João Gama [1]
Bob Henery [2]

[1] LIACC, University of Porto, Rua Campo Alegre 823, 4100 Porto, Portugal.
email: pbrazdil, jgama @ncc.up.pt.

[2] Dept. of Statistics, University of Strathclyde, Livingston Tower, 26 Richmond Street, Glasgow, UK. email: r.j.henery @strathclyde.ac.uk.

Abstract. This paper is concerned with a comparative study of different machine learning, statistical and neural algorithms and an automatic analysis of test results. It is shown that machine learning methods themselves can be used in organizing this knowledge. Various datasets can be characterized using different statistical and information theoretic measures. These together with the test results can be used by a ML system to generate a set of rules which could also be altered or edited by the user. The system can be applied to a new dataset to provide the user with a set of recommendations concerning the suitability of different algorithms and these are graded by an appropriate information score. The experiments with the implemented system indicate that the method is viable and useful.

1 Introduction

Project StatLog carried out perhaps the most comprehensive comparative study of different machine learning, neural and statistical classification (D.Michie, et al., 1994). About 22 different algorithms were evaluated on more than 20 different datasets of industrial interest. It is interesting that no particular algorithm could be considered 'best' when considering the error rates. With some datasets one particular algorithms could be better than other algorithms, but with other datasets this could easily be the other way round. As there was no algorithm which could be considered best overall, a question arises whether one could adopt a method that would identify the promising algorithm(s) on the basis of the existing test results. The purpose of this paper is to show how we can do that.

The aim of our work is to obtain a set of rules characterizing the applicability of different algorithms. It appears that datasets can be characterized using certain features such as number of attributes, proportion of binary, categorical or numeric attributes, unknown values etc. In addition, we can use other more complex statistical or information theoretic measures. It is reasonable to try to match the features of datasets with our knowledge concerning the performance of algorithms. If we select the algorithm that most closely matches the features of the dataset on which the algorithm performed well, then we increase the chances of obtaining useful results. The advantage is that not all algorithms need to be

Organization of this Paper

This paper is organized as follows. Sections 2 describes a set of basic dataset measures used to characterize datasets. Section 3 describes the preprocessing of test results, and in particular, the criteria used to determine whether a particular algorithm can be considered applicable or non-applicable. This section describes also how a particular machine learning algorithm (C4.5) can be used to generate a set of rules on the basis of the available data (dataset measures and classified test results). Section 4 is concerned with the issue of assessing the informativity of the individual rules generated. Section 5 gives an overview of the results and analysis of some of the rules generated. Section 6 shows how the system can provide an advice concerning which algorithm is most suitable for a given dataset. In this section we discuss also the correlation between the advice and the actual performance.

2 Characteristics of Datasets

Our overall aim is to be able to match the features of datasets with our past knowledge concerning the algorithms. In order to achieve this, we need to determine which dataset features are relevant. In this section we will briefly describe some of the features used in this study. The features can be divided into simple measures, statistical measures and information based measures. The simple measures include:

N	Number of examples in the dataset.
p	Number of attributes.
k	Number of classes.
Bin_att	Proportion of binary attributes.
Cat_att	Proportion of categorical attributes.
Un_attrib	Proportion of unknown attributes.
Cost	Cost matrix indicator (it is equal to 1 if costs are used and 0 otherwise)

As for the statistical measures, we have adopted those suggested by R.Henery and C.Taylor (Michie D.et al, 1994). These measures include:

SD_ratio	Standard deviation ratio. Geometric mean ratio of standard deviations of the individual populations to the pooled standard deviation.
Corr.abs	Mean value of correlations between attributes (mean over all pairs of attributes and all populations).
Cancor1	Canonical correlation for the best single linear combination of attributes that discriminates between populations.
Fract1	The first eigenvalue of canonical discriminant matrix divided by the sum of all eigenvalues.
Skewness	Mean of $\mid E(X-\mu)^3 \mid / \sigma^3$.
Kurtosis	Mean of $\mid E(X-\mu)^4 \mid / \sigma^4$.

where $E(X-\mu)$ represents a moment, μ mean and σ standard deviation. The information based measures include:

H(A)	Mean entropy (complexity) of attributes.
H(C)	Entropy (complexity) of class.
M(C,A)	Mean mutual information of class and attributes.
EN.attr	Equivalent number of attributes H(C) / M(C,A)

Each dataset is then simply described using a vector of numeric values.

3 Using Test Results as Data in Meta-level Learning

The test results obtained during the StatLog project were used as raw data which was preprocessed in a particular way. The results for each dataset were analyzed with the objective of determining which algorithms achieved *low error rates* (or *costs*). All algorithms with low error rates were considered *applicable* to this dataset. The other algorithms were considered *inapplicable*.

This categorization of the test results can be seen as preparatory step for the metalevel learning task. Of course, the categorization will permit us also to make predictions regarding which algorithms are applicable on a new dataset.

Of course, the question whether the error rate is *high* or *low* is rather relative. The error rate of 15% may be excellent in some domains, while 5% may be bad in others. This problem is resolved using a method similar to *subset selection* in statistics. First, the best algorithm is identified according to the error rates. Then an acceptable margin of tolerance is calculated. All algorithms whose error rates fall within this margin are considered *applicable*, while the others are labeled as *inapplicable*.

The level of tolerance can reasonably be defined in terms of the standard deviation of the error rate, but since each algorithm achieves a different error rate, the appropriate standard deviation will vary across algorithms. The standard deviation can be estimated by calculating the error margin

$$EM = sqrt(ER * (1 - ER) / NT),$$

where *ER* represents the error rate of the 'best' algorithm, *NT* the number of examples in the test set. Then all algorithms whose error rates fall within the interval <ER, ER + k*EM> are considered *applicable*. Of course we still need to choose a value for k which determines the size of the interval. This affects the confidence that the truly best algorithm appears in the group considered. The larger the value of k, the higher the confidence that the best algorithm will be in this interval. As a rough guide, a value of k=3 corresponds to a 95% confidence level.

For example, let us consider the tests on the Segment dataset consisting of 2310 examples. The best algorithm appears to be ALLOC80 with the error rate of 3% (ER=0.03). Then

$$EM= sqrt(0.03 * (1 - 0.03) / 2310) = 0.0035$$

which is 0.35%. In this example, we can say with high confidence that the best algorithms is in the group with error rates between 3% and k * 0.35%. If k=1, the interval is relatively small - <3%, 3.35%> and includes only two other algorithms (AC2, BayesTree) apart from ALLOC80. All the algorithms that lie in this interval can be considered *applicable* to this dataset, and the others inapplicable. If we enlarge the margin, by considering larger values of k (e.g. 2, 4, 8 or 16), we get a more relaxed notion of applicability. If k=16, for example, the relatively broad band will include most of the "average" algorithms (see Fig.1).

Algorithm	Error rate	Class (k=16)	Margin	Note
ALLOC80	.030	Appl	0.030	Margin for k=0
AC2	.031	Appl		
BayesTree	.033	Appl		
			0.0335	Margin for k=1
NewID	.034	Appl		
			0.037	Margin for k=2
C4.5	.040	Appl		
CART	.040	Appl		
DIPOL92	.040	Appl		
CN2	.043	Appl		
			0.044	Margin for k=4
IndCART	.045	Appl		
LVQ	.046	Appl		
SMART	.052	Appl		
Backprop	.054	Appl		
			0.058	Margin for k=8
Cal5	.062	Appl		
Kohonen	.067	Appl		
RBF	.069	Appl		
kNN	.077	Appl		
			0.086	Margin for k=16
Logdisc	.109	Non-Appl		
CASTLE	.112	Non-Appl		
Discrim	.116	Non-Appl		
Quadisc	.157	Non-Appl		
Bayes	.265	Non-Appl		
ITrule	.455	Non-Appl		
Default	.900	Non-Appl		

Fig. 1 Test Results on *Segment* dataset and Error Margins

The decision as to where to draw the line (by choosing a value for k) is, of course, rather subjective. In this work we had to consider an additional constraint related to the purpose we had in mind. As our objective is to generate rules concerning applicability of algorithms we have opted for the more relaxed scheme of applicability (k=8 or 16), so as to have enough examples in each class (Appl, Non-Appl). This point will be discussed in more detail later.

Some of the tests results analyzed are not characterized using error rates, but rather *costs*. Consequently the notion of error margin discussed earlier has to be adapted to costs. The *standard error of the mean cost* can be calculated from the confusion matrices (obtained by testing), and the cost matrix[1].

---

[1] The values obtained on the basis of some tests were:

Dataset	Algorithm	Mean cost	Standard error (of mean cost)
German credit	Discrim	0.525	0.0327

We notice that the categorization of error rates (into Appl, Non-Appl) seems to be a bit unnatural, but it is necessary, given our aims. We require it simply for the next step, that involves meta-level learning. As we use a classification algorithm we need to introduce such categorization. Had we chosen a regression algorithm, this would not be necessary.

Preprocessing of Test Results

The problem of learning was divided into several phases. In each phase all the test results relative to just one particular algorithm (e.g. CART) were joined, while all the other results (relative to other algorithms) were temporarily ignored. The purpose of this strategy was to simplify the class structure. For each algorithm we would have just two classes (Appl and Non-Appl). This strategy worked better than the obvious solution that included all available data for training. For example, when considering CART algorithm and margin of k =16 we get:

CART-Appl,	Satim	CART-Non-Appl,	KL
CART-Appl,	Vehic	CART-Non-Appl,	Dig44
CART-Appl,	Head	CART-Non-Appl,	Chrom
CART-Appl,	Heart	CART-Non-Appl,	Shut
CART-Appl,	Belg	CART-Non-Appl,	Tech
CART-Appl,	Segm	CART-Non-Appl,	CUT
CART-Appl,	Diab	CART-Non-Appl,	Cr.Man
CART-Appl,	Cr.Ger	CART-Non-Appl,	Letter
CART-Appl,	Cr.Aust	CART-Non-Appl,	Simdat
CART-Appl,	DNA		
CART-Appl,	New-Bel		
CART-Appl,	Faults		
CART-Appl,	Tset		

Fig. 2 Classified test results relative to one particular algorithm (CART)

The classified test results are then modified as follows. The dataset name is simply substituted by a vector containing the corresponding dataset characteristics (measures). Values which are not available or missing are simply represented by "?". This extended dataset is then used in the meta-level learning.

Prior Ordering of Algorithms

The classified test results are interesting per se. They enable us to make quick comparisons among different classification algorithms. Obviously, the more often a particular algorithm is classified as *applicable*, the better.

If we consider the classified test results of CART for k=16 shown earlier, we see that this algorithm can be considered applicable in 13 cases and inapplicable in 9. These numbers

Heart disease	Discrim	0.415	0.0688
Head injury	Logdiscr	18.644	1.3523

In the experiments reported later the error margin was simply set to the values 0.0327, 0.0688 and 1.3523 respectively, irrespective of the algorithm used.

can be used to estimate the probability P(Ai-Appl) that the algorithm Ai is applicable. Here we prefer to calculate the information associated with this probability, suitably normalized. (The method takes into account the overall probability of algorithms falling into the class "applicable". Full description appears in Section 4).

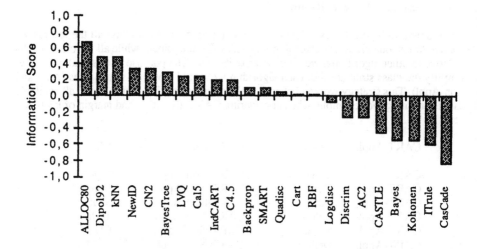

Fig. 3   Information associated with the prior probability of applicability
of different classification algorithms tested in Statlog

Fig. 3 shows the information values for all algorithms tested in StatLog. We have decided to show here the mean of two values, one relative to the error margin k=8 and the other relative to k=16. All values are arranged in a descending order. ALLOC80, for example, is the first place in the ordering. The associated information value is around .7 bits. That is, the information that ALLOC80 is applicable is worth about .7 bits. Similarly the information that Dipol92 or kNN is applicable is worth about .5 bits and so on.

If the information is negative, this can be interpreted as an argument that the algorithm is likely to be non-applicable. This does not mean, of course, that we cannot find situations in which the algorithm could be useful. If we do not have any other information, finding such situations may simply be somewhat less likely.

The information values provide us with useful default decisions which need not be followed. Indeed, the purpose of meta-level learning can be viewed as the process of finding useful rules which enable us to make better decisions than those incorporated in these defaults.

Choice of Algorithm for Meta-Level Learning (C4.5)

A question arises as to which algorithm we should use in the process of meta-level learning. We have decided to use C4.5 (Quinlan, 1992) for the following reasons. First, as our results have demonstrated, this algorithm achieves quite good results overall. Secondly, the decision tree generated by C4.5 can be inspected and analyzed. This is not the case with some statistical and neural learning algorithms.

So, for example, when C4.5 has been supplied with the partial test results relative to CART algorithm, it generated the following decision tree:

```
N > 6435 : Non-Appl (8.0)
N <= 6435:
|  Skew <= 0.57 : Appl (2.0)
|  Skew > 0.57 : Non_Appl (12.0)
```

It has been argued that rules are more legible than trees. The decision tree shown earlier can be transformed into a rule form using a very simple process, where each branch of a tree is simply transcribed as a rule. The applicability of CART can thus be characterized using the following set of rules:

```
CART-Appl      <-- N <= 6435, Skew > 0.57
CART-Non-Appl  <-- N > 6435
CART-Non-Appl  <-- N <= 6435, Skew <= 0.57
```

Quinlan (1992) has argued that rules obtained from decision trees can be improved upon in various ways. For example, it is possible to eliminate conditions that are irrelevant, or even drop entire rules that are irrelevant or incorrect. In addition it is possible to reorder the rules according to certain criteria, introduce a default rule to cover the cases that have not been covered. System C4.5 provides a command that permits to transform a decision tree into a such a rule set. The rules produced by the system are characterized using (pessimistic) error rate estimates.

As is shown in the next section, error rate (or its estimate) is not ideal measure, however. This is particularly evident when dealing with continuous classes. This problem has motivated us to undertake a separate evaluation of all candidate rules and characterize them using a new measure. The aim is to identify those rules that appear to be most informative. The details are given in the following section.

4 Characterizing the Rules Generated

We notice that the amount of data used in generating the rules concerning applicability of one particular algorithm is rather modest. As we used only the StatLog test results, we had only about 22 examples at our disposal (each case represents the results of particular test on a particular dataset). Of these, only a part represented 'positive examples', corresponding to the datasets on which the particular algorithm performed well. Also, the set of dataset descriptors used may not carry too much information. We could thus expect that the rules generated capture a mixture of relevant and fortuitous regularities.

In order to strengthen our confidence in the result the rules generated are evaluated. Our aim is to determine whether the rules could actually be used to make useful predictions concerning its applicability. A rule is considered useful if it appears to make better predictions than the appropriate default rule. The default rule simply states that the algorithm is applicable (with no conditions attached), if the algorithm performs well on relatively many datasets. If the algorithm performs poorly, the default is that the algorithm is non-applicable.

The predictive power of the rules should thus be compared to the default. If a rule appears to be less informative than the default, the default rule should be used instead. All rules (including defaults) are quantified using a measure of how predictive they are. The method of how this is done is given below.

The evaluation of how successful the rules are in predicting the applicability (or non-applicability) of a given algorithm is done using a leave-one-out procedure. Following this procedure *all but one* items is used in training, while the remaining item is used for testing. Of course, the set of rules generated in each pass could be slightly different, but the form of the rules was not our primary interest here.

Let us consider, for example, the problem of predicting applicability of CART. This can be characterized using a confusion matrix, such as the ones shown below, showing results relative to the error margin k=16.

	Appl	Non-Appl
Appl	11	2
Non-Appl	1	8

The rows represent a true class. The columns refer to the predictions made using the rules generated.

The confusion matrix shows that the rules generated were capable of correctly predicting the applicability of CART on a unseen dataset in 11 cases. Incorrect prediction was made only in 1 case. Similarly, if we consider non-applicability, we see that the correct prediction is made in 8 cases, and incorrect one in 2. This gives a rather good overall success rate of 86 %.

Had we decided to use a default rule stating that CART is simply applicable, the number of correct predictions would increase to 13 (11+2), and the number of incorrect ones to 9 (1+8). This gives a success rate of about 59 %. The default stating that CART is inapplicable gives correct predictions in 9 cases, and incorrect one in 13. The corresponding success rate is about 41%.

We notice that success rate is not the ideal measure, however. As the margin of applicability is extended (by making k larger), more cases will get classified as applicable and consequently, the estimates concerning applicability will be easier to make. If we consider an extreme case, when the margin covers all algorithms, we will get an apparent success rate of 100 % (equal to the default). This apparent paradox can be resolved by adopting the measure called *information score* described by Kononenko and Bratko (1991). This measure takes into account prior probabilities.

The information score associated with a definite positive classification[2] is defined as -log P(C), where P(C) represents the prior probability of class C. The information scores can be used to weigh all classifier answers. In our case we have two classes *Appl* and *Non-Appl*.

---

[2] The term 'definite positive classification' is used here to indicate that the classifier affirms that the case belongs to class C with a probability of 1.

The weights can be represented conveniently in the form of a information score matrix as follows:

	Appl	Non-Appl
Appl	- log P(Appl)	- log (1 - P(Appl))
Non-Appl	- log (1 - P(Non-Appl))	- log P(Non-Appl)

The information scores can be used to calculate the total information provided by a rule on the given dataset. This can be done simply by multiplying each element of the confusion matrix by the corresponding element of the information score matrix.

The quantities P(Appl) and P(Non-Appl) can be estimated from the appropriate frequencies. If we consider the frequency of Appl and Non-Appl for *all* algorithms (irrespective of the algorithm in question), we get a kind of absolute reference point. This enables us to make comparisons right across different algorithms.

For example, if we consider tests of 23 algorithms on 22 datasets, we get a dataset consisting of 506 cases (23 x 22). As it happens 307 cases fall into the class *Appl*. The information associated with -logP(Appl) is -log (307 / 506) = 0.721. Similarly, the value of -log P(Non-Appl) is -log (199 /506) = 1.346.

We notice that due to the distribution of data (given by the relatively large margin of applicability of k=16), the examples of applicable cases are relatively common. Consequently, the information concerning applicability has a somewhat smaller weight (.721) than the information concerning non-applicability (1.346).

If we multiply the elements of the confusion matrix for CART by the corresponding elements of the information score matrix we get the following matrix:

	Appl	Non-Appl
Appl	7.93	2.69
Non-Appl	.72	10.77

This matrix is in a way similar to the confusion matrix shown earlier with the exception that the error counts have been weighted by the appropriate information scores. To obtain an estimate of the *average* information relative to *one* case, we need to divide all elements by the number of cases considered (i.e. 22). This way we get:

	Appl	Non-Appl
Appl	.360	.122
Non-Appl	.033	.489

The information provided by classification of *Appl* is .360 - .033 = .327 bits. The information provided by classification of *Non-Appl* is similarly .489 - .122 = .367 bits.

This information obtained in the manner described can be compared to the information provided by the appropriate default rule. If we assume that CART is applicable by default, the corresponding rule will give a correct answer in 13 cases and incorrect one in 9 (we note that as the number of correct answers exceeds the number of errors, this is actually the right default to consider). The number of correct answers and errors can be expressed using a confusion matrix. Then we can calculate the overall information score in a similar way as before. Each answer needs to be weighed using the appropriate information score. In our case we get $(13* -\log P(Appl) - 9* -\log(1-P(Non-Appl)))/22 = 0.131$ bits.

This information score of the default rule can be compared to the information score provided by the rules. A rule can be considered *useful* if it provides us with more information than the default. If we come back to our example, we see that the classification for Appl provide us with .327 bits, while the default classification provides only .131 bits. This indicates that the rules are more informative than the default for CART. In consequence, the actual rule should be kept and the default rule discarded.

5 Rules Generated in Meta-level Learning

This section contains some rules generated using the method described. As we have not used a uniform notion of applicability throughout, each rule is qualified by additional information. The symbol Appl $\downarrow_k$ represents the concept of applicability derived on the basis of the best error rate. In case of Appl Appl $\downarrow_{16}$ the interval of applicability is <Best error rate, Best error rate + 16 STD's> and the interval of non-applicability is <Best error rate + 16 STD's, 1>.

The set of rules generated includes a number of 'default rules' which can be easily recognized (they do not have any conditions on the right hand side of "←"). Each rule included shows also the normalized information score. This parameter gives an estimate of the usefulness of each rule. Only those rules that could be considered minimally useful (with information score > .200) have been included here. In the implemented system we use a few more rules which are a bit less informative (with inf. scores down to .100).

Decision Tree and Rule Base Algorithms:		Inf. score:
C4.5-Appl $\downarrow_{16}$	←	.477
C4.5-Non-Appl $\downarrow_8$	← k > 2	.226
NewId-Appl $\downarrow_{16}$	←	.609
AC2-Non-Appl $\downarrow_8$	←	.447
CART-Appl $\downarrow_8$	← N <= 4999, Kurtosis > 2.92	.186
CART-Appl $\downarrow_{16}$	← N <= 6435, Skew > 0.57	.328
CART-Non-Appl $\downarrow_8$	← N > 4999	.226
CART-Non-Appl $\downarrow_{16}$	← N > 6435	.367
IndCART-Appl $\downarrow_8$	← Cancor1 <= 0.78	.274
IndCART-Appl $\downarrow_{16}$	←	.384
Cal5-Appl $\downarrow_{16}$	← k <= 7	.524
Cal5-Non-Appl $\downarrow_{16}$	← k > 7	.244
CN2-Appl $\downarrow_{16}$	←	.702
ITRule-Non-Appl $\downarrow_8$	← N > 768	.549
ITRule-Non-Appl $\downarrow_{16}$	← N > 1000	.918

Statistical Algorithms:		Inf. score:
Discrim-Appl $\downarrow_8$	← N <= 1000	.247

Discrim-Non-Appl $\downarrow$ 8	$\leftarrow$ N > 1000	.453
Discrim-Non-Appl $\downarrow$ 16	$\leftarrow$ k > 4	.367
QuaDisc-Appl $\downarrow$ 8	$\leftarrow$ N <= 1000	.309
QuaDisc-Appl $\downarrow$ 16	$\leftarrow$ Skew <= 2.56, EnAttr > 2.98	.229
QuaDisc-Non-Appl $\downarrow$ 8	$\leftarrow$ N > 1000, Hx <= 5.58	.226
LogDisc-Appl $\downarrow$ 8	$\leftarrow$ N <= 3186	.495
LogDisc-Non-Appl $\downarrow$ 8	$\leftarrow$ N > 3186	.323
LogDisc-Non-Appl $\downarrow$ 16	$\leftarrow$ k > 4	.367
Alloc80-Appl $\downarrow$ 8	$\leftarrow$	.406
Alloc80-Appl $\downarrow$ 16	$\leftarrow$	.797
kNN-Appl $\downarrow$ 16	$\leftarrow$	.766
Smart-Appl $\downarrow$ 16	$\leftarrow$ Fract1 > 0.63	.262
Bayes-Non-Appl $\downarrow$ 8	$\leftarrow$	.418
Bayes-Non-Appl $\downarrow$ 16	$\leftarrow$	.705
BayTree-Appl $\downarrow$ 16	$\leftarrow$ k <= 7	.557
BayTree-Non-Appl $\downarrow$ 16	$\leftarrow$ k > 7	.305
Castle-Non-Appl $\downarrow$ 8	$\leftarrow$ Cost <= 0, N > 768	.420
Castle-Non-Appl $\downarrow$ 16	$\leftarrow$ Bin_att <= 0	.734

Neural Network Algorithms:		Inf. score:
Dipol92-Appl $\downarrow$ 8	$\leftarrow$	.341
Dipol92-Appl $\downarrow$ 16	$\leftarrow$	.544
Radial-Non-Appl $\downarrow$ 8	$\leftarrow$	.401
LVQ-Appl $\downarrow$ 16	$\leftarrow$	.498
BackProp-Appl $\downarrow$ 8	$\leftarrow$ N <= 3000	.495
BackProp-Appl $\downarrow$ 16	$\leftarrow$ k <= 7, EnAttr > 2.88	.229
BackProp-Non-Appl $\downarrow$ 8	$\leftarrow$ N > 3000, Cancor1 > 0.61	.259
Kohonen-Non-Appl $\downarrow$ 8	$\leftarrow$	.641
Cascade-Non-Appl $\downarrow$ 8	$\leftarrow$	.706
Cascade-Non-Appl $\downarrow$ 16	$\leftarrow$	.866

Fig. 4 Some Rules Generated During Meta-Level Learning

The rules presented could be supplemented by another set generated on the basis of the worst error rate (i.e. the error rate associated with the choice of most common class or worse). In case of Appl $\uparrow$ 16 the interval of applicability is <0, Default error rate - 16 STD's> and the interval of non-applicability is <Default error rate - 16 STD's, 1>.

Discussion

The problem of learning rules for all algorithms simultaneously is formidable. We want to obtain a substantial number rules to qualify each algorithm. In addition, there are perhaps far too many measures given the available data. To limit the complexity of problem we have considered one algorithm at a time. This facilitated the construction of rules. Considering that the problem is difficult, what confidence can we have that the rules generated are minimally sensible?

One possibility is to try to evaluate the rules, by checking whether they are capable of giving useful predictions. This is what we have done and the method was described earlier. Note that measuring simply the success rate has the disadvantage that it does not distinguish between predictions that are easy to make, and those that are more difficult. This is why we have evaluated the rules by examining how informative they are in general. Our analysis showed that the rules generated can indeed provide us with a useful information. For example, the following rule

$$\text{Discrim-Appl} \downarrow_8 \leftarrow N <= 1000$$

provides us with .247 bits of information, if invoked, which is reasonable. On quick glance the condition "N <= 1000" is a bit puzzling, however. Why should Discrim perform simply well, if the number of examples is less than this number?

One possible answer to this question is that the condition shown is simply fortuitous. The rules could contain some fortuitous conditions, given that they were generated on the basis of relatively few data. Unless we have more data, it is difficult to determine which conditions are really relevant. However, it is necessary to note that each condition, such as ""N <= 1000", should be interpreted contextually. The condition cannot be simply interpreted as "Discrim performs will perform well if such and such condition is satisfied". The correct interpretation is something like - "Discrim is likely to compete well under the conditions stated, provided no other more informative rule applies".

However, the condition seems to make sense in the light of the following additional evidence. Some algorithms have a faster learning rate than others. These algorithms compete well with others provided the number of examples is small. The fast learning algorithms may however be overtaken by others later. The experiments with learning curves on the Satellite Image dataset show that Discriminant algorithm is among the first six algorithms in terms of error rate as long as the number of examples is relatively small (100, 200 etc.). This algorithm seems to quickly pick up what is relevant and so we could say, it competes well under these conditions. When the number of examples is larger, however, Discriminant is overtaken by other algorithms. For example, with 3200 examples Discriminant is in the 15th place in the ranking. This supports the view that the system has 'discovered' a new piece of experimental knowledge from the regularities in the data.

There is of course a well recognized problem that should be tackled. Many conditions contain numeric tests which are either true or false. It does not make sense to consider Discriminant algorithm applicable if the number of examples is less than 1000, and inapplicable, if this number is just a bit higher. Obviously a more flexible approach is needed (e.g. using flexible matching). We note, however, that this problem is somewhat attenuated by the fact *different* error margins are used in the process of rule generation. The rules for CART generated by the system were:

CART-Non-Appl $\downarrow_8$	$\leftarrow N > 4999$	.226
CART-Non-Appl $\downarrow_{16}$	$\leftarrow N > 6435$	.367

These rules suggest that there may be a functional dependence between non-applicability and N. It is conceivable that if we used more error margins (e.g. k=4, 8, 12, 16 etc.), we could get a more precise model of this dependence. So we can get some benefits of flexible matching without further work.

6 Giving Advice Concerning Application

Rules generated in the way described permit us to give recommendations as to which classification algorithm could be used with a given dataset. This is done with the help of a kind of expert system called an *Application Assistant (AplAs)*. This system contains a *knowledge base* containing all the rules shown earlier (the actual rule set includes a few extra rules with lower information scores). The interpreter is quite standard, but uses a particular method for resolution of conflicts.

We notice that the knowledge base may contain potentially conflicting rules. In general several rules may apply, some of which may recommend the use of a particular algorithm while others may be against it. Some people believe that knowledge bases should always be cleaned up so that such situations would not arise. This would amount to obliterating certain potentially useful information and so we prefer to deal with the problem in a different way.

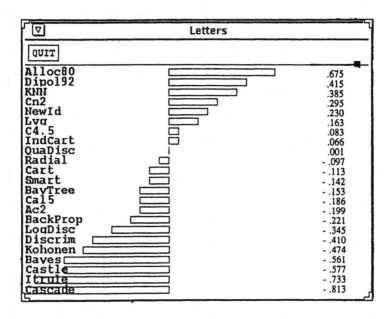

Letters	
QUIT	
Alloc80	.675
Dipol92	.415
KNN	.385
Cn2	.295
NewId	.230
Lvq	.163
C4.5	.083
IndCart	.066
QuaDisc	.001
Radial	- .097
Cart	- .113
Smart	- .142
BayTree	- .153
Cal5	- .186
Ac2	- .199
BackProp	- .221
LogDisc	- .345
Discrim	- .410
Kohonen	- .474
Bayes	- .561
Castle	- .577
Itrule	- .733
Cascade	- .813

Fig. 5 Recommendations concerning applicability of algorithm (for Letters dataset)

For every algorithm we consider all the rules satisfying the conditions, sum all the information scores and then normalize them. The information scores associated with the recommendation to apply an algorithm are taken with a positive sign, the others with a negative one. The sum of information scores is then normalized. In our case, as we use two margins (k=8 and k=16), the mean is divided by 2. The output of this phase is a list of algorithms ordered by their information scores. A positive score can be interpreted as an argument to apply the algorithm. A negative score can be interpreted as an argument against the application of the algorithm. Moreover, the higher the score, the more informative is the recommendation in general. The information score can be then considered as a strength of the recommendation. Figure 5 shows the recommendations obtained for the Letters dataset.

The recommendations given are of course not perfect. They do not guarantee that the first algorithm in the recommendation ordering will have the best performance in reality. However, our results demonstrate that the algorithms accompanied by a strong recommendation do perform quite well in general. The opposite is also true. The algorithms that have not been recommended have a poorer performance in general. In other words, we observe that there is a reasonable degree of correlation between the prediction and the actual test results. This is illustrated in Fig. 6 which shows the correlation between the information score and the success rate for one particular dataset (Letters).

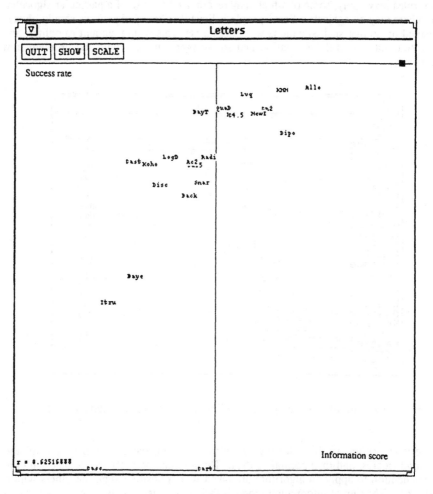

Fig. 6 Correlation between information score and success rate (for Letters dataset)

The top part shows the algorithms with high success rates. The right part shows the algorithms accompanied by a strong recommendation concerning applicability. We notice that several algorithms with high success rates appear there. The algorithm that is most strongly recommended for this dataset is Alloc80 (Inf. score = .601 bits). This algorithm has also the highest success rate of 93.6 %. The algorithms kNN and Dipol92 share the second place in the recommendation ordering. We note that kNN is a very good choice, while Dipol92 is not too bad either.

The correlation between the information score and success rate could, of course, be better. For example, Dipol92 is a bit overvalued, Castle undervalued etc. The correlation could be improved, in the first place, by obtaining more test results. This would give us the opportunity to possibly refine the rule set. It would be beneficial to consider also other potentially useful sets of rules, including the ones generated on the basis of other error margins.

Some Problems and Future Work

Some of the measures used in estimating the performance of algorithms are not too simple to calculate. For example, the programming effort in calculating SD_ratio is greater than that in running the linear discriminant on the available data. Indeed to find SD_ratio requires virtually all the quantities needed in finding the quadratic discriminant. This poses the question: if it is easier to run, say linear discriminants and NewID, why not run them and use the performance of these procedures as yardsticks by which to judge the performance of other algorithms? The similarities evident in the empirical results strongly suggest that the best predictor for logistic regression is linear discriminants (with logistic regression doing that little better on average), and AC2 is very similar to NewID (if there is no hierarchy), and so on. This idea has been followed up and described in (D.Michie, et al., 1994).

There is scope for further work. As almost certainly there are insufficient data to construct reliable rules, it is worth considering an interactive method, capable of incorporating prior expert's knowledge. As one simple example, if it is known that an algorithm can handle cost matrices, this could simply be provided to the system. As another example, the knowledge that the behaviour of NewID and AC2 is likely to be similar could also be useful to the system. The rules for AC2 could be then be constructed from the rules for NewID, by adding suitable conditions concerning e.g. the hierarchical structure of the attributes. Also, some algorithms have in-built checks on applicability, such as linear or quadratic discriminants, and these should be incorporated into the rules constructed by the system.

Despite the fact that there is space for possible improvements, the method is sound in principle and seems to produce very promising results. The user can get a recommendation as to which algorithm could be used with a new dataset. Although the recommendation is not guaranteed to give the best possible advice, it narrows down the user's choice.

Acknowledgements

This work was supported by Esprit II Project StatLog (No.5170). The authors wish to thank Commission of European Communities for this support. Also, we wish to thank the following partners for providing the individual test results:

• Dept. of Statistics, Univ. of Strathclyde, Glasgow, UK; • Dept. of Statistics, Univ. of Leeds, UK; • Aston University, Birmingham, UK; • Forschungszentrum Ulm, Daimler-Benz AG, Germany; • Brainware GmbH, Berlin, Germany; • Fraunhofer Gesellschaft IITB-EPO, Berlin, Germany; • Institut fuer Kybernetik, Bochum, Germany; • ISoft, Gif sur Yvette, France; • Dept. of CS and AI, University of Granada, Spain.

The authors wish to thank Luís Torgo for some corrections, and also, to anonymous referees for their comments.

References ·

Aha D. (1882): Generalizing from Case Studies: A Case Study, in *Proc. of the Ninth International Workshop on Machine Learning (ML92)*, ed. D.Sleeman and P.Edwards, Morgan Kaufmann.

Michie D., Spiegelhalter D.J., Taylor C.C. (1994): *Machine Learning, Neural and Statistical Classification*, Prentice Hall. To be published.

Kononenko I. and Bratko I. (1991): "Information-Based Evaluation Criterion for Classifier's Performance", in *Machine Learning, Vol.6, No. 1*, Kluwer Academic Publishers.

Quinlan R. (1992): *C4.5: Programs for Machine Learning*, Morgan Kaufmann.

Shaffer C. (1993): Selecting a Classification Method by Cross-Validation, in *Machine Learning, Vol.13, No. 1*, Kluwer Academic Publishers.

Appendix

1. Classification Algorithms Used in StatLog

Decision Tree Classifiers:
C4.5	- Inductive Decision Tree
NewID	- New Inductive Decision Tree
AC2	- Decision Trees with Knowledge Acquisition
CART	- Classification and Regression Tree
IndCART	- Classification and Regression Tree
Cal5	- Numeric Decision Tree Classifier

Rule Classifiers:
CN2	- Decision Rule Classifier
ITrule	- Probabilistic Decision Rule Classifier

Classical Statistical Algorithms:
Discrim	- Fisher's Linear Discriminants
Quadisc	- Quadratic Discriminats
Logdisc	- Logistic Discriminants

Non-Parametric Statistical Algorithms:
ALLOC80	- Density Estimation (Kernel Classifier)

kNN	- k-Nearest Neighbour
SMART	- Projection Pursuit (Smooth Additive Regression)
Bayes	- Naive Bayes
BayesTree	- Extension of Naive Bayes
CASTLE	- Causal Networks
DIPOL92	- Discriminate Analysis with Post-Optimisation

Neural Network Classifiers:

RBF	- Radial Basis
LVQ	- Linear Vector Quantizer
Backprop	- Multi Layer Perceptron (Back Propagation)
Kohonen	- Self Organizing Feature Map

Our experiments included one additional algorithm (Cascade) which is officially not included among the algorithms evaluated under StatLog.

2. Datasets Used in StatLog

*	Cr.Aust	- Australian credit		Belg	- Belgian power
*	Cr.Ger	- German credit	*	DNA	- DNA sequence
*	Satim	- Landsat Satellite image		Tech	- Technical
	Dig44	- Handwritten digits (Digits)		Faults	- Finance of maintenance
	KL	- Karhunen-Loeve Digits		New-Bel	- New Belgian power
*	Vehic	- Vehicle silhouttes		Tset	- Tsetse Fly Distribution
*	Segm	- Image Segmentation		CUT	- Character Segmentation
	Chrom	- Chromosomes		Cr.Man	- Credit Management
	Head	- Head injury	*	Letter	- Letter Recognition
*	Heart	- Heart disease		Simdat	- Simulated data
*	Shut	- Shuttle control			(withdrawn later)
*	Diab	- Diabetes of pima-indians			

The dataset marked with "*" were authorized for public distribution and available via ftp (see the next section). The datasets mentioned contain typically several thousands of examples. The largest dataset contains 58000 examples, and the smallest only 270 examples. The datasets are characterized using a varied number of *attributes*. The Australian credit data (Cr.Aust), for example, is characterized using 14 attributes. The number of attributes can be much larger, however. The DNA, Technical and New-Belgian power datasets are characterized by more than 50 different attributes. The number of classes also varies, and is between 2 and 26 for the datasets shown.

3. Support for Further Comparative Testing

LIACC can offer various datasets used in the comparative testing within StatLog as well as some software that has been written during the StatLog project. In particular, LIACC can provide the source code of Evaluation Assistant which can help users to carry out further comparative testing.

General information about this can be obtained from LIACC, University of Porto, from ftp.ncc.up.pt (192.26.239.52), directory pub/statlog, file README. Alternatively, interested parties can contact P.Brazdil or J.Gama, at LIACC, University of Porto, Rua Campo Alegre 823, 4100 Porto, Portugal, Tel.: +351 600 1672, Fax.: +351 600 3654, or by email statlog-adm@ncc.up.pt.

3.1 Datasets

All public domain datasets used in StatLog can be obtained from LIACC, University of Porto, from ftp.ncc.up.pt, directory pub/statlog/datasets. This directory contains several subdirectories, one for each dataset. Each subdirectory contains an associated .doc file with a brief description of the dataset and previous test results on this dataset. Some larger datasets have been split into train and test set (as used in the StatLog project).

The main source of datasets is the UCI Repository of Machine Learning Databases and Domain Theories which is managed by D.W.Aha. Some datasets were processed and the repository mentioned contains both the unprocessed and processed versions. The datasets available from LIACC, contain only the processed datasets. These datasets can also be obtained from University of Strathclyde, via ftp.strath.ac.uk (130.159.248.24), directory Stams/statlog.

3.2 Conducting New Tests with Evaluation Assistant

New tests can be carried out by interested parties with the help of Evaluation Assistant, which is a software tool developed within Project StatLog. Its aim is to facilitate testing of statistical, machine learning and neural algorithms on given datasets and provide standardized performance measures. The Evaluation Assistant is oriented towards classification tasks. Two versions of Evaluation Assistant exist: a command version, and an interactive one.

The command version of Evaluation Assistant consists of a set of basic commands that enable the user to test learning algorithms. This version is implemented as a set of Cshell scripts and C programs. The interactive version of Evaluation Assistant provides an interactive interface that enables the user to set up the basic parameters for testing. The interactive interface is implemented in C and exploits X windows. This version generates a customized version of some scripts which can be examined and modified before execution.

The source code of the Evaluation Assistant is available from LIACC via ftp.ncc.up.pt. The command version is stored in the directory pub/statlog/eac. The source code of the interactive version is stored in the directory pub/statlog/eai. Both versions run on SUN SPARCstation IPC and other compatible workstations.

3.3 Application Assistant

This software prototype analyses previous test results and generates rules concerning applicability of different machine learning, statistical and neural network algorithms. The rules can be used to provide the user with a recommendation concerning which classification method is appropriate for a given dataset.

The rules referred to earlier are generated on the basis of previous test results and dataset characteristics. The semi-automatic analysis of previous test results is done with the help of one particular ML algorithm (C4.5). The result is transcribed in the form of rules which can be altered or edited by the user. The rules constitute, in effect, a knowledge base of an expert system. The system can be applied to a new dataset to provide the user with a set of recommendations concerning the suitability of different algorithms, graded by a score.

3.4 Future Plans Concerning Support

In future database accesible by ftp from LIACC will be organized in such a way that it is easy to add new datasets, classification algorithms, test methods etc., as these become publicly available. The database will be maintained and new test results validated whenever this will be feasible. Datasets will only be added to the database if they are of industrial and/or commercial relevance. One of the principal aims of the database will be to give algorithm developers access to the expersise developed earlier. In this way, the developers of new algorithms will be able to compare results with chosen classification procedures that were used in the StatLog project. This will facilitate the evaluation of new procedures, and should extend the range of algorithms available to potential industrial users.

Inductive Learning of Characteristic Concept Descriptions from Small Sets of Classified Examples

Werner Emde

GMD, FIT.KI
Schloß Birlinghoven
D-53757 St. Augustin
Germany
email: werner.emde@gmd.de

Abstract. This paper presents a novel idea to the problem of learning concept descriptions from examples. Whereas most existing approaches rely on a large number of classified examples, the approach presented in the paper is aimed at being applicable when only a few examples are classified as positive (and negative) instances of a concept. The approach tries to take advantage of the information which can be induced from descriptions of unclassified objects using a conceptual clustering algorithm. The system COLA is described and results of applying COLA in two real-world domains are presented.

1 Introduction

The learning task considered in "learning-from-examples" is to induce a description of a set of objects which are classified by a user or a system as instances (and non-instances) of a general meaningful class, i.e., a concept. The concept description is supposed to help to determine other instances (and non-instances) of the concept. Some examples of well known systems which are able to learn from examples are: AQ [Michalski 73], ID3 [Quinlan 83], FOIL [Quinlan 86], and RDT [Kietz/Wrobel 92].

Although previous research on learning-from-examples has lead to impressive results, the existing approaches are not able to explain an important aspect of human concept learning – namely the ability to learn new concepts from very few examples (see [Carey 85]). We are not interested here in constructing a cognitive model of human learning, but look for some kind of knowledge and/or generalization method which may help us to learn from few examples. However, the problem of learning from a small set of examples is also of great practical relevance. In some application domains, a classification of large number of examples is not available or the acquisistion of the data is too expensive. Also autonomous agents may sometimes be required to improve their behavior from very limited experience.

In the following, it is argued that the use of additional background knowledge (which is often available, but not used in other approaches) enables programs to learn characteristic concept descriptions from small sets of positive and negative examples only. The approach described in this paper tries to take advantage of the information contained in descriptions of unclassified objects (as a kind of additional background knowledge) using a conceptual-clustering algorithm.

In the next section, the consequences of the number of examples available for concept learning on the quality of learning results is analyzed. In the third section of the paper, the general idea of the new approach based on the use of a conceptual-clustering algorithm is described. Section 4 describes an implementation of the new technique in the system COLA. Experimental results obtained by applying COLA to different real-world data sets are presented in section 5. We finish with a discussion of related work (section 6) and some final remarks.

2 Learning from few examples

In the literature two kinds of generalized descriptions are distinguished: *characteristic descriptions* and *discriminant descriptions* [Dietterich/Michalski 81]. A *characteristic description* of a class of objects describes the sufficient conditions for class membership and enables a system to identify all instances of the class and reject all instances of other (disjoint) classes. A *discriminant description* can be applied to discriminate between instances of one class from instances of a pre-defined set of other classes. As a discriminant description needs only to specify properties relevant in the context of a fixed set of other classes, these descriptions are usually more general.

These two kinds of descriptions can be related to two kinds of generalization algorithms: algorithms constructing *most-specific generalizations* and algorithms constructing *most-general generalizations* from a given set of positive and negative examples. A most-general generalization algorithm generalizes the descriptions of the positive examples to the most general description in the hypotheses space such that (only) the negative examples are excluded.[1] A most-specific generalization algorithm generalizes the descriptions of the positive examples to the most-specific description in the hypothesis space covering just all positive examples and excluding all negative examples. Most-general generalizations are built by programs like AQ [Michalski 73], GOLEM [Muggleton/Feng 90][2], RDT [Kietz/Wrobel 92], and FOIL [Quinlan 86]. Examples of programs, which construct most-specific generalizations are ARCH [Winston 75] and OGUST [Vrain 90]. A most-specific generalization algorithm tends to produce characteristic descriptions. A most-general generalization algorithm tends to produce discriminant descriptions.

Whether an intended learning goal can be achieved heavily depends on the number of available learning examples. If the number of examples is large, both kinds of generalizations are likely to deliver descriptions which are complete and

---

[1] It may also be the case that an algorithm searches for a borderline "in the middle" between positive and negative examples.

[2] GOLEM produces first a most specific generalization, which is reduced to a most general generalization in a later step.

correct not only on the training set, but on the future test sets as well. If only a small number of examples is available, a most-specific generalization is still likely to be correct, but will probably be incomplete. All objects predicted as instances of the goal concept are instances, but several instances will not be predicted. A most-general generalization from few examples on the other hand, is still likely to be complete, but will tend to be incorrect.

The consequence of this analysis is that many current learning programs are able to learn from relatively few examples, but the classification accuracy of the concept description is likely to be bad if it is used as a characteristic description. Current inductive learning programs cannot be improved simply by changing their generalization algorithm. What we can do is extend the learning input and improve the algorithms so that they can make use of it. An approach following this direction has already been developed with the system Iou [Mooney 93] which combines empirical and explanation-based learning. This system requires an overly-general domain theory as additional background knowledge in order to be able to learn more accurate concepts from fewer examples than other learning systems (section 6).

3 Conceptual-clustering–based generalization

For concept learning problems where only a relatively small number of positive (and negative) examples is known, but a large set of descriptions of unclassified objects is available, we propose a generalization approach called "conceptual-clustering–based-generalization" (CCG) incorporating a conceptual clustering step.

3.1 Conceptual Clustering

The learning task of a conceptual clustering algorithm can be described as follows. From a given set of descriptions of (unclassified) objects of a domain, a conceptual clustering algorithm is supposed to aggregate the objects into an organized set of meaningful classes and to find (intensional) descriptions of these classes. A class is regarded as meaningful if the organization of knowledge becomes more effective and/or more efficient, e.g., enables a system to infer missing information for partially described objects. Some conceptual clustering programs (e.g., CLUSTER [Michalski/Stepp 83] or COBWEB [Fisher 87]) construct a hierarchy of classes, other programs (e.g., UNIMEM [Lebowitz 87], KBG [Bisson 92b]) construct a directed acyclic graph of classes, which means that the classes are not necessarily disjoint.

An example of a directed-acyclic graph of classes constructed by the conceptual clustering system KBG is shown in figure 1 below. It is a sub-graph of a graph constructed from descriptions of unclassified diseased soybean plants (see section 5), i.e., without the information about the correct diagnoses. The leaves of the graph show the identifier numbers of the different plant disease cases. The nodes are the classes formed by KBG labelled with identifier numbers of the classes. The soybean plant numbered 5 is an instance of class 39, class 38, and class 44. Such non-disjoint classes can be interpreted as capturing different views/similarities on a set of objects.

3.2 A Rough Description of CCG

Following this rough characterization of conceptual clustering, we can now describe the basic idea behind the CCG approach. We assume that the instances of the goal concept are similar to each other and that this similarity can be uncovered in the set of unclassified instances. Thus, we use the set of descriptions of unclassified instances to find a set of classes which capture different similarities among the instances. This is achieved using a conceptual clustering algorithm. The (small) set of classified examples is then used to identify one of the classes produced by the clustering algorithm as the class which captures the similarity of instances of the goal concept. The selection of the class is done after comparing the extensions of all classes with the positive and negative examples. The intensional description of the selected class (produced by the clustering algorithm) is finally proposed as a description of the goal concept. All other classes and class descriptions produced by the clustering system are not incorporated into the knowledge base of the overall system.

The conceptual clustering step can been seen as building a space of possible generalizations. The second step of selecting one class using the examples can been understood as search in the hierarchy (or graph) of generalizations.

The induced concept description covers the positive examples and those unclassified instances used in the clustering step, which are 'similar' to the positive examples. It excludes all negative examples and the unclassified instances, which are not 'similar' to the positive examples. Thus, the induced description of the goal concept is neither a most-specific generalization nor a most-general generalization of the sparse set of examples. The description covers more instances than the most-specific generalization, but less instances than the most-general generalization. In addition, the description produced by the CCG method tends to be intensionally more specific (e.g., the description contains more premises) than a description built by a most general generalization, because the class descriptions built by the clustering algorithm usually need to discriminate between a large number of classes. Therefore, we say that the CCG approach delivers a *characteristic* description of instances of the goal concept.

Before we discuss the details let us state the learning problem this paper deals with more clearly:

Given:

- B: background knowledge in the form of descriptions of objects in a domain,
- C: the name of a goal concept which is not used in the description of the objects in the background knowledge B, but would be helpful in order to complete the descriptions, and

- E: a (small) set of positive (and negative) examples of the instances of the concept C which are already partially described with the background knowledge B.

Find:

- H: an intensional characteristic concept description of the concept C, which covers all (or at least a large number of) the positive examples as well as similar objects described in B and excludes all (or at least most of) the negative examples in E as well as similar objects described in B.

3.3 Details of the CCG Approach

In the above rough description of the CCG approach, several important details are missing. For example, how should a learning system deal with the case that more than one class satisfies the requirement that all positive examples and no negative example is covered? Suppose case 15 (see figure 1) is described as

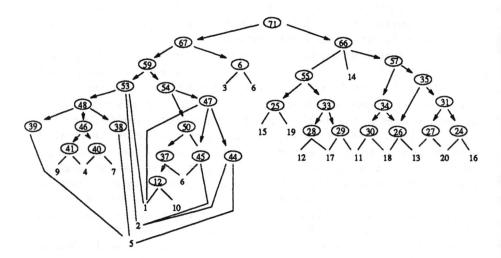

Fig. 1. Classes of diseased soybean plants

positive example and case 3 is described as negative example. The requirement is satisfied by class 25, class 55, and class 66. The first step to deal with this problem is to identify two extreme cases of possible generalizations: the generalization which delivers the *most specific CCG* and the generalization which delivers the *most general CCG*.

The most specific CCG of examples may be computed by climbing the graph from a leaf with a positive example up to the node in the graph covering all other positive examples, the least number of total instances, and no negative examples. This type of generalization is especially appropiate if no negative examples are available to prevent over-generalizations. The most general CCG results from climbing the graph to the top-most class covering all other positive examples, the largest number of total instances, and no negative examples. In the last example, the definition of class 25 would be the most specific CCG and the description of class 66 would be the most general CCG.

It may be interesting to know that class 67 (see figure 1) covers all instances of the soybean disease Diaporthe Stem Canker; furthermore, class 66 covers all soybean plants suffering from Charcoal Rot. This clustering result means that conceptual-clustering-based generalization is able to deliver 100% correct concept descriptions of both soybean diseases from one example per disease only (if the positive examples of one disease is used as negative example for the other class). For example, if case 1 is given as positive example of Diaporthe Stem Canker and case 14 is given as positive example of Charcoal Rot, the most general CCGs of the examples would be the descriptions of class 67 and class 66. On the other hand, the most specific CCGs are class 17 and class 66. In this case, the generalization of case 1 is correct, but extremely incomplete.

The type of generalization a system should perform depends on the intended use of the description and the availability of negative examples. In this paper we assume that the user specifies which kind of generalization the system should perform and discuss in section 5 the classification accuracy of both kinds of generalizations in different domains.

If a clustering algorithm is used which delivers non-disjoint classes, there is still the problem that more than one class fulfills the above requirements. If it is acceptable that a learning system sometimes selects the wrong class, e.g., because the system contains a knowledge revision component able to repair faults in the knowledge base, the system might choose one of the competing class descriptions randomly. Otherwise, the selection should be made interactively with the user of the system.

Up to now we assumed that the conceptual clustering result contains a class covering all positive examples of the target concept. This need not always be the case. If the number of descriptions of unclassified objects is too small, if the described objects represent a non-representative subset of objects in the domain, if the data are noisy, or if the object descriptions are not well suited for the intended use of the descriptions, then a system may run into difficulties. Thus, it can not be assumed, that a class can be found which covers all positive and/or excludes all negative examples. In order to overcome this problem, we propose to use an evaluation function which computes a quality measure for the classes built by the clustering algorithm and enables the system to select one promising class description. The system CoLA (see section 4) uses a evaluation function derived from a function to determine the accuracy of concept descriptions and computes a high quality measure for classes which cover a large number of positive examples and exclude a large number of negative examples. If two (or more) classes have the same quality, one is selected randomly.

However, the use of an evaluation functions is of no help if a target concept can not be described by a conjunctive description. This poses a severe problem, because conceptual clustering systems typically generate only conjunctive class descriptions and the CCG approach described so far is only able to output concept descriptions built by the conceptual clustering algorithm. Although it has been argued that conjunctive descriptions are one of the most common descriptive forms used by humans [Michalski/Stepp 83], it is clear that disjunctive concepts can also be relevant. An obvious solution to this problem is to select a set of classes, which cover together all positive and exclude all negative examples, and to connect the corresponding class descriptions disjunctively.

In this section, the general idea of the CCG approach generalization has been described. The method is independent from a specific choice of a representation formalism and is also independent from a particular conceptual-clustering algorithm. The next section describes the details of an implemention of the method in a system called COLA.

4 COLA: The System

COLA is an inductive learning tool in the knowledge acquisition and machine learning system MOBAL [Morik et al. 93] and makes use of MOBAL's knowledge representation environment. This means that COLA uses an extended function-free Horn-clause representation (paraconsistent with negation) [Morik et al. 93, p. 27ff].

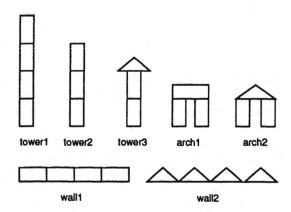

Fig. 2. Various block world objects

The attributes of objects and relations among objects in the domain are described by facts. A set of facts related to one building in a blocks world domain (see figure 2) is shown as an example in table 1.

```
block_world_object(arch2)
part_of(arch2_brick1,arch2)
part_of(arch2_brick2,arch2)
part_of(arch2_wedge,arch2)
brick(arch2_brick1)
brick(arch2_brick2)
wedge(arch2_wedge)
left_of(arch2_brick2,arch2_brick1)
not(touches(arch2_brick2,arch2_brick1))
supports(arch2_brick1,arch2_wedge)
supports(arch2_brick2,arch2_wedge)
on_table(arch2_brick1)
on_table(arch2_brick2)
larger_than(tower1,arch2)
```

Table 1. Facts describing a block world object shown in figure 2

Before the CCG learning algorithm of COLA and the conceptual clustering program used in COLA is described, let us start with an example of a learning result achieved by COLA in the blocks world domain. As background knowledge, facts (like those shown in table 1) about all 'buildings' shown in figure 2 were added to the knowledge base. In addition, the following facts of an instance and a non-instance of the concept is_an_arch were added as positive and negative example to the knowledge base.

```
is_an_arch(arch2)
not(is_an_arch(tower1))
```

The description for the concept is_an_arch induced by COLA from this information is shown below. The description covers both arches and excludes all other buildings shown in figure 2. Note that only one positive and one negative example were necessary to build the description.

```
on_table(X4) & part_of(X1,X2) & ne(X4,X1) &
brick(X4) & supports(X4,X1) & supports(X3,X1) &
ne(X3,X4) & not(touches(X3,X4)) & on_table(X3)
                --->is_an_arch(X2)
```

4.1 KBG-2

COLA uses the conceptual clustering program KBG-2 [Bisson 92b] to perform the conceptual clustering step. The advantage of KBG-2 compared to systems like UNIMEM or COBWEB lies in the fact that KBG's knowledge representation language is based on first-order logic (without negation and function symbols) with some extensions, e.g., for numerical values. Based on this, COLA is able to learn from relational descriptions of objects and to deal with numerical data.

KBG requires as input a case-oriented representation, i.e., a set of object descriptions each in form of a conjunct of ground literals and, optionally, a set of rules as domain theory. The output of KBG consists of a graph of classes and a system of rules enables to predict the instances of the classes.

The conceptual clustering of KBG can be divided into three successive steps. In the first step, the description of the examples are saturated using a domain theory which can be specified optionally. COLA does not need to pass a domain theory to KBG, since (forward-inference) saturation with available rules is performed in MOBAL. In the second learning step, a set of generalization and clustering operators are applied iteratively in a bottom-up fashion guided by similarity measures in order to build a graph of generalizations. The last step aims at building a hierarchical system of rules from the generalization graph. In this step, KBG drops all premises in the class descriptions which are not neccessary to discriminate between the instances of different classes. For a detailed description of the learning step see [Bisson 92a, Bisson 92b]; the rule construction step is described in [Bisson 91].

4.2 Construction of the KBG input

In research on conceptual clustering it is usually assumed that the descriptions of the objects for clustering is given as a conjunction of attribute-value pairs. This assumption makes sense for a lot of applications, because such data is often available from existing databases. The assumption poses difficulties in knowledge based systems using a more powerful representation based on predicate logic, especially if the representation is fact-oriented. If, e.g., a domain is described by a set of facts and rules describing the attributes and relations between several kinds of objects, there is no naturally given input for a clustering algorithm. An obvious answer to this problem is: Collect all facts related to an object to be clustered and make a big conjunction. Unfortunately, this is not a very fruitful idea using a well elaborated knowledge base, because in the worst case it may turn out that each object is related somehow to all other object in the domain. So, each conjunction would contain all facts in the knowledge base.

The system COLA uses currently a language restriction to deal with this problem and to avoid a overly large search space. Using this language restriction COLA is able to learn 1-1 (non)determinate clauses (see [Muggleton/Feng 90]) with conclusions described by one-place predicates. As the restriction is not relevant for the experiments which are described in this paper, we will not go into details of the transformation process here.

4.3 Selection of a class description in COLA

All class descriptions formed by KBG are translated into rules of the MOBAL representation. This translation includes the transformation of the case-oriented representation of the clustering program back into the fact-oriented representation. These resulting rules are applied to all facts stored in knowledge base in order to compute the extension of all classes formed by KBG.

In the next step, COLA searches for disjunctive combinations of the classes constructed by KBG. The maximum number of classes which are combined disjunctively can be specified by the user. As default COLA connects up to 4 class descriptions disjunctively. Only those classes covering at least one positive example and no negative example are taken into account in this step. From these classes COLA creates disjunctive class descriptions and adds them to the class descriptions formed by KBG. In order to avoid a too large search space and to promote the creation of meaningful classes COLA combines only classes whose extensions do not intersect. Furthermore, it is required that the number of covered positive examples is increased by the combination.

In the next step, the following evaluation function is applied to all class descriptions stored in the knowledge base.

ClassQuality(NumCovPos,NumCovNeg,NumPosE,NumNegE) :=
(NumCovPos + NumNegE − NumCovNeg) / (NumPosE + NumNegE)

where:
NumCovPos is the number of covered positive examples
NumCovNeg is the number of covered negative examples
NumPosE is the total number of positive examples
NumNegE is the total number of positive examples

Then, COLA selects the class with the best evaluation. If two or more classes are assigned the same quality, COLA selects the class covering the least number of instances (classified and unclassfied objects) if the system is searching for a most specific generalization. If the system is searching for the most general generalization, the system chooses the class covering more instances. If the same number of instances is covered, COLA selects the class whose class description contains the least number of disjuncts.

The selected class description is used to build the final concept description by renaming the conclusion predicate, e.g., a conclusion like instance_of_class13(X) is changed into is_an_arch(X). This description is added to the knowledge base (while all class descriptions are deleted) and the concept description becomes available to the overall system as well as to following learning processes.

5 Experimental Results

COLA has been applied in several real-world domains in order to test if and under which circumstances the CCG approach improves upon existing methods. In the following we report only about experiments conducted in domains which can also be represented using an attribute-value representation. This has the advantage that the results can also be compared with results achieved by learning programs not able to learn in relational domains (e.g., C4.5 and IBL).[3]

5.1 Test Domains

We present the results of experiments done in two well-known domains which represent extreme cases: the soybean domain with a highly regular data set and the primary tumor domain with a data set known to be relatively incomplete, i.e., not sufficient to induce high quality rules even if a large number of examples is supplied to a learning program. For example, C4.5 and IBL achieve an accuracy between 33%–38% using 275 examples if they are applied to learn 22 class descriptions [Aha et al. 91].

The soybean domain data set [Stepp 84] contains descriptions of 307 diseased soybean plants. Each plant is described by 35 attributes and suffers from one of 19 soybean plant diseases present in the data set. The learning task in this domain was to induce the description of four soybean diseases: Diaphorte Stem Canker (with 10 instances in the data set), Charcoal Rot (10 instances), Rhizoctonia Root Rot (10 instances), and Phytophthora Rot (40 instances). The 18 boolean attributes in the data set and the diagnoses are described in MOBAL using a one-place predicate. All other nominal attributes are represented with a two-place predicate. If the attribute value is missing in the original data set, a corresponding fact is not stored in the knowledge base of MOBAL.

This primary tumor domain data set[4] describes 339 tumor cases. Each case is described by 17 attributes and is assigned to one of 22 possible locations of primary tumor. For our experiments we selected the following four locations covering different numbers of instances as goal concepts: lung (84 instances), head/neck (20 instances), esophasus (9 instances), and breast (24 instances). The data set contains 14 boolean attributes and 3 nominal attributes which are described in the knowledge base using one-place and two-place predicates.

5.2 Learning Programs

In order to be able to make general statements about how the apprach implemented in COLA improves upon existing methods it was necessary to apply also other learning programs to the same learning data. We chose the learning program FOIL-6 [Quinlan 86] as a representative of systems which produce most general generalizations. As a representative of systems performing most specific generalizations we applied a program using the well-known least general generalization rule of Plotkin [71] to the positive examples (without considering the negative examples).

Note that FOIL-6 and the LGG program were no expected to produce learning results which show the best classification accuracy of all applicable learning

---

[3] The learning data stem from the UCI Machine Learning data repository.

[4] The data set was collected by M. Zwitter and M. Soklic at the Ljubljana University Medical Centre in Slovenia.

programs of their class in both test domains and under all test conditions considered in the experiments. Therefore, we were not so much interested in the absolute values of the classification accuracy of their learning results, but the general effect caused by the occurrence of instances of non-goal concepts in the test set.

5.3 Test Method

The learning programs were applied to induce descriptions of the four goal concepts in both domains. In each test run they were supplied with a small number N of randomly selected descriptions of instances of each goal concept including the correct diagnoses. All programs were supplied with the same (MOBAL-) representation of the data. FOIL-6 and COLA used the positive examples of one class as negative examples for the other goal concepts. So, COLA and FOIL-6 used N positive examples and N*3 negative examples to induce a concept description. As additional background, knowledge COLA was supplied with a varying number M of randomly selected descriptions of instances of goal (and sometimes non-goal) concepts in the domain without information about the correct diagnoses.

The accuracy of the learning result was tested using the set of descriptions of instances not given as examples. The concept descriptions induced by a program in one trial were tested one after another. The first concept description was applied to all test instances, the second was applied to all instances not classified as instances of the first concept and so forth. The classification accuracy results discussed below are averaged over 20 to 30 trials.

In a first set of experiments described in the next section we used the learning programs to induce descriptions of the goal concepts which were then applied to classify the remaining unseen instances of the goal concepts. In another set of experiments (section 5.5) we evaluated the classification accuracy of the induced concept descriptions applied to the descriptions of instances of non-goal concepts as well as the remaining unseen instances of the goal concepts.

5.4 Test Data Set Describes Instances of Goal Concepts

The kind of experiments described in this section is similar to the experiments described in other papers in the field of machine learning except that the number of examples supplied to the learning programs is much smaller than usually.

As described above, COLA can be parameterized to output the most general CCG or the most specific CCG. We let COLA build both kinds of generalizations from different numbers N (between 1 and 10) of examples per goal concept and varied the number of descriptions of unclassified instances (of the goal concepts) which were supplied as background knowledge. The goal concepts in the soybean data set cover altogether 70 instances. So, if M is set to 70, all descriptions of instances of all goal concepts are used in the conceptual clustering step. If M is set to 0, the conceptual clustering graph is built only from the N*4 example descriptions. The goal concepts in the primary tumor data set cover altogether

137 instances. Therefore, the maximum number of unclassified descriptions in the backgroud knowledge was 137.

The following hypotheses were tested:

H1 The classification accuracy of the learning result increases with the number of examples N per goal concept. At some point, the number of examples is sufficient to select the best class descriptions in the conceptual clustering graph. If this point is reached, the classification accuracy can not be improved any more using more examples.

H2 The classification accuracy of the learning result increases with the number of descriptions of unclassified instances.

H3 The classification accuracy of a most general CCG is better than the accuracy of the most specific CCG. The most specific CCG covers only instances very similar to the examples. Therefore, a large number of instances will not be predicted as instance of one of the goal concepts. As all cases described in the test data sets are instances of the goal concept, a most specific CCG may be correct, but tends to be very incomplete. The most general CCG may be correct and tends to be complete.

H4 At least in the highly regular soybean data set, COLA will output concept descriptions with a better classification accuracy than FOIL-6 and the LGG program.

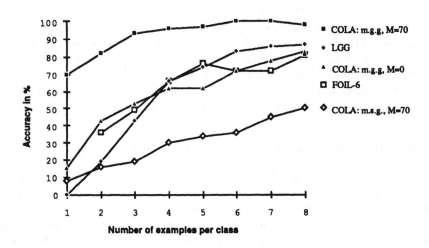

Fig. 3. Test Results in the Soybean domain without Instances of Non-Goal Concepts

The experimental results confirming these hypotheses to a large degree are shown in figure 3 and figure 4. Hypothesis H1 is only partially confirmed by the learning curves, because only two curves clearly show that the accuracy remains

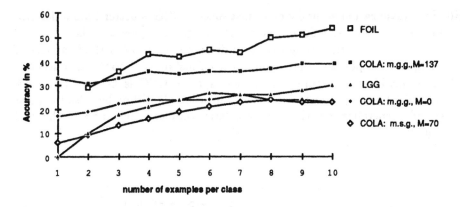

Fig. 4. Test Results in the Primary Tumor Domain without Instances of Non-Goal Concepts

constant after a certain number of examples per class. Hypothesis H2 seems to be correct, but other experiments have shown that the classification accuracy of most specific CCGs can become better if less descriptions of unclassified instances are supplied as background knowledge. This can be explained by the fact that a larger number of descriptions of unclassified instances results in a conceptual clustering graph with more intermediate classes. Although this graph will contain a class covering all instances of a concept, the probability that COLA selects a more specific class increases. The hypotheses H3 and H4 are confirmed by the test results in both domains. As expected, COLA performs better in the soybean data set, but in the primary tumor data set FOIL-6 is the winner.

The conclusion which can be drawn from this first set of experiments is that existing methods should be preferred over the method described in this paper if it is known that the learning result will be applied only to classify instances of goal concepts, because usually it is unknown that a domain is highly regular (as is the case with the soybean domain, where COLA performs much better).

5.5 Test Data Set Describes Instances of Goal and Non-Goal Concepts

In the second set of experiments the concept descriptions built by the learning programs were applied to all descriptions of instances of the goal concepts not supplied as examples and all descriptions of instances of non-goal concepts.

Following hypotheses were tested:

H5 The classification accuracy of a most specific CCG is better than the accuracy of the most general CCG, because there are a large number of instances of non-goal concepts and a most general CCG can cover also instances of non-goal concepts.

H6 The classification accuracy of a most specific CCG is better than a description built by a most general generalization algorithm , because the latter will contain only descriptors necessary to discriminate between the instances of the goal concepts and, thus, tends to cover instances of non-goal concepts.

H7 The classification accuracy of a most specific CCG is better than a description built by a most specific generalization algorithm, because the most specific generalization will exclude a large number of instances of the goal concepts.

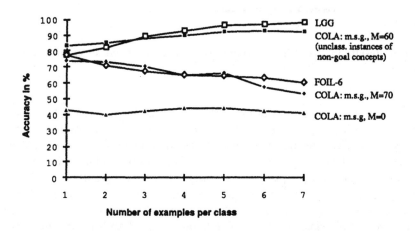

Fig. 5. Test Results in the Soybean domain with Instances of Non-Goal Concepts

Also these hypotheses were confirmed to a large degree (figure 5 and figure 6). Hypothesis 5 is confirmed by experiments in both domains. The classification accuracy of the descriptions built by the most specific CCG in the primary tumor domain (figure 6) is about 30% better than the classification accuracy of the descriptions produced by the most general CCG. A similar result could be observed in the soybean domain. In addition, the experiments have shown that the classification accuracy tends to be better, if the conceptual clustering algorithm is supplied not only with descriptions of (unclassified) instances of goal concepts but also with descriptions of instances of non-goal concepts. In addition, the classification accuracy of COLA decreases with an increasing number of examples, if only descriptions of non-goal concepts are available in the conceptual clustering step. This can be explained by the fact that KBG drops premises not necessary to discriminate between the instances of different classes.

As expected, the classification accuracy of descriptions produced by COLA is significantly better than the results produced by FOIL-6. In contrast to the experiments reported in the last section, the accuracy of the concept description built by FOIL-6 becomes not better with an increasing number of examples.

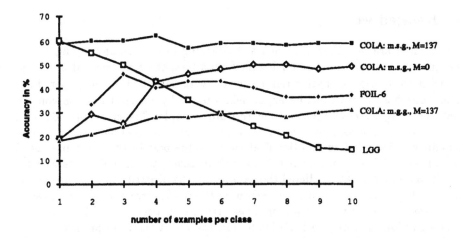

Fig. 6. Test Results in the Primary Tumor Domain with Instances of Non-Goal Concepts

Thus, hypothesis H6 is confirmed by the experiments.

The next hypothesis H7 was confirmed by the experiments in the primary tumor domain, but in the soybean domain, the LGG program performed better than COLA. As the most specific generalization excludes all instances of non-goal concepts the classification accuracy starts with 78% (1 example), all instances (of goal and non-goal concepts) were predicted as non-instances of the goal-concept. In addition, the LLG program is able to take advantage of the regularity in this domain. As the LGG program only constructs conjunctive concept description, the number of correct predicted instances increases with an increasing number of examples (without misclassification of non-goal concept instances). Note that with a decreasing number of descriptions of instances of non-goal concepts in test data set, the classification accuracy of the LLG program will decrease (while the accuracy of the FOIL-6 results will become better). In the primary tumor domain, the classification accuracy of descriptions built by the LGG program decreased with an increasing number of examples.

The conclusion which can be drawn from the second set of experiments is that the CCG approach should be prefered over existing methods, if it is known that the learning result will also be applied to descriptions of non-goal concepts. It is not reasonable to prefer a program which produces most specific generalizations, because usually it is not known that a domain is highly regular. Furthermore, it might be the case that a more sophisticated most specific generalization algorithm (e.g., able to built disjunctive concept descriptions) delivers concept description with a lower classification accuracy.

6 Related work

While there are no other approaches to learning-from-examples trying to use the information contained in unclassified examples, there are several other approaches to concept formation related to the work described in this paper. First of all, one has to mention the experiments made by Fisher using his conceptual clustering system COBWEB to learn from examples [Fisher 87, pp. 161ff]. In contrast to the approach described above, the information about concept membership was included as additional attribute-value pair in the cases presented to COBWEB. After incorporating every fifth instance, the remaining cases were classified and COBWEB predicted the value of the "goal attribute". In one experiment in the soybean domain, it turned out that a 100% correct diagnosis of cases, which were not used in the training phase, requires between 7 and 25 examples. Although COLA performs a little bit better, the result is still impressive.

Such a use of COBWEB is closely related to instance-based learning (IBL) [Aha et al. 91], although the underlying representation of concepts is very different. In both systems, prediction is performed by using the concept membership information of the most similar classified instance. Therefore, IBL and COBWEB can be expected to show a similar classification accuracy as FOIL-6.

An alternative to the use of descriptions of unclassified objects is described by Mooney [93]. His system IOU uses an overly general domain theory as additional background knowledge. The system requires that all features referenced in the domain theory are irrelevant for the induction of additional premises to specialize an over-general concept. This enables IOU to learn more accurate concepts from fewer examples than previous purely inductive systems. Although the assumption made by IOU is very strong, it seems promising to combine the use of information about unclassified objects with the use of an incomplete domain theory in order to learn concepts from small sets of examples.

7 Final remarks

In this paper, a new approach for learning concepts has been described which tries to take advantage of the information contained in unclassified examples. It has been shown that the classification accuracy of concept description can significantly be improved by using this information as additional background knowledge.

It should be emphasize that classification accuracy should not be the only criterion to compare generalization methods. The concept descriptions produced by the CCG approach are more specific than descriptions produced by systems using a most general generalization algorithm, because such systems deliver concept descriptions using only descriptors (e.g., predicates or attributes) necessary to discriminate between the instances of the goal concepts. Therefore, the descriptions produced by a system based on the CCG approach may be more comprehensible.

The computational complexity of the CCG approach is mainly determined by the computational complexity of the conceptual clustering step. Although

KBG searches only for heuristic approximations of most specific generalizations, it was impossible to cluster the whole soybean or primary tumor data set (on a SUN Sparc-10). Therefore, it is necessary to improve our method by a clever strategy for filtering the data passed to the conceptual clustering system.

Experiments with relational data sets and different hypotheses language restrictions are in progress and will be described in another paper.

Acknowledgements: I would like to thank Jörg-Uwe Kietz, Katharina Morik, Edgar Sommer, and Stefan Wrobel for interesting discussions, comments, and suggestions related to the work described in this paper. I would also like to thank Gilles Bisson for his support regarding the use of KBG. Many thanks also to the anonymous referees of this paper (and previous versions of this paper) for their helpful criticism and suggestions. Parts of this work are supported by the European Community ESPRIT program under contract number 6020 "Inductive Logic Programming".

References

[Aha et al. 91] David W. Aha, Dennis Kibler, and Marc K. Albert. Instance-Based Learning Algorithms. *Machine Learning*, 6:37–66, 1991.

[Bisson 91] Gilles Bisson. Learning of rule systems in a first order representation. Rapport de Recherche 628, LRI, University de Paris-Sud, 1991.

[Bisson 92a] Gilles Bisson. Conceptual Clustering in a First Order Logic Representation. In *ECAI92P*, pp. 558–462, 1992.

[Bisson 92b] Gilles Bisson. Learning in FOL with a Similarity Measure. In *AAAI92*, pp. 82–87. AAAI Press, 1992.

[Carey 85] Susan Carey. *Conceptual change in childhood.* MIT Press, Boston, 1985.

[Dieterich/Michalski 81] Thomas G. Dietterich and Ryszard S. Michalski. Inductive Learning of Structural Descriptions. *Artificial Intelligence*, 16:257–294, 1981.

[Fisher 87] Douglas H. Fisher. Knowledge Acquisition Via Incremental Conceptual Clustering. *Machine Learning*, 2:139–172, 1987.

[Kietz/Wrobel 92] Jörg-Uwe Kietz and Stefan Wrobel. Controlling the Complexity of Learning through Syntactic and Task-Oriented Models. In S. Muggleton (ed.), *Inductive Logic Programming*, pp. 107–126. Academic Press, 1992.

[Lebowitz 87] Michael Lebowitz. Experiments with Incremental Concept Formation: UNIMEM. *Machine Learning*, 2:103–138, 1987.

[Michalski 73] R. S. Michalski. Discovering Classification Rules by the Variable-Valued Logic System VL1. In *3rd IJCAI-73, Stanford*, 1973.

[Michalski/Stepp 83] Ryszard S. Michalski and Robert E. Stepp. Learning from Observation: Conceptual Clustering. In R.S. Michalski, J.G. Carbonell, and T.M. Mitchell (eds.), *Machine Learning*, volume I, pp. 331–363. Tioga, Palo Alto, CA, 1983.

[Mooney 93] Raymond J. Mooney. Induction Over the Unexplained: Using Overly-General Domain Theories to Aid Concept Learning. *Machine Learning*, 10:79–110, 1993.

[Morik et al. 93] Katharina Morik, Stefan Wrobel, Jörg-Uwe Kietz, and Werner Emde. *Knowledge Acquisition and Machine Learning: Theory Methods and Applications.* Academic Press, London, New York, 1993. To appear.

[Muggleton/Feng 90] Stephen Muggleton and Cao Feng. Efficient induction of logic programs. In *Proceedings of the 1st Conference on Algorithmic Learning Theory*, 1990.

[Plotkin 71] Gordon D. Plotkin. A further note on inductive generalization. In B. Meltzer and D. Michie (eds.), *Machine Intelligence*, volume 6, chapter 8, pp. 101–124. American Elsevier, 1971.

[Quinlan 83] J. Ross Quinlan. Learning Efficient Classification Procedures and Their Application to Chess End Games. In R.S. Michalski, J.G. Carbonell, and T.M. Mitchell (eds.), *Machine Learning - An Artificial Intelligence Approach*, pp. 463–482. Tioga, Palo Alto, CA, 1983.

[Quinlan 86] J. R. Quinlan. Induction of Decision Trees. *Machine Learning*, 1(1):81–106, 1986.

[Stepp 84] R.E. Stepp. *Conjunctive Conceptual Clustering: A Methology and Experimantation*. Report uiucdcs-r-84-1189, Univ. of Illinois, Urbana, 1984.

[Vrain 90] Christel Vrain. OGUST: A system that learns using domain properties expressed as theorems. In Yves Kodratoff and Ryszard Michalski (eds.), *Machine Learning - An Artificial Intelligence Approach*, volume III, chapter 13, pp. 360–382. Morgan Kaufmann, 1990.

[Winston 75] P. H. Winston. Learning structural descriptions from examples. In P.H. Winston (ed.), *The Psychology of Computer Vision*. McGraw-Hill, 1975.

Fossil: A Robust Relational Learner

Johannes Fürnkranz

juffi@ai.univie.ac.at
Austrian Research Institute for Artificial Intelligence
Schottengasse 3
A-1010 Vienna
Austria

Abstract. The research reported in this paper describes Fossil, an ILP system that uses a search heuristic based on statistical correlation. This algorithm implements a new method for learning useful concepts in the presence of noise. In contrast to Foil's stopping criterion, which allows theories to grow in complexity as the size of the training sets increases, we propose a new stopping criterion that is independent of the number of training examples. Instead, Fossil's stopping criterion depends on a search heuristic that estimates the utility of literals on a uniform scale. In addition we outline how this feature can be used for *top-down pruning* and present some preliminary results.

1 Introduction

Being able to deal with noisy domains is a must for learning algorithms that are meant to learn concepts from real-world data. Significant effort has been made into investigating the effect of noisy data on attribute-value learning algorithms (see e.g. [22, 3, 4, 17]). Not surprisingly, noise handling methods have also entered the rapidly growing field of *Inductive Logic Programming* [15]. Linus [16] relies directly on the noise handling abilities of decision tree learning algorithms, others, like mFoil [9] and REP [5], have adapted well-known methods from attribute-value learning for the ILP framework.

This paper presents Fossil, a Foil-like algorithm [20] that uses a search heuristic based on statistical correlation (Sect. 2). One of the nice features of this heuristic is that it gives a reliable measure of the heuristic value of a literal on an absolute and uniform scale. We show empirically that this feature can advantageously be used to deal with noise by cutting off all literals that have a heuristic value below a certain threshold (Sect. 3). We also present empirical evidence that this threshold is robust, in the sense that a good value for it is independent of the number of training examples and of the amount of noise in the data (Sect. 4). After comparing Fossil to Foil and mFoil we introduce several ideas for adapting pruning methods from decision tree learning in a top-down fashion along with some preliminary results (Sects. 5 and 6) and finally draw some conclusions (Sect. 7).

2 FOSSIL's Search Heuristic

2.1 The Correlation Heuristic

FOSSIL's evaluation function is based on the concept of statistical *correlation*. The *correlation coefficient* of two random variables X and Y is defined as

$$corr(X, Y) = \frac{E((X - \mu_X)(Y - \mu_Y))}{\sigma_X \times \sigma_Y} = \frac{E(X \times Y) - \mu_X \times \mu_Y}{\sigma_X \times \sigma_Y} \tag{1}$$

where μ and σ are *expected value* and *standard deviation*, respectively, of the random variables X and Y.

This *correlation coefficient* measures the degree of dependence of two series of points on a scale from -1 (*negative correlation*) to $+1$ (*positive correlation*). In the following description of its adaptation as a search heuristic for the Inductive Logic Programming algorithm FOIL, we will follow the notational conventions used in [14].

Suppose FOSSIL has learned a partial clause c. Let the set of tuples T_c of size $n(c)$, containing $n^\oplus(c)$ positive and $n^\ominus(c)$ negative instances, be the current training set. We arbitrarily assign the numeric values $+1$ and -1 for the logical values *true* and *false*. The variable X in (1) now represents the truth values $V(c)$ of the tuples in T_c. The variable Y denotes the the truth values $V(L)$ of a candidate literal L. A literal L is said to be *true*, whenever there exists a tuple in T_c that satisfies L; if L introduces new variables, they must have at least one instantiation that makes the literal true. Note that $V(c)$ and $V(L)$ naturally contain the same number of values.

The expected values in (1) will be estimated by the mean values of $V(c)$ and $V(L)$ respectively. Standard deviation will be approximated by the empirical variance. Thus we get

$$\mu_c = \frac{n^\oplus(c) - n^\ominus(c)}{n}, \quad \sigma_c^2 = E(V(c)^2) - E(V(c))^2 = 1 - \mu_c^2,$$

$$\mu_L = \frac{n^\oplus(L) - n^\ominus(L)}{n}, \qquad\qquad \sigma_L^2 = 1 - \mu_L^2 \tag{2}$$

$$\text{with } n = n(L) = n(c) = n^\oplus(c) + n^\ominus(c),$$

The last remaining term to be computed is $E(V(c) \times V(L))$. If both the truth values $v(c)$ and $v(L)$ of a tuple and the literal under scrutiny have the same sign, then $v(c) \times v(L) = 1$. Conversely, if one is positive and the other negative we have $v(c) \times v(L) = -1$. If we denote the number of positive tuples yielding a negative value for the literal L with $n^\oplus(c)^\ominus$ (and analogously define $n^\oplus(c)^\oplus$, $n^\ominus(c)^\oplus$ and $n^\ominus(c)^\ominus$), we get

$$E(V(c) \times V(L)) = \frac{n^\oplus(c)^\oplus + n^\ominus(c)^\ominus - n^\ominus(c)^\oplus - n^\oplus(c)^\ominus}{n} \tag{3}$$

The partial results of above now only need to be substituted into the formula for the correlation coefficient (1). As μ_c and σ_c only need to be evaluated once for each tuple set T_c, evaluation of this formula is not as complicated as it may seem at first sight. Also notice that with this approach no separate calculation for negated literals has to be performed, as a high negative correlation indicates a high dependence on the negated literal.

The literal L_c with the highest absolute value of the correlation coefficient (or $\neg L_c$ if the sign of the coefficient is negative) is then chosen to extend c to form a new clause c'. This is based on the assumption that its high correlation with the current training set T_c indicates some form of causal relationship between the target concept and L_c. The set T_c is then extended to a new set of tuples $T_{c'}$ (which in general will have a different size) and the process continues as described in [20].

2.2 Interesting Features of the Correlation Heuristic

The information gain heuristic used in C4.5 [22] and FOIL has been extensively compared to other search heuristics in decision tree generation [18, 6] and Inductive Logic Programming [14]. The general consensus seems to be that it is hard to improve on this heuristic in terms of predictive accuracy in learning from noise-free data. While our results confirm this, we nevertheless claim that FOSSIL's evaluation function has some important features that distinguish it from the weighted information gain heuristic used in FOIL.

- In FOIL, the heuristic value of each literal and of its negation have to be calculated separately. FOSSIL does this in one calculation, as positive correlation indicates a causal relationship between the tuple set and the literal under scrutiny, while negative correlation indicates a causal relationship between the tuple set and the negation of the literal.
- The correlation function is symmetric and gives equal consideration to covering many positive and excluding many negative examples.
- The correlation between a tuple set and a literal that has at least one true grounding for each tuple is undefined, because μ_L will be 1 and thus σ_L will be 0 (see (2)). Most of these literals are irrelevant, as they do not exclude any negative instances. However, some of them might be very useful, if they introduce new variables. The current version of FOSSIL ignores this problem by treating undefined cases as having correlation 0 and thus has severe problems in learning programs that need *determinate literals* [21]. Setting the heuristic value for the undefined cases to a value $D > 0$ might be a simple solution for *some* of the pathological cases, because in that case FOSSIL would add literals with undefined correlation values whenever no other literal has a correlation $> D$. Irrelevant literals could be removed later in a post-processing phase.[1]

---

[1] Not all of the problematic cases can be taken care of in this way: Quinlan's *determinate literals* are literals that have *exactly* one extension of each positive tuple and *no more* than one extension of each negative tuple. The undefined cases for the correlation value on the other hand are literals that have *at least* one extension for both positive and negative tuples.

- FOSSIL's correlation coefficient — after taking absolute values and choosing the appropriate, positive or negative, literal — allows to compare the candidate literals on a uniform scale from 0 to 1.

How this last property of the correlation heuristic can be used for a simple, but powerful criterion to distinguish noise from useful information will be described in Sect. 3.

3   The Cutoff Stopping Criterion

The value of FOIL's evaluation function is dependent on the size of the tuple set. The same literal will have different information gain values in different example set sizes of the same concept, although its relative merit compared to its competitors will be about the same. FOSSIL on the other hand can judge the relevance of a literal on an absolute basis. This allows the user to require the literals that are considered for clause construction to have a certain minimum correlation value — the *cutoff*.

This can be used as a simple, but robust criterion for filtering out noise, as it can be expected that tuples originating from noise in the data will only have a low correlation with predicates in the background knowledge. If no literal with a correlation above the *cutoff* can be added to the current clause, this clause is considered to be complete. Similarly, if no literal can be found that can start a new clause, the concept definition is considered to be complete. Note that it may happen that FOSSIL "refuses" to learn anything in cases where no predicate in the background knowledge has a significant correlation with the training data.[2]

If a clause that cannot be further extended still covers negative examples, FOSSIL follows a simple strategy: If the clause covers more positive than negative examples, it is retained, and the examples that are covered will be removed from the tuple set. If the clause covers more negative than positive examples, it will not be added to the concept description, and only the positive examples that would have been covered by this clause will be removed. This is in contrast to FOIL, where learning stops entirely as soon as a clause is found that covers less than 80% positive examples. In that case FOIL leaves the remaining positive examples uncovered, while FOSSIL further tries to find clauses that cover some of them. The fact that the learned clauses always have to cover more positive than negative examples guarantees that the algorithm used in FOSSIL can never produce a bigger error on the training set than the method used in FOIL. It was mainly this improvement that lead to a relatively good performance of FOSSIL at tests on the mesh data (32% as opposed to 21% for mFOIL [9])

---

[2] This has actually happened several times, and is evident in the result with 50% Noise (i.e. random classification) in Table 1, where FOSSIL did not learn a single clause in any of the 10 training sets.

4 Experimental Evaluation

4.1 Setup of the Experiments

For the experiments in this paper we have used the domain of recognizing illegal chess positions in the KRK end game [19]. The goal is to learn the concept of an illegal white-to-move position with only white king, white rook and black king on the board. The goal predicate is `illegal(A,B,C,D,E,F)` where the parameters correspond to the row and file coordinates of the pieces in the above order. Background knowledge consists of the predicates X < Y, X = Y and `adjacent(X,Y)`[3]. Recursion was not allowed for efficiency reasons.

Class noise in the training instances was generated according to the *Classification Noise Process* described in [2]. In this model a noise level of η means that the sign of each example is reversed with a probability of η.[4] Noise was added incrementally, i.e. instances which had a reversed sign at a noise level η_1 also had a reversed sign at a noise level $\eta_2 > \eta_1$. Similarly, training sets with n examples were fully contained in training sets with $m > n$ examples.

In all experiments the induced rules were tested against sets of 5000 randomly chosen instances. It also proved useful to record the number of clauses in the induced concept and the average number of literals per clause to measure the complexity of the learned concept description.

4.2 Finding a Good Cutoff Value

The first series of experiments aimed at determining an appropriate value for this parameter for further experimentation. 10 training sets of 100 instances each were used at three different noise levels (5%, 10% and 20%). 6 different settings for the cutoff parameter C were used. The results averaged over the 10 runs are reported in Fig. 1.

The following observations can be made from these graphs:

- A good setting for C in this domain seems to be somewhere around 0.3 for all three noise levels. Coincidentially, the learned concepts are of about equal complexity at this point.
- The curve for the predictive accuracy is U-shaped, similar to some results from Decision Tree learning (see e.g. [4]).
- There is a transition from overfitting the noise to over-generalizing the rules. A low setting of C has a tendency to fit the noise, because most of the literals

---

[3] Because of a misunderstanding our definition of adjacent actually was adjacent_or_equal. However, changing this definition will not change the qualitative results reported in this paper.

[4] Note that this differs from some of the results in the ILP literature, where a noise level of η means that, with a probability of η, the sign of each example is randomly chosen. Thus a noise level of η in our experiments is roughly equivalent to a noise level of 2η in the results reported e.g. in [11, 10].

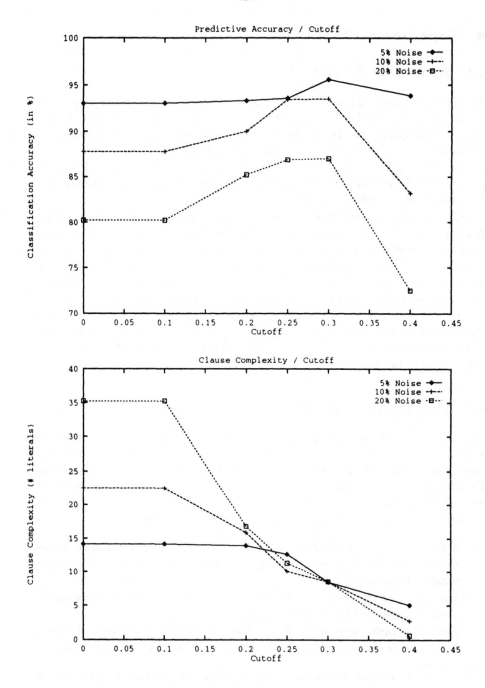

Fig. 1. Experiments with different settings for the *Cutoff*

will have a correlation above the threshold.[5] Conversely, a too optimistic setting of C results in over-generalization as too few literals have a correlation above the threshold.

- The complexity of the learned concepts monotonically decreases with an increase of the cutoff parameter.
- The influence of a bad choice of the cutoff is more significant in data containing a larger amount of noise.

4.3 Comparison with FOIL

We performed two experiments to compare FOSSIL's performance to the performance of FOIL. In the first series we compared the behavior of the two systems with 10 training sets of 100 instances each at different noise levels, which has been the standard procedure for evaluating many ILP systems [20, 11, 10, 19]. In the second experiment we evaluated both programs at a constant noise level of 10%, but with an increasing number of training instances.

According to the results of the previous experiments we set $C = 0.3$ and never changed this setting.

Comparison at Different Noise Levels. In this experiment we compared FOIL4 to FOSSIL at different noise levels. In order to have a fair comparison to FOSSIL where backtracking is not implemented, we used two versions of FOIL, regular FOIL4 and a new version, FOIL-NBT, where FOIL4's extensive mechanisms of backing up and regrowing clauses [23] were not allowed. Surprisingly this version performed better than the original FOIL4 in noisy data as can be seen from the results of Table 1.

An analysis of the result shows that FOSSIL performs best in most of the tests, but no significant difference between FOIL-NBT and FOSSIL can be found. A comparison of the average number of induced clauses and of the average literals per clause shows evidence that FOSSIL over-generalized at the high noise levels. A lower value of the cutoff parameter may result in better performance in the case of 30% noise, although it is unlikely that a useful theory would be learned. An interesting detail is that FOSSIL did not learn anything at a noise level of 50%, i.e. with totally random data. Thus the cutoff mechanism seems to be a primitive, but efficient means of distinguishing noise from useful information.

On the other hand, FOIL4 seems to perform worse than both FOIL-NBT and FOSSIL. The complexity of the concepts learned by FOIL4 increases with the amount of noise in the data, which is clear evidence for over-fitting noise in the data. The next experiment was designed to confirm this hypothesis.

Comparison at Different Training Set Sizes. In this series of experiments we compared FOIL-NBT to FOSSIL at different training set sizes, each having

---

[5] A setting of $C = 0$ results in learning a 100% correct rule for explaining the training set.

Table 1. A Comparison of FOIL and FOSSIL on different levels of noise

Different		Noise							
Noise Levels		0%	5%	10%	15%	20%	25%	30%	50%
FOIL4	Accuracy	98.32	95.26	92.12	90.26	85.21	79.83	71.53	53.00
	# Clauses	3.5	4.2	5.4	5.9	5.7	6.6	8.0	7.9
	Lits/Clause	1.64	1.98	2.41	2.47	2.66	2.98	3.03	3.45
FOIL-NBT	Accuracy	98.11	95.00	92.98	91.76	87.12	79.42	76.32	55.33
	# Clauses	3.5	4.1	4.2	4.2	4.5	5.4	5.0	5.2
	Lits/Clause	1.64	1.98	2.34	2.48	2.67	2.80	2.79	3.08
FOSSIL (0.3)	Accuracy	98.54	95.57	93.52	92.83	87.00	81.63	70.59	(67.07)
	# Clauses	3.7	4.3	3.8	4.2	3.2	2.7	0.7	0.0
	Lits/Clause	1.62	2.02	2.24	2.29	2.67	2.69	0.85	0.0

10% noise. We decided to use FOIL-NBT instead of FOIL4, because it performed better in the previous series of tests. Besides, the version without backing up and regrowing clauses naturally runs faster, which proved to be important. However, we have done a few sample runs with FOIL4 to confirm that its results would not be qualitatively different from those of FOIL-NBT.

Again, we used 10 different training sets and averaged the results. The outcomes of these experiments are summarized in Fig. 2 (the Minimal Error curves will be explained in Sect. 5).

The most important finding is that FOIL clearly fits the noise, while FOSSIL avoids this and learns a slightly over-general, but much more useful theory instead. FOIL's fitting the noise has several disadvantages:

Accuracy: The more examples there are in the noisy training set, the more specialized are the various clauses in the concept description, which decreases the predictive ability of each clause learned by FOIL.[6]

Efficiency: FOIL grows an increasing number of clauses with an increasing number of literals. Also, several of the literals chosen to fit the noise introduce new variables, which leads to an explosion of the size of the tuple set. In fact, the C implementation of FOIL could complete none of the ten experiments with 2000 training examples within 500 minutes of CPU time, while the PROLOG implementation of FOSSIL only needed about 15 minutes of CPU time for each of the training sets, running on the same machine.

Understandability: It is a widely acknowledged principle that the more complex a concept definition is, the less understandable it will be, in particular when both definitions describe the same data set. While the descriptions induced by FOIL for the large training sets were totally incomprehensible

---

[6] This Problem is known as the *Small Disjuncts Problem* [13] and has recently been addressed with an relational learning algorithm using probabilistic concept descriptions [1].

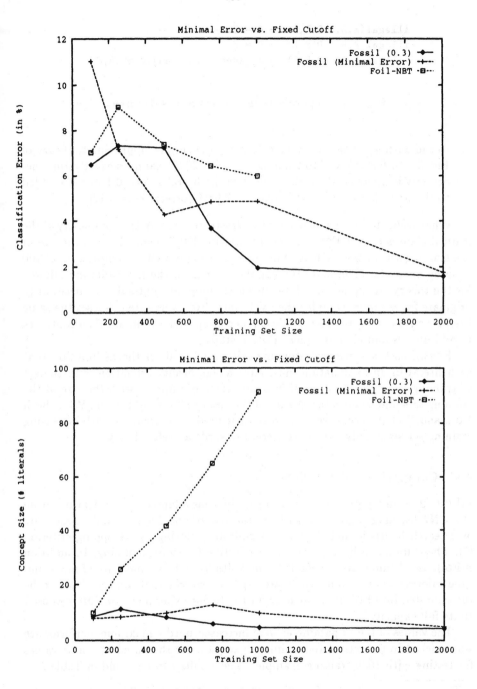

Fig. 2. A Comparison of FOIL and FOSSIL with different training set sizes

```
illegal(A,B,C,D,E,F) :- C = E.
illegal(A,B,C,D,E,F) :- D = F.
illegal(A,B,C,D,E,F) :- adjacent(A,E), adjacent(B,F).
```

Fig. 3. An approximate theory that is 98.45% correct

to the author, FOSSIL converged towards the simple, approximate theory of Fig. 3.[7] In fact, in 8 of 10 training sets with 2000 examples exactly this theory was learned, while in the other two the literal A \== C had been added to the first clause, which still gives a 97.98% correct theory [12].

What seems to be responsible for the drastic increase in the complexity of the learned clauses is that FOIL's stopping criterion [20] is dependent on the size of the training set. In the KRK domain it performs very well on sample sizes of 100 training examples. The more this number increases, the more bits are allowed for the theory to explain the data. However, more examples do not necessarily originate from a more complex theory. In fact, FOIL very often chooses the same literals as FOSSIL for the first clauses of its concept definition, but then continues to add literals and clauses, where FOSSIL stops.

FOSSIL uses a statistical stopping criterion based on the assumption that each literal in an explanation must have a significant correlation with the set of training examples. Statistical measures usually improve with the size of the training sets and so does the quality of the rules induced by FOSSIL. While both FOIL and FOSSIL successively improve their predictive accuracy with increasing training set sizes, only FOSSIL converges towards a useful theory.

4.4 Comparison with mFOIL

mFOIL [9] is an algorithm based on FOIL that has adapted several features from the CN2 learning algorithm, such as the use of the Laplace and m-estimate as a search heuristic and the use of significance testing as a stopping criterion [7]. These methods have proved very effective for noise handling. In addition mFOIL uses beam search (default beam width 5) and can make use of mode and type information to reduce the search space, features that are scheduled to be incorporated into FOSSIL in the near future. In our experiments mFOIL was used to its full capacity.

The values of the m parameter were increased until a maximum performance was reached in the sets of 100 training examples. We then used the same values for testing with 1000 training examples. The results can be found in Table 2.

---

[7] This theory correctly classifies all but 4060 of the 262,144 possible domain examples (98.45%). 2940 positions (1.12%)with WK and WR on the same squares and 1120 positions (0.43%) where the WK is between WR and BK on the same row or file are erroneously classified [12]. (Remember that we have defined adjacent to mean adjacent_or_equal).

Table 2. Comparison with mFOIL

| Training Set Size | mFOIL | | | | | FOSSIL |
	$m = 0.01$	Laplace	$m = 8$	$m = 16$	$m = 32$	$C = 0.3$
100	89.77	89.84	93.03	93.06	91.46	93.52
1000	91.54	92.51	95.70	97.10	98.48	98.05

FOSSIL seems to be at least equal at an example size of 100, unless a considerably better theory has been missed somewhere around $m = 16$. However, mFOIL's strengths come to bear at an example size of 1000. The results reported here are probably not yet the peak of its performance, as with $m = 32$ mFOIL has learned some theories with a predictive accuracy of above 99% which FOSSIL has not achieved so far.[8] Increasing the m further might well improve the bad theories learned, while keeping the good ones.

However, one of the points to make here is that a good value of the m parameter is not only dependent on the amount of noise (as can be seen from the results given in [9] and [10]), but also on the size of the example set. FOSSIL's cutoff parameter on the other hand seems to do reasonably well at different levels of noise and at different training set sizes.

In addition, Sect. 5 illustrates some preliminary results for finding good theories without having to specify a good value for the cutoff parameter.

5 Generating a Series of Concept Descriptions

As we have seen in Sect. 4.4, mFOIL and FOSSIL have many similarities. However, a big disadvantage of mFOIL seems to be that it is not so easy to find the right m. The easiest approach is to try the standard settings used in the literature and choose the m that results in the best theory according to an independent test set. However, with this approach one has no guarantee that one does not miss a better theory with a different m. The results given in [9] also indicate that the choice of a good m depends on the amount of noise in the data, while our experiments in Sect. 4.4 also suggest a dependence on the size of the training set. FOSSIL, on the other hand, achieved reasonable results with one setting of the cutoff parameter on different noise levels as well as different training set sizes.

Another advantage of the cutoff stopping criterion is — besides its efficiency and stability — its close relation to the search heuristic. While FOIL (*encoding length restriction*) and mFOIL (*significance test*) have to do separate calculations to determine when to stop learning, FOSSIL needs to do a mere comparison between the heuristic value of the best candidate literal and the cutoff value. This allows the design of a very simple algorithm that can generate all theories

---

[8] We hope that introducing beam search and using mode and type information will narrow the gap.

that could be learned by FOSSIL with any setting of the Cutoff parameter (see Fig. 4).

$$C = 1.0$$
$$Concepts = \emptyset$$
while $(C > 0.0)$ do
$\quad\quad NewConcept = Fossil(Examples)$
$\quad\quad C = MaxPrunedCorr(NewConcept)$
$\quad\quad Concepts = Concepts \cup NewConcept$
return($Concepts$)

Fig. 4. Algorithm to generate all Concept Definitions learnable by FOSSIL

The basic idea behind the algorithm given in Fig. 4 is the following: Assume that you are trying to learn a theory with a Cutoff of 1.0. Unless there is one literal in the background knowledge that perfectly discriminates between positive and negative examples, we will not find a literal with a correlation of 1.0 and thus learn an empty theory. During this run we can remember the literal with the maximum correlation. If we now set the new cutoff to exactly this maximum value, at least one literal (the one that produced this maximum correlation) will be added to the theory.[9] At this new setting of the cutoff parameter we learn a new theory and again remember the maximum correlation of the literals that have been cut off. Obviously, for all values between the old cutoff and this maximum value, the same theory would have been learned and we can choose this value as the cutoff for the next run. It can also be expected that the new theory will be less general than the previous one. This process is repeated until we have the most specific theory (with $MaxPrunedCorr = 0.0$). An illustration for this process can be found in Fig. 5, where a complete series of theories has been generated from 1000 noise-free examples of the KRK domain.

We have used this simple algorithm in the following way: The training sets were randomly split into two sets of equal size, one for training, one for testing. From the training set a series of theories was learned (all theories down to a cutoff of 0.15[10]) and from these the one with the best predictive accuracy on the test set was selected as the final theory. The results — labeled with *Minimal Error* — can be found in Fig. 2.

It can be seen that this naive and simple method performs better than FOIL,

---

[9] However, as our experience with FOSSIL shows, this is very often not the only change. Usually several more literals that have a correlation value higher than the new cutoff will be added. This is because literals that have a high correlation in the tuple sets covered by an incomplete clause or not covered by an incomplete concept do not necessarily have a high correlation with the tuples in the original training set.

[10] This restriction was only made because of efficiency reasons. From our experience with previous tests we know that theories below 0.15 are usually very specialized and can be expected to give a high classification error.

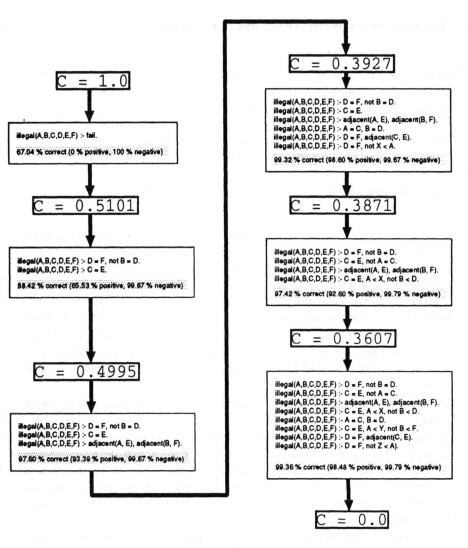

Fig. 5. Generating a series of theories in the noise-free KRK domain

although it practically only learns from half of the training examples. However, it is not as good as FOSSIL with a fixed cutoff. The fact that the minimal error method only uses half of the training examples for learning can also be seen from the graph, where FOSSIL's rather bad learning results at a size of 500 training examples reappear in the curve for the *Minimal Error* method at a training size of 1000 examples, although there is some improvement in the absolute numbers.

An analysis has also shown that the curves for classification accuracy are shaped similar to Fig. 1b, which suggests that some form of hill-climbing can be used to search this series of theories without having to generate all of them. (see Sect. 6).

6   Further Research: Top-Down Pruning

While the naive approach of Sect. 5 might be too crude to be applied in this way, we do think that these preliminary results have some potential for refinement. In particular we see some relationship to pruning methods used e.g. in [5] or [25]. The major difference, however, is that we get a series of different concept descriptions in a general to specific order (*top-down*) as opposed to pruning methods the generate a most specific theory first and then successively generalize it (*bottom-up*).

We believe that the top-down approach has several advantages:

- With increasing example set sizes and increasing noise levels, generating a most specific starting theory for pruning becomes more and more expensive (as can be seen from the results of FOIL in Sect. 4.3). Generating a simple general theory is much less expensive. In the experiments described in Sect. 5, typically less than 5 theories have to be generated to find the optimum and in particular the most specific and most expensive theories need not be learned.
- Efficiency can be further increased, as a clever implementation doesn't have to learn an entirely new theory. It can use the part of the last theory up to the point where the cutoff of the literal with the maximum correlation has occured.
- Pruning and learning are interleaved in this algorithm and can influence each other.
- In Decision Tree Learning several methods for selecting the best tree from a series of trees pruned to a different degree have been developed [17]. We hope that we can adapt some of these methods for relational learning and in particular make them "incremental", i.e. interleave them with the learning process in a way that generates as few unnecessary and expensive theories as possible.
- A weakness of all these algorithms is that they have to use part of the training set for pruning. Due to the robustness of the cutoff parameter we see a chance that a right value for the cutoff might be determined experimentally on parts of the learning set (e.g. with *cross-validation*) and that this information can be used to infer a good value for the parameter for learning from the entire set.

In the light of [24] a method like this may be viewed as automatically shifting the *Overfitting Avoidance Bias*, in some respect similar to CLINT, where a shift of *Language Bias* is realized by learning in increasingly complex representation languages [8]. Both methods try to solve a problem in a simple way first — CLINT by trying to use simpler representation languages first, and Top-Down Pruning by trying to find more general descriptions first — and subsequently switch to more complex solutions if necessary.

7 Conclusion

The system described in this paper uses a new search heuristic based on statistical correlation along with a simple stopping criterion. We see the main advantages of this approach in its

Efficiency: There is no separate calculation of a heuristic function for negated literals and the amount of computing involved in calculating the stopping criterion is reduced to a mere comparison.

Robustness: A good value of the cutoff parameter seems to be independent of the amount of noise and the number of training examples.

Simplicity: In Sects. 5 and 6 we have outlined some promising approaches how the simplicity of the cutoff parameter and its close relation to the search heuristic might be used to interleave learning and pruning in a novel way.

However, mFOIL seems to do a little better in terms of classification error provided that one can find the optimal value of the m-parameter. Here we believe that implementing a simple beam search may help to narrow the gap.

Acknowledgements

This research is sponsored by the Austrian *Fonds zur Förderung der Wissenschaftlichen Forschung (FWF)* under grant number P8756-TEC. Financial support for the Austrian Research Institute for Artificial Intelligence is provided by the Austrian Federal Ministry of Science and Research. I would like to thank J. R. Quinlan and R. M. Cameron-Jones for making FOIL4 ftp-able, Sašo Džeroski for providing mFOIL and a lot of patience, and Gerhard Widmer for a PROLOG implementation of the FOIL algorithm to start with and for encouraging this research. Thanks are also due to two anonymous reviewers for their helpful comments.

References

1. Kamal M. Ali and Michael J. Pazzani. HYDRA: A noise-tolerant relational concept learning algorithm. In *Proceedings of the Thirteenth Joint International Conference on Artificial Intelligence*, pages 1064–1071, Chambèry, France, 1993.
2. D. Angluin and P. Laird. Learning from noisy examples. *Machine Learning*, 2(4):343–370, 1988.
3. Ivan Bratko and Igor Kononenko. Learning diagnostic rules from incomplete and noisy data. In B. Phelps, editor, *Interactions in AI and Statistical Methods*, pages 142–153, London, 1986.
4. L. Breiman, J. Friedman, R. Olshen, and C. Stone. *Classification and Regression Trees*. Wadsworth & Brooks, Pacific Grove, CA, 1984.
5. Clifford A. Brunk and Michael J. Pazzani. An investigation of noise-tolerant relational concept learning algorithms. In *Proceedings of the 8th International Workshop on Machine Learning*, pages 389–393, Evanston, Illinois, 1991.
6. Wray Buntine and Tim Niblett. A further comparison of splitting rules for decision-tree induction. *Machine Learning*, 8:75–85, 1992.

7. Peter Clark and Robin Boswell. Rule induction with CN2: Some recent improvements. In *Proceedings of the 5th European Working Session of Learning*, pages 151–163, Porto, Portugal, 1991.

8. Luc De Raedt and Maurice Bruynooghe. Indirect relevance and bias in inductive concept learning. *Knowledge Acquisition*, 2:365–390, 1990.

9. Sašo Džeroski and Ivan Bratko. Handling noise in Inductive Logic Programming. In *Proceedings of the International Workshop on Inductive Logic Programming*, Tokyo, Japan, 1992.

10. Sašo Džeroski and Ivan Bratko. Using the m-estimate in Inductive Logic Programming. In *Logical Approaches to Machine Learning, Workshop Notes of the 10th European Conference on AI*, Vienna, Austria, 1992.

11. Sašo Džeroski and Nada Lavrač. Learning relations from noisy examples: An empirical comparison of LINUS and FOIL. In *Proceedings of the 8th International Workshop on Machine Learning*, pages 399–402, Evanston, Illinois, 1991.

12. Johannes Fürnkranz. FOSSIL: A robust relational learner. Technical Report TR-93-28, Austrian Research Institute for Artificial Intelligence, 1993. Extended version.

13. R. Holte, L. Acker, and B. Porter. Concept learning and the problem of small disjuncts. In *Proceedings of the 11th International Joint Conference on Artificial Intelligence*, Detroit, MI, 1989.

14. Nada Lavrač, Bojan Cestnik, and Sašo Džeroski. Search heuristics in empirical Inductive Logic Programming. In *Logical Approaches to Machine Learning, Workshop Notes of the 10th European Conference on AI*, Vienna, Austria, 1992.

15. Nada Lavrač and Sašo Džeroski. *Inductive Logic Programming: Techniques and Applications*. Ellis Horwood, 1993.

16. Nada Lavrač, Sašo Džeroski, and Marko Grobelnik. Learning nonrecursive definitions of relations with LINUS. In *Proceedings of the European Working Session on Learning*, Porto, Portugal, 1991.

17. John Mingers. An empirical comparison of pruning methods for decision tree induction. *Machine Learning*, 4:227–243, 1989.

18. John Mingers. An empirical comparison of selection measures for decision-tree induction. *Machine Learning*, 3:319–342, 1989.

19. Stephen Muggleton, Michael Bain, Jean Hayes-Michie, and Donald Michie. An experimental comparison of human and machine learning formalisms. In *Proceedings of the 6th International Workshop on Machine Learning*, pages 113–118, 1989.

20. John Ross Quinlan. Learning logical definitions from relations. *Machine Learning*, 5:239–266, 1990.

21. John Ross Quinlan. Determinate literals in inductive logic programming. In *Proceedings of the 8th International Workshop on Machine Learning*, pages 442–446, 1991.

22. John Ross Quinlan. *C4.5: Programs for Machine Learning*. Morgan Kaufmann, San Mateo, CA, 1993.

23. John Ross Quinlan and R. M. Cameron-Jones. FOIL: A midterm report. In *Proceedings of the European Conference on Machine Learning*, pages 3–20, Vienna, Austria, 1993.

24. Cullen Schaffer. Overfitting avoidance as bias. *Machine Learning*, 10:153–178, 1993.

25. A. Srinivasan, S. H. Muggleton, and M. E. Bain. Distinguishing noise from exceptions in non-monotonic learning. In *Proceedings of the International Workshop on Inductive Logic Programming*, Tokyo, Japan, 1992.

A Multistrategy Learning System and Its Integration into an Interactive Floorplanning Tool

Jürgen Herrmann, Reiner Ackermann, Jörg Peters, Detlef Reipa

Universität Dortmund, Informatik I
44221 Dortmund, Germany
herrmann@ls1.informatik.uni-dortmund.de

Keywords: learning and problem solving, applications of machine learning, multistrategy learning

Abstract. The presented system COSIMA learns floorplanning rules from structural descriptions incrementally, using a number of cooperating machine learning strategies: Selective inductive generalization generates most specific generalizations using predicate weights to select the best one heuristically. The predicate weights are adjusted statistically. Inductive specialization eliminates overgeneralizations. Constructive induction improves the learning process in several ways. The system is organized as a learning apprentice system. It provides an interactive design tool and can automate single floorplanning steps.

1. Introduction

During the last few years the number of reported machine learning applications to real-world problems has grown significantly. ML techniques have been used successfully for tasks from various domains (Morik, 1992), (Kodratoff and Langley, 1993). A main use for the implemented systems is the acquisition of knowledge and data for knowledge-based systems and for conventional software systems.

Many successful machine learning systems acquiring knowledge about complex real-world problems are shaped according to characteristics of the considered domain, i.e. they are tailored to an application. In this context there are two relevant directions of machine learning research:

- The combination of several different machine learning strategies that cooperatively acquire knowledge about the domain (multistrategy learning systems, (Michalski, 1993; Saitta et al, 1993; Morik, 1993))
- The integration of a learning system into a problem solving tool for the domain (van Someren, 1993)

In this paper we present the learning tool COSIMA that combines these two aspects. The system acquires knowledge about floorplanning, a subtask of IC design. The incrementally learned rules are used to automate single design steps performed with an interactive floorplanning tool. For learning the following strategies are used: Selective inductive generalization, inductive specialization, constructive induction and statistical adjustment of parameter weights.

The rest of the paper is organized in following way: To motivate the design decisions for COSIMA, we briefly introduce the floorplanning domain in Section 2. Section 3 gives on overview on the COSIMA system. The combination of the different learning strategies is explained. Our multi-staged inductive generalization algorithm is presented in Section 4. Section 5 deals with the inductive specialization component that is used to eliminate overgeneralizations. The three different uses of constructive induction in COSIMA are described in Section 6. The mechanism for the tuning of predicate weights (which influence all other learning strategies) is the topic of Section 7. Some remarks about the representation of floorplanning knowledge can be found in Section 8. COSIMA's problem solving component that is organized as a floorplanning assistant is explained in Section 9. A description of results and conclusions are presented in the last two sections.

2. Characteristics of the Floorplanning Domain

The system COSIMA acquires knowledge about floorplanning for the early phases of IC design. Floorplanning synthesizes a geometrical hardware description from a structural one (a netlist of functional blocks and their interconnections on register-transfer level). The functional blocks are placed on a two-dimensional area and connected to each other. Typically, the placement is performed by the designer stepwise (see Figure 1).

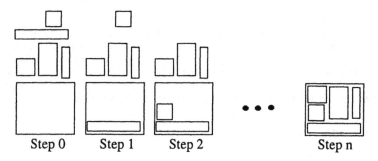

Figure 1: Simplified sequence of steps performed during floorplanning

The objectives of this task are the minimization of the consumed chip-area and the minimization of the total length for the connections. A machine learning system for the floorplanning domain has to be shaped according to the following characteristics:

- There is only *limited and incomplete knowledge* about synthesis and analysis of floorplans. As a consequence machine learning strategies that depend on a strong domain theory cannot be applied. Besides that, the evaluation of a performed floorplanning step is difficult: The effect of an operation on the quality of a floorplan can be evaluated accurately only at the end of a floorplanning process. So a "good-looking" operation can turn out to have a negative effect later. Because of the incomplete knowledge about floorplan analysis, overgeneralizations cannot be avoided.

- The learning and representation of *topological and geometrical properties* is crucial. To represent this information adequately, structural descriptions with typically several hundred facts are required. Therefore, a learning system for floorplanning must scale up - it must be capable to with cope with complex example descriptions. For the same reason, it is not feasible to store old examples - instead incremental learning should be used.

- Depending on the state of the floorplanning process *different aspects of an example have diverging importance*. To represent this fact, we use weighted predicates (see Section 4).

3. Combination of Different Machine Learning Strategies

The floorplanning characteristics described above have led to the selection and combination of the different machine learning strategies for COSIMA described in this section.

Selective inductive generalization is the basic learning strategy used to generate floorplanning rules from examples. An example consists of a floorplanning state (the floorplanning basic area on which some blocks are placed and the list of unplaced blocks) and an operator to be applied to a certain part of this state description. COSIMA uses a fixed set of predefined basic floorplanning operators. A floorplanning rule consists of a right-hand side determining the operator to be applied and a left-hand describing the situations in which the operator can be applied successfully (according to the objectives). Each time a new example becomes available, the corresponding rule is generalized.

Overgeneralizations are eliminated by use of *selective inductive specialization*. An overgenerlization is detected, if a rule matches on a negative example. If an example is rejected by COSIMA's built-in evaluation function or if it is classified by the user accordingly, it is marked as a negative example. The evaluation function can reject an example, if the applied operator leads to an obvious decrease of the floorplan quality.

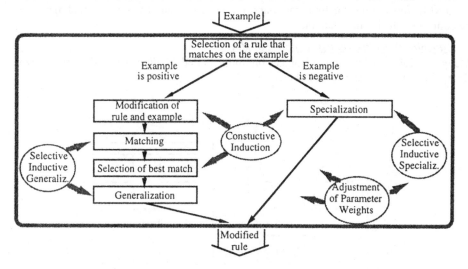

Figure 2: Cooperation of different machine learning strategies in the COSIMA system. Selective inductive generalization and constructive induction cooperatively incorporate a positive example into an existing rule. Inductive specialization and constructive induction are used to eliminate overgeneralizations. Parameter adjustment influences all other strategies.

Constructive induction is used for three different purposes:

1) Before each generalization step, the descriptions of the new example and the corresponding rule are modified to improve generalization.

2) Typically, each generalization step results in several alternative most specific generalizations (MSGs). New predicates are constructed and added to the MSGs to select the best one heuristically.

3) If the selective inductive specialization fails to eliminate an overgenerization, constructive induction is used as an alternative specialization strategy. This situation occurs, if a correct discrimination of a negative example is not possible with current hypothesis language.

Predefined predicate weights guide COSIMA's three different inductive learning strategies. On the basis of statistics about sequences of generalization steps *adjustment of predicate weights* is performed.

The cooperation of the strategies is depicted in Figure 2. In the next sections the different strategies are described with more detail.

4. Selective Inductive Generalization

As COSIMA is learning from examples *incrementally*, each generalization step matches *two* example descriptions (or one rule and one example). Typically each description consists of several hundred facts. As Haussler (Haussler, 1989) has pointed out many MSGs (of different quality) may be created from structural descriptions for complex design tasks. A mechanism is therefore necessary to evaluate (intermediate and final) generalizations and to select the best one. The quality of a generalization depends on the corresponding facts in both input descriptions in accordance with a certain list of consistent object bindings[1]. As far as complex design tasks are concerned, each description typically consists of some important facts and many additional ones describing detail information. A good MSG must prefer the important ones, i.e. the selection of the object bindings must be dominated by the important facts.

Example: Two different lists of object bindings

Many possible combinations of object bindings, called *binding lists*, exist for the two floorplanning examples shown in Figure 3.

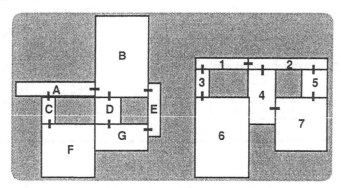

Figure 3: Two simple floorplans that can be matched against each other in *different* ways

Two of them are e.g.

L1: (A:1, B:2, C:3, D:4, E:5, F:6, G:7) or

L2: (A:2, B:6, C:3, D:5, E:1, F:7, G:4)

The first one binds objects according to the structure of the floorplans. Corresponding

---

[1] We only use one-to-one bindings of objects for our generalization strategy. Many-to-one bindings that are used in logic-oriented systems as KBG (Bisson, 1992) are not feasible for the learning of knowledge about *complex design* tasks like floorplanning. Floorplanning operators like the 'placement of BlockA between BlockB and BlockC' require a definite substructure of related objects to be manipulated. In hypotheses with many-to-one bindings this information is lacking.

blocks have the same relative positions and neighbors in both floorplans. For the second list (L2), the areas and shapes of the blocks determine the bindings. If the main aim of the floorplanning process is to minimize the total connection length, the structure of a floorplan is more relevant than the shape of the blocks. Nevertheless, the areas and shapes must be considered too. Therefore, predicate weights are a suitable mechanism to express the importance of each feature and relation.

In COSIMA selective induction is performed by the multi-staged generalization algorithm[2] that uses these numerical weights intensively. They are used to evaluate each (intermediate or final) generalization. A generalization consists of several facts. Each generalized fact F corresponds to a pair of facts from the two considered examples. The similarity of these two facts delivers a weight[3] for F.

Our calculation of the similarity of two facts is somewhat more simple than the formula used in KBG (Bisson 1992). Let $F1 = p(A_1, A_2, \cdots, A_n)$ and $F2 = p(B_1, B_2, \cdots, B_n)$ be the two facts from the two considered examples E1 and E2 that are generalized into F. F1 and F2 are instances of the same predicate p. The weight of F is defined as the similarity between F1 and F2:

$$sim(F1, F2) = weight\ (p) * \prod_{i=1}^{n} sim(A_i, B_i) \qquad (1)$$

The similarity value for any pair of arguments ranges from 0 to 1. The calculation of $sim(A_i, B_i)$ depends on their type. For two *objects* it is equal to 1, for two *numerical values* it is the quotient of their minimum and maximum[4]. If the difference of the values is above a certain limit, the similarity is too low and the fact is dropped from the generalization. Typically this can take place after several generalization steps.

The weight of a generalization is the sum of the weights of its facts being calculated with Formula (1). This method implies that not necessarily the generalizations with the highest number of facts, but those with many important facts, get the highest ratings. In this way the best description that is used for further generalization steps can be determined heuristically.

The multi-staged generalization splits up each example description into two parts: The *important* part consisting of instances of predicates with high weights and the *additional* part consisting of the other facts[5]. During the first stage only the important example parts are matched. This leads to initial, preliminary MSGs. The second stage matches the additional example parts and completes the initial MSGs adding further generalized facts. Each stage is performed by a SPROUTER-like matching procedure (Hayes-Roth and McDermott, 1977). It searches for the best (initial or final) MSGs by stepwise construction of maximal consistent binding lists.

---

[2] This generalization algorithm was first used in the system LEFT (Herrmann and Beckmann, 1992 and 1994), a predecessor of COSIMA. LEFT has the same selective inductive generalization method but no constructive induction or inductive specialization strategies.

[3] We are calculating weights only for *generalized* facts. The weight of a fact in an example description is identical to the weight of the corresponding predicate.

[4] The range of the numerical arguments in our floorplanning domain is relatively small. It is e.g. [1,20] for the numerical argument of the predicate area. The similarity of two areas is expressed by their ratio. According to our point of view, two blocks with areas 1 and 2 are as similar to each other as two blocks with areas 5 and 10. For *large* numerical domains, a normed similarity measure could be more appropriate (e.g. dividing the difference of two values by the maximum possible value).

[5] Alternatively, the example descriptions can be split into several parts. In this case, for *each* part a separate matching phase must be performed.

Example: Binding of objects after the initial matching

Each of the two simple floorplans in figure 4 has 9 blocks. The description language consists of the three predicates

connected(<block>, <block>)	with the weight 40
size(<block>, <integer>)	with the weight 15
shape(<block>, <size-descriptor>)	with the weight 10

The important part of the example description consists of instances of the first predicate. The additional parts describes the size and shape features. After the initial matching (first stage) only the following blocks are bound to each other:

(A:1, B:2, C:3, D:4, E:5, F:6, G:7)

The other blocks are bound during the second matching stage. The initial bindings are not changes during the second stage.

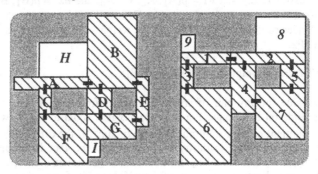

Figure 4: Two simple floorplans after the initial matching: The hatched blocks are already bound to each other

The generalized facts are created by use of the closing interval, climbing generalization tree, turning constants into variables and dropping condition generalization rules (Michalski, 1983). At last the final MSG with the highest rating is selected. A detailed description of the multi-staged generalization algorithm can be found in (Herrmann and Beckmann, 1994). The effects of this algorithm are the following one:

The instance and the hypothesis space are split into 2 disjoint parts. This leads to a significant reduction of the complexity for generalization. On the other hand, few important facts (with high weights) cannot be "outvoted" by many additional (less import) ones. For that reason, our generalization algorithm can find better MSGs for domains like floorplanning that are represented adequately by descriptors with varying importance.

5. Selective Inductive Specialization

The inductive specialization component is applied, if the application of a learned rule, matching on the current floorplanning state, is rejected. The rejection of a rule means that its application would lead to an unfavorable new state according to the floorplanning objectives. The rejection is either initiated by the user or the built-in evaluation function for floorplanning states.

As the floorplanning domain requires an *incremental* learning system (see Section 2), specialization strategies that systematically analyze the whole set of examples at one time cannot be used, e.g. MOBAL's rule discovery tool (Kietz and Wrobel, 1992) or the knowledge refinement component in WHY (Saitta et al, 1993).

One simple method for incremental specialization is the inclusion of exceptional examples into the rule to be specialized, as it is used in the system LEFT (Herrmann and Beckmann, 1994). Using a "without-part" in each rule, negative examples can be excluded easily. Unfortunately this method does not scale up. It blows up the rule description so that the advantages of incremental learning are jeopardized.

An alternative incremental specialization strategy is performed in the system LAIR (Elio and Watanabe, 1991). It compares each new (positive or negative) example with the current hypothesis and uses the differences for the construction and update of a list of candidates for specialization.

LAIR uses a constructive induction method for creation of the fact needed for specialization. It utilizes a set of horn-clauses as background theory. The background knowledge is applied to the candidate list to find the best fact to be added to the rule. Because of the insufficient background knowledge in the floorplanning domain we cannot use this construction method for our system. (COSIMA's alternative constructive induction strategy is explained in the next section.)

Nevertheless a list of candidates can be used for specialization in our domain. The list is constructed and updated in a more distinctive way than in LAIR, which removes a candidate form the list, if it contradicts the current new single example. In COSIMA all facts are stored in the so-called *specialization part* that occurred in at least C % of the examples used for generalization or used during application of a given rule[6]. C is a user selected parameter. Realistic values for C are e.g. 50 or 30. A smaller value for C leads to a bigger specialization part. Each fact in the specialization part is marked with two numeric values:

- The percentage of example descriptions for generalization that comprise the fact
- The percentage of example descriptions the rule has been applied to successfully, i.e. without rejection, that comprise the fact

If a rule matches on a negative example the rule is too general and has to be specialized. Adding a literal to the left-hand side of the rule that *discriminates* the example, this is achieved. In this way a most general specialization (MGS) of the rule is created. In analogy to most specific generalizations (Haussler, 1989) there are many alternative most general specializations, so the selection of the best or at least a good one is crucial. Our specialization strategy uses two different rules for the creation of a MGS (Dietterich and Michalski, 1983), both utilizing the information in the specialization part as bias.

a) The introducing exception specialization rule

The negation of a fact is added to the left-hand side of the rule that occurs in the negative example and in few (at least c %) of the positive ones.

b) The adding condition specialization rule

A fact is added to the left-hand side of the rule that does not occur in the negative example but in most (close to 100%) of the positive ones.

Both rules can lead to a discrimination of old examples that were classified as positive ones. This effect is intended, as the classification of examples is fuzzy in our domain. (There is limited knowledge about the analysis of floorplans, see Section 2.) Therefore, misclassified examples are a major reason for overgeneralizations. Nevertheless, the number of discriminated old examples must be kept small, to minimize the effect of the specialization. The specialization part provides the necessary information to meet this

---

[6] To make the construction of the list less sensitive to the presentation order of the examples, for the fist examples *all* possible candidate facts are included. Only after a number of examples have been used for generalization or application of the rule, the less frequently occuring facts are discharged.

requirement. Other incremental specializations strategies, like e.g. the one in ACT (Anderson, 1986), have a less elaborated discrimination mechanism. The discrimination is based only on the analysis of one positive and one negative example. The influence on the total set of old examples cannot be estimated.

There are several criteria for the evaluation of the alternative specializations created with rule a) and b). The selection of the "best" literal to be added to the rule is based on the following information:

- *Number of positive examples discriminated by the literal*
  As has been mentioned above this number should be minimized to limit the effect of specialization

- *Predicate weight for the instance*
  In our current implementation predicates with high weights are preferred, as they add significant information to the hypothesis

- *Statistics about prior use of the corresponding predicate for discrimination*
  Statistics represent the success of predicates during previous specialization steps. If a predicate has lead to a successful specialization several times, it is a good candidate for the current specialization step according to this heuristic criterion.

- *Number of objects referenced in the rule before and after specialization*
  The addition of a single literal to a hypothesis can increase the number of referenced objects. This is a significant modification of the hypothesis. Therefore, specialization steps that do not increase the number of objects are preferred in COSIMA.

These four criteria provide basic information about the evaluation of the specializations. The way how they should be combined to gain a compound evaluation function depends strongly on the characteristics of the underlying domain.

Besides the rules a) and b) that add a literal to the rule to be specialized COSIMA uses the following specialization rules that are the inverse operations to standard rules of generalization: descending-concept-hierarchy-tree, reducing-interval, turning-variable-into-constant, removing-alternative. A formal description of the corresponding generalization operators can be found in (Michalski, 1983).

Each of these four rules specializes an argument of a fact already existing in the considered floorplanning rule. As the influence of these specializations on the total set of old examples cannot be estimated, the rules a) and b) are the preferred specialization operators in COSIMA.

6. Three Different Ways to Use Constructive Induction

COSIMA's constructive induction strategy combines knowledge-based and syntactical construction of new descriptors. Knowledge-based approaches, e.g. Oxgate (Gunsch, 1991), use domain-dependent knowledge for the construction process. In contrary, syntactical approaches (Wirth and O'Rourke, 1991) are based on domain-independent biases limiting the space of predicates that can be constructed.

In the following the three different uses for constructive induction in COSIMA are explained sequentially.

Modification of Example and Rule Descriptions Before Matching

One purpose of the modification (and the general intention of constructive induction) is to make the descriptions more distinctive, i.e. to make information explicit that is only implicitly represented in the descriptions. For this purpose COSIMA's background knowledge provides several predefined construction operators. They create new predicates, being possibly useful for our domain, from existing "basic" ones. Examples of operators are e.g. the following two ones (Michalski 1983):

- *Counting the instances of a predicate that all have the same constant value at one argument position*
Example: Consider the following basic predicate:
block_state(<block>, <state-value>). The possible values for <state-value> are placed and unplaced. The constructed predicate
#placed_blocks(<number>) makes explicit the number of blocks with the state-value placed.

- *Selecting that instance of a predicate with the maximum numerical value at one argument position*
Example: The constructed predicate maximum_size(<block>) makes explicit that the object <block> is the biggest one.

Each of the construction operators can create a diverse set of different predicates. For instance the maximum-operator can be applied to any predicate with at least one numerical argument type. Some of the operators depend on each other. For the creation of a maximum-predicate a counting-instances-predicate must be used.

The constructed predicates that get a sufficient rating from the predicate evaluation function (see below) are included into the example and the considered rule description. It would not be feasible to add the predicate to the description language for all rules. This would blow the descriptions significantly. Instead, the effect of the construction is limited to the current rule. For different rules different constructed predicates can be relevant.

The second type of modification for example and rule descriptions is the compaction. For this purpose intermediate concepts represented as horn-clauses are induced (Bergadano et al, 1988). An intermediate concept represents a compound property occuring repeatedly in the set of examples.

If the body of a horn-clause (with two ore more literals) matches on an example the unified literals in the example description are substituted with the clause head. (In the system DUCE (Muggleton 1987), this operation, called absorption if the horn-clause is predefined, was used for transformation of propositional descriptions.) Using intermetiate concepts the size of the description is decreased and high-level information about the example is extracted. The left-hand side of Figure 5 shows an example of an intermediate concept used in COSIMA. The right-hand side depicts a geometrical illustration of the concept "corner". A corner consists of three connected blocks that form an "L-shaped" structure. Using intermediate concepts of this kind, several blocks can be combined to substructures of the floorplan topology.

corner(a,b,c) :- on_same_line(a,b,horizontal),
                on_same_line(a,c,vertical),
                direct_neighbour(a,b),
                direct_neighbour(a,c),
                state_connection(a,b,existing),
                state_connection(a,c,existing)

Figure 5: Intermediate concept representing the structure "corner" (left-hand side) and the geometrical representation of a corner in a floorplan example (right-hand side)

COSIMA uses rule-models (Kietz and Wrobel, 1991; Pazzani and Kibler, 1992) for syntactical construction of predicates representing intermediate concepts. The head of a successfully instanciated model forms a new predicate to be included into the considered description. To limit the set of possible new predicates that can be constructed from a rule model, *sorts* are used constraining the instanciations of predicate variables and arguments. In Figure 6 the rule model is depicted that was used to create the intermediate concept for "corner".

new(X,Y,Z) :- $\quad$ P(X,Y,horizontal) $\land$ *Type (P) = IndirectNeighbourhood,*
P(X,Z,vertical),
Q(X,Y) $\land$ *Type (Q) = DirectNeighbourhood,*
Q(X,Z),
R(X,Y,existing) $\land$ *Type (R) = Connection,*
R(X,Z,existing)

Figure 6: Rule model in COSIMA. "new" stands for a predicate identifier to be created automatically during instanciation of the model. (Meaningful predicate names have to be inserted by the user.) The italic terms denote the sort restrictions.

COSIMA's two different construction methods can be combined. A new predicate constructed from a *predefined construction operator* can be included into the body of an *intermediate concept*. Besides that, intermediate concepts can be created hierarchically: More complex intermediate concepts are defined by use of existing ones.

To make the creation of intermediate concepts less dependent on the existing rule models, COSIMA has a method for the creation of new models based on past successful instanciations of existing ones. If there are several instanciations of the same model, a new clause is created with a body consisting of the corresponding literals in all instanciations. A new rule model is abstracted from this clause. For a more detailed description of the constructive induction mechanisms see (Reipa, 1993).

Evaluation of the Constructed Predicates

This is a crucial task for any constructive induction strategy. Typically, a flexible construction mechanism results in a big number of *irrelevant* new predicates. COSIMA's evaluation function is based on the following criteria:

* number of literals in the rule model used
* number of instances of the new predicate in the two considered descriptions
* degree of compaction achieved with the new predicate
* past success of the rule model

From these criteria a heuristic numerical value is calculated for each new predicate. Only the predicates with a high rating are included into example and rule descriptions.

Selection Among Alternative MSGs

This is the second use for constructive induction in COSIMA. From structural description many different alternative most specific generalizations (MSGs) can be created. The *weight* of each MSG is the sum of the weights for the facts. If there are several MSGs with the same highest rating, constructive induction is used to select the best one.

If applicable, COSIMA adds instances of constructed predicates to an MSG making it more specific in that way. A fact is added, if it is valid for the corresponding objects in all examples[7]. This increases the weights for some MSGs and makes a selection possible.

---

[7] This condition already limits the number of accepted constructed predicates significantly. For this reason the threshold value for the acceptance of new predicates, that reduces this number further, is now lower than during the modification of descriptions (see above).

During this stage of the generalization process new facts are only *added* to the MSGs, no compaction takes place.

Specialization of Rules

If the inductive specialization strategy mentioned above fails to select a discriminating fact, constructive induction is used as an alternative specialization strategy. A new fact is constructed that discriminates the negative example from the positive ones.

COSIMA's constructive induction strategy is incremental. For the creation of a new predicate the two current descriptions (rule and example) are analyzed. When a new positive example becomes available and is generalized with the rule the utility of the new instances is checked. If they are not valid for the new example, they are dropped.

7. Adjustment of Parameter Weights

Experts know what information is absolutely necessary for a certain operation in the considered domain. They can therefore divide the set of predicates into the two required subsets (important predicates and additional ones) and deliver possibly a partial ordering for each set. From this information initial predicate weights can be determined. A modification of these weights is performed by a statistical parameter adjustment mechanism. Analyzing the generalization and specialization steps regularly it evaluates the relevance of the different predicates for the learning process and adjusts the weights incrementally.

8. Representation of Floorplanning Knowledge in COSIMA

Floorplanning may be divided into two steps: The *topology planning* which performs a rough, relative placement of the blocks, and the *geometry planning* which determines the exact floorplan geometry based on this topology.

COSIMA incrementally acquires rules which create a floorplanning *topology*.[8] The topology is represented as a *grid-graph* (Watanabe, 1987), a graph with (square) nodes which are marked with positions on a two-dimensional grid. The nodes represent the floorplan blocks; grid-positions stand for the relative placement of the blocks. Two blocks are connected by an edge if there is a corresponding connection in the circuit description COSIMA gets as an input. Four rectangles represent the boundary of the floorplan. The upper left part of Figure 7 show a grid graph with some blocks that have already been placed.

A logic-based description is not well suited for the representation and manipulation of structural and geometrical knowledge. For this reason we use a hybrid representation for COSIMA. The manipulation of the current floorplanning state is performed by a set of predefined floorplanning operators that operate on an object-oriented representation, implemented in the CommonLisp Object System CLOS. Each operator is implemented using quite a complex CommonLisp procedure. After each manipulation, the new state is translated into the predicate description which the learning component can work on.

---

[8] The geometry planning is more straight-forward and can be calculated by a conventional algorithm (Watanabe, 1987).

9. Integration of the Learning System into a Floorplanning Tool

The learning strategies described above are embedded in an interactive floorplanning system that assists the designer. LEFT has a graphical interface that shows the current floorplanning state and which is used by the designer to initiate the application of an operator (see Figure 7).

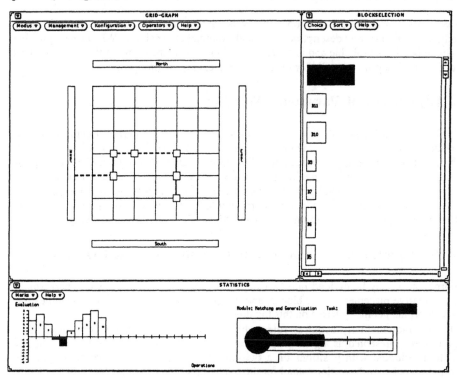

Figure 7: User Interface of COSIMA. The upper right window shows the ordered list of blocks to be placed. The blocks are placed onto the positions of the grid shown in the upper left window. In this way the topology of the floorplan is designed. The lower window depicts performance statistics. The graph on the left-hand side shows the quality of the most recent floorplanning operations. The user can take back unfavorable operations. The bar on the right hand side informs about the state of current matching and generalization process.

The system operates as a learning apprentice (Mitchell et al, 1985). The user can select from the list of possible operations an appropriate floorplanning operator for the next design step. The performance component executes the operator. This leads to a new floorplanning state. The old state description and the operator form a positive example. It is used to construct a new rule or to generalize an existing one. The learned rules are used in the following way: To make the selection of a well-suited operator easier, each time a rule matches on the current state the execution of the operator in the right-hand side is proposed to the user. If the user rejects the proposed operator the current state forms a negative example for that rule and it is specialized accordingly.

10. Experimental Results

We are currently evaluating the quality and capability of COSIMA's different strategies. This includes for instance the selection of appropriate parameters for the different evaluation functions.

The effect of the multi-staged generalization algorithm on the speed of matching and generalization has already been evaluated and is illustrated in Figure 8. The algorithm is compared to another version that is limited to a single stage, i.e. all predicates are considered during one single generalization stage. Both versions used the same predicate weights. The results show that the multi-staged generalization algorithm can significantly improve the run time for inductive generalization taken from real-world design examples. (The single-staged generalization is only quicker for very small examples.)

On top of which, the tests show that the multi-staged generalization improves the quality of the gained learning result. It selects the appropriate MSGs for several test cases, which could not be generalized correctly by the single-staged generalization algorithm.

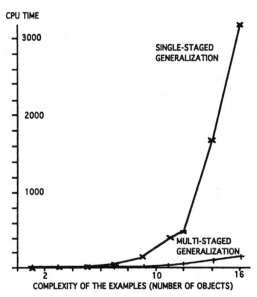

Figure 8: Comparison of Run-Times for the
Single- and the Multi-Staged Generalization

There are some preliminary results about the effects of the other machine learning strategies, based on a limited number of tests we have already performed[9]. Figure 9 depicts the results of one test series. In each of the floorplan examples used for this series at least one corner occurred (see Figure 5 for a description of the intermediate concept corner). The example size varied from 250 to 520 facts.

We have investigated how the description length of a rule created from these examples changed during multi-staged generalization with and without constructive induction. It is the typical case for realistic floorplanning examples that only a smaller part of the example description is significant for the concept to be learned. Therefore, the dropping condition generalization rule is the most important one.

---

[9] Therefore, at the moment our interpretation of the experimental results is somewhat fuzzy.

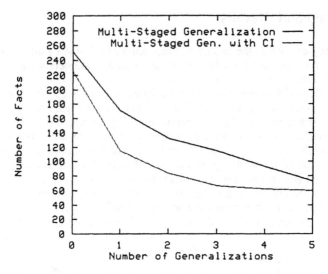

Figure 9: Comparison of rule sizes for multi-staged generalization without constructive induction (upper line) and with constructive induction (lower line)

The combination of constructive induction with multi-staged generalization had several effects. From the beginning it decreased the rule size, and it lead to an earlier convergence of the number of facts. This combination of the two machine learning strategies does also influence the quality oft the learned rules, as has been confirmed by several other series of tests, too. It decreases the error rate of the rules significantly.

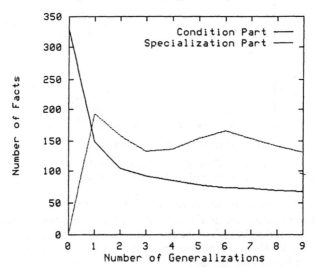

Figure 10: Comparison of number of facts for the specialization part and the condition part of a rule that is generalized several times

Another series of tests analyzed the development of the specialization part during a number of successive generalizations (see Figure 10). In this series the size of the specialization part was always somewhat larger than the size of the condition part, but the specialization part did not grow significantly during generalization. There is no combinatorial explosion of the specialization part. This is an important difference to the simple specialization strategy of the system LEFT (Herrmann and Beckmann, 1994) that blew up the size of the specialization part after learning from a few negative examples.

Another aspect that has still to be analyzed and is relevant for all incremental systems is the influence of the example order on the learning results.

11. Conclusion

The implemented system COSIMA combines different machine learning strategies. It demonstrates how selective inductive generalization, inductive specialization, constructive induction and statistical adjustment of parameter weights can be integrated into a multi-strategy machine learning system that acquires knowledge about a real-world problem - floorplanning for integrated circuits.

Another important aspect of machine learning applications is the integration of a learning system into the daily work of the user. The organization of the user interaction has a great impact on the acceptance for the software tool. Considering this aspect, COSIMA has been organized as a learning apprentice system that is integrated into an interactive floor-planning tool. COSIMA does not require a teaching mode. It learns from examples that the user generates during his/her normal work with the floorplanning tool.

Acknowledgements: We would like to thank Siegfried Bell for useful comments on an earlier version of this paper.

References

Anderson, J.R. (1986). Knowledge Compilation. In Machine Learning: An Artificial Intelligence Approach Vol II, eds. R. S. Michalski, J. G. Carbonell, T. M. Mitchell, 289-310. Morgan Kaufmann..

Bergadano, F., Giordana, A. & Saitta, L. (1988). Automated Concept Acquisition in Noisy Domains. IEEE Transactions on Pattern Analysis and Machine Intelligence.

Bisson, G. (1992). Conceptual Clustering in a First Order Logic Representation. Proc. 10th ECAI, August 3-7, Vienna.

Dietterich, T.G., & Michalski, R.S. (1983). A Comparative Review of Selected Methods for Learning from Examples. In Machine Learning: An Artificial Intelligence Approach, eds. R. S. Michalski, J. G. Carbonell, T. M. Mitchell, pp 41-81. Palo Alto: Tioga Press.

Elio, R., & Watanabe, L. (1991). An Incremental Deductive Strategy for Controlling Constructive Induction in Learning from Examples. Machine Learning Journal. Vol 7, 7-44, Boston: Kluver Academic Publishers.

Gunsch, G.H. (1991). Opportunistic Constructive Induction: Using Fragments of Domain Knowledge to Guide Construction. PhD Thesis, University of Illinois at Urbana-Champaign.

Haussler, D. (1989). Learning Conjunctive Concepts in Structural Domains. Machine Learning Journal. Vol 4, 7-40, Boston: Kluver Academic Publishers.

Hayes-Roth, F., & McDermott, J. (1977). Knowledge Acquisition from Structural Descriptions. Proc. 5th IJCAI, 356-362.

Herrmann, J., & Beckmann, R. (1992). LEFT - A Learning Tool for Early Floorplanning. Proc. 18th Euromicro Conference, pp 587-594, September 14-17, Paris.

Herrmann, J., & Beckmann, R. (1994). LEFT - A System that Learns Rules about VLSI-Design from Structural Descriptions. (to appear) In Y. Kodratoff (Guest Ed.), Applied Artificial Intelligence, Special Issue on Real-World Applications of Machine Learning Techniques . London: Taylor and Francis Ltd.

Kietz, J.U., & Wrobel, S. (1992). Controlling the Complexity of Learning in Logic Though Syntactic and Task-Oriented Models. Arbeitspapiere der GMD Nr. 503, GMD, Schloß Birlinghoven.

Kodratoff, Y., & Langley, P. (Eds.), (1993). Real-World Applications of Machine Learning. Workshop Notes on the ECML-93 Workshop. Vienna.

Michalski, R.S. (1983). A Theory and Methodology of Inductive Learning. In R.S. Michalski, T.M. Mitchell and J.G. Carbonell (eds.), Machine Learning: An Artificial Intelligence Approach. Palo Alto, CA: Tioga Publishing.

Michalski, R.S. (1993). Inferential Theory of Learning as a Conceptual Basis for Multistrategy Learning. Machine Learning Journal. Vol 11, 111-152, Boston: Kluver Academic Publishers.

Mitchell, T.M., Mahadevan, S., & Steinberg, L. (1985). LEAP - A Learning Apprentice for VLSI Design. Proc. 9th IJCAI, pp 573-580, August 18-23, Los Angeles.

Morik, K. (1992). Applications of Machine Learning. Proceedings of the Sixth European Knowledge Acquisition Workshop (pp 9-13). Springer.

Morik, K. (1993). Balanced Cooperative Modeling. Machine Learning Journal. Vol 11, 217-236, Boston: Kluver Academic Publishers.

S. Muggleton (1987). DUCE, an Oracle Based Approach to Constructive Induction, Proc of the 10th Int. Joint Conference on Artificial Intelligence, IJCAI87

Pazzani, M., & Kibler, D. (1992). The Utility of Knowledge in Inductive Learning. Machine Learning Journal. Vol 9, 57-95, Boston: Kluver Academic Publishers.

Reipa, D. (1993). Konstruktive Induktion für eine strukturelle Beschreibungssprache. Diploma Thesis, University of Dortmund.

Saitta, L., Botta, M., & Neri, F. (1993). Multistrategy Learning and Theory Revision. Machine Learning Journal. Vol 11, 153-172, Boston: Kluver Academic Publishers.

van Someren, M. (Ed.) (1993). Learning and Problem Solving. Workshop Notes on the MLnet Workshop. Blanes.

Wirth, R., & O'Rourke, P.O. (1991). Constraints for Predicate Invention. Proc. of the 8th Int. Machine Learning Conference, Evanston: Morgan Kaufmann.

Watanabe, H. (1987). FLUTE - An Expert Floorplanner for Full-Custom VLSI Design. IEEE Design & Test, pp 32-41. New York: Computer Society of the IEEE.

Bottom-Up Induction of Oblivious Read-Once Decision Graphs

Ron Kohavi

Computer Science Department, Stanford University
Stanford, CA. 94305
E-mail: Ronnyk@CS.Stanford.EDU

Abstract. We investigate the use of *oblivious, read-once decision graphs* as structures for representing concepts over discrete domains, and present a bottom-up, hill-climbing algorithm for inferring these structures from labelled instances. The algorithm is robust with respect to irrelevant attributes, and experimental results show that it performs well on problems considered difficult for symbolic induction methods, such as the Monk's problems and parity.

1 Introduction

Top down induction of decision trees [25, 24, 20] has been one of the principal induction methods for symbolic, supervised learning. The tree structure, which is used for representing the hypothesized target concept, suffers from some well-known problems, most notably the replication problem and the fragmentation problem [23]. The replication problem forces duplication of subtrees in disjunctive concepts, such as $(A \land B) \lor (C \land D)$; the fragmentation problem causes partitioning of the data into fragments, when a high-arity attribute is tested at a node. Both problems reduce the number of instances at lower nodes in the tree — instances greatly needed for statistical significance of tests performed during the tree construction process.

The smallest decision trees for most symmetric functions, such as parity and majority, have exponential size; consequently, programs that look for small trees tend to generalize poorly on such functions. One notable advantage of decision trees over other representations, such as neural nets, is the fact that the learned structures are readable by human experts who can confirm, reject, or modify the given hypothesis (*i.e.*, the tree), aided by background knowledge.

In this paper we investigate the use of *Oblivious, read-Once Decision Graphs* (**OODGs**) as a structure for representing concepts over discrete domains, and present a bottom-up, hill-climbing algorithm for inferring these structures from instances. OODGs have a *different bias* from that of decision trees, and thus some concepts that are hard to represent as trees are easy to represent as OODGs and vice-versa (although the latter seems rare). Since OODGs are graphs, they are easy for humans to perceive, and should be preferred over other representations (*e.g.*, neural nets) whenever it is important to comprehend the meaning and structure of the induced concept.

OODGs (see Sect.2 for a formal definition) are rooted, directed acyclic graphs (DAGs) that can be divided into levels. All nodes at a level test the same attribute, and all the edges that originate from one level terminate at the next level. See Fig.1(a) for an example of an OODG representing the exclusive-or (denoted by $\oplus$) of three variables, X_1, X_2, and X_4, with a fourth variable, X_3, being irrelevant.

The restriction that all nodes of a given level must test the same attribute gives the structure many nice properties (see Sect.2.1), and has proven to be very useful in the engineering community, where it is used in Ordered Binary Decision Diagrams (OBDDs). This bias, while constraining the class of decision graphs, still allows the "compression" of circuits with up to 10^{120} states into manageable structures, which are then used in automatic verification of correctness.

In the next section we formally define the OODG structure and present some basic properties. Section 3 introduces the basic algorithm, which is nondeterministic and assumes that the full instance space is available. Section 4 presents a hill-climbing version of the algorithm using one level of lookahead to resolve both the nondeterminism and the problem of generalization from an incomplete instance space. An important observation is the ability of the algorithm to discover irrelevant attributes, helping to decrease the size of the hypothesis space, and making the generalization much easier. Section 5 reports preliminary experiments. Section 6 describes related work, and Section 7 concludes with future work.

2 Oblivious Read-Once Decision Graphs

In this section we formally define the OODG structure and describe some basic properties. The name OODG is a combination of the terms "Oblivious" and "read-Once" that are used in theoretical complexity analysis of branching programs, and the term "Decision Graph" that is used in the artificial intelligence community, most notably the recent use of the term by Oliver, Dowe, and Wallace in [22, 21].

Given n discrete variables (or attributes), $X_1, X_2, \ldots, X_n$, with domains $D_1, \ldots, D_n$ respectively, the **instance space** $\mathcal{X}$ is the cross-product of the domains, *i.e.*, $D_1 \times \cdots \times D_n$. A **$k$-categorization function** is a function f mapping each instance in the instance space to one of k categories, *i.e.*, $f : \mathcal{X} \mapsto \{0, \ldots, k-1\}$. Without loss of generality, we assume that for each category there is at least one instance in $\mathcal{X}$ that maps to it.

2.1 The OODG Structure

We begin by describing a general decision graph, then specialize it to be read-once and oblivious.

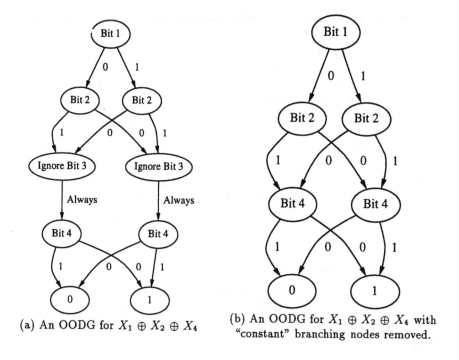

(a) An OODG for $X_1 \oplus X_2 \oplus X_4$

(b) An OODG for $X_1 \oplus X_2 \oplus X_4$ with "constant" branching nodes removed.

Fig. 1. An OODG for 3-bit parity with one irrelevant attribute ($\oplus$ denotes exclusive-or).

A **decision graph** for a k-categorization function over variables $X_1, X_2, \ldots,$ X_n with domains $D_1, D_2, \ldots, D_n$, is a directed acyclic graph (DAG) with the following properties:

1. There are exactly k nodes, called **category nodes**, that are labelled $0, 1, \ldots,$ $k - 1$, and have outdegree zero.
2. Non-category nodes are called **branching nodes**. Each branching node is labelled by some variable X_i and has $|D_i|$ outgoing edges, each labelled by a distinct value from D_i.
3. There is one distinguished node — the **root** — that is the only node with indegree zero.

The category assigned by a decision graph to a given variable assignment (an instance), is determined by tracing the (unique) path from the root to a category node, branching according to the labels on the edges.

A **read-once** decision graph is a graph where each variable occurs at most once along any computation path. A **levelled** decision graph is a graph where the nodes are partitioned into a sequence of pairwise disjoint sets, the levels, such that outgoing edges from each level terminate at the next level. An **oblivious** decision graph is a levelled graph such that all nodes at a given level are labelled by the same variable. An oblivious graph thus defines a total ordering on the variables. (The name "oblivious" denotes the fact that testing of variables depends only on their order within the levels, independent of the input itself.) An oblivious decision graph is **reduced** if there do not exist two distinct nodes at the same level that branch in exactly the same way on the same values. If two such nodes exist, they can be united.

An **OODG** is an oblivious read-once decision graph. Unless otherwise noted, the OODG is assumed to be reduced. The **size** of an OODG is the number of nodes in the graph, and the **width** of a level is the number of nodes at that level.

When displaying OODGs, if all edges emanating from a node terminate at the same node, we either replace the edges by one edge labelled "always," as shown in Fig.1(a), or remove such "constant" nodes altogether, as shown in Fig.1(b).

2.2 Properties of OODGs

We now describe some properties of OODGs. These properties help us understand the strengths and weaknesses of the OODG structure. Proofs of these properties for OBDDs can be found in [7, 6, 17], and can be generalized to OODGs.

- An OODG can represent any k-categorization function.
- For any k-categorization function f, and for a given ordering of the variables for the levels, there is a unique (up to isomorphism) reduced OODG implementing f.
  This is not surprising, as an OODG is very similar to a deterministic finite automaton that has been "unrolled" to avoid cycles.
- There exist functions that have a polynomial (or even linear) size OODG representation under one variable ordering, and an exponential size OODG under another ordering. One such example for Boolean variables is

$$(X_1 \wedge X_2) \vee (X_3 \wedge X_4) \vee \cdots \vee (X_{2n-1} \wedge X_{2n}).$$

  The ordering $X_1, X_2, \ldots, X_{2n}$ gives a graph with $O(n)$ nodes, while the ordering $X_1, X_{n+1}, X_2, X_{n+2}, \ldots, X_n, X_{2n}$ requires $O(2^n)$ nodes.
- There are functions for which no variable ordering results in a polynomial size OODG representation (the Shannon effect). Wegener [28] has shown that almost all Boolean functions result in exponentially sized branching programs (and hence OODGs) under all orderings. Bryant [6] showed that at least one of the $2n$ bits of integer multiplication is an inherently complex function, requiring exponential sized OBDD (and hence OODG) for all orderings.
- All symmetric Boolean functions — functions which yield the same value for all permutations of the input variables — have OODGs of size $O(n^2)$. Examples of symmetric Boolean functions are parity, "exactly k-of-n", and "at least k-of-n".

We now present a theorem that gives an upper bound on the width of different levels of an OODG, given an instance space of Boolean variables. This theorem shows that the width bounds on OODGs are asymmetric; the graph grows much faster from the bottom than from the top. In Fig.2, the width of the "kite" at each level is proportional to the maximum number of nodes possible at that level. The kite is thus an envelope bounding both the overall size and the specific width of every OODG with the given number of levels. This theorem is one of the motivations for growing the graphs bottom-up — a wrong ordering will "explode" fast, and a lookahead of $\log n$ levels, will get us to the level where the graph can be the widest.

Theorem 1 Kite Theorem. *The width of level i of a reduced OODG with m levels implementing a k-categorization function over Boolean inputs is bounded by*

$$\min\left\{2^i, k^{2^{(m-i)}}\right\}$$

Proof (sketch): The first term is a top-down bound; each Boolean variable can cause the number of branching nodes to grow by a factor of at most two. The second term is a bottom-up bound; if a level has k nodes, the level above it must have at most k^2 nodes, since there are only k^2 mappings from $\{0,1\} \mapsto \{0,\ldots,k-1\}$. If two nodes branch the same way on both values of the Boolean variable, and the OODG is not reduced. $\square$

3 Bottom-Up Construction of OODGs

In this section we present an algorithm for constructing a reduced OODG given the full (labelled) instance space. The algorithm is recursive and nondeterministic. For simplicity of notation, we assume Boolean variables and an arbitrary number of categories. Our current implementation allows general discrete variables.

The input to the algorithm is a set of sets, $\{C_0, C_1, \ldots, C_{k-1}\}$, where each set C_i is the set of all instances labelled with category i. The output of the algorithm is a reduced OODG that correctly categorizes the instance space.

The algorithm, shown in Fig.3, works by creating sets of instances, such that each set corresponds to one node in the graph (the input sets corresponding to the category nodes). Intuitively, we want an instance in a set C_i to reach node V_i corresponding to it, when the instance's path is traced from the root of the completed OODG, branching at branching-nodes according to the attribute values.

Given the input, the algorithm nondeterministically selects a variable X to test at the penultimate level of the OODG. It then creates new sets of instances (corresponding to the nodes in the penultimate level of the final OODG) which are projections of the original instances with variable X deleted. The sets are created in such a way that all instances in a set C_{xy} (which matches a branching node) are a subset of the instances of some input set C_x when augmented with

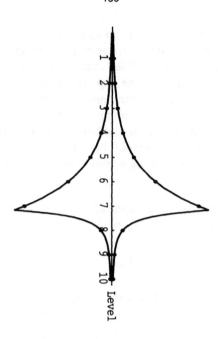

Fig. 2. The diagram's width at a level is proportional to the maximum number of nodes possible in an OODG at that level.

variable $X = 0$, and similarly, they are a subset of the instances of some set C_y when augmented with variable $X = 1$. In the graph, the branching node corresponding to C_{xy} will have the edge labelled 0 terminating at node x, and the edge labelled 1 terminating at node y.

The new sets now form a smaller problem over $n - 1$ variables, and the algorithm calls itself recursively to compute the rest of the OODG with the sets of the new level serving as the input. The recursion stops when the input to the algorithm is a single set, possibly consisting of the *null* instance (0 variables).

It can be shown that the algorithm always terminates with a reduced OODG (proof omitted).

Example 1. Executing the Algorithm on Parity In this example we show how to run the algorithm for the 3-bit odd parity function with one irrelevant attribute, i.e., $f = X_1 \oplus X_2 \oplus X_4$ (X_3 being irrelevant). To resolve the nondeterminism, we will select attributes in reverse numerical order, that is, X_4, X_3, X_2, X_1.

The input to the algorithm is $\{C_0, C_1\}$. All instances in C_0 have a label 0, and all elements in C_1 have label 1

$$C_0 = \{0000, 0010, 0101, 0111, 1001, 1011, 1100, 1110\}$$
$$C_1 = \{0001, 0011, 0100, 0110, 1000, 1010, 1101, 1111\}$$

Deleting attribute X_4 from each instances gives us the following projected in-

---

Input: k sets $C_0, \ldots, C_{k-1}$ such that $\mathcal{X} = \bigcup_{i=0}^{k-1} C_i$ (the whole instance space).
Output: Reduced OODG correctly categorizing all instances in $\mathcal{X}$.

1. If $(k = 1)$ then return the graph with one node.
2. Nondeterministically select a variable X to be deleted from the instances.
3. Project the instances in $C_0, \ldots, C_{k-1}$ onto the instance space $\mathcal{X}'$, such that variable X is deleted. Formally, if X is the ith variable,

$$\mathcal{X}' \leftarrow \pi_{(X_1, \ldots, X_{i-1}, X_{i+1}, \ldots, X_n)} \bigcup_{i=0}^{k-1} C_i$$

4. For all $i, j \in \{0, \ldots, k-1\}$ let C_{ij} be the set containing instances from $\mathcal{X}'$ s.t. the instances belong to set C_i when augmented with $X = 0$, and to the set C_j when augmented with $X = 1$.
5. Let k' be the number of non-empty sets from $\{C_{ij}\}$. Call the algorithm recursively with the k' non-empty sets, and let G be the OODG returned.
6. Label the k' leaf nodes of G, corresponding to the non-empty sets C_{ij} with the variable X. Create a new level of k nodes corresponding to the sets $C_0, \ldots, C_{k-1}$. From the node corresponding to each C_{ij}, create two edges: one labelled 0, terminating at the (category) node corresponding to C_i, and the other labelled 1, terminating at the (category) node corresponding to C_j.
7. Return the augmented OODG G.

Fig. 3. A nondeterministic algorithm for learning OODGs.

---

stance space

$$\mathcal{X}' = \{000, 001, 010, 011, 100, 101, 110, 111\}$$

Because we started with the full instance space, each of these projections has a defined **destination** (a set name shown after the right-arrow below) for each possible value of X_4. Creating sets from all projected instances in $\mathcal{X}'$ that have the same destinations for the same values of X_4, we get

$$C_{01}(0 \rightarrow C_0, 1 \rightarrow C_1) = \{000, 001, 110, 111\}$$
$$C_{10}(0 \rightarrow C_1, 1 \rightarrow C_0) = \{010, 011, 100, 101\}$$

Note that out of four possible sets, only two were needed. We now construct the OODG recursively using the two non-empty sets C_{01} and C_{10} as our input sets. Selecting variable X_3 to delete gives us the following projection

$$\mathcal{X}'' = \{00, 01, 10, 11\}$$

Creating the appropriate sets from the projected instances in $\mathcal{X}''$ yields

$$C_{00}(0 \rightarrow C_{01}, 1 \rightarrow C_{01}) = \{00, 11\}$$
$$C_{11}(0 \rightarrow C_{10}, 1 \rightarrow C_{10}) = \{01, 10\}$$

Note that each of the two new sets implements a constant function that ignores the value of the given attribute (*i.e.*, it branches to the same node regardless of the attribute value). A level for which all implemented functions are constant implies that the variable is irrelevant. Continuing the execution yields the OODG depicted in Fig.1.

4 HOODG: A Hill Climbing Algorithm For Constructing OODGs

In this section we address the two main problems ignored in the algorithm described in the previous section:

1. Deciding where to place projected instances (Step 4 of the algorithm) for which we have more than once choice. This can happen if a projection does not have all possible augmentations because we do not have the full instance space.
2. Ordering the variable for selection in Step 2.

4.1 Placing Projected Instances

If we do not have the full instance space, there will be projections of instances for which some values of the deleted attribute will be missing (*e.g.*, we know that a projected instance must branch to some node on values 0 and 2, but do not know where it should branch on values 1 and 3). Call such projections *Incomplete Projections*, or **IPs.** A decision on where to place these instances constitutes a bias, since it determines how unseen instances will be classified.

Following Occam's razor principle, we would like to find the smallest OODG consistent with the data (since we assume no noise, we will not overfit the data). We are thus looking for a minimal set of branching nodes that "covers" all projections, *i.e.*, a minimal cover.

An IP is **consistent** with another projection, P, (at the same level of the graph) if they do not have conflicting destinations on the same value of the deleted variable. An IP **agrees** with another projection, P, if they are consistent, and all destinations defined for the IP are also defined for the projection P (note that *agrees* is an asymmetric relation).

The placement strategy used in our implementation is to start creating projection sets (branching nodes) with projections having the greatest number of known destinations (values of the deleted variable), then for projections with fewer known destinations. Each projection is placed in a projection set where it agrees with all instances whenever possible; otherwise, it is placed in a set where it is consistent with all instances, if possible; otherwise, a new projection set is created, consisting of the single projection. Ties are broken in favor of projection sets with more destinations.

4.2 Ordering the Variables

There are $n!$ possible orders in which to select the variables in Step 2 of the algorithm. Given the full instance space, it is possible to find the optimal ordering using dynamic programming by checking "only" 2^n orderings, as described in [11, 12].

In our implementation, we chose to greedily select the variable that yields the smallest width (minimal number of nodes) at the next level (equivalent to a one-ply lookahead). We consider each variable in turn, compute the width of the level that would be formed if we were to select that variable in Step 2 of the algorithm, and then select the one that minimizes the width. Tie-breaking for variables with the same resultant width favors those with the greater number of "constant" nodes, $i.e.$, nodes that ignore the variable value. This tends to favor irrelevant attributes early, increasing the ratio of the training set size to the projected instance space. Equality is possible only if each projected instance has exactly $|D|$ instances in the sets before the projection, where $|D|$ is domain size of the irrelevant variable.

Example 2. The Monk's Problems The Monk's problems are three artificial problems that allow comparison of algorithms. In [27], 24 authors have compared 25 machine learning algorithms on these problems. In the given domain, robots have six different nominal attributes as follows:

$$Head\text{-}shape \in \{round, square, octagon\}.$$
$$Body\text{-}shape \in \{round, square, octagon\}.$$
$$Is\text{-}smiling \in \{yes, no\}.$$
$$Holding \in \{sword, balloon, flag\}.$$
$$Jacket\text{-}color \in \{red, yellow, green, blue\}.$$
$$Has\text{-}tie \in \{yes, no\}.$$

In the first problem, Monk 1, the target concept is

$$(Head\text{-}shape = Body\text{-}shape) \text{ or } (Jacket\text{-}color = red)$$

The standard training set for this problem has 124 instances out of 432 possible instances. Running our algorithm on this problem shows the significance of discovering irrelevant attributes. The three irrelevant attributes are selected first, and after constructing three levels of constant nodes, we are left with a problem of inducing an OODG for the remaining three attributes. There are 36 possible instances for the three remaining attributes, and the projections of the specific training set given in this problem yield 35 different instances (the expected number is 34.91, so this is not a fortuitous training set). The missing instance agrees with only one of the two nodes at the level at which it is projected, so we do not have a choice of where to put it. After discovering the irrelevant attributes, the problem becomes trivial. Fig.4 shows the resulting OODG, after removing constant nodes.

Target concept is: (Head-shape = Body-shape) or (Jacket-color = red).

Fig. 4. Resulting OODG for Monk's problem 1 (constant nodes removed).

In the second problem, Monk 2, the concept is

Exactly two of the attributes have their *first* value.

The standard training set for this problem has 169 instances. This problem has no irrelevant attributes which makes it very hard, given the original encoding of six nominal attributes. However, if we encode it using a *local representation*, where each attribute value is represented by one Boolean indicator variable, many attributes become irrelevant. This is the encoding scheme used by Thrun and Fahlman when neural nets were tested.

Under a local-representation encoding, there are 17 attributes, but 11 of them are irrelevant. Projecting the instances on the six relevant attributes yields 52 different instances out of 64 possible ones.

There is a subtle problem when running our hill-climbing algorithm. In the first stage, each of the 17 attributes is redundant (*i.e.*, the penultimate level has only constant nodes when each is selected), making it a candidate for being an irrelevant attribute. Intuitively, deleting any *one* such Boolean attribute still allows us to solve the problem; in the local representation, the missing attribute can be reconstructed from the other attributes, since for every variable in the original encoding, *exactly* one of the new indicator variables must be set to 1 (and the others to zero). Note of course that once one variable is deleted, other variables that were "candidates" become relevant. Our heuristic for choosing the "best" attribute is to do one level of lookahead for redundant attributes. The attribute that creates the most number of redundant attributes at the *next* level is selected.

With the lookahead procedure described above, and using local representation, HOODG correctly generalizes the training set to get 100% accuracy on the test set. Fig.5 shows the resulting OODG, which is the smallest one possible for the given target concept.

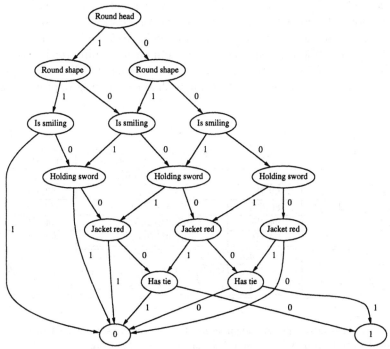

Target concept is: Exactly two of of the following attributes must have the value 1 {round-head, round-shape, is-smiling, holding-sword, jacket-red, has-tie}.

Fig. 5. Resulting OODG for Monk's problem 2

5 Experimental Results

The complexity of our algorithm as implemented is $O(ns^2 + is^2(n-1))$ per level, where i is the number of irrelevant attributes at the given level, and s is the number of projected instances at that level. Running on a a SPARCstation ELC, the execution time varies from about 3 seconds for Monk 1, 10 seconds for parity 5+5 (described below) to four and a half minutes for Monk 2 in the local representation (mostly due to the large number of irrelevant attributes).

Table 1 shows the accuracy results for some classical datasets and some artificial ones. The datasets Monk 1,2,3, and Vote, were taken from Quinlan's C4.5 data files (Monk3 has 5% noise); each has one training set and one test set. The vote database is a real-world database that includes votes for each of the U.S. House of Representatives Congressmen on the 16 key votes identified by the Congressional Quarterly Almanac Volume XL (the votes are simplified to yes, no, or unknown). The data set consists of 300 instances and the test set consists of 135 instances.

The second part of the table depicts the average of 10 runs, each with a randomly chosen training set. Each training set for Monk 1* is of size 124 (as is the original training set); each training set for Parity5, which is the XOR of 5 bits, consists of 50% of the instance space; and each training for Parity 5+5, which is the XOR of 5 bits with 5 irrelevant bits, consists of 10% of the instance space. The systems compared are ID3, C4.5, with and without grouping (-s flag), and HOODG.

Data Set	ID3	C4.5 / C4.5 (grouping)	HOODG
Monk 1	81.7%	75.7%/100.0%	100.0%
Monk 2	69.2%	65.0%/74.1%	83.1%
Monk 2 (local repr.)	86.6%	70.4%/75.9%	100.0%
Monk 3	94.4%	97.2%/100.0%	94.4%
Vote	94.1%	97.0%/93.3%	94.1%
Monk 1*	92.3% ± 4.6%	86.1% ± 3.7%/92.9% ± 7.0%	100% ± 0.0%
Parity 5 (50%)	60.6% ± 3.0%	50.0% ± 0.0%/50.0% ± 0.0%	100% ± 0.0%
Parity 5+5 (10%)	55.2% ± 4.5%	52.5% ± 4.7%/52.5% ± 4.7%	100% ± 0.0%

Table 1. Comparison of different algorithms. Results in the second part of the table are averaged over 10 runs with standard deviation after the ± sign.

It is interesting to note that while C4.5 gets 100% on the original training set for Monk 1, it has a large variance when executed on different training sets of the same size.

6 Related Work

Lee [15] introduced *binary decision programs* that are evaluated by executing a series of instructions that test a variable and make a two way branch. He showed that it is possible to represent any switching function in $O(\frac{2^n}{n})$ such instructions.

Akers [1] described binary decision diagrams, and gave a top-down procedure for building them using the Boole-Shannon expansion [3, 26]:

$$f = x_i \cdot f|_{x_i=1} + \overline{x_i} \cdot f|_{x_i=0}$$

where $f|_{x_i=b}$ is the restriction, or cofactor, of the function f

$$f|_{x_i=b}(x_1, \ldots, x_n) = f(x_1, \ldots, x_{i-1}, b, x_{i+1}, \ldots, x_n)$$

Moret [20] gives an excellent survey of work on decision trees and diagrams, with over 100 references.

Bryant [6] introduced Ordered Binary Decision Diagrams (OBDDs), which spawned a plethora of articles and a whole subcommunity dealing with OBDDs [7, 5, 19, 13]. OBDDs are a restriction of Binary Decision Diagrams (BDDs), where a total ordering is defined over the set of variables and all paths must test variables in accordance with the given ordering. Note that OBDDs are *not* necessarily levelled. Bryant describes the advantages of OBDDs over the common representations like CNF and DNF (these advantages apply to OODGs too):

- Operations like complementation may yield exponential growth for DNF and CNF, while they do not change the size of OBDDs.
- Common operations such as reduction, $f_1 < \text{op} > f_2$ (where op is any binary function), restriction, and composition, are bounded by the product of the graph sizes for the functions being operated on.
- Satisfiability testing takes constant time (check if the OBDD is the single category node 0), while finding a satisfying assignment for n variables takes $O(n)$ Counting the number of satisfying assignments if $O(|G|)$ where $|G|$ is the size of the graph, and finding all satisfying assignments is $O(n \cdot |S_f|)$ where $|S_f|$ is the number of such satisfying assignments.

OBDDs have been used for automatically verifying finite state machines, including 64-bit ALUs, with up to 10^{120} states by representing the state space symbolically instead of explicitly [9, 8]. These applications show, at least empirically, that many functions occurring in engineering domains seem to be representable in small (polynomial) OBDD structures (and hence in OODGs).

In the computer science theory community, binary decision graphs have been called **branching programs,** and have been extensively studied in the hope of separating some complexity classes and for studying the amount of space needed to compute various functions [4]. Two important theorems tell us that an algorithm in $\text{SPACE}(S(n))$ for $S(n) \geq \log n$ has a branching program complexity of at most $c^{S(n)}$ for some constant c [16], and that constant-width branching programs are very powerful, being able to accept all NC^1 languages [2].

In the machine learning community, general decision graphs were investigated by Oliver [21, 22] whose algorithm constructs the graphs top-down, by doing a hill-climbing search through the space of graphs, estimating the usefulness of each graph by Wallace's MMLP (minimum message length principle). At each stage a decision is made whether to split a leaf (and which), or whether to join to leaves. Operations that increase the message-length are never performed, hence the algorithm is guaranteed to terminate. The algorithm is (heuristically) able to overcome the replication and fragmentation problem associated with decision-trees.

Dvorak independently discovered the bottom-up technique we have used here to minimize OBDDs [10]. Although his work resembles ours, his motivation is to minimize functions with Don't Cares, while ours is to induce structures with high predictive power.

The relations between the different models, that is, OBDD, Branching Programs, and Decision Trees are summarized by Meinel in [17]. Translating Meinel results to the terms used in this paper, we get the following lemmas:

- There exists a Boolean function for which the smallest decision tree representing it has size $O(2^n)$, while there is an OODG representing it of size $O(n)$.
- There exists a Boolean function for which the smallest OODG representing it has size $O(2^{(n/\log n)})$, while there is a tree of size $O(n^2/\log n)$ representing it. (This lemma shows the different bias of the two structures.)
- There exist a Boolean function for which the smallest OODG has size size $2^{\Omega(n)}$, while an oblivious decision graph of depth linear in n that is not read-once, can represent it in $n^{O(1)}$.

An interesting point, first mentioned by Lee and Akers and studied in [19], is that a decision diagram actually represents more than one function. Entering the diagram at a different node allows *sharing* functions.

7 Future Work

Since our algorithm is essentially a hill-climbing algorithm, it may not find a global minimum. Researchers working on OBDDs (cf. [18, 14]) have experimented with exchanging variables after building the graph, and have achieved good results.

Deeper lookahead for variable selection is an obvious possible extension, especially since one motivation for growing the graph from the bottom is the asymmetric shape (the kite shape depicted in Fig.2) bounding the OODG.

We have shown promising preliminary results of using this structure with a simple hill-climbing heuristic. Looking further down the road, we need a method of dealing with noise, possibly by pruning the OODG. We need to extend the variable domains from discrete to real-valued, and to conduct more experiments on the generalization power.

Acknowledgements We would like to thank Nils Nilsson and Yoav Shoham for their continued support for this idea, and for supporting the MLC++ project at Stanford. Thanks to everyone who contributed to MLC++, especially George John, Richard Long, David Manley, Ofer Matan, and Karl Pfleger. Thanks to Ronen Brafman, Pat Langley, John Oliver, Ron Rymon, and Tomas Uribe for their comments on the first draft of this paper, and to James Kittock for carefully reading drafts of this paper. Our implementation was written using the MLC++ library, and the OODGs depicted in this paper are actual outputs generated by library routines that interface with AT&T's **dot** program written by Koutsofios and North.

References

1. Sheldon B. Akers. Binary decision diagrams. *IEEE Transactions on Computers*, C-27(6):509–516, 1978.
2. David A. Barrington. Bounded-width polynomial-size branching programs recognize exactly those languages in NC^1. *Journal of Computer and System Sciences*, 38(1):150–164, 1989.
3. George Boole. *An investigation of the laws of thought, on which are founded the theories of logic and probabilities*. London, Walton and Maberly; Macmillan and Co., 1854. Reprinted by Dover Books, New York, 1954.
4. Ravi B. Boppana and Michael Sipser. The complexity of finite functions. In J. van Leeuwen, editor, *Handbook of Theoretical Computer Science*. Elsevier, 1990.
5. Karl S. Brace, Richard L. Rudell, and Randal E. Bryant. Efficient implementation of a BDD package. In *27th ACM/IEEE Design Automation Conference. Proceedings*, pages 40–45, 1990.
6. Randal E. Bryant. Graph-based algorithms for boolean function manipulation. *IEEE Transactions on computers*, C-35(8):677–691, 1986.
7. Randal E. Bryant. Symbolic boolean manipulation with ordered binary-decision diagrams. *ACM Computing Surveys*, 24(3):293–318, 1992.
8. J. R. Burch, E. M. Clarke, and D. E. Long. Representing circuits more efficiently in symbolic model checking. In *28th ACM/IEEE Design Automation Conference. Proceedings*, pages 403–407, 1991.
9. J. R. Burch, E. M. Clarke, K. L. McMillan, D. L. Dill, and L. J. Hwang. Symbolic model checking: 10^{20} states and beyond. In *Fifth Annual IEEE Symposium on Logic in Computer Science.*, pages 428–439. IEEE Comput. Soc. Press, 1990.
10. Vaclav Dvorak. An optimization technique for ordered (binary) decision diagrams. In P. Dewilde and J. Vandewalle, editors, *Compeuro Proceedings. Computer Systems and Software Engineering*, pages 1–4. IEEE Comput. Soc. Press, 1992.
11. Steven J. Friedman and Kenneth J. Suppowit. Finding the optimal variable ordering for binary decision diagrams. In *24th ACM/IEEE Design Automation Conference*, pages 348–355, 1987.
12. Steven J. Friedman and Kenneth J. Suppowit. Finding the optimal variable ordering for binary decision diagrams. *IEEE Transactions On Computers*, 39(5):710–713, 1990.
13. Masahiro Fujita, Hisanori Fujisawa, and Jusuke Matsunaga. Variable ordering algorithms for ordered binary decision diagrams and their evaluation. *IEEE Transactions On Computer-Aided Design of Integrated Circuits and Systems*, 12(1):6–12, 1993.
14. Nagisa Ishiura, Hiroshi Sawada, and Shuzo Yajima. Minimization of binary decision diagrams based on exchanges of variables. In *IEEE International Conference On Computer-Aided Design. Digest of Technical Papers*, pages 472–475. IEEE Comput. Soc. Press, 1991.
15. C. Y. Lee. Representation of switching circuits by binary-decision programs. *The Bell System Technical Journal*, 38(4):985–999, 1959.

16. William J. Masek. A fast algorithm for the string editing problem and decision graph complexity. Master's thesis, Massachusetts Institute of Technology, 1976.
17. Christoph Meinel. Branching programs — an efficient data structure for computer-aided circuit design. *Bulletin of the European Association For Theoretical Computer Science*, 46:149–170, 1992.
18. Shin-ichi Minato. Minimum-width method of variable ordering for binary decision diagrams. *IEICE Transactions On Fundamentals of Electronics, Communications and Computer Sciences*, E75-A(3):392–399, 1992.
19. Shin-ichi Minato, Nagisa Ishiura, and Shuzo Yajima. Shared binary decision diagram with attributed edges for efficient boolean function manipulation. In *27th ACM/IEEE Design Automation Conference. Proceedings*, pages 24–28, 1990.
20. Bernard M. E. Moret. Decision trees and diagrams. *ACM Computing Surveys*, 14(4):593–623, 1982.
21. J.J. Oliver, D.L. Dowe, and C.S. Wallace. Inferring decision graphs using the minimum message length principle. In A. Adams and L. Sterling, editors, *Proceedings of the 5th Australian Joint Conference on Artificial Intelligence*, pages 361–367. World Scientific, Singapore, 1992.
22. Jonathan J. Oliver. Decision graphs — an extension of decision trees. In *Proceedings of the fourth International workshop on Artificial Intelligence and Statistics*, pages 343–350, 1993.
23. Giulia Pagallo and David Haussler. Boolean feature discovery in empirical learning. *Machine Learning*, 5:71–99, 1990.
24. J. R. Quinlan. Induction of decision trees. *Machine Learning*, 1:81–106, 1986. Reprinted in Shavlik and Dietterich (eds.) Readings in Machine Learning.
25. J. Ross Quinlan. *C4.5: Programs for Machine Learning.* Morgan Kaufmann, Los Altos, California, 1992.
26. C. E. Shannon. The synthesis of two-terminal switching circuits. *The Bell System Technical Journal*, 28(1):59–98, 1949.
27. S.B. Thrun, J. Bala, E. Bloedorn, I. Bratko, B. Cestnik, J. Cheng, K. De Jong, S. Dzeroski andS.E. Fahlman, D. Fisher, R. Hamann, K. Kaufman, S. Keller, I. Kononenko, J. Kreuziger, R.S. Michalski, T. Mitchell, P. Pachowicz, Y. Reich, H. Vafaie, W. Van de Weldel, W. Wenzel, J. Wnek, and J. Zhang. The monk's problems: A performance comparison of different learning algorithms. Technical Report CMU-CS-91-197, Carnegie Mellon University, 1991.
28. Ingo Wegener. *The Complexity of Boolean Functions.* B. G. Tuebner, 1987.

Estimating Attributes: Analysis and Extensions of RELIEF

Igor Kononenko

University of Ljubljana, Faculty of Electrical Engineering & Computer Science,
Tržaška 25, SLO-61001 Ljubljana, Slovenia
e-mail: igor.kononenko@ninurta.fer.uni-lj.si

Abstract. In the context of machine learning from examples this paper
deals with the problem of estimating the quality of attributes with and
without dependencies among them. Kira and Rendell (1992a,b) developed an algorithm called RELIEF, which was shown to be very efficient
in estimating attributes. Original RELIEF can deal with discrete and
continuous attributes and is limited to only two-class problems. In this
paper RELIEF is analysed and extended to deal with noisy, incomplete,
and multi-class data sets. The extensions are verified on various artificial
and one well known real-world problem.

1 Introduction

This paper deals with the problem of estimating the quality of attributes with
strong dependencies to other attributes which seems to be the key issue of machine learning in general. Namely, for particular problems (e.q. parity problems
of higher degrees) the discovering of dependencies between attributes may be
unfeasible due to combinatorial explosion. In such cases efficient heuristic algorithms are needed to discover the dependencies.

Information gain was proposed as a measure for estimating the attribute's
quality by Hunt et al. (1966) and later used by many authors (Quinlan, 1986).
The idea is to estimate the difference between the prior entropy of classes C and
posterior entropy, given values V of an attribute:

$$Gain = -\sum_C P(C) \log_2 P(C) - \sum_V \left(-P(V) \times \sum_C P(C|V) \log_2 P(C|V) \right) \quad (1)$$

Information gain and similar estimates like gini index (Breiman et al., 1984),
distance measure (Mantaras, 1989), and j-measure (Smyth & Goodman, 1990)
assume that attributes are independent and therefore are not applicable in domains with strong dependencies between attributes.

Kira and Rendell (1992a,b) developed an algorithm called RELIEF, which
was shown to be very efficient in estimating attributes. The key idea of RELIEF
is to estimate attributes according to how well their values distinguish among
instances that are near each other. For that purpose RELIEF for a given instance
searches for its two nearest neighbours: one from the same class (called *nearest*

hit) and the other from different class (called *nearest miss*). In fact, RELIEF's estimate $W[A]$ of attribute A is an approximation of the following difference of probabilities:

$$W[A] = P(\text{different value of A}|\text{nearest instance from different class})$$
$$- P(\text{different value of A}|\text{nearest instance from same class}) \qquad (2)$$

The rationale is that good attribute should differentiate between instances from different classes and should have the same value for instances from the same class.

Original RELIEF can deal with discrete and continuous attributes and is limited to only two-class problems. It is not clear how RELIEF could be extended to deal with incomplete data and to deal with problems with more than two classes. Straightforward extensions do not give satisfactory results. In this paper RELIEF is analysed and extended to deal with noisy, incomplete, and multi-class data sets. The extensions are verified on various artificial and one well known real-world problem.

In the next section RELIEF is described and extended to k-nearest neighbours search. In section 3, we extend relief to deal with missing data and in section 4 to deal with multi-class problems. Results of experiments with extended versions of RELIEF on artificial data sets and one real world problem are discussed in section 5.

2   Estimating Probabilities with RELIEF

The original algorithm of RELIEF (Kira & Rendell, 1992a,b) is the following

```
set all weights W[A] := 0.0;
for i := 1 to m do
    begin
        randomly select an instance R;
        find nearest hit H and nearest miss M;
        for A := 1 to all_attributes do
        W[A] := W[A] - diff(A,R,H)/m + diff(A,R,M)/m;
    end;
```

where *diff(Attribute,Instance1,Instance2)* calculates the difference between the values of Attribute for two instances. For discrete attributes the difference is either 1 (the values are different) or 0 (the values are equal), while for continuous attributes the difference is the actual difference normalized to the interval $[0, 1]$. Normalization with m guarantees that all weights are in the interval $[-1, 1]$.

Function *diff* is used also for calculating the distance between instances to find the nearest neighbours. The total distance is simply the sum of differences over all attributes.

Obviously, the algorithm tries to approximate the difference (2). Parameter m represents the number of instances for approximating probabilities. The larger

m implies more reliable approximation. However, m cannot exceed the number of available training instances. The obvious choice for relatively small number of training instances is to set m to the upper bound and run the outer loop of the learning algorithms over all available training instances. In all our experiments we used this simplification of the algorithm.

The selection of the nearest neighbours is of crucial importance in RELIEF. The purpose is to find the nearest neighbours with respect to important attributes. Redundant and noisy attributes may strongly affect the selection of nearest neighbours and therefore the estimation of probabilities on noisy data becomes unreliable. To increase the reliability of probability approximation RE-LIEF can be extended to search for k-nearest hits/misses instead of only one near hit/miss. The extended version of the algorithm, called RELIEF-A, averages the contribution of k nearest hits/misses.

To estimate the contribution of more nearest neighbours we generated 3 data sets. All attributes in these data sets are binary with equal prior probabilities for both values ($P(V1) = P(V2) = 0.5$) except for random attributes which have various prior probability of values, which are however independent of the class. There are two equally probable classes ($P(C1) = P(C2) = 0.5$) and each data set has 200 instances. We compared the *intended information gain* of attributes with the estimates generated by RELIEF-A by calculating the standard linear *correlation coefficient*. The correlation coefficient can show how close are the intended quality and the estimated quality of attributes.

The intended information gain is the one calculated from probabilities that were used to generate artificial data sets. Note that due to random generator (and in later sections due to added noise and incomplete data) the factual information gain may differ from the intended information gain. However, in all our experiments the correlation between the intended information gain and the factual information gain was greater than 0.95. Besides, as we are interested in the "true" probability distribution that was "responsible" for generation of the data, we should consider the intended information gain as the target for an ideal estimator.

First data set contained 5 random binary attributes with different prior probability of values ($P(V1) = 0.5, 0.4, ..., 0.1$) and 5 independent informative attributes. The degrees of information gains were determined with the probability of value $V1$ given class $C1$ ($P(V1|C1) = 0.95, 0.85, ..., 0.55$) and given class $C2$ ($P(V1|C2) = 1 - P(V1|C1)$).

The second data set was obtained from the first data set by replacing each informative attribute with 2 binary attributes (altogether $5 + 5 \times 2 = 15$ attributes). The values of each pair of new attributes were determined by the value of the original attribute using parity relation of second order (EXOR relation). For example, if original attribute has value $V1$ then two new attributes have equal values, otherwise different values. Therefore, the *intended* information gain of two new attributes together is equal to the information gain of the original attribute. Note that information gain calculated with (1) is zero for all new attributes while the intended information gain for the new attribute is half of the information gain of the original attribute.

The third data set was obtained from the first data set by replacing each informative attribute with 3 binary attributes (altogether 20 attributes), the values of which were determined by the value of the original attribute using parity relation of third order. Therefore, each new attribute in this data set has one third of the information gain of the original attribute. Each data set was also corrupted with 0%, 10% and 20 % class noise. X% of noise means that class was changed for X% of randomly selected instances.

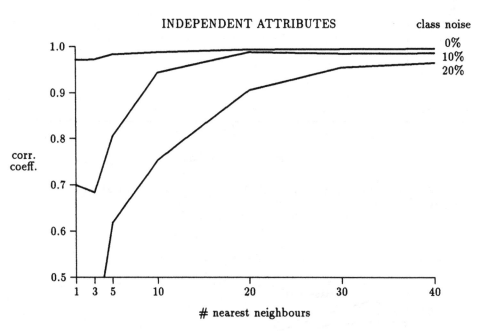

Figure 1: Results of experiments with RELIEF-A using the data set with independent and informative attributes.

The results for each data set are presented on figures 1-3. The results clearly show that the higher number of nearest neighbours in RELIEF-A improves the estimates of attributes even for noise free data sets. However, the improvement is more drastic for data sets with noise.

For independent attributes (figure 1) the quality of estimate monothonously increases with the number of nearest neighbours. This can be formally explained with the following derivation. When the number of nearest neighbours increases, equation (2) becomes:

$$W[A] = P(\text{different value of A}|\text{different class})$$

$$- P(\text{different value of A}|\text{same class}) \qquad (3)$$

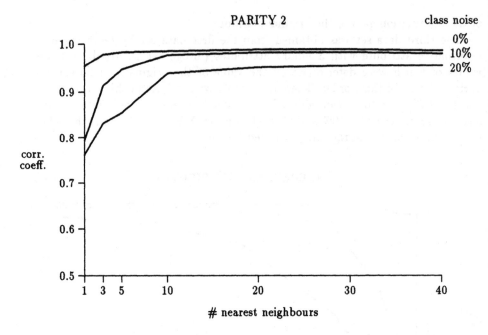

Figure 2: Results of experiments with RELIEF-A using the data set with pairwise informative attributes.

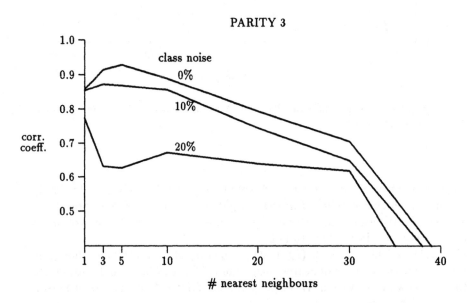

Figure 3: Results of experiments with RELIEF-A using the data set with triplets of informative attributes.

$$= P(\text{equal value of A}|\text{same class})$$

$$-P(\text{equal value of A}|\text{different class})$$

If we rewrite

$$P_{eqval} = P(\text{equal value of A})$$

$$P_{samecl} = P(\text{same class})$$

and

$$P_{samecl|eqval} = P(\text{same class}|\text{equal value of A})$$

we obtain using Bayes rule:

$$W[A] = \frac{P_{samecl|eqval}P_{eqval}}{P_{samecl}} - \frac{(1 - P_{samecl|eqval})P_{eqval}}{1 - P_{samecl}}$$

Using equalities

$$P_{samecl} = \sum_C P(C)^2$$

$$P_{samecl|eqval} = \sum_V \left(\frac{P(V)^2}{\sum_V P(V)^2} \times \sum_C P(C|V)^2 \right)$$

we obtain:

$$W[A] = \frac{P_{eqval} \times Gini'(A)}{P_{samecl}(1 - P_{samecl})} \tag{4}$$

where

$$Gini'(A) = \sum_V \left(\frac{P(V)^2}{\sum_V P(V)^2} \times \sum_C P(C|V)^2 \right) - \sum_C P(C)^2 \tag{5}$$

is highly correlated with gini-index (Breiman et al., 1984) for classes C and values V of attribute A. The only difference is that instead of factor

$$\frac{P(V)^2}{\sum_V P(V)^2}$$

gini-index uses

$$\frac{P(V)}{\sum_V P(V)} = P(V)$$

Gini index is one of impurity functions that is in turn highly correlated with information gain as defined with (1). The denominator of equation (4) is constant for all attributes and therefore does not influence the correlation factor. Factor P_{eqval} is a kind of normalization factor for multi valued attributes. In our experiments all attributes were binary with equal prior probabilities for both values, which gives constant $P_{eqval} = 0.5$. Therefore, with increasing number of nearest neighbours, the estimates of RELIEF-A are highly correlated with gini-index and information gain.

For dependent attributes the quality increases up to a maximum but later decreases as the number of nearest neighbours exceeds the number of instances that belong to the same peak in the distribution space for a given class. This effect can be seen on figure 3 while for PARITY-2 problem we observed this effect for larger number of nearest neighbours.

It is interesting that, for smaller number of nearest hits/misses used by the algorithm, noise more drastically affects results on independent data sets than results on data sets with dependent attributes. This may be explained by the fact that an incorrect class label implies incorrect attribute values for only one half/third of attributes for parity-2/parity-3 problems. Again, using higher number of nearest neighbours helps: it drastically reduces this effect.

3   Incomplete Data Sets

To enable RELIEF-A to deal with incomplete data sets, the function

$$diff(Attribute, Instance1, Instance2)$$

should be extended to missing values of attributes. We compared 3 versions of RELIEF:

RELIEF-B: If at least one of two instances has unknown value for a given attribute, the diff is set to $1 - \frac{1}{\#\_values\_of\_attribute}$.

RELIEF-C: Same as RELIEF-B except that during updating the estimates $W[A]$ the contributions of such differences (calculated from instances with at least one unknown value for the given attribute) are ignored, with appropriate normalization. The idea is that unknown values should be ignored from the estimates and if enough training instances is provided, the resulting estimates should converge to correct estimates.

RELIEF-D: Calculate the probability that two given instances have different values for the given attribute:

− if one instance (e.g. I1) has unknown value:

$$diff(A, I1, I2) = 1 - P(value(A, I2)|class(I1))$$

− if both instances have unknown value:

$$diff(A, I1, I2) = 1 - \sum_{V}^{\#values(A)} \big(P(V|class(I1)) \times P(V|class(I2)) \big)$$

The conditional probabilities are approximated with relative frequencies from the training set.

To estimate the performance of three algorithms 0%, 10%, 20 % and 30% of values of informative attributes were replaced with unknown values. It turned out that for noise free data, there was no significant difference between the performance of above three algorithms. However, for incomplete and noisy data,

RELIEF-D performed significantly better. A typical picture is shown on figure 4 for the data set with independent informative attributes. The number of nearest hits/misses was set to 10 and there were 30% of unknown values. For other data sets and other values of parameters the pictures of results are similar.

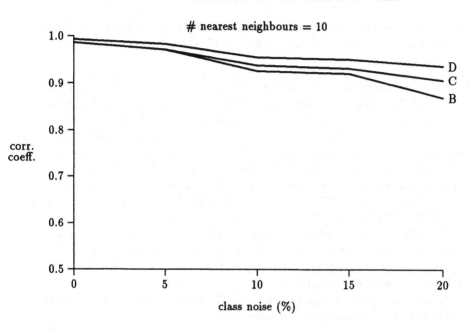

INDEPENDENT ATTS with 30% UNKNOWN VALS

Figure 4: Results of different versions of RELIEF on incomplete data set (30% of unknown attribute values) with independent attributes. The number of nearest hits/misses is 10.

4 Multi-Class Problems

Kira and Rendell (1992a,b) claim that RELIEF can be used to estimate attributes of data sets with more than two classes by splitting the problem into a series of 2-class problems. This solution seems unsatisfactory. In order to use RELIEF in practice it should be able to deal with multi class problems without any prior changes in knowledge representation that could affect the final outcomes.

We experimented with two extensions of RELIEF-D for multi-class problems:

RELIEF-E: Near miss of the given instance I is defined as the nearest neighbour from different class. This is straightforward generalization of RELIEF.

RELIEF-F: Instead of finding one near miss M from different class, the algorithm finds one near miss $M(C)$ for each different class and averages their contribution for updating estimates $W[A]$. The average is weighted with the prior probability of each class:

$$W[A] := W[A] - diff(A, R, H)/m + \sum_{C \neq class(R)} [P(C) \times diff(A, R, M(C))]/m$$

The idea is that the algorithm should estimate the ability of attributes to separate each pair of classes regardless of which two classes are closest to each other.

In order to compare the performance of above two algorithms we generated four additional data sets. First two data sets have 3 and 4 equally probable classes, respectively, 3 random attributes, and 3 informative attributes for each pair of classes. The data set with 3 classes has $3 + 3 \times \frac{3 \times 2}{2} = 12$ binary attributes, and the one with 4 classes have $3 + 3 \times \frac{4 \times 3}{2} = 21$ attributes. The attributes were made informative by means of the prior probability of one of the attribute's values given the class. E.g. for attribute that is informative for separating class 1 and 3 we have $P(V1|C1) = 0.95, 0.75, 0.55$, $P(V1|C3) = 1 - P(V1|C1)$ and $P(V1|C2) = P(V1|C4) = 0.5$.

The other two data sets were obtained from the first two by replacing each informative attribute with 2 binary attributes in the same way as in the second data set described in section 2. Therefore, the third data set has 21 attributes and the last one has 39 attributes.

Results are given in figures 5 and 6. The results show clear advantage of RELIEF-F both in noise free and noisy data.

5 Discussion

RELIEF is efficient heuristic estimator of attributes that is able to deal with data sets with dependent and independent attributes. Its extensions incorporated in RELIEF-F enable it to deal with noisy and incomplete data sets and, what is probably the most important contribution of RELIEF-F, it can efficiently deal with multi class problems.

To verify this conclusions, drawn from experiments with artificial data sets, we ran different versions of RELIEF on one well known medical data set. However, for real world data sets the intended (true) information gain of attributes is unknown. For "primary tumor" data set physicians claim, that attributes are independent, and this was also confirmed with the experiments with semi-naive Bayesian classifier (Kononenko, 1991). Therefore, for this data set, it is acceptable to use information gain calculated with (1) as an estimate of the target attribute quality.

To estimate the performance of different versions of RELIEF, we calculated the correlation coefficient between factual information gain of attributes and RELIEF's estimates $W[A]$. Results are given in figure 7. Results on the real

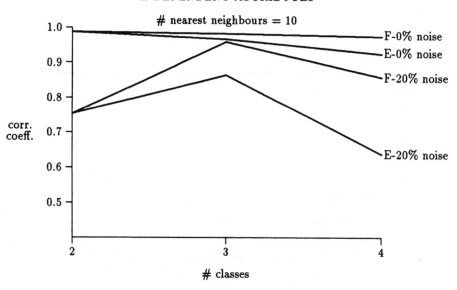

Figure 5: Results of different versions of RELIEF in multi-class problems with independent attributes without noise and with 20% class noise. The number of nearest hits/misses is 10.

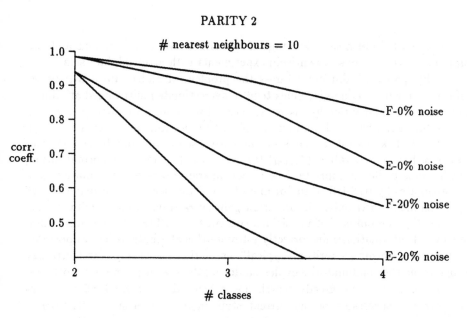

Figure 6: Results of different versions of RELIEF in multi-class problems with dependent attributes without noise and with 20% class noise. The number of nearest hits/misses is 10.

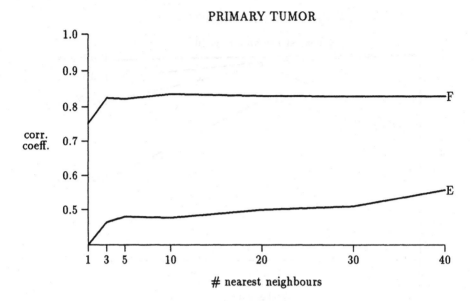

Figure 7: Results of different versions of RELIEF on "primary tumor" medical data set. Versions of RELIEF-E with the same algorithm for unknown values as RELIEF-B and RELIEF-C have all their correlation coefficients less than 0.4.

world data set confirm the advantage of RELIEF-F over other versions and also support the conclusions drawn from experiments with artificial data sets.

In this paper we did not address the problem of multi valued attributes. Information gain (1) and gini-index tend to overestimate multi valued attributes and various normalization heuristics are needed to avoid this tendency (e.g. gain ratio (Quinlan, 1986) and binarization of attributes (Kononenko et al., 1984)). RELIEF with k-nearest hits/misses implicitly uses prior probability that two instances have equal values (P_{eqval}) (see equation (4)) for such normalization, which seems to be appropriate. The major difference between information gain and estimates by RELIEF-F in "primary tumor" problem is in estimates of two most significant attributes. Information gain overestimates one attribute with 3 values (by the opinion of physicians specialists). RELIEF-F and normalized versions of information gain correctly estimate this attribute as less important.

Inductive learning algorithms typically use variants of greedy search strategy to overcome the combinatorial explosion during the search for good hypotheses. The major role in the greedy search has a heuristic function that estimates the potential successors of the current state in the search space. RELIEF-F seems to be very promising heuristic function that may overcome the myopy of current inductive learning algorithms. Kira and Rendell used RELIEF as a preprocessor to eliminate irrelevant attributes from the data description before learning. RELIEF-F is general, efficient and reliable enough that can be used inside the learning process to guide the search.

Acknowledgements

Part of this work was done during the author's stay at California Institute of Technology in Pasadena, CA. I would like to thank Padhraic Smyth and Prof. Rodney Goodman for enabling my work in their Micro Systems Research Laboratory. This work was supported by Slovenian Ministry of Science. I thank Matevž Kovačič and Uroš Pompe for comments on earlier versions of the paper. One of the reviewers was slightly imprecise when suggesting me to read strongly related papers in journals IEEE Trans. on PAMI, Pattern Recognition and Pattern Recognition Letters in years 1978-1990. I would appreciate if any reader can make this information more precise.

References

1. Breiman L., Friedman J.H., Olshen R.A., Stone C.J.: Classification and Regression Trees. Wadsforth International Group 1984
2. Hunt E., Martin J & Stone P.: Experiments in Induction. New York: Academic Press 1966
3. Kira K. & Rendell L.: A practical approach to feature selection. In: Proc. Intern. Conf. on Machine Learning. (Aberdeen, July 1992) D.Sleeman & P.Edwards (eds.), Morgan Kaufmann 1992, pp.249-256
4. Kira K. & Rendell L.: The feature selection problem: traditional methods and new algorithm. In: Proc. AAAI'92. San Jose, CA, July 1992
5. Kononenko I., Bratko I., Roškar E.: Experiments in inductive learning of medical diagnostic rules. In: Proc. International School for the Synthesis of Expert Knowledge Workshop. Bled, Slovenia, August 1984
6. Kononenko I.: Semi-naive Bayesian classifier. In: Proc. European Working Session on Learning, (Porto, March 1991), Y.Kodratoff (ed.), Springer Verlag 1991, pp.206-219
7. Mantaras R.L.: ID3 Revisited: A distance based criterion for attribute selection. In: Proc. Int. Symp. Methodologies for Intelligent Systems. Charlotte, North Carolina, U.S.A., Oct. 1989
8. Quinlan R.: Induction of decision trees. Machine learning 1, 81–106 (1986)
9. Smyth P. & Goodman R.M.: Rule induction using information theory. In. G.Piatetsky-Shapiro & W.Frawley (eds.): Knowledge Discovery in Databases. MIT Press 1990

BMWk Revisited

Generalization and Formalization of an Algorithm for Detecting Recursive Relations in Term Sequences

Guillaume Le Blanc*

LRI, URA 410 du CNRS, Bâtiment 490, Université de Paris-Sud,
F-91405 Orsay Cedex, France
E-mail : Guillaume.Le-Blanc@lri.fr

Abstract. As several works in Machine Learning (particularly in Inductive Logic Programming) have focused on building recursive definitions from examples, this paper presents a formalization and a generalization of the BMWk methodology, which stems from program synthesis from examples, ten years ago. The framework of the proposed formalization is term rewriting. It allows to state some theoretical results on the qualities and limitations of the method.

1 Introduction

Detecting recursive relations in term sequences is likely to have a number of applications in Machine Learning, Theorem Proving and other fields. During the last seventies and early eighties, an algorithm called BMWk (for Boyer-Moore-Wegbreit-Kodratoff) came out to be very fruitful in the field of program synthesis from examples [5, 7, 8, 19]. Unfortunately, this topic has sunk into oblivion mainly as its protagonists decided to investigate new ways of automatic programming since program synthesis from examples seems too difficult.

Recently, many Machine Learning research workers – especially in the field of Inductive Logic Programming – have come to the conclusion that it is essential to be able to learn recursive definitions [14].

This background compels us to examine the previous works in program synthesis. We studied the two last implementations of the BMWk algorithm [3, 17]. It appears that the methodology is very interesting and in some way close to the work of Lapointe and Matwin [1, 11].

Nevertheless, the BMWk methodology as it is exposed by Fargues [3] and Papon [17] suffers from some drawbacks (no distinction between operators and utilization strategy, unjustified heuristics, limited framework, conception errors) so that a formalization is absolutely necessary.

* This work is supported by the Esprit project BRA ILP n° 6020 and the french MRT through PRC-IA

Moreover, the BMWk algorithms, as opposed to most of those coming from Inductive Logic Programming [16, 18] follow strong directing rules and as LOP-STER [1] or as the algorithm of Idestam-Almquist [4] use fewer examples. These qualities are very interesting since the search space is gigantic.

In the light of works published during the last decade, it is possible to reformulate the BMWk methodology, building a solid formalization and even generalizing it so that it can handle the Inductive Logic Programming usual bench marks. The aim of this paper is to present a formalization and a generalization of the BMWk methodology. As we state in Sect. 6 this results in a powerful methodology able to synthesize complicated functions with several embedded level of recursivity directly from examples built with constructors (e.g. synthesize polynomial functions or exponential functions from examples built with 0 and s, without any other knowledge).

2 Preliminaries

In this Sect., we shall give the notations, definitions and the theoretical requisite propositions. Most vocabulary of this Sect. is defined and exemplified in a survey on term rewriting by Dershowitz and Jouannaud [2].

Let $\mathcal{F} = \{f, g, h, \ldots\}$ be a finite set of function symbols and let $\mathcal{X} = \{u, v, w, x, y, z, \ldots\}$ be a set of variables. Let $T(\mathcal{F}, \mathcal{X})$ be the set of terms constructed using $\mathcal{F}$ and variables in $\mathcal{X}$ and $T(\mathcal{F})$ the set of *ground terms* (i.e. terms without variables). Let $Var(T)$ be the set of all the variables which appear in the term T. Let $\mathcal{C}$, $\mathcal{C}'$ and $\mathcal{C}''$ be disjoint subsets of $\mathcal{F}$ which are designated to be sets of *constructor* symbols. Usually constructors are named with letters from the beginning of the alphabet $\{b, c, e, \ldots\}$. Constructors stand to represent data types and non-constructors represent functions (e.g. 0 and s are constructors for the natural integers 0, $s(0)$, $s(s(0))$,...). Lists are built with two constructors cons and nil, the empty list. Instead of $cons(x, y)$ and nil, we prefer the notation $[x|y]$ and $[]$.

A *substitution* σ or θ is a function from terms to terms which replaces the variables of a term by other terms (e.g. if $\sigma = \{x/a, y/f(x)\}$ and $T = g(x, g(x, y))$ then $T\sigma = g(a, g(a, f(x))))$. A substitution ρ which replaces variables for variables and which is bijective is called a *variable renaming*. Given two terms M and T, if there exists a substitution θ such that $M\theta = T$ we say that the *pattern M recognizes* the term T or that M *subsumes* T or that M is a *generalization* of T. The subsumption relation defines an ordering on terms. Given two terms S and T, G is a *least general generalization* (lgg) if G subsumes S and T and if all term which subsumes S and T also subsumes G. Two terms S and T *unify* if there exists a substitution σ such that $T\sigma = S\sigma$.

If L_i and R_i are terms in $T(\mathcal{F}, \mathcal{X})$, the set of *equations* $\{L_i = R_i\}$ defines a *congruence* on $T(\mathcal{F}, \mathcal{X})$ if $f(S_1, \ldots, S_n) = f(T_1, \ldots, T_n)$ whenever $S_i = T_i$ for all i, if for all substitution θ, $S\theta = T\theta$ whenever $S = T$ and if it is reflexive, transitive and symmetric. Equations define functions from constructors. For example, the addition can be recursively defined by $s(x) + y = s(x + y)$ and $0 + y = y$. A *destructor* is a function which extracts the nth argument of a constructor term; **car** and **cdr** are the destructors of the constructor term **cons**. We use the notation a and d instead of **car** and **cdr**; a and d defined by $a([x|y]) = x$ and $d([x|y]) = y$. We also use the notation $adddd(x)$ for $a(d(d(d(d(x)))))$.

Term rewriting gives a way to calculate equalities. If L_i and R_i are terms in $T(\mathcal{F}, \mathcal{X})$, the set of *rewrite rules* $\{L_i \rightarrow R_i\}$ defines a *rewrite relation* on $T(\mathcal{F}, \mathcal{X})$ if $f(S_1, \ldots, S_n) \rightarrow f(T_1, \ldots, T_n)$ whenever $S_i \rightarrow T_i$ for all i, if for all substitution θ, $S\theta \rightarrow T\theta$ whenever $S \rightarrow T$ and if it is reflexive and transitive (the notation for the reflexive and transitive closure of $\rightarrow$ is $\xrightarrow{*}$). A *rewrite system* (namely a set of rewrite rules) *terminates* if for any term T there is no infinite chain of rewriting from T. A rewrite system is *confluent* if for any terms T, U and V, there exists a term S such that $U \xrightarrow{*} S$ and $V \xrightarrow{*} S$ whenever $T \xrightarrow{*} U$ and $T \xrightarrow{*} V$.

A well-founded ordering is an ordering with no infinite decreasing chain. A *reduction ordering* is a well-founded ordering $\prec$ on $T(\mathcal{F}, \mathcal{X})$ such that for all substitution σ and all terms T and T', if $T \prec T'$ then $T\sigma \prec T'\sigma$ and such that for all terms T_i, T and T', if $T \prec T'$ then $f(T_1, \ldots, T_{i-1}, T, T_{i+1}, \ldots, T_n) \prec f(T_1, \ldots, T_{i-1}, T', T_{i+1}, \ldots, T_n)$. The termination of a rewrite relation $\rightarrow$ is proved if it is included into a reduction ordering. The sub-term relation defines a reduction ordering. The sub-term ordering is a particular case of a more powerful class of reduction ordering called *recursive path ordering* [2].

3 Function Synthesis from Examples

First and foremost, we have to expose precisely the problem we want to solve. The BMWk methodology provides a way to compare terms in order to discover recursive relations among them. The main mechanisms that it uses are term matching and least general generalization calculus for two terms. Until now, the framework of BMWk was the LISP language for historical reasons. The examples have been defined as pairs of LISP lists and the solution of the synthesis as a LISP function. Since the BMWk algorithms in fact operate on terms we prefer to avoid this formalism. We use instead the notion of term rewriting [2] which supplies a more general background and which is closer to logic programming.

Given some examples of a function defined on terms by a congruence

reverse$([]) = []$
reverse$([a'']) = [a'']$
reverse$([a'', b'']) = [b'', a'']$
reverse$([a'', b'', c'']) = [c'', b'', a'']$
reverse$([a'', b'', c'', d'']) = [d'', c'', b'', a'']$

the BMWk algorithms generates a recursive definition of that function.

reverse$(x) \rightarrow f(x, x)$
$f([], v) \rightarrow []$
$f([x|y], v) \rightarrow f_1'([x|y], d(v), [a(v)])$
$f_1'([x], u, z) \rightarrow z$

$$f_1'([x_1, x_2|y], u, z) \rightarrow f_1'([x_2|y], d(u), [a(u)|z])$$
$$a([x|y]) \rightarrow x \quad \text{and} \quad d([x|y]) \rightarrow y$$

Since it does not allow the constant a'', b'', c'' or d'' to appear in the definition of the function and since this problem can not always be solved by variabilizing the constants a'', b'', c'' or d'' as we will see later, the examples are written $f(I\sigma) = O\sigma$, where σ is a substitution which contains all the parts of the example which must not appear in the definition of f. For example, we write $\{x_1/a'', x_2/b''\}, \texttt{reverse}([x_1, x_2]) \mapsto [x_2, x_1]$ instead of $\texttt{reverse}([a'', b'']) = [b'', a'']$. C'' will be the set of constructors $\{a'', b'', c'', d''\}$, C the set of the other constructors of the "inputs" $\{[\_|\_], []\}$ and C' the remaining constructors of the "outputs" (this set is empty in our example).

Definition 1 Input/Output example. Given C, C' and C'' three sets of constructor symbols and $\mathcal{X}$ a set of variable symbols, an example (or Input/Output example) of a function f is a triple (σ, I, O) where σ is a ground substitution on $T(C \cup C' \cup C'', \mathcal{X})$, I is a term from $T(C, \mathcal{X})$ and O a term from $T(C \cup C', \mathcal{X})$ such that $Var(O) \subset Var(I)$. We write $\sigma, f(I) \mapsto O$ for an Input/Output example.

Definition 2 function synthesis from example. Given $\{\sigma_j, I_j \mapsto O_j\}_{j \in J}$ a finite set of Input/Output examples from a function f (which defines a congruence $=$ on terms), synthesizing f from the examples means to build a term rewrite system $\mathcal{R}$ such that for all j, $f(I_j\sigma_j) \rightarrow_\mathcal{R} O_j\sigma_j$.

The term rewrite system $\mathcal{R}$ is consistent with respect to f if for all ground terms I and O from $T(C \cup C' \cup C'')$ such that $f(I) \xrightarrow{*}_\mathcal{R} O$ then $f(I) = O$.

The term rewrite system $\mathcal{R}$ is complete if for all ground terms I and O from $T(C \cup C' \cup C'')$ such that if $f(I) = O$ then there exists a ground term O' such that $f(I) \xrightarrow{*}_\mathcal{R} O'$.

The term rewrite system $\mathcal{R}$ is correct if it is complete and consistent.

Given a set of examples $\{\sigma_j, I_j \mapsto O_j\}_{j \in J}$ it would be nice to be able to consider the rewrite system $\{f(I_j) \rightarrow O_j\}_{j \in J}$. Alas, this rewrite system is not necessarily consistent with respect to f. In particular, it can be inconsistent with respect to the examples. Let us see an example. Given two examples from $\texttt{member}$, with $\sigma = \{x/a'', y/b'', z/c''\}$:

$$\sigma, \texttt{member}(x, [y, x]) \mapsto \texttt{true} \quad \text{and} \quad \sigma, \texttt{member}(z, [x, y]) \mapsto \texttt{false}$$

the rewrite rule $\texttt{member}(z, [x, y]) \rightarrow \texttt{false}$ is contradictory to the examples (because the first example implies that $\texttt{member}(a'', [b'', a'']) = \texttt{true}$).

The method exposed in this paper only handles the case where the rewrite system is consistent with respect to the example.

Restriction 3. Given two examples $\sigma, f(I) \mapsto O$ and $\sigma', f(I') \mapsto O'$ and $=$ the syntactic equality, if there exists θ such that $f(I'\theta) = f(I\sigma)$ then $O'\theta = O\sigma$.

The functions $\texttt{reverse}, \texttt{plus}, \texttt{times}$ among others (as opposed to $\texttt{member}$) meet this restriction ($\texttt{reverse}([x, y]) = [y, x]$ no matter if $x = y$ or $x \neq y$).

In order to apply the BMWk methodology, the examples need a last transformation which consists in replacing the variables of O by their position in I. This position is given by the destructors. For example, $\mathtt{reverse}([x, y]) \rightarrow [y, x]$ is turned into $\mathtt{reverse}(x) \rightarrow f(x, x)$ and $f([x, y], v) \rightarrow [a(d(v)), a(v)]$ (since $ad([x, y]) = y$ and $a([x, y]) = x$). Since this transformation is not necessarily unique, we state a new restriction.

Restriction 4. Given an example $\sigma, f(I) \mapsto O$ the variables of O must have a single position in I.

Generally this restriction holds when the previous one holds. Also the functions $\mathtt{reverse}$, $\mathtt{plus}$, $\mathtt{times}$ bear this restriction.

If both restrictions hold, the example $\sigma, f(I) \mapsto O$ is turned into $f(I, v) \rightarrow O\theta$, where θ replaces each variable of O with its position in I. Assume, now, we have a set of rewrite rules $\{f(C_i, v) \rightarrow F_i\}_{i \in I}$.

4 Recursivity

Given a set of rewrite rules $\{f(C_i, v^m) \rightarrow F_i\}_{i \in I}$, where v^m is the variable vector $v_1, \ldots, v_m$, applying the BMWk methodology roughly consists in *"matching two consecutive terms."* The most important restriction of the algorithms described ten years ago was to only deal with linearly ordered examples. As Jouannaud and Kodratoff pointed out, the inputs of the examples (i.e. the C_i) have to belong to an *ascending linear domain* [5]. This condition still remains when they propose a methodology for two variables functions [6]. In his Ph. D. thesis, Papon [17] considers recursive relations with a step greater than one but still retains the linearity condition.

Because of these restrictions, the methodology was only able to handle recursive relations such that $f(s^k(n))$ is a function of $f(n)$ or $f([x|l])$ is a function of $f(l)$.

We would like to deal with more complicated definitions. For example, the Fibonnacci function is given by $f(ss(n)) = f(s(n)) + f(n)$, $f(s0) = s0$ and $f(0) = s0$. We can improve the methodology by defining the notion of *recursive scheme*.

Definition 5 recursive scheme. Given $\preceq$ a reduction ordering on $T(\mathcal{C}, \mathcal{F}, \mathcal{X})$, a recursive scheme with respect to $\preceq$ is a finite set $\{M_\alpha \mapsto \{R_{\alpha\beta}\}_{1 \leq \beta \leq m_\alpha}\}_{\alpha \in A}$ where the M_α and the $R_{\alpha\beta}$ are terms from $T(\mathcal{C}, \mathcal{X})$ such that for all α and all β, $R_{\alpha\beta} \prec M_\alpha$. The M_α are called the patterns of the recursive scheme and the $R_{\alpha\beta}$ the recursive calls of M_α.

The notion of recursive scheme specifies which kind of recursive relations will be investigated by the BMWk methodology. The ordering condition is necessary to ensure that the relation given by the method can be calculated (i.e. the calculus terminates). The recursive scheme for the Fibonnacci function is $\{ss(x) \mapsto \{s(x), x\}, s(0) \mapsto \emptyset, 0 \mapsto \emptyset\}$.

Given a set of examples, it is not possible to detect a relation corresponding to any recursive scheme. So, it is necessary to adapt in some way the recursive scheme to the examples.

Definition 6 recursive scheme compatibility. Given a set of terms $\{C_i\}_{i \in I}$, C_i is recursively recognized by a pattern if it is recognized and if the recursive calls also recognize some C_j with the same substitution up to a variable renaming.

A recursive scheme is compatible with a set of terms if each pattern recursively recognizes at least one C_i.

This definition is necessary because a relation like $f(ss(x)) = f(s(x)) + f(x)$ can not be established without some examples like $f(s^{n+2}(0))$, $f(s^{n+1}(0))$ and $f(s^n(0))$.

Recall that a synthesis problem is a finite set of rewrite rules $\{f(C_i, v^m) \to F_i\}_{i \in I}$ (Cf. Sect. 3). Given a recursive scheme $\mathcal{RS} = \{M_\alpha \mapsto \{R_{\alpha\beta}\}_{1 \leq \beta \leq m_\alpha}\}_{\alpha \in A}$, I_α is a subset of the set of the indexes of the C_i that M_α recursively recognizes. We also assume that i belongs to some I_α if C_i is recursively recognized by some pattern.

We say that $\mathcal{RS}$ is complete with respect to $\{C_i\}_{i \in I}$ if each C_i is recursively recognized by at least one pattern and that it is consistent if each C_i is recursively recognized by at most one pattern. If $\mathcal{RS}$ is complete and consistent, the I_α form a partition[2] of I.

5 The BMWk Methodology

Now, we can expose the mechanisms of the BMWk algorithms. It can be stated as four operators or inference rules.

5.1 Example

Let us consider first a simple case, the synthesis of the **reverse** function which reverses the order of the items in a list. After the preliminary transformation exposed in Sect. 3 the problem becomes:

$$f([], v) \to []$$
$$f([x_1], v) \to [a(v)]$$
$$f([x_2, x_1], v) \to [ad(v), a(v)]$$
$$f([x_3, x_2, x_1], v) \to [add(v), ad(v), a(v)]$$
$$f([x_4, x_3, x_2, x_1], v) \to [addd(v), add(v), ad(v), a(v)]$$
$$f([x_5, x_4, x_3, x_2, x_1], v) \to [adddd(v), addd(v), add(v), ad(v), a(v)]$$

with $\mathbf{reverse}(x) \to f(x, x)$.

Let us call $F_0, F_1, \ldots, F_5$ the right hand sides of the rules. Given the recursive scheme $\{[x|y] \mapsto \{y\}, [] \mapsto \phi\}$ we try to find $f([x|y], v)$ as a function of $f(y, v')$.

---

[2] All index $i \in I$ belongs to one and a single I_α

This can be achieved if there exists a substitution θ_i such that $F_{i+1} = F_i\theta_i$. Alas the matching between F_i and F_{i+1} fails because there is no substitution θ such that $[] = [a(v)]\theta$.

The generalizing rule (see Sect. 5.2 for technical details) is designed for this kind of situation. Let $G_{i+1} = \text{lgg}(F_i, F_{i+1})$, where "lgg" means the least general generalization ($G_4 = \text{lgg}(F_3, F_4) = [add(u_1), ad(u_1), a(u_1)|u_2]$). Since F_{i+1} is an instance of G_{i+1}, it is sufficient to find a recursive relation among the G_i to have a recursive definition for the function f. Now, the G_i sequence is more simple than the F_i sequence and it is probably possible to find a recursive relation among the G_i even if it is not possible among the F_i.

When generalizing new variables appear which are a priori different for each of the G_i because the least general generalization is defined up to a variable renaming. Their renaming (so that they become the same for each G_i) is quite complex and although Papon [17] and Kodratoff have studied it, it needs further work.

In our example, the new variables are called u_1 and u_2. Let f_1' be the function which calculates the generalizations and let h_1 and h_2 be the functions which calculate the substitutions on u_1 and u_2. The calculus of f can be decomposed into the set of rules:

$$
\left\{
\begin{array}{l}
h_1([x_1], v) \to d(v) \\
h_1([x_2, x_1], v) \to d(v) \\
h_1([x_3, x_2, x_1], v) \to d(v) \\
h_1([x_4, x_3, x_2, x_1], v) \to d(v) \\
h_1([x_5, x_4, x_3, x_2, x_1], v) \to d(v)
\end{array}
\right.
\quad
\left\{
\begin{array}{l}
h_2([x_1], v) \to [a(v)] \\
h_2([x_2, x_1], v) \to [a(v)] \\
h_2([x_3, x_2, x_1], v) \to [a(v)] \\
h_2([x_4, x_3, x_2, x_1], v) \to [a(v)] \\
h_2([x_5, x_4, x_3, x_2, x_1], v) \to [a(v)]
\end{array}
\right.
$$

which defines the substitutions on u_1 and u_2,

$$f_2'([], v) \to []$$
$$f_1'([x_1], u_1, u_2) \to u_2$$
$$f_1'([x_2, x_1], u_1, u_2) \to [a(u_1)|u_2]$$
$$f_1'([x_3, x_2, x_1], u_1, u_2) \to [ad(u_1), a(u_1)|u_2]$$
$$f_1'([x_4, x_3, x_2, x_1], u_1, u_2) \to [add(u_1), ad(u_1), a(u_1)|u_2]$$
$$f_1'([x_5, x_4, x_3, x_2, x_1], u_1, u_2) \to [addd(u_1), add(u_1), ad(u_1), a(u_1)|u_2]$$

which corresponds to the generalized part (using the new variables u_1 and u_2),

$$f([x|y], v) \to f_1'([x|y], h_1([x|y], v), h_2([x|y], v))$$
$$f([], v) \to f_2'([], v)$$

the recursive definition for f.

The previous transformation consists in applying the generalizing rule. Now, since h_1 and h_2 are constant it is possible replace their rules with:

$$h_1(x, v) \to d(v)$$
$$h_2(x, v) \to [a(v)]$$

this process is called identifying.

The only remaining problem is the synthesis of f_1'. Following the new recursive scheme $\{[x_1, x_2|y] \mapsto \{[x_2|y]\}, [x] \mapsto \emptyset\}$, it is possible to match F_i' with F_{i-1}' (the right hand sides of the rules defining f_1') since F_i' is an instance of F_{i-1}'. This yields the constant substitution $\{u_1/d(u_1), u_2/[a(u_1)|u_2]\}$. The functions

g_1' and g_2' calculate these substitutions. Since they are constant, the identifying rule applies and leads to the rewrite system :

$g_1'(x, u_1, u_2) \rightarrow d(u_1)$

$g_2'(x, u_1, u_2) \rightarrow [a(u_1)|u_2]$

$f_1'([x], u_1, u_2) \rightarrow u_2$

$f_1'([x_1, x_2|y], u_1, u_2) \rightarrow f_1'([x_2|y], g_1'([x_1, x_2|y], u_1, u_2), g_2'([x_1, x_2|y], u_1, u_2))$

$h_1(x, v) \rightarrow d(v)$

$h_2(x, v) \rightarrow [a(v)]$

$f_2'([], v) \rightarrow []$

$f([x|y], v) \rightarrow f_1'([x|y], h_1([x|y], v), h_2([x|y], v))$

$f([], v) \rightarrow f_2'([], v)$

Finally, replacing constant functions by their values and adding the definition of the destructors a and d, the system becomes more readable :

reverse$(x) \rightarrow f(x, x)$

$f([], v) \rightarrow []$

$f([x|y], v) \rightarrow f_1'([x|y], d(v), [a(v)])$

$f_1'([x], u_1, u_2) \rightarrow u_2$

$f_1'([x_1, x_2|y], u_1, u_2) \rightarrow f_1'([x_2|y], d(u_1), [a(u_1)|u_2])$

$a([x|y]) \rightarrow x$ and $d([x|y]) \rightarrow y$

The algorithm described in the thesis of Papon [17] synthesizes this program since the examples have an *ascending linear domain* [5] (i.e. a domain which is described by some predicates $\pi_i(x) = \pi_0(d^i(x))$ where d is made up of destructors).

Notice finally that the methodology needs a minimum number of four examples to yield this result.

5.2 Inference Rules

This section is rather technical and can be skipped by the reader who does not need a deep understanding of the BMWk methodology.

Assume that we have a set of rewrite rules and a set of recursive schemes (see the notations Sect. 4). When necessary we will choose a compatible recursive scheme to apply one of the following inference rules :

Identifying to synthesize the constant function on some domains.

Given a recursive scheme without recursive calls.

$$\frac{\{f(C_i, v^m) \rightarrow F_i\}_{i \in I}}{\{f(M_\alpha, v^m) \rightarrow F_\alpha\}_{\alpha \in A}} \text{ if } \forall \alpha, i \quad i \in I_\alpha \Rightarrow F_\alpha = F_i$$

This means that if it is possible to group some C_i in a set where $f(C_i, v^m)$ is constant and has the value F_α and if the pattern M_α recognizes these C_i (e.g. M_α is the least general generalization of the C_i) then it is possible to replace the rules $f(C_i, v^m) \rightarrow F_\alpha$ by a single one $f(M_\alpha, v^m) \rightarrow F_\alpha$. This corresponds to infer by induction that $f(C, v^m)$ is constant for all term C recognized by M_α. In particular, if f is constant on all the examples it is possible to infer that f is constant on any entry.

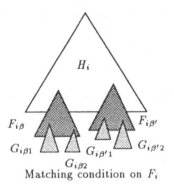

Matching condition on F_i

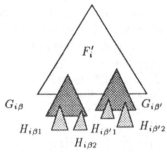

Generalizing condition on F_i

Matching to detect recursive relations and synthesize a recursive definition. If it is possible to find some instances of $F_{i\beta}$ and $F_{i\beta'}$ into each term F_i (Cf. the figure *"Matching condition on F_i"*) and if C_i is greater than $C_{i\beta}$ and $C_{i\beta'}$ then some recursive relation like $f(n) = h(n, f(n-1, g_{\beta 1}(n), g_{\beta 2}(n)), f(n-2, g_{\beta' 1}(n), g_{\beta' 2}(n)))$ holds. The purpose of the matching rule is to detect such a recursive relation.

Given a recursive scheme complete with respect to $\{C_i\}_{i \in I}$, if for all α and all i in I_α, $F_i = H_i[u_\beta/F_{i\beta}[v_1/G_{i\beta 1}, \ldots, v_m/G_{i\beta m}]]_{1 \le \beta \le m_\alpha}$ (Cf. figure), then the following inference rule applies:

$$\frac{\{f(C_i, v^m) \to F_i\}_{i \in I}}{\begin{array}{l} \{h_\alpha(C_i, v^m, u^{m_\alpha}) \to H_i\}_{\alpha \in A, i \in I_\alpha} \\ \{g_{\alpha\beta k}(C_i, v^m) \to G_{i\beta k}\}_{\alpha \in A, i \in I_\alpha, 1 \le \beta \le m_\alpha, 1 \le k \le m} \\ \{f(M_\alpha, v^m) \to h_\alpha(M_\alpha, v^m, f(R_{\alpha\beta}, g_{\alpha\beta}(M_\alpha, v^m))^{m_\alpha})\}_{\alpha \in A} \end{array}}$$

with $\mathbf{g}_{\alpha\beta}(x, v^m) = g_{\alpha\beta 1}(x, v^m), \ldots, g_{\alpha\beta m}(x, v^m)$ and $f(R_{\alpha\beta}, \mathbf{g}_{\alpha\beta}(M_\alpha, v^m))^{m_\alpha}$ $= f(R_{\alpha 1}, \mathbf{g}_{\alpha 1}(M_\alpha, v^m)), \ldots, f(R_{\alpha m_\alpha}, \mathbf{g}_{\alpha m_\alpha}(M_\alpha, v^m))$. This rule applies each time the $F_{i\beta}$ match some disjoint subterms of F_i. Such a matching does not always exist. If it fails only on few examples it is possible to slightly modify the recursive scheme in order to deal with the failure cases as particular cases.

Generalizing to prepare the examples before applying the matching rule when it does not apply. It is not always possible to find embedded instances of $F_{i\beta}$ in F_i in order to apply the matching rule. But it could be possible to find some term $F'_{i\beta}$ "which looks like" $F_{i\beta}$. In that case it is possible to eliminate the differences between $F'_{i\beta}$ and $F_{i\beta}$ when replacing $F'_{i\beta}$ by $G_{i\beta}$, the least general generalization of $F'_{i\beta}$ and $F_{i\beta}$ (Cf. the figure *"Generalizing condition on F_i"*). The idea beyond this technique is to replace the wrong F_i sequence by the better sequence obtained when elimating the subterms H_{ijk} (Cf. figure). This very important idea has been discovered by Kodratoff [7]. Given a recursive scheme complete with $\{C_i\}_{i \in I}$, for all α and all i in I_α let $F_i = F'_i[u_\beta/F'_{i\beta}]_{1 \le \beta \le m_\alpha}$. Given $G_{i\beta}$ the least general generalization of $F_{i\beta}$

and $F'_{i\beta}$, and $F'_{i\beta} = G_{i\beta}[u_1/H_{i\beta 1}, \ldots, u_p/H_{i\beta p}]$, the following inference rule applies:

$$\frac{\{f(C_i, v^m) \to F_i\}_{i \in I}}{\begin{array}{l} \{h_{\alpha\beta k}(C_i, v^m) \to H_{i\beta k}\}_{\alpha \in A, i \in I_\alpha, 1 \leq \beta \leq m_\alpha, 1 \leq k \leq p_\alpha} \\ \{f'_\alpha(C_i, v^m, u^{p_\alpha}) \to F'_i[u_\beta/G_{i\beta}]_{1 \leq \beta \leq m_\alpha}\}_{\alpha \in A, i \in I_\alpha} \\ \{f(M_\alpha, v^m) \to f'_\alpha(M_\alpha, v^m, h_{\alpha\beta}(M_\alpha, v^m)^{m_\alpha})\}_{\alpha \in A} \end{array}}$$

with notations similar to those of the matching rule. This rule applies when the matching rule does not, so that it constitutes in some way an attempt to force the matching. When generalizing, new variables appear. The renaming of these variables is a real problem that Papon explains in his thesis [17].

Composing to cut a complex problem into two sub-problems.

$$\frac{\{f(C_i, v^m) \to F_i\}_{i \in I}}{\begin{array}{l} \{g(C_i, v^m, u) \to G_i\}_{i \in I} \\ \{h(C_i, v^m) \to H_i\}_{i \in I} \\ f(x, v^m) \to g(x, v^m, h(x, v^m)) \end{array}} \quad \text{if } F_i = G_i[u/H_i]$$

This inference rule splits the terms F_i into two subterms G_i and H_i. This rule is difficult to use because many cuts are a priori possible, whereas most of them lead nowhere.

6 Results

Now, we shall state a few general results about the qualities and limitations of the BMWk methodology. All the following results apply to any implementation of the method. The formalization we gave has the advantage to yield to very precise results on synthesized functions. We state below the most important ones.

Proposition 7 inference termination. *For all sets of examples and all choices of recursive schemes there is no infinite chain of inferences.*

Proof. Build a well-founded ordering which decreases with the inferences.

This result is very interesting because it ensures that the choice of a *"wrong"* inference or a *"wrong"* recursive scheme has no other consequence than delaying the final result. We can also show that the number of recursive schemes compatible with the domain is finite, that the number of variable renamings for the generalization is finite and that the number of uses of the composing rule is also finite thus there is a finite number of choices. Alas the search space is quite big.

Proposition 8 correction on the example. *Given $\sigma, I \mapsto O$ an example and $\mathcal{R}$ a rewrite system calculated by the BMWk methodology, $I\sigma \xrightarrow{*}_{\mathcal{R}} O\sigma$.*

Proof. Show that if $\mathcal{R} \vdash \mathcal{R}'$ then the relation $\xrightarrow{*}_{\mathcal{R}}$ is a subset of $\xrightarrow{*}_{\mathcal{R}'}$.

This means that the examples can be calculated from the recursive definition given by the method. It was not always the case with the algorithm of Fargues [3] and Papon [17].

Proposition 9 termination. *The rewrite system given by the BMWk methodology terminates if all the recursive schemes are valid with respect to the same recursive path ordering (in particular if it is the subterm ordering).*

Proof. Expand the ordering so that it decreases on the calculated rewrite rules.

According to the last proposition, the BMWk methodology restricted to subterm ordering generates term rewrite systems which terminate (i.e. for all possible evaluation strategies, the use of the calculated recursive definitions always leads to a value).

Proposition 10 confluency. *Given a recursive scheme $\mathcal{RS}$ used by the methodology, if there does not exist any pair of patterns which unify and if there does not exist any variable which has more than one position in a given pattern then the term rewrite system built by the BMWk methodology is confluent.*

Proof. Technical, show that the term rewrite system is *orthogonal* (a class of rewrite systems which are known to be confluent).

The confluency property ensures that the rewrite rules define a function (i.e. given an input the calculated recursive definition leads to at most one output). The hypothesis on the recursive scheme is not very restrictive so that it can hold in most cases.

Proposition 11 class of the synthesized functions. *The BMWk algorithm restricted to subterm ordering and natural integers can not synthesize a function which increases faster than the exponential functions but it can synthesize exponential functions.*

This means that for any function f synthesized by the BMWk algorithm restricted to subterm ordering and natural integers, there exists a constant c such that $|f(x)| \leq c^{|x|}$. The methodology restricted to unary functions on natural integers synthesizes exactly the functions $f(n) = \sum_i P_i(n)c_i^n$ where P_i is a polynomial with positive rational coefficients and c_i a positive natural integer constant. This result is very intuitive because of the analogy between matching and substraction so that $f(n)$ is a solution of some linear equation $f(n + k) = \sum_{i < k} a_i f(n + i)$ where a_i is an integer.

The methodology is able to synthesize other functions like Ackermann's function. But it is quite improper to insist on this fact because only the recursive scheme of Ackermann's function is complicated and the methodology gives no indication of how to choose the recursive scheme. More important is the fact that functions such as $f(x) = x^x$ can not be synthesized with the subterm ordering restriction (the definition $x^{y+1} = x \times x^y$ is validated by the subterm ordering).

It is quite difficult to define in the general case the class of the synthesized functions even with the subterm ordering restriction. Generally, when the subterm ordering restriction holds, BMWk can not synthesized functions which increase faster than the exponential functions but there exists some pathological cases (functions which increase arbitrarily fast). Moreover, BMWk can not synthesized functions which increase too slowly (logarithm,square root,...).

7 Related Works

In program synthesis from example, Summers [19] was the first to introduce the idea of comparing two terms F_i and F_{i+1} in order to discover that the first one is an instance of the second one ($F_{i+1} = F_i\theta$). Then Fargues showed that the substitution θ may be considered i dependent so that the same search process should apply with θ instead of F and Kodratoff refines the method considering G_i the least general generalization of F_i and F_{i+1} in order to deal with the case where θ does not exist [3, 7]. Then Kodratoff and Papon introduced a variable renaming algorithm for the G_i set [8, 17] to implement the idea of Fargues and Kodratoff.

Up to now, there exists only two implementations of BMWk [3, 17]. These implementations contain a conception error concerning the generalizing rule (see Sect. 5.2) which entails that the synthesized program does not always calculate all the examples. Despites this problem these algorithms are usually able to synthesize unary functions on linear domains (lists, integers, stacks,...). Introducing the notion of recursive scheme, we made a strong generalization of the method which allows to synthesize functions of any arity and needing several recursive calls so that it is now possible to synthesize functions on other data types such as trees, heaps, terms,...Nevertheless, this is not.yet implemented. Moreover, our formalization (Sect. 5.2) allows to correct the conception error in the algorithms of Fargues and Papon (Proposition 8).

Recently, in Inductive Logic Programing several works came close to the BMWk methodology. Ling pointed out the necessity of learning recursive predicates[3] [14] and several algorithms have been proposed to achieve this task ([16, 18] among others). Most of these algorithms need numerous examples and even more counter-examples. Also, Ling has proposed an algorithm to learn from "good examples" [12, 13]. The notion of "good examples" is very close to our work since the BMWk methodology is able to learn from very small sets of examples. The algorithm of Lapointe and Matwin [1, 9, 10] could be seen in some way as a particular case of the work of Fargues although they now develop it in a different way. Finally, Idestam-Almquist [4] showed how to use subterm positions to discover recursive relations. This is close to the idea of Summers which consists in replacing output constants by their position in the input.

Among all the Inductive Logic Programing works, those of Lapointe and Matwin are the closest to BMWk. These algorithms are strongly driven by the

---

[3] Following the work of Kleene, Ling emphasized that some theories are not finitelly axiomatisable without using recursive definitions.

examples so that they avoid useless calculus and also use the notion of subterm unification. BMWk is more powerful since the class of the functions it synthesizes is larger. For example, it can synthesize all the polynomial functions from examples only containing the constructors 0 and s (this entails that the definitions BMWk built could contain an arbitrary number of recursivity levels) whereas the algorithm of Lapointe and Matwin can not synthesizes such functions without using some background knowledge. The BMWk methodology restricted to natural integer is based on the principle that if f is a polynomial function of degre d then $f(n+1) - f(n)$ is a polynomial of degre $d-1$. This analogy is possible since $u = v\theta$ entails $|u| = |v| + |\theta|$. It is the original idea which is behind the BMWk methodology.

All the functions that can be synthesized with the algorithms of Lapointe and Matwin [1, 9, 10] can be synthesized by BMWk. The main difference between their work and BMWk is rather technical. With the notations of Sect. 5.2, their algorithms try to find some relations of the form $F_i = H_i[F_{i-k}]$ with $H_i = H_i'\theta^k$ and $H_i' = \sigma^l[H_{i-l}']$ where θ and σ correspond to what they call some generating terms. BMWk search for relations of the form $F_i = H_i[F_{i-1}\theta_i]$ where H_i and θ_i could verify some similar relations or may be constant, which is obviously more general. The reasons why BMWk use the substitution θ_i which does not appear in the work of Lapointe and Matwin are described in Sect 3 (non-instanciated examples, positions of input variables in the output). The other differences are that some of the algorithms of Lapointe and Matwin can use background knowledge whereas BMWk does not[4] and that they usually does not need consecutive examples whereas BMWk does.

The last important difference between BMWk and the Inductive Logic Programming usual methods is that it can not use instanciated examples (see Sect. 3) whereas the later usually only use instanciated ones.

8 Conclusion

Our work confers a new youth to the old BMWk algorithms. This is achieved by separating four fundamental operators from the calculus strategy. Introducing the notion of recursive scheme, we have done a strong generalization with respect to the *"state of the art"* of the BMWk methodology. This results in gain of power. Since our formalization uses the framework of term rewriting, we are able to state precise results on the calculated recursive definitions. Last, but not least, the BMWk methodology supplies a restricted search space and needs very few examples so that it is likely to be very useful in Machine Learning (in particular in Inductive Logic Programming).

The methodology is also interesting because it can be improved. First, to handle example sets which contain $\sigma, I \mapsto O$ and $\sigma', I' \mapsto O'$ such that there exists θ, $I\theta = I'\theta$ and $O\theta \neq O'\theta$ (our current work). This allows to deal with the **member** predicate, for example. By the way, it is probably possible to supply

---

[4] Nevertheless BMWk is able to synthesize the auxilliary knowledges that it needs.

background knowledge to the methodology in order to synthesize functions like **sort** which use the knowledge of the predifined $<$ predicate. Finally, it is very easy to extend the methodology to the synthesis of relations (more than one output is associated to a given input, $in([a'', b'', c'']) = a''$ or b'' or c'').

Acknowledgements

I would like to gratefully thank Céline Rouveirol, Jean-François Puget and José de Siqueira for their helpful advices and Yves Kodratoff my thesis advisor.

References

1. David W. Aha, Charles X. Ling, Stan Matwin, and Stephane Lapointe. Learning singly-recursive relations from small datasets. In F. Bergadano, Luc De Raedt, Stan Matwin, and S. Muggleton, editors, *Proceedings of the IJCAI workshop on inductive logic programming*, Chambéry, France, 1993.
2. Nachum Dershowitz and Jean-Pierre Jouannaud. *Handbook of Theorical Computer Science*, volume B, chapter Rewrite Systems, pages 243–320. MIT Press, 1990.
3. Jean Fargues. Une méthodologie pour la synthèse de programme : application à la synthèse à partir d'exemples. Thèse, Université Pierre et Marie Curie (Paris VI), June 1978.
4. Peter Idestam-Almquist. Recursive anti-unification. In Stephen Muggleton, editor, *Proceedings of the third international workshop on Inductive Logic Programming*, pages 241–253, Ljubljana, Slovenia, March 1993. J. Stefan Institute.
5. Jean-Pierre Jouannaud and Yves Kodratoff. Characterization of a class of functions synthesized from examples by a SUMMER's like method using a BMW matching technique. In *Proceedings of the 6th IJCAI*, pages 440–447, 1979.
6. Jean-Pierre Jouannaud and Yves Kodratoff. *A methodology for two variable functions synthesis from examples*. CRIN université de Nancy, 1979.
7. Yves Kodratoff and Jean Fargues. A sane algorithm for the synthesis of LISP functions from example problems : the Boyer and Moore algorithm. In *Proceedings of the AISB meeting*, pages 169–175, Hamburg, 1978.
8. Yves Kodratoff and Éric Papon. A system for program synthesis and program optimization. In *Proceedings of the AISB meeting*, pages 1–10, Amsterdam, 1980.
9. Stéphane Lapointe, Charles Ling, and Stan Matwin. Constructive inductive logic programming. In Stephen Muggleton, editor, *Proceedings of the third international workshop on Inductive Logic Programming*, pages 255–264, Ljubljana, Slovenia, March 1993. J. Stefan Institute.
10. Stéphane Lapointe, Charles Ling, and Stan Matwin. Constructive inductive logic programming. In Ruzena Bajcsy, editor, *Proceedings of the 13th IJCAI*, volume Vol. 2, pages 1030–1036. Morgan-Kaufmann, August 1993.
11. Stéphane Lapointe and Stan Matwin. Induction de programmes logiques récursifs fondée sur la sous-unification. In PRC-IA GRECO, editor, *Actes des 1ères Journées Francophones d'Apprentissage et d'Explication des Connaissances*, pages 3–14. AFIA AFCET, PRC-IA GRECO, April 1992.
12. Charles Xiaofeng Ling. Inductive learning from good examples. In *Proceedings of the 12th IJCAI*, volume Vol. 2, pages 751–756, Sydney, Australia, August 1991. Morgan-Kaufmann.

13. Charles Xiaofeng Ling. *Inductive Logic Programming*, chapter Inductive learning from good examples, pages 113–129. APIC. Turing Institute Press, academic press edition, 1992.

14. Charles Xiaofeng Ling. Inventing necessary theoretical terms to overcome representation bias. In *Proceedings of the ML92 workshop on biases in inductive learning*, Aberdeen, Scotland, July 1992.

15. Stephen Muggleton, editor. *Inductive Logic Programing*. APIC. Turing Institute Press, academic press edition, 1991.

16. Stephen Muggleton and C. Feng. *Inductive Logic Programming*, chapter Efficient induction of logic programs, pages 281–298. APIC. Turing Institute Press, academic press edition, 1992.

17. Éric Papon. Algorithmes de détection de relations de récurrence – application à la synthèse et à la transformation de programmes. Thèse, Université de Paris-Sud, April 1981.

18. Ross J. Quinlan. Learning logical definition from relations. *Machine Learning Journal*, Vol. 5(3):239–266, 1990.

19. P.D. Summers. A methodology for LISP program construction from examples. *Journal of the ACM*, Vol. 24:161–175, 1977.

An Analytic and Empirical Comparison of Two Methods for Discovering Probabilistic Causal Relationships

Donato Malerba, Giovanni Semeraro and Floriana Esposito

Dipartimento di Informatica, Università degli Studi di Bari
via Orabona 4, 70126 Bari, Italy
{malerbad I semeraro I esposito}@vm.csata.it

Abstract. The discovery of causal relationships from empirical data is an important problem in machine learning. In this paper the attention is focused on the inference of probabilistic causal relationships, for which two different approaches, namely Glymour et al.'s approach based on constraints on correlations and Pearl and Verma's approach based on conditional independencies, have been proposed. These methods differ both in the kind of constraints they consider while selecting a causal model and in the way they search the model which better fits to the sample data. Preliminary experiments show that they are complementary in several aspects. Moreover, the method of conditional independence can be easily extended to the case in which variables have a nominal or ordinal domain. In this case, symbolic learning algorithms can be exploited in order to derive the causal law from the causal model.

1 Introduction

Both a fortune-teller and a financial planner can make a forecast on the result of an investment in stocks. The former will use a pack of cards while the latter will base his/her prediction on his/her knowledge about the present economical situation as well as the economical, social and psychological processes which control the state of the Stock Exchange. Although it may happen that the fortune-teller's prediction is more accurate than that made by a financial planner, few people would be inclined to entrust a fortune-teller with their own savings. The reason for such a distrust is that a fortune-teller relates the result of the investment to the obscure meaning of the arrangement of the cards while the financial expert is able to *explain* why he/she made a certain prediction.

Generally speaking, the *explanatory* knowledge of a phenomenon allows us not only to make a forecast just like the *declarative* knowledge, but also to explain the reasoning followed in order to reach some conclusions. Since causality plays an important role in human understanding, it can be fairly stated that causal knowledge is a fundamental part of any intelligent system. For instance, Steels [12] pointed out that the major problem of the first expert systems was their inability to provide effective explanations of why an observed phenomenon happened rather than very simple explanations based on the chain of heuristic rules used to reach a conclusion.

In recent years, the exigency of disposing of deep knowledge on the application domain has been raised in machine learning as well. In particular, the importance of disposing of a domain theory which controls the inferential process of a learning system has been stressed, since it would be better to find generalizations which can explain the learned concepts themselves other than correctly classify new observations. The increasing interest towards explanation-based learning is just due to its ability of generalizing concepts by using an appropriate domain theory [6, 3]. Nevertheless, the real applicability of this learning paradigm is strongly conditioned by the possibility of defining a domain theory, often comprising a *causal model*, which is complete, consistent and tractable.

As to the completeness property, the definition of a complete theory can be made easier by means of systems which can inductively discover causal relations from data, that is a theory which can explain every example from the domain theory under study.

A cause-effect relationship can be deterministic or probabilistic. A deterministic relationship can be established when the description of all the variables involved in a phenomenon is sufficiently detailed, while a probabilistic relationship exists when some relevant variables cannot be measured or when some measurements are not sufficiently accurate. As Suppes [13] has already emphasized, most of the causal relationships that humans use in their reasoning are probabilistic.

In this paper, we compare two statistical approaches to discovering causal relationships, namely Glymour et al.'s method of constraints on correlations [4, 11] and Pearl and Verma's method of conditional independencies [7]. Preliminary experiments indicate that these methods are complementary since they show very different results for diverse causal models. Moreover, these methods can only discover a causal dependence between variables in the model and not the causal law. When the variables in the model are numerical (interval or ratio level measurements), coefficients of the linear models can be estimated by means of regression analysis. However, the method based on conditional independence can also be applied to nominal or ordinal variables, in which case symbolic inductive learning algorithms can help to find the causal rules of the phenomenon. Thus, inductive learning algorithms together with statistical causal inference systems can be exploited in order to discover causal relationships which can be subsequently used as a part of the domain theory of an analytic learning system.

2 Preliminaries

A *causal model* is the abstraction of a set of cause-effect relationships from a statistical model in which we ignore the equations and most of the statistical assumptions. A causal model of a set of variables V can be represented by a directed graph, whose nodes are distinct elements of V and whose edges denote direct causal relationships between pairs of variables (see Figure 1). Henceforth, we will consider only the case of acyclic causal models, which can be represented by directed acyclic graphs (*dags*). Moreover, we assume

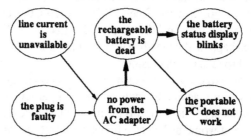

Figure 1. A causal model referring to power problems in a portable PC. Bold arrows indicate a trek between the two effects "the battery status display blinks" and "the portable PC does not work."

that the reader is familiar with some basic notions on dags, so we limit ourselves to introduce only the following concepts:

An *acyclic (open) path* is a path which contains no cycle. A *trek* between two distinct nodes v and w is a pair of acyclic paths, p and q, from a node u to v and w respectively, such that they intersect only in u. The trek is denoted by $<p,q>$ and u is called *source* of the trek. Bold arrows in Figure 1 show a trek between the nodes "the battery status display blinks" and "the portable PC does not work." The source of the trek is the variable "no power from the AC adapter." Henceforth, T_{uv} will denote the set of treks between u and v, while P_{uv} will denote the set of acyclic paths from u to v. Note that when u and v coincide, then $T_{uv}=P_{uv}$. For any node v of a dag, *indegree(v)* is equal to the number of edges directed into v, while *outdegree(v)* is equal to the number of edges directed out of v.

Definition 1 *(stochastic causal theory)*

A *stochastic causal theory* (SCT) is a triple $(<V,E>, (\Omega,P), X)$ where:
1) $<V,E>$ is a causal model;
2) (Ω,P) is a probability space for the random variables in V. Every variable in V has a non-zero variance. If there is no trek between two variables $u,v \in V$, then u and v are statistically independent. Moreover, each variable $v \in V$ having a causal predecessor *(indegree(v)>0)* is associated with one *error variable* e_v which takes into account external sources of variance.
3) X is a set of independent equations in V. For each $v \in V$ such that *indegree(v)>0* the equation:

$$v = f_v(w_{v1}, w_{v2}, ..., w_{vn}, e_v)$$

is a member of X, *where wv1, wv2, ..., w_{vn}* are all variables adjacent to v.

A variable v is said to be *independent* iff *indegree(v)=0*, otherwise it is *dependent*. Dependent variables are the effects of some causes, and they are associated with some disturbance terms, that is, the error variables. These latter represent the increment by which any individual v may fall off the regression line:

$$v = f_v(w_{v1}, w_{v2}, ..., w_{vn}, 0)$$

According to definition 1, stochastic causal theories may differ in the form of the relationship between a set of causes (variables adjacent to v) and an effect (v itself), that is, in the form of f_v. SCTs in which f_v is a linear function are of peculiar interest.

Definition 2 *(stochastic linear causal theory)*

A *stochastic linear causal theory* (SLCT) is a 4-tuple $(<V,E>, (\Omega,P), X, L)$ where:
1) $(<V,E>, (\Omega,P), X)$ is a stochastic causal theory;
2) L is a *labelling function* for the edges in E taking values in the set of non-null real numbers. For any edge e from u to v, we will denote $L(e)=a_{vu}$. The label of a path p, $L(p)$, is defined as the product of the labels of each edge in p. The label of a trek $t=<p,q>$ is defined as $L(t)=L(p)L(q)$.
3) X is a set of independent homogeneous linear equations in V. For each $v \in V$ such that *indegree(v)>0* the equation:

$$v = \sum_{w \in Adj(v)} a_{vw}w + e_v$$

is a member of X, where $Adj(v)=\{w \in V \mid w$ is adjacent to $v\}$.

The label associated to an edge from u to v summarizes the total impact on v of a unit change in u after it has rippled through the causal model. Such an impact on v can be positive or negative according to the sign of the label. Consequently, given a path p from u to v, the associated label represents the total impact on v of a unit change of u when only the causal relationships in p are considered. Figure 2 shows an example of labelled causal model and the set of linear equations derived from it. Here λ is a *latent* variable, that is a not measured variable which represents a cause of the phenomenon described by the causal model and has a possible theoretical explanation. Also error variables e_i are not measured, but differently from latent variables they do not carry with them any theoretical interpretation and do not represent a common cause of two or more variables. All the other variables, denoted by Latin characters, are *measured* or *observed*, that is a sample is available for all them.

3 The Method of Constraints on Correlations

Explaining observed data is the main reason for which a theory is built. In the case of statistical linear theories, the aim is usually the explanation of correlations or covariances between random variables whose values have been collected in a sample. In particular, for stochastic linear causal theories, the goal is that of discovering causal relationships by exploiting the information coming from correlations between measured variables. However, it is generally raised the following question: how can a correlation (or a covariance), which is a symmetric piece of information, provide hints on the direction of causality? Of course, if we knew which variable temporally precedes which we could also define univocally the causal direction. When temporal information is unavailable, temporal constraints can be replaced by constraints on correlations. However, by using a simple correlation between two variables no one can discriminate the concomitant variation due to a common (hidden) cause from a real causal influence of a variable on the other one. On the contrary, the causal relationship between two variables can be determined by examining the covariances of a larger set of variables. For instance, if we are given two variables, x="line current is unavailable" and y="no power from the AC adapter", we can conclude that x causes y only if we consider a further *control* variable z, say "the plug is faulty", such that z is correlated to y but not to x (see Figure 1).

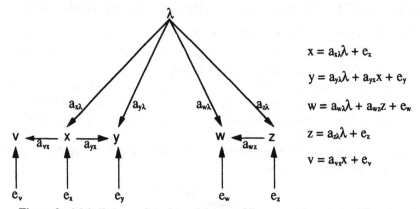

$$x = a_{x\lambda}\lambda + e_x$$

$$y = a_{y\lambda}\lambda + a_{yx}x + e_y$$

$$w = a_{w\lambda}\lambda + a_{wz}z + e_w$$

$$z = a_{z\lambda}\lambda + e_z$$

$$v = a_{vx}x + e_v$$

Figure 2. A labelled causal model and the set of linear equations derived from it.

Symmetrically, we can also conclude that z causes y by taking x as control variable.

Given a SLCT $T = (<V,E>, (\Omega,P), X, L)$, Glymour et al. [4, pp. 285-286] have proven the following formula for the covariance γ_{xy} between two variables x and y:

$$\gamma_{xy} = \sum_{w \in T_{xy}} L(t)\, \sigma^2_{s(t)}$$

where $\sigma^2_{s(t)}$ is the variance of the variable $s(t)$, the source of a trek t between x and y.

Note that, if variables are standardized apart, then $\sigma^2_v = 1$ for any variable $v \in V$ and the covariance γ_{xy} equals the correlation ρ_{xy}. Thus, the correlation between two measured variables is equal to the sum, over all treks connecting the variables, of the product of the coefficients corresponding to the directed edges in the trek [5]. Indeed, in the case of variables that are standardized apart, the label associated to an edge from u to v denotes the correlation between u and v.

Covariances computed according to the previous formula are said to be *implied* by the theory, in order to distinguish them from the sample covariances. Unfortunately, the computation of γ_{xy} for any two variables x and y requires knowledge about the edge labels and the variances of the independent variables. Instead of estimating coefficients and variances in order to compare the *values* of implied correlations with the corresponding values of sample correlations, Glymour et al. prefer to compare *constraints* on covariances (or correlations) implied by the model with constraints on covariances (or correlations) which hold in the data. Thus, the problem is to *search for the causal model which implies the set of constraints that best fits to the set of constraints which hold in the data.*

There are several kinds of constraints on covariances which could be taken into account, but some considerations on computational complexity drive Glymour et al. to consider only two kinds of constraints: *tetrad* and *partial equations*. They are enough to choose among several alternative causal models and can be easily tested as well.

Definition 3 *(tetrad equation)*

Let $M = <V,E>$ be a causal model, and x, y, w, z four distinct measured variables in V. A *tetrad equation* between x, y, w, z is one of the following equations:

$$\rho_{xy} \cdot \rho_{wz} = \rho_{xw} \cdot \rho_{yz}$$
$$\rho_{xy} \cdot \rho_{wz} = \rho_{xz} \cdot \rho_{yw}$$
$$\rho_{xw} \cdot \rho_{yz} = \rho_{xz} \cdot \rho_{yw}$$

where ρ_{ij} is the correlation between i and j.

The above equations represent constraints on a foursome of variables, while *partial equations* define constraints on a triplet of variables.

Definition 4 *(partial equation)*

Let $M = <V,E>$ be a causal model, and x, y, z three distinct measured variables in V. A *partial equation* between x, y, z is the following equation:

$$\rho_{xz} = \rho_{xy} \cdot \rho_{yz}$$

This equation can be equivalently written as:

$$\rho_{xz.y} = 0$$

since:

$$\rho_{xz.y} = (\rho_{xz} - \rho_{xy} \cdot \rho_{yz}) / [(1 - \rho^2_{xy}) \cdot (1 - \rho^2_{yz})]^{1/2}.$$

Such constraints on covariances are particularly interesting since it can be shown that in linear causal models their satisfaction depends *on the causal model alone*, that is, the dag, and not on the distribution of variables neither on particular numerical values of the coefficients a_{vu}. Thus, it is not necessary to estimate either the coefficients or the variances of the independent variables, since we can know which equations are satisfiable (or implied) by a SLCT $T= (<V,E>, (W,P), X, L)$ by simply looking at the causal model $<V,E>$. In fact, the following two theorems can be proven [4 pp. 265-288, 293-310]:

Theorem 1

Let $T=(<V,E>,(W,P),X,L)$ be a SLCT, $<V,E>$ an acyclic graph, and u, v, w, x four distinct measured variables in V. Then the following propositions are equivalent:

a) T implies the tetrad equation $\rho_{uv} \cdot \rho_{wx} = \rho_{ux} \cdot \rho_{vw}$

b) $\displaystyle\sum_{t \in T_{uv}} L(t) \cdot \sum_{t \in T_{wx}} L(t) \equiv \sum_{t \in T_{ux}} L(t) \cdot \sum_{t \in T_{vw}} L(t)$

where $\equiv$ means that the left expression identically equals the right expression, that is the two expressions are equal for all possible values of their linear coefficients.

For instance, the model in Figure 2 implies the following tetrad equation:

$$\rho_{xw} \cdot \rho_{zy} = \rho_{xz} \cdot \rho_{wy}$$

since the left expression of condition b) in theorem 1, that is:

$$(a_{w\lambda}a_{x\lambda} + a_{wz}a_{z\lambda}a_{x\lambda})(a_{y\lambda}a_{z\lambda} + a_{z\lambda}a_{y x}a_{z\lambda}) = a_{w\lambda}a_{x\lambda}a_{y\lambda}a_{z\lambda} + a_{w\lambda}a^2_{x\lambda}a_{yx}a_{z\lambda} + a_{wz}a_{z\lambda}a_{y\lambda}a^2_{z\lambda} + a_{wz}a^2_{z\lambda}a_{yx}a^2_{z\lambda}$$

identically equals the right expression, which is:

$$a_{x\lambda}a_{z\lambda}(a_{y\lambda}a_{w\lambda} + a_{w\lambda}a_{x\lambda}a_{yx} + a_{y\lambda}a_{z\lambda}a_{wz} + a_{z\lambda}a_{yx}a_{z\lambda}a_{wz})$$

Theorem 2

Let $T=(<V,E>, (W,P), X, L)$ be a SLCT, $<V,E>$ an acyclic graph, and x, y, z three distinct measured variables in V. Then the following propositions are equivalent:

a) $\rho_{xz.y} = 0$

b) y is a vertex in any trek connecting x to z, and either any trek between y and z is reduced to an acyclic path or any trek between y and x is reduced to an acyclic path. Formally:
$(\forall\, t \in T_{xz} : y \in t) \wedge [(\forall\, t \in T_{yz} : t \in P_{yz}) \vee (\forall\, t \in T_{yx} : t \in P_{yz})].$

For instance, the model in Figure 2 implies the following partial equation:

$$\rho_{vz.x} = 0$$

since x is a node of the only trek connecting v and z, $< <\lambda,x,v>, <\lambda,z> >$, and the only trek connecting x and v is $< <x,v>, <x> >$, which is an acyclic path.

In conclusion, the problem of checking whether a constraint (tetrad or partial equation) is satisfied by a SLCT is reduced to a search problem for some trek sets. Then the problem is moved to verifying constraints which hold in the data. In order to establish whether a tetrad equation holds, an asymptotic test is performed on the *tetrad difference*:

$$H_0 : \hat{\rho}_{uv} \cdot \hat{\rho}_{wx} - \hat{\rho}_{ux} \cdot \hat{\rho}_{vw} = 0$$

where $\hat{\rho}_{ij}$ is the sample correlation between the variables i and j. It can be proven that, as the sample size grows, the distribution of a tetrad difference converges in probability to a normal distribution having mean zero and variance given by Wishart's formula [1].

As to the partial correlation, the following test:

$$H_0: \hat{\rho}_{xy.z} = 0$$

can be easily performed by taking into account the fact that the *Fisher's* z statistics:

$$z = \frac{1}{2} \ln \left(\frac{1+\hat{\rho}_{xy.z}}{1-\hat{\rho}_{xy.z}} \right)$$

converges in probability to a normal distribution with mean zero and variance given by $\sigma^2 = 1/(N-3)$, where N is the sample size [1].

When a certain causal model has been hypothesized, it is necessary to compare constraints which hold in the data to constraints implied by the model. Therefore, we need some *criteria* in order to evaluate how much a model fits to the data. Such criteria can also be exploited when comparing different alternative causal models. Glymour et al. [4] propose three criteria:

1) *H-I* (or *incompleteness* criterion): the number of constraints which hold in the data but are not implied by the model;

2) *I-H* (or *inconsistency* criterion): the number of constraints implied by the model but not holding in the data;

3) *simplicity* criterion: the previous criteria being equal, prefer the simplest model, that is the causal model with the lowest number of edges.

Obviously, the set H of constraints which hold in the data depends on the significance level used for the hypothesis tests presented above. Thus, when a significance level is fixed, the only way to change H-I and I-H is that of modifying the set I of implied constraints. In particular, the *specialization* of a causal model by adding an edge may decrease the number of implied constraints, in which case the model incompleteness (H-I) may increase while the model inconsistency (I-H) may decrease.

All these ideas have been implemented in a program, called TETRAD [4], that helps the user to search for good models of correlation or covariance data. The program operates in two modes: *manual* and *automatic*. In the former mode, the user can ask the program to provide information on the possible elaborations of a given causal model. For each elaboration, only one edge is added to the causal model, so that the user is given in charge of the task of making the best choice and then analyzing new possible elaborations of the modified causal model. On the contrary, TETRAD's automatic search procedure starts with an initial causal model and suggests the addition of *sets* of treks to the *initial* causal model in order to provide an *extended* model which better fits to the data according to the above criteria. The initial model must be an acyclic graph such that:

a) there are no edges between measured variables;

b) all measured variables are effect of a latent cause;

c) all latent variables are connected each other.

For each foursome of measured variables, a particular subgraph of the causal model is selected. Such subgraph consists of:

1) the foursome of measured variables;

2) all latent variables, named *parents*, which are adjacent to any variable in the foursome;

3) all edges from the parents to any variable in the foursome;
4) all treks, including latent variables which are not parents, between the parents.

According to the type of subgraph, TETRAD suggests the addition of sets of treks defeating the implication of constraints which do not hold in the data at a significance level α. However, some of the suggested treks may also increase the incompleteness of the model, in which case they will be excluded from further processing. The remaining suggested treks form *locally minimal* sets LM_i, since their addition to the model is evaluated by considering only a subgraph of the causal model. As search proceeds from foursome to foursome, it forms *globally minimal* sets GM_i of suggested treks such that GM_i will defeat as many implied constraints involving all foursomes considered so far as is possible without increasing incompleteness. At the end of the automatic search, TETRAD outputs the sets GM_i and the minimum significance level at which these sets are non-empty. Even if it is not explicitly stated in [4], tetrad equations are the only constraints considered by TETRAD when it builds the sets GM_i.

TETRAD's automatic procedure is heuristic since the addition of treks to the initial model is based only on local information, that is the type of subgraph built for each foursome. Thus, if the initial model satisfies the conditions a-c) listed above, the sets of suggested treks are probably, but not certainly, correct. However, if one of those conditions is violated, the sets of suggested trek additions are not even probably correct.

4 The Method of Conditional Independencies

This method builds the causal model explaining sample data by analysing the conditional independence which holds in the sample. It is based on a clear theory of causality which classifies several types of causal relationships. This is done in the light of Reichenbach's principle [10] according to which every dependence between two variables x and y has a causal explanation, so either one causes the other or there is at least a third variable z influencing both of them (z is the source of a trek between x and y). Moreover, also in this approach, temporal information is not considered essential, but it can be easily exploited when available.

Let O be a set of random variables with a joint probability distribution P, and $x, y, z_1, z_2, ..., z_n \in O$. Then x and y are said to be (*conditionally*) *independent in the context* $\{z_1, z_2, ..., z_n\}$ if it happens that:

$$P(x,y \mid z_1, ...,z_n) = P(x \mid z_1, ...,z_n) \cdot P(y \mid z_1, ...,z_n)$$

Henceforth, $I(P)$ will denote the set of conditional independencies between the variables in O when P is the joint probability distribution. Moreover, we will write $I(x,y/\{z_1, z_2, ..., z_n\})$ if x and y are conditionally independent in the context $\{z_1, z_2, ..., z_n\}$, otherwise we will write $\neg I(x,y/\{z_1, z_2, ..., z_n\})$.

Given a causal model $M = <V,E>$ and its subset of observed variables $O \subseteq V$, we define *latent structure* the pair $S = <M,O>$. In other terms, S is a structure explaining which variables are observed in a causal model M.

Definition 5 (*implication of a probability distribution*)
A latent structure $S = <M,O>$ *implies* a joint probability distribution P^* on O iff there exists a SCT $T = (<V,E>, (\Omega,P), X)$ such that $P_{[O]} = P^*$, where $P_{[O]}$ denotes the marginal distribution for the variables in O.

Henceforth, the set of probability distributions implied by a latent structure S will be denoted by P_S.

Definition 6 *(consistency with a probability distribution)*

A latent structure $S=<M,O>$ is *consistent* with a given probability distribution P^* on the variables in O iff $P^* \in P_S$.

For a given sample distribution P^* on a set O of observed variables, we could try to find a latent structure $S=<M,O>$ that is consistent with P^*. However, the problem of estimating P^* is very hard, especially in the case of a large number of observed variables, even when the form of the probability distribution is known a priori. In order to simplify the problem, Pearl and Verma [7] reduce it to finding a latent structure that is consistent with the set of conditional independencies of P^*, $I(P^*)$, rather than P^* itself.

Definition 7 *(implication of a conditional independence)*

A latent structure $S=<M,O>$ *implies* a conditional independence I between some variables in O, if for each $P \in P_S$ we have $I \in I(P)$, that is I is a conditional independence for each probability distribution implied by the latent structure.

Henceforth, the set of conditional independencies implied by a latent structure S will be denoted by $I(S)$. Formally, we can write:

$$I(S) = \bigcap_{P \in P_S} I(P)$$

The set $I(S)$ can be derived by simply looking at the causal model. Indeed, the following theorem can be proven:

Theorem 3

Given a latent structure $S=<M,O>$, and two variables $x,y \in S$, then there is a conditional independence between two variables x and y in a given context C iff
1. $\forall\, t \in T_{xy}\ \exists\, z \in C : z \in t$, and
2. $\forall z \in C\quad [(\ \forall t \in T_{zx}$ such that t does not contain variables in $C-\{z\} : t \in P_{zx})\ \vee$
   $(\forall t \in T_{zy}$ such that t does not contain variables in $C-\{z\} : t \in P_{zy}\ )]$

Figure 3a shows a latent structure and the corresponding set of conditional independencies which could be derived according to Theorem 3. It is worthwhile to observe that such a set of conditional independencies can be observed for the latent structure S' in Figure 3b, as well. However, this is possible for only some, not all, probability distributions with which the latent structure is consistent. Therefore, $I(x,y/\varnothing)$ is implied by S and not S' according to definition 7.

Definition 8 *(consistency with a set of conditional independencies)*

A latent structure $S=<M,O>$ is consistent with a given set $I(P^*)$ of conditional independencies between the variables in O iff $I(P^*)=I(S)$.

As stated above, Pearl and Verma move the goal to finding a latent structure $S=<M,O>$ such that $I(S)=I(P^*)$. However, there is no guarantee that independencies observed on the sample distribution P^* are not *accidental* but they actually reflect the true *(structural)* independencies in the underlying causal model M. For this reason the two authors assume that P^* is a *stable distribution* generated by the underlying SCT.

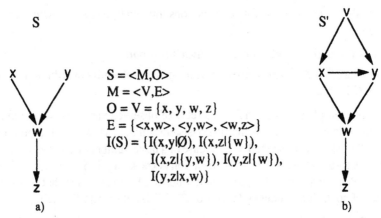

Figure 3. a) Latent structure and corresponding set of implied conditional independencies. The conditional independence $I(x,y|\varnothing)$ can be observed for some, but not all, particular probability distributions with which the latent structure S' in b) is consistent. Thus, it is not implied by S'.

Definition 9 *(stable distribution)*

Let $S=<M,O>$ be a latent structure. A SCT $T=(M,(W,P),X)$ generates a *stable distribution* $P_{[O]}$ on O iff $I(P_{[O]}) \subseteq I(S)$, that is $P_{[O]}$ does not contain extraneous independencies.

Since by definition of $I(S)$ we have that $I(S) \subseteq I(P_{[O]})$, then for a stable distribution we can conclude that $I(S) = I(P_{[O]})$. Therefore, under the assumption of stability it is reasonable to restrict the search of a causal model to the latent structures that are consistent with $I(P^*)$. In this way we have assumed that Nature does not show a sample distribution P^* which implies accidental independencies but It can still hide some variables. Thus, the problem of finding a causal model is still under-constrained, since there could be an infinite number of dependency-equivalent latent structures $S=<M,O>$ *with* different numbers of latent variables and such that $I(S) = I(P_{[O]})$. Pearl and Verma restrict their search to particular latent structures called *projections*.

Definition 10 *(projections)*

A latent structure $S=<<V,E>,O>$ is a *projection* on O of another latent structure $S'=<<V',E'>,O>$ iff
1) for each latent variable $\lambda \in V$ we have:
   a) indegree(λ)=0, that is λ is independent;
   b) outdegree(λ)=2;
   c) $\lambda \rightarrow v$, $\lambda \rightarrow w$ are in E, where $v,w \in O$ and v, w are not connected by any edge in E';
2) $I(S)=I(S')$.

Therefore, the maximum number of latent variables which can be added to a graph is given by the number of pairs of observed variables not connected by any edge. An example is shown in Figure 4. Pearl and Verma [7] have proven that each latent structure has at least one projection, therefore it is reasonable to search a causal model only in the space of projections. For projections it is convenient to use hybrid graphs as representation formalism.

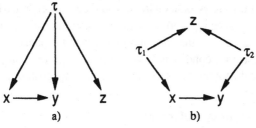

Figure 4. The latent structure in b) is a projection of the latent structure in a).

Definition 11 *(hybrid graph)*

An *hybrid graph* is a couple $G=<V,E>$ where V is the set of nodes and $E=<E_N, E_U, E_B>$ is a triple of three disjunct sets of edges:

E_N is a set of *non-directed* edges (u—v);
E_U is a set of *uni-directed* edges (u→v);
E_B is a set of *bi-directed* edges (u↔v).

By extension, for each pair $u,v \in V$ we write that the edge $<u,v> \in E$ iff $(u—v) \in E_N$ or $(u→v) \in E_U$ or $(u↔v) \in E_B$. According to the above definition, a directed graph is a particular hybrid graph in which $E_N = E_B = \varnothing$. Projections are represented by means of hybrid graphs in which $E_N = \varnothing$, moreover, a latent cause λ for two observed variables u and v is represented by eliminating the variable λ and adding a bi-directed edge between u and v. Thus the graph of a projection will have only observed variables. The intersection of the hybrid graphs representing all the possible projections of latent structures consistent with the sample distribution is called *core* of P^*.

The IC-algorithm (Inductive Causation algorithm) proposed by Pearl and Verma [7] builds the core of a sample distribution P^*, that is the intersection of the hybrid graphs representing all the possible projections of the minimal latent structure consistent with P^*. The input to the program is the set of conditional independencies which hold in P^*. The output core has four kinds of edges:

a) *marked uni-directed edges* representing genuine causal relationships;
b) *unmarked uni-directed edges* representing potential causal relationships;
c) *bi-directed edges* representing spurious associations;
d) *non-directed edges* representing those causal relationships that cannot be classified by using the only independencies in O (there would need different constraints).

Below, the definitions of genuine and potential causal relationships as well as the definition of spurious association are provided.

Definition 12 *(potential causal influence)*

A variable x has a *potential causal influence* on another variable y if
1) x and y are dependent in every context (for each context $C : \neg I(x,y|C)$);
2) there exists a variable z and a context C such that:
   a) $I(x, z | C)$;
   b) $\neg I(z, y | C)$.

If there are no latent variables, the only cases satisfying definition 12 are those shown in Figure 5a. Indeed, if it were y←x, then there would be a dependence between x and z, in contrast with a). But what can guarantee that x and y have no latent common cause, that is, x↔y ? If we were sure that all the variables involved in the phenomenon under study had been taken into account, condition 1) would be enough to avoid this eventuality. Nevertheless, since we do not have this certainty we can only postulate a *potential* cause of x on y.

Definition 13 *(genuine causal influence)*

A variable x has a *genuine causal influence* on y if there exists another variable z such that:
1) x and y are dependent in every context and there is a context C such that:
    a) z has a potential causal influence on x;
    b) $\neg I(z,y \mid C)$;
    c) $I(z,y \mid C \cup \{x\})$
or
2) x and y are in the transitive closure of rule 1.

Figure 5b shows the only two cases satisfying condition 1) when there are only three measured variables. Condition 2) covers those cases in which there is a path from x to y whose edges represent genuine causal relationships oriented in the direction from x to y.

Definition 14 *(spurious association)*

Two variables x and y have a *spurious association* if they are dependent in some context S $(\neg I(x,y \mid C))$ and there exist two variables z_1 and z_2 such that:
1) $\neg I(z_1, x \mid C)$;
2) $I(z_1, y \mid C)$;
3) $\neg I(z_2, y \mid C)$;
4) $I(z_2, x \mid C)$.

In this definition, conditions 1) and 2) prevent x from causing y, while conditions 3) and 4) prevent y from causing x, thus the dependence between x and y can only be explained by a spurious association. An example of spurious association is shown in Figure 5c. In this case the context C is the empty set.

5   Empirical Comparison of the Two Methods

In this section, Glymour et al.'s and Pearl and Verma's approaches to causal inference are empirically compared. The first three experiments have been performed by using models in which the assumptions of linearity, normality, acyclicity and stability are made. Note

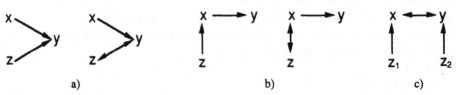

Figure 5. a) the two cases of potential causal influence; b) the two cases of genuine causal influence; c) a case of spurious association.

that when independent variables of a linear model are normal, then all random variables in the model are normal as well as the joint probability distribution. Thus, tests on independence between two variables, say x and y, in the context $\{z_1, z_2, ..., z_n\}$ are reduced to tests of Fisher's z statistics computed for the correlation coefficient $\rho_{xy.z_1, z_2, ..., z_n}$.

Obviously when all the variables involved in the phenomenon are observed, then the method of conditional independencies is by far the best. Indeed, since the sample distribution is stable, there is a causal connection between two variables in the graph only when they are dependent in each context. It could happen that some of these connections are not explained (not directed edges) or not precisely defined (potential causes) due to the lack of further control variables. However, when there are no latent variables and we know it, we can clearly claim that all potential causes are genuine causes, since there cannot be any spurious association without latent variables.

Experiment 1

Let us consider the model in Figure 6a. All independent variables have a standard normal distribution, $N(0,1)$, the significance level for all the test is $\alpha=0.05$ and the sample size is $N=1000$. In Table I, all the sample correlations are reported. From these correlations we find the following conditional independencies:

$$I(x,w \mid \varnothing) \qquad\qquad I(x, z \mid \varnothing) \qquad\qquad I(y, z \mid \{w\})$$

In Figure 6b, the output of the IC-algorithm is shown. Initially, the connections x—y, y—w and w—z are recovered, since the pairs of variables (x,y), (y,w) and (w,z) are dependent in every context. Then, by applying twice the definition of potential causal inference at each pair of variables, the connections x→y and w→y are recovered, for x can be a control variable for the pair (y,w) and w can be taken as a control variable for the pair (x,y). The connection w—z cannot be explained due to the lack of control variables. The connections x→y, w→y labelled as potential causes can be considered genuine causes if we assume a priori that there are no latent variables.

By trying to analyse this sample with TETRAD's automatic search procedure, we soon meet a problem: what is the initial model? In Figure 6c the simplest initial model is presented. Such a model is evidently wrong since the latent variable τ does not exist in reality. However, we will ignore connections with τ, since we are interested in finding causal relationships between observed variables alone.

The automatic search procedure suggests an addition of either a trek between x and y or a trek between w and z at the significance level $\alpha=0$. Indeed, the only tetrad equation that holds in the data is:

$$\rho_{xw} \cdot \rho_{yz} = \rho_{xz} \cdot \rho_{yw}$$

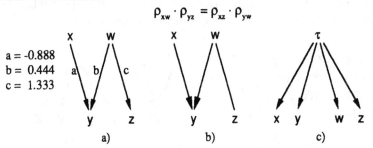

$$a = -0.888$$
$$b = 0.444$$
$$c = 1.333$$

Figure 6. a) True causal model of experiment 1. b) Causal model inferred by means of the IC-algorithm. Bold arrows represent potential causes. c) TETRAD's initial causal model.

Table I			
	x	y	w	z
x	1			
y	-0.6299	1		
w	-0.05351	0.3253	1	
z	-0.0566	0.2872	0.7930	1

Table II			
	x	y	w	z
x	1			
y	0.5322	1		
w	0.4741	0.8659	1	
z	0.0057	0.0182	0.2471	1

while the other two tetrad equations implied by the model, that is:

$$\rho_{xy} \cdot \rho_{wz} = \rho_{xw} \cdot \rho_{yz}$$
$$\rho_{xy} \cdot \rho_{wz} = \rho_{xz} \cdot \rho_{yw}$$

do not. The addition of the a of either a trek between x and y or a trek between w and z improves the consistency criterion, but when we add the edges $x \rightarrow y$ and $w \rightarrow z$ at the initial model we get a model in which no further improvement is possible. To sum up, the method of constraints on correlations is not able to discover the causal relation $w \rightarrow y$.

Experiment 2

When there are latent variables, the goodness of final results strongly depends on the topology of the initial causal model. For instance, let us consider the true causal model in Figure 7a, where τ is a latent variable. Once again the a sample is generated by imposing all independent variables to have a standard normal distribution. Table II shows the correlations between observed variables for a sample of 1000 observations. According to such correlations the following independencies are found:

$$I(x,w \mid \{y\}) \qquad\qquad I(x,z \mid \varnothing) \qquad\qquad I(y,z \mid \varnothing)$$

By applying the IC-algorithm, the model in Figure 7b is built. This result is undoubtedly better than that obtained by TETRAD's automatic search procedure when the initial causal model is that shown in Figure 7c. Once again, this model includes a latent variable τ that does not exist in reality, but it is the simplest initial model we can provide. Since we are interested in finding causal relationships between observed variables we will ignore connections with τ. TETRAD suggests the addition of either a trek between x and y or a trek between z and y, even though there is no trek between z and y in the original model (z and y are independent in any context). Such treks could be realized by adding the following connections: $x \leftrightarrow y$ and $z \rightarrow y$. However, the final model is not better than the initial one, neither can we discover the causal relationship $y \rightarrow w$.

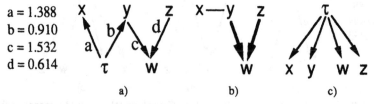

$a = 1.388$
$b = 0.910$
$c = 1.532$
$d = 0.614$

a)   b)   c)

Figure 7. a) True causal model of experiment 2. b) Causal model inferred by means of the IC-algorithm. Bold arrows represent potential causes. c) TETRAD's initial causal model.

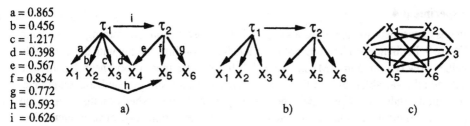

Figure 8. a) True causal model of experiment 3. b) TETRAD's initial causal model. c) Causal model inferred by means of the IC-algorithm.

Experiment 3

In this experiment we generated a sample of 5000 observations for the model in Figure 8a and we ran TETRAD with the initial model of Figure 8b. Correlations are given in Table III. In this case a trek between x_2 and x_5 is suggested and by asking a detailed analysis of the initial model augmented with the edge $x_2 \rightarrow x_5$ we are provided with further suggestions, namely:

$$x_4 \rightarrow x_5 \qquad x_4 \leftrightarrow x_5 \qquad \tau_1 \rightarrow x_4 \qquad x_6 \rightarrow x_5 \qquad \tau_1 \rightarrow x_6 \qquad x_6 \leftrightarrow x_5$$

By testing all these additions to the augmented model, we find that the best models are the following:

initial model + $x_2 \rightarrow x_5$ + $\tau_1 \rightarrow x_4$
initial model + $x_2 \rightarrow x_5$ + $x_6 \rightarrow x_5$
initial model + $x_2 \rightarrow x_5$ + $x_6 \leftrightarrow x_5$

among which there is the true causal model.

The method of conditional independencies provides poor results since no independencies hold in the data. In fact, it is possible to discover independencies only between observed variables, but having excluded latent variables from consideration all couples of variables are determined to be dependent (see Figure 8c).

To sum up, the method of conditional independencies is not good to study those phenomena in which there are some latent variables controlling many observed variables which have no spurious association. Indeed, this method can only discover projections of the real model, where a latent variable can only control two observed variables.

Table III

	x1	x2	x3	x4	x5	x6
x1	1					
x2	0.25120	1				
x3	0.49724	0.30191	1			
x4	0.36036	0.20448	0.42635	1		
x5	0.32524	0.51905	0.38348	0.48400	1	
x6	0.23871	0.12966	0.27900	0.44256	0.47144	1

Experiment 4

In this experiment we generated a sample of 1000 observations concerning the model in Figure 9. Each independent observed variable has an ordinal domain with three possible values: low (L), medium (M) and high (H). In this case there is no linear dependence between the variables, even if the causal relationships are still probabilistic. Of course, conditional independencies cannot be tested by means of the Fisher's z statistics as in the previous experiments, since the variables are not integer or ratio level measurements. We built a contingency table for each pair of variables in order to test the independence in the empty context, and we used a χ^2 test on each table. For testing conditional independence for non-empty contexts we had to generate as many subtables as the number of possible values that variables in the context can take. At the significance level $\alpha=0.05$ we detected the following independencies:

$$I(x_1, x_2 \mid \varnothing) \quad I(x_1, x_4 \mid \varnothing) \quad I(x_1, x_5 \mid \{x_3\}) \quad I(x_2, x_4 \mid \varnothing) \quad I(x_2, x_5 \mid \{x_3\}) \quad I(x_3, x_4 \mid \varnothing)$$

The IC-Algorithm builds the original model with the only difference that all the causal relationships but $x_3 \rightarrow x_5$ are potential and not genuine.

At this point, having discovered the causal dependencies between the variables, we used a learning system in order to induce the causal rules from the data. In particular, two learning problems were defined: the first for learning the causal law which relates the study level and the intelligence of a student with his/her preparation, and the second for learning how the preparation and the leniency of the examiner can affect the final result of the examination. In order to solve both problems we used C4.5 [9], a learning system that induces decision trees from examples. In particular, in the first problem examples are described by means of x_1, x_2 and the class (target) attribute x_3, while in the second problem examples are described by means of x_3, x_4 and the class (target) attribute x_5. Results are shown in Figure 10. The composition of the training cases at a leaf F gives a probability $P(K \mid F)$ that a case at F belongs to class K, where the probability can be estimated as a relative frequency [8]. For instance, in the case of a moderately lenient examiner and an insufficiently prepared student, the probability of having a low score is $71/(71+16) = 0.82$ while the probability of having a medium score is $16/(71+16) = 0.18$. From tree b) in

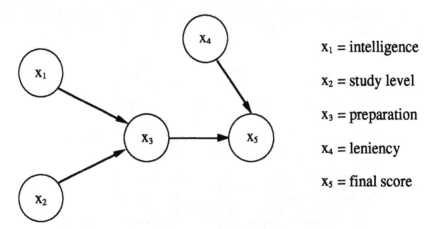

Figure 9. Causal model of experiment 4. All variables have an ordinal domain.

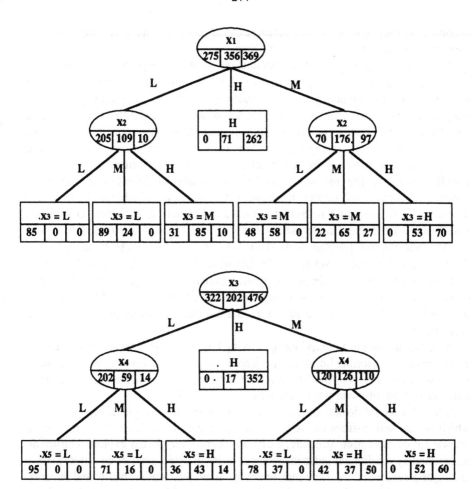

Figure 10. The two decision trees generated by C4.5 for the model in Figure 9. Together, they explain the causal law that rules the sociological model. Leaves are represented in boxes. Triplets of numbers in each node represent the distribution of examples reaching the node with respect to the values taken by the target attribute, namely L, M, and H.

Figure 10, we can also draw the conclusion that even students with an insufficient or moderately good preparation can get a high score when the examiner is particularly lenient. These and other rules can be directly derived in an explicit form by transforming each decision tree into a set of production rules.

6 Conclusions

Inferring causal models from empirical data is an arduous but exciting task. In fact, causal knowledge is a relevant part for any intelligent system that aims at explaining its decisions, predictions or even the behaviour of another intelligent system [2]. However, most of the causal relationships that humans use in their reasoning are probabilistic.

In this paper an analytic and empirical comparison between two different approaches to statistical causal inference has been presented. These approaches differ both in the kind of constraints they consider while selecting a causal model and in the way they search for the model which better fits to the sample data.

In Glymour et al.'s approach, constraints on correlation implied by the model are compared with those that hold in the data. Two kinds of constraints are considered: tetrad and partial equations, involving foursomes and triplets of variables respectively. TETRAD is a program that helps to discover causal models by testing tetrad differences and partial correlations. It can work in two different modes: manual and automatic. In the automatic mode a heuristic search strategy is performed in order to find an elaboration of the initial causal model that improves the completeness and consistency criteria with respect to tetradic constraints. The automatic procedure is heuristic since the addition of treks to the initial model is based only on local information, that is, the type of subgraph built for each foursome. TETRAD simply helps to discover causal models but it neither performs any statistical test of the causal model as a whole nor it estimates the coefficients of the model.

However, the true problem with TETRAD is just in the asymptotic test of tetrad differences and partial correlations. As Glymour et al. themselves admit, tests are performed on each tetrad difference or partial correlation as though it were independent of the others, even if this is almost never correct. In fact, there is no well-known test for the whole set of tetrad differences or partial correlations involving the very same variables.

Note that the strong assumptions underlying Glymour et al.'s approach are linearity and normality. The former limits the applicability to datasets containing only interval or ratio level measurements. Another limitation is the necessity of disposing of a complete initial model that involves latent variables.

These limitations do not concern the approach based on conditional independencies which in turn suffers from the very opposite problem of not exploiting partial initial knowledge of the causal structure. Pearl and Verma's approach exploits constraints determined by conditional independencies in order to detect genuine causal influences among observed variables. Note that, under the assumptions of normality and linearity, a test on the partial equation $\rho_{xz.y} = 0$ is equivalent to a test of the conditional independence $I(x, z \mid \{y\})$. Thus, this approach exploits some of the constraints used in the other one. Nevertheless, tetrad equations are constraints peculiar of Glymour et al.'s approach, while conditional independencies with contexts having a cardinality different from one are constraints exploited only in Pearl and Verma's approach.

There are a bias and a basic assumption in the method of conditional independencies: the former is towards projections while the latter concerns the stability of the underlying distribution. As already shown in the third experiment, such a bias can prevent the IC-algorithm from discovering the correct underlying model. On the contrary, stability seems a reasonable assumption that helps to reduce the search space. The applicability of Pearl and Verma's approach to variables of any level of measurement is simply limited by the availability of statistical tests for independence between variables of different levels of measurement.

Some preliminary experiments show that the two methods are complementary. Nevertheless, they share some common aspects. Firstly, both approaches require a large sample of data. Indeed, tests on tetrad differences are positively biased for small samples while several tests on conditional independencies may lead to unpredictable results if we use high significance levels. Secondly, it is possible to cast the search performed by both methods as a constraint satisfaction problem, where constraints are determined by the approaches themselves. This last aspect will be investigated in future work.

Finally, we have pointed out that both methods investigated in the paper can only discover causal dependencies between variables in the model but they are not able to define the causal laws. In the fourth experiment we have shown how, using an inductive learning algorithm, it is possible to fill this gap. In particular, we generated probabilistic decision trees which can effectively represent probabilistic causal relationships.

Acknowledgments

Thanks to Michael Pazzani for his helpful comments on an earlier draft of the paper and to Francesco Colasuonno for his precious collaboration on conducting the experiments. Also, a special thank to the anonymous reviewers whose comments helped to make this paper clearer.

References

1. T. W. Anderson: An introduction to multivariate statistical analysis. New York: Wiley 1958
2. P.R. Cohen, A. Carlson, L. Ballesteros, R. St. Amant: Automating path analysis for building causal models from data. In Machine Learning: Proceedings of the Tenth International Conference. San Mateo: Morgan Kaufmann 1993, pp. 57-64
3. G. DeJong, R. Mooney: Explanation-based learning: an alternative view. Machine Learning 1, 145-176 (1986)
4. C. Glymour, R. Scheines, P. Spirtes, K. Kelly. Discovering causal structure. Orlando: Academic Press 1987
5. D. Heise. Causal analysis. New York: Wiley 1975.
6. T.M. Mitchell, R.M. Keller, S.T. Kedar-Cabelli: Explanation-based generalization: a unifying view, Machine Learning 1, 47-80 (1986).
7. J. Pearl, T. S. Verma: A theory of inferred causation. In: J. A. Allen, R. Fikes, E. Sandewall (eds.): Principles of Knowledge Representation and Reasoning: Proceedings of the Second International Conference. San Mateo: Morgan Kaufmann 1991, 441-452
8. J. R. Quinlan: Probabilistic Decision Trees. In: Y. Kodratoff, R.S. Michalski (eds): Machine learning: an artificial intelligence approach, vol III. San Mateo: Morgan Kaufmann 1990, 140-152
9. J. R. Quinlan: C4.5: programs for machine learning. San Mateo: Morgan Kaufmann 1993
10. H. Reichenbach: The direction of time. Berkley: University of California Press 1956
11. P. Spirtes, C. Glymour, R. Scheines: Causation, prediction and search. Berlin: Springer 1993
12. L. Steels: Second Generation Expert Systems. Future Generation Computer Systems 1, 213-221 (1985)
13. P. Suppes: A probabilistic theory of causation. Amsterdam: North Holland 1970

Sample PAC-Learnability in Model Inference

S.H. Nienhuys-Cheng[1] and M. Polman[1,2]

[1] Dept. of Computer Science, Erasmus University of Rotterdam,
P.O.Box 1738, 3000 DR Rotterdam, The NetherLands.
[2] Tinbergen Institute.

Abstract. In this article, PAC-learning theory is applied to model inference, which concerns the problem of inferring theories from facts in first order logic. It is argued that uniform sample PAC-learnability cannot be expected with most of the 'interesting' model classes. Polynomial sample learnability can only be accomplished in classes of programs having a fixed maximum number of clauses. We have proved that the class of context free programs in a fixed maximum number of clauses with a fixed maximum number of literals is learnable from a polynomial number of examples. This is also proved for a more general class of programs.

1 Introduction and Preliminaries of PAC-Learning

In the field of machine learning, two important paradigms are PAC-learning [15] and Inductive Logic Programming (ILP) [9]. Both paradigms are concerned with learning from examples within some domain. In this paper we will try to apply some of the theory developed around the sample (PAC-)learnability of concept classes to classes of 'models' in first order logic, by considering least Herbrand models of logic programs as concepts in PAC-learning. Now, establishing results about the sample learnability of model classes (globally, the number of examples required to PAC-learn them) requires information about their so-called *Vapnik-Chervonenkis dimension*. Specifically, we want to find an upper bound on this dimension, following Lemma 1 (see below). This upper bound involves the number of equivalence classes of programs, i.e. groups of programs behaving identically, on the set of examples of some maximal length. As we will show, for certain classes this number can be estimated by counting programs of a specific form. We performed this method on two model classes, thus proving that they are PAC-learnable from a polynomial number of examples (polynomial sample learnable). An algorithm that actually learns these classes is given by a slight adaptation of an algorithm by Shapiro [14].

Besides polynomial sample learnability, there is another learnability criterion, called uniform sample learnability. This criterion is more stringent and we will show, by a property of prime numbers, that it is too strict for the really 'interesting' classes of logic programs.

In the rest of this section and Section 2 we will state the basic notions in both PAC-learning and model inference, necessary for the results presented later on. The definitions used in this section mostly come from [10].

Basic notions Let Σ be some finite alphabet. Let X be the domain of our interest, namely, a set of finite strings over Σ. A subset f of X is called a *concept*. A number of concepts with distinct features can be grouped in a *class* of concepts $\mathcal{F}$.

Example. As an example, consider the class of the *monotone monomials* over the domain of the (0,1)-strings. These are concepts representable by boolean functions consisting of the conjunction of a number of boolean variables. A concept contains those and only those strings for which its corresponding monomial formula returns true (e.g. the concept of strings of length 4 corresponding to the formula $a_1 \wedge a_4$ would be the set $\{1001, 1011, 1101, 1111\}$).

An example for some concept f is a pair (α, V), where $\alpha \in X$ and $V = 1$ if $\alpha \in f$ and $V = 0$ if $\alpha \notin f$. Finally, $X^{[n]}$ is the set of all domain elements of *length* at most n.

Probabilistic issues In the PAC-learning paradigm, we are concerned with finding, with tunable probability, a concept in a concept class that is tunably close to the 'intended' concept, using examples for the latter concept to guide our actions. More specifically, examples for some *target concept* f in class $\mathcal{F}$ are generated according to some unknown probability distribution P on $X^{[n]}$, for some given n, and fed to a learning algorithm. Eventually, the algorithm should output a concept $g \in F$, such that with probability at least $1 - \delta$, $P(f \triangle g) \leq \varepsilon$ [3], where δ and ε (*and* n) are the input parameters of the algorithm. A formal definition of a PAC-algorithm is as follows:

Definition PAC-learning algorithm. A learning algorithm A is a *PAC-algorithm* for a class of concepts $\mathcal{F}$ over X if

1. A takes as input $\varepsilon, \delta > 0$ and $n \in \mathbb{N}$, where ε is the *error* parameter, δ is the *confidence* parameter and n is the *length* parameter.
2. A may call the procedure **example**, which returns examples for some concept $f \in \mathcal{F}$, according to an arbitrary and unknown probability distribution P on $X^{[n]}$.
3. For all concepts $f \in \mathcal{F}$ and for all probability distributions P on $X^{[n]}$, A outputs a concept $g \in \mathcal{F}$, such that with probability at least $1 - \delta$, $P(f \triangle g) \leq \varepsilon$.

As will be clear from the discussion below, the internal behavior of PAC-learning algorithms, i.e. the way in which examples are processed by the algorithms, is of less importance to us. We only require that the output concept is a member of the specified concept class.

Learnability criteria We are interested in the number of examples needed to learn concepts from a class probably approximately correctly. The following complexity measure for learning-algorithms plays an important role.

Definition sample complexity. Let A be a learning algorithm for concept class $\mathcal{F}$. The *sample complexity* of A is a function s with parameters ε, δ and n. It returns the maximum number of calls of **example** by A, for all runs of $A(\varepsilon, \delta, n)$, for all $f \in \mathcal{F}$ and all P on $X^{[n]}$. The value of s is infinite if no finite maximum exists.

---

[3] The symbol $\triangle$ is used to represent the symmetric difference between two concepts.

Using the above definition, the following learnability criterion for classes can be defined:

Definition PSL. Class $\mathcal{F}$ is said to be *polynomial sample learnable* (PSL) if there exists a PAC-learning algorithm for $\mathcal{F}$, with a sample complexity that is bounded by some polynomial p in $\frac{1}{\epsilon}$, $\frac{1}{\delta}$ and n.

Another learnability criterion for classes is that of *uniform* sample learnability. This notion uses a definition of a PAC-algorithm in which the parameter n is not included. A class is called uniformly sample learnable if there exists an algorithm for it, having a sample complexity that is an integer-valued function in $\frac{1}{\epsilon}$ and $\frac{1}{\delta}$ only.

Vapnik Chervonenkis dimension It appears ([1]) that a class $\mathcal{F}$ is PSL if and only if it has a polynomial *Vapnik Chervonenkis dimension* [16]. This is a number associated with a class, which involves the notion of *shattering*:

Definition shattering. A class of concepts $\mathcal{F}$ on X *shatters* a set $S \subseteq X$ if the set given by $\{f \cap S | f \in \mathcal{F}\}$ is the power set of S, denoted by 2^S.

Now, the Vapnik Chervonenkis dimension (VC-dimension) of a class is defined as follows:

Definition VC-dimension. The VC-dimension of a concept class $\mathcal{F}$ on X is the greatest integer d (if it exists) such that there exists a set $S \subseteq X$ of cardinality d that is shattered by $\mathcal{F}$. It is denoted by $\mathbf{D_{VC}}(\mathcal{F})$.

If for each concept f in $\mathcal{F}$, $f^{[n]}$ denotes $f \cap X^{[n]}$ and if $\mathcal{F}^{[n]}$ is defined as $\{f^{[n]} | f \in \mathcal{F}\}$, then we say that $\mathcal{F}$ is of polynomial dimension if $\mathbf{D_{VC}}(\mathcal{F}^{[n]})$ is bounded from above by a polynomial in n.

The following lemma [10] concerns the relation between the VC-dimension of a class and the number of concepts in it.

Lemma 1. Let $\mathcal{F}$ be a class of concepts on domain X. Then

$$2^{d_{vc}} \leq |\mathcal{F}^{[n]}| \leq (|X^{[n]}| + 1)^{d_{vc}}$$

where $d_{vc} = \mathbf{D_{VC}}(\mathcal{F}^{[n]})$.

So, by finding a tight enough upper bound on $|\mathcal{F}^{[n]}|$, one can prove that $\mathcal{F}$ has a polynomial VC-dimension from which it would follow that $\mathcal{F}$ is PSL.

Uniform sample learnability has a significant link to the VC-dimension as well. In [1] it is proved that in order for a class to be uniformly sample learnable, it has to have a finite VC-dimension and vice versa. This will come up again in Section 6.

2 Model Inference

It appears that PAC-learning theory can be applied to what is known as *model inference* in first order logic. Specifically, we can consider least Herbrand models of programs as concepts in classes of models, for which the existence of a polynomial VC-dimension can be sought. In this section, we will give some basic notions in model inference.

Notations In the following, we will denote the predicates in a first order language by $Even$, P, etc. Functions will be denoted by f, g, s, etc., and variables by a capital X_1, Y etc. We will denote constants by lower-case characters a, b or digits 0, 1,... Also, to represent terms we use t, t_1, t_2 etc., for literals we use L_1, L_2, etc., and for clauses C, C_1,...

An example We will start off with an example to grasp the intuitive idea of model inference. Consider a first order language $\mathcal{L}$, consisting of the predicate $Even$, the function s (successor), and the constant 0. Let $\mathcal{L}_o$ be the set of ground (variable-free) atoms of $\mathcal{L}$ and $\mathcal{L}_h$ be the set of Horn-Clauses over $\mathcal{L}$. Suppose, that the ground atoms $Even(0)$, $Even(s(s(0)))$, etc. are true and $Even(s(0))$, $Even(s(s(s(0))))$, etc. false. Then we would like to find, for example, the following set of clauses in $\mathcal{L}_h$:

$Even(0)$.

$Even(s(s(X))) \leftarrow Even(X)$.

These clauses imply all true ground atoms and no false ones.

Model inference problem The model inference problem in first order logic is defined as follows ([14]):

Definition model inference problem. Suppose we are given some unknown model M for a first order language $\mathcal{L}$. Can we find a finite set of clauses (a theory), all true in M, that imply all true sentences in $\mathcal{L}_o$ and no false ones? We call such a theory an $\mathcal{L}_o$-*complete axiomatization* of M. The clauses from which the theory is allowed to be constructed are contained in a subset $\mathcal{L}_h$ of $\mathcal{L}$, called the hypothesis language.

Remark. In the rest of this article we will, given a first order language $\mathcal{L}$, let $\mathcal{L}_o$ consist of the ground atoms of $\mathcal{L}$ and $\mathcal{L}_h$ of the Horn-clauses of $\mathcal{L}$.

3 PAC-learning and Model Inference

Classes of concepts in PAC-learning are determined by the way the concepts are represented, e.g. monotone monomials. We say that a program T represents a set M of ground atoms (a concept) if $M = \{\alpha \mid T \vdash \alpha\}$. Now, it is known that any consistent set (program) T of Horn-clauses (!) in language $\mathcal{L}$ has the least Herbrand model, which is unique for T. The least Herbrand model for a program T is identified by a set of ground atoms, corresponding exactly with the set of ground atoms that are logical consequences of T. So, we can also say that a set of Horn-clauses T represents a set of ground atoms (concept) M if M corresponds with the least Herbrand model of T.

Thus, a class of concepts $\mathcal{M}$ in $\mathcal{L}_o$ contains sets of ground atoms, such that for each M in $\mathcal{M}$ there is a program T (of some class-specific type) of Horn-clauses having a least Herbrand model that corresponds with M.

Remark. In the following, we will also use the term (Herbrand) 'model' where we actually mean the concept/set of ground atoms corresponding to it. This is to indicate that we are dealing with concepts of ground atoms in first order logic. Similarly, we will speak of classes of *models*. This should not give rise to confusion considering the above discussion.

PAC-learnability of model classes If we use the class notion defined above, we expect a PAC-algorithm for a model class $\mathcal{M}$ to receive as input examples of a model $M \in \mathcal{M}$, according to some probability distribution P over $\mathcal{L}_o$ and output a finite set of clauses in $\mathcal{L}_h$ (a program) having a least Herbrand model (also in $\mathcal{M}$) such that the PAC-requirements are fulfilled.

Now, suppose that our first order language $\mathcal{L}$ consists of the following symbols:

- predicates $P_1, ..., P_p$.
- functions $f_1, ..., f_m$.
- constants $c_1, ..., c_k$.

Other symbols in atoms in $\mathcal{L}_o$ are '(', ')', and ','. Let K denote the total number of symbols: $K = p + m + k + 3$ and let the *length* of an atom α in $\mathcal{L}_o$ equal the number of symbols in α. Then it can be proved that any *consistent* model inference algorithm for a class $\mathcal{M}$ over $\mathcal{L}_o$, will after $\frac{1}{\epsilon}\left((n+1)\mathbf{D_{VC}}(\mathcal{F}^{[n]})\ln K + \ln\frac{1}{\delta}\right)$ calls of **example**, output a set of clauses in $\mathcal{L}_h$ such that the PAC-requirements are met. Therefore, it is a PAC-algorithm. (By 'consistent' we mean that the algorithm always outputs a concept consistent with the examples seen so far.) The proof of the above statement is analogous to [10] pp. 22-23.

Notice, that if $d = \mathbf{D_{VC}}(\mathcal{M}^{[n]})$ is bounded by a polynomial in n, then the number of facts/examples needed is bounded by a polynomial in n, $\frac{1}{\epsilon}$ and $\frac{1}{\delta}$. In other words (as we saw in Section 1), if $\mathcal{M}$ is of polynomial dimension, it is polynomial sample learnable.

From the following example, a restriction on the type of classes for which PSL is possible follows:

Example. Let $\mathcal{M}$ be the class of all models in some first order language $\mathcal{L}$, representable by a program in a finite number of clauses. Consider $\mathcal{L}_o^{[n]}$, the domain of ground atoms of length $\leq n$. Clearly, every subset of $\mathcal{L}_o^{[n]}$ has a finite program to represent it, namely a listing of the subset itself. Therefore, it is a member of $\mathcal{M}$. From this, it follows that the whole of $\mathcal{L}_o^{[n]}$ is shattered by $\mathcal{M}$. This implies, since the number of ground atoms in $\mathcal{L}_o^{[n]}$ is not polynomial in n, that the VC-dimension of $\mathcal{M}^{[n]}$ is not polynomial in n. Thus, $\mathcal{M}$ is not polynomial sample learnable. Also, if we require the models in a class all to contain a finite number of ground atoms, PSL cannot be achieved.

Thus, it seems reasonable to concentrate on classes of models, representable by a program in some fixed maximum number of clauses. Classes of models representable by programs in some maximum number c of clauses having some maximum number l of literals, for some fixed c, l, will from now on be denoted by $\mathcal{M}_{c,l}$. This is the type of classes we will focus on.

An algorithm In [14], Shapiro suggests an algorithm for model inference, referred to by him as a naive learning algorithm. It is based on arranging all possible theories over a language $\mathcal{L}$ in a sequence, which is possible if we are dealing with a finite number of predicate-, function- and constant symbols in $\mathcal{L}$. As positive and negative examples come by, the current theory is kept as long as it is consistent with the examples seen so far. If it becomes inconsistent, the next theory becomes the current theory etc. So, if we can find a class of models $\mathcal{M}$ of polynomial VC-dimension, then this algorithm learns $\mathcal{M}$ with a polynomial sample complexity.

It should be noted, that Shapiro's algorithm is adapt for models having the property of *h-easyness*, which is, basically, a minor restriction on their complexity and has to do with the number of computational steps within which one can conclude whether a theory is consistent with a set of examples or not. In the rest of this paper we will assume *h*-easyness as an additional property for the discussed model classes, without going into the matter further. For the interested reader, we refer to [14].

4 How to Prove Polynomial Sample Learnability

The real challenge after defining the boundaries of the discussion is to actually identify specific classes of concepts as being or not being polynomial sample learnable. All classes we are going to consider will be of the type $\mathcal{M}_{c,l}$, with some additional restrictions regarding the form of the clauses. Now, in order to prove whether or a class $\mathcal{M}_{c,l}$ is PSL, information is needed regarding its VC-dimension. By Lemma 1 this information can be obtained from the inequality $2^d \leq |\mathcal{M}_{c,l}^{[n]}|$, where $d = \mathbf{D_{VC}}(\mathcal{M}_{c,l}^{[n]})$. We want to find an upper bound on $|\mathcal{M}_{c,l}^{[n]}|$ of the form $2^{p(n)}$ where p is some polynomial in n.

Problems Unfortunately, simply counting the intersections of all models in $\mathcal{M}_{c,l}$ with $\mathcal{L}_0^{[n]}$ is out of the question. We need to count the expressions (programs) that have the concepts in $\mathcal{M}_{c,l}^{[n]}$ as their least Herbrand models. Of course we only need those programs structured according to the definition of $\mathcal{M}_{c,l}$. Unfortunately (again!), for every intersection of a model with $\mathcal{L}_o^{[n]}$, there will probably still be a vast number of programs all equally qualified to represent it. Including all these programs in establishing our upper bound is very likely to result in disaster.

Equivalence classes Now, consider the following: we call two programs equivalent if they behave the same on $\mathcal{L}_o^{[n]}$, i.e. if their least Herbrand models have the same intersection with $\mathcal{L}_o^{[n]}$. This gives us an equivalence class of programs for every intersection of a model in $\mathcal{M}_{c,l}$ with $\mathcal{L}_o^{[n]}$. What we need, in theory, is the number of equivalence classes. What we will do, actually, is trying to find an acceptably small number of programs for each equivalence class, such that we only have to count programs instead of intersections of models with $\mathcal{L}_o^{[n]}$.

Representative program Our hope is that we only have to consider programs of a certain form. In fact, we hope that: if M is a model in $\mathcal{M}_{c,l}$, then $M^{[n]}$ can be represented by a program containing only literals of length at most $h(n)$, for some polynomial h. In that case we would only have to count the number of programs in our class consisting of literals of less than n characters, which is a relatively easy job. This number would be an upper bound on the number of equivalence classes, which is the number of intersections of models in $\mathcal{M}_{c,l}$ with $\mathcal{L}_o^{[n]}$. Formally:

Question. Let $\mathcal{M}_{c,l}$ be a class of models over $\mathcal{L}$ and let $M \in \mathcal{M}_{c,l}$. Suppose that M can be represented by a program T. Is there a program T' giving the same output as T on examples of length $\leq n$, and containing only literals of length $\leq h(n)$, where h is a polynomial in n?

Polynomial sample learnability Suppose that this is true for some class $\mathcal{M}_{c,l}$. Now, let K be $p + m + k + 3 + 1$, where k, m and p are defined as in Section 3 (the '1' is included to count the empty symbol). Then, in a clause of at most l literals of length $\leq h(n)$, there are $l \cdot h(n)$ places to put symbols. We can choose from the K symbols (as above) *and* variables. The number of different variables in such a clause is limited by $l \cdot h(n)$. So, the number of different clauses of maximally l literals of length $\leq n$ is bounded from above by

$$((K + l \cdot h(n))^{l \cdot h(n)}$$

The number of programs in clauses of this form is bounded by

$$((K + l \cdot h(n))^{c \cdot l \cdot h(n)}$$

So, according to Lemma 1, we have:

$$2^d \leq (K + l \cdot h(n))^{c \cdot l \cdot h(n)}$$

It follows, that

$$d \leq c \cdot l \cdot h(n)^2 \log(K + l \cdot h(n))$$

This means that class $\mathcal{M}_{c,l}$ is polynomial sample learnable.

5   The Class of Context Free Models

Consider the following program T:

$P(X, 0, X)$.

$P(s(X), Y, s(Z)) \leftarrow P(X, Y, Z)$.

$P(s(s(s(X))), s(Y), s(s(s(Z)))) \leftarrow P(X, Y, Z)$.

If we want to derive the ground atom $\alpha = P(s(0), 0, s(0))$ from this program by SLD-resolution (essentially, we derive the empty clause from $T \wedge \neg\alpha$), then we can see that the third clause will not be used in the process. In fact, this clause will not be used to derive any atom in $\mathcal{L}_o$ of smaller length than its positive literal. We can use this kind of property in proving that the classes $\mathcal{M}_{c,2}$ of context free models are

PSL. Context free models are models representable by a program, in which every clause is an atom or a two-literal clause of the form

$$P(t_1, ..., t_m) \leftarrow P(X_1, ..., X_m).$$

where each variable X_i occurs in t_i. The notion of context free programs was first defined in [13].

Example. As an example, consider the notion of 'plus'. This can be captured by a context free program in a language with 3-ary predicate *Plus*, constant 0 and 1-ary function s (the successor function) as follows:

$$Plus(0, X, X).$$

$$Plus(s(X), Y, s(Z)) \leftarrow Plus(X, Y, Z).$$

Size and length Before we formalize the above and give the proof, we will adopt an alternative for the *length* function. We suggest the use of the *size* operator:

Definition size. The *size* of a term in a first order language is the total number of variable-, function-, and constant symbols appearing in it. The size of an atom is the sum of the sizes of the terms it contains as arguments.

As an example, consider the the ground atom $P(s(s(X)), 0)$. The size of this atom is 4.

It is easy to prove that *length* and *size* are equivalent, i.e. in establishing a polynomial VC-dimension for a class, it does not matter whether it is polynomial in the size or in the length of the ground atoms. The set of sentences in $\mathcal{L}_o$ of size at most n will be denoted by $\mathcal{L}_o^{(n)}$. Analogous notations go for classes and concepts.

We have the following result concerning context free model classes:

Theorem 2. The classes $\mathcal{M}_{c,l}$ of context free models are PSL.

Proof. We will prove that the function $h(n)$, mentioned in the question of Section 4 equals n for this class. Let $M \in \mathcal{M}_{c,l}$ and let T be a program having M as its least Herbrand model. Let α be any ground atom in M, with $size(\alpha) \leq n$ for some n. Since M is the least Herbrand model of T and α is in M, it is known, by the *refutation completeness* of SLD-resolution, that there is a finite derivation of the empty clause from $\{\neg\alpha\} \cup T$ by SLD-resolution. Now, α cannot be unified with a positive literal in T of size $> n$. If α can be unified with the positive literal L from clause $C = (L \leftarrow L_1)$ by substitution σ, then

1. $L_1\sigma$ will be ground, since all variables of L_1 are in L and they are instantiated by ground terms according to σ.
2. The size of $L_1\sigma$ will not exceed n. This follows from the fact that in negative literals no function symbols or constants occur and each variable in L_1 occurs in its corresponding term in L.

So, in the next resolution step, where we derive $L_1\sigma$ from T, we have a similar situation as in deriving α itself. Again no unification can take place with any positive literal of size $> n$, and after unification with some positive literal, the negative literal (if present) will, after substitution, not have size $> n$. It follows that in the resolution procedure for α, the clauses in T containing literals of size $> n$ will not be needed. If we delete from T all such clauses, we are left with a program T', equivalent to T with regard to the atoms in $\mathcal{L}_o^{(n)}$, containing only literals of size $\leq n$. This is true for every model in $\mathcal{M}_{c,l}$ and for every n. It follows that $h(n) = n$ for this class. Thus, $\mathcal{M}_{c,l}$ is PSL, by the arguments used in Section 4. □

Shapiro Recall Shapiro's suggestion for an implementation of a model inference algorithm. This can become a PAC-algorithm for the above class, having a polynomial sample complexity. To make it suitable for this class the only adaptation needed is having the sequence of all possible theories in $\mathcal{L}$ replaced by the sequence of all possible theories within the context free class. This argument is valid for every class of models that is PSL.

6 Another Learnable Class

The class of context free models is significant, but has limited possibilities. We want to generalize it to some extent, such that the arguments used in the previous section to prove PSL, are still valid. We have arrived at: the class $\mathcal{M}_{c,l}$ for some fixed c, l, with the additional requirement, that in any clause $C = (L \leftarrow L_1, ..., L_m)$ of a program in $\mathcal{M}_{c,l}$, any argument in one of the L_i must be contained in an argument in L.

Example. A program in this class will contain clauses of the form:

$$P(f(g(X)), f(Y)) \leftarrow Q(g(X), f(Y), Y), R(f(g(X))).$$

every argument on the right of the '$\leftarrow$' is a subterm of an argument in the positive literal.

Theorem 3. Class $\mathcal{M}_{c,l}$ is polynomial sample learnable.

Proof. Let the maximum arity of all predicates in $\mathcal{L}$ be A. We will prove that for the class $\mathcal{M}_{c,l}$, $h(n) = nA$, where h is again the function from the question in Section 4. We can use arguments similar to those used for the context free models. Suppose that we have a program T for some $M \in \mathcal{M}_{c,l}$ and a ground atom α in M of size $\leq n$ for some n. Notice that all terms in α must be of size $\leq n$. If we want to derive a contradiction from $\neg\alpha \wedge T$ then α cannot be unified with positive literals containing terms of size $> n$. So α will not unify with any positive literal of size $> nA$. Also, if α unifies with positive literal L in clause $C = (L \leftarrow L_1, ..., L_m)$ by substitution σ, then any negative literal L_i in C will, after substitution, be ground and not contain terms of size $> n$. This is because for all i the terms in $L_i\sigma$ will be subterms of terms in $L\sigma$. It follows that the size of $L_i\sigma$ will not exceed nA. The same arguments are valid if we want to derive $L_i\sigma$ from T. It follows that in deriving α

from T, clauses with literals containing terms of size $> n$ will not be needed. Thus, by deleting such clauses from T, we have a program T', equivalent to T with regard to $\mathcal{L}_o^{(n)}$, containing only terms of size $\leq n$, so every literal has size $\leq nA$. This can be done for all $M \in \mathcal{M}_{c,l}$ and all n. It follows that $h(n) = nA$ for this class and thus $\mathcal{M}_{c,l}$ is PSL. $\qquad\square$

Remark. In the above class, we can relax the restrictions regarding constants, appearing in a program in $\mathcal{M}_{c,l}$ slightly, while preserving PSL. There are two possibilities: the first is to require that in any clause, the constant term of the largest size always appears in the positive literal. Notice that this does not imply that any constant term in a negative literal is contained in a term in the positive literal. The second option is to restrict the maximum size of any constant term appearing in a program. In both cases, the function $h(n)$ will still be bound by a polynomial in n.

7 Uniform Sample Learnability of Model Classes

We have proved the fact that the class $\mathcal{M}_{c,l}$ of context free models is PSL. In the introduction we also mentioned uniform sample learnability. Now, uniform sample learnability is a more stringent complexity criterion than PSL. Is the class of context free models uniformly sample learnable? From the following, we can see that it is not.

The interesting classes In this section we will briefly discuss uniform sample learnability of model classes. We will prove that most of the 'interesting' classes of models are not uniformly sample learnable. As was stated in Section 1, this can be done by proving that these classes do not have a finite VC-dimension.
The classes we are particularly interested in are again those classes containing models representable by a program in at most c clauses of at most l literals, for some fixed c, l.
Now, let $\mathcal{L}$ be a language containing at least one predicate P, one function f and one constant a. then:

Proposition 4. $\mathcal{M}_{c,l}$ for $\mathcal{L}$ is not uniformly sample learnable, for all $c, l > 1$.

Proof. We will show that $\mathcal{M}_{2,2}$ does not have a finite Vapnik Chervonenkis dimension and is therefore not uniformly sample learnable. From this it follows that every superclass of this class (i.e. a class with greater c and/or l) is also not uniformly sample learnable.
Suppose P and f are of arity 1. We will denote an n times nested function by f^n, e.g. $f(f(f(a)))$ is denoted by $f^3(a)$. Now, if we want anything in $\mathcal{L}_o$ to be deducible from a program of 2 clauses of maximally 2 literals, then it has to contain at least one one-literal clause. Consider the situation where this clause is ground and that the other one is a two-literal clause containing a variable, say X. Let $x_1 = 210$, $x_2 = 330$, $x_3 = 462$, $x_4 = 770$, $x_5 = 1155$. Notice, that every x_i is the product of 4 out of the 5 first prime integers: $2, 3, 5, 7, 11$. Now consider the following set S of ground atoms: $\{P(f^{x_1}(a)), P(f^{x_2}(a)), P(f^{x_3}(a)), P(f^{x_4}(a)), P(f^{x_5}(a))\}$. Suppose

that model M contains $P(f^{x_2}(a))$, $P(f^{x_4}(a))$ and $P(f^{x_5}(a))$ but not $P(f^{x_1}(a))$ and $P(f^{x_3}(a))$. Consider the following program:

$P(a)$.

$P(f^{55}(X)) \leftarrow P(X)$.

From this program, all three true atoms can be derived and no false one. The reason for this is that 55 is the greatest common divisor of x_2, x_4 and x_5, and is the product of the two primes 11 and 5 by which resp. x_1 and x_3 are not divisible. Actually, we can construct a similar program for every mapping of the five ground atoms to $\{true, false\}$: we just replace the number 55 by the greatest common divisor of the x_i's of the true atoms. Therefore, such an S is shattered by $\mathcal{M}_{2,2}$.

Indefinitely larger shattered sets of ground atoms can be constructed, if we increase the number of x_i's by using more consecutive primes. Therefore, the Vapnik Chervonenkis dimension of even this simple class is not finite. We only have to modify the proof slightly if we want it to be valid for classes over languages in more predicates and functions having larger arity as well. Now, since this class is a subclass of every class described in the proposition, the validity of the proposition follows immediately. □

As we can see, the programs constructed to prove non-uniform sample learnability are all context free. From this it follows that, as was mentioned before, the class $\mathcal{M}_{c,l}$ of context free models is not uniformly sample learnable.

8 Conclusions

In this paper we have attempted to combine PAC-learning with model inference. The second can be seen as a subject in the field of Inductive Logic Programming. Looking upon Herbrand models as concepts in the domain of all ground atoms enables us to consider the VC-dimension of classes of models. We can find an upper bound on this dimension by counting the number of different programs fit to represent the models in a class restricted to $\mathcal{L}_o$. For two classes, among which the class of context free models, this upper bound is tight enough to establish PSL. Uniform sample learnability, which is a stronger requirement than PSL, is out of the question for the more 'interesting' classes.

Open Problems Frankly, all additional restrictions on $\mathcal{M}_{c,l}$-type classes bother us: we would like to drop them without losing PSL. However, consider the following program.

$P(s(s(s(a))))$.

$P(X) \leftarrow P(s(X))$.

If we want to derive $P(s(s(a)))$ from this program then the first clause will be used: this clause cannot be omitted to get a program equivalent with regard to atoms of size ≤ 3. We have similar problems when allowing for variables in the body of a clause that do not appear in the head. So, in proving PSL for more general classes than the ones described above, the old arguments are no longer valid. New proof methods will have to be found.

Furthermore, interesting problems arise when considering the so-called one-sided learnability of model classes, which means that one only allows mistakes in the output of a specific type: inclusion-only errors or exclusions-only errors. This has a significant link to the question, whether or not the intersection (or union) of two models in a class, is a model in the class as well. Our expectation is that the intersection of two context free models in a class $\mathcal{M}_{c,l}$ is a model in this class as well.

9 Related Work

Applying the PAC-learning paradigm to classes of logic programs is a subject that has received considerable attention in the last few years. A lot of authors doing research in this area discuss the subject of polynomial *time learnability*, which involves the number of *computational steps* needed to PAC-learn a class of concepts, thus implicitly including sample learnability (polynomial sample learnability, which we discuss as a separate issue, is a prerequisite for polynomial time learnability), the *consistency* problem and the *evaluation* problem. The consistency problem concerns the number of steps to compute a logic program (in some class) consistent with a set of examples, and evaluation problem concerns the number of steps to classify an example using some output theory. We will give a brief overview of some of the results in these areas.

In [8] the idea of feeding PAC-learning algorithms for model classes with 'good' data to speed up convergence, is proposed. In this way, the quality of the examples, which is believed to be essential in human learning, is included in the paradigm. Indeed, positive learnability results can be achieved if the requirement of random example-generation is replaced by so-called generative representative sets of examples.

In [11] the approach is to have a learning algorithm, given some fixed background theory T, generate one sentence S, such that $T \cup S$ will behave similarly to $T \cup S'$ (S' being the 'target' sentence). The term 'similarly', of course, can be filled in to contain PAC-requirements. It is proved, that under certain restrictions, the class of constrained atoms is polynomial time learnable. Constrained atoms are Horn clauses in which each variable in the body also appears in the head of the clause, which was also the case in the classes for which we proved PSL.

In [4], it is shown that the class of *ij-determinate* Horn clauses is polynomial time learnable, where an ij-determinate Horn clause is a clause in which the body can contain variables not appearing in the head under the restriction that these variables have a unique binding, that the so-called *depth* of the clause is bounded by a constant (i) and that the arity of the body literals is bounded by a constant j. These clauses are in some respects more general than those in the program classes we studied, because new variables may appear in the body of a clause. However, the results are still concerned with learning one clause. PAC-learnability of *non-recursive, function-free* programs of maximally c ij-determinate Horn clauses, for some constant c, can be proved under the condition of so-called 'simple distributions'.

Very recently, Cohen [2], proved PAC-learnability results for a number of classes, among which are also several one-clause program classes. It is proved that log-depth (instead of constant depth) j-determinate clauses are not polynomial time learnable. The class of non-recursive, function-free programs in any number of clauses with a maximum of l literals in the body is proved to be polynomial time learnable from negative examples only. It is also shown that allowing for recursion in the programs of a class introduces severe learnability problems. These can be (partially) solved by allowing only for so-called *linear* recursion, where only one literal in the body of a clause is allowed to cause recursion (see also [3]).

In [7] some negative learnability results are proved. It is shown that dropping the requirement of ij-determinacy leads to non-polynomial time learnability. Dropping only the fixed depth requirement or only the determinacy requirement will also render non-polynomial time learnable classes.

Finally, in [5] it is shown that the class of programs of maximally c clauses (for some constant c), which are constrained, non-recursive and function free, is polynomially learnable.

As the reader will have noticed, most research in this area is aimed at finding efficiently learnable model classes with as much expressive power as possible. However, polynomial time learnability, as a criterion, imposes quite stringent restrictions of the definition of learnable classes. In concentrating solely on sample learnability, thus to some extent ignoring the consistency problem, these restrictions can be partly removed. The most important issue then becomes a polynomial VC-dimension, a topic we did not find discussed explicitly very often in work about classes of logic programs.

A lot of positive results in polynomial time learnability do, however, involve classes of programs in which the requirement of constraind-ness is replaced by bounded depth or determinacy. This is an interesting topic that we have not addressed so far.

References

1. Blumer, A., Ehrenfeucht, A., Haussler, D., Warmuth, M.: Learnability and the Vapnik-Chervonenkis Dimension. Journal of the Association for Computing Machinery **36** No. 4 (1989) 929-965
2. Cohen, W.: Learnability of Restricted Logic Programs. Proceedings of the Third International Workshop on Inductive Logic Programming (ILP'93) (1993) 41-71
3. Cohen, W.: PAC-Learning a restricted Class of recursive Logic Programs. Proceedings of the Third International Workshop on Inductive Logic Programming (ILP'93) (1993) 73-86
4. Dzeroski, S., Muggleton, S., Russel, S.: PAC-Learnability of Determinate Logic Programs. Proceedings of the Fifth ACM Workshop on Computational Learning Theory (1992) 128-135
5. Dzeroski, S., Muggleton, S., Russel, S.: Learnability of Constrained Logic Programs. Proceedings of ECML'93 (1993) 342-347
6. Ehrenfeucht, A., Haussler, D., Kearns, M., Valiant, L.: A General Lower Bound on the Number of Examples Needed for Learning. Information and Computation **82** (1989) 247-261
7. Kietz, J.: Some Lower Bounds for the Computational Complexity of Inductive Logic Programming. Proceedings of ECML'93 (1993) 114-123

8. Ling, X.: Inductive Learning from Good Examples. Proceedings of IJCAI'91 (1991) 751-756

9. Muggleton, S.: Inductive Logic Programming. Muggleton S. (ed.), Inductive Logic Programming, Academic Press (1992) 3-27

10. Natarajan, B.: Machine Learning, a Theoretical Approach. Morgan Kaufman Publishers, Inc (1991)

11. Page, C.D., and Frish, A.M.: Generalization and Learnability: A study of Constrained Atoms. Muggleton (ed.), Inductive Logic Programming, Academic Press (1992) 29-61

12. Polman, M., Nienhuys-Cheng, S.-H.: PAC-Learning and Model Inference. Benelearn '93, Collection of work reports, Vrije Universiteit Brussel (1993)

13. Reynolds, J.C.: Transformational Systems and the Algebraic Structure of Atomic Formulas. Machine Intelligence 5 (1970) 135-153

14. Shapiro, E.: Inductive Inference of Theories from Facts. Technical Report 192, Dept. of Computer Science, Yale University, USA (1981)

15. Valiant, L.G.: A Theory of the Learnable. Communications of the ACM 27 No. 11 (1984) 1134-1142

16. Vapnik, V., and Chervonenkis, A.: On the uniform convergence of relative frequencies of events to their probabilities. Theory of Probability and its Applications 16 No. 2 (1971) 264-280

Averaging Over Decision Stumps

Jonathan J. Oliver and David Hand

Department of Statistics, Open University
Walton Hall, Milton Keynes, MK7 6AA, UK

Abstract. In this paper, we examine a minimum encoding approach to the inference of decision stumps. We then examine averaging over decision stumps as a method of generating probability estimates at the leaves of decision trees.

1 Introduction

We discuss the supervised learning problem with particular emphasis on small data sets. Supervised learning involves constructing a rule from a training set of examples, where each example has a set of measurements and a class associated with it. We then use the constructed rule to make predictions of the class for future examples.

It is our experience that very simple rules may produce quite high predictive accuracy on many data sets. For example, a Bayes classifier [14] which assumes that the attributes are statistically independent, can perform well even in those cases when the independence assumption is clearly inappropriate.

In this paper, we focus on classification rules that take the form of decision trees [3, 15]. It has been found that decision tree like rules, that only consider one or two attributes, can perform surprising well [11, 12, 25]. In particular, Holte [11] and Iba and Langley [12] considered rules that only considered one attribute. These simple rules are in effect severely pruned decision trees and have been termed *decision stumps* [12].

The majority of machine learning systems determine a model to explain some data by considering a range of models, and selecting a single model that satisfies some criterion. Some authors argue that in some circumstances, a set of models can explain data better than a single model [7]. Within the field of decision trees, pruning is equivalent to selecting a single tree, which can then be used for making predictions for future examples. Tree averaging [2, 4, 5, 8, 10, 13, 16] involves making predictions using a set of trees.

This paper is organised in the following way. Section 2 defines decision stumps. In Sections 3 and 4, we examine the relationship between pruning and tree averaging. Section 5 demonstrates how MML can be used to assign weights for tree averaging. In Section 7, we replace each leaf of a decision tree with a weighted set of decision stumps. In some cases this improves predictive accuracy of a decision tree, without the computational cost associated with option trees.

2 Decision Stumps

We identify height 1 (a single leaf) and height 2 decision trees as decision stumps. Consider the LED data set described by Breiman et al. [3]. This data set has 10 classes representing whether the LED is showing the digits 0-9. The LED has 7 elements (A1 — A7), as shown in the key in Figure 1, each of which has a 10% chance of being faulty. Figure 1 depicts the 8 decision stumps for the LED data set and shows where a non faulty display would categorise each digit.

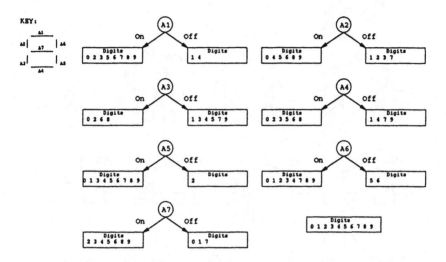

Figure 1: Decision stumps for the LED data set

When we consider decision stumps for data sets with continuous attributes, then we may construct multiple decision stumps for the one attribute. We restrict ourselves in this paper, to one decision stump for each continuous attribute, by selecting the cut point which minimises a minimum encoding metric.

3 Pruning

Constructing a decision tree is traditionally performed in 2 phases, a *Growing Phase*, and a *Pruning Phase*. The Growing Phase grows a *complete* decision tree by recursively splitting each leaf until each leaf is either class pure, or considered too small to split. The Pruning Phase takes as input the complete tree T. Its task is to select a single "best" tree from the *set of pruned trees* of T, { PT_1, PT_2, ..., PT_n }. The set of pruned trees contains each tree that has 0 or more decision nodes transformed into leaves. For example, the set of pruned trees for the tree T in Figure 2 = { PT_1, PT_2, ..., PT_{13} }.

The measures used for pruning are typically statistical estimates of the error rate, and pruning involves finding the pruned tree that minimises this estimate. The estimates of error are typically calculated by *cross validation* [3].

4 Tree Averaging

Tree averaging or *smoothing* is a generalization of pruning that has recently been receiving more attention. Buntine [4, 5], Kwok and Carter [13], Hastie and

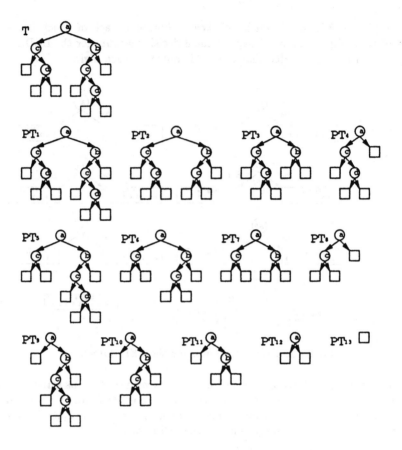

Figure 2: The set of pruned trees for Tree T

Pregibon [10] and Clark and Pregibon [8] consider averaging over decision trees. Bahl et al. [2] smooth down decision pylons, and Quinlan [16] smoothes down Model Trees. A variety of methods are used to perform averaging, including cross validation [2, 10, 8] and a Bayesian approach [4, 5]. Experiments performed by Buntine [4, 5] and Quinlan [16] suggest that tree averaging is superior to pruning.

Tree averaging involves calculating a set of weights $\{\ w_1,\ w_2,\ \ldots\ ,w_n\ \}$, for each tree in the set of pruned trees. We normalize the set of weights such that $\sum_{i=1}^{i=n}\ w_i\ =\ 1$. A new object, O, can be classified by a smoothed tree by:

1. Determining the probability given to each class by each tree:

$$Pr(O_i^k)\ =\ Prob(O\ belongs\ to\ class\ k\ according\ to\ PT_i).$$

2. Calculating the probability distribution over classes for object O, by summing over the set of pruned trees.

$$Prob(O\ belongs\ to\ class\ k)\ =\ \sum_{i=1}^{i=n}\ w_i\ \times\ Pr(O_i^k).$$

3. Assigning O to the class with maximum probability.

4.1 Option Trees

Buntine [4, 5] took the idea of tree averaging one step further. Tree averaging considers the set of pruned trees of a single tree. *Option trees* represent a large set of trees, and average over the set of pruned trees for each tree in this set. The result off this is that option trees use more computational resources than traditional decision trees. However, this is offset by the improved predictive ability of option trees [4, 5].

5 MML Inference

The minimum encoding learning paradigms were developed during the 1960s and 1970s. There are two schools of minimum encoding inference: Minimum Message Length (MML) — developed by Wallace et al. [9, 22, 23, 24], and Minimum Description Length (MDL) — developed by Rissanen [17, 18, 19, 20]. These learning paradigms are applicable to a wide range of problems, since they were developed to "fit models to data". An introduction is given by Georgeff and Wallace [9].

These approaches turn the problem of finding a good hypothesis into the problem of minimizing an encoding of the data. Given a hypothesis, we can calculate the length of encoding the hypothesis and the data given the proposed hypothesis. Thus, these approaches offer a clear answer to the bias problem, i.e., searching for the hypothesis that has the smallest encoding of the hypothesis and data.

Decision trees can be regarded as a theory about a domain, mapping objects to classes. We define an *explanation* of the class vector as a message encoded as a binary string and consisting of two parts. The first part states the decision tree, T, and the second part states the class vector using a code that gives the minimum expected message length using T.

Quinlan and Rivest [17] and Wallace and Patrick [24] have presented encoding scheme for decision trees. In this paper, we use a slightly modified form of the code used by Wallace and Patrick [24]. We note that an encoding of decision stumps should use the fact that we are willing to split only the root node.

5.1 Averaging over Theories Using MML

When given a set of trees, $\{ T_1, T_2, \ldots T_n \}$, about some data, we may calculate the message length, ML_i of the explanation provided by each tree, T_i. We may establish a posterior probability distribution over trees:

$$Prob(T_i|D) \propto Prob(D\&T_i) = 2^{-ML_i}$$

We may use the posterior distribution over the theories, in 2 ways: (1) we may select that tree with the highest posterior probability, or (2) we may use the posterior distribution over trees to estimate expectations for new objects, as done by Allison et al. [1] and Buntine [4, 5]. We determine the expected probability of object x

belonging to class c as:

$$E(Prob(Class = c|x)) = \sum_{T_i \in models} Prob(T_i|D) \times Prob(Class = c|x, D, T_i) \quad (1)$$

Equation 1 can be rewritten as

$$E(Prob(Class = c|x)) = \sum_{T_i \in models} w_i \times Prob(Class = c|x, D, T_i) \quad (2)$$

where each tree has weight $w_i = 2^{-ML_i}$. In practical applications there is an infeasible number of decision trees to calculate this sum. Tree averaging and option trees restrict the *models* set, and attempt to approximate this sum.

5.2 Weighting Schemes for Decision Stumps

We consider 3 weighting options for decision stumps:

1. Weighting each stump equally. Hence if their are N available decision stumps, then we weight each stump with $w_i = \frac{1}{N}$

2. Assigning weight 1.0 to the decision stump with minimum message length, and weight 0.0 to the other decision stumps.

3. Weighting each stump according to the posterior implied by the MML encoding scheme. If decision stump i has message length ML_i then we weight stump i with weight $w_i = 2^{-ML_i}$

To classify a test object, O we construct the expected frequency distribution over classes, and assign the most frequent class to object O.

$$E(Freq(class_j \mid O)) = \sum_{i=1}^{nstumps} w_i \times Freq(class_j \mid O, stump_i)$$

6 Empirical Evaluation of Decision Stumps

We consider the following data sets [1]: Geographic (described by Wallace and Patrick [24]), Glass (described by Buntine [6]) LED (described by Breiman et al. [3]), Mushroom (described by Schlimmer and Granger [21]) and Pole (described by Buntine [6]). A summary of some properties of these data sets is given in Table 1. The base accuracy is the proportion of cases that have the most common class.

6.1 Results

We implemented the 3 weighting options for decision stumps described in Section 5.2. Table 2 gives the percentage accuracy for decision trees [24] and the 3 decision stump schemes on the data sets summarised in Table 1. These results were averaged over 10 runs. For each run a training set was randomly created, and the accuracy was calculated using the remainder of the data set as the test set.

---

[1] The majority of these data sets come from from the UCI repository.

Data Set	Cont Attr	Binary Attr	Multi val. Attr	Total Attr	No. Class	Size	Base Acc.
Geographic	8	-	-	8	4	106	37.7 %
Glass	9	-	-	9	6	214	35.5 %
Heart Disease	5	3	5	13	2	303	54.1 %
LED	-	7	-	7	10	3000	10.0 %
Mushroom	-	4	18	22	2	8124	51.8 %
Pole	4	-	-	4	2	1847	51.0 %

Table 1: A summary of the data sets considered

Data Set	Items	Decision Tree Accuracy %		Equal Weights Accuracy %		Best Stump Accuracy %		MML Weights Accuracy %	
Geo	10	33.3	±8.0	42.1	±8.7	33.3	±8.0	36.9	±3.9
	20	36.3	±11.2	39.2	±8.3	36.3	±11.2	39.1	±8.2
	30	42.0	±7.3	41.7	±7.7	41.7	±6.3	45.5	±10.2
	40	53.9	±11.2	40.5	±7.4	46.1	±7.5	49.5	±10.7
p-value		0.80		0.58		0.057		—	
Glass	10	29.0	±10.6	34.4	±6.5	29.0	±10.6	29.0	±10.6
	20	34.7	±3.4	34.6	±5.4	34.7	±3.4	35.3	±4.7
	30	39.7	±6.0	40.0	±9.1	38.6	±6.3	42.0	±6.3
	40	41.4	±3.7	36.1	±4.4	41.3	±3.8	43.0	±4.4
p-value		0.21		0.12		0.21		—	
Heart Disease	10	51.7	±6.5	62.4	±13.3	53.6	±9.6	62.4	±15.2
	20	58.0	±11.5	66.8	±13.6	63.4	±10.7	66.6	±10.8
	30	68.8	±10.5	67.4	±10.5	73.0	±3.2	75.7	±3.0
	40	71.9	±3.2	70.0	±12.0	71.9	±3.2	73.3	±3.1
p-value		3.0×10^{-6}		1.00		1.5×10^{-5}		—	
LED	10	10.2	±0.4	19.4	±7.6	10.2	±0.4	18.0	±9.5
	20	21.9	±5.0	20.2	±5.8	18.4	±0.5	22.1	±5.3
	30	30.9	±9.6	20.5	±3.1	18.1	±0.6	24.1	±5.6
	40	43.0	±9.6	23.5	±7.2	18.1	±0.6	24.1	±6.7
p-value		NEG 0.62		1.0		3.7×10^{-9}		—	
Mushroom	10	67.3	±17.7	72.6	±15.3	67.3	±17.7	77.5	±16.2
	20	89.1	±5.4	77.1	±17.0	89.1	±5.4	89.9	±6.0
	30	95.5	±2.7	81.4	±13.1	94.9	±3.8	96.0	±2.1
	40	95.6	±3.8	80.1	±17.2	95.0	±4.7	95.2	±5.0
p-value		0.0013		5.4×10^{-9}		0.00054		—	
Pole	10	60.5	±17.2	63.9	±10.8	60.5	±17.2	64.4	±17.7
	20	70.5	±18.2	63.8	±9.6	70.5	±18.2	76.4	±14.6
	30	80.5	±11.5	64.3	±12.9	80.5	±11.5	80.5	±11.3
	40	85.1	±0.2	67.0	±15.0	85.1	±0.2	85.1	±0.2
p-value		0.031		0.0019		0.031		—	

Table 2: The accuracy of decision trees and decision stumps on some data sets

In Table 2, the standard deviation of the accuracy is indicated after the "±" symbol. The p-values give the statistical significance of the 40 simulations performed for each domain when each method is compared with the MML weighted stump scheme. The p-value for the LED domain is labelled "NEG" since decision trees outperformed MML weighted stumps (but not significantly). The method used to obtain these p-values is described in the next section.

6.2 Analysing the Simulation Outcomes

For a given data set, to compare the accuracy of two classification rules we need to take into account the fact that the ten observations at each training set size are matched (the same ten training samples were used to design both classifiers). This means that the standard deviations of the differences are in fact much smaller than those derived from the standard deviations given in Table 2. We could perform matched paired t-tests (or nonparametric equivalents) at each training set size but, with only ten runs at each size, these tests would not be very powerful. Attempts to combine the four training set sizes into a single analysis (by analysing the forty results in a single paired comparison test or by using analysis of variance with training set size as a factor) are complicated by the fact that the variances in the four training set size groups are different. This invalidates paired comparison tests because it breaks the iid assumption and it invalidates the analysis of variance because it breaks the homoscedasticity assumption. A proper formal analysis would involve an appropriately weighted analysis of variance. To avoid such complications in this paper, we have simply computed the signs of each of the forty differences and conducted a sign test for those differences which are non-zero. (Even this is not perfect since it makes the latent assumption that the medians of the population distributions of differences do not change sign over the range of training set sample sizes we have analysed.) We did this for each data set (six) and for the comparison of the MML weighted decision stump classifier with each of the other classifiers (three). This results in 18 tests in all.

At the 5% level you expect approximately one of these tests to be significant by chance alone, if the null hypothesis of no difference between classifiers is true. We, however, have obtained 9 out of 18 showing a significant difference favouring the MML weighted scheme.

7 Fanned Decision Trees

The decision stump scheme has another possible use. Traditional decision trees classify a new object using the class distribution at the leaf associated with that object. We can construct all the stumps at each leaf of a decision tree as shown in Figure 3. We term such a structure as a *fanned decision tree*. We may classify a new object, O, using a fanned decision tree by identifying the leaf, L, that we would associate with O, and classifying O using the decision stumps associated with L.

A fanned decision tree is a restricted option tree [4, 5]. The approach we take in this paper has some advantages over option trees:

1. Option trees take up to a magnitude more space and time than decision trees. The additional computational complexity with fanned decision trees is virtually insignificant.

2. Option trees requires considerable skill to set the search parameters.

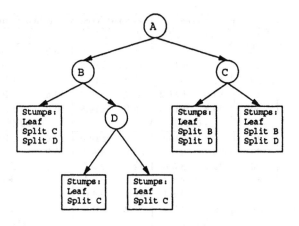

4 Binary Atrributes (A, B, C, D)

Figure 3: A fanned decision tree

We implemented fanned decision trees and repeated the empirical evaluation performed in Section 6. Table 3 gives the percentage accuracy for MML decision trees [24], fanned decision trees and MML weighted decision stumps. The p-values give the statistical significance of the 60 (or 50 in the Geographic domain) simulations performed for each when each method is compared with fanned decision trees. In five out of the six domains, fanned trees performed significantly better than decision trees. The comparison of fanned trees and MML weighted stumps was inconclusive.

8 Analysis of Results and Conclusions

The decision stump scheme described is limited to very small training sets and decision trees (and other classification schemes) will outperform decision stumps with larger training sets. In some cases (such as rare medical conditions) we may only have very small data sets available.

The results in Table 2 and Table 3 lead us to the following conclusions:

- The MML weighted stumps classifier outperformed the equally weighted stumps and the best stump classifiers.

- Over the data sets considered, fanned decision trees outperformed decision trees. Fanned trees significantly outperformed MML weighted stumps in 3 domains, but in the Mushroom domain MML weighted stumps significantly outperformed fanned trees. Of course, these results should be interpreted in the light of the relatively large number of significance tests that have been conducted. In general, fanned trees were similar to MML weighted stumps for small training sets (< 50 items say), and then slightly superior to decision trees for larger training sets.

- Once there was sufficient data for decision trees to grow beyond height 2,

Data Set	Items	Tree Accuracy %		Fanned Tree Accuracy %		MML Stump Accuracy %	
Geo	10	33.3	±8.0	36.9	±3.9	36.9	±3.9
	20	36.3	±11.2	41.2	±11.8	39.1	±8.2
	30	42.0	±7.3	47.5	±10.7	45.5	±10.2
	40	53.9	±11.2	57.7	±10.3	49.5	±10.7
	50	60.4	±13.8	60.9	±14.5	50.2	±13.8
p-value		0.00012		—		0.00028	
Glass	10	29.0	±10.6	29.0	±10.6	29.0	±10.6
	20	34.7	±3.4	35.4	±4.9	35.3	±4.7
	30	39.7	±6.0	42.8	±8.7	42.0	±6.3
	40	41.4	±3.7	42.6	±2.1	43.0	±4.4
	50	43.6	±3.4	47.6	±8.0	43.5	±3.5
	100	56.9	±9.6	57.9	±10.2	40.9	±3.3
p-value		0.0013		—		0.0046	
Heart Disease	10	51.7	±6.5	61.4	±14.5	62.4	±15.2
	20	58.0	±11.5	65.7	±10.2	66.6	±10.8
	30	68.8	±10.5	74.4	±2.6	75.7	±3.0
	40	71.9	±3.2	72.2	±2.9	73.3	±3.1
	50	73.3	±2.3	73.3	±2.3	74.7	±1.9
	100	73.5	±2.3	74.2	±1.7	71.9	±4.6
p-value		9.5×10^{-7}		—		NEG 0.071	
LED	10	10.2	±0.4	18.0	±9.5	18.0	±9.5
	20	21.9	±5.0	27.9	±7.8	22.1	±5.3
	30	30.9	±9.6	34.4	±9.0	24.1	±5.6
	40	43.0	±9.6	43.7	±10.4	24.1	±6.7
	50	45.8	±6.1	47.0	±5.6	22.5	±6.4
	100	56.8	±6.8	57.6	±6.2	18.5	±2.0
p-value		6.7×10^{-8}		—		1.0×10^{-7}	
Mushroom	10	67.3	±17.7	77.8	±16.3	77.5	±16.2
	20	89.1	±5.4	89.1	±5.4	89.9	±6.0
	30	95.5	±2.7	95.5	±2.7	96.0	±2.1
	40	95.6	±3.8	95.6	±3.8	95.2	±5.0
	50	96.7	±2.3	96.7	±2.3	97.1	±2.4
	100	98.4	±0.5	98.4	±0.5	98.5	±0.1
p-value		0.25		—		NEG 3.8×10^{-5}	
Pole	10	60.5	±17.2	64.4	±17.7	64.4	±17.7
	20	70.5	±18.2	76.4	±14.6	76.4	±14.6
	30	80.5	±11.5	80.5	±11.3	80.5	±11.3
	40	85.1	±0.2	85.1	±0.2	85.1	±0.2
	50	83.7	±3.1	83.7	±3.1	84.1	±3.0
	100	84.7	±0.9	84.7	±0.9	84.7	±0.9
p-value		0.031		—		1.0	

Table 3: The accuracy of decision trees, fanned trees, and decision stumps

decision trees can outperform decision stumps. However, in half of the domains considered the behaviour between stumps and trees was almost identical.

9   Acknowledgments

We would like to thank the anonymous referees, Andrew Webb and Dave Signorini for their helpful comments. This work has been carried out with the support of the Defence Research Agency, Malvern.

References

[1] L. Allison, C.S. Wallace, and C.N. Yee. Finite-state models in the alignment of macromolecules. *Journal of Molecular Evolution*, 35:77–89, 1992.

[2] L.R. Bahl, P.F. Brown, P.V. deSouza, and R.L. Mercer. A tree-based statistical language model for natural language speech recognition. *IEEE Transactions on Acoustics, Speech, and Signal Processing*, 37:1001–1008, 1989.

[3] L. Breiman, J.H. Friedman, R.A. Olshen, and C.J. Stone. *Classification and Regression Trees*. Wadsworth, Belmont, 1984.

[4] W.L. Buntine. *A Theory of Learning Classification Rules*. PhD thesis, School of Computing Science in the University of Technology, Sydney, February 1990.

[5] W.L. Buntine. Learning classification trees. *Statistics and Computing*, 2:63–73, 1992.

[6] W.L. Buntine and T. Niblett. A further comparison of splitting rules for decision-tree induction. *Machine Learning*, 8:75–85, 1992.

[7] P. Cheeseman. In defense of probability. In *Proceedings of IJCAI-85*, pages 1002–1009, 1985.

[8] L.A. Clark and D. Pregibon. Tree-based models. In J.M. Chambers and T.J. Hastie, editors, *Statistical Models in S*, pages 377–420. Wadsworth and Brooks, California, 1992.

[9] M.P. Georgeff and C.S. Wallace. A general criterion for inductive inference. In *Proceedings of the 6th European Conference on Artificial Intelligence*, pages 473–482, 1984.

[10] T. Hastie and D. Pregibon. Shrinking trees. Technical report, AT&T Bell Laboratories, Murray Hill, New Jersey 07974, USA, 1990.

[11] R.C. Holte. Very simple classification rules perform well on most commonly used datasets. *Machine Learning*, 11:63–91, 1993.

[12] W.F. Iba and P. Langley. Induction of one-level decision trees. In *Machine Learning: Proceedings of the Ninth International Workshop*, pages 233–240, 1992.

[13] S.W. Kwok and C. Carter. Multiple decision trees. In R.D. Schachter, T.S. Levitt, L.N. Kanal, and J.F. Lemmer, editors, *Uncertainty in Artificial Intelligence 4*, pages 327–335. Elsevier Science, Amsterdam, 1990.

[14] P. Langley, W.F. Iba, and K. Thompson. An analysis of bayesian classifiers. In *Proceedings of AAAI-92*, pages 223–228, 1992.

[15] J.R. Quinlan. Induction of decision trees. *Machine Learning*, 1:81–106, 1986.

[16] J.R. Quinlan. Learning with continuous classes. In A. Adams and L. Sterling, editors, *Proceedings of the 5th Australian Joint Conference on Artificial Intelligence*, pages 343–348. World Scientific, Singapore, 1992.

[17] J.R. Quinlan and R.L. Rivest. Inferring decision trees using the minimum description length principle. *Information and Computation*, 80:227–248, 1989.

[18] J. Rissanen. A universal prior for integers and estimation by minimum description length. *Annals of Statistics*, 11:416–431, 1983.

[19] J. Rissanen. Stochastic complexity. *Royal Statistical Society Journal*, 49:223–239, 1987.

[20] J. Rissanen. *Stochastic Complexity in Statistical Inquiry*. World Scientific, Singapore, 1989.

[21] J. Schlimmer and R. Granger. Incremental learning from noisy data. *Machine Learning*, 1:317–354, 1986.

[22] C.S. Wallace and D.M. Boulton. An information measure for classification. *Computer Journal*, 11:185–194, 1968.

[23] C.S. Wallace and P.R. Freeman. Estimation and inference by compact coding. *Royal Statistical Society Journal*, 49:240–252, 1987.

[24] C.S. Wallace and J.D. Patrick. Coding decision trees. *Machine Learning*, 11:7–22, 1993.

[25] S.M. Weiss and I. Kapouleas. An empirical comparison of pattern recognition, neural nets, and machine learning classification methods. In *Proceedings of IJCAI-89*, pages 781–787, 1989.

Controlling Constructive Induction in CiPF: An MDL Approach

Bernhard Pfahringer

bernhard@ai.univie.ac.at
Austrian Research Institute for Artificial Intelligence
Schottengasse 3
A-1010 Vienna
Austria

Abstract. We describe the propositional learning system CiPF, which tightly couples a simple concept learner with a sophisticated constructive induction component. It is described in terms of a *generic architecture for constructive induction*. We focus on the problem of controlling the abundance of opportunities for constructively adding new attributes. In CiPF the so-called *Minimum Description Length* (MDL) principle acts as a powerful control heuristic. This is also confirmed in the experiments reported.

1 Introduction

In learning concept descriptions from preclassified examples, simple concept learners typically make strong assumptions about the way these examples are represented. For effectively learning a concept its examples must populate one or a few regions of the hypothesis space expressible in the description language. For example, decision trees encode axis-parallel nested hyper-rectangles. Two different problems may cause irregular distributions of learning examples in the original representation space: *noise* and/or an *inadequate description language*. Both phenomena lead to complex, convoluted induced concept descriptions which will be hard to understand and will perform poorly at predicting concept membership of unclassified examples.

As a remedy for the latter problem constructive induction has been introduced, e.g. in [Dietterich & Michalski 81] and [Mehra et al. 89]. The basic idea is to somehow transform the original representation space into a space where the learning examples exhibit (more) regularities. Usually this is done by introducing new attributes and forgetting old ones. So constructive induction is searching for an adequate representation language for the learning task at hand.

In this paper we report on CiPF, a generic constructive induction system, and on how search in the representation space is controlled in CiPF. Section 2 briefly describes a generic architecture for constructive induction and discussed CiPF in these terms. In section 3 will focus on how the problem of controlling search for useful representation changes is solved in CiPF by means of the powerful *Minimum Description Length (MDL) Principle* [Rissanen 78]. Section

4 reports experiments and compares results to C4.5 [Quinlan 93], a well-known sophisticated decision tree learner. Section 5 summarizes related work, gives conclusions and talks about further research directions we are pursuing within CiPF.

2   A Generic Architecture and an Introduction to CiPF

This section will briefly describe a generic architecture for constructive induction and use this architecture to introduce CiPF. We will also discuss some important design rationales of CiPF.

Figure 1 depicts a possible generic architecture for describing constructive learners. Most implemented systems can be described in terms of this architecture or a subset of it, if one supplies proper instantiations for the different processes (boxes in the model). The three different processes working together are:

- The CI module: Given examples and attribute descriptions and possibly already some descriptions/hypotheses, this module constructs new attributes according to some methodology. Output of this module are new attribute descriptions and the augmented and transformed learning examples.
- The Selective Learner: Any (classical) propositional learning algorithm can be used to induce rules from the transformed learning data. Output of this module is a set of rules forming a hypothesis that compresses and explains the learning data.
- The Evaluator: This current hypothesis must be evaluated in some way to decide whether it is of good enough quality to serve as a final result, or if it should be input into another cycle of induction. It might also be the case that no good hypothesis is found, but computation nonetheless terminates due to exhausted resources like maximal number of cycles or heuristically/statistically based doubt about the possibility of finding any better hypothesis.

Actual systems not only differ in their choices for the different parameters (e.g. which methods they select for doing CI or what algorithm lies at the heart of their respective learner), they may even omit modules and/or pathways at all; for instance, some systems do not run in cycles, but perform sequential one-shot learning only.

The main goal in building CiPF is designing a practical system for constructive induction that minimizes the number of user-settable parameters. So we try to identify principled choices or automated ways of choosing good values for necessary decisions where other systems rely on user-specified parameter values. This was one reason for choosing the *Minimum Description Length Principle* as an evaluator. This will be described in more detail in the next section.

CiPF borrows heavily from existing systems in that we have tried to collect useful features of known machine learning systems. We try to combine these in a synergetic fashion in CiPF. CiPF is a true instance of the generic architecture

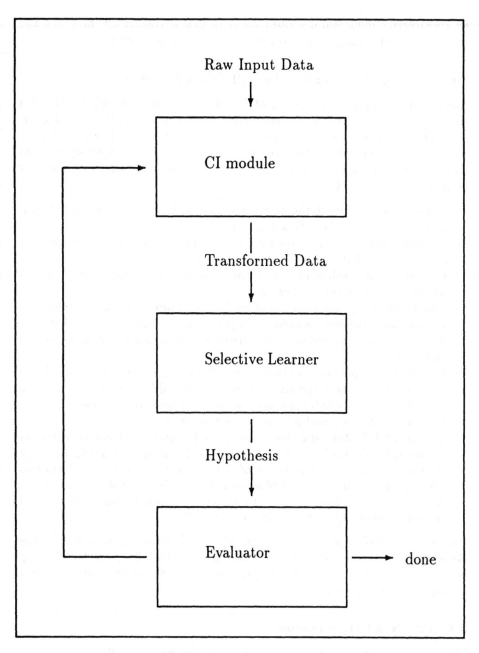

Fig. 1. Constructive induction: a generic architecture

for constructive induction described above in that it realizes all the boxes and pathways. CiPF's components will be detailed in the following.

2.1 Constructive Induction in CiPF (the CI Module)

Just like the multi-strategy system AQ17-MCI [Bloedorn et al. 93], CiPF takes an operator-based approach to constructive induction. It supplies a (still growing) list of generally useful CI operators plus an interface allowing for user-supplied special operators. For instance, these might encode possibly relevant background knowledge. We have currently implemented the following generally useful CI operators in CiPF:

- Compare attributes of the same type: is attribute A1 *Equal to/Different from/Greater than/Less than* attribute A2.
- Discretize numeric attributes into several intervals using Chi-Merge techniques [Kerber 92].
- Conjoin possible values of nominal attributes into sets using modified Chi-Merge as proposed in [Kerber 92].
- Count how many of a given set of boolean attributes are true (or false).
- Conjoin two attributes occuring in a good rule [Matheus & Rendell 89].
- Perform intra-construction [Muggleton 87, Muggleton & Buntine 88] of good rules.
- For the set of positive examples covered by a good rule: compute intervals/subsets for the respective numerical/nominal base-level attributes, so that these intervals/subsets exactly cover these positive examples.
- Drop attributes not used by any of the good rules. [1]
- The medical 3σ-*heuristic*: for numerical attributes construct an attribute testing if this numerical value is in a plausible range. This *healthy* range is operationally defined in terms of mean values and standard deviations derived from the healthy part of a population as the interval $[\mu - 3\sigma, \mu + 3\sigma]$. A value outside such a range is a strong indicator for pathological test results in medical applications [2] (see also section 4.2).

Recursive application of these operators may yield complex new attributes like *the number of numerical attributes being off more than 3σ from the 'healthy' mean is zero or one* . It is the user's task to choose the appropriate operators for any learning problem.

2.2 CiPF's Selective Learner

We have implemented a simple propositional FOIL-like learner [Quinlan & Cameron-Jones 93], i.e. our selective learner is a simplified cousin

---

[1] One might argue whether *dropping an attribute* really is a *constructive induction* operator or not. Anyway it being a very useful operator we have chosen to include it in the above list. Furthermore the terminology used in [Bloedorn et al. 93] defines set of *constructive induction operators* as the union of *constructors* and *destructors*.

[2] Personal communication from a lab physician

of FOIL dealing with propositional horn clauses only. So we are using ideas from *Inductive Logic Programming* and translate them back (specialize them) for propositional problems. We prefer direct induction of rules over decision trees for various reasons. The two most important ones are:

- Unknown values can be dealt with pragmatically: never incorporate tests for *unknown* in a rule.
- Induction focuses on one class at a time. At least in relational learning this approach seems to be superior to decision trees [Watanabe & Rendell 91] and we suspect that the same might be true for propositional learning.

Currently the learner is a quick-and-dirty custom implementation, as we want to focus on constructive induction, but still like to have the possibility of working on the internals of the learner. We will of course have to address the serious shortcomings of this module in further research. Right now this learner in CiPF uses the *Laplace expected error estimate* as a search heuristic, because [Lavrac et al. 92] shows that accuracy estimators outperform information gain criteria when learning rules instead of decision trees. [3] The only stopping criterion used is *no improvement of the estimate*. There is currently no other form of pruning in the learning component.

3 Using MDL to Control Constructive Induction (the Evaluator Module)

CiPF takes a rather eager approach to constructive induction: at every step all possible new attributes are added. This over-abundance in the representation space combined with the simplistic learner quickly results in unwieldy, overly complex induced rule sets when learning without appropriate control. These rule sets may be both difficult to comprehend for the user and yield mediocre results when classifying unseen examples. In analogy to *noise fitting* [Anguin & Laird 87] this phenomenon could be called *language fitting*. Typical examples of such behaviour are published in the section on AQ17-HCI in the *Monk report* [Thrun et al. 91], which describes three artificial learning problems for evaluating and comparing different algorithms. We have made similar experiences with early versions of CiPF lacking sophisticated control.

To prevent CiPF from *language fitting* we have devised the following simple, yet effective control regime:

- Every time the CI module is called, it is allowed to construct an unlimited number of new attributes.
- These attributes will be input to the next learning step. There they will *compete* with each other for being used in induced rules.
- Only the *fittest* attributes will be allowed to survive.

---

[3] Use of the more general *M-estimate* also discussed in that paper instead of the *Laplace estimate* would introduce one of those parameters we are trying to avoid if possible.

So how are the *fittest* attributes determined in CiPF? We pragmatically equate them with the set of attributes being used by *good* rules. How CiPF determines the set of *good* rules for a class is one of its major innovations. Instead of using some ad-hoc measures of accuracy and quality or some user-supplied evaluation functions we have identified the so-called *Minimum Description Length Principle* [Rissanen 78, Quinlan & Rivest 89] as a very well-performing evaluator.

In a nutshell, MDL is a concept from information theory that takes into account both a theory's simplicity and a theory's predictive accuracy simultaneously. MDL is disarmingly simple: concept membership of each training example is to be communicated from a sender to a receiver. Both know all examples and all attributes used to describe the examples. Now what is being transmitted is a theory (set of rules) describing the concept and, if necessary, explicitly all positive examples not covered by the theory (the false-negative examples) and all negative examples erroneously covered by the theory (the false-positive examples). Now the cost of a transmission is equivalent to the number of bits needed to encode a theory plus its exceptions in a sensible scheme. The MDL Principle states that the best theory derivable from the training data will be the one requiring the minimum number of bits.

So for any set of rules generated by the learner and for subsets of these rules a *cost* can be computed. The rule-set with minimum cost is the best theory for the training data. Only rules of this set will be called *good* rules and will be used as input for the constructive induction module. The precise formula used to apply the MDL Principle in CiPF is the same one as used by C4.5 [Quinlan 93] for simplifying rule sets:

$$Cost = TheoryCost + log_2\left(\binom{C}{FP}\right) + log_2\left(\binom{NC}{FN}\right)$$

In this formula TheoryCost is an estimate for the number of bits needed to encode the theory. C is the total number of training examples covered by the theory, FP is the number of false-positive examples, NC is the total number of training examples not covered by the theory, and FN is the number of false-negative examples. So the second and the third term of the formula estimate the number of bits needed to encode all false-positive and all false-negative examples respectively. In summary this formula approximates the total cost in number of bits for transmitting a theory and its exceptions.

A slight modification necessary for constructive induction is to take into account also the different complexities of *constructed attributes*. This can easily be achieved in a uniform manner by adding attribute-defining rules to the rule set, one for each *constructed* attribute used in the original rule set. Thus using a *constructed* attribute entails a kind of penalty or cost, which will be amortized either if this attribute offers superior compression or if it is used in more than one rule.

Furthermore, CIPF differs in the way the above MDL estimate is utilized algorithmically. For complexity reasons it is of course impossible to evaluate all possible subsets of rules. [Quinlan 93] reports serious difficulties using greedy hill-climbing and therefore resorts to expensive simulated annealing. In contrast, in our setting a hill-climbing strategy seems to work quite satisfactorily in combination with a preprocessing step as follows:

- Sort all rules induced by the learner in descending order of their estimated accuracy.
- Starting with an empty theory, always add the next best rule to the current theory as long as the MDL estimate improves, i.e. a better compression is achieved.

The output of this algorithm is a subset of all the originally induced rules which will be a good, if not the best theory for the training data in terms of the currently available attributes. Exactly this subset will be used to determine which attributes are to be kept and which are to be dropped for the next cycle of induction: exactly those (original and constructed) attributes are kept which appear in at least one rule of the selected theory. This subset of rules is also used as input for the constructive induction module.

Globally, CIPF does a kind of hill-climbing in the representation space, computing new attributes and new sets of rules utilizing these attributes as long as the overall cost estimate (as measured by the above MDL formula) improves. This last theory is then the overall output of CIPF. Empirically this simple strategy seems to produce good results, as indicated by the experiments reported in the next section and it is effectively computable. Also, to repeat its two main advantages, the strategy includes no user-settable parameters, and also it does not require a secondary training set (*train-test set*), like e.g. AQ17-MCI, to evaluate the quality of constructed attributes.

4 Experiments

In the experiments reported here, CIPF's performance was compared to C4.5 on the same training and test sets. C4.5 is a very sophisticated, production quality selective learner. It was run with default settings and the results reported are for pruned decision trees [4] on the test set.

4.1 Monk's Problems

The *Monk's problems* [Thrun et al. 91] are three artificially constructed problems in a space formed by six nominal attributes having from two to four possible values. These three problems are abbreviated to Monk1, Monk2, and Monk3 in the following. CIPF in its current status gives mixed results for the Monk's

---

[4] Typically pruned trees yielded better accuracy than both unpruned trees and rule sets generated from the tree.

problems. From table 1 we see that Monk1 was solved without problems. CiPF finds the correct theory:

```
true <= (jacket_color = red)

true <= (head_shape = body_shape)
```

This is no surprise as this example is simple and CiPF has the necessary constructive operator *compare attributes of the same type* at its disposal. C4.5 achieves only 72.4% accuracy for the pruned decision tree, but is able to reach the full 100% for the rules extracted from this tree.

Performance on Monk2 is far from optimal, though. Comparison with C4.5, which is better, but also far from optimal, seems to indicate missing constructive operators. We believe that full negation and disjunction (currently not available in CiPF) may solve Monk2. Alternatively a student at our department is currently finishing work [Kramer 93] on an interesting general constructive operator computing *extensional products* of nominal attributes. This operator seems to be able to solve Monk2 very well.

Results for Monk3 are quite good, but seem to indicate that CiPF has a problem with noise. Potential answers to noise in CiPF will be briefly discussed in the next major section. For C4.5 the unpruned tree is slightly better than the pruned tree, which is not what we expected knowing that the training set exhibits 5% class noise.

To give an impression of both the inferiority of the simple learner currently used in CiPF and the strong abilities of the CI component we have included into table 1 accuracies of the theories induced in the first step (just before the first constructive induction step is taking place). Typically these values are significantly worse than those of C4.5, but with the help of the strong CI component CiPF is able to reach and sometimes even outperform C4.5's predictive performance!

Additionally we would like to mention that some learning system exhibit a much better performance than C4.5 on the *Monk's problems*, e.g. AQ17-HCI achieves 100%, 93.1%, and 100% on Monk1, Monk2, and Monk3 respectively, and a specialized form of Backpropagation yields 100%, 100%, and 97.2% respectively. As already mentioned above we interpret this as an indication for missing constructive operators appropriate for especially the Monk2 problem. [5]

4.2 Two Medical Datasets

For another set of experiments we used two medical datasets, one being the hepatitis data available from the Machine Learning Archive at Irvine, the second being numerical descriptions extracted from cardiac thallium scintigrams recorded at the University of Vienna Medical School [Prem et al. 93]. The first

---

[5] AQ17-HCI has at its disposal a very special CI operator which perfectly fits the Monk2 problem, thus explaining its impressive performance on this problem.

Table 1. Monk's Problems: accuracies (percentages) for CɪPF after the first and the final cycle of induction and for C4.5.

	CɪPF first	CɪPF final	C4.5
MONK1	70.78	100	72.4
MONK2	66.92	80.7	83.3
MONK3	92.36	97.2	97.2

set exhibits a good mixture of numerical and boolean attributes with a few values missing. The second set is of comparable size (159 examples total), but uses 45 numerical attributes, which we strongly believe to be redundant. The classification task for both datasets is to separate *ill* from *healthy* patients. Experiments were performed with the examples split randomly into equally sized training and test sets for ten runs. Tables 2 and 3 show the respective results of these experiments.

Table 2. Hepatitis data: average number of errors and average accuracy for ten test runs for CɪPF and C4.5.

	#Errors	Accuracy
CɪPF	14.6	81.29
C4.5	13.3	82.95

Table 3. Scan data: absolute number of errors and their average for ten test runs for CɪPF and C4.5.

Run	1	2	3	4	5	6	7	8	9	10	Average #Errors
CɪPF	19	15	20	22	16	14	20	20	19	18	18.3
C4.5	23	22	25	22	20	21	29	30	19	22	23.3

The absolute number of errors translate into an average error of 18.71% and 17.05% for CɪPF and C4.5 for the hepatitis data, and into 22.87% and 29.13% average error respectively for the scan data. So CɪPF performs slightly worse than C4.5 on the first set, but significantly better on the second set. We attribute C4.5's better performance on the hepatitis data to both C4.5's sophisticated handling of noise and to the fact that CɪPF's general medical heuristic is not applicable here. [6] For the scan data, in almost all cases CiPF is significantly better than C4.5. This is a direct consequence of CiPF's constructive abilities. In all these test runs CiPF either constructs an attribute *at most one attribute value is "out of the healthy range"* (see above description of the 3σ-heuristic), which is a good way of characterizing healthy people. Or CiPF constructs the opposite attribute *more than a certain number of attribute values (typically 5) are "out of the healthy range"*, which is well-suited for characterizing people exhibiting serious health problems.

4.3 Inductive Logic Programming Exercises

Encouraged by the original INDUCE system [Dietterich & Michalski 81], which was able to learn *structural* descriptions from examples, and by the current success of LINUS [Dzeroski & Lavrac 91], which essentially translates ILP problems into an attribute-value representation for efficient induction, we started to examine two classical ILP exercises: illegal king-rook-king (KRK) chess endgame positions [Fuernkranz 93] and finite element mesh design [Dolsak & Muggleton 92], [Dzeroski & Bratko 92].

KRK is very easily represented in CiPF. The example tupels of the relation `illegal/6` are transformed into six basic attributes encoding rank and file of all three pieces. Background knowledge in the original formulation consists of definitions for `=/2`, `less_than/2` and `adjacent/2`. Only the last predicate `adjacent/2` had to be encoded as a CI operator, as both `Equal-To` and `Less-Than` are presupplied CI operators in CiPF. Induced theories usually resemble the approximate theories given in [Fuernkranz 93]. A sample theory derived by CiPF from 100 training examples looks as follows:

```
[1] illegal <= (BLACK-KING-FILE = WHITE-ROOK-FILE)

[2] illegal <= (BLACK-KING-RANK = WHITE-ROOK-RANK)

[3] illegal <= (adjacent BLACK-KING-FILE WHITE-KING-FILE) and
               (adjacent BLACK-KING-RANK WHITE-KING-RANK)

[4] illegal <= (adjacent BLACK-KING-FILE WHITE-KING-FILE) and
               (BLACK-KING-RANK = WHITE-KING-RANK)
```

This approximate theory was tested with 5000 test examples yielding an accuracy of 98.4%. This is consistent with [Fuernkranz 93] which proves a theory consisting of the first three clauses 1,2,3 to be 98.451% correct.

For the mesh design domain we did a manual translation along the lines implicitly suggested in [Dolsak & Muggleton 92]. All the one-argument predicates were translated into three nominal attributes with the appropriate sets

---

[6] Still CiPF discovers regularities missed by C4.5, like that all female patients are healthy. This can be attributed to directly learning rules instead of decision trees.

of possible values. Ignoring all two-argument attributes encoding structure (**neighbor/2**, **opposite/2** and **same/2**) CIPF achieves the surprising results shown in table 4 (results for FOIL,MFOIL,and GOLEM were taken from [Dzeroski & Bratko 92]). One sample rule induced covering 22 positive and no

	FOIL	MFOIL	GOLEM	CIPF
A	17	22	17	21
B	5	12	9	13
C	7	9	5	10
D	0	6	11	23
E	5	10	10	26
SUM	34	59	54	93

Table 4. Mesh Design: Number of Correctly Classified Examples.

negative example looks like the following:

```
N=1 <= (LOAD = ONE_SIDE_LOADED or NOT_LOADED) and
       (EDGE-TYPE  = NOT_IMPORTANT)
```

The ability to form appropriate subsets of possible values of an attribute (called *internal value disjunction* in AQ17-derived systems) seems to provide useful contructed attributes for this learning task. So CIPF without any structural information performs almost twice as well as FOIL, MFOIL, or GOLEM. Still even 93 correctly classified examples translate to only 33.5% accuracy. So there probably is a good chance of achieving much better results by means of a more careful analysis of the mesh design problem itself.

For translating and using the complete original specification automatically we will have to encode constructive operators capable of recursively inspecting objects linked to the object in focus and of summarizing properties of these objects. We are currently designing such operators. These would allow constructing attributes like *this node has a neighbor node with the property* (**edge-type = fixed**) or *this node has at least two* **opposite** *nodes*. Naturally the property to be learned - *number of finite elements for this node* in the mesh domain - could also be represented as an attribute of the example available for inspection by constructive operators. Thus for the mesh domain attributes like *number of finite elements of my* **same** *neighbor* could be constructed which effectively represent a kind of recursive definition. Once such recursive definitions are allowed, additional control will be needed, e.g. to prevent the construction of *cyclic* attributes useless for effective prediction. For instance an attribute *the number of finite elements of my* **same** *neighbor's* **same** *neighbor* would not make sense for prediction, as it references the node in question itself. Pitfalls of recursion in ILP are dealt with at length in [Cameron-Jones & Quinlan 93].

A constructive induction system equipped with such operators might offer an alternative perspective [7] on ILP, possibly providing a more natural fit for data in object-oriented representations or databases.

5 Conclusions, Related Work, and Further Research

Incorporating the MDL Principle into CIPF as the single, uniform heuristic for evaluating theories and thereby implicitly guiding constructive induction proved valuable. The MDL Principle combines both accuracy and complexity of a theory into a single uniform measure. Thus CIPF does not require any ad-hoc measurements or user-defined evaluation functions of possibly questionable quality and can nonetheless use *all* of the available training data for induction. Other approaches (e.g. AQ17-MCI) have to resort to splitting the training data into two or more sub-parts performing some sort of cross-validation on these sub-parts. Such an approach may be more expensive computationally and may miss regularities in the data. Nonetheless, on a systems level, CIPF certainly is most closely related to and influenced by the multi-strategy system AQ17-MCI. The main difference is the way control is imposed on constructive induction. CIPF eagerly tries to use every opportunity for constructive induction until the MDL principle stops this cycling process. AQ17-MCI takes a different approach: relying on a set of meta-rules [Aha 92], it tries to identify the need (*when*) and the directions (*how*) for a change in the representation space. On the operator side AQ17-MCI seems to be more mature especially regarding so-called *deconstructors*. It would certainly be interesting to compare both systems on some tasks using the same set of operators in both systems. A further difference is our aiming at emulating and extending ILP in a constructive induction framework.

Principled Constructive Induction is an interesting concept introduced in [Mehra et al. 89]. Geometric interpretation of the various constructors and the notion of *linear separability* is used to guide the selection of appropriate constructors. These ideas might have interesting implications for CIPF, too.

The problem of *language fitting* is also mentioned and discussed in [Matheus 90] in the context of the CITRE system and a framework for constructive induction. This approach uses additional background knowledge in two different ways when constructing attributes. Domain-knowledge constraints are used to eliminate less desirable new attributes beforehand and domain-dependent transformations generalize newly constructed attributes even further in ways meaningful to the current problem. Though these ideas do not currently fit directly into CIPF's schema for constructive induction, they might still point to valuable further improvements possible for CIPF.

Our further research directions for CIPF include:

- Replacing all other heuristics currently employed by CIPF (e.g. the Laplace estimate as a search heuristic guiding the selective learner) by the MDL principle [Tangkitvanich & Shimura 93]. We have already implemented a simple

---

[7] at least at the level of implementation

selective learner guided by MDL instead of some accuracy estimator plus stopping criterion. Preliminary experiences seem to suggest robustness regarding noise but a bias towards over-general theories.

- Identifying and implementing additional generally useful constructive operators.
- Improving the selective learner: for instance, the stopping criterion could be modified to take into account the results of the evaluator. From the worst rule still included in the current rule set according to the MDL principle a stronger stopping criterion (like *minimal accuracy*) could be estimated.

An additional endeavour is the search for learning problems at the right level of difficulty. Unfortunately, most of the public machine learning databases at Irvine seem to be easy [Holte 93]. Therefore the best one can hope for for a system like CiPF (and other constructive learners) is to be on a par with sophisticated selective learners (e.g. C4.5) for such databases. We are looking for more difficult and complex learning tasks (tasks where it is hard to define an adequate representation language beforehand), which will allow constructive induction systems to really show their abilities.

Acknowledgements

This research is sponsored by the Austrian *Fonds zur Förderung der Wissenschaftlichen Forschung (FWF)* under grant number P8756-TEC. Financial support for the Austrian Research Institute for Artificial Intelligence is provided by the Austrian Federal Ministry of Science and Research. I would like to thank Gerhard Widmer for constructive discussion and help with this paper.

References

[Aha 92] Aha D.W.: Generalizing from Case Studies: A Case Study, in Sleeman D. and Edwards P.(eds.), Machine Learning: Proceedings of the Ninth International Workshop (ML92), Morgan Kaufmann, San Mateo, CA, pp.1-10, 1992.

[Angluin & Laird 87] Angluin D., Laird P.: Learning from Noisy Examples, Machine Learning, 2(4), 343-370, 1987.

[Bloedorn et al. 93] Bloedorn E., Wnek J., Michalski R.S.: Multistrategy Constructive Induction: AQ17-MCI, in Michalski R.S. and Tecuci G.(eds.), Proceedings of the Second International Workshop on Multistrategy Learning (MSL-93), Harpers Ferry, W.VA., pp.188-206, 1993.

[Cameron-Jones & Quinlan 93] Cameron-Jones R.M., Quinlan J.R.: Avoiding Pitfalls When Learning Recursive Theories, in Bajcsy R.(ed.), Proceedings of the Thirteenth International Joint Conference on Artificial Intelligence, Morgan Kaufmann, San Mateo, CA, pp.1050 -1057, 1993.

[Dietterich & Michalski 81] Dietterich T.G., Michalski R.S.: Inductive Learning of Structural Descriptions: Evaluation Criteria and Comparative Review of Selected Methods, Artificial Intelligence, 16(3), 257-294, 1981.

[Dolsak & Muggleton 92] Dolsak B., Muggleton S.: The Application of Inductive Logic Programming to Finite-Element Mesh Design, in Muggleton S., Inductive Logic Programming, Academic Press, London, U.K., 1992.

[Dzeroski & Lavrac 91] Dzeroski S., Lavrac N.: Learning Relations from Noisy Examples: An Empirical Comparison of LINUS and FOIL, in Birnbaum L.A. and Collins G.C.(eds.), Machine Learning: Proceedings of the Eighth International Workshop (ML91), Morgan Kaufmann, San Mateo, CA, pp.399-402, 1991.

[Dzeroski & Bratko 92] Dzeroski S., Bratko I.: Handling Noise in Inductive Logic Programming, Proceedings of the 2nd International Workshop on Inductive Logic Programming, 1992.

[Fuernkranz 93] Fuernkranz J.: A numerical analysis of the KRK domain. Working Note, 1993. Available upon request.

[Holte 93] Holte R.C.: Very Simple Classification Rules Perform Well on Most Commonly Used Datasets, Machine Learning, 11(1), 1993.

[Kerber 92] Kerber R.: ChiMerge: Discretization of Numeric Attributes, in Proceedings of the Tenth National Conference on Artificial Intelligence, AAAI Press/MIT Press, Menlo Park, pp.123-128, 1992.

[Kramer 93] Kramer S.: CN2-MCI: Ein zweistufiges Verfahren für konstruktive Induktion, Master's thesis in preparation, Vienna, 1993.

[Lavrac et al. 92] Lavrac N., Cestnik B., Dzeroski S.: Search heuristics in empirical Inductive Logic Programming, in Workshop W18, Logical Approaches to Machine Learning, ECAI-92, Vienna, 1992

[Matheus & Rendell 89] Matheus C.J., Rendell L.A.: Constructive Induction On Decision Trees, in Proceedings of the Eleventh International Joint Conference on Artificial Intelligence (IJCAI-89), Morgan Kaufmann, Los Altos, CA, 645-650, 1989.

[Matheus 90] Matheus C.J.: Adding Domain Knowledge to SBL Through Feature Construction, in Proceedings of the Eighth National Conference on Artificial Intelligence (AAAI -90), AAAI Press/MIT Press, Menlo Park, CA, pp.803-808, 1990.

[Mehra et al. 89] Mehra P., Rendell L.A., Wah B.W.: Principled Constructive Induction, in Proceedings of the Eleventh International Joint Conference on Artificial Intelligence (IJCAI-89), Morgan Kaufmann, Los Altos, CA, 651-656, 1989.

[Muggleton 87] Muggleton S.: Duce, An Oracle-based Approach to Constructive Induction, in Proceedings of the 10th International Joint Conference on Artificial Intelligence (IJCAI-87), Morgan Kaufmann, Los Altos, CA, p.287-292, 1987.

[Muggleton & Buntine 88] Muggleton S., Buntine W.: Machine Invention of First Order Predicates by Inverting Resolution, in Laird J.(ed.), Proceedings of the Fifth International Conference on Machine Learning, Univ.of Michigan, Ann Arbor, June 12-14, Morgan Kaufmann, San Mateo, CA, pp.339-352, 1988.

[Prem et al. 93] Prem E., Mackinger M., Dorffner G., Porenta G., Sochor H.: Concept Support as a Method for Programming Neural Networks with Symbolic Knowledge, in Ohlbach H.J.(ed.), GWAI-92: Advances in Artificial Intelligence, Springer, Berlin, Lecture Notes in AI, Vol.671, 1993.

[Quinlan & Rivest 89] Quinlan J.R, Rivest R.L.: Inferring Decision Trees using the Minimum Description Length Principle, in Information and Computation, 80:227-248, 1989.

[Quinlan & Cameron-Jones 93] Quinlan J.R., Cameron-Jones R.M.: FOIL: A Midterm Report, in Brazdil P.B.(ed.), Machine Learning: ECML-93, Springer, Berlin, pp.3-20, 1993.

[Quinlan 93] Quinlan J.R.: C4.5: Programs for Machine Learning, Morgan Kaufmann, San Mateo, CA, 1993.

[Rissanen 78] Rissanen J.: Modeling by Shortest Data Description, in Automatica, 14:465-471, 1978.

[Tangkitvanich & Shimura 93] Tangkitvanich S., Shimura M.: Learning from an Approximate Theory and Noisy Examples, in Proceedings of the Eleventh National Conference on Artificial Intelligence (AAAI -93), AAAI Press/MIT Press, Menlo Park, CA, pp.466-471, 1993.

[Thrun et al. 91] Thrun S.B., et.al.: The MONK's Problems: A Performance Comparison of Different Learning Algorithms, CMU Tech Report, CMU-CS-91-197, 1991.

[Watanabe & Rendell 91] Watanabe L., Rendell L.: Learning Structural Decision Trees from Examples, in Proceedings of the 12th International Conference on Artificial Intelligence, Morgan Kaufmann, San Mateo, CA, pp.770-776, 1991.

Using Constraints to Building Version Spaces

Michèle Sebag

LMS-CNRS URA 317, Ecole Polytechnique, 91128 Palaiseau Cedex, France

Abstract. Our concern is building the set G of maximally general terms covering positive examples and rejecting negative examples in propositional logic.

Negative examples are represented as constraints on the search space. This representation allows for defining a partial order on the negative examples and on attributes too. It is shown that only minimal negative examples and minimal attributes are to be considered when building the set G. These results hold in case of a non-convergent data set.

Constraints can be directly used for a polynomial characterization of G. They also allow for detecting erroneous examples in a data set.

1 Introduction

The Version Space frame defines two bounds in the search space in empirical inductive learning [7] : the upper bound, set G, includes terms maximally general rejecting negative examples ; the lower bound, set S, includes terms maximally specific covering positive examples. Many works in the machine learning field shows how inspiring this frame is : to mention but a few, Smith and Rosenbloom [11] show that in propositional logic, in the case of a convergent data set (leading to $S = G$), learning only needs to consider those negative examples that are near-misses, in the sense defined by Winston [12]. H. Hirsh [5] defines a set of operations on Version Spaces and studies their computational complexity within a propositional formalism.

This paper focuses on building set G from positive and negative examples in propositional logic. Our motivations for building set G are both cognitive and pragmatic. From a cognitive point of view, human learning seems to perform specialization only when forced to by negative examples or instructors [9]. The practical advantages of such doing are clear : when learning from a few examples[1], specific learning leads to concepts of little further applicability.

But building set G is critical [2] : within a formalism as simple as the boolean one, its size may be exponential with respect to the number of attributes [4]. We propose, following the line of [5] and [8], a new formalization of the negative examples so to deal with the exponential size problem. Negative examples are formalized as constraints on the generalization ; a partial order on the negative examples is then derived. Therefore this formalisation results in extending the notion of near-miss and the polynomial results of [11] to a *non* convergent data

---

[1] This is the case for children ; this is the case also for many industrial problems where gathering examples is expensive.

set. It also allows for pruning the attributes of the problem domain. Moreover, it allows detection of erroneous examples in a ML-Smart -like way [1].

This paper is organized as follows. Section 2 formalizes negative examples as constraints on generalization. A partial order on negative examples is derived from the constraints ; it is shown that only minimal negative examples are necessary to learning. Section 3 defines the partial order on attributes derived from the constraints and shows that only minimal attributes are to be explored when building G. Section 4 focuses on expressing G and classifying a further case. The complexity of the proposed classification is in $\mathcal{O}(K \times P \times N)$, where K is the number of attributes, P the number of positive examples and N the number of negative examples. Section 5 describes how to detect erroneous examples by using constraints. Last, section 6 briefly reviews some related works.

2 From negative examples to constraints

The problem domain is described by K attributes $x_1, .., x_K$; attributes are linear i.e. integer- or real-valued [6], or valued in a tree-structured domain. Given a conjunctive term S and a set of negative examples $Ce_1, \ldots Ce_N$, the solution space is that of conjunctive terms covering S and rejecting any negative example. In this section, our goal is to propose a representation of the negative examples enabling ordering and pruning of both the negative examples (2.4) and the attributes (in section 3).

2.1 A negative example induces a constraint

Let us consider a toy problem for the purpose of illustration. The concept to learn is that of *Hero* ; attributes are the name of the person, its favorite color and the number of questions s/he asks :

	Name	Color	Nb Questions
Ex	*Arthur*	*Blue*	*3*
Ce_1	*Ganelon*	*Grey*	*7*
Ce_2	*Iago*	*Yellow*	*4*
Ce_3	*Bryan*	*Green*	*10*
Ce_4	*Triboulet*	*Cream*	*5*

Attribute *Nb_Questions* is linear; *Name* and *Favorite Color* are tree-structured :

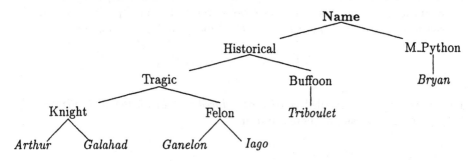

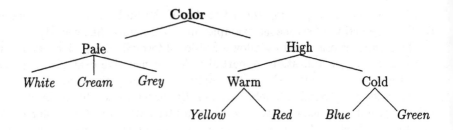

Any discriminant generalization of example Ex must reject negative example Ce_1. In the case of attribute *Color*, the most general value covering *Blue* and rejecting *Grey* is *High*. The corresponding selector [6] rejecting Ce_1 thus is : $[Color = High]$. The disjunction of the most general selectors covering Ex and rejecting Ce_1 is :

$$[Name = Knight] \bigvee [Color = High] \bigvee [Nb\_Questions = [0, 6]]$$

This disjunction can be thought of as a constraint upon the generalization of Ex : any term in the solution space must satisfy this logical constraint.

More generally, such a constraint upon the generalization of any positive term can be derived from any negative example. After proposing a representation of such constraints, we focus on their pruning (2.4) and handling in order to express G (4.1) or classify a further case (4.2).

2.2 Formalizing Constraints

In the following, the notation $x(T)$ stands for the value of attribute x in term T ; $x(T)$ thus is a qualitative value in the case of a tree-structured attribute, and an interval or a single value in the case of a linear attribute. The G set associated to a positive term S and negative examples $Ce_1, \ldots, Ce_N$ is noted $G(S, Ce_1, ..Ce_N)$.

Now, for any negative example Ce_j, for any attribute x_i,
- Let $E_{i,j}$ be, if it exists, the most general value (respectively the widest interval) such that it covers (resp. includes) value $x_i(S)$ and does not cover (resp. include) value $x_i(Ce_j)$ if attribute x_i is qualitative (resp. linear).
- Let $I(j)$ be the set of attributes such that value $E_{i,j}$ is defined. $I(j)$ denotes the set of possibly guilty attributes, according to the terminology of [11].

By definition, the most general selectors covering S and rejecting Ce_j (if we restrict to operator '='), are the $[x_i = E_{i,j}]$, for x_i in $I(j)$. So, one has :

$$G(S, Ce_j) = \bigvee_{x_i \in I(j)} [x_i = E_{i,j}]$$

The above expression, called *constraint induced by Ce_j on the generalization of S*, is given an extensional representation.

Let O_i be the domain of attribute x_i, and let Ω denote the cross product of domains $O_i : \Omega = O_1 \times \ldots \times O_K$. A constraint may then be represented as a subset of Ω.

Definition (constraint) :
Given term S, one associates to any negative example Ce_j the subset of Ω denoted $Constraint(S, Ce_j)$, defined by :

$$Constraint(S, Ce_j) = (V_{i,j})_{i=1}^K$$

$$where\ V_{i,j} = \begin{cases} E_{i,j} \ if\ E_{i,j}\ is\ defined & (\Leftrightarrow x_i \in I(j)) \\ \phi & otherwise \end{cases}$$

The empty value ϕ is assumed more specific than any value V_i in any domain O_i.

The negative examples described in 2.1 give rise to the following constraints :

	Name	Color	Nb Questions
$Constraint(Ex, Ce_1)$	$Knight\_Name$	$High\_Color$	$[0, 6]$
$Constraint(Ex, Ce_2)$	$Knight\_Name$	$Cold\_Color$	$[0, 3]$
$Constraint(Ex, Ce_3)$	$Historical\_Name$	$Blue$	$[0, 9]$
$Constraint(Ex, Ce_4)$	$Tragic$	$High\_Color$	$[0, 4]$

2.3 Ordering Constraints and Negative Examples

The partial order relations defined on domains O_i classically induce a partial order relation on their cross-product Ω, denoted $\leq_\Omega$. One has :

$$((V_i)_{i=1}^K \leq_\Omega (W_i)_{i=1}^K) \Longleftrightarrow (\forall i = 1..K,\ V_i \leq W_i)$$

where $V_i \leq W_i$ means that value V_i is covered by value W_i, if attribute x_i is tree-structured, and that interval V_i is included in interval W_i if x_i is linear.

This order relation enables comparing constraints and thus, negative examples.

Definition (nearest-miss) :
Given term S and negative examples $Ce_1, \ldots Ce_N$, Ce_i is called nearest miss to S iff $Constraint(S, Ce_i)$ is minimal with respect to the order relation $\leq_\Omega$ among $Constraints(S, Ce_j)$, $j = 1..N$.

Negative example Ce_2 is a nearest miss ; Ce_4 is not for we have :

$$Constraint(Ex, Ce_2) \leq_\Omega Constraint(Ex, Ce_4)$$

(*Knight* is less general than *Tragic* ; *Cold* is less general than *High* ; last, one has $[0, 3] \subset [0, 4]$). This shows that a nearest-miss is not necessarily a near-miss: Ce_2 is discriminated from Ex by more than one attribute.

2.4 Pruning negative examples

Given the above definition, a result parallel to that of [11] holds : bottom-up learning only needs positive examples and nearest-miss negative examples.

Proposition 1 :

Given positive term S and negative examples $Ce_1, \ldots Ce_N$, assume without loss of generality that nearest-misses are examples $Ce_1, \ldots Ce_L, L \leq N$. Then

$$G(S, Ce_1, \ldots Ce_N) = G(S, Ce_1, \ldots Ce_L)$$

Proof.

- We first associate to any ω in Ω, $\omega = (V_i)_{i=1}^{K}$, the disjunction of selectors $[x_i = V_i]$, for V_i not empty :

$$\omega \in \Omega \rightarrow g(\omega) = \bigvee_{i \, / \, V_i \neq \phi} [x_i = V_i]$$

It is straightforward to show that (where $\leq$ stands for 'less general than') :

$$\forall \, \omega_1, \, \omega_2 \, \in \, \Omega, \, (\, \omega_1 \, \leq_\Omega \, \omega_2 \,) \iff (\, g(\omega_1) \, \leq \, g(\omega_2) \,) \qquad (1)$$

- By definition, one has

$$G(S, Ce_i) = g \, (Constraint(S, Ce_i))$$

and

$$G(S, Ce_1, \ldots, Ce_N) = \bigwedge_{i=1}^{N} (\, g \, (Constraint(S, Ce_i)))$$

- For any negative example Ce_j which is not a nearest-miss, $(j \geq L)$, there is a nearest-miss Ce_i with $Constraint(S, Ce_i) \leq_\Omega Constraint(S, Ce_j)$. Hence from (1), one has $g(Constraint(S, Ce_i)) \leq g(Constraint(S, Ce_j))$. So

$$g(Constraint(S, Ce_i)) \bigwedge g(Constraint(S, Ce_j)) = g(Constraint(S, Ce_i))$$

And

$$G(S, Ce_1, ..Ce_L) = G(S, Ce_1, ..Ce_L) \bigwedge G(S, Ce_{L+1}, ..Ce_N) = G(S, Ce_1, ..Ce_N)$$

$\square$

This proposition then extends the result of [11] in case of a non convergent data set[2]. Therefore, negative examples that are not near-misses can be pruned without any loss of information.

---

[2] From [11], we have then : a data set is convergent iff there are at most N minimal constraints, each of them involving a single attribute.

2.5 Complexity

The notations used are that of Smith and Rosenbloom [11] : K denotes the number of attributes, P the number of positive examples and N the number of negative examples. It is assumed that exploring the domain hierarchy of any attribute can be done in constant time ; then

- Following [11], the complexity of building set S is in $\mathcal{O}(P \times K)$. Storing S requires a $\mathcal{O}(K)$ memory size.
- The constraints building is in $\mathcal{O}(N \times K)$ according to 2.2 ; their update when S is generalized is in $\mathcal{O}(N \times K)$ too[3]. The incremental building of the constraints so is in $\mathcal{O}(P \times N \times K)$. Their storage is in $\mathcal{O}(N \times K)$.
- The constraints pruning, according to definition 2.3, is in $\mathcal{O}(N^2 \times K)$.

3 Ordering and Pruning Attributes

A partial order on the attributes $x_1, \ldots x_K$ of the problem domain can be derived from a set of constraints. It is shown that only minimal attributes with respect to this order are to be explored when building the G set.

3.1 Definition

Given constraints $C_1, \ldots, C_L$, for any attribute x_i, we denote O_i^* the set of values $x_i(C_m)$ for $m = 1..L$. This set O_i^* induces a partition over the set of constraints, denoted $\mathcal{P}_i$: two constraints belong to the same subset if they have same value for attribute x_i. Subset $\mathcal{E}_{i,k}$ in partition $\mathcal{P}_i$ is the set of constraints C_m such that $x_i(C_m)$ equals value $U_{i,k}$, belonging to O_i^*.

So, if we consider the set of minimal constraints $C_1, \ldots C_3$:

	Name	Color	Nb Questions
C_1	$Knight$	$High$	$[0, 6]$
C_2	$Knight$	$Cold$	$[0, 3]$
C_3	$Historical$	$Blue$	$[0, 9]$

we have $O_1^* = \{Knigt, Historical\}$, which induces the partition $\mathcal{P}_1 = \{\{C_1, C_2\}, \{C_3\}\}$

The partitions over a given domain are partially ordered ; their order relation noted $\leq$, classically is defined by :

$$(\mathcal{P}_1 \leq \mathcal{P}_2) \Leftrightarrow (\forall\, \mathcal{E}_{1,i} \in \mathcal{P}_1, \ \exists\, \mathcal{E}_{2,j} \in \mathcal{P}_2 \ /\ \mathcal{E}_{1,i} \subset \mathcal{E}_{2,j})$$

If two partitions $\mathcal{P}_i$ and $\mathcal{P}_j$ are such that $\mathcal{P}_i \leq \mathcal{P}_j$, we can define an application $\varphi_{i,j}$ from O_i^* to O_j^* which associates to value $U_{i,k}$ value $U_{j,l}$ such that for

---

[3] For every attribute x_i, for every constraint C_j, if x_i is in $I(j)$ (value $E_{i,j}$ is defined), it is checked whether $E_{i,j}$ still is more general than $x_i(S)$. If not, x_i is removed from set $I(j)$. If set $I(j)$ is empty for a constraint C_j, negative example Ce_j is no longer discriminated from S, and the version space fails.

any constraint C_m, $x_i(C_m) = U_{i,k} \Rightarrow x_j(C_m) = U_{j,l}$.

For instance, the partition $\mathcal{P}_3 = \{\{C_1\}, \{C_2\}, \{C_3\}\}$ derived from attribute *Nb_Questions* is finer than the partition $\mathcal{P}_1$. The corresponding application $\varphi_{3,1}$ is defined by :
$$\varphi_{3,1}([0,6]) = \varphi_{3,1}([0,3]) = Knight$$
$$\varphi_{3,1}([0,9]) = Historical$$

This partial order allows for defining a partial order on attributes :

Definition (finer attribute) :
Given a set of constraints $C_1, \ldots, C_L$, attribute x_i is finer than attribute x_j, noted $x_i \leq_{att} x_j$ iff :
- *Sets O_i^* and O_j^* are totally ordered with respect to set inclusion[4].*
- *The partition induced by x_i is finer than the partition induced by x_j : $\mathcal{P}_i \leq \mathcal{P}_j$*
- *Function $\varphi_{i,j}$ defined above is monotonic from O_i^* into O_j^**

$$\forall U_1, U_2 \in O_i^*, ((U_1 < U_2) \Rightarrow (\varphi_{i,j}(U_1) \leq \varphi_{i,j}(U_2)))$$

- *For every k, constraint C_k involves attribute x_i ($x_i(C_k) \neq \phi$) iff it also involves attribute x_j.*

Attribute *Nb_Questions* is finer than attribute *Name* : the set of values $O_3^* = \{ [0,3], [0,6], [0,9] \}$ is ordered and $\varphi_{3,1}$ is monotonic.

3.2 Pruning attributes

The partial order defined on the attributes enables a result parallel to that of the section 2.4 : only minimal attributes with respect to this order are to be explored when building G.

Proposition 2 :

Let x_i and x_j be two attributes such that $x_i \leq_{att} x_j$.

Let $G(S, C_1, \ldots C_L)$ denote the set of maximally general terms covering term S and satisfying constraints $C_1, \ldots C_L$. Let G' be the subset of G given by the terms not involving attribute x_j.

For any term T in G', one defines term T^* by :
- if T does not involve attribute x_i, $T^* = T$.
- Otherwise, let $[x_i = V_i]$ be the selector involving x_i in T[5].

  - If V_i is such that $V_i = sup\{ V_k \ / \ \phi_{i,j}(V_k) = \phi_{i,j}(V_i) \}$, then T^* is the term obtained by replacing selector $[x_i = V_i]$ in T by selector $[x_j = \varphi_{i,j}(V_i)]$.
  - Otherwise $T^* = T$.

---

[4] If x_i is a tree-structured attribute then O_i^* is totally ordered : all values in O_i^* can be compared for they all are more general than $x_i(S)$ by construction. If x_j is a linear attribute, O_j^* is not necessarily totally ordered w.r.t. set inclusion.

[5] This selector is unique : only the most specific value V_i is retained.

Then any term in G either belongs to G', or is a T^* for some T in G'.

The proof is given in appendix.

In practice, set G' is obtained by considering minimal attributes only. (The attributes pruning thus only takes place during the expensive phase of the G building.) Then, G is obtained from G' by making straightforward use of functions $\varphi_{i,j}$. In the example, only attributes *Color* and *Nb_Questions* are considered to build G' ; the terms in set G' are :

$T_1 = [Color = Blue]$
$T_2 = [Color = Cold] \bigwedge [Nb\_Questions = [0, 9]]$
$T_3 = [Color = High] \bigwedge [Nb\_Questions = [0, 3]]$

Terms T_2 and T_3 give rise to terms T_2^* and T_3^*

$T_2^* = [Color = Cold] \bigwedge [Name = Historical\_Name]$
$T_3^* = [Color = High] \bigwedge [Name = Knight\_Name]$

3.3 Complexity

Pruning attributes involves, for any (ordered) pair of attribute (x_i, x_j) :

- Building application $\varphi_{i,j}$ from O_i^* into O_j^* ; the size of O_i^* is upper bounded by the number of constraints, (which is upper bounded by the number of negative examples N) and by the number of values in O_i. Hence, if L denotes the maximum number of values in any O_i, this step is in $\mathcal{O}(min(N, L))$. The storage of $\varphi_{i,j}$ also is in $\mathcal{O}(min(N, L))$.
- Checking the monotonicity of $\varphi_{i,j}$, which is in $\mathcal{O}(min(N, L)log(min(N, L)))$.

Finally, the complexity of the attributes pruning is in
$\mathcal{O}(K^2 \times min(N, L)log(min(N, L)))$.

4 Building G or Classifying ?

This section addresses the characterization of G from the constraints.

4.1 Building G

In a first step, S is built from the set of positive examples ; constraints are built and updated as detailed in 2.2 and 2.5.

Constraints are then explored in order to build the terms in G. Here is the pseudo-code of the constrained generalization algorithm[6]. Array *Selector[i]* stores the active selector of constraint C_i ; i_0 is the index of the current constraint.

Initialize()
     For i = 1..N

---
[6] This algorithm is implemented in C++.

```
        Selector[i] = 0;
     G = { } ; T = true ; i₀ = 1.
```

Main()
        Initialize();
        While $(0 < i_0 \leq N)$,
            If (constraint C_{i_0} is not yet satisfied by term T)
                If $(Selector[i_0] \neq 0)$
                    Remove from T the $Selector[i_0]$-th selector of C_{i_0};
                Increment $Selector[i_0]$;
                Continue :
                If (C_{i_0} has $Selector[i_0]$ selectors)
                    $T = T \bigwedge$ the $Selector[i_0]$-th selector of C_{i_0};
                Else
                    $Selector[i_0] = 0$;
                    If (Backtrack()) goto Continue;
                    Else stop.
            Increment i_0;
        EndWhile
        $G = G \bigcup T$;// Term T is a solution
        if (Backtrack()) goto Continue; // to find other solutions.
        else stop.
Backtrack()
Let j be the index of the last active constraint (with Selector[j] $\neq$ 0);
        While $(j > 0)$
            Remove from T the $Selector[j]$-th selector of C_j;
            Increment $Selector[j]$;
            If (C_j has $Selector[j]$ selectors)
                $i_0 = j$;
                return $True$;
            Else
                $Selector[j] = 0$;
                Decrement j;
        EndWhile
        return $False$;
```

This procedure allows to find all terms in G ; however, terms found may be not all maximally general : a selector added to satisfy a given constraint may become useless because of a selector added further on and satisfying also this constraint.

So one has to check whether a term $T$ is maximally general or not. This is done by building $G(T, Ce_1, ..Ce_N)$ ; T is maximally general iff $G(T, Ce_1, ..Ce_N) = T$.

In spite of the pruning of the search space enabled by constraints, the number of conjunctive terms in G may still be exponential with respect to the number
```

of attributes. However, the constraints are sufficient to characterize G with a polynomial complexity.

4.2 Using constraints to classify

Let E be the description of a further case. The diagnosis function is as usual given by

$$Diagnosis(E) = \begin{cases} True & if\ E \leq S \\ False & if\ E \nleq G \\ Unknown\ otherwise \end{cases}$$

The only point is checking whether E belongs to G, i.e. whether E satisfies all constraints $Constraint(S, Ce_i)$. This can be done with a complexity $\mathcal{O}(K \times N)$ (still assuming that exploring the generalization hierarchy of any attribute is done in constant time).

Therefore, the proposed formalization provides the user with a polynomial characterization of G, even in case of a non-convergent data set. This result is discussed with reference to that of H. Hirsh [5] in the last section.

5 Detecting erroneous examples

Dealing with noisy data has long been recognized an unavoidable task in machine learning [3]. However, detecting and rejecting outliers and/or erroneous examples could ease greatly the learning task [10]. This section deals with detecting erroneous examples in the data set. More precisely, it gives sufficient conditions for an example to be erroneous. An example is said to be erroneous if either its description or its conclusion differ from what it should be.

Negative examples are represented as constraints with respect to a positive term to generalize ; this representation holds, be this positive term either the actual S, or any positive example Ex_i in the data set. Let $C(E_i, Ce_k)$ denote the constraint put by negative example Ce_k upon the generalization of positive example E_i. This constraint is a boolean function computable on the problem domain. Should positive example E_j satisfy constraint $C(E_i, Ce_k)$? Yes : if E_j belongs to concept C, then E_j belongs to set G, and then it belongs to any set $G(E_i, Ce_1, \ldots, Ce_N)$ in case of a conjunctive concept C. So, let us denote $\delta(i, j, k)$ the boolean value $C(E_i, Ce_k)(E_j)$; this boolean should be true for any positive example E_j.

Assume now that $\delta(i, j, k)$ is false : then, according to the above discussion, either E_i or E_j or Ce_k is erroneous, i.e. has a corrupted description or conclusion. This fact only gives a hint ; but one can appreciate where the problem eventually comes from, by aggregating hints and considering all $\delta(i, j, k)$.

The procedure is inspired from the one exposed in [1]. Bergadano et al. state that along the specialization process, the number of examples belonging to the extension of the current term is to decrease ; the point is that, when specialization is based on a litteral defined by the domain theory - and *if this definition is too specific*, then this decreasing is much higher than the average decreasing of the extension size, averaged along the specialization process. When an unusual decrease is observed, the current predicate and its definition are submitted for correction to the expert. In the same line, we associate to example Ex_i the number of booleans $\delta(i, j, k)$ that are false, for j ranking from 1 to P and k from 1 to N. Let $\sigma(Ex_i)$ denote this sum. This allows to order positive examples by ascending order of "suspicion" : the greater $\sigma(Ex_i)$, the more likely Ex_i is erroneous. Similarly, one can associate to a negative example Ce_k the number of $\delta(i, j, k)$ that are false, for i and j ranking from 1 to P. This quantity allows for ordering negative examples by ascending order of suspicion.

Of course, the final decision to reject an example as erroneous belongs to the expert ; the only crisp information provided by our approach is to state that, given a boolean $\delta(i, j, k)$ false, one at least among examples Ex_i, Ex_j and Ce_k, is erroneous. In practice, we proceed as follows : the expert provides the system with a rate of erroneous examples. Then, until this rate of examples has been rejected, or until the stack is empty, the positive and negative examples maximizing function σ are proposed to the expert. If they are discarded by the expert, function σ is updated; otherwise, the next positive and negative examples maximizing σ are considered.

6 Related works

6.1 An exponential size

Among the related works, we must first mention Haussler [4] who showed that the number of conjunctive terms in set G could be exponential with respect to the number of attributes. The example is as follows :
The problem domain is $\{0,1\}^{2m}$. One is given positive example Ex, whose all components are true, and m negative examples Ce_i, $i = 1..m$; components of Ce_i are all true, except the i-th and the $(m + i)$-th.

Any negative example Ce_i leads to specialise set G ; this specialization may be done along any feature discriminating Ce_i from $Ex = S$, i.e. one of attributes i or $m + i$. The number of choices (and of conjunctive terms in G) is multiplied by 2 at each negative example. The final number of elements in G is thus 2^m.

Many strategies have been proposed so to deal with that number of choices and terms.

6.2 Using near-misses

Smith and Rosenbloom [11] first consider the negative examples which are discriminated from S by only one attribute (so there is no choice for specialization). Such negative examples are called near-misses, according to Winston [12]. A major result of [11] is to show that when the data set is convergent, learning only needs positive examples and near-miss negative examples to converge. Accordingly, they propose an algorithm linear with respect to the number of attributes K, the number of positive examples P and the number of negative examples N:

Negative examples are stocked in a waiting list.

When set S is generalized from a positive example, the waiting list is scanned : if there is a negative example which is a near-miss (i.e. with exactly one attribute discriminating this example from S), then G is specialized with respect to this guilty attribute so to reject the negative example.

This way, the memory size required is in $\mathcal{O}((N+2) \times K)$ (stocking of S, G and the waiting list).

This process leads to G = S if the data set is convergent. Otherwise, after having considered all positive examples and near-miss negative examples, the usual *Candidate Elimination Algorithm* [7] is used to update set G from the remaining negative examples.

6.3 Another representation of the G set

H. Hirsh [5] proposes to represent a Version Space by $[S,\mathcal{N}]$ where $\mathcal{N}$ stands for the list of negative examples. For conjunctive tree-structured languages, this representation supports a polynomial computation of some functions defined on a Version Space :

• *Collapse* : when data are inconsistent, or the description langage does not allow to describe the concept to learn ; *Collapse* is true if S is empty ; (see *Update* below);

• *Converge* : in case of convergence, from [11] there is a near-miss for any attribute in list $\mathcal{N}$;

• *Update* given new example E : if E is negative it is added to list $\mathcal{N}$ and elements in S covering it are removed ; otherwise E is used to generalize S, and resulting terms covering some example in $\mathcal{N}$ are removed ;

• *Classify* a new case E : if E satisfies any term in S, then it belongs to the concept ; otherwise, compute the Version Space that would result if E were a positive example ; if this new Version Space collapses, E does not actually belong to the concept ; otherwise, the diagnosis is unknown.

The drawback of this representation is that maintaining the list of negative examples gives few hints to what G could be. Addressing this remark, J. Nicolas [8] proposes a disjunctive formalization such that the G set induced by a single negative example is represented by a single term. The trouble comes from intersecting several Version Spaces when several negative examples are considered. This operation is very expensive ; the actual number of (disjunctive) terms may still be exponential.

6.4 Discussion

Our approach is very near from that of H. Hirsh, with a slightly higher complexity of our update (learning) phase ; the complexity of the classifying phase is equivalent to that of Hirsh : it is equivalent to check whether case E satisfies

Constraint (S, Ce_i), or whether the generalization of E and S covers negative example Ce_i.

From the intelligibility standpoint the constraint derived from a negative example is more general and thus understandable by the expert than the negative example itself (furthermore, by pruning the constraints the number of useful informations can be much decreased). So, the presented approach achieves some trade-off between efficiency and understandability. But the major advantage of our formalization compared to that of H. Hirsh, it that it enables to detect the erroneous examples by an all-at-once handling of the data.

Compared to the approach of J. Nicolas [8], the final expensive phase of the G building is performed in a reduced search space : constraints allow for pruning both negative examples and attributes. This phase can also be completely escaped as shown in 4.2.

7 Summary and Perspectives

Representing the negative examples as constraints on the generalization of a positive term enables to prune the negative examples and the attributes to be explored when building the G set.

This representation also allows for a computable polynomial characterization of G ; whatever the actual number of conjunctive terms in G, this characterization is linear with respect to the number of attributes, the number of positive examples and the number of negative examples. The price to pay lies in the fact that a set of constraints is less understandable by the expert than a set of conjunctive terms. Last, our approach enables detecting erroneous examples.

Further research aims at extending this approach to learning a disjunctive concept. The constraints building applies, be the positive term considered the S set or any positive example Ex_i. One may then consider the G set derived from a positive example Ex_i and the negative examples $Ce_1, \ldots Ce_N$, (the *star of* Ex_i by analogy with the star algorithm [6]). A next step is to cluster these stars, so to identify the (conjunctive) subconcepts involved in a disjunctive concept.

References

1. F. Bergadano, A Giordana, *A Knowledge Intensive Approach to Concept Induction*, ICML 1988, pp 305-317.
2. A. Bundy, B. Silver, D. Plummer, *An analytical Comparizon of Some Rule Learning Programs*, Artificial Intelligence, 27, 1985, pp 137-181.
3. P. Clark T. Niblett *Induction in noisy domains* Progress in machine learning, Proc. EWSL 1987, I. Bratko N. Lavrac Eds, Sigma Press.
4. D. Haussler, *Quantifying Inductive Bias : AI Learnign Algorithms and Valiant's Learning Framework*, Artificial Intelligence, 36, 1988, pp 177-221.
5. H. Hirsh, *Polynomial-Time Learning with Version Spaces*, Proc. National Conference on Artificial Intelligence, 1992 pp 117-122.

6. Michalski R.S. *A theory and methodology for inductive learning* Machine Learning: An Artificial Intelligence Approach, I, R.S. Michalski, J.G. Carbonnell, T.M. Mitchell Eds, Springer Verlag, (1983), p 83-134.

7. T.M. Mitchell, *Generalization as Search*, Artificial Intelligence Vol 18, pp 203-226, 1982.

8. J. Nicolas, *Une Représentation Efficace pour les Espaces de Version*, JFA 1993.

9. J. Piaget, *Six études de psychologie*, Denoel 1964.

10. R. Quinlan, *The effect of noise on concept learning* Machine Learning: An Artificial Intelligence Approach, I, R.S. Michalski, J.G. Carbonnell, T.M. Mitchell Eds, Vol 2, Morgan Kaufman, 1986.

11. B. Smith, P. Rosenbloom, *Incremental non-backtracking focussing : A polynomially- bounded generalization algorithm for version space*, Proc. National Conference on Artificial Intelligence, 1990, pp 848-853.

12. P.H. Winston, *Learning Structural Descriptions from Examples* The Psychology of Computer Vision, P.H. Winston Ed, Mc Graw Hill, New York, 1975, pp 157-209.

Appendix

Proposition 2 :

Let x_i and x_j be two attributes such that $x_i \leq_{att} x_j$.

Let $G(S, C_1, \ldots C_L)$ denote the set of terms maximally general covering term S and satisfying constraints $C_1, \ldots C_L$. Let G' be the subset of G given by the terms not involving attribute x_j.

For any term T in G', one defines term T^* by :
- if T does not involve attribute x_i, $T^* = T$.
- Otherwise, let $[x_i = V_i]$ be the selector involving x_i in T.

  - If V_i is such that $V_i = sup \{ V_k \ / \ \phi_{i,j}(V_k) = \phi_{i,j}(V_i)\}$, then T^* is the term obtained by replacing selector $[x_i = V_i]$ in T by selector $[x_j = \phi_{i,j}(V_i)]$.
  - Otherwise $T^* = T$.

Then any term in G either belongs to G', or is a T^* for some T in G'.

Proof.

A preliminary remark is the following : as set O_l^* is totally ordered for $l = i$ or j[7], it induces a total order on partition $\mathcal{P}_l$ too. So selector $[x_l = U_{l,m}]$ enables to satisfy any constraint C_k such that $U_{l,m} \leq x_l(C_k)$, and more generally, any constraint belonging to some $\mathcal{E}_{l,j}$ in $\mathcal{P}_l$, with index j greater than m.

$$Let \ G'' = \bigvee_{T \in G'} (T \bigvee T^*)$$

A.1 $G \subset G''$

Let Z be a maximal term in G.

- We first show that Z involves at most one among attributes x_i or x_j. Let us suppose that Z includes two selectors $[x_i = V_i]$ and $[x_j = V_j]$. Compare V_j and $\varphi_{i,j}(V_i)$:

  - If $V_j \leq \varphi_{i,j}(V_i)$, then from the preliminary remark, all constraints satisfied by selector $[x_i = V_i]$ are satisfied by selector $[x_j = V_j]$ too. Hence selector $[x_i = V_i]$ can be suppressed - which contradicts the fact that Z is maximal.
  - Similarly if $\varphi_{i,j}(V_i) \leq V_j$, then all constraints satisfied by $[x_j = V_j]$ are satisfied by $[x_i = V_i]$, which contradicts the fact that Z is maximal.

---

[7] By definition, if $x_i \leq_{att} x_j$ then sets O_i^* and O_j^* are totally ordered.

So Z involves at most one among attributes x_i and x_j.

• Suppose that Z does not involve x_j. Then by construction, Z belongs to G', and to G".

• Suppose that Z involves x_j and includes selector $[x_j = V_j]$. Let V_i be such that

$$V_i = sup \ \{V_k \ / \ \varphi_{i,j}(V_k) = V_j\}$$

Let T be the term defined from Z by replacing selector $[x_j = V_j]$ by $[x_i = V_i]$, which satisfies the same constraints by construction. We show that T belongs to G'. In opposition, suppose that there exists T' in G' such that $T' > T$.

  • If T' does not involve x_i, (as T' does not involve x_j neither for T' belongs to G'), then from $T' > T$ one has $T' > Z$; this contradicts the fact that Z is maximal.
  • So T' must involve attribute x_i ; assume that T' includes selector $[x_i = W_i]$; then $T' > T$ implies $W_i \geq V_i$.
  Consider now term Z', built by replacing in T' selector $[x_i = W_i]$ by $[x_j = \varphi_{i,j}(W_i)]$. By definition of $\varphi_{i,j}$, $W_i \geq V_i$ implies $\varphi_{i,j}(W_i) \geq V_j$; hence $Z' \geq Z$; however, Z' satisfies the same constraints as Z, and so belongs to G. But, Z being maximal in G, one has $Z = Z'$, so $\varphi_{i,j}(W_i) = V_j$; by definition of V_i, this implies $V_i \geq W_i$, which contradicts the fact $T' \neq T$.

Then there exists a term T in G' such that $Z = T^*$. So, all terms in G are obtained from G' by the procedure given in the proposition 2.

A.2 $G" \subset G$

We show now that any term in G" belongs to G. By construction, if T belongs to G' then it belongs to G. It remains to show that all terms T^* as defined in proposition 2 eventually belong to G. Let T be a term in G' including selector $[x_i = V_i]$, with V_i such that :
$$V_i = sup\{V_k \ / \ \varphi_{i,j}(V_k) = \varphi_{i,j}(V_i)\}$$

Let T^* be the term built from T by replacing $[x_i = V_i]$ by $[x_j = \varphi_{i,j}(V_i)]$.
  Suppose that there exists Z in G such that $Z > T^*$.
• If Z does not involve x_j, as Z does not involve x_i neither (for $Z > T^*$ and T^* does not involve x_i), Z belongs to G'. Hence $Z > T^*$ implies $Z > T$, which contradicts the fact that T is maximal.
• If Z involves x_j, then there exists in G' a term S such that $Z = S^*$ (from A.1). It is straightforward to show that $Z = S^* > T^*$ implies $S \geq T$; now, as T is maximal, $T = S$; so $Z = T^*$, and T^* is maximal.
□

On the Utility of Predicate Invention in Inductive Logic Programming

Irene Stahl

Fakultät Informatik, Universität Stuttgart, Breitwiesenstr. 20-22, D-70565 Stuttgart

Abstract. The task of predicate invention in ILP is to extend the hypothesis language with new predicates in case that the vocabulary given initially is insufficient for the learning task. However, whether predicate invention really helps to make learning succeed in the extended language depends on the bias that is currently employed.

In this paper we investigate for which commonly employed language biases predicate invention is an appropriate shift operation. We prove that for some restricted languages predicate invention does not help in case that the learning task fails, and characterize the languages for which predicate invention is useful as bias shift operation.

1 Introduction

Inductive logic programming (ILP) [Mug92] aims to learn logic programs from examples in the presence of background knowledge. As opposed to propositional frameworks, this setting leads to a generally infinite space of possible target programs systems have to consider.

Biases are used to search and restrict this hypothesis space. *Algorithmic* biases guide the search of a system, whereas *absolute* biases restrict the space of potential solutions that is considered at all. The absolute bias determines the target language of inductive inference by constraining the *vocabulary* to be used in hypotheses, that is the available predicate, function and constant symbols, and the *form* and *complexity* of potential target programs. The aim of using a language bias is to consider fewer, ideally only finitely many well-structured or understandable hypotheses.

However, the restrictions imposed by the absolute bias might be too strong such that the hypothesis space does not include a correct target program. In that case, it needs to be relaxed such that the enlarged hypothesis space contains a solution. Extending the given vocabulary with *newly invented predicates*, for short *predicate invention (PI)*, is one possibility to shift the bias. Besides overcoming the limitations of the insufficient vocabulary, the new predicates might also allow for the formulation of simpler hypotheses that conform to the complexity restrictions of the target language.

However, the appropriatness of PI depends on its prior utility for the current language bias. In some languages it is the only possibility to make learning succeed, whereas in others it is useless in case that the learning task fails.

In this paper, we investigate the utility of PI as bias shift operation in ILP. We give a formal definition of the usefulness of PI with respect to the absolute bias, and recall a general result that motivates the introduction of new predicates to overcome the limitations of the given language. In the following sections, we show for which language biases PI is an appropriate shift operation. Finally, we characterize the languages for which PI is useful, and the contribution of the new predicates to the resulting target programs.

2 Definitions

The task of ILP is defined formally as follows. Given ground facts $E^{\oplus}$ and $E^{\ominus}$, the positive and negative examples, a logic program B as background knowledge, and a target language L, the system is to find a logic program $P \in L$ such that $B \cup P \vdash E^{\oplus}$ (*completeness*) and $B \cup P \not\vdash E^{\ominus}$ (*consistency*). The quadruple $(E^{\oplus}, E^{\ominus}, B, L)$ is called the *learning problem*.

It is based on an *intended interpretation* of the user that satisfies at least B and $E^{\oplus}$. In the limit, all ground facts true and false in the intended interpretation are given as positive and negative examples. In this setting, the learning task means to construct a *finite axiomatisation* of the intended interpretation. In more realistic scenarios $E^{\oplus}$ and $E^{\ominus}$ are *finite* subsets of the facts true and false in the intended interpretation. In that case there is always a solution to the learning problem if not explicitly excluded by L, namely $P = E^{\oplus}$. As these *trivial definitions* prevent the investigation of the utility of any bias shift operation, we assume some mechanism to exclude them from the hypothesis space, as e.g. cross validation. This technique splits $E^{\oplus}$ and $E^{\ominus}$ in training and test examples. The target program is constructed from the training examples, and verified on the test examples. Though cross validation leads to programs the predictiveness of which exceeds the given training examples, it is not completely satisfactory for excluding trivial definitions. This issue needs a further, more thorough investigation.

If a learning task fails in the given language L, L is too restrictive to finitely axiomatize the intended interpretation. PI is useful if extending L with finitely many new predicates makes a learning task succeed that fails otherwise. Utility is defined with respect to the class of target languages, that is the absolute bias[1].

Definition 1. Let $\mathcal{L}$ be a class of first order languages. PI is *useful* in $\mathcal{L}$ if there exists a learning problem $(E^{\oplus}, E^{\ominus}, B, L)$, $L \in \mathcal{L}$, such that learning fails in L, but succeeds in a language $L' \in \mathcal{L}$ that extends L with finitely many new predicates.

Definition 1 is relatively weak in as much as only the *existence* of a learning problem that succeeds through PI is required for PI to be useful. A stronger definition would demand that *every* learning problem could be solved by means of PI. Kleene [Kle52] has proved this strong utility of PI in the framework of identification in the limit with unrestricted first order logic as target language.

---

[1] A separate problem we do not investigate in this paper is the utility of PI with respect to the shift of algorithmic biases.

Theorem 2. *Any recursively enumerable set C of formulas in a first order language L is finitely axiomatizable in a first order language L' that extends L with finitely many additional predicate symbols.*

If C is set to the set $E^{\oplus}$ of facts that are true in the intended interpretation, this theorem proves that *every* first order learning problem can be solved by inventing appropriate new predicates, provided that $E^{\oplus}$ is recursively enumerable.

However, in the more restricted framework of ILP this strong view of usefulness is unsuitable because both the target language L and the extended language L' are subject to the same restrictions. As there are learning tasks that fail not because of missing predicates in L, but because of the restrictions that also apply to each extension L', there is no chance to prove strong usefulness results. For example, in section 3.7 we show that PI is very useful for regular unary logic programs [YS91]. It allows to detect recursive substructures in the examples. However, if learning fails because non-regular predicates are given as examples, PI does not help. Therefore, we adopt the weak definition 1 of usefulness.

3 Usefulness Results

To prove usefulness results according to definition 1 it suffices to give examples of learning problems that succeed through PI and fail otherwise. There are two different classes of hypothesis languages for which PI is useful. The first is unrestricted or weakly restricted Horn logic. The second class contains languages restricted to a fixed size by size bounds, schemes or language parameters. Here, PI mainly serves to extend the language without violating the specified parameters or schemes.

In the following, we shortly recall the definition of each language, and present an example that proves the usefulness of PI.

3.1 Unrestricted and Weakly Restricted Horn Logic

In Horn logic, all clauses are restricted to contain at most one positive literal. Though this restricts full clausal logic, first order Horn logic is still very expressive. Accordingly, logical implication is undecidable as in case of first order logic.

PI is useful to recover from the failure of a learning task $(E^{\oplus}, E^{\ominus}, B, L)$ for Horn clause languages L. For example, given facts about the multiplication of natural numbers, there is no solution of the learning problem using only the predicate *multiply/3*, the function *s/1* and the constant 0 (cf. [Lin91]). Only introducing a new predicate *add* will make learning succeed.

The usefulness of PI as bias shift operation is passed on to weak restrictions of Horn logic, namely *connected* and *generative* clauses. The body variables of connected clauses [Rou91, Rae91] must be related to the head of the clause. Vice versa, the head variables of generative clauses [MF90] must occur in the body. As each arbitrary clause can be made connected, respectively generative, by adding body literals, neither of both is a real restriction. Therefore, inducing connected or generative clauses is as hard as inducing arbitrary clauses. Likewise, PI is useful as bias shift operation.

3.2 Size and Complexity Measures

Heuristic size- or complexity measures place a fixed or application-dependent size- or complexity bound on the hypotheses. They realize Ockham's razor principle that prefers the simplest complete and consistent program. There are different approaches to measure the simplicity of a program. Some use only syntactic properties of the hypotheses as criterion, either independently of the examples [MB88, Wro] or when compared to them [Qui90]. Others take into account the complexity of proofs from the theory [Sha83, Mug88, Wir89, SMB92, MSB92].

PI is useful if no solution of the learning problem exists within the specified bounds. New predicates can be employed to factor out common parts of clauses, or to express recursive subrelations and exceptions intensionally. The resulting theory might fit the given size and complexity bounds and make learning succeed.

3.3 Schemes

Schemes describe the structure of the hypothesis clauses at an abstract level. They allow to express prior knowledge about the expected structure of hypothesis clauses in certain application domains, for example DCG clauses for grammar learning. As only finitely many schemes are given, the search space is finite.

SIERES [Wir91a] and CAN [Tau92] use graphs to represent the number of literals and the argument dependencies between them. RDT [Kie91] and CIA [Rae92] employ function-free second-order clauses with predicate variables to describe the allowed structure of hypothesis clauses. The instantiations of the available schemes with respect to the background knowledge constitute the search space for learning.

If no solution instantiating the given schemes exists, PI helps to overcome the limitations imposed by them.

Example 1. Let the available scheme be

SIERES, CAN (graph)	RDT, CIA (second order clause)
S:	$S : P(X) \leftarrow Q(X), R(X)$

and let the target definition be

$$C \ : \ p(X) \leftarrow q(X), r(X), s(X)$$

Then there is no complete and consistent instantiation of S. If a new predicate is introduced, two clauses instantiating S that are equivalent to C can be found:

$$p(X) \quad \leftarrow q(X), newp(X)$$
$$newp(X) \leftarrow r(X), s(X)$$

That is, PI extends the hypothesis language without requiring more complex schemes. Additionally it allows to express recursive subrelations.

3.4 Language Series

Language series [Rae92, Rae91] are sets of parametrized languages. For each instantiation of the parameters the resulting hypothesis language is finite. CLINT [Rae92] orders its parametrized languages according to generality. If the system fails to detect a complete and consistent definition within the current language, it shifts to a more general one.

As in the case of schemes, PI is useful to replace the shift to a more complex language. For example, CLINT's language series 3 restricts the depth of existential quantification within the target clauses:

$$\forall i_1, .., i_k \geq 0 \; : \; L_{i_1,..,i_k} = \{ \; C \mid head(C) = p(X_1, .., X_n), \; X_j \neq X_k \; \forall \, j \neq k$$
$$\wedge \; body(C) \subseteq B_{i_1,..,i_k}(X_1, .., X_n)$$
$$\wedge \; C \text{ linked and range restricted}^2 \; \}$$
$$\text{where } B_i(X_1, .., X_n) = \{ \; q(Y_1, .., Y_k) \mid |\{Y_1, .., Y_k\} - \{X_1, .., X_n\}| \leq i \; \wedge$$
$$\{Y_1, .., Y_k\} \cap \{X_1, .., X_n\} \neq \phi \; \}$$
$$B_{i_1,..,i_k}(X_1, .., X_n) = \{ \; q(Y_1, .., Y_k) \in B_{i_k}(Z_1, .., Z_l) \mid$$
$$\{Z_1, .., Z_l\} = vars(B_{i_1,..,i_{k-1}}(X_1, .., X_n)) \; \}$$

If no solution exists in the given language $L_{i_1,..,i_k}$, PI does the same job as shifting to a more complex language.

Example 2. A target clause

$$C = p(X) \leftarrow r(X, U), q(U, V), p(U, W), r(V, W)$$

is not in $L_{1,0}$, but in $L_{1,1,0}$. With a new predicate it can be rewritten to two clauses in $L_{1,0}$:

$$p(X) \quad \leftarrow r(X, U), newp(U)$$
$$newp(U) \leftarrow q(U, V), p(U, W), r(V, W).$$

However, as in the case of schemes PI is a more powerful operation than the pure language shift, as recursive subrelations might be detected.

---

^{2} Both linked and connected, and range restricted and generative, are synonymous. The formers are more usual in the deductive data base literature.

Example 3. Suppose a set of clauses

$$p(X) \leftarrow s(X, U), r(U)$$
$$p(X) \leftarrow s(X, U), q(U, V), r(V)$$
$$p(X) \leftarrow s(X, U), q(U, V), q(V, W), r(W)$$

.....

is needed to describe the target concept. Without PI, shifts from $L_{1,0}$ to $L_{1,1,0}$ and $L_{1,1,1,0}$ are necessary, whereas introducing a recursively defined new predicate allows a definition in $L_{1,0}$:

$$p(X) \quad\;\; \leftarrow s(X, U), newp(U)$$
$$newp(U) \leftarrow q(U, V), newp(V)$$
$$newp(U) \leftarrow r(U)$$

3.5 Determinate Clauses

Similar to language series 3 of CLINT, the determinacy restriction [MF90] is used to constrain the maximum depth of existential quantification. Additionally, a semantic restriction is placed on the the number of instantiations of the existentially quantified variables with respect to the background knowledge.

Definition 3. Let B be a logic program and $E^{\oplus}$ a set of ground atoms. Every unit clause is $0j$-*determinate*. An ordered clause $A \leftarrow B_1, .., B_m, B_{m+1}, .., B_n$ is ij-*determinate* iff $A \leftarrow B_1, .., B_m$ is $(i-1)j$-determinate, and every literal $B_k \in \{B_{m+1}, .., B_n\}$ contains only determinate terms and has degree at most j. A term t found in B_k is *determinate* with respect to B_k iff for every substitution θ such that $A\theta \in E^{\oplus}$ and $\{B_1, .., B_m\}\theta \subseteq \mathcal{M}(B)^3$ there is a unique ground atom $B_k\theta\sigma \in \mathcal{M}(B)$. The *degree* of B_k with respect to t is the number of variables in B_k which must be instantiated to determine t.

In case that no ij-determinate solution of the learning problem exists, PI is useful to overcome the limitations of ij-determinacy, at least for the parameter i.

Example 4. Given functional predicates $q(+, -)$, $r(+, -)$ and $s(+, -)$, the clause

$$C = p(X, Y) \leftarrow q(X, U), r(U, V), s(V, W)$$

violates the constraint $i = 2$ as the variable W is found at depth $i = 3$. With a new predicate it can be rewritten to two $2j$-determinate clauses:

$$p(X, Y) \quad\; \leftarrow q(X, U), r(U, V), newp(V)$$
$$newp(V) \leftarrow s(V, W).$$

However, in case that the j-parameter is violated, the situation is more complicated. In general, PI is not capable of decreasing the degree of literals from $k > j$ to $\leq j$.

---

[3] $\mathcal{M}(B)$ is the set of all ground atoms derivable from B.

Example 5. Given functional predicates $q(+,-)$, $r(+,-)$ and $t(+,+,-)$, the clause

$$C = p(X,Y) \leftarrow q(X,N1), r(X,N2), t(N1,N2,Y)$$

violates the constraint $j = 1$ in the last literal. It cannot be rewritten in $i1$-determinate clauses.

If the determinacy constraint itself is violated, the non-determinate background knowledge $\mathcal{M}(B)$ has to be transformed into functional form. As the functional parts of a non-determinate predicate must be named differently, PI is involved.

Example 6. The clause

$$ancestor(Anc, Desc) \leftarrow \underline{parent(Z, Desc)}, ancestor(Anc, Z)$$

is not determinate because of the *parent*-literal. In order to express *ancestor* with determinate clauses, the *parent*-relation in the background must be transformed into functional form, e.g. by inventing the determinate *mother* and *father* predicates. Then, the clauses

$$ancestor(Anc, Desc) \leftarrow father(Z, Desc), ancestor(Anc, Z)$$
$$ancestor(Anc, Desc) \leftarrow mother(Z, Desc), ancestor(Anc, Z)$$

are determinate and equivalent to the target clause.

This kind of PI involves detecting dependencies between the arguments of a predicate, and restructuring the knowledge base. It is employed in the context of inductive data engineering [Fla93].

3.6 Constrained Clauses

Constrained clauses are a special case of determinate clauses with the depth of existential quantification restricted to zero. That is, constrained clauses C contain no existential variables, more formally $vars(body(C)) \subseteq vars(head(C))$. As for determinate clauses, PI is useful to make learning succeed when the initial vocabulary was insufficient. This can be shown by the following example.

Example 7. Let $B = \phi$ and

$$E^{\oplus} = \{ rev([],[]), rev([a],[a]), rev([a,b],[b,a]), \ldots \}$$
$$E^{\ominus} = \{ rev([a,b],[a,b]), rev([c],[c,e]), rev(a,[a]), \ldots \}$$

Then there is no constrained solution of the learning problem that uses only $rev/2$, $[\_|\_]$ and $[]$ (though there is one with existential variables, cf. [Bun90]). However, using an additional 3-place predicate *newp* allows a constrained definition:

$$rev(L, LR) \leftarrow newp(L, [], LR)$$
$$newp([], L, L)$$
$$newp([X|R], L, L1) \leftarrow newp(R, [X|L], L1)$$

3.7 RUL-programs

Regular unary logic (RUL) programs [YS91] are a special case of constrained programs. They contain only unary predicates, and allow for non-variable argument terms only in the clause heads. The head arguments of clauses of the same predicate must differ in their function symbol. Additionally, every variable in a clause must occur exactly once in the head and once in the body.

The extensions of predicates defined by RUL-programs are regular sets particularly suited to describe argument types. RUL-programs allow for very efficient induction methods [STW93]. In case that the example set is regular, PI is useful to make the learning task succeed.

Example 8. Let $B = \phi$,

$$E^{\oplus} = \{\, t(f(g([a]))),\qquad E^{\ominus} = \{\, t(g([a])), t([a]), t([])$$
$$t(f(g([a,a]))),\qquad\qquad t(g([a,a])), t([a,a]),$$
$$t(f(g([a,a,a]))))\}\qquad\qquad t(g([a,a,a])), t([a,a,a])\}$$

Then there is no complete and consistent RUL-program P using only $t/1$. Using an additional predicate symbol $q/1$ allows a definition

$$t(f(g([a|Y]))) \leftarrow q(Y).$$
$$q([]).$$
$$q([a|Y]) \leftarrow q(Y).$$

However, if $E^{\oplus}$ exemplifies non-regular predicates, e.g.

$$E^{\oplus} \subseteq \{\, t(f(L_1, L_2)) \mid L_1, L_2 \text{ lists of the same length } \},$$

only the introduction of n-ary new predicates might help. The algorithm described in [STW93] allows to decide whether $E^{\oplus}$ can be defined by a RUL-program at all. If yes, the necessary new predicates are introduced, otherwise the algorithm fails. As the examples for the new predicates are structurally less complex than the examples in $E^{\oplus}$, infinite loops of new predicates cannot occur.

4 Uselessness Results

In spite of the general utility of PI as bias shift operation for fixed size languages, there are language biases for which even PI fails to extend the range of expressible concepts. In particular, function-free languages exhibit this kind of weakness.

Proving the uselessness of PI according to definition 1 is more difficult than proving its usefulness. Instead of simply giving examples for successful applications of PI, we have to show that no extension of the target language with new predicates makes the learning task succeed.

4.1 Function-Free Constrained Clauses

Function-free constrained clauses are constrained clauses without any functors except for finitely many constants. In contrast to the general case of constrained clauses, PI is useless to recover from a failure of the learning task.

Example 9. Let examples about $grandparent(X, Y)$ be given for a set of persons, and let the background knowledge contain all *parent*-relations between them. Then there is no non-trivial constrained program that covers the examples. Furthermore, PI is useless as it cannot help to introduce the necessary existential variable.

The following theorem proves this assertion.

Theorem 4. If there is no function-free constrained solution P to the learning problem $(E^\oplus, E^\ominus, B, L)$, then there is also no function-free constrained solution P' in L' for each extension L' of L with finitely many new predicate symbols.

Proof. We assume that a solution P' in L' exists. New predicates in P' can be eliminated without changing the success set, because recursive calls of them are applied to permutations of the head arguments. As there are only finitely many, non-recursive definitions can be determined that allow to eliminate the new predicates in P'. This results in a complete and consistent P'' in L, in contradiction to the precondition of the theorem.
Construction of P'' from P': Let

$$P' = \underbrace{C_{newp}}_{\substack{\text{clauses with new} \\ \text{predicates as} \\ \text{positive literals}}} \cup \underbrace{C_{def}}_{\substack{\text{clauses that do not} \\ \text{contain a new} \\ \text{predicate positively}}}$$

$$\text{Let } A_0 = C_{newp}$$
$$A_{i+1} = A_i \cup \{C \mid \exists C_1, C_2 \in A_i \ (C = (C_1 \cdot C_2 \sigma)^4) \land \neg \exists C' \in A_i \ (C'\theta \subseteq C)\}$$

As there are only finitely many clauses in each constrained function-free language L', there is an integer n such that $A_{n+1} = A_n$. Let

$$A = A_n - \{C \in A_n \mid C \text{ contains a new predicate negatively}\}$$

Then A has the same success set as C_{newp}, that is $A \vdash a$ iff $C_{newp} \vdash a$:

$\Rightarrow$: Let $A \vdash a$ be true. For each clause $C \in A - C_{newp}$ used in the proof, there is a resolution derivation from C_{newp}. Therefore, there is a resolution proof $C_{newp} \vdash a$.

$\Leftarrow$: Let $C_{newp} \vdash a$ be true. If a clause C used in the proof is not in A, it contains new predicate literals in the body. For each possibility to resolve them away, there is a corresponding clause in A. Therefore, there is a resolution proof $A \vdash a$.

---

[4] Here, $(A \cdot B\sigma)$ is the result of resolving A and B with substitution σ.

The set A contains only non-recursively defined new predicates the definitions of which can be used to unfold the new predicate literals in C_{def}. This results in the desired program P'' in L.

That is, in function-free constrained Horn logic PI is useless in case that the learning task fails. The same is true for the more restricted case of completely bound clauses C where $vars(head(C)) = vars(body(C))$.

4.2 Monadic Horn Logic

Monadic Horn logic is function-free Horn logic restricted to unary predicates. In contrast to RUL-programs, monadic logic programs need not to be constrained, but might contain existential variables. However, we can show that for each monadic logic program there is an equivalent one without existential variables.

Theorem 5. *Given an arbitrary monadic logic program P' in a language L, there exists a program P in L with the same success set without existential variables.*

Proof. Body literals with an existential variable as argument are always true or always false, regardless of the current proof. Therefore they can be eliminated from P' without changing the success set. A detailed description of the construction of P from P' can be found in [STU1].

That is, only constrained clauses need to be considered when learning in monadic Horn logic. Therefore, PI is useless if learning fails.

4.3 Function-Free Horn Logic

Function-free logic programs contain no functors except for finitely many constants. Excluding arbitrary functors leads to the decidability of logical implication, in contrast to full first order Horn logic.

This decidability accounts for the uselessness of PI. In [Sta93] we prove that, given $(E^{\oplus}, E^{\ominus}, B, L)$ with a function-free language L, only clauses with at most n different variables need to be considered for the target program P. The parameter n depends on the number of constants in B and L, and the arity of the available predicates. This property accounts on the one hand for the decidability of the learning problem, but on the other hand for the uselessness of PI. As only clauses with up to n different variables need to be considered, recursively defined new predicates can be eliminated by a method similar to that for constrained clauses.

Theorem 6. *If there is no function-free solution P to the learning problem $(E^{\oplus}, E^{\ominus}, B, L)$, then there is also no function-free solution P' in L' for each extension L' of L with finitely many new predicate symbols.*

Proof. As in the proof of theorem 4, we assume that a complete and consistent P' in L' exists, and construct a complete and consistent P'' in L, in contradiction to the precondition of the theorem. The crucial difference from theorem 4 is in the inductive construction of the set A of non-recursive new predicate definitions:

$$A_0 = C_{newp}$$
$$B_{i+1} = A_i \cup \{C \mid \exists C_1, C_2 \in A_i \; (C = (C_1 \cdot C_2 \sigma)) \wedge \neg \exists C' \in A_i \; (C'\theta \subseteq C)\}$$

B_{i+1} might contain clauses with $> n$ variables, where n is the bound on the number of variables. By the method we describe in [Sta93], an extensionally equivalent set A_{i+1} of clauses with at most n variables is constructed from B_{i+1}. As there are only finitely many clauses with $\leq n$ variables, there is an integer k such that $A_{k+1} = A_k$. The set

$$A = A_k - \{C \in A_k \mid C \text{ contains a new predicate negatively}\}$$

can be proved to be extensionally equivalent to C_{newp}. As it contains only non-recursive definitions of new predicates, it can be used to unfold the new predicates in C_{def}, resulting in the desired program P''.

That is, if the learning method fails to find a function-free solution, PI is useless to recover from the failure. However, if the validity and predictiveness of the induced program is to exceed the given constants, new predicates might be necessary for the learning task.

Example 10. Let examples about $male\_ancestor(X, Y)$ be given for a set of persons, and let the background knowledge contain the $parent(X, Y)$- and $male$-relations for them. Then a correct function-free target program can be found that uses only $parent$ and $male$ within the clause bodies. However, this program will fit exactly the family relations between the known people. For arbitrary persons, it will generally produce no predictions. Therefore, if arbitrary many persons are to be considered, only the introduction of a new recursively defined predicate as e.g. $ancestor$ might help.

However, the example refers to a fundamentally stronger success criterion for learning. The induced program is to cover not only the given examples with respect to the given background knowledge, but arbitrary examples with respect to an augmented background knowledge. This violates in fact the restriction to function-free programs, as potentially infinitely many constants need to be considered.

5 Characterizing Languages with respect to Predicate Invention

In the previous sections we discussed the usefulness of PI for different language biases. The results are summarized in figure 1. It shows that the more restricted the target language is, the less useful is PI.

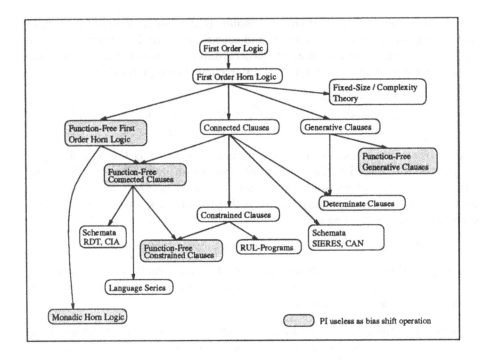

Fig. 1. Usefulness of PI as bias shift operation

Especially for function-free languages, the introduction of new predicates does not increase the expressiveness of the the original language. Function-free languages are quite weak as the inductive inference method can never leave the space of what is expressible with the given constants and predicates. If the validity of the induced program is to exceed the given constants, PI might be useful. However, in that case the learning task is as difficult as in unrestricted Horn logic.

The languages for which PI is a useful bias shift operation can be distinguished in two classes. The first is the class of unrestricted or weakly restricted Horn clause languages. If learning fails in a language of that kind, PI might help to overcome the limitations of the given vocabulary. Necessary new predicates must be defined recursively in these languages, as else the original learning task would not have failed. That is, PI really has the capability to introduce new predicates missing in the original vocabulary. However, this capability comes at the price of the undecidability of the problem when to introduce a new predicate. In [STU1] we prove that it is undecidable whether a learning task $(E^\oplus, E^\ominus, B, L)$ fails in an unrestricted or weakly restricted Horn clause language L, that is whether L should be extended to make learning succeed.

The second class of languages for which PI is useful contains languages restricted to a fixed size by language parameters, schemes or size bounds. For each learning problem, these languages result in a finite hypothesis space. In this framework, new predicates mainly serve the task of extending the given fixed-size language without violating the specified parameters or schemes. They do the same job as shifts to a more general language as e.g. in CLINT [Rae92], increasing parameters as e.g. for ij-determinacy [MF90], or supplying more complex schemes. In the strict logical sense, most of these predicates are not necessary as they can be eliminated by unfold-operations. However, in contrast to the pure language shifts, new predicates allow additionally for expressing recursive subrelations as e.g. in example 3. Therefore, PI is a more powerful bias shift operation.

A special case of PI is the transformation of non-determinate background literals in functional form. It involves detecting dependencies between arguments of the literals, and restructuring the knowledge base accordingly. This kind of PI is employed in the context of inductive data engineering [Fla93], where a relational data base is restructured according to inductively detected attribute dependencies.

6 Conclusions

The central aim of PI in ILP is to extend the given vocabulary in case it is insufficient for the learning task. The utility of PI as bias shift operation depends on its prior utility for the current language bias. The theoretical results presented in this paper mark the boundaries of appropriatness for PI in ILP. Though they give no practical algorithms for efficiently deciding when PI is actual necessary, they indicate for which language biases it is useful at all.

Three classes of language biases can be identified with respect to the utility of PI. For function-free languages, PI can be proved as useless. These languages are restricted so strongly that PI cannot increase their expressiveness. Only allowing negation by failure leads to a useful form of PI, the so-called closed world specialisation [BM92].

For unrestricted or weakly restricted Horn clause languages, PI is useful and really capable of introducing predicates missing in the original language. However, inductive inference is unfeasible in these frameworks.

The remaining class of fixed-size languages allows for tractable induction procedures. Additionally, PI is useful both for shifting the language bias syntactically and extending the vocabulary with necessary new predicates. That is, for these languages PI integrates two different bias shift operations in one. The capabilities of PI when compared to changing the language parameters or supplying more complex schemes need to be explored further.

Furthermore, the utility of PI with respect to algorithmic biases evidenced in the work on constructive induction in propositional learning has to be studied separately. This might lead to more practical results that those in this paper.

Acknowledgements

This work has been supported by the European Community ESPRIT BRA 6020 ILP (Inductive Logic Programming).

References

[BM92]   Bain, M., Muggleton, S. (1992): *Non-Monotonic Learing* in S. Muggleton (ed): Inductive Logic Programming, Academic Press

[Bun90]   Buntine, W. (1990): *Constructive Induction in Definite Clause Logic*, draft

[Fla93]   Flach, P. A. (1993): *Predicate Invention in Inductive Data Engineering*, Proceedings of the European Conference on Machine Learning, Vienna

[Kie91]   Kietz, J., Wrobel, S. (1991): *Controlling the Complexity of Learning in Logic through Syntactic and Task-Oriented Models*, in S. Muggleton (ed): Inductive Logic Programming, Academic Press

[Kle52]   Kleene, S. C. (1952): *Finite Axiomatizability of Theories in the Predicate Calculus Using Additional Predicate Symbols* in S. C. Kleene: Two Papers on the Predicate Calculus, Memoirs of the American Mathematical Society No. 10

[Lin91]   Ling, C. X. (1991): *Inventing Necessary Theoretical Terms in Scientific Discovery and Inductive Logic Programming*, Report No. 302, Dept. of Computer Science, University of Western Ontario, London, Ontario

[Mug88]   Muggleton, S. (1988): *A Strategy for Constructing New Predicates in First Order Logic*, in Proceedings of the Third European Working Session on Learning, Pitman

[MB88]   Muggleton, S., Buntine, W. (1988): *Machine Invention of First-Order Predicates by Inverting Resolution*, Proceedings of the 5th International Conference on Machine Learning, Morgan Kaufman

[MF90]   Muggleton, S., Feng, C. (1990): *Efficient Induction of Logic Programs*, Proceedings of the 1st Conference on Algorithmic Learning Theory, Tokyo, OHMSHA

[Mug92]   Muggleton, S. (1992): *Inductive Logic Programming*, in S. Muggleton (ed): Inductive Logic Programming, Academic Press

[MSB92]   Muggleton, S., Srinivasan, A., Bain, M. (1992): *Compression, Significance and Accuracy*, in Proceedings of the Ninth International Machine Learning Conference, Morgan Kaufmann

[Qui90]   Quinlan, J. R. (1990): *Learning Logical Definitions from Relations*, Machine Learning 5

[Rae91]   De Raedt, L. (1992): *Interactive Theory Revision: an Inductive Logic Programming Approach*, Academic Press

[Rae92]   De Raedt, L., Bruynooghe, M. (1992): *Interactive Concept-Learning and Constructive Induction by Analogy*, Machine Learning 8(2)

[Rou91]   Rouveirol, C. (1991): *ITOU: Induction of First Order Theories*, in S. Muggleton (ed): Inductive Logic Programming, Academic Press

[Sha83]   Shapiro, E. Y. (1983): *Algorithmic Program Debugging*, MIT Press, Cambridge Mass.

[SMB92]   Srinivasan, A., Muggleton, S., Bain, M. (1992): *Distinguishing Exceptions from Noise in Non-Monotonic Learning*, in Proceedings of ILP'92, Tokyo

[STW93]   Stahl, I., Tausend, B., Wirth, R. (1993): *Two Methods for Improving Inductive Logic Programming Systems*, Proceedings of the European Conference on Machine Learning, Vienna

[STU1]   Stahl, I. (1993): *Predicate Invention in ILP – Decidability, Utility and Decision Criteria*, Deliverable STU1 of the ESPRIT BRA 6020 ILP, September 1993

[Sta93] Stahl, I. (1993): *Properties of Inductive Logic Programming in Function-Free Horn Logic*, this volume

[Tau92] Tausend, B. (1992): *Using and Adapting Schemes for the Induction of Horn Clauses*, ECAI-92 Workshop on Logical Approaches to Machine Learning, Vienna

[Wir89] Wirth, R. (1989): *Lernverfahren zur Vervollständigung von Hornklauselmengen durch inverse Resolution*, Dissertation, Universität Stuttgart, Institut für Informatik

[Wir91a] Wirth, R., O'Rorke, P. (1991): *Constraints on Predicate Invention* in Proceedings of the Eighth International Workshop on Machine Learning, Morgan Kaufmann

[Wro] Wrobel, S.: *Exploiting a Problem-Solving Context to Focus Concept Formation*, to appear in Machine Learning Journal

[YS91] Yardeni, E., Shapiro, E. (1991): A Type System for Logic Programs, *Journal of Logic Programming 10*.

Learning Problem-Solving Concepts
by Reflecting on Problem Solving

Eleni Stroulia and Ashok K. Goel

College of Computing, Georgia Institute of Technology
Atlanta, GA 30332-0280

Abstract. Learning and problem solving are intimately related: problem solving determines the knowledge requirements of the reasoner which learning must fulfill, and learning enables improved problem-solving performance. Different models of problem solving, however, recognize different knowledge needs, and, as a result, set up different learning tasks. Some recent models analyze problem solving in terms of generic tasks, methods, and subtasks. These models require the learning of problem-solving concepts such as new tasks and new task decompositions. We view reflection as a core process for learning these problem-solving concepts. In this paper, we identify the learning issues raised by the task-structure framework of problem solving. We view the problem solver as an abstract device, and represent how it works in terms of a structure-behavior-function model which specifies how the knowledge and reasoning of the problem solver results in the accomplishment of its tasks. We describe how this model enables reflection, and how model-based reflection enables the reasoner to adapt its task structure to produce solutions of better quality. The Autognostic system illustrates this reflection process.

1 Motivation and Background

That which is commonly known as "intelligence" is surely the result of the interaction of a great number of cognitive abilities such as motor control, vision, learning, problem solving, and language use, just to name a few. Yet most AI research does not fully exploit the constraints that these faculties impose on one another. For example, research on problem solving often assumes the existence of rich domain knowledge for solving complex problems but it typically ignores the issue the acquisition of the assumed knowledge. Similarly, research on learning often views the learner as an entity unto itself, and focuses on developing strategies to learn simple concepts without much regard to their usefulness in reasoning. For example, much of learning research has focused on the issue of acquisition of *domain concepts*, e.g., [32, 11, 20]. The task most commonly used for evaluating the products of concept learning has been classification. While the learning of new concepts may expand the range of objects a classification system may recognize, it has little or no effect on the *internal mechanism* of classification. Improving the classification mechanism requires the learning of *problem-solving concepts,* i.e. concepts that affect the problem-solving mechanism as opposed to domain concepts which simply refer to classes of objects and relations in the world.

When learning research has aimed towards improving the performance of a problem solver, it has adopted a narrow view of problem-solving. For example, some studies have investigated learning in the context of tasks such as game-playing [27], automatic programming [28], symbolic integration [22], and scheduling [21]. These systems view problem solving as search in a problem space. The search begins at either the initial or the goal state in the problem space, and ends with a sequence of operators that connects the two states. These systems assume the availability of a "complete" set of operators. The only type of information not completely specified is the heuristic rules for selecting the operators. In this framework, the only problem-solving concepts that the problem solver may learn are rules for selecting an appropriate operator to apply at a given state in the problem space. Since these systems can learn only one kind of concept, the impact of learning on problem solving is limited to improving the efficiency of the problem solver. Moreover, for realistically complex tasks, such as planning in a complex environment, it is unreasonable to assume a complete operator set; in such environments, it would be desirable that the system can learn new operators depending on the environmental structure and the task requirements.

Recent work on problem solving has led to a family of theories [6, 33, 19, 5, 29] that describe problem solving at a level higher than that of states, operators, heuristics etc. These theories analyze problem solving in terms of different kinds of generic tasks and generic methods. A task is specified in terms of the kinds of information it takes as input and gives as output. A method is characterized by the kinds of knowledge it uses, and the subtasks it sets up, when applied to some task. Different methods may use different kinds of knowledge, e.g., associative, episodic, or causal knowledge, and set up different subtasks for the same task.

These theories of problem solving use a richer vocabulary of problem-solving concepts. They admit different kinds of concept learning that go beyond learning heuristics for operator selection, for example, learning new tasks and new task decompositions. Note that since these theories posit several different kinds of problem-solving concepts, which play different roles in problem solving, they introduce the issue of what *kind* or kinds of concept to learn in addition to what concept to learn.

Despite the recent popularity of these theories of problem solving, relatively little work has been done on the learning of the problem solving concepts they postulate. We view *reflection* as a core process for recognizing the needs of problem solving, learning the knowledge that can fulfill these needs, and effectively integrating it in the current problem-solving process. We endow the problem solver with a model of its own task structure and with a process capable of monitoring its reasoning on a specific problem, assigning blame, upon failure, to some element in its task structure, and appropriately redesigning its task structure. In this paper, we sketch an architecture for reflective learning, describe a language for specifying the problem-solver's knowledge and reasoning, and discuss the process for performance-driven reflective learning as a model-based redesign task. We illustrate the learning process using an example from the Autognostic system, a reflective path planner.

2 Reflection for Concept Learning

A Perspective on Problem Solving We adopt Chandrasekaran's [1989] task structures as the framework for analyzing and modeling problem solving. A task consumes some type(s) of information as input and produces as output some other type(s) of information. A task may be accomplished by one or more methods, each of which may decompose the task into a set of simpler subtasks. A method is specified by the kinds of knowledge it uses, the subtasks it sets up, and the control it exercises over the processing of these subtasks. The subtasks into which a method decomposes a task can, in turn, be accomplished by other methods, or, if the appropriate knowledge is available, they may be solved directly. The task structure of a problem solver thus provides a recursive decomposition of its overall task in terms of methods and subtasks.

The tasks and subtasks in the task structure of a problem solver may be instances of generic tasks [4]. A generic task is a task instances of which can be encountered in several domains, such as classification and plan synthesis, and whose methods are applicable to all its instantiations.

A task, in our framework, is specified by the information it takes as input, the information it produces as output, a prototypical task of which it is an instance, and a set of conceptual relations between the input and output information. These conceptual relations constitute a partial description of the correct performance of this task. If the task is accomplished by a method, then the conceptual relations of its subtasks and the ordering relations that the method imposes over these subtasks constitute a partial description of a correct internal mechanism for this task.

The task structure of a problem solver is non-deterministic. Firstly, a task may be accomplished by more than one methods; if more than one method is applicable to a given task in the task structure, then the problem solver opportunistically selects a given method based on some criteria. Secondly, a method may itself be non-deterministic, in that it may specify only a partial ordering for the subtasks it sets up, and some subtasks may not be necessary under specific conditions.

Concept Learning Revisited The task-structure framework of problem solving identifies several problem-solving concepts, and gives rise to corresponding learning tasks, including the following:

1. the criteria for the applicability of a particular method for a given task,
2. the conditions which determine whether and when a subtask of a method is necessary for the progress of the problem solving, and
3. the conceptual relations between the types of information a task takes as input and produces as output.

Thus the products of concept learning may be of several different kinds and may result in different kinds of modifications to the problem-solving process. Learning the applicability criteria of a method to some task is roughly similar to learning heuristic rules for selecting among operators in the problem-solving-as-search framework. Learning the conditions under which to perform a subtask, and learning the conceptual relations between the input and output of a subtask, do not really have equivalents in the problem-solving-as-search framework. If, however, we were to paraphrase them in that framework, then, the former (learning the conditions under which a task needs to be performed in order to contribute to the progress of problem solving) would be roughly equivalent to learning when the application of an operator contributes to the progress towards the goal state, and the latter (learning the conceptual relations that a task imposes between its input and output) would be roughly equivalent to revising the preconditions and post-conditions of an operator or learning a new operator.

3 Reflective Concept Learning

The task-structure view of problem solving compounds the difficulty of concept learning because it raises the issue of deciding "what kind or kinds of concept to learn" in addition to the question of deciding "which concept to learn". In our work, we adopt reflection as the core process for learning problem-solving concepts. We view the reflection process as composed of three abilities:

1. recognizing the need for a new concept of a specific kind in the task structure,
2. identifying the specific concept to be integrated in the task structure, and
3. integrating the new concept so that it results in a valid modified task structure and improved performance.

To enable reflection, we need a well-defined language for representing the task structure of the problem solver. We have adapted the language of structure-behavior-function (SBF) models for describing how physical devices work [12] for this purpose. Adapting the SBF language for modeling how a problem solver works, we express tasks as transitions between information states: the input and output information states of a task describe the types of information that the task takes as input and produces as output correspondingly. Each information-transformation task is annotated by a set of conceptual relations between the task's input and output information, and a set of conditions under which its accomplishment contributes to the progress of problem solving. Moreover, each information transformation is annotated by a pointer to a prototypical task of which it is an instance, and a set of pointers to the methods that can be used to accomplish it. Methods are expressed as partially-ordered sequences of state transformations which specify in detail how they accomplish the task for which they are applicable. Each method in turn is annotated by a set of conditions under which it is applicable to the task. Tasks which are not decomposable by any methods point to the program modules that can directly accomplish them.

The comprehension of a problem solver of its own reasoning in terms of this SBF model enables the problem solver to improve its performance

1. by specifying a "road map" for problem solving which allows the problem solver to *monitor* the progress of its reasoning on a specific problem,
2. by specifying "correctness" criteria for the results of each of the problem-solver's subtasks, so that, when it fails, the problem solver can *assign blame* for its failure to these subtasks whose results are not consistent with their corresponding criteria, and
3. by guiding the problem solver to consistently *redesign* its own problem solving and thus improve its performance.

Monitoring When presented with a new problem, the problem solver uses the model of its reasoning to *monitor* its process for solving this problem. As it solves a given problem, the problem solver records which method it uses for a specific task, which of the resulting subtasks it performs, in which order, by which method, and their corresponding results. The model generates expectations regarding the information states the problem solver goes through as it solves the problem. Each information state in the problem solving should be related to the preceding one according to the conceptual relations of the task carrying out the transformation between them. Also, a task should be performed only when it contributes to the progress of the reasoning.

As the problem solver monitors its reasoning on a given problem, some of these expectations may fail. For example, a conceptual relation of some task may not hold true between the actual values of its input and output information. If, in spite of this failure, the problem solver produces an acceptable solution for the given problem, then the problem solver may recognize the need to modify its understanding of the conceptual relations of task that generated the failed expectations. That is, it may recognize the need to learn a new conceptual relation that can appropriately describe the transformation that this task imposes between its input and output. This is an instance of recognizing the need for learning a type-3 concept.

Another type of expectation failure that may occur during monitoring is that the information produced by some intermediate subtask may not get used by any other subtask. In this case, the problem solver may recognize the need to refine its understanding about the conditions under which the performance of this task contributes to the progress of problem solving. This is an instance of recognizing the need for learning a type-2 concept.

Blame Assignment Even if the problem solving proceeds without expectation failures, the problem solver may produce an incorrect or suboptimal solution. If the problem solver receives the correct solution as feedback from the world, then this too may present another opportunity for learning. In this case, the problem solver can use the record of its failed reasoning process, and the model of its problem solving to *assign blame* for the failure to some element(s) in its task structure and propose modifications which can potentially remedy the problem.

The task-structure view of problem solving gives rise to a taxonomy of learning tasks each one corresponding to a different type of potential cause of failure that the problem solver can identify [30]. In this paper we focus on the learning tasks that involve learning of a new problem-solving concept.

One possible cause for the failure of the problem solver to produce the desired solution to the given problem may be that it did not use the appropriate method to solve it. Often the applicability criteria of some methods may overlap. If the known applicability criteria do not enable the problem solver to discriminate between the methods, then it may choose one arbitrarily. As different methods decompose the overall task into different sets of subtasks, the sets of conceptual relations that describe the transformation of the input problem to the output solution differ from one method to another. Thus, in general, the solutions that each method produces are characterized by different properties. The properties and attributes of the desired solution may suggest that the problem solver should have been used some method, say, $M_{alternative}$, different from the one actually used, say M_{used}. In such a case, the problem solver may recognize that it should modify the applicability criteria of the available methods such that it gives precedence to $M_{alternative}$ over M_{used} in similar situations. This is an instance of recognizing the need for learning a type-1 concept.

Another possible cause for the failure of the problem solver to produce the desired solution may be that as it transforms its input information to produce a solution, it does not "pay attention" to the "right properties" of its problem domain. Often there may be enough information in the problem-solver's knowledge of the world to enable the production of the desired type of solutions. But the problem solver may produce an incorrect solution because it does not make use of the available knowledge. The problem-solver's model of its reasoning and knowledge may lead it to recognize the need for introducing a new subtask in the task structure, such that it uses the knowledge needed for the production of the desired solution type. In this case, the problem solver has to learn the conceptual relations that specify the new task. This is an instance of recognizing the need for learning a type-3 concept.

Redesign After having recognized the need for learning a problem-solving concept of a specific type, the problem solver must employ a learning strategy to actually learn the concept and subsequently *redesign* its task structure to integrate the new concept in it. In the cases of revising the conditions of a method's applicability to a task, or the conditions of a task's usefulness in problem solving, the integration of the new concept does not involve any non-local consequences to the task structure. However, in the case of introducing a new task in the task structure (type-3 concept learning), the consequences to the task structure are non-local. This is because the introduction of a new task implies modifications to the flow of control and information among the existing tasks in the task structure. The semantics of the SBF models can guide the problem solver in its modification process so that the result is a valid task structure as we illustrate below.

Evaluation of Learning There is no a priori guarantee that learning will result in an improved problem solver. However, learning can be evaluated through subsequent problem solving. If the problem that triggered the modification can now be solved and the appropriate solution produced, then this is strong evidence that indeed the modification was appropriate. If not, the problem solver may try other modifications or it may try to evaluate why the modification did not bring the expected results. The latter assumes a model of the reflection process: reflection is a reasoning task, and it too can be modeled in terms of SBF models just like any other task.

4 Router: A Case-Study Problem Solver

In our work, we use Router, [13], a path planning system, as a case-study problem solver. Router's task is to find a path from an initial location to a goal location in a physical space. Router was not developed specifically for the purposes of this work; thus, originally it did not have a model of its own problem solving. On top of Router, we have developed Autognostic which has a SBF model of Router's reasoning and which is also capable of the reflection process described above. Router and Autognostic together constitute a reflective reasoner and learner.

Figure 1 diagrammatically depicts the architecture we have developed for reflective learning. In this architecture, the reasoner has both reasoning and meta-reasoning capabilities. In Figure 1 tasks are depicted as solid-line, tilted boxes, knowledge is depicted as dashed-line boxes, control flow is shown by double arrows, input and output information flow is depicted by simple arrows, and access and use of knowledge by tasks is depicted by double-headed arrows.

At the reasoning level, Router has domain knowledge. It has a world model which contains knowledge about objects in the world and the relations between them. It also has a case memory which consists of experiences of solving specific problems in the world. Router knows two methods that can achieve this task: a model-based method, and a case-based method. When Router is presented with a problem, it chooses one of these methods based on a set of heuristic rules which evaluate their applicability and utility on the particular problem at hand. At the reasoning level the reasoner, Router, does not have explicit understanding of its knowledge or reasoning.

At the meta-reasoning level, however, the reasoner, Autognostic, understands Router's problem solving in terms of a SBF model. The SBF model of the problem-solver's reasoning captures the interdependencies between the different tasks it can perform, its problem-solving methods, and its knowledge. Autognostic understands that it knows two methods that can be used to achieve the path-planning task. Each one of these methods decomposes the overall problem-solving task in different sets of subtasks, and uses different types of knowledge. One method uses the world model and the other uses the case memory. The problem solver has also explicit knowledge about the ontology on which its world model and case memory are based and their respective organizations. The problem solver uses the knowledge it has at the meta-reasoning level to monitor its

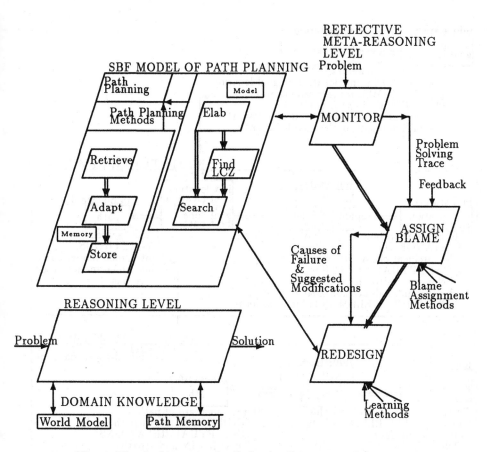

Fig. 1. The Architecture of a Reflective Reasoner and Learner

reasoning, assign blame to some element of its reasoning process it when it fails, redesign it, and thus learn and improve its performance.

Figure 2 depicts a part of the SBF model of Router's problem solving, more specifically a part of its model-based path-planning method. Since the example we discuss in this paper involves the model-based method only, we do not describe in detail Router's case-based method [14]. In the language of SBF models, problem-solving process is viewed as a sequence of transformations between information states. In Figure 2, each information state is depicted as a rectangular box, and contains the information available at the state; each state transformation is depicted by a double arrow, and is annotated by the description of the task which accomplishes the transformation.

Router model of its world is a hierarchically organized topographical model. The model contains knowledge about pathways, their directions and the intersections between them. The pathways are grouped into neighborhoods and the neighborhoods are organized in a space-subspace hierarchy. The higher-level neighborhoods contain knowledge of major pathways, and cover large spaces.

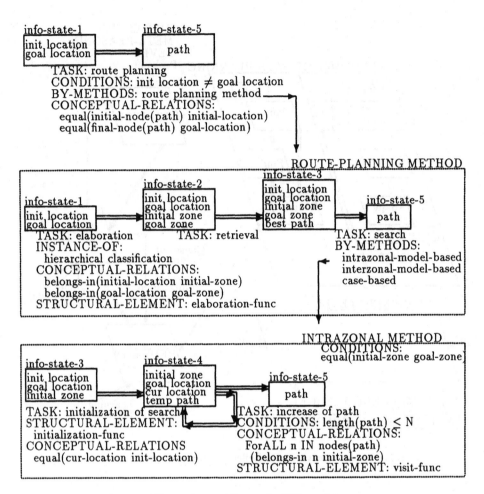

Fig. 2. Part of Router's SBF model

Each neighborhood gets decomposed into several neighborhoods at the immediately lower level. These lower-level neighborhoods contain knowledge of minor pathways but cover spaces smaller than the neighborhood that subsumes them.

When Router is presented with a problem, it first finds the neighborhoods of the initial and goal intersections, `initial-zone` and `goal-zone` correspondingly, with the `elaboration` subtask. Then, the `retrieval` subtask searches in Router's path memory, for a path that is close to the current problem. The conceptual relations of the `retrieval` subtask specify that the retrieved path should connect some intersection in the `initial-zone` to some intersection in the `goal-zone`, to be similar enough to the current problem. If the two problem intersections belong in the same neighborhood, Router may use the `intrazonal-model-based` method to `search` for a path between the two given locations. The `intrazonal-model-based` search method is essentially a breadth-

296

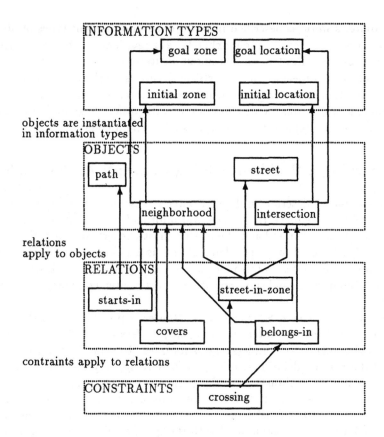

Fig. 3. Fragment of Autognostic's meta-model of Router's world knowledge

first search within the common neighborhood of the two intersections. If the two intersections do not belong in a single neighborhood, Router has two other options for solving the **search** subtask: it can either perform a hierarchical search its neighborhood organization, **interzonal-model-based** method, or it can use the path it retrieved from its memory, as the basis for solving the current problem (**case-based** method). The SBF model of the **intrazonal-model-based** method, is shown in the bottom dashed-line box, in Figure 2. Initially, Router sets up its **current-location** to be the **initial-location**, and initializes its **temporary-path** to contain only this intersection. Then, by repeating the **increase-of-path** subtask, it incrementally adds additional intersections to the **temporary-path**. This subtask is repeated under the condition that the length of the temporary path does not exceed N. If, at some point, Router reaches the **goal-location** Router assigns the value of the **temporary-path** to the **path** and returns it as the desired solution.

Figure 3 depicts part of Autognostic's meta-model of Router's world knowledge. Router's world is described in terms of several different types of **objects**, such as **intersections, neighborhoods, streets** and **paths**. The **types of information** that Router reasons about in its route-planning process are instances of these objects. The objects in Router's world are related through **relations**, such as **belongs-in** which relates intersections to neighborhoods, and **covers** which relates neighborhoods with other neighborhoods. Finally, some relations are related to each other with domain **constraints**.

5 Learning a Problem-Solving Concept: An Example

In this section we describe in detail Router's reasoning for a specific problem. In this problem, feedback from the world informs Router that there is a better solution to the problem at hand. Thus Autognostic reflects on Router's reasoning using the SBF model of its problem solving as a guide, identifies the cause of the failure and proposes to introduce a new task to Router's task structure. We discuss the adaptation and show how it improves Router's planning performance.

Monitoring the Problem Solving Process Router is presented with the problem of connecting *(10th & center)* with *(dalney & ferst-1)*. Autognostic monitors Router's planning process and generates its trace. The trace is a partial instantiation of the SBF model of Router's problem solving; only the part of the model which explains the subtasks actually performed during the specific problem-solving process gets instantiated. For this example, the trace is the instantiation of the part of the SBF model depicted in Figure 2, where each one of the different types of information is instantiated with the specific values produced during the particular planning session.

Router uses its **route-planning** method to solve the task, and sets up its corresponding subtasks. The **elaboration** subtask produces as output $z1$ as the value of both the **initial-zone** and the **goal-zone**. The **retrieval** task returns no path similar enough to the current problem from Router's memory. Since its applicability test, i.e., equality of the initial and goal zones is true, Router chooses to solve the **search** task with **intrazonal-model-based** method. The repeated execution of the **increase-of-path** subtask produces the path *(center 10th East atlantic) (10th atlantic South ferst-1) (atlantic ferst-1 East dalney)* which is returned as the output **path** of the overall **route-planning** task.

Assigning Blame for Producing a Suboptimal Solution The path that Router produced is correct. However it is suboptimal, because it is longer than the path *(center 10th East dalney) (10th dalney South ferst-1)* which is presented to Router as feedback.

Autognostic uses the feedback, the trace of Router's reasoning on the specific problem, and the SBF model of Router's problem solving, to identify the cause of its failure. This model-based method for blame-assignment searches through the task structure of Router's problem solving, and the search is guided by the feedback and the problem-solving trace.

The blame-assignment process first identifies the highest task in the task structure whose output is the information for which the problem solver produced an undesirable value. In this example, it identifies the route-planning task because this is the highest task producing the suboptimal path. The process then uses the conceptual relations of the task under inspection to investigate whether the desired value given as feedback could have been produced by the task. If the desired output value and the input of this task are verified by the conceptual relations, then the desired value could indeed have been produced by the task under inspection. The blame-assignment method thus infers that the reason why this value was not actually produced must lie within the internal mechanism of the task, that is, it must be due to some of the subtasks which were performed to accomplish the task under inspection. From the trace of the problem solving, the blame-assignment process infers which method was actually used to solve this task, and, as above focuses the assignment of the blame to the subtask which produced the undesired value. In this example, the blame-assignment process focuses initially to route-planning and subsequently to increase-of-path.

If at some point, the conceptual relations of a task do not hold true between the input of this task and the desired value, then Autognostic tries to infer alternative input values which would satisfy the failing conceptual relations. This is possible when the task's input information is not part of the overall problem specification, in this example { initial-location goal-location }, but is produced by some intermediate task in the task structure. Autognostic is able to infer alternative values for the input of the task under inspection in two ways: (a) if the failing conceptual relation is a domain relation exhaustively described in an association table, (Autognostic's meta-level understanding of Router's domain relations, 3, includes a pointer to the data structure holding the relation's association table), then Autognostic can search for the inverse mappings; alternatively (b) Autognostic may know the domain of the desired value (Autognostic's meta-level understanding of Router's domain objects, 3, includes a pointer to the data structure holding the set of the instances of this object known to Router) and it can try to find these values in the domain that would satisfy the conceptual relations of the task. If Autognostic infers an alternative value for some intermediate type of information, the focus of the blame-assignment process shifts to identifying why this value was not produced.

In this example, the conceptual relation of the increase-of-path fails for the desired value for path and the actual input value for the information initial-zone. The relation belongs-in is a domain relation, and from its association table, Autognostic infers that the value of initial-zone should have been za. Thus, the blame-assignment process focuses on identifying why za was not produced as the value for initial-zone.

If the blame-assignment process reaches a leaf task (that is, a task not further decomposable by a method) whose input is part of the overall problem specification, then there are two possible situations: the desired output value and the actual input values may or may not be consistent with the conceptual relations of that task. In the latter case, Autognostic infers that another method should probably have been used for the production of the desired value. If there is no alternative method known, then this is an indication that the role of the task under inspection in the task structure, that is its conceptual relations, should be reevaluated.

On the other hand, a leaf task which can produce two alternative values, both of them consistent with its conceptual relations, with one of them however leading to the desired overall problem solution and the other leading to an unacceptable solution, is an indication that the task structure is not sufficiently tailored to producing the right kind of solutions.

```
ASSIGN-BLAME-SUBOPTIMAL-VALUE(path,
                    actual value (center 10th East atlantic)
                                 (10th atlantic South ferst-1)
                                 (atlantic ferst-1 east dalney)
                    desired value (center 10th East dalney)
                                  (10th dalney South ferst-1) )
PRODUCED(path) = { increase of path }
CONCEPTUAL-RELATIONS(increase of path):
    ForAll n IN nodes(path) belongs-in(n initial-zone)
    Conceptual-Relations hold TRUE for actual values of path and initial-zone
    Conceptual-Relations DO NOT hold TRUE for desired value of path
                                and actual value of initial-zone
INFERRING ALTERNATIVE VALUE FOR initial-zone
    ForAll n IN nodes(desired path) belongs-in(za) ⇒
                            desired value(initial-zone) = za


ASSIGN-BLAME-SUBOPTIMAL-VALUE(initial-zone,
                    actual value z1
                    desired value za )
PRODUCED(initial-zone) = {elaboration }
CONCEPTUAL-RELATIONS(elaboration):
    belongs-in(initial-intersection initial-zone)
    Conceptual-Relations hold TRUE for actual values of initial-zone
                                and initial-intersection
    Conceptual-Relations hold TRUE for desired value of initial-zone
                                and actual value of initial-intersection

⟹ elaboration can produce either za or z1 for value of initial-zone
```

Fig. 4. Blame Assignment using the SBF model of Router's Path-Planning process

Part of the blame-assignment process for this example is shown in detail in Figure 4. From the desired value of the **path** and the conceptual relation of the producing subtask **increase-of-path**, Autognostic infers that the value of the information **initial-zone** should have been za. Both the actual z1 and the alternative *za* values of this information meet the conceptual relation of its producing subtask **elaboration**. At this point, Autognostic knows that the **elaboration** subtask can potentially produce either *za* or *z1* as values for the **initial-zone**, because the domain relation **belongs-in(intersection zone)** is not one-to-one.

In this case, Autognostic has two possible modifications actions to choose from: (i) modification to domain relation, that is deletion from the domain relation of the unacceptable mapping, so that it allows only the preferred mapping, and (ii) insertion of selection task, in order to enable the problem solver to select the preferred one mapping when multiple ones are possible. We discuss the first adaptation in [30]; in this paper we describe how the insertion of a selection task affects Router's problem solving.

Redesigning the Problem Solver: Inserting a Selection Task The motivation behind inserting a selection task after the elaboration task in Router's task structure is to enable Router to reason about the two possible values for **initial-zone** and select the most appropriate one. This way, Autognostic can "tailor" Router's task structure towards producing the kind of solutions represented by the feedback.

The SBF model of the problem-solver's reasoning explicitly specifies the ontology of the problem-solver's domain. For each type of information that its tasks consume and produce, the SBF model specifies what type of world object it is. Moreover, for each type of world object, among other things, the model specifies the domain relations which are applicable to it. Autognostic uses this knowledge, along with the specific values (actual and preferred) of the information type to be selected, to discover a relation which can be used to differentiate between these values. If there is such a relation, then Autognostic can use it as a conceptual relation for the new task to be inserted in the task structure.

In our example, Autognostic knows that one domain relation applicable to neighborhoods is the **covers** relation. Given the actual and the alternative values for the **initial-zone**, *z1* and *za* correspondingly, Autognostic notices that *covers(z1 za)*. It then hypothesizes that this can be used as a differentiating criterion between possible alternative values for the **initial-zone**. Thus it inserts in the set of subtasks of the **route-planning** method, after **elaboration**, the **selection-after-elaboration** subtask, with input **intermediate-initial-zone**, (a new information type produced by the elaboration subtask, which does not produce anymore "the" initial zone but all the possible alternatives) output **initial-zone**, and conceptual relation **covers(intermediate-initial-zone initial-zone)**. The new task has as a goal, given a specific path-planning problem, to reason about the possible values of the **initial-zone** in the context of this problem, and select the one which is covered by the rest of them, that is the most specific one.

In more general terms, a newly inserted task in the problem-solver's task structure has as a goal to reason about the possible values of some type of information in the context of a specific problem and select the most appropriate one for the given problem. Thus, the selection-task insertion implies the discovery of a characteristic property of the information type to be selected which will enable the problem solver to discriminate among the possible values of this information, and select the most appropriate one for a given problem. In our example, selecting the most specific value for the `initial-zone` results in the selection of a low-level neighborhood. Given that lower-level neighborhoods describe smaller spaces in more detail, Router's search becomes very local, and the two problem locations are connected through small pathways instead of major ones, which, in general, results in shorter paths.

In order for the problem solving task structure to be consistent after this modification, Autognostic needs to perform some more modifications in addition to the insertion of the `selection-after-elaboration` task: (i) introduce a new type of information `intermediate-initial-zone` to hold the intermediate results of the `elaboration` task and to be the input of the new task, (ii) create a function to carry out the transformation of the new task, (iii) change (reprogram) the function `elaboration-func` to actually return appropriately a list of values instead of a single one, (iv) modify the description of `initial-zone` in the SBF model to describe as producing task the `selection-after-elaboration` task, and (v) modify the `route-planning` method to include the new task after the `elaboration` task. Autognostic can autonomously perform modifications (i) (ii) and (iv) but not (iii), which is currently performed by a human programmer, at the suggestion of Autognostic.

Evaluating the modified Problem Solver After Router's process is modified, Autognostic evaluates the appropriateness of the revision by presenting Router with the problem that led to failure before. As Router solves the same problem once again Autognostic goes back again to its monitoring task. In our example, Router produces the desired path this time, so the modification can be evaluated as successful. Had Router failed, once again, to deliver the desired path, Autognostic would have another learning opportunity, and it would repeat its blame-assignment-and-learning task.

6 Related and Further Research

Reflection has received much attention in psychological research on metacognition. The main results of this research are that reflection upon own's problem solving enables the problem solver to select particular strategies in particular situations [9], reformulate the course of its own "thinking" to improve performance and meet the varying demands of the task at hand [2], and improve its performance capabilities by monitoring and careful evaluation of its own thinking [17]. Our work on Autognostic is inspired by these results and is consistent with them.

In parallel with research in psychology, AI researchers recognized the usefulness of meta-knowledge, that is knowledge about what they know and how they reason, in intelligent systems [3]. Many AI systems have used descriptions of their own problem solving for several different tasks. These descriptions have taken a variety of forms depending on the view they adopt for problem-solving and on the task they are used for. Teiresias [7, 8], for example, views problem solving as recursive rule activation. It models its rule base in terms of meta-rules that describe which rules can be used as evidence for or against inferences on domain objects. Teiresias uses its meta-rules to guide the domain expert in identifying erroneous rules in the rule base and acquiring new ones.

Castle and Meta-Aqua are recent systems that use reflection for failure-drive learning. Castle [10] views problem solving as a sequence of interacting components. For each of its components it has a description of its correct performance and a set of intended behavior properties which are important to the effectiveness of this component in the overall architecture. Castle's components are similar to Autognostic's tasks. However, Castle's functional architecture is not hierarchical (a problem solver is a sequence of components) and deterministic (it uses a single sequence of components) which limits its expressiveness. In addition, this limits Castle's blame-assignment task to finding a fault in a single linear component sequence. Moreover, Castle lacks the concept of generic (prototypical) tasks which enables Autognostic to transfer the results of its learning from one point of its task structure to another. Meta-Aqua [26] views understanding as a cycle of explaining its input using XPs, cases and domain knowledge, and modifying its knowledge when anomalies are encountered. It uses a set of special explanation patterns, IMXPs (introspective meta XPs), to parse its trace of reasoning and recognize reasoning failures. Unlike Autognostic, Meta-Aqua does not have explicit descriptions for the "correct" behavior of its reasoning elements (i.e. XP-instantiation, case-interpretation).

NOOS [25] views reasoning as transfer from precedents and uses reflection for learning by memorization of episodes. In NOOS reasoning and learning are modeled in a framework similar to task structures. MAX [18] uses a explicit description of a robot's capabilities to enable deliberative, and consequently more effective, integration of these capabilities. It focuses on self-monitoring rather than recovery from failure.

Failure recovery analysis [15] is another technique for planner modification. It uses statistical analysis of long traces of the planner actions to infer correlation between action patterns and failures. This technique is more appropriate to rapidly changing domains where planning tends to be more reactive to the environment and less deliberative, and where there is no good understanding of the interactions between the different planning strategies.

Functional models, similar to SBF models, have also been used for software program verification [1], knowledge-base validation [31], and student modeling in the context of a tutoring system [16].

Both Router and Autognostic are operational systems. We have evaluated Autognostic for several learning tasks in Router's task domain, for example, the acquisition of new world knowledge, certain kinds of reorganization of the world knowledge, and some kinds of modifications to the task structure along the lines described above. In order to evaluate the generality of Autognostic's language for describing how a problem solver works and its process for reflective reasoning, we are presently using it in the task domain of engineering design. In the future, we are interested in validating our process-model of reflection against existing psychological data, integrating Autognostic with an autonomous robot and investigating the acquisition of SBF models from source code.

7 Conclusions

We believe that theories of intelligence that artificially divorce learning and problem solving are often under-constrained. Problem solving determines the knowledge needs of the reasoner which learning must fulfill, and learning enables improved problem-solving performance - improvement in problem-solving performance is one way of evaluating the quality of learning. However, different models of problem solving recognize different kinds of knowledge needs, and, as a result, set up different learning tasks and enable different kinds of performance improvement.

The task-structure framework of problem solving gives rise to three different types of problem-solving concepts:

1. the criteria for the applicability of a particular method for a given task,
2. the conditions which determine whether and when a subtask of a method is necessary for the progress of the problem solving, and
3. the conceptual relations between the types of information a task takes as input and produces as output.

We view reflection as a core process for learning these problem-solving concepts. The capability of reflection raises, itself, a set of issues:

1. How to assign the blame for the undesirable properties of the overall problem-solving behavior to some element of the problem-solver's reasoning
2. How to modify elements of the problem-solver's reasoning while maintaining its overall consistency
3. How to represent the elements of the problem-solver's reasoning and the interactions between them, in order to support the previous two tasks, and in such a way, that it is possible to model problem solvers with complex hierarchical, multi-strategy reasoning capabilities

Our work has led us to identify some types of knowledge which must be captured in a framework for modeling problem solving. Such a framework should describe:

1. the subtasks that the problem solver can accomplish and their information needs,
2. the alternative strategies which can potentially accomplish the overall task of the problem solver, and the information and control interactions of the subtasks these strategies consist of
3. the ontology on which the problem-solver's domain knowledge is based

We adapted the language of structure-behavior-function (SBF) models for specifying the functioning of a physical device to develop a modeling framework which satisfies the above knowledge needs. The SBF model enables a reasoner to monitor its problem solving, and, upon failure, to assign blame to some element (subtask or domain knowledge) in its task structure and redesign it appropriately. In this paper, we showed how this process enables the problem solver to

1. recognize the need for a new concept of a specific kind in the task structure,
2. identify the specific concept to be integrated in the task structure, and
3. integrate the new concept so that it results in a valid modified task structure and improved performance.

In addition to improving problem-solving efficiency, which is the general result of learning problem-solving concepts of the first and second kinds, learning concepts of the third kind enables the reasoner to tailor the problem-solving mechanisms to produce solutions of better quality.

Acknowledgements

This work has been supported by the National Science Foundation (research grant IRI-92-10925), the Office of Naval Research (research contract N00014-92-J-1234), and the Advanced Projects Research Agency. In addition, Stroulia's work has been supported by an IBM graduate fellowship.

References

1. D. Allemang: Understanding Programs as Devices, PhD Thesis, The Ohio State University (1990)
2. L. Baker, A.L. Brown: Metacognitive skills of reading. In: D. Pearson (ed.): A Handbook of reading research, New York: Longman (1984)
3. A. Barr: Meta-Knowledge and Cognition. Proceedings of the Sixth International Joint Conference on AI 31:33 (1979)
4. B. Chandrasekaran: Towards a functional architecture for intelligence based on generic information processing tasks. In Proceedings of Tenth International Joint Conference on Artificial Intelligence, 1183-1192, Milan (1987)
5. B. Chandrasekaran: Task Structures, Knowledge Acquisition and Machine Learning. Machine Learning 4:341-347 (1989)
6. W.J. Clancey: Heuristic Classification, Artificial Intelligence 27:289:350 (1985)
7. R. Davis: Interactive transfer of expertise: Acquisition of new inference rules, Artificial Intelligence 12:121-157 (1977)
8. R. Davis: Meta-Rules: Reasoning about Control. Artificial Intelligence 15:179-222 (1980)
9. J.H. Flavell: First discussant's comments: What is memory development the development of? Human Development 14:272-278 (1971)
10. M. Freed, B. Krulwich, L. Birnbaum, G. Collins: Reasoning about performance intentions. In Proceedings of the Fourteenth Annual Conference of the Cognitive Science Society, 7-12 (1992)

11. D. Fisher, M. Pazzani: Computational Models of Concept Learning. In D.H. Fisher, M.J. Pazzani, and P. Langley (eds.): Concept Formation: Knowledge and Experience in Unsupervised Learning. Morgan Kaufmann. (1991)

12. A. Goel: Integration of Case-Based Reasoning and Model-Based Reasoning for Adaptive Design Problem Solving, PhD Thesis, The Ohio State University (1989)

13. A. Goel, T. Callantine, M. Shankar, B. Chandrasekaran: Representation, Organization, and Use of Topographic Models of Physical Spaces for Route Planning. In Proceedings of the Seventh IEEE Conference on AI Applications. 308-314, IEEE Computer Society Press (1991)

14. A. Goel, T. Callantine: An Experience-Based Approach to Navigational Route Planning. In Proceedings of the IEEE/RSJ International Conference on Intelligent Robotics and Systems (1992)

15. A. Howe: Analyzing Failure Recovery to Improve Planner Design. In Proceedings of the Tenth National Confrence on AI, 387-392 (1992)

16. K. Johnson: Exploiting a Functional Model of Problem Solving for Error Detection in Tutoring, PhD Thesis, The Ohio State University (1993)

17. R.H. Kluwe: Cognitive Knowledge and Executive Control: Metacognition. In D. R. Griffin (ed.): Animal Mind - Human Mind. Springer-Verlag, Berlin (1982)

18. D.R. Kuokka: The Deliberative Integration of Planning, Execution, and Learning, Carnegie Mellon, Computer Science, Technical Report CMU-CS-90-135 (1990)

19. J. McDermott: Preliminary steps toward a taxonomy of problem-solving methods, In Sandra Marcus (ed.): Automating Knowledge Acquisition for Expert Systems, Kluwer Academic Publishers (1988)

20. R.S. Michalski: Inferential learning theory as a basis for multi-strategy adaptive learning. In R.S. Michalski and G. Tecuci (eds.): Proceedings of the First International Workshop on Multistrategy Learning, 3-18, Harpers Ferry, WV (1991)

21. S. Minton: Qualitative results concerning the utility of explanation-based learning. Artificial Intelligence 42:363-392 (1990)

22. T.M. Mitchell, P.E. Utgoff, B. Nudel, R.B. Banerji Learning problem-solving heuristics through practice. In Proceedings of the Seventh International Joint Conference on AI 127-134 (1981)

23. T. Mitchell, J. Allen, P. Chalasani, J. Cheng, O. Etzioni, M. Ringuette, J. Schlimmer: Theo: A Framework for Self-Improving Systems. In K. VanLehn (ed.): Architectures for Intelligence, Lawrence Erlbaum (1989)

24. J. Piaget: Biology and Knowledge. University of Chicago Press (1971)

25. E. Plaza, J.L. Arcos: Reflection and Analogy in Memory-based Learning. In R. S. Michalski and G. Tecuci (eds.): Proceedings of the Second International Workshop on Multistrategy Learning (1993)

26. A. Ram, M.T. Cox: Introspective Reasoning Using Meta-Explanations for Multistrategy Learning. In R. S. Michalski and G. Tecuci (eds.): Machine Learning: A Multistrategy Approach IV. Morgan Kaufmann, San Mateo, CA (1992)

27. A. Samuel: Some studies in machine learning using the game of checkers. IBM Journal of R&D. (1959) Reprinted in Feigenbaum and Feldman (eds.): Computers and Thought (1963)

28. J.G. Sussman: A Computational Model of Skill Acquisition, American Elsevier, New York, (1975)

29. L. Steels: Components of Expertise. AI Magazine 11:30-49 (1990).

30. E. Stroulia, A. Goel: Functional Representation and Reasoning for Reflective Systems. Applied Artificial Intelligence: An International Journal (to appear). (1993)

31. M. Weintraub: An Explanation-Based Approach to Assigning Credit, PhD Thesis, The Ohio State University (1991)
32. P. Winston: Learning New Principles from Precedents and Exercises. Artificial Intelligence 19 (1982)
33. B.J. Wielinga, A.Th. Schreiber, J.A. Breuker: KADS: A modelling approach to knowledge engineering. In Knowledge Acquisition 4(1). Special issue "The KADS approach to knowledge engineering" (1992)

Existence and Nonexistence of Complete Refinement Operators

Patrick R. J. van der Laag[1,2] and Shan-Hwei Nienhuys-Cheng[1]

[1] Department of Computer Science, Erasmus University of Rotterdam,
P.O.Box 1738, 3000 DR Rotterdam, the Netherlands
[2] Tinbergen Institute

Abstract. Inductive Logic Programming is a subfield of Machine Learning concerned with the induction of logic programs. In Shapiro's Model Inference System – a system that infers theories from examples – the use of downward *refinement operators* was introduced to walk through an ordered search space of clauses. Downward and upward refinement operators compute specializations and generalizations of clauses respectively. In this article we present the results of our study of *completeness and properness* of refinement operators for an *unrestricted search space* of clauses ordered by *θ-subsumption*. We prove that locally finite downward and upward refinement operators that are both complete and proper for unrestricted search spaces ordered by θ-subsumption do not exist. We also present a complete but improper upward refinement operator. This operator forms a counterpart to Laird's downward refinement operator with the same properties.

1 Introduction

Inductive Logic Programming (ILP) is a subfield of machine learning concerned with the induction of logic programs that are consistent with examples of an unknown concept, i.e. programs that can derive all positive examples and none of the negative ones. Within ILP, generalization and specialization of theories and clauses play important roles.

Whereas logical implication between theories or clauses are conceptually most desirable, θ-subsumption, a weaker version of it, is widely used since it is more manageable and we use it as our notion of generality w.r.t. which we study refinement. Clause C *θ-subsumes* clause D if there is a substitution $θ$ such that $Cθ \subseteq D$, where C and D are represented as sets of literals. If C θ-subsumes D and D θ-subsumes C then C and D are called *(subsume) equivalent*.

Shapiro [15] has introduced the use of downward refinement operators in model inference. A *downward refinement operator* $ρ$ can be used to derive a set of specializations of a clause C, denoted by $ρ(C)$. We also consider *upward refinement operators*, denoted by $δ$, that return sets of generalizations. In our opinion, ideal refinement operators are *locally finite*, *complete* and, less important, *proper* for search spaces of clauses that are not restricted beforehand. Local finiteness means that $ρ(C)$ or $δ(C)$ is finite and computable. Properness means that C is not equivalent with any element of $\rho(C)$ or $\delta(C)$, and completeness that every proper specialization or generalization of a clause can be found.

Although θ-subsumption is simpler and easier to understand than logical implication, there are still some simple looking but unanswered questions related to refinement w.r.t. θ-subsumption. They will be answered in this article.

1. Can we define locally finite, complete and proper downward or upward refinement operators for unrestricted search spaces ordered by θ-subsumption?
2. If not, can we define locally finite and complete downward or upward refinement operators for such search spaces if we drop the condition of properness?

The following example illustrates the problems of completeness and properness of refinement operators for unrestricted search spaces.

Example 1. Consider the following clauses that represent that node X is in a cycle of length 3 and 1 respectively:

$$C = cycle(X) \leftarrow con(X, Y), con(Y, Z), con(Z, X)$$
$$D = cycle(X) \leftarrow con(X, X)$$

Then clause C θ-subsumes clause D as can be verified by the substitution $\{Y/X, Z/X\}$. A downward refinement operator like Laird's ρ_0 [7] can derive D from C in two refinement steps: applying the variable unifications $\{Y/Z\}$ and $\{Z/X\}$. We say that there is a ρ_0-*chain* from C to D via E.

$$E = cycle(X) \leftarrow con(X, X), con(X, Z), con(Z, X) \in \rho_0(C)$$
$$D' = cycle(X) \leftarrow con(X, X), con(X, X), con(X, X) \in \rho_0(E) \subseteq \rho_0^2(C)$$

In ILP, clauses are usually interpreted as sets of literals, hence the duplicate literals in D' can be removed to get D. When we want to derive C from D using an upward refinement operator, anti-unification of variables in D can only result in C if we first duplicate the literal $con(X, X)$ in D twice. Note that the clauses D and E are subsume equivalent. Still it seems useful to derive E from D first, since it can be used to derive C later on. We will prove that this kind of equivalent refinement steps are necessary for completeness.

In this example, two literal duplications were sufficient to derive C. But how many duplications are necessary to derive other clauses in an unrestricted search space, for example cycles of arbitrary length n? Even if we drop the condition of properness, problems with local finiteness of a complete upward refinement operator arise if the required number of literal duplications cannot be determined.

The results in this article provide a negative answer to Question 1. We prove that complete and proper refinement operators for unrestricted search spaces ordered by θ-subsumption do not exist.

Question 2 is already partly answered by Laird's [7] improper, complete downward refinement operator for unrestricted sets of clauses. In this article we complete the affirmative answer by defining an upward counterpart to Laird's downward refinement operator. We will show that the number of required literal duplications in upward refinement is finite and computable. Using this observation we will come to our positive result,

In practice these results imply that under the restriction of local finiteness and completeness, any attempt to modify an improper refinement operator into a proper one or to construct a new proper refinement operator is doomed to fail.

Related work. Refinement operators for clauses ordered by θ-subsumption are also described by Shapiro [15], Laird [7], and Ling and Dawes [9]. Shapiro intended to define a downward refinement operator for finite search spaces such that every reduced clause was derivable from the empty clause. We have shown that his operator did not satisfy this weak completeness property[3] and proposed another proper and complete downward refinement operator for finite search spaces of reduced clauses [6]. Laird's modified version of Shapiro's downward refinement operator is complete but improper for unrestricted search spaces as will be discussed in Section 4. Ling and Dawes have proposed an upward refinement operator for clauses that is, using our definitions, neither complete nor proper and operates on finite search spaces. It lacks the, in our opinion vital (cf. Example 1), ability of increasing the number of literals in generalization. In [12], the authors and Leon van der Torre presented a deconstruction of logical implication that resulted in six downward and upward refinement operators for finite search spaces ordered by six increasingly strong orderings. In this last article the use of the substitution and set ordering to define refinement operators for the θ-subsumption ordering was introduced. This approach will also be taken in Section 5, in which we develop our complete upward refinement operator for unrestricted search spaces. This last refinement operator is presented before as a working paper in [5].

The difference between θ-subsumption and logical implication between clauses can be characterized by self-resolution. When a clause is resolved $n-1$ times with itself then the resulting clause is called an n-th power of the original clause. The original clause is also called an n-th root of the resulting clause [10]. Operators that compute n-th powers and roots of a clause can be used to extend downward and upward refinement operators for θ-subsumption to logical implication. For example, the complete upward refinement operator for θ-subsumption that will be presented in this article becomes complete for logical implication when we incorporate Idestam-Almquist's [1] *expansions* of clauses. Incomplete but more efficient operators that compute n-th roots of clauses are described in [2] and [8].

Outline of the article. In Section 2 we give some basic definitions concerning orderings and refinement operators. In Section 3 we prove the nonexistence of complete and proper refinement operators for unrestricted search spaces ordered by θ-subsumption. In Section 4 we briefly discuss Laird's complete downward refinement operator for such search spaces. A complete upward refinement operator will be defined in three steps in Section 5. Finally, in Section 6, we will present our conclusions and suggest some future research directions.

---

[3] This incompleteness is described independently by Niblett [11]

2 Notation and Definitions

2.1 Notation

Given a language of first order logic $\mathcal{L}$ with finitely many function and predicate symbols we use the following notation. Clauses are denoted by $C, D, \ldots$, function symbols by f, g, constants by a, b, predicate symbols by p, q, r and literals by L, M. All these symbols can occur with subscripts.

In this article we make an explicit distinction between the representation of a clause as a set and as a sequence of literals. This is necessary since we need to describe the operation of duplicating a literal in Section 5. In the four preceding sections the difference is not important. Whenever we say 'clause C' we mean a *sequence* of literals: $C = L_1, \ldots, L_m \leftarrow M_1, \ldots, M_n$.

The *set* representation is common in ILP and will, in this article, sometimes be used to facilitate definitions. By writing $\dot{C}$ we mean that clause C is considered as a set of literals and thus the internal ordering and repetition of literals play no role. For example, the clauses

$C = even(X) \leftarrow odd(Y), odd(Y), plus(Y, Y, X)$, and
$D = even(X) \leftarrow plus(Y, Y, X), odd(Y)$

have the same set representation

$\dot{C} = \dot{D} = \{even(X), \neg plus(Y, Y, X), \neg odd(Y)\}$.

All definitions and properties of refinement operators in this article will be described in terms of general first order clauses but they can easily be adapted for (definite) Horn-clauses.

2.2 Definitions

In the following definitions S can be any set of clauses and $\succeq$ can be any ordering.

Given two literals L and M, we use the following notions:

- L and M are called *compatible* iff they have the same predicate name and sign [13].
- A literal is called *most general w.r.t. a clause* C iff it contains only distinct variables as arguments that do not occur in C [15].

Given a set of clauses S and clauses $C, D, E \in S$, we use the following notions:

- S is called *unrestricted* iff all clauses of some language $\mathcal{L}$ are in it.
- A binary relation $\succeq$ on S is called a *quasi-ordering* on S iff it is reflexive $(C \succeq C)$ and transitive $(C \succeq D$ and $D \succeq E$ imply $C \succeq E)$. For every quasi-ordering $\succeq$ we can define an *equivalence* relation $\sim$ by $C \sim D$ iff $C \succeq D$ and $D \succeq C$.
- Quasi-ordering $\succeq_1$ is *stronger* than $\succeq_2$ if $C \succeq_2 D$ implies $C \succeq_1 D$. If also for some C, D, $C \not\succeq_2 D$ and $C \succeq_1 D$ then $\succeq_1$ is *strictly stronger* than $\succeq_2$.

- If $C \succeq D$ holds then C is called a *generalization* of D and D a *specialization* of C. If $C \succ D$ holds, meaning $C \succeq D$ and $D \nsucceq C$, than C is a *proper generalization* of D and D is *proper specialization* of C. If $C \succeq D$ or $D \succeq C$ then C and D are called *comparable*.
- If $C \succ D$ and there exists no E such that $C \succ E \succ D$, then C is called an *upward cover* of D and D is called a *downward cover* of C.

Given a set of clauses S ordered by $\succeq$,

- ρ is a *downward refinement operator* iff $\forall C \in S$: $\rho(C) \subseteq \{D \in S | C \succeq D\}$
- δ is an *upward refinement operator* iff $\forall C \in S$: $\delta(C) \subseteq \{D \in S | D \succeq C\}$

All definitions regarding refinement operators will be presented in terms of downward refinement but are defined similarly for upward refinement.

- ρ is called *locally finite* iff $\forall C \in S$: $\rho(C)$ is finite and computable.
- ρ is called *proper* iff $\forall C \in S$: $\rho(C) \subseteq \{D \in S | C \succ D\}$
- The sets of *one-step refinements*, *n-step refinements* and *refinements* of a clause $C \in S$ are defined respectively as
$\rho^1(C) = \rho(C)$
$\rho^n(C) = \{D | \exists E \in \rho^{n-1}(C) \text{ and } D \in \rho(E)\}$
$\rho^*(C) = \rho^1(C) \cup \rho^2(C) \cup \ldots \cup \rho^i(C) \cup \ldots$
- ρ is called *complete* iff $\forall C, D \in S$ if $C \succ D$ then $\exists E \in \rho^*(C)$ and $E \sim D$[4].

3   Complete and Proper Refinement

Before we present our nonexistence results we motivate our interest in complete and proper refinement operators for an unrestricted search space. First of all, it should be clear that any refinement operator that is not locally finite is of no practical use. All refinement operators in this article will be locally finite.

Completeness of refinement operators is an important property since without it it is hard to make any statement concerning the performance of the systems in which they are used. Properness is a nice property for reasons of efficiency. If a clause is refuted because it is too general or too specific then we are not interested in clauses that are equivalent with this refuted clause. These clauses will also be too general or too specific. Still some refinement operators do return equivalent clauses. It will appear that improper refinement steps are sometimes necessary as a bridge to reach proper specializations or generalizations.

Since the clauses in the theory to learn are not known in advance, any restriction to the search space might exclude these clauses. Shapiro [15] solves this problem by incrementally expanding the search space. This, however, brings a lot of extra work. Furthermore, even if a clause and a proper specialization of it are both in a restricted search space, problems with finding a refinement chain between them can still occur if intermediate clauses are not in this search space.

---

[4] Our notion of completeness is stronger than Shapiro's [15] notion of completeness that is defined for downward refinement operators only by $\rho^*(\square) = S$, where $\square$ denotes the empty clause.

3.1 Nonexistence Conditions

Example 2. Consider the clauses

$$D_2 = q(X_1) \leftarrow p(X_1, X_2), p(X_2, X_1)$$
$$D_n = q(X_1) \leftarrow p(X_1, X_2), p(X_2, X_1) \ldots, p(X_{n-1}, X_n), p(X_n, X_{n-1})$$
$$C = q(X_1) \leftarrow p(X_1, X_1)$$

D_n contains every literal $p(X_i, X_j)$, where $1 \leq i, j \leq n$ and $i \neq j$. In the following subsection we will show that if these clauses are ordered by θ-subsumption they satisfy $D_2 \succ D_3 \succ \ldots \succ D_n \succ D_{n+1} \succ \ldots \succ C$, and no clause E satisfies $D_n \succeq E \succ C$ for all n. Lemma 2 states for ordered search spaces that contain clauses like these, no locally finite, complete and proper upward refinement operator exists. The problems are illustrated in Figure 1b. The arrows illustrate proper generalization relations. Using a locally finite and proper upward refinement operator, all filled dots can be derived from C, whereas the open dots can not. Hence it can not be complete.

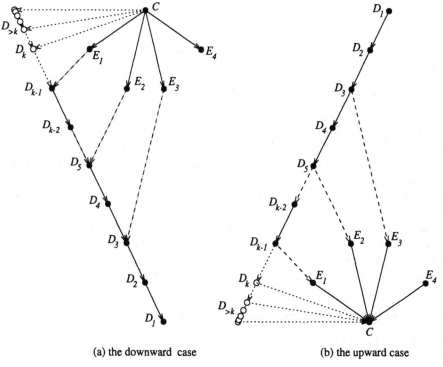

(a) the downward case   (b) the upward case

Fig. 1. Nonexistence conditions for locally finite, complete and proper refinement operators.

The following lemma states sufficient condition to conclude that locally finite, complete and proper downward refinement operator does not exist.

Lemma 1. *Let S be ordered by $\succeq$. If S contains clauses C and D_n, $n \geq 1$ such that*

1. $C \succ \ldots \succ D_{n+1} \succ D_n \succ \ldots \succ D_2 \succ D_1$, *and*
2. $\nexists E$ *such that for all* $n \geq 1$: $C \succ E \succeq D_n$.

Then a locally finite, complete and proper downward refinement operator for S ordered by $\succeq$ does not exist.

Proof. Assume that such a ρ exists. Let $\rho(C) = \{E_1, \ldots, E_m\}$, then $C \succ E_i, 1 \leq i \leq m$. For every E_i, let $n_i = \min\{n | E_i \not\succeq D_n\}$. Because of condition 2 these n_i's exist. Let $k = \max\{n_i\}$. Then $C \succ D_k$ and $E_i \not\succeq D_k$, $1 \leq i \leq m$. Thus, D_k is not in $\rho(C)$ itself nor is D_k derivable from any E_i. We conclude that ρ is not complete. □

An analogous proof holds for the upward version of Lemma 1:

Lemma 2. *Let S be ordered by $\succeq$. If S contains clauses D_n, $n \geq 1$ and C such that*

1. $D_1 \succ D_2 \succ \ldots \succ D_n \succ D_{n+1} \succ \ldots \succ C$, *and*
2. $\nexists E$ *such that for all* $n \geq 1$: $D_n \succeq E \succ C$.

Then a locally finite, complete and proper upward refinement operator for S ordered by $\succeq$ does not exist.

We will apply these lemma's that are valid for arbitrary ordered search spaces to unrestricted search spaces ordered by θ-subsumption. Example clauses that fit the lemma's can already be found in a logical language with one binary predicate p and no function symbols. The nonexistence results of the succeeding subsections are valid for any logical language that contains infinitely many variables, one or more predicate symbols of arity> 1 and any number of function symbols.

For simplicity we use only positive literals in the construction of our example clauses. By changing these examples a little they can be transformed to program clauses. For example, if we use $\{p(X_1, X_2), p(X_2, X_1)\}$ then the same problems occur with the program clause $p(a, a) \leftarrow p(X_1, X_2), p(X_2, X_1)$.

3.2 Nonexistence for Upward Refinement

Throughout this subsection we use the clauses with the following underlying sets:

$$\dot{K}_n = \bigcup \{p(X_i, X_j) | 1 \leq i, j \leq n, i \neq j\}$$
$$\dot{C} = \{p(X_1, X_1)\}$$

$\dot{K}_n$ represents a structure that is known as a complete graph of size n, for example

$$\dot{K}_3 = \{p(X_1, X_2), p(X_1, X_3), p(X_2, X_1), p(X_2, X_3), p(X_3, X_1), p(X_3, X_2)\}.$$

Throughout this section $\dot{C}$ will be used whenever set properties are used, such as in $\dot{C} \subseteq \dot{D}$. Otherwise we write C, where C is a clause that contains one occurrence of every literal in $\dot{C}$. Until Section 5 the difference between the two notations is not important and can be ignored.

We adopt from Plotkin's definition of reducedness [13]. A clause C is called *reduced* iff $\dot{D} \subseteq \dot{C}$ and $D \sim C$ imply $\dot{C} = \dot{D}$. In words, C is reduced iff it equivalent to no proper subset of itself.

Lemma 3. *For all $n \geq 2$, K_n is reduced.*

Proof. Assume K_n is not reduced for some n. Then for some substitution θ, $\dot{K}_n\theta \subset \dot{K}_n$. This implies that two literals $p(X_{i_1}, X_{i_2})$ and $p(X_{j_1}, X_{j_2})$ in K_n are mapped to the same literal $p(X_{k_1}, X_{k_2})$ in $K_n\theta$. If $i_1 \neq j_1$ then $p(X_{i_1}, X_{j_1})$ in K_n is mapped to $p(X_{k_1}, X_{k_1})$. Otherwise, $i_2 \neq j_2$ and $p(X_{i_2}, X_{j_2})$ in K_n is mapped to $p(X_{k_2}, X_{k_2})$. Both cases contradict $\dot{K}_n\theta \subset \dot{K}_n$. □

Lemma 4. $K_2 \succ K_3 \succ \ldots \succ K_n \succ K_{n+1} \succ \ldots \succ C$.

Proof. For every K_n we can define a θ that maps every X_i in K_n to X_1. This gives $\dot{K}_n\theta \subseteq \dot{C}$. Since $p(X_1, X_1)$ in C cannot be mapped to any literal in any K_n we get $K_n \succ C$.

Using the trivial substitution we can prove $K_n \succeq K_{n+1}$. Since K_{n+1} is reduced (Lemma 3) and $\dot{K}_n \subset \dot{K}_{n+1}$, K_{n+1} and K_n cannot be equivalent, and $K_n \succ K_{n+1}$. □

Lemma 5. *Let C and K_n be defined as above. Then there is no E such that for all $n \geq 2$, $K_n \succeq E \succ C$.*

Proof. Assume that E satisfies $K_n \succeq E \succ C$ for all $n \geq 2$. Let $X_1, \ldots, X_m$ be all variables in E. By $\dot{E}\theta \subseteq \dot{C}$, E can contain only literals $p(X_i, X_j)$. In these literals $X_i \neq X_j$ must hold, otherwise E is equivalent with C. But then $\dot{E} \subseteq \dot{K}_m$ which implies $E \succeq K_m \succ K_{m+1}$. This contradicts $K_n \succeq E$ for $n = m + 1$. □

Theorem 6. *A locally finite, complete and proper upward refinement operator for unrestricted search spaces ordered by θ-subsumption does not exist.*

Proof. Follows directly from Lemma 2, Lemma 4 and Lemma 5. □

3.3 Nonexistence for Downward Refinement

Throughout this subsection clauses with the following underlying sets are used:

$\dot{C} = \{p(X_1, X_2), p(X_2, X_1)\}$
$\dot{C}_n = \{p(Y_1, Y_2), p(Y_2, Y_3), \ldots, p(Y_{n-1}, Y_n), p(Y_n, Y_1)\}$
$\dot{D}_n = \dot{C} \cup \dot{C}_{3^n}, n \geq 1$

We state without proof that

Lemma 7. *For all $n \geq 1$, D_n is reduced.*

Lemma 8. *Let C and D_n be defined as above. Then $C \succ \ldots \succ D_{n+1} \succ D_n \succ \ldots \succ D_2 \succ D_1$.*

Proof. $C \succ D_n$ follows directly from $\dot{C} \subset \dot{D}_n$ and the reducedness of D_n (Lemma 7). Let θ be the substitution that maps every Y_j, $1 \leq j \leq 3^{n+1}$, in D_{n+1} to Y_k in D_n, where $k = 3^n$ iff $j \bmod 3^n = 0$ and $k = j \bmod 3^n$ otherwise. Then $\dot{D}_{n+1}\theta = \dot{D}_n$, and hence $D_{n+1} \succeq D_n$. Assume $D_n \succeq D_{n+1}$. Then for some σ, $\dot{D}_n\sigma \subseteq \dot{D}_{n+1}$ and since $|\dot{D}_n| < |\dot{D}_{n+1}|$, $\dot{D}_n\sigma \subset \dot{D}_{n+1}$. But then $\dot{D}_{n+1}\theta\sigma = \dot{D}_n\sigma \subset \dot{D}_{n+1}$, which contradicts that D_{n+1} is reduced (Lemma 7). We conclude $D_n \not\succeq D_{n+1}$, and hence $D_{n+1} \succ D_n$. $\square$

Lemma 9. *Let C and D_n be defined as above. Then there is no E such that for all $n \geq 1$, $C \succ E \succeq D_n$.*

Proof. Assume that E is a clause that satisfies $C \succ E \succeq D_n$ for all $n \geq 1$. Choose an m such that $3^m > |\dot{E}|$. Then, for some θ, $\dot{E}\theta \subseteq \dot{D}_m$. Since $|\dot{E}\theta| < 3^m$ and $|\dot{D}_m| = 3^m + 2$, we know that at least one of the literals of the C_{3^m}-part of D_m does not occur in $E\theta$. Without loss of generality we may assume that $p(Y_n, Y_1) \in \dot{D}_m - \dot{E}\theta$.

Consider the clause $\dot{F} = \dot{D}_m - \{p(Y_n, Y_1)\}$. Then $\dot{E}\theta \subseteq \dot{F}$ implies $E \succeq F$. Let σ map every Y_i in F to X_1 if i is odd, and to X_2 if i is even. Then $\dot{F}\sigma \subseteq \dot{C}$ and hence $F \succeq C$. So $E \succeq F \succeq C$, which contradicts $C \succ E$. $\square$

Theorem 10. *A locally finite, complete and proper downward refinement operator for unrestricted search spaces ordered by θ-subsumption does not exist.*

Proof. Follows directly from Lemma 1, Lemma 8 and Lemma 9. $\square$

4   Complete Downward Refinement

Laird has presented a generalized version of Shapiro's [15] refinement operator for reduced clauses in [7], where he referred to Shapiro's (incorrect) proof of (weak) completeness. We repeat the definition of Laird's downward refinement operator in our notation:

Refinement operator ρ_0. Let $C = L_1, \ldots, L_m \leftarrow M_1, \ldots, M_n$ be a clause. Then $D \in \rho_0(C)$ when exactly one of the following holds:

1. $D = C\theta$, where $\theta = \{X/Y\}$ and both variables X and Y occur in C.
2. $D = C\theta$, where $\theta = \{X/f(Y_1, \ldots, Y_n)\}$, f is an n-ary function symbol, X occurs in C and $Y_1, \ldots, Y_n$ are distinct variables not occurring in C.
3. $D = L_1, \ldots, L_{m+1} \leftarrow M_1, \ldots, M_n$, where L_{m+1} is a most general atom w.r.t. C.
4. $D = L_1, \ldots, L_m \leftarrow M_1, \ldots, M_{n+1}$, where M_{n+1} is a most general atom w.r.t. C.

Where Shapiro needed to restrict the search space to a finite set, Laird's ρ_0 operates on unrestricted search spaces.

Theorem 11. ρ_0 *is a locally finite, complete but improper refinement operator for unrestricted search spaces ordered by θ-subsumption.*

Proof. Local finiteness of ρ_0 follows directly from the finite number of variables in a clause and the definition of ρ_0. A proof of completeness can be found in [4]. Improperness is easy to verify. Consider for example the clauses $C = p(f(X)) \leftarrow p(X)$ and $D = p(f(X)) \leftarrow p(X), p(Y)$. They satisfy $C \sim D$, and $D \in \rho_0(C)$ by item 4. □

5 Complete Upward Refinement

Our intention is to define an upward refinement operator δ_0 with the same properties as ρ_0. The different problems involved in the definition of such an upward refinement operator arise in different weaker orderings. We therefore consider three increasingly weak orderings: the θ-subsumption, set, and substitution ordering, denoted by $\succeq, \succeq_1$, and $\succeq_2$ respectively. The corresponding complete upward refinement operators will be denoted by $\delta_0, \delta_1, \delta_2$. Since refinement operators for weaker and simpler orderings can be used to define refinement operators for stronger, more complex orderings, δ_0, δ_1 and δ_2 will be defined in reverse order. The weak to strong approach was also used in [12], where we investigated proper refinement in restricted, finite search spaces. δ_1 and δ_2 that will be defined later on could already be found in that article.

5.1 The Substitution Ordering

In the *substitution ordering* $\succeq_2$, clauses are treated as sequences of literals, the number of the literals and their position in a clause are fixed. It is defined by
$C \succeq_2 D$ iff $\exists \theta : C\theta = D$

Example 3. Consider
$$C = even(X) \leftarrow odd(Y), plus(Y, Y, X) \text{ and}$$
$$D = even(Z) \leftarrow plus(3, 3, Z), odd(3).$$
C and D are incomparable in the substitution ordering because no substitution can map $odd(Y)$ to $plus(3, 3, Z)$ or the other way around. If the places of the body literals in either C or D were swapped then $C \succeq_2 D$ would hold by $\theta = \{X/Z, Y/3\}$ (in fact, $C \succ_2 D$).

In the substitution ordering, substitutions that are not renamings determine proper refinements [12]. In all clauses comparable with a clause C, predicate symbols appear in the same place as in C and no literals can be removed or added. We can speak of clauses being treated as atoms, $L_1, \ldots, L_m \leftarrow M_1, \ldots, M_n$ can be viewed as $\vee(L_1, \ldots, L_m, \neg M_1, \ldots, \neg M_n)$ where the ordering of the arguments of $\vee$ is fixed. Reynolds [14] has described a (downward) cover relation for atoms which corresponds with items 1 and 2 in the definition of ρ_0. This relation can be used as a downward refinement operator for clauses w.r.t. the substitution ordering directly.

Our first upward refinement operator is obtained by inverting these substitutions. The dual of item 2 in ρ_0 has to be described seperately for constants and function symbols of arity > 0. Replacing some or all occurences of a constant c by a new variable X always inverts a ρ_0-substitution $\{X/c\}$. Replacing some but not all occurences $f(Y_1, \ldots, Y_n)$ by a variable X does not invert a ρ_0-subsitition $\{X/f(Y_1, \ldots, Y_n)\}$ since it results in a clause in which Y_i still occurs.

Refinement operator δ_2. Let C be a clause, then

$D \in \delta_2(C)$ iff one of the following holds:

1. D is C after some (not all) occurrences of a variable Y in C are replaced by a variable X not in C.
2. D is C after all occurrences of a term $f(Y_1, \ldots, Y_n)$ are replaced by a variable X, where f is a n-ary function symbol $(n > 0)$, X does not occur in C and all Y_i's are distinct variables not occurring elsewhere in C besides in terms $f(Y_1, \ldots, Y_n)$.
3. D is C after some or all occurrences of a constant c are replaced by a variable X, where X does not occur in C.

Lemma 12. *δ_2 is a locally finite refinement operator.*

Proof. Every clause contains a finite number of term occurrences. Therefore the number of possible inverse substitutions is finite and δ_2 is locally finite. ☐

Lemma 13. *δ_2 is a complete refinement operator for unrestricted search spaces w.r.t. the substitution ordering.*

Proof. It is proved by Reynolds [14, Theorem 4] that for every pair of atoms A and B, if $A \succ_2 B$ then there is a finite chain $A = A_0, \ldots, A_n = B$ such that A_i is a downward cover of A_{i-1} and A_i can be derived from A_{i-1} through item 1 or 2 of ρ_0. Since A is a downward cover of B iff B is an upward cover of A we can use δ_2 in the upward case. Since clauses are treated as atoms, this result can be generalized to unrestricted search spaces of clauses ordered by $\succeq_2$. ☐

5.2 The Set Ordering

In the *set ordering* $\succeq_1$, permutation of literals and addition or removal of duplicate literals in a clause no longer influence generality relations. The set ordering is strictly stronger than the substitution ordering [12]. It is defined by $C \succeq_1 D$ iff $\exists \theta : \dot{C}\theta = \dot{D}$.

Set reduction of a clause is the removal of all duplicate literals in it. A clause is *set reduced* iff it contains no duplicate literals. If set reduction of C results in C', then clearly $C \sim_1 C'$. We might therefore call C' the set reduced equivalent of C.

In the set ordering, the necessity of adding literals in generalization steps arises:

Example 4. We repeat the clauses of Example 1:

$$D = cycle(X) \leftarrow con(X, X)$$
$$D' = cycle(X) \leftarrow con(X, X), con(X, X), con(X, X)$$
$$E = cycle(X) \leftarrow con(X, X), con(X, Z), con(Z, X)$$
$$C = cycle(X) \leftarrow con(X, Y), con(Y, Z), con(Z, X)$$

In the set ordering, $C \succ_1 E \succ_1 D' \sim_1 D$. These clauses illustrate a ρ_0-chain of downward refinement steps, $E \in \rho_0(C), D \in \rho_0(E)$. At every step two variables are unified and duplicate literals are removed. In the case of upward refinement, $C \in \delta_2(E)$ holds. However, δ_2 can not be used to derive E from D, since the number of literals must increase. If we duplicate $con(X, X)$ twice in D before applying δ_2, then we would obtain D' and $E \in \delta_2(D')$. This motivates our definition of δ_1 later on.

In the case of downward refinement operators, equal literals are of no use since they remain equal after substitution. Hence there is no need to duplicate literals at any time and clauses can be set reduced as soon as duplicate literals appear.

As the last example showed for the case of upward refinement, literals sometimes should be repeated before inverse substitutions are applied by δ_2. We can easily define an operator that duplicates a literal:

Let $C = L_1, \ldots, L_m \leftarrow M_1, \ldots, M_n$ be a clause, then $D \in eq_1(C)$ iff
$$D = L_1, \ldots, L_m \leftarrow M_1, \ldots, M_i, M_i, \ldots, M_n \text{ or}$$
$$D = L_1, \ldots, L_i, L_i, \ldots, L_m \leftarrow M_1, \ldots, M_n.$$
By applying eq_1 zero or more times, $eq_1^*(C)$ contains infinitely many clauses of the form $L_1, \ldots, L_1, L_2, \ldots, L_2, \ldots, L_m, \ldots, L_m \leftarrow$
$$M_1, \ldots, M_1, M_2, \ldots, M_2, \ldots, M_n, \ldots, M_n.$$

In his description of the inversion of θ-subsumption Jung [3] also incorporated the addition of arbitrary many copies of body literals to a clause. Later on in this section we will show that only a finite part of eq_1^* is needed for computing one-step upward refinements.

Refinement operator δ_1. Let C be a set reduced clause, then

$$D \in \delta_1(C) \text{ iff there are } C' \in eq_1^*(C), D \in \delta_2(C') \text{ and } D \text{ is set reduced.}$$

Note that clauses with duplicate literals are hard to describe when clauses are represented as sets of literals. We therefore need the sequence of literals representation of clauses for clauses that are obtained by eq_1^* and submitted to δ_2.

The proof of the following lemma contains the solution for the main problem of defining a locally finite complete upward refinement operator for unrestricted search spaces ordered by $\succeq_1$ or $\succeq$. It shows that the number of necessary literal repetitions is finite and computable.

Lemma 14. δ_1 *is a locally finite refinement operator.*

Proof. We show that, no matter how many times every single literal of C is repeated before δ_2 is applied, $\delta_1(C)$ contains finitely many nonequivalent clauses.

Given a clause C, if $C' \in eq_1^*(C)$ and $D \in \delta_2(C')$, then D contains exactly one variable, say X, that is not in C' and C. Suppose that δ_2 replaces some or all of the occurrences of a constant c in C' by X (the cases of anti-unification and functional terms can be proved similarly). Let c occur in the literals $L_1, \ldots, L_m$ of C. In every such literal L_i, c occurs finitely many times, say n_i times. When δ_2 is applied to C' every single occurrence of c is either replaced by X or not. For a single literal L_i this results in 2^{n_i} possible different literals. Hence there is no need to repeat L_i more than 2^{n_i} times.

For each literal L in C we can thus compute an upper bound of the sufficient number of repetitions of L in C'. Hence we only have to consider a finite and computable part of $eq_1^*(C)$ in the definition of δ_1. $\qquad\square$

The following example illustrates the local finiteness of δ_1.

Example 5. Consider the clause

$$C = q(b) \leftarrow p(a, a)$$

We describe the case in which δ_2 replaces some or all occurrences of a by a new variable X. Then $L = p(a, a)$ can either become $p(X, X)$, $p(X, a)$, or $p(a, X)$, or remain unchanged. We claim that no more than $2^2 = 4$ occurrences of L in C' are useful. Consider

$$C' = q(b) \leftarrow p(a, a), p(a, a)$$
$$C'' = q(b) \leftarrow p(a, a), p(a, a), p(a, a), p(a, a)$$
$$D_1 = q(b) \leftarrow p(a, X), p(X, a)$$
$$D_2 = q(b) \leftarrow p(a, X), p(X, a), p(a, X), p(X, a)$$
$$D_3 = q(b) \leftarrow p(a, X), p(X, a), p(X, X), p(a, a)$$

Then D_1 is one of the clauses in $\delta_2(C')$ and D_2 and D_3 are two of the many possible clauses in $\delta_2(C'')$. D_2 contains the literals $p(a, X)$ and $p(X, a)$ twice and is not set reduced. D_2 is therefore not a member of $\delta_1(C)$.

Proper generalizations of C with more than five literals do exist. But they all have at least two variables that are not in C. Consider for example the clause

$$E = q(b) \leftarrow p(a, X), p(X, a), p(X, X), p(X, Y), p(Y, X),$$

then E is not derivable from C in one step. It is however derivable in two steps.

Lemma 15. δ_1 *is a complete upward refinement operator for unrestricted search spaces w.r.t. the set ordering.*

Proof. Let C and D be set reduced clauses such that $D \succ_1 C$. Then there exists a substitution θ such that $\dot{D}\theta = \dot{C}$.

$D \succeq_2 D\theta$, so by the completeness of δ_2 there exists a finite δ_2-chain from $D\theta$ to a clause $D' \sim_2 D$.

$D\theta$ possibly differs from C in the repetition of literals and a permutation of literals. Since in the definition of δ_1 all necessary literals are repeated before δ_2 is applied and the ordering of literals does not influence the applicability of δ_2, there exists a δ_1-chain from C to $D'' \sim_1 D$ containing all δ_2 steps of the δ_2-chain from $D\theta$ to D', possibly preceded by literal duplications. □

Example 6. We will illustrate the proof of Lemma 5.7 using the following clauses:

$$C = even(X) \leftarrow odd(3), plus(3,3,X)$$
$$D = even(U) \leftarrow plus(V,W,U), odd(V), odd(W)$$

$\dot{D}\theta = \dot{C}$ by $\theta = \{U/X, V/3, W/3\}$. Hence there exists a δ_2-chain from $D\theta$ to a clause $D' \sim_1 D$:

$$D\theta = even(X) \leftarrow plus(3,3,X), odd(3), odd(3)$$
$$E = even(X) \leftarrow plus(Z,Z,X), odd(Z), odd(Z) \in \delta_2(D'\theta)$$
$$D' = even(X) \leftarrow plus(Z,W,X), odd(Z), odd(W) \in \delta_2(E)$$

This δ_2-chain from $D\theta$ to D' can indeed be transformed to a δ_1-chain from C to D'' by adding the necessary literal duplications:

$$C = even(X) \leftarrow odd(3), plus(3,3,X)$$
$$E' = even(X) \leftarrow odd(Z), plus(Z,Z,X) \in \delta_1(C)$$
$$E'' = even(X) \leftarrow odd(Z), odd(Z), plus(Z,Z,X) \in eq_1^*(E')$$
$$D'' = even(X) \leftarrow odd(Z), odd(W), plus(Z,W,X) \in \delta_2(E'') (D'' \in \delta_1(E'))$$

Note that every literal modification in the δ_2-chain $D\theta, E, D'$ returns in the δ_1-chain C, E', D''. The literal $odd(Z)$ is duplicated once in E' in order to derive D''.

5.3 The θ-Subsumption Ordering

The θ-subsumption ordering is strictly stronger than the set ordering [12]. To transform our upward refinement operator for the set ordering ($\dot{C}\theta = \dot{D}$) to one for the θ-subsumption ordering ($\dot{C}\theta \subseteq \dot{D}$) is relatively easy. We only have to incorporate an operation for removing literals. We therefore invert the operation of adding a most general literal:

Refinement operator δ_0. Let C be a set reduced clause, then

$$D \in \delta_0(C) \text{ iff } D \in \delta_1(C) \text{ or}$$
$$D \text{ is } C \text{ after removing a literal that is most general w.r.t. } D.$$

Theorem 16. *δ_0 is a locally finite, complete but improper upward refinement operator for unrestricted search spaces ordered by θ-subsumption.*

Proof. Local finiteness. Every clause C contains finitely many literals, hence finitely many one-step refinements can be added by the new operation of removing a literal. Local finiteness of δ_0 then follows from the local finiteness of δ_1.
Completeness (outline). Let $D \succeq C$, then for some θ, $\dot{D}\theta \subseteq \dot{C}$. First we prove that there exists a finite δ_0-chain from C to $D\theta$. Let $\{M_1, \ldots, M_n\} = \dot{C} - \dot{D}\theta$.

Let $\dot{C}_i = \dot{D}\theta \cup \{M_1, \ldots, M_i\}$, then $\dot{C}_n = \dot{C}$. We will show that we can successively derive $\dot{C}_{n-1}, \ldots, \dot{C}_0 = \dot{D}\theta$.

For $i = n - 1$ downto 1:
We start with $\dot{C}_{i+1} = \dot{C}_i \cup \{M_{i+1}\}$.
Let L_{i+1} denote a literal that is compatible with M_{i+1} and most general
    w.r.t. $\dot{C}_i$. Then $\dot{C}_{i+1} = (\dot{C}_i \cup \{L_{i+1}\})\theta$ for some θ.
-By the completeness of δ_1, we can derive $\dot{C}_i \cup \{L_{i+1}\}$ from $\dot{C}_{i+1}$.
-Since L_{i+1} is most general w.r.t. $\dot{C}_i$, we can remove L_{i+1} from $\dot{C}_i \cup$
    $\{L_{i+1}\}$, which results in $\dot{C}_i$.

Since there are finitely many literals M_i, all these operations can be performed in a finite number of refinement steps. We now have a finite δ_0-chain from C to $D\theta$. By the completeness of δ_1, there exists a finite δ_1-chain from $D\theta$ to $D' \sim D$. Since all operations of δ_1 are operations of δ_0 too, this δ_1-chain can be used to complete the δ_0-chain from C to $D' \sim D$.

Improperness. Consider the clauses

$$C = p(f(X)) \leftarrow p(X), p(Y)$$
$$D = p(f(X)) \leftarrow p(X)$$

As can be verified, $C \sim D$, but $D \in \delta_0(C)$.   □

6   Conclusions and Future Research

In this article we have presented some new results regarding refinement in unrestricted search spaces ordered by θ-subsumption. A localy finite, complete but improper upward refinement operator has been defined, a downward refinement operator with these properties already existed. We have proven that locally finite downward and upward refinement operators that are both complete and proper for these search spaces do not exist.

Our current and future research involves a logical framework in which all refinement operators that we know of find their place. Operators are classified according to being upward or downward and properties such as local finiteness, properness, weak and strong completeness w.r.t. an (un)restricted search space and its generality ordering. Using this framework we try to fill the categories in which no refinement operators are known.

Acknowledgment. We thank Leon van der Torre for reading and commenting the article as well as for his moral support.

References

1. P. Idestam-Almquist. Generalization under Implication by Using Or-Introduction. In P.B. Brazdil, editor, *ECML-93*, pages 56–64, Vienna, Austria, April 1993. LNAI-667, Springer-Verlag.
2. P. Idestam-Almquist. Recursive Anti-unification. In S. Muggleton, editor, *ILP'93*, pages 241–253, Bled, Slovenia, March 1993. Technical Report IJS-DP-6707, J.Stefan Institute.

3. B. Jung. On Inverting Generality Relations. In S. Muggleton, editor, *ILP'93*, pages 87–101, Bled, Slovenia, March 1993. Technical Report IJS-DP-6707, J.Stefan Institute.

4. P.R.J. van der Laag. Een Meest Algemene Verfijningsoperator voor Gereduceerde Zinnen. In *NAIC-92*, pages 29–39. Delftse Universitaire Pers, 1992. In Dutch, English version has appeared as Technical Report EUR-CS-92-03, Erasmus Univerity of Rotterdam, Dept. of Computer Science.

5. P.R.J. van der Laag and S.H. Nienhuys-Cheng. A Locally Finite and Complete Upward Refinement Operator for θ-Subsumption. In *Benelearn-93*. Artificial Intelligence Laboratory, Vrije Universiteit Brussel, Brussels, 1993.

6. P.R.J. van der Laag and S.H. Nienhuys-Cheng. Subsumption and Refinement in Model Inference. In *ECML-93*, pages 95–114, Vienna, Austria, April 1993. LNAI-667, Springer Verlag.

7. P.D. Laird. *Learning from Good and Bad Data*. Kluwer Academic Publishers, 1988.

8. S. Lapointe and S. Matwin. Subunification: A Tool for Efficient Induction of Recursive Programs. In *ML-92*, pages 273–280, Aberdeen, 1992. Morgan Kaufmann.

9. C. Ling and M. Dawes. SIM the Inverse of Shapiro's MIS. Technical report, Department of Computer Science, University of Western Ontario, London, Ontario, Canada., 1990.

10. S.H. Muggleton. Inverting Implication. In Muggleton, S.H., editor, *Proceedings of the International Workshop on Inductive Logic Programming*, 1992.

11. T. Niblett. A Note on Refinement Operators. In *ECML-93*, pages 329–335. LNAI-667, Springer Verlag, 1993.

12. S.H. Nienhuys-Cheng, P.R.J. van der Laag, and L.W.N. van der Torre. Constructing Refinement Operators by Decomposing Logical Implication. In P. Torasso, editor, *AI*IA'93*, pages 178–189, Torino, Italy, October 1993. LNAI-728, Springer-Verlag.

13. G.D. Plotkin. A Note on Inductive Generalization. *Machine Intelligence*, 5:153–163, 1970.

14. J.C. Reynolds. Transformational Systems and the Algebraic Structure of Atomic Formulas. *Machine Intelligence*, 5:135–153, 1970.

15. E.Y. Shapiro. Inductive Inference of Theories from Facts. Technical Report 192, Department of Computer Science, Yale University, New Haven. CT., 1981.

A Hybrid Nearest-Neighbor and Nearest-Hyperrectangle Algorithm

Dietrich Wettschereck

Dearborn Hall 303
Department of Computer Science
Oregon State University
Corvallis, OR 97331-3202
USA
wettscd@cs.orst.edu

Abstract. Algorithms based on Nested Generalized Exemplar (NGE) theory [10] classify new data points by computing their distance to the nearest "generalized exemplar" (i.e. an axis-parallel multidimensional rectangle). An improved version of NGE, called BNGE, was previously shown to perform comparably to the Nearest Neighbor algorithm. Advantages of the NGE approach include compact representation of the training data and fast training and classification. A hybrid method that combines BNGE and the k-Nearest Neighbor algorithm, called KBNGE, is introduced for improved classification accuracy. Results from eleven domains show that KBNGE achieves generalization accuracies similar to the k-Nearest Neighbor algorithm at improved classification speed. KBNGE is a fast and easy to use inductive learning algorithm that gives very accurate predictions in a variety of domains and represents the learned knowledge in a manner that can be easily interpreted by the user.

1   Introduction

Salzberg [10] describes a family of learning algorithms based on nested generalized exemplars (NGE). In NGE, an exemplar is a single training example and a generalized exemplar is an axis-parallel hyperrectangle that may cover several training examples. These hyperrectangles may overlap or nest. The NGE algorithm grows the hyperrectangles incrementally as training examples are processed. Once the generalized exemplars are learned, a test example can be classified by computing the distance between the example and each of the generalized exemplars. If an example is contained inside a generalized exemplar, the distance to that generalized exemplar is zero. The class of the nearest generalized exemplar is assigned to the test example.

The NGE approach can be viewed as a hybrid of nearest neighbor methods and propositional Horn clause rules. Like nearest neighbor methods, a distance metric is applied to match test examples to training examples. But like Horn clause rules, training examples can be generalized to be axis-parallel hyperrectangles. Advantages of the NGE approach over other methods include fast training, few user-defined parameters (one for NGE and none for BNGE, see below), compact representation of the training data, and the ability to interpret hyperrectangles as prototypes of the task. These prototypes can be used to justify or explain decisions made by the classifier. The NGE algorithm, as described in this paper, differs from Nearest Neighbor methods, including those with reduced exemplar sets [3, Chapter 6], through its rectangular bias and its ability to distinguish queries that fall inside of some hyperrectangles from those that are not covered by any hyperrectangle. It differs from Parzen Windows [9] in that hyperrectangles can be of varying sizes and edge lengths may be unequal.

Salzberg [10] achieved promising classification results with NGE in three domains. However, Wettschereck & Dietterich [14] have reported that when tested in 11 additional domains, NGE does not perform as well as the nearest neighbor (NN) algorithm in 6 out of the 11. Wettschereck & Dietterich [14] point out some weaknesses of NGE and suggest ways to improve its performance. The single most successful improvement in predictive accuracy can be achieved by elimination of overlapping hyperrectangles. A weakness of the NGE algorithm is the need for expensive cross-validation to estimate the best value for the one user-defined parameter of NGE. This necessity for cross-validation can be avoided by training NGE in batch mode. This improved version of NGE, called BNGE ("Batch" NGE), is either superior to or indistinguishable from NGE in all domains tested. It was concluded that creation of overlapping hyperrectangles should be avoided when training NGE and that BNGE should be employed in place of NGE in any situation where batch learning is appropriate. The main advantages of BNGE over NGE are that BNGE often yields better data compression and has no user-specified parameters thus making it easier to use. BNGE compares favorably to approaches based on neural networks in training time and experimenter's effort required to construct a classifier. For example, it takes only approximately 1 hour on a Sparc-2 workstation to construct a BNGE classifier for the 16000 training examples of the Letter Recognition domain described in Table 1. A classifier constructed by BNGE is generally faster than a Nearest Neighbor approach while neural networks often find more compact representations of the training data thus making them faster at classification time.

The potential advantages of NGE algorithms (data compression, fast learning and classification, interpretability of exemplars) are significant, but classification accuracy is still not satisfactory. This paper proposes and tests two additional modifications to the NGE algorithm. First, the amount of memory required by NGE algorithms can be further reduced after the classifier is constructed by pruning hyperrectangles that were not generalized during the training period. These trivial hyperrectangles contribute little to NGE's predictive accuracy, but they consume memory and increase the time needed for classification. Second, to achieve better classification accuracy, a hybrid algorithm that uses BNGE in areas of the input space that are covered by hyperrectangles and that uses kNN otherwise, is introduced and evaluated. We call this algorithm KBNGE. It is shown that, while BNGE is significantly inferior to the kNN algorithm in 6 out of 11 domains, KBNGE is inferior to the kNN algorithm in only 1 domain and yields better predictive accuracy in 2 other domains. Furthermore, KBNGE is shown to be faster than kNN in all domains. The KBNGE algorithm can be seen as a generalized Nearest Neighbor algorithm. Nearest Neighbor algorithms play an important role in inductive machine learning because of their simplicity and their ability to give highly accurate predictions after a short learning phase. The KBNGE algorithm shares these advantages and offers, in addition, fast classification and a compact representation of the most salient parts of the task learned.

1.1 The NGE Algorithm

Figure 1 summarizes the NGE algorithm following closely Salzberg's definition of NGE. NGE constructs hyperrectangles by processing the training examples sequentially. It is initialized by randomly selecting a user-defined number of seed training examples and constructing trivial (point) hyperrectangles for each seed. Each subsequent training example is first classified according to the existing set of hyperrectangles by computing the distance from the example to each hyperrectangle. If the class of the nearest hyperrectangle and the training example coincide, then the nearest hyperrectangle is extended to include the training example, otherwise the second nearest hyperrectangle is tried (this is called the second match heuristic). Should both the first and second nearest hyperrectangles have different classes than the training example, then the training example is stored as a new (trivial) hyperrectangle. A query is classified according to the class of the nearest hyperrectangle. Distances are computed as follows: If an example lies outside of all existing hyperrectangles, a distance is computed according to a distance metric. If the example falls inside a hyperrectangle, its distance to that hyperrectangle is zero. If the example is equidistant to several hyperrectangles, the smallest of these is taken to be the "nearest" hyperrectangle.

In our implementation of NGE, we first make a pass over the training examples and normalize the values of each feature into the interval [0,1] (linear normalization [1]). Features of values in the test set are normalized by the same scaling factors (but note that they may fall outside the [0,1] range). Aside from this scaling pass, the algorithm is entirely incremental.

The original NGE algorithm was designed for continuous features only. Discrete and symbolic features require a modification of the distance computation for NGE. We adopted for NGE the policy that for each symbolic or discrete feature the set of covered feature values is stored for each hyperrectangle (analogous to storing the range of feature values for continuous features). A hyperrectangle then covers a certain feature value if that value is a member of the covered set. If a hyperrectangle is generalized to include a missing discrete or symbolic feature, then a flag is set such that the corresponding feature of the hyperrectangle will cover any feature value in the future.

Each hyperrectangle H^j is labeled with an output class. The hyperrectangle is represented by its lower left corner (H^j_{lower}) and its upper right corner (H^j_{upper}) for continuous features and by the set of values (H^j) covered for symbolic or discrete features. The distance between H^j and an example E with features f_1 through $f_{nFeatures}$ is defined as follows:

$$D(E, H^j) = \sqrt{\sum_{i=1}^{nFeatures} d_{f_i}(E, H^j)^2}$$

where:

if (f_i continuous)
$$d_{f_i}(E, H^j) = \begin{cases} E_{f_i} - H^j_{upper,f_i} & \text{if } E_{f_i} > H^j_{upper,f_i} \\ H^j_{lower,f_i} - E_{f_i} & \text{if } H^j_{lower,f_i} > E_{f_i} \\ 0 & \text{otherwise} \end{cases}$$

else
$$d_{f_i}(E, H^j) = \begin{cases} 1 & \text{if } E_{f_i} \in H^j \\ 0 & \text{otherwise} \end{cases}$$

Choice of the distance metric can significantly influence the performance of any distance-based machine learning algorithm in domains with continuous features [15]. Euclidean distance (L^2-norm) is used in this paper for NGE. Note that the decision whether a query is inside or outside of a hyperrectangle is independent of the metric. On the other hand, the metric may heavily influence the number and shape of hyperrectangles constructed.

1.2 The Nearest Neighbor Algorithm

One of the most venerable algorithms in machine learning is the nearest neighbor algorithm (NN, see [3] for a survey of the literature). The entire training set is stored in memory. To classify a new example, the Euclidean distance (possibly weighted) is computed between the example and each stored training example, and the new example is assigned the class of the nearest neighboring example. Better classification accuracy can often be achieved by using more than the first nearest neighbor to classify a query. The number k of neighbors to be considered is usually determined via leave-one-out cross-validation [13]. Aha [1] describes several space-efficient variations of nearest-neighbor algorithms.

1.3 Experimental Methods and Test Domains

To measure the performance of the NGE and nearest neighbor algorithms, we employed the training set/test set methodology. Each data set was randomly partitioned into a training set containing approximately 70% of the patterns and a test set containing the remaining patterns (see also Table 1). After training on the training set, the percentage of correct classifications on the test set was measured. The procedure was repeated a total of 25 times to reduce statistical variation. In each experiment, the algorithms being compared were trained (and tested) on identical data sets to ensure that differences in performance were due entirely to the algorithms.

1. **Build an NGE classifier (input: number s of seeds):**
2. Initialization: /* assume training examples are given in random order */
3.   for each of the first s training examples E^s call createHyperrectangle(E^s)
4. Training:
5.   for each remaining training example E:
6.   find the two H^j with $D(E, H^j)$ minimal
7.   /* in case of ties, choose the two H^j with minimal area */
8.   call these hyperrectangles $H^{closest}$ and $H^{second\ closest}$
9.   if (class(E) == class($H^{closest}$))   generalize($H^{closest}, E$)
10.   else if (class(E) == class($H^{second\ closest}$)) generalize($H^{second\ closest}, E$)
11.   else   createHyperrectangle(E)

12. **Generalize a hyperrectangle:**
13.   generalize(H, E)
14.   for all features of E do:
15. $H_{upper, f_i} = \max(H_{upper, f_i}, E_{f_i})$
16. $H_{lower, f_i} = \min(H_{lower, f_i}, E_{f_i})$
17.   replMissFeatures(H, E)

18. **Create a hyperrectangle:**
19.   createHyperrectangle(E)
20. $H_{upper} = E$
21. $H_{lower} = E$
22.   replMissFeatures(H, E)

23. **Replace missing features in a hyperrectangle:**
24.   replMissFeatures(H, E)
25.   for all features of E do:
26.   if (feature i of E is missing)
27. $H_{upper, f_i} = 1$
28. $H_{lower, f_i} = 0$

29. **Classification of a test example:**
30.   classify(E)
31.   output: class(H^j) with $j = \text{argmin}_i\ D(E, H^i)$
32.   /* in case of ties, choose H^j out of all ties with minimal area */

Fig. 1. Pseudo-code describing construction of an NGE classifier and classification of test examples. H generally denotes a hyperrectangle and E an example.

We have reported the average percentage of correct classifications and its standard error. Two-tailed paired t-tests were conducted to determine the level of significance at which one algorithm outperformed another. A performance difference was considered significant when the p-value was smaller than 0.05.

Eleven domains of varying size and complexity were used to compare the performance of NGE to nearest neighbor. The first three data sets are two dimensional data sets especially constructed in Wettschereck & Dietterich [14] to evaluate NGE. The decision boundaries in Tasks A and C are rectangular, while in Task B the boundary is diagonal. The data sets for the other eight domains were obtained from the UC-Irvine repository [1, 6] of machine learning databases. Table 1 describes some of the characteristics of the domains used. There are a few important points to note: (a) the Waveform-40 domain is identical to the Waveform-21 domain with the addition of 19 irrelevant features (having random values), (b) the Cleveland database [4] contains some missing features, and (c) many input features in the Hungarian database [4] and the Voting Record database are missing.

Table 1. Domain characteristics (modified from Aha (1990)). B = Boolean, C = Continuous, N = Nominal.

Domain	Training Set Size	Test Set Size	Number and Kind of Features	Number of Classes
Task A	350	150	2 C	2
Task B	350	150	2 C	2
Task C	350	150	2 C	10
Iris	105	45	4 C	3
Led-7 Display	200	500	7 B	10
Waveform-21	300	100	21 C	3
Waveform-40	300	100	40 C	3
Cleveland	212	91	5 C, 3 B, 5 N	2
Hungarian	206	88	5 C, 3 B, 5 N	2
Voting	305	130	16 B	2
Letter recog.	16000	4000	16 C	26

2 Pruning

One of the main advantages of NGE and its variations when compared to the Nearest Neighbor algorithm is that NGE often finds a more compact representation of the data. For example, if all training patterns of one class can be described by a single rectangle, then BNGE will find that rectangle. Often, however, NGE and BNGE store trivial point-hyperrectangles. Since these hyperrectangles cover no significant part of the input space, they may contribute little to the generalization accuracy of NGE while using up memory and slowing down the classifier during classification. Figure 2 describes the effect on the performance of BNGE if hyperrectangles that cover only one training example ($BNGE_{p1}$), at most two training examples ($BNGE_{p2}$), or at most five training examples ($BNGE_{p5}$) were removed from the classifier prior to classification of the test examples. Pruning of exemplars that cover only one training example (i.e. were never generalized) significantly decreased the performance of BNGE only in the Cleveland domain. However, in the remaining ten domains, pruning of un-generalized hyperrectangles had little effect on the predictive accuracy of BNGE (and NGE, experiments not shown). The largest reduction in memory was achieved by removal of un-generalized exemplars in the Waveform domains. BNGE stored approximately 140 hyperrectangles in these domains. On average, 4 hyperrectangles remained after pruning in these domains, while no loss in predictive accuracy was observed. More than 75% of the hyperrectangles could be pruned in the Letter Recognition domain, also with no significant loss in predictive accuracy. A significant reduction in storage was observed in all domains except in Task A, where BNGE had found the smallest possible representation of the training data without pruning. The slight improvement in performance in the Hungarian and Voting domains indicates that un-generalized exemplars may often represent noisy training examples. Pruning could therefore be used to filter out noisy exemplars to improve speed and accuracy of the classifier.

It is important to note that the main purpose of the pruning technique described here is to find a more compact BNGE classifier with somewhat similar classification accuracy. Since this approach is a modification of BNGE's bias, it may also suffer from the same problems as other pruning techniques [11] with respect to classification accuracy. However, pruning never increases the amount of storage required by BNGE.

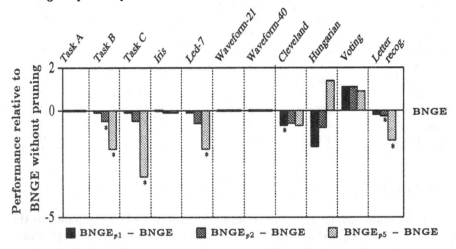

Fig. 2. Performance differences between BNGE without pruning and BNGE with different levels of pruning on the test set. The subscript px indicates that hyperrectangles which cover at most x training examples were removed before the classifier was tested. Performance relative to BNGE without pruning is shown. These differences (*) are statistically significant ($p < 0.05$).

Through inspection of hyperrectangles that were constructed by $BNGE_{p5}$ in the Hungarian domain, we could, for example, determine that 4 of the 13 input features in this domain are completely irrelevant and that the typical patient who is likely to suffer from heart disease can be described as a middle-aged male experiencing atypical angina or asymptomatic chest pains with exercise-induced angina and a medium to high ST depression induced by exercise relative to rest. After pruning in the Voting Records domain only one hyperrectangle for Republicans and one for Democrats was left to describe the voting patterns of the members of the US congress in the legislative period described in that data set. In particular, the votes on adoption of the budget and the physician fee freeze were most informative, and 11 of the 16 features were irrelevant.

3 A Hybrid Algorithm – KBNGE

Figure 3 (and Table 4) compares the performances of the Nearest Neighbor algorithm (NN), BNGE, and KBNGE (see below) to those of the k-Nearest Neighbor algorithm (kNN, k determined via leave-one-out cross-validation [13]) in eleven domains. Shown are relative performance differences between kNN and the other algorithms compared. An asterisk appears when the difference is statistically significant. BNGE (without pruning) outperforms the first Nearest Neighbor algorithm (NN) in 3 domains and is outperformed by NN in 4 other domains. The k-Nearest Neighbor algorithm outperforms NN and BNGE in 6 domains, and BNGE shows better generalization performance than kNN in Tasks A and C.

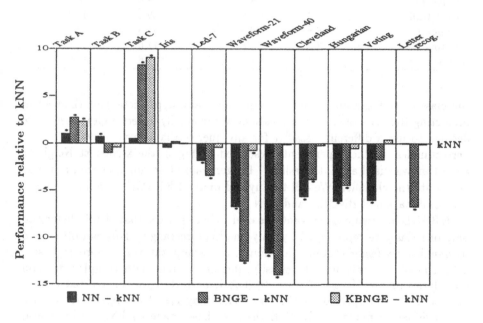

Fig. 3. Performance of NN, BNGE, and KBNGE relative to kNN. An * indicates that the performance difference between kNN and the other algorithms is statistically significant (p < 0.05). See Table 4 in appendix for detailed numbers.

Table 2 shows results from a set of experiments that were conducted to determine where BNGE would commit most of its errors. Displayed are the percentages of test examples that were covered by at least one hyperrectangle (column 2), the percentage of these test examples that were misclassified (column 3), the percentage of test examples that were outside of all hyperrectangles (column 4), and the percentage of these "outside"-test examples that were misclassified (column 5). BNGE commits significantly more errors when predicting

331

Table 2. Comparison of correctness of classifications made by BNGE inside of hyperrectangles versus outside. Numbers are based on a single repetition.

	Percentage of test examples			
	classified		classified	
Domain	inside	of these incorrect	outside	of these incorrect
Task A	93.3	0.0	6.7	20.0
Task B	80.7	4.1	19.3	10.3
Task C	76.0	0.9	24.0	38.9
Iris	80.0	0.0	20.0	22.2
Led-7	89.4	26.0	10.6	56.6
Wave-21	26.0	11.5	74.0	33.8
Wave-40	12.0	8.3	88.0	35.2
Cleveland	30.8	3.6	69.2	33.3
Hungarian	45.5	12.5	54.5	22.9
Voting	83.0	2.8	17.0	13.6
Letter recogn.	68.4	1.0	31.6	32.8

the class of test examples that are not inside any hyperrectangles than when predicting the class of test examples that are inside hyperrectangles. Hence, we decided to use a different classifier for any queries that are not covered by hyperrectangles. In the experiments described in Fig. 3, the k-Nearest Neighbor algorithm was used as that classifier.[1] Un-generalized exemplars were pruned to accelerate the classifier. We call this hybrid method KBNGE to indicate that it is a combination of $BNGE_{p1}$ and kNN.

KBNGE has two main advantages over kNN: 1) Areas that clearly belong to only one class are represented by only one hyperrectangle. This can often lead to significantly faster classification times. The computationally more expensive kNN classifier is only used to classify queries in areas with complex decision boundaries or high levels of noise. 2) The hyperrectangles constructed can be inspected and interpreted by the user. This may lead to a higher acceptance of the decisions made by KBNGE than of those made by kNN or by neural networks, for example. Figure 3 indicates that KBNGE has the same predictive accuracy as kNN in 8 domains, is outperformed by kNN in the Cleveland domain, and outperforms kNN in Tasks A and C (level of significance p < 0.05). KBNGE is faster than kNN at classification time if the following rough formula is satisfied:

$$\#(training\ examples) >$$
$$2 \times \#(hyperrectangles) + (1 - x) \times \#(training\ examples) \qquad (1)$$

where x is the percentage of test cases classified by BNGE. All other $(1 - x)\%$ of the test cases are classified by the kNN classifier. The value of x differs from domain to domain (see Table 3) and must be determined empirically. The justification for the formula is that kNN has to compare each query to all training

---

[1] Once again, k values were determined via leave-one-out cross-validation [13]. Values of k varied significantly across domains and for different random partitions of the training data within most domains (see also Table 5).

examples, while KBNGE must compare each query to all hyperrectangles (a comparison to a hyperrectangle is approximately twice as expensive as a comparison to a training example), and if the query is not covered by any hyperrectangles (which happens in $(1-x)\%$ of the cases), KBNGE must compare the query to all training examples.[2] Formula (1), evaluated with the data displayed in Table 3, shows that KBNGE is faster than kNN in all domains tested. It can also be seen from that table that in domains with large amounts of noise (Waveform, Cleveland, and Hungarian), kNN is used very often, which indicates that a noise tolerant version of BNGE should help to improve the speed of KBNGE even further.

The number of training (and test) examples covered by any hyperrectangle differs significantly within and across domains. For example, a single hyperrectangle is always constructed in the Iris domain to cover all instances of Iris Setosa, while in the Cleveland and Hungarian domains a single hyperrectangle never covers more than approximately 30% of the training (20% of the test) examples of its class.

Table 3. Complexity of KBNGE. Shown are the number of hyperrectangles constructed by the BNGE part of KBNGE, the ratio of the number of hyperrectangles to the number of training examples (in parentheses), and the average percentage of test examples which were covered by at least one hyperrectangle. Numbers are means ($\pm$ standard error) over 25 experiments.

Domain	Number of hyperrectangles constructed by $BNGE_{p1}$		Percentage of test examples classified by $BNGE_{p1}$[*]
Const A	4.0 ± 0.0	(1%)	96.7%
Const B	18.2 ± 0.6	(6%)	82.6%
Const C	22.4 ± 0.7	(7%)	83.8%
Iris	4.6 ± 0.3	(4%)	77.9%
Led-7	31.0 ± 0.6	(16%)	77.0%
Wave-21	4.0 ± 0.1	(1%)	22.7%
Wave-40	3.1 ± 0.1	(1%)	14.4%
Cleveland	23.0 ± 0.8	(11%)	35.8%
Hungarian	25.3 ± 0.5	(12%)	49.8%
Voting	12.3 ± 0.7	(4%)	78.0%
Letter recogn.	663.5 ± 2.7	(4%)	68.3%

[*] All other test examples were classified by kNN

---

[2] Formula (1) assumes that retrieval of training data is not conducted more efficiently with methods such as k-d trees [5] or box-trees [7]. In domains with many relevant features, neither k-d trees nor box-trees provide significant speedups over serial search. In domains where they do provide speedups, KBNGE could also be accelerated by storing the hyperrectangles in a box tree.

4 Conclusions and Discussion

A batch version of NGE without overlapping hyperrectangles, called BNGE, was introduced in Wettschereck & Dietterich [14] and shown to significantly outperform NGE in most domains tested. A simple pruning technique, which significantly reduces the amount of storage required by NGE and BNGE, is introduced in this paper. This significant simplification of the classifier had no negative effect on the predictive accuracy of BNGE (and NGE) in 10 of the 11 domains tested. A very compact representation of the training data is found after a classifier is constructed with BNGE and pruned. This representation can be used to do the following:

- Re-evaluate the representation. For example, we were able to determine in several domains through inspection of the hyperrectangles after training and pruning that some of the input features were irrelevant.
- Learn about the task. If only a few hyperrectangles are necessary to describe a task, then it can be said that it has a low level of noise and that one might be able to construct a rule-based system from the hyperrectangles to solve the task. If a large number of small hyperrectangles is necessary, then the task at hand is either extremely complex or the input representation is not powerful enough and should be modified.
- Assign levels of confidence to decisions. Queries that fall inside of hyperrectangles constructed by BNGE are significantly more likely to be classified correctly than queries outside of all hyperrectangles.
- Determine which regions of the input space are not adequately covered by training examples. This could prompt the experimenter either to collect more data or to clearly define which inputs can be processed by the system and which should be rejected. The ability for the user to easily interpret exemplars as prototypes of the task to be learned is a significant advantage of hyperrectangular based methods over such methods as kNN, neural networks, or decision trees.

A hybrid method, called KBNGE, that uses BNGE in areas that clearly belong to one output class and kNN otherwise was introduced and shown to have accuracy similar to kNN at improved classification speed in a large number of applications. In the majority of the domains tested, over 70% of the test examples were classified by the hyperrectangular based part of KBNGE, thus making it significantly faster than kNN at classification time and enabling the system to justify most of its decisions in a manner that can be easily understood by the user. Note that the pruning technique used by KBNGE (un-generalized hyperrectangles are removed) influences the classification accuracy of KBNGE only for queries that perfectly match a given trivial hyperrectangle and only if $k \neq 1$. In all other cases, pruning only affects the speed of KBNGE.

A flaw of the current version of BNGE is that it constructs hyperrectangles only in those parts of the input space that contain no noisy patterns. Future work will introduce noise tolerance into the BNGE algorithm by introducing a mechanism for accepting merges of hyperrectangles even if examples of other classes would be covered. A conceivable approach would be Omohundro's bottom-up model merging approach [8], for example.

The KBNGE algorithm exhibits classification accuracies comparable to the best known accuracies, it is fast in training and testing time, and it is easy to use. We believe KBNGE is an important tool to include in the set of commonly used machine learning algorithms.

Acknowledgements

I thank Steven Salzberg for providing assistance during the implementation of NGE. I also thank Thomas Dietterich, Kathy Astrahantseff, Bill Langford, and the anonymous reviewers for comments made on earlier drafts of this manuscript. This research was supported in part by NSF Grant IRI-8657316, NASA Ames Grant NAG 2-630, and gifts from Sun Microsystems and Hewlett-Packard.

References

1. Aha, D.W.: A Study of Instance-Based Algorithms for Supervised Learning Tasks. Technical Report, University of California, Irvine (1990)
2. Carpenter, G.A., Grossberg, S., Markuzon, N., Reynolds, J.h., Rosen, D.B.: Fuzzy ARTMAP: A Neural Network Architecture for Incremental Supervised Learning of Analog Multidimensional Maps. IEEE Transactions on Neural Networks 3 (1992) 698–713
3. Dasarathy, B.V.: Nearest Neighbor (NN) Norms: NN Pattern Classification Techniques. IEEE Computer Society Press (1991)
4. Detrano, R., Janosi, A., Steinbrunn, W., Pfisterer, M., Schmid, K., Sandhu, S., Guppy, K., Lee, S., Froelicher, V.: Rapid searches for complex patterns in biological molecules. American Journal of Cardiology 64 (1989) 304–310
5. Friedman, J.H., Bentley J.L., Finkel, R.A.: An Algorithm for Finding Best Matches in Logarithmic Expected Time. ACM Transactions on Mathematical Software. 3 (1977) 209–226
6. Murphy, P.M., Aha, D.W.: UCI Repository of machine learning databases [Machine-readable data repository]. Technical Report, University of California, Irvine (1991)
7. Omohundro, S.M.: Five Balltree Construction Algorithms. Technical Report, International Computer Science Institute, Berkeley, CA (1989)
8. Omohundro, S.M.: Best-First Model Merging for Dynamic Learning and Recognition. Neural Information Processing Systems 4 San Mateo California: Morgan Kaufmann Publishers, INC. (1992) 958–965
9. Parzen, E.: An estimation of a probability density function and mode. Ann. Math. Stat. 33 (1962) 1065–1076
10. Salzberg, S.: A Nearest Hyperrectangle Learning Method. Machine Learning 6 (1991) 277–309
11. Schaffer, C.: Overfitting Avoidance as Bias. Machine Learning 10 (1993) 153–178
12. Simpson, P.K.: Fuzzy min-max neural networks: 1. Classification. IEEE Transactions on Neural Networks 3 (1992) 776–786
13. Weiss, S.M., Kulikowski, C.A.: Computer Systems that learn. San Mateo California: Morgan Kaufmann Publishers, INC. (1991)

14. Wettschereck, D., Dietterich, T.G.: An Experimental Comparison of the Nearest-Neighbor and Nearest-Hyperrectangles Algorithms. Machine Learning (to appear)
15. Wettschereck, D.: A Study of Distance-Based and Local Machine Learning Algorithms. Ph.D. Thesis. Oregon State University, OR (to appear)

Appendix

Table 4. Percent accuracy ($\pm$ standard error) on test set. Shown are mean performances over 25 repetitions, standard error. These ($\star$ $\dagger$ $\bullet$) differences to kNN are statistically significant.

Domain	Performance			
	NN	kNN	BNGE	KBNGE
Const A	97.7±0.4*	96.7±0.4	99.4±0.1†	99.0±0.2†
Const B	97.9±0.3$^\bullet$	97.2±0.5	96.2±0.4	96.8±0.3
Const C	83.5±0.7	83.0±0.7	91.3±0.4†	92.1±0.3†
Iris	95.2±0.4	95.6±0.5	95.8±0.4	95.6±0.4
Led-7	70.5±0.6†	72.3±0.6	68.9±0.6†	71.9±0.6
Wave-21	75.2±1.1†	81.9±0.9	69.4±1.1†	81.2±0.7$^\bullet$
Wave-40	69.1±0.8†	80.7±1.1	66.8±1.1†	80.6±1.0
Cleveland	77.8±0.9†	83.4±0.5	79.6±1.1*	83.2±0.6
Hungarian	75.9±0.8†	82.0±1.0	77.6±1.1†	81.5±1.0
Voting	87.3±0.7†	93.3±0.5	91.6±1.7	93.7±0.5
Letter recognition	95.8±0.1	95.8±0.1	89.1±0.1†	95.7±0.0

†: $p < 0.001$, *: $p < 0.005$, $^\bullet$: $p < 0.05$

Table 5. Values of k used by KBNGE.

Domain	k value		
	min	max	average
Const A	1	99	24.7±6.7
Const B	1	27	6.5±1.5
Const C	1	5	1.6±0.2
Iris	1	18	8.0±0.8
Led-7	2	7	4.3±0.4
Wave-21	7	92	34.4±4.2
Wave-40	14	93	43.3±5.0
Cleveland	3	57	18.6±3.5
Hungarian	21	57	37.2±2.3
Voting	3	10	6.1±0.5
Letter recognition	1	1	1.0±0.0

Chapter 3

Extended Abstracts

Automated Knowledge Acquisition for PROSPECTOR-like Expert Systems

Petr Berka, Jiří Ivánek

Dept. of Information and Knowledge Engineering, Prague University of Economics,
W. Churchill Sq. 4, 130 67 Prague, CR

Abstract. The method for automatic knowledge acquisition from categorical data is explained. Empirical implications are generated from data according to their frequencies. Only those of them are inserted to created knowledge base whose validity in data statistically significantly differs from the weight composed by the PROSPECTOR like inference mechanism from the weights of the implications already present in the base. A comparison with classical machine learning algorithms is discussed. The method is implemented as a part of the Knowledge EXplorer system.

1 Knowledge Acquisition task

The aim of an particular application of a diagnostic expert system is to weight each diagnosis (goal of the consultation) using values of input attributes. A knowledge base of such a system contains for each goal a set of weighted rules leading from combinations of values of input attributes to this goal.

In our sence, PROSPECTOR-like expert systems are based on rules in the form

$$Ant \Longrightarrow Suc \ (weight)$$

where

$Ant = j_1c_1...j_kc_k$ is a combination (conjunction of attribute-value pairs, also called *categories*) of length k,

Suc is a single category (goal),

$weight$ from the interval $< 0, 1 >$ expresses the uncertainty of the rule.

During a consultation, all the rules which match the values of input attributes of a particular case are found and their weights are combined (composed) using following pseudobayesian combining function $\oplus$: $x \oplus y = (x * y)/(x * y + (1 - x) * (1 - y))$. Since the knowledge base can contain both a rule $Ant \Longrightarrow Suc \ (weight)$ and its subrule $Ant' \Longrightarrow Suc \ (weight')$, where $Ant' \subset Ant$, this operation is used with respect to the correction principle suggested by Hájek [6].

The result of a consultation is a list of goals (diagnoses, recommendations, etc.) ordered according to their composed weights.

Our idea of *knowledge acquisition* is to construct the knowledge base as a minimal set of rules, which describes given data and can directly be used for consultations. The essential question is which of empirical implications $Ant \Longrightarrow Suc$ (where Suc is the goal diagnosis) hidden in data are to be inserted into the resulting knowledge base and with which weight. The answer depends not only on the data (i.e. on the validity of each implication computed as conditional probability $P(Suc/Ant)$) but also on the inference mechanism used (i.e. in our case that of PROSPECTOR), and on the requirement of accuracy with which the resulting knowledge base corresponds to the data. The predictive power of the knowledge base is controlled by the employed statistical test of the hypotheses that results obtained from knowledge base during consultations (expressed as composed weights) correspond to empirical implications in data (expressed as validities).

2 Algorithm

Input: Data, goal Suc
Output: Knowledge base KB

Initialisation:

    Set KB to be a list containing the empty implication $\emptyset \Longrightarrow Suc$ with the weight computed from the relative frequency of Suc in data;

    Set CAT to be a list of categories jc sorted in descending order of their frequencies in data;

    Set OPEN to be a list of implications $jc \Longrightarrow Suc$ sorted in descending order according to the frequencies of jc in data ;

Computation:

    while OPEN is not empty do

1 select the first implication $Ant \Longrightarrow Suc$ from OPEN;

2 test of the implication $Ant \Longrightarrow Suc$:

    2.1 compute the *validity* of the implication;

    2.2 compute the *composed_weight* from the weights of all the subrules of $Ant \Longrightarrow Suc$ which are already in KB, using composition function $\oplus$;

    2.3 if the validity significantly differs from the composed weight (we use the χ^2 goodness-of-fit test) then add $Ant \Longrightarrow Suc$ to KB with the weight w such that $w \oplus composed\_weight = validity$;

3 expansion of the implication $Ant \Longrightarrow Suc$:

    3.1 for each jc from CAT such that jc precedes in CAT all the categories from Ant do

        3.1.1 generate a new combination $Ant \& jc$;

        3.1.2 insert the implication $Ant \& jc \Longrightarrow Suc$ into OPEN just after the last implication $C \Longrightarrow Suc$ such that the frequency of C is greater or equal than the frequency of $Ant \& jc$;

    enddo;

4 delete the implication $Ant \Longrightarrow Suc$ from OPEN;

    enddo;

If required, the expansion of implications (Step 3) can be controlled by a required maximal length of Ant, a minimal required frequency of Ant and a minimal required validity of $Ant \Longrightarrow Suc$.

3 Experiments

The presented algorithm of knowledge base acquisition is implemented as a part of the Knowledge EXplorer system. [1, 7]. The knowledge acquisition component has been tested in the framework of the ALEX system [10] and for evaluation of virological hepatitis tests [2].

We also compared our approach with CN2 and KnowlewdgeSeeker (KS)[1] on data taken from Machine Learning Repository [8]. "Japanese Credit data" consists of 125 objects and 11 attributes; the task is to learn knowledge when to grant a credit. The whole set was used for training. "Monk's data" are three artificial problems used for testing different ML algorithms [9]. The results are summarized below. The table gives number of the obtained rules and the accuracy of classification (on training set for data CREDIT, on testing sets for data MONK):

	data CREDIT		data MONK1		data MONK2		data MONK3	
system	rules	accuracy	rules	accuracy	rules	accuracy	rules	accuracy
CN2	35	100%	8	100%	51	66%	19	91%
KS	15	80%	3	75%	1	67%	12	94%
KEX	86	97%	4	50%	59	66%	10	99%

The accuracy 50% for KEX on MONK1 data is caused by missing rules for negative examples; so these examples remained unclassified. On the other hand, all positive examples were classified correctly. In this case KEX learned exactly the hidden concept.

4 Concluding remarks

Knowledge EXplorer performs symbolic empirical learning from examples (cases), where the induced concept description is in the form of weighted decision rules. Our algorithm can deal with noisy data, unknown values, redundancy and contradictions.

The generalisation (done by selecting implications using the χ^2 test and removing of redundant rules) is usually very high. Typically, the resulting knowledge base consists only of a small fraction (several percents) of all implications that fulfil the parameters.

When visually interpreting the knowledge base, sometimes some "obvious" piece of knowledge cannot be found. This is because the effect of the corresponding "missing" rule can be composed from its (more general) subrules, which are already in the knowledge base. So this rule is redundant and thus not inserted. Therefore, the knowledge base has to be taken into account as a whole and only within an expert system.

---

[1] Commercial TDIDT system developed at FirstMark Technologies, Canada [3].

When comparing Knowledge EXplorer to well known learning algorithms (TDIDT-like and AQ-like) we can find the following differences:

1. KEX can create more than one rule covering a specific example,
2. the knowledge base of KEX can contain both a rule and its subrule,
3. during consultation, the system can recommend (infer with positive weight) more than one concept.
4. because of used statistical test, KEX requires reasonable amount of input data,

The resulting set of rules obtained by KEX is usually larger then that obtained by ID3-like or AQ-like algorithms. This fact gives more possibilities for explanation and allows us to handle incompletely described cases since more then one rule is applicable during consultation. But the obtained knowledge base is closely related to PROSPECTOR-like inference mechanism.

References

1. Berka, P.: Knowledge EXplorer. A Tool for Automated Knowledge Acquisition from Data. TR-93-03, OeFAI Technical Report, Vienna, 1993.
2. Berka, P.: A Comparison of Three Different Methods for Acquiring Knowledge about Virological Hepatitis Tests. TR-93-10, OeFAI Technical Report, Vienna, 1993.
3. Biggs,D. - de Ville,B - Suen,E.: A method of choosing multiway partitions for classification and decision trees. Journal of Applied Statistics, Vol. 18, No. 1, 1991, 49-62.
4. Clark,P.: Functional Specification of CN and AQ. TI/P2154/PC/4/1.2, Turing Institute, 1989.
5. Duda,R.O. - Gasching,J.E.: Model Design in the Prospector Consultant System for Mineral Exploration. in: Michie,D. (ed.), Expert Systems in the Micro Electronic Age, Edinburgh University Press, UK, 1979.
6. Hájek,P.: Combining Functions for Certainty Factors in Consulting Systems. Int.J. Man-Machine Studies 22,1985, 59-76.
7. Ivánek,J. - Stejskal,B.: Automatic Acquisition of Knowledge Base from Data without Expert: ESOD (Expert System from Observational Data), in: Proc. COMPSTAT'88 Copenhagen (Physica-Verlag Heildelberg 1988), 175-180.
8. Murphy,P.M. - Aha,D.W.: UCI Repository of Machine Learning Databases. Irvine, University of California, Dept. of Information and Computer Science.
9. Thrun S.B. et al: The Monk's problems. A Performance Comparision of Different Learning Algorithms, Carnegie Mellon University 1991, 154p.
10. Winkelbauer,L. - Berka,P.: New Algorithms for ALEX: Expanding An Integrated Learning Environment. in: Proc. ECML93 workshop on integrated learning architecture, 1993.

On the Role of Machine Learning in Knowledge-Based Control

Werner Brockmann

University GH Paderborn
FB 14, FG Datentechnik
D-33095 Paderborn, Germany

Abstract. Knowledge-based methods gain increasing importance in automation systems. But many real applications are too complex or there is too little understanding to acquire useful knowledge. Therefore machine learning techniques like the directed self-learning which is used here may help to bridge this gap. In order to point out the advantages of machine learning in process automation, we applied the directed self-learning method to the control of an inverted pendulum. Through a comparison between a knowledge-based and a machine learning version of the controller, both based on the knowledge of the same expert, results were achieved which demonstrate the usefulness of machine learning in control applications.

1 Introduction

Knowledge-based control systems, hereinafter called KBC, offer an important alternative to conventional controllers especially because of their ability to implement nonlinear controllers in an intuitive and model-free way. A KBC therefore evaluates the state of the process by linguistic variables. The relation between concrete, numerical feature values and the corresponding terms of the linguistic variable may be described by fuzzy sets via membership functions, as in fuzzy controllers, or in a crisp manner, like the ARON-technique [1]. Both allow very complex nonlinearities, but knowledge based methods are normally limited by an overwhelming amount of rules in complex applications. So machine learning is a very promising approach to cope with complex applications. In this paper we therefore try to work out the advantages of the self-organizing process itself over a direct specification by expert knowledge. Thus we compared an online machine learning technique relying on a knowledge-based law of adaptation to a knowledge-based controller which is specified by control knowledge of the same expert. Here we use the ARON-technique (Alternatives Regularly Organized and Numbered) [1] in conjunction with the directed self-learning technique [2] because they are as simple as possible and offer a very intuitive way of learning. In order to work out the advantages of machine learning clearly, we used the simple and popular example of controlling an inverted pendulum.

2 Knowledge-Based Control of an Inverted Pendulum

Based on the experience of a human expert, a KBC was designed using the angle of distortion θ and its velocity θ' as features. Each feature is subdivided by 7 non-linear linguistic terms. On the output side, the motor voltage is specified directly in the control actions. The control rules were tuned to optimize the response to an initial distortion of 30°.

Fig. 2 shows the control results of the KBC. The first swing in the Fig. 2 is the control response to the initial distortion. The pole is raised with a small overshoot and is standing after 0.25 seconds. This result is optimal in the expert´s notion because it reflects his individual idea of what the controller is capable of. The second swing additionally demonstrates the control response to a temporary (50 ms) force which tries to knock down the pole. Although the KBC was not tuned to meet disturbing forces, it keeps the pole upright with a satisfactory transient phase. The state plane representation of the KBC is shown in Fig. 6 in order to illustrate the control characteristics as an input-output relation. It clearly indicates the stepped, nonlinear control actions of the KBC which are typical for the ARON-technique.

3 Self-Learning Control of an Inverted Pendulum

The directed self-learning we used operates similar to self-organizing controllers and is described further in [2]. As Fig. 1 shows, it uses a second knowledge based system, the so-called hyper-system which is also implemented by the ARON-technique and incorporates a knowledge based law of adaption. In this case, the hyper-knowledge is also based on θ and θ′ for they are needed to rate the performance of the controller. They are differentiated by 10 and 11 linguistic terms. The rules describing the hyper-knowledge were spezified by the same expert as above. Such rule sound like *'IF θ is positive large AND θ′ is positive large THEN the responsible control action has to be increased by an amount of 3 Volts'*. The latency time we used to access a control actions of the basic-system was 2 sampling periods.

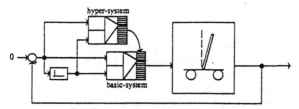

Fig. 1. Scheme of self-learning control of an inverted pendulum

The basic-system is the same as desribed in chapter 2, except that only 4 coarse rules were implemented to prevent the pole from falling down. They are only triggered when θ or θ′ is extremely large, as Fig. 6 illustrates. Due to these rules, the KBC only performs some strong control actions, making the pole to swing back and forth. This can be seen during the first 0.9 seconds in Fig. 3. At 0.9 seconds the hyper-system is activated. Its effect is clearly seen in Fig. 3 as well as in Fig. 8 because the control actions get more and more elaborated. Thus the pole is stabilized without any human interaction in the upper position within 1.3 seconds. The convergence is so quick because the basic-system uses a small amount of terms which therefore have a large range of applicability. Thus they are addressed and modified frequently.

The self-learning controller also had to cope with initial distortions. The results of distortions of ±30° are shown in Fig. 4 for applying the distortion for the first time in the first half of the figure and after 20 times in the second half. The corresponding state space representation is given in Fig. 9. It demonstrates that the hyper-system also improves these situations immediately although the hyper-knowledge was not designed for this case. Apparently a performance is yielded which is much better than that of the KBC. Only 0.13 seconds are needed to stabilize the pole, even without an overshoot. Although the controller is based on a coarsely quantized feature space, this is the best result we obtained by investigating many different kinds of controllers, like linear, fuzzy and adaptive ones. The reason becomes evident when comparing Fig. 7 and Fig. 9.

The a priori given control knowledge is much more diversified, but doesn't reach the strength of the knowledge-based version if compared to Fig. 6. Thus, the reason for the improved control results is the elevation and the valley which occur within in the state space near to $\theta = 0$ and to $\theta' = 0$ (Fig. 9). This non-monotonic behavior is completely new and unecpexted at first. But considering the pole's moment of inertia it becomes evident that it is useful to apply a control action into the opposite direction in order to get a very fast stabilization, even though the pole is not yet in an upright position. Thus the machine learning version of the controller had detected a strategy which makes real sense.

The same effect is emphasized by applying an external force which tries to knock down the pole. So the first swing in Fig. 5 is based on the knowledge after the first trial of Fig. 3. The control response is still comparable to that of the knowledge-based control, see Fig. 2. The second swing shows the effect of the external force to the self-learned controller after training the intial distortions for 20 times. The tipping movement is reduced significantly and an overshoot is avoided although the disturbing force was not applied during the training phase so far. The third swing of Fig. 5 finally demonstrates the effect of considering the external force within the learning process for only 3 times. The tipping movement is reduced drastically so that it is even nearly negligible. The reason are the strong control actions which compensate the external force almost immediately which also can be seen in the state space representation of Fig. 10.

4 Concluding Remarks

In this paper we used the example of the self-learning control of an inverted pendulum to demonstrate the usefulness of machine learning techniques in process control. It turned out that techniques like the directed self-learning may lead to a significant improvement, even in applications for which a knowledge-based solution exists. The reason is that the machine learning version is not limited by the imagination of an expert, but is directly evaluating the process behavior instead. It further turned out that self-learning systems act flexible even in unforeseen situations. This may lead to a control behavior which differs from ordinary or knowledge-based control systems. Thus some unforeseen solutions may be derived automatically, as the effect of a disturbing force demonstrates.

References

1. Brockmann, W.: Combining Real-Time with Knowledge Processing Techniques. 5th Int. Conf. on Industrial and Engineering Applications of Artificial Intelligence and Expert Systems IEA-AIE, Springer Verlag, Berlin, 1992, 594-603
2. Brockmann, W.: Online Machine Learning for Adaptive Control. IEEE Int. Workshop on Emerging Technologies and Factory Automation ETFA, CRL Publishing Ltd., London, 1992, 190-195
3. Mandic, N.J., Scharf, E.M. et. al.: Practical Application of a Heuristic Fuzzy Rule-Based Controller to the Dynamic Control of a Robot Arm. IEE Proc., Vol. 132, Pt. D, No. 4, 1985
4. Shao, S.: Fuzzy Self-Organizing Controller and its Application for Dynamic Processes. Fuzzy Sets and Systems, 26(1998), 151-164
5. Stender, J.: SOL - Second Order Learning. Brainware GmbH, Berlin, 1990
6. Yamakawa, T.: Stabilization of an Inverted Pendulum by a High-Speed Fuzzy Logic Controller Hardware System. Fuzzy Sets and Systems 32(1989), 161-180
7. Zhang, B., Grant, E.: Experiments in Adaptive Rule-Based Control. 3rd Int. Conf. on Industrial and Engineering Appl. of Art.Int. and Expert Systems, 1990, 563-568

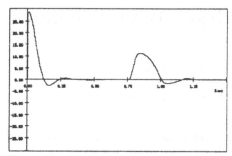

Fig. 2. Knowledge-based control of an inverted pendulum

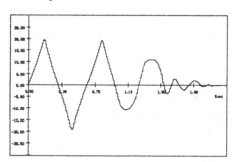

Fig. 3. Initial learning of the self-learning control of an inverted pendulum

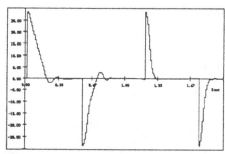

Fig. 4. Response to a distortion of ±30°

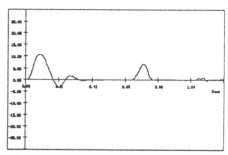

Fig. 5. Response to an external force

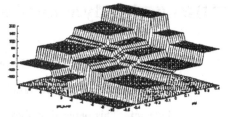

Fig. 6. State space representation of knowledge based controller

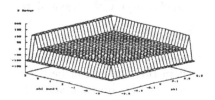

Fig. 7. State space representation of initial self-learning controller

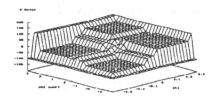

Fig. 8. Self-learning controller after first trial (Fig. 3)

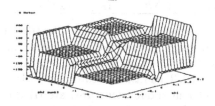

Fig. 9. Self-learning controller after 20 cycles of distortion

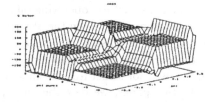

Fig. 10. Self-learning controller after applying an external force 3 times

Discovering dynamics with genetic programming

Sašo Džeroski and Igor Petrovski

Institut Jožef Stefan, Jamova 39, 61111 Ljubljana, Slovenia

Abstract. This paper describes an application of the genetic programming paradigm to the problem of structure identification of dynamical systems. The approach is experimentally evaluated by reconstructing the models of several dynamical systems from simulated behaviors.

1 Introduction

The task of identification of dynamical systems (discovering dynamics), as addressed in this paper, can be defined informally as follows: Given an example behavior of a dynamical system, find a set of laws that describe the dynamics of the system. More precisely, a set of real-valued system variables is measured at regular intervals over a period of time, as illustrated in Table 1. The laws to be discovered (also called model of the dynamical system) are typically a set of differential equations $dX_i/dt = f_i(X_1, \ldots, X_n)$, $i = 1, \ldots, n$.

Table 1. A behavior trace of a dynamical system.

Time	System variables			
	X_1	X_2	$\ldots$	X_n
t_0	x_{10}	x_{20}	$\ldots$	x_{n0}
$t_1 = t_0 + h$	x_{11}	x_{21}	$\ldots$	x_{n1}
$\vdots$	$\vdots$	$\vdots$	$\ddots$	$\vdots$
$t_N = t_0 + Nh$	x_{1N}	x_{2N}	$\ldots$	x_{nN}

In mainstream system identification, as summarized by Ljung [4], the assumption is that the model structure (i.e. the functional form of each f_i) is known. The task is then to determine suitable values for the parameters in the model. This task is accordingly called *parameter identification*. In practice, many different model structures are tried out and the process of identification really becomes the process of evaluating and choosing between the resulting models in these different structures [4]. We refer to this task as *structure identification*.

Genetic algorithms [2] can be used to optimize the values of parameters in a fixed model structure, operating on parameter values encoded as bit strings. Genetic programming [3], on the other hand, can operate on populations of models (expressions) of different structure, which can also contain parameters. While genetic algorithms can be used for parameter identification, genetic programming can be used for structure identification.

In this paper, we describe the application of genetic programming to the problem of structure identification of dynamical systems. Section 2 presents in detail the implementation of the genetic programming paradigm intended for structure identification. The experimental evaluation of the approach is described in Section 3. Finally, Section 4 gives a brief discussion and concludes.

2   Structure identification with genetic programming

In the following, we describe our implementation of the genetic programming paradigm intended for discovering dynamics (GPDD). `Parameters` will be written in `teletype` font and their default values given in brackets.

An initial population of `pop_size` (300) individuals is first randomly generated. For a predefined number of `generations` (30) the population is evolved in the following manner. The fitness of each individual is calculated and track is kept of the individual with best fitness seen so far. The new population is created from the current one by applying fitness-proportionate reproduction and crossover. `perc_crossover` % (90 %) of the new population is formed by crossover and (100 - `perc_crossover`) % (10 %) by reproduction. Offspring that are already in the new generation or are too large (i.e. have more than `max_nodes` (30) nodes) are not inserted in the new population. Finally, after the predefined number of generations, the fittest individual (over all generations) is returned.

During the generation of the initial population, trees are randomly generated by choosing internal nodes from the set of available operators and terminal (leaf) nodes from the set of system variables. Terminal nodes can also be constants. `perc_full_tr` % (50 %) of the generated trees are full (i.e. have all leaves at the same depth), with depth ranging from 1 to `size_tr` (3). Operators are chosen according to a pre-specified probability distribution (default operators $\{+xy, -xy, /xy, *xy, \mathtt{square}(x)\}$, probabilities $(0.24, 0.24, 0.24, 0.24, 0.04)$).

When generating random (non-full trees) an internal node is created with probability `perc_node_tr` % (40 %), and a terminal node (leaf) otherwise. `perc_const` % (50 %) of the leaf nodes are constants, `perc_blocks` % (20 %) of the remaining are building blocks if any are provided, and the rest are variables. We discuss building blocks below. Constants are assigned random initial values from the interval $[-5, 5]$; their values are optimized during the calculation of the fitness. Finally, duplicates are not inserted in the initial population.

Building blocks are subexpressions that can appear in the model sought. The user can specify them as a kind of background knowledge. They may contain generic variables (standing for any system variable), system variables, generic constants and operators. The values of the generic constants are optimized in the context of the tree in which the building block appears. Building blocks are treated as single units (leaves) during crossover (i.e. are not split).

When searching for a formula $dY/dt = f_i(X_1, \ldots, X_n)$, $Y \in \{X_1, \ldots, X_n\}$, trees in the population are candidate functions for f_i. The fitness of a tree T is calculated as $F(T) = (1 + E(T))^{-1} \times (1 + 0.01 \times \mathtt{size\_in\_fit} \times logS(T))^{-1}$, where $E(T) = \sum_{i=1}^{N} (y_i - y_0 - \int_{t_0}^{t_0+ih} T(X_1, \ldots, X_n)dt)^2$, `size_in_fit` (20) is a parameter, and $S(T)$ is the size of the tree T (total number of nodes of T). The integral $\int_{t_0}^{t_0+ih} T(X_1, \ldots, X_n)dt$ is calculated numerically from the measured values of the system variables. The accuracy term dominates the fitness function, but tree size can still have considerable influence in favor of smaller trees.

We use the iterative Levenberg-Marquardt nonlinear optimization method [5] to fit (optimize) the constants in the candidate trees. The total number of iterations used (consumption of computational resources) is fixed and equals `first_iters` × `pop_size` + `total_iters` ($3 \times 300 + 1000$).

3 Experimental evaluation

Three domains (Population dynamics, Brusselator, Monod) from Džeroski and Todorovski [1] were used. Simulated behaviors were given to GPDD, which was run once for each system variable, producing one differential equation each time. This was repeated 10 times. The parameter settings for GPDD were as described in Section 2. The number of generations was lowered from 30 to 20 and 15 when fast convergence to the correct model was obtained in a preliminary experiment.

Population dynamics. The model of population dynamics consists of two equations: $dN_1/dt = k_1 N_1 - s N_1 N_2$ and $dN_2/dt = s N_1 N_2 - k_2 N_2$.

Ten runs were conducted for both system variables, and the genetic programming algorithm was given 20 generations.

Formulae equivalent to the correct one were found in eight of the ten runs for dN_1/dt. Among these, six are variants of $dN_1/dt = (160 - N_2)(N1/100)$ and have the same fitness. The formulae $dN_1/dt = N_2 N_1(1.6/N_2 - 0.01)$ and $dN_1/dt = (N_1/N_2)(1.6 N_2 - 0.01 N_2 N_2)$ are larger and have smaller fitness. In the remaining two cases, formulae with large error (low fitness) were produced.

In seven of the ten runs for dN_2/dt correct formulae were found, all with the same fitness and of the form $dN_2/dt = 0.01 N_2(N_1 - 20)$. In two cases, formulae with large error were produced. The remaining formula has 29 nodes and can be simplified to $dN_2/dt = 0.001 - 0.00005 N_1 - 0.2 N_2 + 0.01 N_1 N_2$. It has low error.

Brusselator. The Brusselator is described by the following equations: $dX/dt = A - (B + 1)X + X^2 Y$ and $dY/dt = BX - X^2 Y$.

The ten runs of the genetic programming algorithm were given 15 generations each. The best tree for dX/dt is $dX/dt = X(Y(X - 0) - 3) + 1$, which is equivalent to the first equation in the model. It is worth noting that several formulae have lower error, but much larger size, and consequently lower fitness than the above.

Nine of the ten formulae produced for dY/dt are equivalent to the correct one, three of them being of the form $dY/dt = (2 - YX)X$ and having the highest fitness. For illustration, one of the remaining six formulae has the form $dY/dt = YX(-1 \times X) - (-2 \times X)$, and a fitness of 0.68 (the best formula has fitness 0.72). The tenth formula is both longer and has higher error.

Monod. Equations $dc/dt = -\frac{\mu_{max}}{y} \frac{c}{c+k_s} x$ and $dx/dt = \left(\mu_{max} \frac{c}{c+k_s} - k_d\right) x$ describe the growth of bacteria x given nutrient c.

Ten runs of 30 generations each were conducted. The best formulae for dc/dt and dx/dt are quite complicated and not obviously related to the above equations, although the equation for dx/dt contains the term $\frac{c}{c+100}$ which is the maximum growth rate of the bacteria. They also have relatively high error as compared to the errors of the best equations for previous domains.

The maximum growth rate is a known quantity in ecological modeling and can be used as a background (domain) knowledge in the form of the building block $\frac{c}{c+C}$, where C is a generic constant. Another ten runs of 30 generations each were conducted using the building block $\frac{c}{c+C}$. This time, the two best formulae, $dc/dt = x/(-6/(c/(c+100)))$ and $dc/dt = (x(c/(c+100))) \times (-0.167)$, are equivalent to the correct formula. The three best formulae for dx/dt are also correct. The errors of these formulae are comparable to the ones for the best formulae in the other domains. The building block thus helps significantly towards building more accurate and understandable models.

4 Discussion and further work

As compared to Koza's symbolic regression approach [3], several improvements have been made in our approach. First, parameter identification is carried by the Levenberg-Marquardt method. This gives better parameter values than the entirely evolutionary manipulation of randomly introduced constants done by Koza. Second, our fitness function takes into account the size of the formulae, imposing a bias towards simpler formulae. Finally, our approach allows for the use of background knowledge in the form of building blocks.

In addition, the fitness function takes into account the nature of the problem of discovering dynamics. Namely, instead of numerically introducing derivatives, as done in LAGRANGE [1] (which can produce highly inaccurate results), the fitness function in GPDD integrates the candidate function numerically. Another advantage over the LAGRANGE approach is the more expressive space of models. Furthermore, GPDD avoids the problem of redundancy present in LAGRANGE. Finally, while GPDD can use background knowledge, it is not obvious how this can be done in LAGRANGE.

We applied GPDD to simulated behaviors of several dynamical systems. For the simpler systems, GPDD reconstructed models equivalent to the original even without the use of domain knowledge. For the Monod model, better results were achieved when background knowledge was available. These results illustrate the potential of our approach for discovering dynamics. However, much more experimental evaluation is needed. In particular, a thorough study over a variety of domains, both real and artificial, is needed. In this respect, the sensitivity of GPDD to noisy (erroneous) measurements should be investigated. This is easiest to carry out on artificial data with synthetical noise. An analysis is also needed of the influence of unnecessary (irrelevant) operators and background knowledge (building blocks). Finally, the approach should be applied to real-life domains.

Acknowledgement. This research was supported in part by the Slovenian Ministry of Science and Technology.

References

1. S. Džeroski and L. Todorovski. Discovering dynamics. In *Proc. 10th Int. Conference on Machine Learning*, pp. 97-103. Morgan Kaufmann, San Mateo, CA, 1993.
2. D.E. Goldberg. *Genetic Algorithms in Search, Optimization and Machine Learning.* Addison-Wesley, Reading, MA, 1989.
3. J.R. Koza. The genetic programming paradigm: Genetically breeding populations of computer programs to solve problems. In B. Souček, editor, *Dynamic, Genetic, and Chaotic Programming*, pp. 203-321. John Wiley & Sons, 1992.
4. L. Ljung. Modelling of industrial systems. In *Proc. 7th Int. Symposium on Methodologies for Intelligent Systems*, pp. 338-349. Springer, Berlin, 1993.
5. W. H. Press, B. P. Flannery, S. A. Teukolsky, and W. T. Vetterling. *Numerical Recipes.* Cambridge University Press, Cambridge, MA, 1986.

A Geometric Approach to Feature Selection

Tapio Elomaa and Esko Ukkonen

Department of Computer Science, P. O. Box 26 (Teollisuuskatu 23)
FIN-00014 University of Helsinki, Finland
{elomaa, ukkonen}@cs.helsinki.fi

Abstract. We propose a new method for selecting features, or deciding on splitting points in inductive learning. Its main innovation is to take the positions of examples into account instead of just considering the numbers of examples from different classes that fall at different sides of a splitting rule. The method gives rise to a family of feature selection techniques. We demonstrate the promise of the developed method with initial empirical experiments in connection of top-down induction of decision trees.

1 Introduction

Traditional feature selection methods are based on statistical evaluation heuristics, which base their ranking solely on the observed frequencies of instances. I.e., some information content measure (e.g., entropy) is computed for the splitting of the training set a feature introduces if applied [1, 4]. Typically, no other information, except an example's value for the feature is utilized in this decision-making. Alternative methods are given in [2, 3]. In this paper we introduce a method that also considers the position of examples in the instance space as the basis of its decision-making. We concentrate on decision tree learning in this paper, even though our method can be applied to other inductive learning schemes, like "separate-and-conquer" rule learners, as well.

The main idea of our technique is to take pairs of examples that lie (roughly) perpendicularly to a splitting boundary into account when ranking the splitting rule. We try to avoid dispersing example clusters in which the members are all of the same class. On the other hand, we try to place the boundary in between examples from different classes. Empirical comparison with the information gain heuristic demonstrates that the new method can improve the prediction accuracy and reduce the size of the produced decision trees in some domains.

2 Rationale for inspecting the frontiers

Consider the two-dimensional space of the following figure, where we have two choices of a linear separator to be applied as splitting rule: A and B. The two features X and Y are of ordered type. Using only frequencies there is no way to discriminate between A and B. However, we can easily see that A would be a much better choice than B, since it readily clusters the examples in the 'opposite' direction, while B breaks such clusters needlessly. If split B is chosen, then there does not exist any linear division along the dimension Y leading to a perfect clustering.

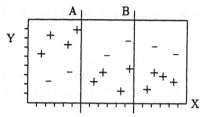

How could we tell A apart from B without breaking promising clusters in the dimension Y? Our approach is to compute the number of pairs of examples that fall at different sides of a splitting rule. Every pair of examples from the same class that the rule breaks up diminishes its goodness count, while breaking up a pair of examples of different classes is rewarded. We do not count all example pairs but, rather, limit our attention to certain regions of the space. These regions of our interest are the *frontiers* of a splitting rule.

3   A geometric approach to feature selection

Let us now define the evaluation function for features based on the geometric properties of the data. An *instance* is an n-dimensional vector of feature values. An *example* is an instance with an associated classification. Let a be an example and X a feature. Then, by $a(X)$ we denote the projection of vector a into the dimension X, i.e., the value of feature X in the example a, and by a_X we denote the vector a excluding its dimension X.

We are considering only binary splits on ordered features at the moment. Hence, a splitting rule S concerning the value of feature X is of the form $X \leq$ constant. Geometrically the inequality defines a halfspace in the instance space. Let $S(a)$ be the truth value of applying the splitting rule S to the example a. By $S(X)$ we denote the constant appearing in the splitting rule S.

We define that a pair of examples (a, b) is an *internal pair* (of class C) if both a and b are of the same class (C), otherwise (a, b) is an *external pair*. The pair (a, b) belongs to the (k, l)-*frontier* of a splitting rule S concerning the value of feature X if

$$d(a_X, b_X) \leq l \text{ and } |S(X) - a(X)| \leq k \text{ and } |S(X) - b(X)| \leq k \text{ and } S(a) \neq S(b).$$

The function d approximates the examples' deviation from the perpendicular direction. In other words, a pair of examples belongs to the (k, l)-frontier of a splitting rule if the line connecting the two examples (as determined by the function d) deviates from the direction of the normal of the splitting boundary by at most an angle l, both are within the distance k from the splitting boundary in the dimension under consideration, and they fall at different sides of the hyperplane. Varying the distance bound k and the angle bound l gives rise to a family of techniques for frontier inspection.

There are several possible ways to choose the distance measure d. We elect to use threshold $(m\text{-of-}n)$ functions; that is, we require that m features out of the total n features under consideration must be equal. Then the first condition of (k, l)-frontier takes the form $d(a_X, b_X) \leq n - m$, where $n = \|a\| - 1$. Threshold functions let us circumvent the problem of nonuniformity of feature ranges. They remove the need of normalizing the feature ranges.

A splitting rule S interfears with a cluster of examples in the direction of its normal least when it breaks up as few internal pairs in its (k, l)-frontier as possible. Furthermore, segmentation along the dimension under consideration is at greatest when as many external pairs as possible are broken up. To evaluate a splitting rule S we subtract the number, $I_{k,l}(S)$, of internal pairs within the (k, l)-frontier of S from the number, $E_{k,l}(S)$, of external pairs within its (k, l)-frontier. We try to maximize this difference. That is, the splitting rule S registering the largest value for the function

$$Q(S) = E_{k,l}(S) - I_{k,l}(S)$$

is chosen as the new branching rule.

4 Discussion

Multiway splitting does not pose a major problem in case of ordered features, since the subsets introduced by the splitting rule will also be ordered along the dimension under consideration. Hence, if the data is split into n subsamples we apply the binary splitting procedure to the $n-1$ pairs of adjoining subsets and sum together all values $Q(S_i)$, where S_i is one of the $n-1$ splitting boundaries of the rule.

With nominal features we cannot set any bounds to the distance of two examples. Moreover, we cannot tell which of the subsets of the training data introduced by the splitting lie next to each other when there are more than two possible values. However, computing the deviance of an example from the normal of the split is not problematic when threshold functions are applied.

Since the distance of two examples cannot be bound on nominal features we elect to treat them as a special case: we do not try to bind the distance but, rather, treat the (k, l)-frontier as if it was (∞, l)-frontier for nominal features. Deciding on the adjacency of subsets introduced by splitting on a nominal feature is a bit more difficult problem. We could choose a random order of the subsamples and treat it as a set of ordered subsamples, or we could go through all the possible orders, count the value of function Q for each of them and choose a suitable measure out of the function values (e.g., the best function value, the average over all function values). The random ordering scheme is applied in the subsequent experiments.

5 Experiments

The algorithms in the following experiments are an implementation of ID3 [4] with information gain as the feature selection heuristic, ID3G is the basic ID3 with the addition of the geometric heuristic to resolve ties of the gain heuristic, and finally, in IDG the geometric heuristic has replaced the information gain; otherwise the program is unchanged, in particular the χ^2 test is still in action.

The domains are two Boolean functions: six-bit multiplexor and four-bit exclusive-or with four irrelevant bits; the difficult (the second) domain of the MONK's problems [5]; a breast cancer domain from the Helsinki University Central Hospital and four of the standard UCI repository databases.

Table 1. The average (over 20 runs) accuracies and sizes of the trees built by the three algorithms on test data and the time taken to build the tree.

DOMAIN	ACCURACY (%)			SIZE (# of nodes)			TIME (1/100 s.)		
	ID3	ID3G	IDG	ID3	ID3G	IDG	ID3	ID3G	IDG
6-Multiplexor	78.6	80.0	98.1	35.0	34.4	21.2	1.5	2.8	4.1
XOR 4+4	70.3	81.2	100.0	156.7	116.9	31.0	10.3	21.5	57.3
MONK 2	69.2	69.7	78.2	173.0	171.0	179.0	6.0	8.5	38.4
LED	68.9	67.0	67.6	103.3	103.0	111.1	6.2	7.5	35.3
Voting	94.4	94.8	92.8	25.5	25.9	90.2	8.0	12.4	291.3
Hepatitis	78.7	73.7	84.1	45.4	47.1	66.5	3.5	8.3	176.9
Tumor	25.7	25.0	29.5	199.3	205.7	437.9	21.7	69.6	665.7
Breast cancer	54.2	53.0	54.5	399.1	381.9	992.4	29.8	69.6	374.3
AVERAGE	67.5	68.1	75.6	142.2	135.7	241.2	10.9	25.0	205.4

From Table 1 we observe that in the first three domains, which contain all possible feature value combinations, the geometric approach achieves significant advantage over the information gain in prediction accuracy. The induced decision trees are either optimal or close to optimal in size for these concepts. IDG takes only some 3–6 times the construction time of ID3 in tree building. No angle relaxation is required in these complete domains; i.e., the angle bound $l = 0$.

IDG's behavior in the remaining five test domains is determined by the characteristics of the domain. In LED and Tumor domains, which have many possible classes (10 and 22, respectively), it is neither able to increase the classification accuracy significantly nor able to reduce the classifier size by relaxing the angle bound. In the Hepatitis domain good results in both respects are achieved, while in the Voting domain only the tree size reduces by angle relaxation. What is the significant difference of these two domains is not yet clear to us. In the Breast cancer domain, on the other hand, some advantage in tree accuracy can be achieved by angle relaxation at the expense of increased classifier complexity.

Our initial experiments with the new method clearly demonstrate the potential of it. However, further analysis and development is required before consistent behavior can be expected.

References

1. Breiman, L., Friedman, J., Olshen, R., Stone, C.: *Classification and Regression Trees.* Wadsworth, Pacific Grove, CA, 1984
2. Fayyad, U., Irani, K.: The attribute selection problem in decision tree generation. *Proc. Tenth National Conference on Artificial Intelligence* (pp. 104–110). Morgan Kaufmann, San Mateo, CA, 1992
3. Kira, K., Rendell, L.: A practical approach to feature selection. *Proc. Ninth Intl. Workshop on Machine Learning* (pp. 249–256). Morgan Kaufmann, San Mateo, CA, 1992
4. Quinlan, R.: Induction of decision trees. *Mach. Learn.* 1 (1986) 81–106
5. Thrun, S. *et al.*: The MONK's problems – a performance comparison of different learning algorithms. Report CMU-CS-91-197. Carnegie Mellon University

Identifying Unrecognizable Regular Languages by Queries

Claudio Ferretti – Giancarlo Mauri

{ferretti,mauri}@imiucca.csi.unimi.it

Dipartimento di Scienze dell'Informazione
via Comelico 39, 20135 Milano – Università di Milano, ITALY

Abstract. We describe a new technique useful in identifying a subclass of regular trace languages (defined on a free partially commutative
monoid). We extend an algorithm defined by Dana Angluin in 1987 for
DFA's and using equivalence and membership queries. In trace languages
the words are equivalence classes of strings, and we show how to extract,
from a given class, a string that can drive the original learning algorithm.
In this way we can identify a class of regular trace languages which includes languages which are not recognizable by any automaton.

1 Introduction

Considering the problem of learning formal languages from examples, and specifically regular languages, [An87] gave an efficient algorithm to learn deterministic
finite automata by membership and equivalence queries with counterexamples.
We call this algorithm DFAL, and we will show how to extend it to learn other
classes of languages, even not representable by automata. Other extensions to
DFAL are, e.g., in [BR87, Sa90].

Recently, researches on formal models for concurrent processes underlined the
importance of trace languages [Ma85], defined as subsets of a free partially commutative monoid (f.p.c.m.), and a theory of trace languages has been developed
[BMS89, AR86], parallel to that of classical languages on free non-commutative
monoids (string languages).

A fundamental difference between trace and string languages is that regular
trace languages are in general not recognized by a finite state automaton on the
f.p.c.m., i.e. Kleene's theorem cannot be generalized to them. As known results
about the identification of regular languages are based on automata, here we
discuss some modifications to use them on regular trace languages.

2 Definitions and Notations

Given a finite alphabet Σ and the free monoid $\Sigma^\star$, a *concurrence relation* θ is
a subset of $\Sigma \times \Sigma$ and $\equiv_\theta$ denotes the congruence relation on $\Sigma^\star$ generated by
the set $C_\theta = \{(ab, ba) \mid (a, b) \in \theta\}$. The quotient $M(\Sigma, \theta) = \Sigma^\star / \equiv_\theta$ is the *free
partially commutative monoid* associated with the concurrence relation θ.

An element of $M(\Sigma, \theta) = \Sigma^\star / \equiv_\theta$ is a *trace*, and can be seen as a set of
strings. Given a string s, $[s]_\theta$ is the trace containing s; given a string language
L, $[L]_\theta$ is the set of traces containing at least one string from L.

Any $T \subseteq M(\Sigma, \theta)$ is a *trace language*. As in the sequential case, the class RTL_θ of *regular* trace languages on $M(\Sigma, \theta)$ can be defined as the least class containing finite trace languages and closed with respect to set-theoretic union, concatenation and $(\cdot)^*$ closure of languages, being the concatenation of two traces the equivalence class of the concatenations of their strings. I.e., these languages are defined by regular expressions on finite sets. Moreover, it can be shown that a trace language T is regular if and only if there is a regular string language L such that $T = [L]_\theta$ [BMS89].

We will consider only the case in which θ is a transitive relation. As a consequence, the maximal cliques of the graph associated to the concurrence relation induce a partition on Σ. Two letters will be in the same element of this partition if and only if they are nodes of the same maximal clique in the graph associated to θ, i.e., if and only if they commute in C_θ. So we can define the alphabet as the partition: $\Sigma = \bigcup_{i=1}^n c_i$, where n is the number of maximal cliques in the graph of θ. The term *clique* is from now on extended to the elements c_i of the partition on Σ, when not explicitly referred to the graph of θ. Given this, we can prove a useful result, where letters from Σ are grouped as the variables in a usual algebraic monomial:

Theorem 1. *Each trace t in $M(\Sigma, \theta)$ can be uniquely represented as a sequence of monomials $t_1 \ldots t_m$, where all the letters of each monomial t_i are from the same clique, and any two adjacent monomials are for different cliques.*

Proof. (Sketch) Any string is divided in groups of letters that never mix together.

Given a monomial t_i, $|t_i|_{a_j}$ denotes the degree of a_j in t_i, and $MCD(|t_i|_\Sigma)$ denotes the Maximum Common Divisor of the degrees of the letters in t_i.

3   Main Results

Our results apply to the restricted class of regular trace languages defined by a transitive θ and by regular expressions where, when an operation of the expression joins two different traces, the trailing letters of the first don't commute in θ with the leading letters of the second. This means that in such a regular expression the joining of different traces never mix letters, while this is still allowed when concatenating one or more copies of the same trace. We call them *isolating* regular expressions and *isolating* regular trace languages. This subclass of RTL_θ offers a way to extract strings with interesting properties from each trace. Given $\Sigma = \{a, b, x\}$ and $\theta = \{(a, b)\}$, isolating languages are: $[ax \cdot \{axb\}^*]_\theta$, $[\{ab\}^*]_\theta$.

3.1   Choosing a String

Given the monoid $M(\Sigma, \theta)$, with θ transitive, we can choose from any trace t, represented by the sequence of monomials $t_1 \ldots t_m$, the string $s = s_1 \ldots s_m$ made in the following way: for each t_i write the string $s_i = a_1^{p_1} a_2^{p_2} \ldots a_1^{p_1} a_2^{p_2} \ldots$, where a_i is a letter and $p_j = |t_i|_{a_j}/MCD(|t_i|_\Sigma)$. Let's call these strings *ordered* strings. E.g., given that (a, b) is in θ, the trace $[aaabbbbbb]_\theta$ can be represented by $a^3 b^6$, and the corresponding ordered string is *abbabbabb*.

The first key property of this rule is that the ordered string of a trace, obtained concatenating an unbounded number of times the same unknown trace, is the concatenation of the ordered strings of the repeated trace.

Lemma 2. *If the trace t is represented by a single monomial, and $os(t)$ is the ordered string of t, then $os(t \cdot t) = os(t) \cdot os(t)$.*

Proof. The single monomial representing $t \cdot t$ will have each letter with twice the degree it has in t. Therefore also the MCD is doubled, and the exponents p_i in the resulting ordered string will be the same. Then this string will be the concatenation of two copies of the ordered string of t. $\square$

When the concatenated trace is more complex we can state a weaker property: from any trace generated by the closure of a regular language, the ordered string we choose belongs to a slightly bigger regular language generating the same traces.

Lemma 3. *If θ is transitive, $s = s_1 s_2 s_3$ is a string on Σ, with strings s_1 and s_3 containing letters from the same clique, and s_2 an ordered string with trailing and leading letters from cliques different from that of s_1 and s_3:*

$$[\{L \cup \{s_1 s_2 s_3\}\}^\star]_\theta = [\{L \cup \{s_1 s_2 \{s' s_2\}^\star s_3\}\}^\star]_\theta,$$

where s' is the ordered string of $[s_3 s_1]_\theta$.

Proof. Clearly, $[s']_\theta = [s_3 s_1]_\theta$, and the inner closure adds strings to the language between square brackets, but doesn't add new traces to the trace language. Any trace $[\ldots s_1 s_2 s_3 s_1 s_2 s_3 \ldots]_\theta$, generated by the first language, will contain also the string $\ldots s_1 s_2 s' s_2 s_3 \ldots$, which belong to the second language and that is its ordered string. $\square$

Given any regular expression for T we can find an equivalent, w.r.t. θ, regular expression on $\Sigma^\star$ containing the ordered strings. This means that the ordered strings of traces of T belong to a regular trace language L such that $[L]_\theta = T$.

Theorem 4. *Given an isolating regular trace language T over a transitive concurrence relation θ, there exists a regular language L on $\Sigma^\star$ such that $[L]_\theta = T$ and any ordered string extracted from $t \in M(\Sigma, \theta)$ belongs to L if and only if t belongs to T.*

Proof. (Sketch) Consider the regular expression that defines T as being built from finite trace languages, applying to them many subsequent union, concatenation, and closure operations. We will build a regular expression on $\Sigma^\star$, that defines a language L which satisfies our statement, by induction on the structure of the regular expression for T, using the properties stated for ordered strings over regular operations.

E.g., when $T = T'^\star$, being it a union of concatenations, we consider different cases of joined traces, and cover this unbounded operation using Lemma 3. $\square$

3.2 Identifying Isolating Languages

We can identify an isolating target language T using membership and equivalence queries with counterexamples using DFAL on Σ^* [An87] to identify a regular language L such that $[L]_\theta = T$. DFAL identifies an automaton, but in this way it represents L and then an isolating regular trace language, and some of these have no finite automaton recognizing them, as it is for $[\{ab\}^*]_\theta$ (otherwise one could obtain by regular operations $\{a^n b^n \mid n \geq 0\}$, which is not regular).

Given any regular expression for T, by Theorem 4 we know that there exists an equivalent, w.r.t. θ, regular expression made of ordered strings. This means that the ordered strings of traces of T belong to a regular trace language L such that $[L]_\theta = T$. This same L is the real target of DFAL. The interactions between teacher and learner are filtered substituting counterexamples traces by their ordered strings, and strings from DFAL with the traces that are their equivalence classes in the f.p.c.m. This operation requires polynomial time in the relevant parameters, except when substituting a negative counterexample, where the best known method requires exponential time.

Given the regular expression for T, n the number of states of the minimal DFA recognizing a regular string language L such that $[L]_\theta = T$. Our operations enlarge the corresponding regular expression but this additions cannot require more than a polynomial, in n, number of new states in the automaton recognizing the new regular language.

We can then apply the results of [An87] on learning with DFAL a DFA of p states, with p polynomial in n and, together with the observation on the time required to process a negative counterexample, we can state the following

Theorem 5. *Isolating regular trace languages with transitive concurrence relation, and generated by a language recognized by a DFA of n states, can be exactly identified in polynomial time in n and in the length of positive counter examples.*

It would be interesting to refine the algorithm making use of the information we have about the structure of the extracted regular language, trying to reduce the exponential dependence on the length of negative counterexamples.

References

[AR86] IJ.Aalbersberg, G.Rozenberg. Theory of traces. *Theor. Comp. Sci.*, 60:1–, 1986.

[An87] D.Angluin. Learning regular sets from queries and counterexamples. *Information and Computation*, 75:87–, 1987.

[BR87] P.Berman, R.Roos. Learning one-counter languages in polynomial time. In *Proc. of the Symp. on Found. of Comp. Sci.*, 61–, 1987.

[BMS89] A.Bertoni, G.Mauri, N.Sabadini. Membership problems for regular and context-free trace languages. *Information and Computation*, 82:135–, 1989.

[Ma85] A.Mazurkiewicz. Semantics of concurrent systems: A modular fixed point trace approach. *Lect. Notes in Comp. Sci.*, vol. 188, 353–, Springer-Verlag, 1985.

[Sa90] Y.Sakakibara. Inductive inference of logic programs based on algebraic semantics. *New Generation Computing*, 7:365–, 1990.

Intensional Learning of Logic Programs

D. Gunetti and U. Trinchero

Università di Torino, Dip. di Informatica
Corso Svizzera 185, 10149 Torino, Italy
{gunetti,trincher}@di.unito.it

Abstract

In this paper we investigate the possibility of learning logic programs by using an intensional evaluation of clauses. Unlike learning methods based on extensionality, by adopting an intensional evaluation of clauses the learning algorithm presented in this paper is correct and sufficient and does not depend on the kind of examples provided. Since searching a space of possible programs (instead of a space of independent clauses) is unfeasible, only partial programs containing clauses successfully used to derive at least one positive example are taken into consideration. Since clauses are not learned independently of each others, backtracking may be required.

1 Introduction

Inductive Logic Programming (ILP) is the field of Machine Learning concerned with the problem of learning logic programs from ground examples of their input-output behavior.

Since learning logic programs is in general hard, many systems (such as Foil [2]) try to achieve efficiency by adopting an *extensional* evaluation of candidate clauses. However, since clauses are learned extensionally, but then the whole program is interpreted intensionally (i.e. it is run on a Prolog interpreter), extensional methods are, in general, not correct nor sufficient[1][1], unless some (or even many) special examples are given to the system. Since all these examples must be covered, this can strongly slow the learning task.

The above problems are particularly serious if we want propose ILP also as a tool for Logic Programming and for Software Engineering at large. Especially in this case, the potential ILP user should be able to get a logic program each time it exists in the designed hypothesis space (and not only sometimes or even often), and the synthesized program should be correct (and not only "approximately" correct) at least on the seen examples. Moreover, the user should not be compelled to provide

---

[1] A program is *complete* if it derives all the positive examples, and it is *consistent* if it does not derive any of the negative examples. A learning system is *correct* if it only outputs complete and consistent programs, and it is *sufficient* if it finds a complete and consistent program if it exists in the hypothesis space.

an extensionally complete list of examples, since otherwise it could be simpler and/or faster to write down directly the required program.

In this paper we wish to investigate the possibility of fulfilling the above requirements with an alternative approach to the ILP problem. We present an ILP algorithm (actually, two slightly different versions of the same algorithm) which is correct and sufficient. The originality of the approach is that it adopts an intensional evaluation of candidate clauses. That is, clauses are checked against positive and negative examples by running them with a Prolog Interpreter. In this way the problems of extensionality are automatically overcome, since a logic program is learned in the same way as it will be used. The learning algorithm is automatically suitable for multiple predicate learning and it can work with any number of positive and negative examples. In particular, in no sense it requires an extensionally complete set of positive examples.

2 The Learning Algorithm

The induction procedure described in this section is called *Intensional Learner* (IL for short). First, given a set of clauses S and an example e such that $S \vdash_{SLD} e$, let us define a clause of S as *successful* (w.r.t. e) if it used in the proof of e. IL works as follows. Candidate clauses (CC) are produced from a description of the hypothesis space (HS), until a set of successful clauses (a partial program) deriving some positive example e^+ is found. The partial program p is added to the partial programs discovered previously, and the covered examples are removed, until no more positive examples remain. At every step, the whole set of clauses learned up to that point is checked against the negative examples, and if some of them are derived the learning task backtracks to a different derivation for e^+. If no consistent set of clauses can be found in CC, a new clause from the hypothesis space is generated and added to CC, and a different possible solution is sought. Here is an informal description of IL (algorithm 1):

input: a set of positive and negative examples E+ and E-
    a description of the hypothesis space HS
    a background knowledge BK
CC $\leftarrow \emptyset$; P $\leftarrow \emptyset$
while E+ $\neq \emptyset$ do
   $c \leftarrow$ generate_one_clause(HS)
   CC $\leftarrow$ CC $\cup c$
   for each e^+ such that CC $\cup$ BK $\vdash_{SLD} e^+$ do
     let $p \subseteq$ CC be the set of clauses successfully used to derive e^+
     P $\leftarrow$ P $\cup p$
     if $\exists e^-$ such that P $\cup$ BK $\vdash_{SLD} e^-$ then backtrack
     E+ $\leftarrow$ E+ - e^+

We note that each p is learned by simply running CC $\cup$ BK as a normal logic program on a Prolog interpreter on one of the positive examples, and maintaining a trace of the clauses effectively used in the derivation of that example. In the same way the current P is checked against the negative examples.

We immediately notice that there is a major drawback in the above algorithm. If a set of partial programs consistent with the given examples cannot be found in the current CC, a new clause is added to CC from the hypothesis space, and the search starts again. However, a lot of time can be wasted by learning again the same partial programs as before (i.e. those not involving the new clause) and found inconsistent. A solution to this problem is to search from the very beginning the entire hypothesis space, i.e. by immediately assigning to CC all the clauses in HS (let's call this version of Intensional Learner as algorithm 2). Clearly, a serious drawback of this solution is that the hypothesis space must be finite, and it must be completely generated before the beginning of the learning task.

Since we can also define a hypothesis space containing clauses with different consequents, multiple predicate learning is automatically achieved. We note that both for making the learning procedure terminate, and to guarantee the termination of learned programs, we must require that candidate recursive clauses satisfy some well-ordering relation, such as in [2].

3 Discussion and Conclusion

We begin this section by addressing some major issues about the properties of the induction procedure.

First, if we suppose that the set of generated clauses CC forms a terminating program, then the following property holds:

Theorem 1: *IL is correct and sufficient.*
Proof: Trivial, as it is a consequence of the definition of the induction procedure. Obviously, in the case of algorithm 2 we must assume HS to be finite.

A second major point is about the computational complexity of the learning task. Extensional methods explore a hypothesis space HS of independent clauses, and hence they have a complexity which is linear in $|HS|$. On the contrary, an exhaustive search in the space of possible programs (i.e. pick up a subset of HS and check it against the given examples) would be exponential in $|HS|$, and practically unfeasible. Our approach stands between these two, as it only takes into consideration (partial) programs which derive at least one positive example, and where each clause is successful. To estimate the computational complexity of intensional learner (algorithm 1), consider a positive example e^+ such that $CC \cup BK \vdash_{SLD} e^+$ for some set CC. Let the *depth* of e^+ be the maximum number of clauses used in its derivation[2]. For practical program induction tasks, it is often the case that the depth of an example is related to its complexity, and not to the set of candidate clauses CC. As a consequence, if we have n positive examples, d is the maximum depth on all the examples, S is the size of the first subset of the hypothesis space containing a

---

[2]For example, if we are working with sets or lists, and we can guarantee that all recursive calls in CC ∪ BK are on a smaller set or on a shorter list, then the depth of an example is the size of the sets or lists it contains.

complete and consistent program w.r.t. the examples, and we can assure that each partial program is discovered only once, the complexity of our method will be of the order of S^{nd}. For algorithm 2, since here a partial program can be derived at most once, we have a computational complexity of the learning task of the order of $|HS|^{nd}$ (to which we must add the time required to generate the hypothesis space).

Third, it is clear that the complexity of the learning task can be improved by controlling the number and kind of given examples. Unlike in extensional systems, in IL there is not *any* relationship between the given examples and the possibility to learn a program complete and consistent w.r.t. those examples. Simply, if such a program exists in the hypothesis space, it is found. This means that with an intensional evaluation of clauses, a positive example is sufficient to learn all the clauses necessary to derive it. By limiting the number (n) and the depth (d) of the positive examples, it it possible to improve the performance of the system without affecting its ability to learn.

We conclude by observing that the induction procedure we have presented is rather simple and expectable, and it could be improved in many way. Nevertheless, even as it is, it shows that learning logic programs by adopting an intensional evaluation of clauses is feasible if 1) we avoid searching a space of possible programs and limit ourselves to set of successful clauses and 2) we limit the size of the hypothesis space by some form of prior information and strong constraints. Even if the intensional approach is, in general, less efficient if compared with the extensional approach, it seems particularly suitable for software engineering applications, where the requirements for complete and consistent programs, and the ability to find them whenever they exist in the hypothesis space are a primary demand. Moreover, an intensional system can work with very few and simple examples of the target concept(s). This is important to limit the computational cost of the system, and it is fundamental if no more examples are available. We believe that a careful choice of the examples, together with a judicious design of the hypothesis space can make the efficiency of intensional systems comparable with the one of extensional systems.

Acknowledgement: This work was in part supported by BRA ESPRIT project 6020 on Inductive Logic Programming.

References

[1] F. Bergadano. Inductive database relations. *IEEE Trans. on Data and Knowledge Engineering*, 5(6), 1993.

[2] R. Quinlan. Learning Logical Definitions from Relations. *Machine Learning*, 5:239–266, 1990.

Partially Isomorphic Generalization and Analogical Reasoning*

Eizyu Hirowatari ** and Setsuo Arikawa

Research Institute of Fundamental Information Science,
Kyushu University 33, Fukuoka 812, Japan
e-mail: {eizyu, arikawa}@rifis.sci.kyushu-u.ac.jp

Abstract. Analogical reasoning is carried out based on an analogy which gives a similarity between a base domain and a target domain. Thus the analogy plays an important role in analogical reasoning. However, computing such an analogy leads to a combinatorial explosion. This paper introduces a notion of partially isomorphic generalizations of atoms and rules which makes it possible to carry out analogical reasoning without computing the analogy, and gives a relationship between our generalization and the analogy. Then we give a procedure which produces such a generalization in polynomial time.

1 Introduction

Analogical reasoning is an important paradigm of machine learning. It acquires unknown knowledge by computing an analogy which gives a similarity between a base domain and a target domain. In analogical reasoning, we first detect an analogy, and then project the well-known knowledge in the base domain into the target domain under the analogy. Thus essentials of analogical reasoning are computing an analogy which is a mapping from a base domain to a target domain. However, there often arises a problem of combinatorial explosion in computing analogies. We solve this problem by using a new concept of partially isomorphic generalizations of atoms or rules.

Our partially isomorphic generalization is a method to generalize an atom or a rule as general as possible without destroying its syntactical structure. We show that the facts, i.e., grand atoms, derived from the atoms thus generalized are also derived by the ordinary analogical reasoning by Haraguchi and Arikawa [1, 2]. Hence our generalization can be justified by their theory of analogical reasoning.

2 Analogical Reasoning

Analogical reasoning is carried out by projecting some of a base domain to a target domain under an analogy. Hence we take an analogy as a mapping from the base to the target.

---
* This work is partly supported by Grants-in-Aid for JSPS fellows and Scientific Research on Priority Areas from the Ministry of Education, Science and Culture, Japan.
** JSPS Fellowship for Japanese Junior Scientists.

In this paper we deal with logic programs (programs, for short) as the domains for analogical reasoning. Let P_1 and P_2 be base and target programs, respectively, on which analogical reasoning is carried out. Let U_i be the Herbrand universe for P_i ($i = 1, 2$). For a finite subset φ of $U_1 \times U_2$, we define a set φ^+ as the smallest set that satisfies the following conditions:

(a) $\varphi \subseteq \varphi^+$,

(b) $\langle t_1, s_1 \rangle, \ldots, \langle t_n, s_n \rangle \in \varphi^+ \Rightarrow \langle f(t_1, \ldots, t_n), f(s_1, \ldots, s_n) \rangle \in \varphi^+$,

where f is a function symbol occurring in both P_1 and P_2. We say that φ is an *analogy* if we can take φ as a function such that $\varphi^+(t) = s$ if $\langle t, s \rangle \in \varphi^+$.

An analogy can be extended from terms to atoms in a natural way. For atoms $\alpha = p(t_1, \ldots, t_n)$ and $\beta = p(s_1, \ldots, s_n)$, and for an analogy φ, we say that α is *analogous to* β *under* φ, if $\varphi^+(t_i) = s_i$ holds for $1 \leq i \leq n$.

3 Partially Isomorphic Generalization

For atoms α and β, we write $\alpha \leq \beta$ when $\beta\theta = \alpha$ for a substitution θ, and $\alpha \simeq \beta$ when $\beta \leq \alpha$ and $\alpha \leq \beta$. Let S be the set of all generalizations of an atom. By $[S]$ we denote the set of equivalence classes of all atoms in S induced by $\simeq$. From now on we identify an atom with its equivalence class. Then $\leq$ is a partial order on $[S]$. We define two binary functions $\sqcap$ and $\sqcup$ on $[S]$ as follows: For $[\alpha]$ and $[\beta]$ in $[S]$, $[\alpha] \sqcap [\beta]$ and $[\alpha] \sqcup [\beta]$ are the greatest common instance and the least common generalization of $\{[\alpha], [\beta]\}$ w.r.t. $\leq$, respectively [5]. Hence $[S]$ is a lattice with a partial order $\leq$, a meet operator $\sqcap$, and a join operator $\sqcup$. We call the lattice $[S]$ a *normal lattice*.

Now we introduce a new concept of partially isomorphic generalizations of atoms. Let α be an atom and t be a term occurring in α. Then we say that t is a *quasi-replaceable term* of α, if t is a constant or a term of the form $f(X_1, \cdots, X_n)$, where f is a function symbol and each X_i is a variable symbol. For u, a term or an atom, let V_u be the set of all variables occurring in u. Let $\alpha[t]$ be the atom obtained by replacing each occurrence of a quasi-replaceable term t in α by a new variable Z. If $V_t \cap V_{\alpha[t]} = \emptyset$ holds, we write $\alpha \to \beta$ for each variant β of $\alpha[t]$, and then we say that t is a *replaceable term* of α. The relation $\to$ is a binary relation on a set of atoms. We define $\to^*$ as the reflexive and transitive closure of $\to$. Then we say that β is a *partially isomorphic generalization* (PIG, for short) of α, if $\alpha \to^* \beta$.

Let S be the set of all PIGs of an atom. We consider the set $[S]$ of equivalence classes of all atoms in S induced by $\simeq$. Just as we have done with $\leq$, we have the following theorem.

Theorem 1. *Let S be the set of all PIGs of an atom. Then $[S]$ is a lattice with a partial order $\to^*$, a meet operator $\sqcap$, and a join operator $\sqcup$.*

We call the lattice $[S]$ a *PIG lattice*. There exists an atom γ such that $\beta \to^* \gamma$ holds for each PIG β of α. We say such an atom γ to be the *greatest PIG* of α. The difference of the PIG lattice from the normal lattice is shown in Figure 1.

Let α be a ground atom and φ be an analogy. Then we define $Ana(\alpha, \varphi)$ as the set of all ground atoms to which α is analogous under φ, and $G(\alpha)$ as the

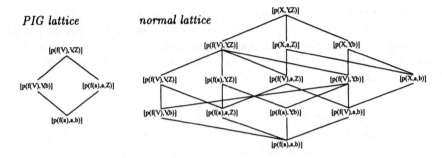

Fig. 1. The PIG lattice and the normal lattice for $p(f(a), a, b)$.

set of all ground instances of the greatest PIG of α. Then we have the following theorem.

Theorem 2. *Let α be a ground atom. For each atom β in $G(\alpha)$, there exists an analogy φ such that β is in $Ana(\alpha, \varphi)$.*

A ground atom α is analogous to all ground instances of the greatest PIG of α under analogies. Hence, in order to obtain an analogy φ and a grand atom to which α is analogous under φ, it suffices to compute the greatest PIG of α. Now we show an algorithm which computes the greatest PIG of an atom.

> **Algorithm:** G_{PIG}
> > **input:** an atom α
> > **output:** the greatest PIG A of α
> > **begin**
> > > $A := \alpha;\quad N := 0;$
> > > **while** there exists the $(N + 1)$-st quasi-replaceable term t
> > > > from the right in A **do**
> > > > **if** t is a replaceable term **then**
> > > > > replace each occurrence of t in A by a new variable Z
> > > > > **else** $N := N + 1$;
> > > > output A and halt
> > **end.**

The *length* of an atom α is the number of occurrences of constant, variable and function symbols in α. Then the numbers of nodes in the PIG lattice and the normal lattice for the atom of length n is at most 2^n and $en!$, respectively, where e is Napier's number.

The following theorem guarantees that we can compute the greatest PIG of an atom in polynomial time.

Theorem 3. *Let α be an atom of length n. The greatest PIG of α can be computed in time $O(n^2)$.*

We have realized the PIG system as a Prolog program which takes an atom α as input, constructs PIGs of α in an ordering by the relation $\rightarrow$, and then returns the greatest PIG of α as output. It works based on the algorithm G_{PIG}. The system has been implemented by K-Prolog on Spark Station 10. For example, if the question to our PIG system is ``?- pig(p(f(a),a,g(b),g(b)),Atom).'', then the answer from the system is ``Atom = p(f(_222),_222,_218,_218)''.

4 Reasoning by PIG

Just as we have done with PIGs of atoms, we can define PIGs of rules with bodies, and we have the same results on rules as those of atoms.

Now we discuss reasoning by PIGs. Let P_1 and P_2 be programs. For each rule C in $P_1 \cup P_2$, we compute the greatest PIG R of C in polynomial time, and then learn a new program P obtained by replacing each C in $P_1 \cup P_2$ by R. Thus we can acquire the fact derived from P without computing an analogy which often leads to a combinatorial explosion. The fact thus acquired can be derived from P_1 and P_2 by analogical reasoning. Hence reasoning by PIGs of rules is more useful than the analogical reasoning as far as time complexity is concerned.

5 Conclusion

The ordinary methods of generalization [4] of examples often cause non-valid and over generalization, and sometimes they need vast search-spaces. To overcome these difficulties we have considered syntactic analogies and introduced the notion of PIG. Our PIGs are all valid generalizations in the sense that they are justified by the theory of analogical reasoning. Moreover each PIG can be computed in polynomial time.

We are now considering a declarative definition of PIGs, and a kind of completeness of PIGs with respect to the analogical reasoning. Also we are improving our previous work on EBG by analogical reasoning [3] using PIGs.

References

1. Haraguchi, M., Arikawa, S.: A foundation of reasoning by analogy – analogical union of logic programs. In Proceedings of Logic Programming Conference (1986), Lecture Notes in Computer Science **264** (1987) 58–69

2. Haraguchi, M., Arikawa, S.: Reasoning by analogy as a partial identity between models. In Proceedings of First International Conference on Analogical and Inductive Inference, Lecture Notes in Computer Science **265** (1987) 61–87

3. Hirowatari, E., Arikawa, S.: Explanation-based generalization by analogical reasoning. In Proceedings of International Workshop on Inductive Logic Programming (1992)

4. Plotkin, G. D.: A note on inductive generalization. Machine Intelligence **5** (1970) 153–216

5. Reynolds, J. C.: Transformational systems and the algebraic structure of atomic formulas. Machine Intelligence **5** (1970) 135–151

Learning from Recursive, Tree Structured Examples

P. Jappy, M.C. Daniel-Vatonne, O. Gascuel, and C. de la Higuera
DIF - LIRMM, 161 rue Ada, 34392 - Montpellier - FRANCE

Abstract In this paper, we propose an example representation system that combines a greater expressive richness than that of the Boolean framework and an analogous treatment complexity. The model we have chosen is algebraic, and has been used up to now to cope with program semantics [4]. The examples are represented by labelled, recursive typed trees. A signature enables us to define the set of all allowed (partial or complete) representations. This model properly contains Boolean representations. We show that in the PAC framework defined by Valiant [10], the extensions to this model of two Boolean formula classes: k-DNF and k-DL, remain polynomially learnable.

1 Introduction

This paper deals with data representation, in Inductive Learning. Two main trends are found in the literature:

The first and older one uses an attribute-values type language. When the attribute values are symbolic, this type of language is very close to propositional logic and to the Boolean framework. Learning from these attribute-values representations is "often" "quite" easy. This was shown from a theoretical point of view within the COLT. For instance k-DNF, k-CNF [10] and k-DL [9] are three Boolean formula classes that are polynomially learnable as defined in [10]. Practically, the successful applications of the attribute-values representation (in Machine Learning, but in Statistics and Pattern Recognition also) are extremely numerous. Of course, and that is the tradeback for efficiency, this type of representation is relatively poor.

The second trend tends to use a "structural" representation close to predicate logic or to semantic networks. For the main part, this approach comes from Artificial Intelligence and in particular the work of Winston [11]. This type of representation is richer than the previous one. Not only can we give the global characteristics of the example (e.g. *the colour, the shape*...), but also the relations that link its components (e.g. it is composed of a sphere *on top of* a cube...). The drawback is the algorithmic complexity problems inherent in this type of representation. This was shown by Haussler [6] within the framework of the COLT. However, recent work in Inductive Logic Progamming [3,8] has produced positive results on some very restricted FOL classes.

This paper proposes an "in between" way. We try to combine a complexity similar to that of the Boolean framework with a greater expressive power. The model we have chosen to represent the data has been used so far in algebraic program semantics [4]. The examples are represented by labelled, recursive typed trees called typed terms. A signature enables us to define the set of all allowed representations (be they partial or complete). The idea of using trees stems from the fact that they are close to the "limit of polynomiality". Forest matching, for instance, is already NP-complete. The fact that we dispose of a generation mechanism, rather than simple tree-like representations, enables us to better comprehend the language and its properties. For example, it allows us to define, and eventually generate, all specialisations of a given description. This representation model and its relation to the Boolean one are sketched in Section 2. Our goal is to dispose of a representation system that is richer than the Boolean one, yet remains of similar algorithmic complexity. Proving that this is the case cannot be done out of a precise context. This is why we focus on PAC learning and show (in Section 3) that the natural extensions of two of the main Boolean formula classes, k-DNF and k-DL, stay polynomially learnable.

2 Typed Terms

Typed terms are built using an algebraic structure called a *signature* which determines the set of authorised representations. This contains the allowed symbols along with their types and argument types. With such a structure, terms are constructed recursively in a similar manner to mathematical functions. This endows them with a tree structure having good complexity properties and a natural intuitive graphic representation.

A **signature** is a quadruple (S, F, σ, α) where :
• S is a finite set of types (also called *sorts*).
• F is a finite set of symbols.
• $\sigma : F \longrightarrow S$ is a many-to-one mapping. For any ϕ in F, $\sigma(\phi)$ is called type of ϕ.
• $\alpha : F \longrightarrow S^*$ is a mapping (where S^* is the free monoid generated by S). For any symbol ϕ in F, $\alpha(\phi)$ gives the order and type of ϕ's arguments, with $\alpha(\phi) = \varepsilon$ the empty word when ϕ has no arguments. $/\alpha(\phi)/$ the length of $\alpha(\phi)$, is called ϕ's arity.

Furthermore, to each type s, is implicitly added a special symbol Ω_s meaning "unknown" such that $\alpha(\Omega_s) = \varepsilon$. Terms containing one or more of these symbols are partial descriptions of objects and the others are said to be completely specified. In the following, we assume that all the examples used for learning are completely specified.

The **set of terms** of type s (noted T_s) is the smallest set such that:
$$\forall \phi \in F, \sigma(\phi) = s \text{ and } \alpha(\phi) = \varepsilon \Rightarrow \phi \in T_s \quad \text{and}$$

$$\forall \phi \in F, \sigma(\phi) = s, \alpha(\phi) = s_1...s_n \text{ and } \forall i \in [1,n] \ t_i \in T_{s_i} \Rightarrow \phi(t_1, ... ,t_n) \in T_s$$

Note that this definition is recursive and so allows direct implementation.

The **generalisation relation** between terms is defined by : t is more general than t' (noted $t \leq t'$) iff t is Ω or both terms have the same root ϕ and all arguments of ϕ in t are more general than those in t'. Relation $\leq$ is a partial order of minimal element Ω_s. The generalisation test $t \leq t'$ is linear in the size of t.

The **size of a term** is the sum of all its non Ω symbols. This size is a measure of the information content of the term. This allows us to compute N_k, the number of terms of a given type s and of size at most k, which is needed for learnability results. This value is :

$$N_k \leq k! \ a^k f^k \qquad \text{where } a = max\{/\alpha(\phi)/, \phi \in F\} \text{ and } f = /F/$$

Example: The following signature can be used to describe the origins of present day Americans, tracing through the genealogy of a person until it reaches one of the following possibilities: a Native American ancestor, or an immigrant from one of the continents.

$S = \{r\}$ where r stands for race.

F	σ	α	F	σ	α
American	r	rr	African	r	ε
Asian	r	ε	European	r	ε
Hispanic	r	ε	Native	r	ε

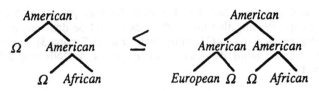

Remark: This simplified signature admits only one type. The need for multisortedness appears when one wishes to add extra characteristics. Furthermore, the order of the arguments isn't commutative and in this example the left son of a node describes (by convention) the ancestors on the father's side and the right son those on the mother's.

Typed terms and Boolean representations

Any Boolean term can be simulated by a typed term using the following signature: each variable V_i is assigned a type and two literals (v_i and $\neg v_i$) plus the corresponding Ω, all having the same common root. So any literal can be true, false or unknown, the root representing their conjunction. This shows that our model generalises the Boolean one.

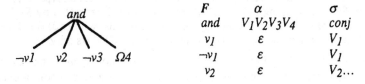

	F	α	σ
	and	$V_1 V_2 V_3 V_4$	conj
	v_1	ε	V_1
	$\neg v_1$	ε	V_1
	v_2	ε	$V_2...$

It follows that the extension of non learnable Boolean function classes to typed terms will not be polynomially learnable either. This argument is in no way incompatible with the one stating that the superset of a non learnable class can be learnable : we simply translate a Boolean learning problem into another in the typed term framework and get our result through reduction. So, we will only concentrate on two learnable Boolean classes, namely k-DNF and k-DL. We define their natural extensions by replacing Boolean terms by their typed counterparts, and note these new classes k-TDNF and k-TDL respectively (where k now represents the maximum size of terms rather than the number of literals). In doing so, we have to extend Valiant's definition of polynomial learnability [10] by replacing the complexity parameter n (the number of Boolean variables) by a, the maximum arity of a symbol and f the number of symbols in the signature. Note that this extrapolation is consistent since using the above transformation, we have $a = n$ and $f = 2n+1$.

3 Polynomial learnability of k - TDNF and k - TDL

We must assume that the examples are randomly sampled from a population on which a fixed but unknown probability measure is defined. Then the two new concept classes defined above can be shown to fit in Valiant's definition of polynomial learnability. To prove this, we will use the theorem by Blumer *et al.* [1] which splits this task into two easier problems. The first is to show that each concept class is polynomial sized - that is the logarithm of its size is a polynomial in the complexity parameters a and f mentioned above. The second is to produce an indentification algorithm which finds a function consistent with the training data or detects its non existence, and is polynomial in a, f and in the size of the learning set. We get [7] :

- $|k\text{-}TDNF| = 2^{N_k} \le 2^{k!a^k f^k}$. So $log(|k\text{-}TDNF|) \in O(N_k) = O((af)^k)$

- $|k\text{-}TDL| = 3^{N_k}(N_k!)$. So $log(|k\text{-}TDL|) \in O(N_k log (N_k)) = O((af)^{k+1})$

This shows that both classes are polynomial sized. Furthermore, the identification algorithms are very similar to those used by Valiant [10] and Rivest [9] and have similar complexity (this is detailed in [7]). So these two new classes are polynomially learnable, an important contribution to this result being the polynomiality of the generalisation test.

4 Discussion and conclusion

This paper studies the characteristics of a new example representation language and shows that from a PAC learning point of view, it leads to a complexity similar to that of the Boolean framework. Several points deserve to be discussed :

In our model, the number of possible representations is sometimes infinite (as in our example) which is never the case with Boolean terms. Yet, some aspects of the Boolean framework are preserved, which explains our results concerning PAC learning.

Signatures and grammars have several similarities. Both rest on analogous algebraic construction systems [2]. But our use of signatures is very different to that usually made of grammars. When we place ourselves in a grammatical framework, derivation trees are not essential. Here, on the contrary, we are interested in the trees themselves and give the interior nodes a meaning. Furthermore, the goal of grammatical induction is to learn "the grammar", whereas here we already dispose of the signature. This difference in approach explains our reaching a polynomial learnability result when most problems regarding grammars have a much greater difficulty [5].

We also feel that terms can represent an alternative approach to ILP in the study of recursive rules. Similarities and differences between both approaches remain to be investigated.

References :
1. Blumer, A., Ehrenfeucht, A., Haussler, D. and Warmuth, M.K. (1986). Classifying learnable geometric concepts with the Vapnik-Chervonenkis dimension. *Proceedings of the Eighteenth Annual ACM Symposium on Theory of Computing.* 273-282.
2. Courcelle, B. (1986). Equivalences and transformations of regular systems - applications to recursive program schemes and grammars, *Theoretical Computer Science* 42 (1), 1-122.
3. Cohen, W.W. (1993). Pac-Learning a Restricted Class of Recursive Logic Programs. *Proceedings of the Tenth National Conference on Artificial Intelligence.* 86-92.
4. Goguen, J.A., Thatcher, J.W., Wagner, E.G. and Wright, J.B. (1977). Initial algebra semantics and continuous algebras, *Journal A.C.M.* 24 (1), 68-95.
5. Gold, M. (1978). Complexity of automaton identification from given data, *Information and control* 37, 302-320.
6. Haussler, D. (1989). Learning conjunctive concepts in structural domains, *Machine Learning* 4, 7-40.
7. Jappy, P., Daniel-Vatonne, M.C., Gascuel, O. and de la Higuera., C. (1993). Learning from Recursive, Tree Structured Examples. *Rapport de Recherche LIRMM.* No 93040.
8. Muggleton, S.H. (1992). *Inductive Logic Programming.* Academic Press.
9. Rivest, R.L. (1987). Learning decision list, *Machine Learning* 2(3), 229-246.
10. Valiant, L.G. (1984). A theory of the learnable. *ACM Com.* 27, 1134-1142.
11. Winston, P.H. (1975). Learning Structural descriptions from Examples, in *The psychology of computer vision,* Winston P. H. (Ed.), Mc Graw Hill, New York, 157-209.

Concept Formation in Complex Domains

A. Ketterlin and J.J. Korczak

Centre de Recherche en Informatique – Université Louis Pasteur
7, rue René Descartes, 67000 Strasbourg, France
e-mail: {alain,jjk}@dpt-info.u-strasbg.fr

Abstract. Most empirical learning algorithms describe objects as a list of attribute-value pairs. A *flat* attribute-value representation fails, however, to capture the internal structure of real objects. Mechanisms are therefore needed to represent the different levels of detail at which an object can be seen. A common structuring method is reviewed, and new principles of evaluation are proposed. As another way of enriching the representation language, a formalism is also proposed for multi-valued attributes, allowing the representation of sets of objects.

1 Introduction

Concept formation is the task of building a hierarchical organisation of concepts from a sequential presentation of unclassified objects. It is often called *categorization*, and has a central importance in many machine learning theories and applications. The basic COBWEB algorithm, for instance, maintains a conceptual hierarchy by incrementally integrating new observations [1]. It performs a hill-climbing search through a space of conceptual hierarchies. The heuristic measure used, called *category utility*, is based on the average increase of predictivity for individual attributes. In fact, nodes in a conceptual hierarchy are labelled with a global predictivity score, which averages individual attributes' predictivity. This predictivity score, noted $\Pi(C)$, increases monotonically on any path from the root to a leaf, and quantifies a generalization partial ordering.

The aim of this work is to extend the space of representable observations for concept formation systems based on attribute-value representation formalism, since, it is largely restricted to low-level *flat* objects, i.e. objects with no internal structure. Complex domains require mechanisms to represent objects that can be viewed at different levels of detail [5]. In the case of the attribute-value representation formalism, values have to be allowed to be objects themselves, are observed and can be clustered on their own. In fact, little work has been done on the clustering of sets of objects. The easiest way to model sets is to allow multi-valued attributes. Such attributes take their value in a typed space of objects.

In both cases, embedded objects may be of any structural complexity. The fundamental assumption made throughout this paper is that they can be found in one single concept hierarchy. In essence, this means that objects of the same type can be compared and clustered, and leading us to a component-first strategy, since embedded objects must have been clustered for the englobing objects to be clustered. The reason for this restriction is that, in both cases, embedded objects are replaced by their conceptual signature (the concept that best describes it).

Section 2 introduces structured attributes. In Section 3, multi-valued attributes are described. In conclusion, the current position and some areas for future work are identified.

2 Structured Attributes

An important issue in representing complex objects is to be able to represent their internal structure. Real-world objects are often perceived as *structured*, i.e. decomposed into smaller, independent, embedded components. These are linked to the englobing object (the *composite*) by a PART-OF relation, the composite object being the *aggregation* of its components. The structure of instances can thus be described with a tree (a *partonomy*), where leaf-nodes represent *primitive* attributes (i.e. continuous or nominal) and internal nodes represent structured attributes, the root representing the object as a whole.

Values for structured attributes are objects. For any structured attribute, noted A_s, there exists a concept hierarchy, noted Γ_s, which partially orders the instance space, i.e. the space where values of A_s reside. Suppose a concept C, covering the set of objects $\{O_1, \ldots, O_N\}$, the object O_n taking value O_{ns} for A_s. A predictivity measure for A_s must evaluate the cohesiveness of the set $\{O_{1s}, \ldots, O_{Ns}\}$, which is the set of A_s' values in C. This evaluation is performed in three steps[1]:

1. The embedded objects $O_{1s}, \ldots, O_{Ns}$ are located in the concept hierarchy Γ_s.
2. The most specific common ancestor, noted γ_{gs}, of the reached concepts is computed. According to the concept hierarchy Γ_s, this node is the most specific generalization of the set of embedded objects.
3. The predictivity score of γ_{gs} is used as the predictivity score of A_s in C.

The process of estimating predictivity for a structured attribute is equivalent to repeated applications of a *climb-generalization-tree* operator: the concept used to characterize a set of objects covers them all, and there are no more specific concepts having the same property.

At the object level, the representation of a structured attribute is an (embedded) object. At the concept level, structured attributes are represented with an embedded concept. The memory structure required to manipulate structured objects and concepts looks like a forest of conceptual hierarchies, where nodes of some trees *point to* nodes in other, more basic hierarchies: more precisely, it may be seen as a hierarchy of hierarchies.

The task of concept formation is defined as incremental unsupervised empirical learning. The mechanism for finding the conceptual representation of an

---

[1] Thompson & Langley's LABYRINTH system [5] is designed to deal with structured objects: their evaluation strategy also relies on the conceptual signature of embedded objects, but treats these as nominal values.

attribute described above may be used in a totally incremental manner. When incorporating a new instance into a concept, the new most specific common ancestor of the covered values can be easily computed from its previous state and the conceptual signature of the incoming value. Moreover, seen values need not be kept, thus leaving memory space spare.

3 Multi-Valued Attributes

Multi-valued attributes allow the representation of properties whose values are sets of objects. Just as a structured attribute admits its own conceptual hierarchy, a multi-valued attribute A_m is associated to a concept hierarchy Γ_m, where the elements of its values are clustered. Let us suppose a concept C, with an extensional definition of N objects, each having a set $S_n = \{O_{n1}, \ldots, O_{nm_n}\}$ as its value for A_m.

When examining the concept hierarchy Γ_m according to the sets S_n, one can distinguish three kinds of nodes. Firstly, there may be nodes in Γ_m that cover no object from any set S_n: these are said to be *empty*, and are ignored. Secondly, there may be nodes that cover objects from only one set: these are said to be *homogenous*, and characterize the difference between a set and all the others. The third type of node, the most informative, is called a *heterogenous*, or *mixed*, node[2]. It is always possible to find nodes in Γ_m that cover objects from at least two distinct sets S_i and S_j.

Intuitively, a predictive characterization of a set of sets of objects relies on highly predictive (specific) mixed nodes. Since a mixed node's parent is also mixed, a good characterization of a set of multiple values can be found at the interface between mixed and homogenous nodes in Γ_m. This means that the more informative mixed nodes are the most specific ones. On the other hand, informative homogenous nodes are the most general ones. This leads us to the definition of *central* nodes. Central nodes are mixed nodes with no mixed subnode, i.e. the most specific mixed nodes. The set of central nodes in a concept hierarchy Γ_m, according to the set of values $\{S_1, \ldots, S_N\}$, forms a generalization of these values. Moreover, predictivity scores of central nodes give an evaluation of the predictivity of this generalization. All central nodes do not, however, cover the same proportion of sets, nor the same proportion of objects. It seems intuitive to weight contributions of central nodes according to these factors. The exact formula to compute A_m's predictivity is:

$$\sum_{l=1}^{L} \frac{n_e(S, \gamma_l)}{N} \cdot \frac{n_o(S, \gamma_l)}{N_o} \cdot \Pi(\gamma_l)$$

where L is the number of central nodes (noted $\gamma_1, \ldots, \gamma_L$), S is the set of values $\{S_1, \ldots, S_N\}$, $n_e(S, \gamma_l)$ is the number of sets in S having a non-empty intersection with the extensionnal definition of γ_l, $n_o(S, \gamma_l)$ is the total number of objects from $S_1, \ldots, S_N$ covered by γ_l, and $N_o = \sum_{n=1}^{N} |S_n|$.

---

[2] The formal definitions of the empty, homogenous and mixed node can be found in [3].

In the case of a structured attribute A_s, the conceptual representation of A_s was a single concept from Γ_s. For a multi-valued attribute A_m, the conceptual representation of A_m is a set of concepts from Γ_m. Thus, a concept described with multi-valued attributes *points* to several other, more basic, concepts.

4 Conclusions

The motivation for these new types of attributes is to extend the concept representation formalism. They do not entail any modification of the original control structure of COBWEB, nor do they fundamentally change its evaluation function. Structured and multi-valued attributes may be seen as *type-constructors*, and can be contrasted with continuous and nominal attributes, which are called *primitive* attributes. Measures of predictivity for primitive attributes are part of the background knowledge. In contrast, in the case of structured and multi-valued attributes, predictivity measures are based on self-made concept hierarchies. The two *type-constructor* attributes allow concept formation to take place in many domains [3]. In particular, several data models use the same mechanisms to represent complex data [2].

Another aspect of structured concepts is their relation to abstraction, as defined in [4]. In this framework, abstraction is a knowledge *transmutation* that decreases the level of detail at which objects are observed. This was exactly the motivation for structured objects, i.e. to capture the different levels of detail. Knowledge transmutations like *concretion* would be, in our framework, to *split* a structured attribute into its descendants in the partonomy. In contrast, abstraction, would be to *merge* nodes of the partonomy to form a new, intermediate, structured attribute. Such transformations of the partonomy carry out some form of constructive induction. Moreover, heuristics to decide when to perform abstraction or concretion are available, through examination of relative predictivity variations at different levels in the partonomy. The result would be a concept formation system that, at the same time, learns the best representation for objects.

References

1. Fisher, D.H. (1987). Knowledge Acquisition via Incremental Conceptual Clustering. *Machine Learning, 2*, pp 139–172.
2. Hull, R., & King, R. (1987). Semantic Database Modeling: Survey, Applications, and Research Issues. *ACM Computing Surveys, 19*, pp 201–260.
3. Ketterlin, A., & Korczak, J.J. (1993). Concept Formation in Complex Domains: Structured and Multi-Valued Attributes. *Research Report*, Centre de Recherche en Informatique, Université Louis Pasteur, Strasbourg.
4. Michalski, R.S. (1993). Inferential Theory of Learning as a Conceptual Basis for Multistrategy Learning. *Machine Learning, 11*, pp 111–151.
5. Thompson, K., & Langley, P. (1991). Concept Formation in Structured Domains. In D.H. Fisher, M.J. Pazzani, & P. Langley (Eds.), *Concept Formation: Knowledge and Experience in Unsupervised Learning*, pp 127–161. Morgan Kaufmann.

An Algorithm for Learning Hierarchical Classifiers

Jyrki Kivinen, Heikki Mannila, Esko Ukkonen, Jaak Vilo

Department of Computer Science; P.O. Box 26 (Teollisuuskatu 23)
FIN-00014 University of Helsinki, Finland
email: {jkivinen,mannila,ukkonen,vilo}@cs.helsinki.fi

1 Introduction. In [4] an Occam algorithm ([1]) was introduced for PAC learning certain kind of decision lists from classified examples. Such decision lists, or *hierarchical rules* as we call them, are of the form shown in Fig.1. The purpose of the present paper is to discuss the practical implementation of the algorithm, to present a linguistic application (hyphenation of Finnish), and compare the learning result with an earlier experiment in which Angluin's k-reversible automata were used.

> **if** $x \in C_1$ or $x \in C_2$ or ...or $x \in C_n$ **then** σ_1
> **else** **if** $x \in C_{n+1}$ or $x \in C_{n+2}$ or ...or $x \in C_{n+m}$ **then** σ_2
> ...
> **else** **if** $x \in C_{n+m+...+1}$ or $x \in C_{n+m+...+2}$ or ...or $x \in C_p$ **then** σ_k
> **else** <default> σ_{k+1}

Fig. 1. Hierarchical rule of depth k.

The rule in Fig. 1 has k *levels*. Each level contains an *if*-statement that tests whether or not the instance x to be classified belongs to the union of some *basic concepts* C_i and if so, then gives a classification $\sigma_j \in \{+, -\}$ for x. There are k such levels and after them the default level with classification σ_{k+1} which is taken if x does not belong to any C_i appearing on the k ordinary levels. The number of basic concepts tested on each level is not restricted and the classifications σ_j alternates between consecutive levels.

2 Algorithm. To explain the intuition behind the algorithm, consider first the cases $k = 0$ and $k = 1$. For $k = 0$, the hierarchical rule consists of the default rule only. Such a rule can be consistent with the training examples only if all examples are positive or all are negative. Normally this is not the case. Rather, there are *exceptions* to any default rule. Our algorithm tries to classify the exceptions correctly using *exception rules* that are applied before the default rule. If $k = 1$, each consistent basic concept forms an exception rule. From such rules a minimal cost subset is selected such that it (exactly) covers all the exceptions. This gives a hierarchical rule of depth 1

$$\text{if } x \in C_1 \text{ or } x \in C_2 \text{ or ...or } x \in C_n \text{ then } \sigma_1 \text{ else } \sigma_2,$$

where the exception rules are **if** $x \in C_1$ **then** σ_1, **if** $x \in C_2$ **then** $\sigma_1, \ldots$, **if** $x \in C_n$ **then** σ_1. These exception rules are of depth 0. Concepts $C_1, C_2, \ldots, C_n$ are the *bases* of the rules.

A hierarchical rule of depth k is formed by covering the exceptions to the default rule by exception rules of depth $k - 1$. An exception rule of depth $k - 1$ is like a hierarchical rule of depth $k - 1$, with the default rule (which can be understood as rule **if** $x \in$ **true** **then** σ) replaced by rule **if** $x \in C$ **then** σ.

Concept C is the base of the exception rule. The rule has to be consistent with the examples it covers.

To get an Occam learning algorithm, we should find a *shortest* hierarchical rule that is consistent with the training sample. This is an NP-hard problem in general, but a good enough approximation can be found in polynomial time using the standard greedy heuristics for the set cover problem. This together with dynamic programming allows us to construct approximately shortest exception rules of depth $0, 1, \ldots$ for all basic concepts until enough rules are found to form a short consistent global rule.

Recall that a *weighted set cover problem* is defined by a domain D, an index set I and corresponding sets $D_i, i \in I$, with positive real costs $cost(D_i)$. A solution to the problem is the subset $J \subseteq I$ such that $\bigcup_{j \in J} D_j = D$ and the sum $\Sigma_{j \in J} cost(D_j)$ of costs for sets D_j is minimized. Chvatal ([2]) showed that if the minimal solution has cost M, then the greedy method obtains in polynomial time a solution with a cost at most $M \cdot H(|D|)$, where $H(n) = \sum_{i=1}^{n} \frac{1}{i} = \Theta(\log n)$. Greedy algorithm builds the approximately minimal set cover incrementally adding one set (that covers some of the remaining elements of D by the lowest cost per element) at a time to the cover. We denote by *Weighted_Set_Cover*(D,I,$\{D_i\}$,$\{cost(D_i)\}$) a function that gives the greedy solution to the set cover problem.

We use this algorithm for finding a minimum cost set of exception rules of depth $k-1$ that covers the exceptions to the default rule. The cost of an exception rule is the sum of the costs of the basic concepts appearing in the rule, and the rule is assumed to cover the examples covered by its base. The same principle is also used for generating the exception rules of depths $0, 1, 2, \ldots, k - 1$. The resulting algorithm is given in detail in Fig. 2. The exception rules are implicitly represented in table Exception_Rules. The final result is traced starting from entry Exception_Rules[$k + 1$][true].

It can be shown that $T = O(k \cdot |R|^2 \cdot |S|^2)$ is an upper bound for the running time of the algorithm in Fig. 2. Here k is the number of levels, R is the set of the basic concepts and S the set of the training examples. Thus we can gain speed by decreasing the number of basic concepts (for example, often actually the same concepts can have different names in R; we can eliminate all except one) and the number of training examples (by standard windowing approach as in [6]). A memory-saving alternative is to re-compute the exception rules when the solution of finite cost is known to exist.

3 Empirical results.
We have implemented and tested our algorithm for learning the hyphenation rules for a natural language. In this application the substrings of the training examples define basic concepts C as follows. Let w be any substring occurring in some training example. Then the concept with name w covers all strings that are representable as xwy, where x and y are arbitrary strings. In the hyphenation problem we are given a totally hyphenated word, as 'hy–phen–a–tion', for example. This word defines actually 10 classified examples:

```
h-yphenation -    hyph-enation -    hyphena-tion +    hyphenatio-n -
hy-phenation +    hyphe-nation -    hyphenat-ion -
hyp-henation -    hyphen-ation +    hyphenati-on -
```

INPUT: $S = S_+ \bigcup S_-$ // A sample: positive and negative examples
              integer k   // Depth of the hierarchical rule to be constructed
OUTPUT: Consistent, near minimal hierarchical rule of depth at most k

$R :=$ set of basic concepts $\cup$ {**true** } // Concepts that cover a nonempty subset of S
Rule_Cost: **array** $[1..k+1][R]$ **of real**   // Computed costs for rules
Exception_Rules: **array** $[2..k+1][R]$ **of set** of concepts
D_+, D_-: **array**$[R]$ **of set of** examples
for $r \in R$ compute:
    $D_+[r] := S_+ \cap r;\ \ D_-[r] := S_- \cap r;\ \ Cost(r) :=$ the cost of r

for $\tau \in \{+, -\}$ // Choose the type of the highest level
    $\sigma := \tau$ // In the following: $\bar{\sigma} \equiv$ if $(\sigma = +)$ then $-$ else $+$
    for $r \in R$ // Initialize the first level. It can't have exception rules
        if $(D_{\bar{\sigma}}[r] = \emptyset)$ **then** Rule_Cost[1][r] := $Cost(r)$
                          else Rule_Cost[1][r] := ∞ // Inconsistent rule
    for level := 2 **to** k+1
        $\sigma := \bar{\sigma}$ //Alternate the classification of the level
        if (level=k+1) **then** H:={**true**} **else** H:=R
        for $r \in H$
            J := *Weighted_Set_Cover*$(\ D_{\bar{\sigma}}[r],\ R,\ D_{\bar{\sigma}},$ Rule_Cost[level-1] $)$
           Exception_Rules[level][r] := J
           if no finite cover J exists **then** Rule_Cost[level][r] := ∞
           else Rule_Cost[level][r] := $\sum_{j \in J}$ Rule_Cost[level-1][j] + $Cost(r)$

if (Rule_Cost[k+1][**true**] $< \infty$)   // Output the rule
then
    Concepts_at_Level[k+1] := { **true** }; Class_at_Level[k+1] := σ
    for q := k **downto** 1
        Concepts_at_Level[q] := $\bigcup_{r \in \text{Concepts\_at\_Level}[q+1]}$ Exception_Rules[q+1][r]
        Class_at_Level[q] := $\bar{\sigma}$; $\sigma := \bar{\sigma}$
else Fail // No consistent rule of depth k and first level labeled by τ exists

Fig. 2. Algorithm that constructs a consistent, near-minimal hierarchical rule.

One possible rule that is consistent with these examples,

    if –ph **or** n–a **or** a–t **then** + **else** <default> –,

says, for example, that there is a correct hyphenation point between n and a.

We have experimented with the hyphenation of Finnish. The training data, correctly hyphenated words from a lecture containing computer science oriented technical language (1706 words), has been used earlier also to learn the hyphenation rule by Angluin's synthesis algorithm for k-reversible finite-state automata (see [3]). The hyphenation automata had very high accuracy for proposed hyphenation points (about 98%), though they might miss some of the possible hyphens. Unfortunately the automata were large: in average 100 states and 250 transitions for 3-reversible language. That is too much for easy understanding by humans.

In our experiments to learn the hyphenation by hierarchical rules, each example contained one hyphen and was classified as either positive or negative depending from whether the hyphen was allowable in that position or not. As the basic concepts we used the substrings found from the examples as well as the same substrings transformed so that all original characters were mapped to consonants (K) and vowels (E). Then, for example, concept '–KE' covers all the possible strings where consonant-vowel pair is preceded by a hyphen. We used the windowing approach and started from 0.1 fraction of all the 14880 examples. The algorithm constructed the rule that was consistent with that window. Then the window was enlarged by the examples from remaining part of examples that were misclassified by constructed rule. After 5 such iterations the method resulted 1, 2 and 3-level hyphenation rules that were consistent with all 14880 examples. The final sample consisted of 1378 positive examples and 2397 negative ones. Our algorithm produced an easy to read and understand rule that contained 100 patterns with average length of 4 characters:

```
if
    -ene, -eni, -est, -nas, -nomai, -notta, -salg, -sets, -sos, -täk, -x,
    -yd, ama-, e-no, eru-, g-, i-sar, it-r, ite-o, ity-, la-u, mu-s, p-r,
    tu-s, vyy-, yvi-
then -
else if
    äe-, ö-ym, -alg, -arvo, -d, -ets, -g, -j, -lex, -ma, -omai, -ong, -osa,
    -po, -pr, -rar, -spi, -ti, -to, -v, a-aske, a-e, a-ilm, a-o, a-uks, a-us,
    ais-a, bs-, e-ä, e-a, e-o, e-uks, e-us, e-utt, e-y, ea-as, en-o, i-ä, i-a,
    i-en, i-es, i-o, i-tr, intö-, k-k, k-t, kom-, mus-, n-as, n-kr, n-otta,
    n-st, o-a, o-e, rus-, s-s, t-äk, t-t, ta-aj, ttö-ä, tu-it, tus-, u-a,
    u-e, umo-, y-ä, y-e, E-EEKE, E-KE, E-KEE, EK-KE, KE-KEKK, KEEK-KE, KEK-KE
then +
else default -
```

The hyphenation algorithm (for English) of TₑX [5] is a 5-level hierarchical classifier that in some respects is similar to our rules. The synthesis algorithm of [5] for finding the classifier counts probabilities for patterns that allow or prohibit the hyphens, and the resulting rule doesn't have to be totally consistent with the data.

References

1. A. Blumer, A. Ehrenfeucht, D. Haussler, and M. K. Warmuth. Occam's razor. *Information Processing Letters*, 24:377–380, April 1987.
2. V. Chvátal. A greedy heuristic for the set-covering problem. *Mathematics of the Operation Research*, 4(3):233–235, August 1979.
3. R. Kankkunen, H. Mannila, M. Rantamäki, and E. Ukkonen. Experience in inductive inference of a hyphenation algorithm for Finnish. In *Proceedings of the Finnish Artificial Intelligence Symposium (STEP'90)*, pages 183–193. Oulu, Finland, 1990.
4. J. Kivinen, H. Mannila, and E. Ukkonen. Learning hierarchical rule sets. In *Proc. of the 5th Annual ACM Workshop on Computational Learning Theory.*, pages 37–44. Pittsburgh, Pennsylvania, July 27–29 1992.
5. M. F. Liang. *Word Hy-phen-a-tion by Com-put-er.* PhD thesis, Stanford University, 1983.
6. J.R. Quinlan. Induction of decision trees. *Machine Learning*, 1:81–106, 1986.

Learning Belief Network Structure from Data Under Causal Insufficiency

Mieczyslaw A. Klopotek

Institute of Computer Science, Polish Academy of Sciences
PL 01-237 Warsaw, 21 Ordona St., Fax: (48-22) 37-65-64
Phone: (48-22) 36-28-85 ext. 45, e-mail: klopotek@plearn.bitnet

Abstract. Hidden variables are well known sources of disturbance when recovering belief networks from data based only on measurable variables. Hence models assuming existence of hidden variables are under development. This paper presents a new algorithm exploiting the results of the known CI algorithm of Spirtes, Glymour and Scheines [4]. CI algorithm produces partial causal structure from data indicating for some variables common unmeasured causes. We claim that there exist belief network models which (1) have connections identical with those of CI output, (2) have edge orientations identical with CI (3) have no other latent variables than those indicated by CI, and (4) and the same time fit the data. We present a non-deterministic algorithm generating the whole family of such belief networks.

1 Introduction

It is a well known phenomenon of human mind to think in terms of causality. The background behind this paradigm is a strong belief that an event may in fact have only few causes so that reasoning about real world events may be kept from explosion of alternative explanations by identifying intrinsic causality. Belief networks (BN), bayesian networks, causal networks, or influence diagrams, or (in Polish) cause-effect networks (terms frequently used interchangeably) are quite popular for expressing causal relations under multiple variable setting both for deterministic and non-deterministic (e.g. stochastic) relationships in domains like statistics, philosophy, artificial intelligence.

Various expert systems, dealing with uncertain data and knowledge, possess knowledge representation in terms of a belief network (e.g. knowledge base of the MUNIM system, ALARM network [1] etc.). A number of efficient algorithms for propagation of uncertainty within belief networks and their derivatives have been developed, e.g. [2].

2 Causal Inference Algorithm

Hidden (latent) variables are source of trouble both for identification of causal relationships (well-known confounding effects) and for construction of a belief network (ill-recognized direction of causal influence may lead to assumption of independence of variables not present in the real distribution). Hence much research has been devoted to construction of models with hidden variables. It is a trivial task to construct a belief network with hidden variables correctly reflecting the measured joint distribution. One can consider a single hidden variable upon which all the measurables depend on. But such a model would neither meet the requirements put on belief network (space saving representation of distribution, efficient computation of marginals and conditionals) nor those for causal networks (prediction capability under control of some variables). Therefore, criteria like minimal latent model [3] or maximally informative partially oriented path graph [4] have been proposed. As the IC algorithm for learning minimal latent model [3] is known to be wrong, let us consider the CI algorithm from [4].

In [4] the concept of including path graph is introduced and studied. Given a directed acyclic graph G with the set of hidden nodes V_h and visible nodes V_s representing a causal network CN, an including path between nodes A and B belonging to V_s is a path in the graph G such that the only visible nodes (except for A and B) on the path are those where edges of the path meet head-to-head and there exists a directed path in G from such a node to either A or B. An including path graph for G is such a graph over V_s in which if nodes A and B are connected by an including path in G ingoing into A and B, then A and B are connected by a bidirectional edge $A < - > B$. Otherwise if they are connected by an including path in G outgoing from A and ingoing into B then A and B are connected by an unidirectional edge $A- > B$. As the set V_h is generally unknown, the including path graph (IPG) for G is the best we can ever know about G. However, given an empirical distribution (a sample), though we may be able to detect presence/absence of edges from IPG, we may fail to decide uniquely orientation of all edges in IPG.

Therefore, the concept of a partial including path graph was considered in [4]. A partially oriented including path graph contains the following types of edges: unidirectional $A- > B$, bidirectional $A < - > B$, partially oriented $Ao- > B$ and non-oriented $Ao-oB$, as well as some local constraint information $A*-*B*-*C$ meaning that edges between A and B and between B and C cannot meet head to head at B. (Subsequently an asterisk (*) means any orientation of an edge end: e.g. $A*- > B$ means either $A- > B$ or $Ao- > B$ or $A < - > B$). A partial including path graph (PIPG) would be maximally informative if all definite edge orientations in it (e.g. $A - *B$ or $A < - *B$ at A) would be shared by all candidate IPG for the given sample and vice versa (shared definite orientations in candidate IPG also present in maximally informative PIPG), the same should hold for local constraints.

Recovery of the maximally informative PIPG is considered in [4] as too complex and a less ambitious algorithm CI has been developed therein producing a PIPG where only a subset of edge end orientations of the maximally informative PIPG are recovered. Authors of CI claim such an output to be still useful when considering direct and indirect causal influence among visible variables as well as some prediction tasks.

3 From CI Output to Belief Network

From the point of view of BN construction the output of CI is not satisfactory. Though it indicates necessity of inclusion of hidden variables at some places (as a parentless parent of nodes at ends of bidirectional edges), it leaves open the question of necessity of inclusion of other latent variables into the model (e.g. as parent of nodes at ends of undecided edges $Ao - oB$ or partially decided edges $Ao- > B$). Though we can clearly include as many hidden variables as we want and the model may be as correct as ever, however such procedure would impose unnecessary space and computation time burden for applications exploiting the belief network (probability distributions of hidden variables are to be saved, and the space required for saving conditional distribution at a visible node grows about exponentially with the number of ingoing edges). On the other hand, incorrect orientation of edges left unoriented may result in introducing independencies not really present in the data, so that belief network would not reflect the true underlying probability distribution. Therefore, it is of vital importance to answer the question if the output of CI is sufficient to construct a belief network, if further hidden variables need to be included, and how to construct this BN.

As an answer to this question we propose the following algorithm and the accompanying theorem. First we introduce the notion of legally removable node.

In a partially oriented including path graph π, a node A is called *legally removable* iff there exists no local constraint information $B * - *A* - *C$ for any nodes B and C and there exists no edge of the form $A * - > B$ for any node B.

CI-to-BN Algorithm
Input: Result of the CI algorithm (a partial including path graph)
Output: A belief network

A) Accept unidirectional and bidirectional edges obtained from CI.
B) Orient every edge $Ao- > B$ as $A- > B$.
C) Copy the partially oriented including path graph π onto π'.
   Repeat:
   In π' identify a legally removable node A. Remove it from π' together with every edge $A * - * B$ and every constraint with A involved in it. Whenever an edge $Ao - oB$ is removed from π', orient edge $Ao - oB$ in π as $A < -B$. Until no more node is left in π'.
D) Understand every bidirectional edge $A < - > B$ as indicator of parentless hidden variable H_{AB} being parent of exactly A and B $A < -H_{AB}- > B$ with no edge between A and B.
End of CI-to-BN

Theorem i *By the CI-to-BN algorithm, a belief network can always be obtained.*
(ii) The obtained belief network keeps all the dependencies and independencies of the original underlying including path graph.

Please notice that no other hidden variables are introduced than those indicated by CI. Notice also that the step C) is non-deterministic: at a given moment more than one legally removable node may exist. A change in order of node removal may lead to change of orientation of some edges of the resulting BN. Hence a whole family of BN compatible with the CI output and not introducing additional hidden variables is generated.

4 Discussion, Summary and Outlook

Within this paper an algorithm of recovery of belief network structure from data has been presented. It relies essentially on exploitation of the result of the known CI algorithm of Spirtes, Glymour and Scheines [4]. The edges of partial including path graph, not oriented by CI, are oriented to form a directed acyclic graph. We claim that such an orientation of edges always exists without necessity of adding auxiliary hidden variables, and that this BN captures all dependencies and independencies of the intrinsic underlying including path graph.

The algorithm presented will provide with belief networks with provably minimal number of parentless latent variables with two unconnected children so that the computational and spatial complexity of the resulting belief network will be as small as possible. Also the precise location of hidden variables to be included will be provided - contrary to the proposal of [1] sect.3.2.2. where most probably location of hidden variables is identified. It will (non-deterministicly) yield a whole statistically indistinguishable family of such belief networks.

The CI-to-BN algorithm will suffer from very same shortcomings as the CI algorithm, that is it is tractable only for a small number of edges (< 10). It will be interesting task to examine the possibility of such an adaptation of the Fast CI algorithm [4]. It may not be trivial as the product of CI differs from that of FCI. It is worth trying as FCI can realistically handle networks with 30 and more variables. Another path of research would be to elaborate a version of CI-to-BN assuming only with a restricted number of variables participating in d-separation, which would also bind the exponential explosion of search space.

References

1. Cooper G.F., Herskovits E.: *A Bayesian method for the induction of probabilistic networks from data*, Machine Learning **9** (1992), 309-347.
2. Pearl J.: *Probabilistic Reasoning in Intelligent Systems:Networks of Plausible Inference*, Morgan Kaufmann, San Mateo CA, 1988
3. Pearl J., Verma T.: A theory of inferred causation,, [in:] Principles of Knowledge Representation and Reasoning, Proc. of the Second International Conference, Cambridge, Massachusetts, April 22-25, 1991, Allen J., Fikes R., Sandewell E. Eds,, San Mateo CA:Morgen Kaufmann, 441-452.
4. Spirtes P., Glymour C., Scheines R.: Causation, Prediction and Search, Lecture Notes in Statistics 81, Springer-Verlag, 1993.
5. Verma T., Pearl J.: Equivalence and synthesis of causal models, Proc. 6th Conference on Uncertainty in AI, 220-227, 1990.

Cost-Sensitive Pruning of Decision Trees

Ulrich Knoll[1] and Gholamreza Nakhaeizadeh[1] and Birgit Tausend[2]

[1] Daimler-Benz AG, Research and Technology, F3W, Wilhelm-Runge-Str. 11,
D-89013 Ulm, Germany
[2] Fakultät Informatik, Universität Stuttgart, Breitwiesenstr. 20-22,
D-70565 Stuttgart, Germany

Abstract. The pruning of decision trees often relies on the classification accuracy of the decision tree. In this paper, we show how the misclassification costs, a related criterion applied if errors vary in their costs, can be intregrated in several well-known pruning techniques.

1 Introduction

Many algorithms for the induction of decision trees from classified examples based on ID3 [Qui86] have been implemented in learning tools, e.g. CART [BFOS84], C4.5 [Qui92], and NEwID [Bos90]. As noisy, sparse or incomplete data sets often cause overly complex decision trees, pruning methods are applied to obtain a best tree with respect to criteria as the classification accuracy, the complexity of the tree, or the criteria of the methods evaluated in [Min89].

A related criterion, the misclassification costs, applies if errors vary in their costs. For example, granting a credit to an unreliable applicant may be more expensive for a bank than refusing it to a good applicant. In this paper, we first show in section 2 how pruning methods can be adapted to use this criterion, and evaluate them in section 3. In section 4, we outline goals of further research.

2 Misclassification Costs as a Pruning Criterion

Given a set of classified examples in an attribute-value representation, the induction of decision trees results in a classifier that can be used to determine the class of new examples. Although the learning algorithm generally produces optimum trees, overly complex decision trees might result from noisy, sparse or incomplete data. The error rate of a tree is determined by estimating its error rate for all examples by an appropriate criterion, or by splitting the data set in disjunctive sets of training and test examples.

A tree can be pruned during or after its construction. Postpruning approaches first construct a complete decision tree, which is pruned afterwards. Either particular pruning criteria determine how to prune it best, or a series of alternative pruned trees is constructed among which the best one is selected.

Given $p(j|t)$, the probability that an object in node t is in class j with $\sum_j p(j|t) = 1$, and the costs $C(i|j)$ of classifying an object of class j falsely in class i, where $C(i|j) \geq 0$ if $i \neq j$ and $C(i|j) = 0$ otherwise, the costs of t are

$$r_c(t) = \sum_j C(i|j)p(j|t).$$

The class of a node is the class i minimizing these costs. Given $p(t)$, i.e. the probability for selecting node t, the costs $R_c(t)$ and $R_c(T)$ for a tree T with the set $\widetilde{T}$ of leaves are

$$R_c(t) = r_c(t)p(t), \text{ and } R_c(T) = \sum_{t \in \widetilde{T}} R_c(t) = \sum_{t \in \widetilde{T}} r_c(t)p(t) \qquad (1)$$

In minimal-cost-complexity pruning [BFOS84], both the construction of a series of pruned trees and the selection of the best tree depends on the error rate and the complexity of the tree. Replacing the error rates $R(T)$ of the tree and $R(t)$ of a node by the misclassification costs $R_c(T)$ and $R_c(t)$ of equation (1) results in a new criterion taking into account the misclassification costs. Similarly, the best tree can be selected by evaluating the test examples, e.g by the test sample estimate ts or the cross validation estimate cv. Estimating the ratio of examples in a class j by $N_j^{(1)}/N^{(1)}$ in the test sample estimate ts, and by N_j/N in the cross validation estimate cv results in

$$R^{ts}(T) = \frac{1}{N^{(1)}} \sum_{i,j} C(i|j)N_{ij}^{(1)}, \text{ and } R^{cv}(T_k) = \frac{1}{N} \sum_{i,j} C(i|j)N_{ij},$$

where the test set contains $N^{(1)}$ examples, $N_j^{(1)}$ examples of class j, and N_{ij} examples of class j wrongly classified in i by the tree T.

In contrast, reduced-error pruning [Qui87] is a single-stage approach, i.e. the construction of the series of pruned trees stops with the best tree. A subtree S with root node t_s of S is pruned in T if $R(S) \geq R(t_s)$, and S does not include a subtree with the same property. The misclassification costs can be integrated by replacing $R(S)$ and $R(t_s)$ by $R_c(S)$ and $R_c(t_s)$ of equation (1).

The pessimistic pruning [Qui87] does not split the data set in training and test examples, but replaces subtrees S with $L(S)$ leaves by their root node t, if the error rate $E(t)$ is in the standard error SE of $E(S)(L(S)/2)$. This is done until no further subtrees can be pruned. Replacing the error rate E by the misclassification costs EK results in

$$EK(S) = (E' + \frac{L(S)}{2} + SE(E' + \frac{L(S)}{2})) * C_{avg}$$

where S is a subtree, $E' = \sum_{k \in L(S)}(EF(k) + \frac{1}{2})$, $EF(t) = E + \frac{1}{2}$, E is the error rate, and $C_{max}(t) = \max_j C(j|i)$. The average costs are given by

$$C_{avg}(T) = \frac{\sum_{k \in L(T)} N(k) * C_{max}(k)}{N(t)},$$

where $N(k)$ is the number of examples in a node k. Obviously, this criterion is equal to the criterion E in [Qui87] if the misclassification costs do not vary.

In minimum-error pruning [BK87], the misclassification costs can be included as in pessimistic pruning, i.e. given k classes, n examples of which n_c are in class c, and $C_{max} = \max_j C(j|i)$, the cost-sensitive criterion is

$$EK(t) = \frac{n - n_c + k - 1}{n + k} * C_{max}.$$

The NEWID pruning method is similar to pessimistic pruning except that it allows to prune a subtree S of a node t even if its classification accuracy exceeds the accuracy of the node without the subtree by tr percent. Replacing the error rates $R(S)$ and $R(t)$ by the cost-sensitive error rates $R_c(S)$ and $R_c(t)$ leads to the cost-sensitive NEWID-method, i.e.

$$R_c(t) \leq (1 + \frac{tr\ in\ percent}{100}) * R_c(S)$$

The variable-threshold NEWID-method replaces the fixed threshold by a variable one computed by

$$tr \geq 100 * (\frac{R_c(t)}{R_c(S)} - 1).$$

3 Empirical Results

In contrast to the studies in [Qui87] and [Min89], we focus on the evaluation of the pruning methods that rely on the misclassification costs, and compare the results of each method evaluated on the same data sets [Kno93].

The evaluated data sets are part of the applications analysed in the Esprit-Project StatLog [STA93]. The default costs are given by the users, i.e.

1. *Credit:* prediction of the creditability of bank clients. It consists of 1000 examples with 20 attributes and 2 classes, and the default costs are 87.5.
2. *Diabetes:* prediction whether a patient is a diabetic. It includes 768 examples with 6 attributes and 2 classes, and the default costs are 125,
3. *Heart Disease:* prediction of heart diseases. It includes 270 examples with 12 attributes, and 2 classes, and the default costs are 18.8.

Using eight-fold cross validation, each data set is split randomly in a training, a pruning and a testing set with a share of 65%, 22% and 13%, respectively. If no pruning data set is needed, pruning and training sets are combined, i.e. the share of the training data is 87%. The cost matrices including a column nc with costs of unclassified examples are provided by the users as shown in table 1.

Credit	no risk	risk	nc
no risk	0	1	1
risk	13.29	0	13.29

Diabetes	neg	pos	nc
neg	0	2	2
pos	5	0	5

Heart Disease	yes	no	nc
yes	0	1	1
no	5	0	5

Table 1. Default costs of the data sets

The average results of a 8-fold cross validation of NEWID, C4.5 [Qui92], and the misclassification costs and the accuracy rates of the cost-sensitive pruning methods evaluated on the three data sets are shown in table 2.

There are several observations holding for all data sets. First, using misclassification cost as pruning criterion improves the results in comparison to the methods NEWID and C4.5. The reduction of the costs of pruning approaches without a pruning data set exceeds that of the other approaches. The reason may be that the set of examples in the training is larger in the former methods.

Concerning the credit data, the cost matrix is strongly asymmetric. As a consequence, the pruning methods tried to classify almost all test examples as "risk", i.e. granting no credit at all. Obviously, such a classifier is useless in practice. This data set shows the importance of a precise cost matrix, i.e. emphasizing the costs of particular classes might give unacceptable results. As the cost matrix of the diabetes data set is too symmtric, the changes of the costs and accuracy rates are very small. In contrast, evaluating the cost-sensitive pruning methods on the heart disease data results in cost reductions of 33% to 43%.

	NewID	NewID Cost Sensitiv	NewID Variable Thresh.	Cost Complex. Pruning	Error Reduced Pruning	Pessim. Pruning	Minimum Error Pruning	C4.5
Credit								
Costs	498.5	117.5	133.6	92.5	121.9	87.5	97.5	320.5
Accuracy	70%	46.8%	52.1%	34.8%	51.9%	30%	50.4%	71%
Diabetes								
Costs	105.4	75.1	79.8	75.6	77.1	74	70.9	74.1
Accuracy	72.8%	69.8%	70.4%	70.4%	71.1%	74.0%	70.9%	71.1%
Heart Disease								
Costs	29.5	20.5	20.0	20.6	21.0	18.8	22.6	27.9
Accuracy	73.5%	60.3%	70.6%	67.1%	67.8%	44.3%	70.3%	72.3%

Table 2. Results of pruning with misclassification costs

4 Conclusions

As shown by the empirical evalution, cost-sensitive pruning methods result in improved decision trees with respect to the costs. However, the improvement strongly depends on the cost matrix provided. On the one hand, asymmetry in the matrix is necessary to achieve lower costs, on the other hand, the results might be not useful if the asymmetry is too strong. Thus, studying the influence of the matrices and determining suitable matrices is subject of further research. Current work is concerned with the integration of misclassification costs in other pruning methods, e.g. critical value pruning [Min87], or minimum-error pruning using m-estimate [CB91], and with the adaption of algorithms constructing decition trees in order to take into account misclassification costs in this stage.

References

[BFOS84] L. Breiman, J. H. Friedman, R. A. Olshen, and C. J. Stone. *Classification and Regression Trees.* The Wadsworth and Brooks, Belmond, 1984.

[BK87] I. Bratko, and I. Kononenko. Learning diagnostic rules from incomplete and noisy data. London Buisness School: Unicom Seminars Ltd, 1987.

[Bos90] R. Boswell. *Manual for NEWID, Version 4.1.* Turing Institute, Glasgow,1990.

[CB91] B. Cestnik, and I. Bratko. On Estimating Probabilities in Tree Pruning. In *Machine Learning – EWSL-91 Learning* . Springer, 1991.

[Kno93] U. Knoll. Kostenoptimiertes Prunen in Entscheidungsbäumen. Diplomarbeit Nr. 924, Fakultät Informatik, Universität Stuttgart, 1993.

[Min87] J. Mingers. Expert systems - rule induction with statistical data. *Journal of the Operational Research Society*, 38, 1987.

[Min89] J. Mingers. An empirical comparison of pruning methods for decision tree induction. *Machine Learning*, 4, 1989.

[Qui86] J.R. Quinlan. Induction of Decision Trees. *Machine Learning*, 1, 1986.

[Qui87] J.R. Quinlan.Simplifying decision trees.*Int. J. Man-Machine Stud.*, 27, 1987.

[Qui92] J.R. Quinlan.*C4.5: Programs for Machine Learning.* Morgan Kaufmann,1992.

[STA93] StatLog: Comparative Testing of Statistical and Logical Learning. Deliverable 4.1, 1993.

An Instance-Based Learning Method for Databases: An Information Theoretic Approach

Changhwan Lee

Department of Computer Science and Engineering
University of Connecticut, Storrs, CT 06269

Abstract. A new method of instance-based learning for databases is proposed. We improve the current similarity measures in several ways using information theory. Similarity is defined on every possible attribute type in a database, and also the weight of each attribute is calculated automatically by the system. Besides, our nearest neighbor algorithm assigns different weights to the selected instances. Our system is implemented and tested on a typical machine learning database.

1 Introduction

Instance-based learning(IBL) algorithms have shown high classification accuracies, and its power has been demonstrated in a number of important real world domains (e.g. [2] [5]). As each instance is represented by a set of attribute-value pairs, instance-based learning algorithms, which learn by storing examples as points in a feature space, require some means of measuring similarity between instances [1]. When the feature values are numeric, Euclidean distance can be used to compare examples. However, in a database environment, there exist other types of attributes including categorical or pointer type. Due to this problem, a more sophisticated treatment of the feature space is required. Recently there have been several attempts to define similarity for categorical domains [3] [7]. However, these methods can not be used directly in the database environment either due to the lack of the similarity measure for pointer type or due to the lack of the weights for attributes. In this paper, we point out some problems that current similarity measures contain and propose a new improved method of measuring similarity between instances in databases. We define similarity measures for every attribute type in the database, and provide methods to calculate the weights for both attributes and selected instances. Our method has been implemented and tested on a typical machine learning database. Our classification accuracy is compared with that of other well known methods.

2 Information Theoretic Similarity Measure

We improve the current similarity measures in a number of ways. Firstly, we take into account the weights of attributes, and the weights will be calculated automatically by the system. Secondly, our learning program handles variables which take any data type: binary, continuous, categorical, or pointer. Pointer types are different from categorical types with respect to the way they store information. With current similarity measure, we would lose part of the information given by pointer types. Thirdly, some stored instances are more reliable classifier than others. Intuitively, one would like these trustworthy examplars to have more drawing power than others. We accomplish this by giving reliable instances higher values, making them appear closer to a new example.

Now we will describe the detailed method of calculating similarity metrics. Suppose we compare the similarity between two instance X and Y, and let x_i and y_i, for $i = 1, \ldots, k$, be the values of i-th attribute for X and Y, respectively. Let a_i be a value of an attribute A, and its target attribute is denoted as T. Let $\Theta_T(X, Y)$ denote the similarity function between X and Y with respect to attribute T. $\Theta_T(X, Y)$ will be defined in the following manner.

$$\Theta_T(X, Y) = \omega_1 \Theta(x_1, y_1) + \omega_2 \Theta(x_2, y_2) + \cdots + \omega_k \Theta(x_k, y_k) \tag{1}$$

where ω_i is the weight of attribute A_i, and $\Theta(x_i, y_i)$ denotes the similarity between values x_i and y_i. The computation of similarity between two instances consists of two steps: calculating the weights of attributes and calculating value similarity between two attribute values. Each step will be explained in detail in the following.

The basic idea for calculating the weight of each attribute is that the more information an attribute gives to the target attribute, the more weight the attribute is to have. For one value assignment of the attribute, its corresponding information content will be calculated using entropy function. For discrete attribute types such as binary, categorical or pointer, we calculate the information content for each separate discrete value and their average value becomes the weight of the attribute. For numeric attributes, we assume that the values are discretized in advance, and the same procedure will be applied. Now the critical part is how to measure the amount of information a value assignment gives to the target attribute. Suppose we are to estimate the amount of information that a value assignment of an attribute A gives to the target attribute T. Kullback [4] has proposed the following measure for the information content of a value assignment.

$$Ent(T|A = a) = \sum_t p(t|a) \cdot \log \frac{p(t|a)}{p(t)} \tag{2}$$

where t, a represent value assignments of T, A, respectively. This measure is interpreted as the average mutual information between the events t and a with the expectation taken with respect to the a posteriori probability distribution of T. It can be viewed as a similarity between two probability distributions. Summation of formula (2) with respect to a may serve as the weight of attribute A. However, in that case, attributes with a large number of category are to have larger weights since the weights increase monotonically as the number of category increases. To avoid this problem, formula (2) is multiplied by the probability that each category can happen, $p(a)$. Furthermore, because the value of this measure can grow indefinitely, using $Ent(T|A)$ as the weight of an attribute may provide anomalous similarity values. By dividing the current $Ent(T|A)$ value by the total summation of $Ent(T|A)$, we have the following formula which ranges from zero to one. Therefore, the final formula for an attribute A is given as

$$\frac{Ent(T|A)}{\sum_A Ent(T|A)} = \frac{\sum_a p(a) \, Ent(T|A=a)}{\sum_A Ent(T|A)} \, . \tag{3}$$

The second step for calculating instance similarity is to compute the similarity between two attribute values. In the following, a new method for calculating similarity between two values, $\Theta(x_i, y_i)$ of equation 1, is defined for each data type: binary, categorical, numeric, and pointer.

For binary values, we just check whether they match with each other.

$$\Theta(x_i, y_i) = \begin{cases} 1 & : \quad x_i = y_i \\ 0 & : \quad x_i \neq y_i \end{cases} \tag{4}$$

For categorical(nominal) values, we first measure the amount of information that x_i or y_i gives about the target attribute. Formally, the similarity is given as

$$\Theta(x_i, y_i) = 1 - \frac{|Ent(T|A=x_i) - Ent(T|A=y_i)|}{Ent(T|A)} \, . \tag{5}$$

For numeric values, the distance between values x_i and y_i is defined as the ratio of absolute value of $|x_i - y_i|$ to the total range of A. Therefore, the similarity between these two values is defined as

$$\Theta(x_i, y_i) = 1 - \frac{|x_i - y_i|}{|A_{max} - A_{min}|} \tag{6}$$

where A_{max}, A_{min} denote the maximum and minimum values of attribute A, respectively.

For pointer attribute type, since a value of pointer type refers to another instance, the difference between two pointer values can be regarded as the difference between those two which are being referred to. The formal definition of similarity for pointer value is defined in recursive form as follows: In case either or both of x_i, y_i refer to instances which does not exist in the database, the similarity is defined as zero. Otherwise,

$$\Theta(x_i, y_i) = \begin{cases} \Theta_T(x_i, y_i) & : \quad x_i \neq y_i \\ 1 & : \quad x_i = y_i \end{cases} \tag{7}$$

3 Algorithm and Experimental Results

Our instance-based learning algorithm stores a series of training instances in its memory, and uses a similarity metric to compare new instances to those stored. The algorithm requires two passes of the training set. During the first pass, the weights of feature will be calculated. The second pass is to calculate a standard similarity metric for measuring the similarity between two examples in a multi-dimensional feature space. Another different feature of our system from other instance-based learners is that we give different weights to the selected instances. In our system, closer instances are assigned larger weight values. Among the instances selected from the database, the similarity values of instances with the same class value will be accumulated, and the class value which has the highest collected similarity values will be the final classification value.

Tic-tac-toe game database has been selected for the purpose of tesing our algorithm. It encodes the complete set of possible board configurations at the end of tic-tac-toe games. Each of the nine attributes in the database corresponds to one tic-tac-toe square. It contains 958 instances of legal tic-tac-toe endgame boards. Figure 1 shows the attributes and their corresponding weights calculated by applying our algorithm. As we can see in Figure 1, the attribute number 5 has the highest weight among others, which is intuitively correct. When we play the tic-tac-toe game and we mark the center square in the first place, we are supposed to win ! In addition, we can see that the squares of 2, 4, 6, and 8 have the same weight, which is correct because they are symmetric. Similarly, the weights of 1, 3, 7, and 9 also show the same weight as well. The results of other algorithms are shown in Figure 2. Our system has shown excellent performance in this database.

0.0800	0.0413	0.0800
(1)	(2)	(3)
0.0413	0.5145	0.0413
(4)	(5)	(6)
0.0800	0.0413	0.0800
(7)	(8)	(9)

Fig. 1. Weights of tic-tac-toe attributes

ID3	CN2	IB3	Proposed Method
84.0%	98.1%	99.1%	99.5%

Fig. 2. Success rates for tic-tac-toe data

References

1. D. Aha, D. Kibler and M. Albert Instance-based Learning Algorithms. *Machine Learning*, 6(1) pp. 37-66, 1991.
2. L. W. Bradshaw. Learning about speech sounds: The NEXUS project. *Proceedings of the Fourth Int'l Workshop on Machine Learning*, Irvine, CA: Morgan Kaufmann, pp. 1-11, 1987.
3. S. Cost and S. Salzberg. A Weighted Nearest Neighbor Algorithm for Learning with Symbolic Features, *Machine Learning*, Vol. 10, pp. 57-78, 1993.
4. S. Kullback, *Information Theory and Statistics*, New York: Dover Publications, 1968.
5. J. M. Kurtzberg. Feature analysis for symbol recognition by elastic matching. *IBM Journal of Research and Development*, 31:91-95, 1987.
6. P. Smyth and R. M. Goodman. Rule Induction Using Information Theory, in G. P. Shapiro and W. J. Frawley, editor, *Knowledge Discovery in Databases*, MIT Press, 1991.
7. C. Stanfill and D. Waltz. Toward Memory-based Reasoning, *Communications of the ACM*, 29(12), pp. 1213-1228, 1986.

Early Screening for Gastric Cancer Using Machine Learning Techniques

W.Z. Liu, A.P. White & M.T. Hallissey

Birmingham University, Edgbaston, P.O. Box 363, Birmingham B15 2TT,U.K. [1]

Abstract. The feasibility of using machine-learning techniques to screen dyspeptic patients for those at high risk of gastric cancer was demonstrated in this study. Data on 1401 dyspeptic patients over the age of 40, consisted of 85 epidemiological and clinical variables and a gold-standard diagnosis, made by upper gastrointestinal endoscopy. The diagnoses were grouped into two classes — those at high risk of having (or developing) gastric cancer and those at low risk. A machine-learning approach was used to generate a cross-validated sensitivity-specificity curve in order to assess the power of the discrimination between the two groups.

Acknowledgement. This work was partially supported by the Cancer Research Campaign under grant no. SP2229/0101.

1 Introduction

Gastric cancer is an extremely serious condition and those unfortunate enough to suffer from it stand little chance of survival unless a diagnosis is made and an operation performed at an early stage in the development of the disease. The problem is that, in the early stages of the condition, the patient suffers from a variety of dyspeptic symptoms which could easily indicate the presence of any of about a dozen different gastric complaints. The only way to be sure of the diagnosis is to make use of an endoscope to carry out an internal examination of the patient. Unfortunately, endoscopic examination of *all* dyspeptic patients is too expensive for the National Health Service to support. Therefore, the goal was to use machine learning techniques to identify a *subset* of dyspeptic patients at high risk of having gastric cancer, so that they could undergo endoscopic examination. The immediate objective was to generate a cross-validated sensitivity-specificity curve in order to assess the discriminative power of the technique.

2 Variable Classification Thresholds

Typically, machine learning software produces estimated posterior probabilities of class membership of new cases undergoing classification. These are obtained from

---

[1] W.Z. Liu is in the School of Mathematics and Statistics, where A.P. White is an Associate Member. M.T. Hallissey is in the Department of Surgery.

Predicted Class

		1	0
Actual Class	1	a (hit)	b (miss)
	0	c (FP)	d (CR)

Table 1: Frequency table for the classification outcomes in a two-class discrimination task. FP represents false positive and CR represents correct rejection.

the frequency counts of the cases in the training set found at the terminal nodes. In the field of medical diagnosis, it is often the case that a test for a particular disease does not operate with perfect accuracy. This leads to the possibility of two different types of error — false positive error in which the disease is predicted when it is actually absent and false negative error (or 'miss') where the test result is negative when the disease is present. It is clear that, in this application, the second type of error is more serious than the first. Consequently, the usual approach of classifying according to the largest posterior probability found at the terminal node is not satisfactory in such a situation. A more flexible approach to such situations is to adopt classification *threshold* probabilities. With the diagnosis of serious medical conditions, the classification threshold would typically be set at a lower value for predicting the presence of the disease, than for predicting its absence. Of course, the ability to vary the classification threshold means that, as the error rate for false negatives is decreased, the error rate for false positives increases. 'Hits' and correct rejections are similarly inversely related. Table 1 displays the four possible outcomes for a two-class discrimination task. From this table, some important quantities can be defined. In the terminology of medical diagnosis, *sensitivity* and *specificity* are defined as follows. Sensitivity is the conditional probability of correct classification, given that the disease is present and specificity is the conditional probability of correct classification, given that the disease is absent. Algebraically, from Table 1, sensitivity is given by $a/(a+b)$ and specificity is defined as $d/(c+d)$. As the classification threshold for the disease is reduced, sensitivity will *increase* and specificity will *decrease*, i.e. there is a trade-off between the two. If the classification threshold probability is varied from 0 to 1, values for sensitivity and specificity are generated as a series of number-pairs, which can be plotted on a graph. Another quantity of interest for two-class discrimination tasks is the *odds ratio*. From the foregoing table, this is defined as ad/bc. It is a measure of the magnitude of association in a 2×2 table. In the current context, it is useful because it can be used as a measure of discrimination power.

Sensitivity-specificity curves run from coordinates $(0, 1)$ to $(1, 0)$. A straight line corresponds to an odds ratio of one (i.e. absence of any effective discrimination). In general, a sensitivity-specificity curve will 'bulge' into the upper-right quadrant of the graph. The more extreme the curve, the larger the corresponding odds ratio (i.e. the better the discrimination). Sensitivity-specificity curves are useful because they show the relationship between these two quantities throughout the range of threshold values and, with the use of odds ratio contours, indicate the discrimination power at different threshold settings.

3   Method

Part of the database of dyspeptic patients described by Hallissey et al. (1990) was used for the study. Briefly, this consisted of records on 1401 patients over the age of 40 who were referred to dyspepsia clinics because of symptoms of dyspepsia.

The data on each patient comprised a gold-standard diagnosis (made by upper gastrointestinal endoscopy) and a total of 85 epidemiological and clinical variables. The diagnoses were grouped into two classes. Class 1 (the high risk group) consisted of those patients diagnosed as either having gastric cancer, or belonging to any of three other diagnostic categories regarded as being at risk for developing the disease because of the mucosal changes typically associated with these conditions. These were gastric ulcer, atrophic gastritis and gastric polyp. A total of 370 cases fell into the high risk group. Class 2 (the low risk group) comprised the remaining cases.

Classification was performed by Predictor. Various aspects of Predictor have been described elsewhere by White & Liu (1993), Liu (1993) and Liu & White (to appear) and will not be described here in detail. Briefly, Predictor operates by a recursive binary partitioning of the data space, under a form of statistical control which branches preferentially on the more important variables. A stopping rule based on significance testing principles (White & Liu, to appear) guards against excessive branching and the specification of a minimum terminal node frequency provides additional control against overfitting. Missing values are dealt with by dynamic path generation, as described in the references just cited. Cross-validation is provided as an option. This is a well-established statistical technique, whose purpose is to provide a fair assessment of the performance of a predictive system. It involves testing each case separately, using a model derived from the other cases.

In order to produce the cross-validated sensitivity-specificity curve, the significance level in Predictor was set at 0.5 and the minimum terminal node frequency at 5. Cross-validation mode was used. Another option in Predictor produces the posterior probabilities of class membership for each case classified. This feature was employed and the resulting probabilities were post-processed by separate software to produce the data required for the sensitivity-specificity graph.

4   Results and Discussion

Part of the cross-validated sensitivity-specificity curve is displayed in Figure 1. It should be noted that a large proportion of spurious missing values was discovered on some of the variables, due to problems encountered in the data before they were transferred to the computer used for running Predictor. Nevertheless, the machine learning algorithm was able to perform competently in spite of this difficulty.

Some idea of the power of the discrimination may be gained by looking closely at the graph in Figure 1. Most of the curve corresponds to criterion settings giving odds ratios (for the cross-validated classification matrix) of 5 or more. Better discrimination is apparent at the high-sensitivity end of the curve, which is beneficial because of the greater interest in performing discrimination with a high-sensitivity criterion because of the seriousness of gastric cancer if diagnosis is missed in the early stages.

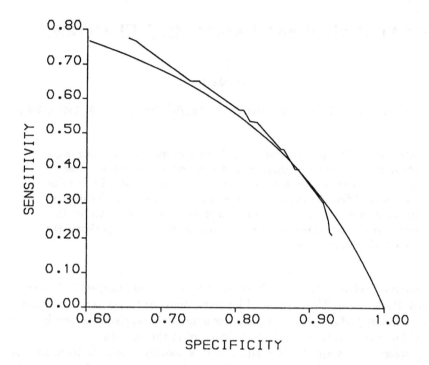

Figure 1: Part of the cross-validated sensitivity-specificity curve for detection of those at high risk for gastric cancer. The smooth curve represents a contour line for an odds ratio of 5. See text for further explanation.

For example, one particular point on this curve (obtained by classifying cases as high-risk if the cross-validated estimated posterior probability of membership of this class is greater than or equal to 0.2) gives a sensitivity of 0.768 and a specificity of 0.664, with an odds ratio of 6.54 for the cross-validated classification matrix. With this criterion setting, 45.0% of the sample are classified as high-risk.

References

Hallissey, M.T., Allum, W.H., Jewkes, A.J., Ellis, D.J. and Fielding, J.W.L. (1990). Early detection of gastric cancer. *British Medical Journal*, **301**, 513-515.

Liu, W.Z. (1993). *Aspects of Machine Learning*. Unpublished PhD thesis.

Liu, W.Z. & White, A.P. (to appear). The importance of attribute selection measures in decision tree induction. *Machine Learning*.

White, A.P. and Liu, W.Z. (1993). Fairness of attribute selection in probabilistic induction. In *Research and Development in Expert Systems* IX, edited by M.A. Bramer. Cambridge: Cambridge University Press.

White, A.P. and Liu, W.Z. (to appear). Bias in information-based measures in decision tree induction. *Machine Learning*.

DP1: Supervised and Unsupervised Clustering

Joel D. Martin

Dept. of Computer Science, University of Pittsburgh, Pittsburgh, PA, 15260, USA

Abstract. This paper presents DP1, an incremental clustering algorithm that accepts a description of the expected performance task — the goal of learning — and uses that description to alter its learning bias. With different goals DP1 addresses a wide range of empirical learning tasks from supervised to unsupervised learning. At one extreme, DP1 performs the same task as does ID3, and at the other, it performs the same task as does COBWEB.

There is a traditional contrast between supervised and unsupervised learning (Duda & Hart, 1973). The supervised learner is told one target variable that will be important at performance. On the other hand, unsupervised learners have no such guidance and learn all predictive structure in the domain.

We present an integrated algorithm that smoothly varies its learning bias depending upon a description of the anticipated performance task. DP1 can be made to address the same task as ID3 (Quinlan, 1986), COBWEB (Fisher, 1987), or Anderson and Matessa's (1992) method (Bc).

1   Expected distribution of prediction tests

A performance task is supervised if a particular variable has a special status. In such tasks, the probability that the learner will know the value of a non-target variable at prediction time is 1.0 and 0.0 for the target variable. These probabilities are the *availability probabilities* (Table 1). Conversely, the probability that the learner will have to guess the value of a non-target variable is 0.0 and is 1.0 for the target variable. These probabilities are called *goal probabilities* (Table 1).

Alternatively, a learning task is unsupervised if no variable has a special status. In other words, the probability that the learner will know a variable value at prediction time is some uniform value. Similarly, the probability that the learner will have to guess the value of a certain variable is uniform across the values.

2   The Model: DP1

The DP1[1] algorithm is an incremental concept formation method that is a descendant of COBWEB (Fisher, 1987) and Bc (Anderson & Matessa, 1992). It

---

[1] Directed Partitioning, Version 1.

performs a beam search (with a beam size of two) to find a single set of mutually exclusive partitions that is expected to lead to highly accurate predictions. Each partition is a subset of the encountered instances. As each instance arrives, it is added to one of the existing concepts or a new concept is created. This is done for each of the two hypotheses in the beam. DP1 assigns the instance to a concept if by doing so, the measure of predictive accuracy is improved more than by assigning the instance to any other concept.

There are several novel characteristics of DP1 as compared with other incremental partitioning algorithms. Many of these result from adding supervision to a partitioning algorithm. First, instead of performing a simple hill-climbing search, DP1 uses a beam search with a beam size of two. That is, it keeps track of two alternative partitions of the instances at any time. This is less expensive than the merging and splitting used by COBWEB (Fisher, 1987). DP1 only maintains two partitionings whereas COBWEB maintains several.

Second, DP1 evaluates a partition based on the current instance and a set of test instances. The test instances provide a domain dependent measure of when the current instance is different enough to belong to a new concept. A small set of previous instances is retained to correctly reflect the dependencies between variables. In DP1 every concept keeps track of the instances that are the most and least probable examples of that concept.

DP1's algorithm is as follows:

1. The model is initialized to contain no concepts.
2. Given a model that partitions $n - 1$ instances, for each concept calculate estimate of predictive accuracy when the n-th instance is classified to the concept.
3. Assign the n-th instance to the concept with the maximum estimate.
4. When predicting the value of variable i, do the following,
   (a) Classify the instance to the most probable concept given F,
   (b) Choose the most probable value given the concept.

2.1 The calculations

The accuracy score used in DP1 captures the two intuitions, a) that the probability of being correct is higher if the goal variables have highly probable values for the concept; and b) the probability of being correct is higher if the available variables have distinctive values for the concept.

The score used is equal to:

$$\sum_h \sum_k (\sum_i P(goal_{A_i}) P(V_{ij}|C_k)) \sum_l P(available_{F_{hl}}) \frac{P(C_k)P(F_{hl}|C_k)}{\sum_m P(C_m)P(F_{hl}|C_m)}$$

(1)

The quantities referred to are calculated as follows.

$$P(C_k|F_{hl}) = \frac{P(C_k)P(F_{hl}|C_k)}{\sum_m P(C_m)P(F_{hl}|C_m)}$$

(2)

Table 1. Predictive accuracy. Standard dev. in parentheses.

Dataset - Task	DP1	DP1 US	COBWEB/CLASSIT	ID3
Hepatitis	0.83 (0.06)	0.79 (0.05)	0.77 (0.05)	0.78 (0.05)
XOR-3	0.96 (0.08)	0.44 (0.02)	0.51 (0.28)	0.69 (0.36)

$$P(F_{hl}|C_k) = \prod_i P(V_{ij}|C_k) \tag{3}$$

For discrete variables:

$$P(V_{ij}|C_k) = \frac{n_{ij} + \alpha_i}{n_i + \alpha_0} \tag{4}$$

For continuous or ordered variables:

$$P(V_{ij}|C_k) = Normal(V_{ij}, \mu_{C_k}, \sigma_{C_k}) \tag{5}$$

In these equations, V_{ij} refers to the jth value of the ith variable. F_l refers to a partial instance. C_k refers to the classification of an instance to the kth concept. The quantities, α_i, are parameters of a Dirichlet distribution and α_0 is the sum over those parameters. We set all the α_i's to be 1.0 and never vary them.

3 Application to machine learning datasets

DP1 was applied to one natural domain, hepatitis, and one artificial domain called the XOR-3 domain that has three independent XOR relationships.

We ran each of five learning systems, DP1 in supervised mode, DP1 in unsupervised mode, COBWEB/CLASSIT (Gennari, Langley, & Fisher, 1990), and ID3 (Quinlan, 1986). When unsupervised, DP1 had availability probabilities set uniformly to 1.0 and goal probabilities set uniformly to 1/16. In supervised mode, DP1 had availability probabilities set to 1.0 for all variables but the 'lives' variable and goal probabilities set to 0.0 except for 'lives' variable which was 1.0.

For the hepatitis dataset, in each of ten trials, each of the systems was taught a randomly selected set of 116 (75%) instances and then tested on a separate set of 39 (25%) instances. In all the empirical studies below, testing a system on an instance meant removing a variable value from the instance, allowing the system to predict the value of that variable, and then checking if the prediction was correct. Average prediction performance for whether a patient lives or dies is shown in Table 1.

For this dataset, performance was significantly better (ANOVA, $P < .05$) for the supervised DP1 than for the unsupervised. Further, the supervised performance was significantly better than that for the other systems.

Finally, all systems were applied to the XOR-3 dataset in which there are nine

Table 2. Accuracy for all variables, XOR-3. Standard dev. in parentheses.

Dataset - Task	DP1	DP1 US
XOR-3	0.441 (0.09)	0.635 (0.05)

variables. These variables are partitioned into three sets of three variables. The values for each set of three variables are interrelated by the XOR relationship.

In each of ten trials, each system was taught a randomly selected set of 50 instances and then tested on a separate set of 14 instances. The average prediction performance for predicting the value of the first variable is shown in Table 1.

For this dataset, performance was significantly better (ANOVA, $P < .05$) for the supervised DP1 than for the unsupervised and significantly better than for any other system.

In addition, the extra work done by DP1 in unsupervised mode translates to better average prediction for all attributes. To test this, we ran DP1 in supervised and unsupervised modes, testing its ability to predict the value of any of the last six (of nine) variables. In each of ten trials, the system received 50 training instances and 14 test instances (means in Table 2).

4 Discussion

This paper presents DP1 that can perform both supervised and unsupervised learning and introduces a notation to describe the expected distribution of prediction tests. DP1 performs best when it expects the performance task that it later receives.

Bibliography

Anderson, J. R. & Matessa, M. (1992). Explorations of an incremental, Bayesian algorithm for categorization. *Machine Learning, 9*, 275–308.

Duda, R. O. & Hart, P. E. (1973). *Pattern classification and scene analysis*. New York: Wiley & Sons.

Fisher, D. H. (1987). Knowledge acquisition via incremental conceptual clustering. *Machine Learning, 2*, 139–172.

Gennari, J., Langley, P., and Fisher, D. (1990). Models of incremental concept formation. *Artificial Intelligence, 40*, 11–61.

Quinlan, J. R. (1986). Induction of decision trees. *Machine Learning, 1*, 81–106.

Using machine learning techniques to interpret results from discrete event simulation

Dunja Mladenić[1], Ivan Bratko[1,2], Ray J. Paul[3], Marko Grobelnik[1]

[1] J. Stefan Institute, Dept. of Computer Sc., Jamova 39, Ljubljana, Slovenia
[2] Faculty of Electr. Eng. and Computer Sc., Tržaška 25, Ljubljana University
[3] Brunel University, Dept. of Computer Sc., Uxbridge, England
e-mail: dunja.mladenic@ijs.si

Abstract. This paper describes an approach to the interpretation of discrete event simulation results using machine learning techniques. The results of two simulators were processed as machine learning problems. Interpretation obtained by the regression tree learning system RETIS was intuitive but obviously expressed in a complicated way. To enable a more powerful knowledge representation, Inductive Logic Programming (ILP) system MARKUS was used, that also highlighted some attribute combinations. These attribute combinations were used as new attributes in further experiments with RETIS and ASSISTANT. Some interesting regularities were thereby automatically discovered.

1 Introduction

Discrete simulation involves several stages: design and implementation of a model for the system under study, performing experiments with the simulator, analysis and presentation of experimental results (Paul and Balmer 1991). Analysis and presentation of experimental results is usually done intuitively. Deriving useful conclusions from the simulation results is a demanding task. In this paper we propose to automate this task by means of machine learning techniques. It should be emphasised that in this application of Machine Learning tools the prediction accuracy is not the main goal. After all, if the user is interested in prediction, she or he can always use the simulator for that. The real goal here is to find interpretation of simulation data and discover regularities, thus helping the user to develop intuitive understanding of the domain.

Discrete event simulation produces example situations that can be used as examples for machine learning. Section 2 describes discrete event simulation domains used in our experiments with machine learning. Section 3 describes three machine learning algorithms used to interpret the results of discrete event simulation. Results are discussed in Section 4.

2 Domains description

In our experiments we used two discrete event simulators, the Supermarket and the Pub. They were suggested and generated by the domain expert as simple and commonly used example domains in the simulation theory.

Each discrete event simulator has input parameters (attributes) that can be changed by the user (our domain expert) and output some statistical indicators (classes) calculated by the simulator. For each simulator and for each output value, a machine learning domain was constructed and experiments with it performed.

In the Supermarket domain, customers arrive and spend some time shopping. After shopping, they have to wait to be served by a cashier. A customer who on arrival sees a queue of more than QWSize people waiting to be served, leaves without entering the supermarket. In the described process, there are some attributes whose influence we want to investigate: number of cashiers in the supermarket, Cashiers (varied from 1 to 5); maximum queue size tolerated by a customer, QWSize (varied from 1 to 10); time between two arrivals, Arrival (exponentially distributed with a mean of 1 to 10 minutes). We considered as interesting the following statistical outputs, used as classes in learning: customer "utilisation" (ratio between the number of customers that enter the shop and the number of customers that arrive); cashier utilisation (fraction of cashier's time spent actually serving customers); length of the customers wait queue. Each combination of attribute values corresponds to a run of simulator producing a machine learning example. In this way, domains for all possible attribute values were generated, having $5 \times 10 \times 10 = 500$ examples.

In the pub simulator, customers arrive and wait for the barmaid to pour them a glass of drink. After drinking, they leave or return to the queue for another drink. The barmaids just pour beer and wash glasses. A glass can be either clean (and empty), full (in use) or dirty. Problems, experiments and domain expert's comments for this domain are similar to the Supermarket domain.

3 Machine learning algorithms used

This section gives brief description of machine learning algorithms used to interpret the results of discrete event simulation.

ASSISTANT (Cestnik, Kononenko and Bratko 1987) is an attribute-value learning algorithm for the construction of binary classification trees. RETIS (Karalič 1992) is an attribute-value learning algorithm for the construction of regression trees. Regression trees are similar to binary classification trees constructed by the ASSISTANT algorithm. MARKUS (Grobelnik 1992) is an Inductive Logic Programming (ILP) system designed for inferring Prolog programs from examples and counter examples of there behaviour. The MARKUS algorithm has its basis in Shapiro's MODEL INFERENCE SYSTEM (Shapiro 1983), but extends it in several ways. A Prolog program induced by MARKUS uses background-knowledge predicates defined by the user.

4 Experiments and results

Experiments were performed on six learning domains (three for the shop and three for the pub simulator).

As an example of regression trees generated by RETIS, let us consider the tree for customer utilisation (which we can not include here for space reasons). In the part of regression tree with `Cashiers = 1` and `Arrival < 4`, customer utilisation monotonically increases between 0.31 and 0.63 and is independent of customer tolerance (`QWSize`). This can be explained as follows: for a small number of cashiers and a high arrival rate of customers (attribute `Arrival` small), the waiting queue in the steady state of the system is always long and occasionally drops below `QWSize` thus not influencing customer utilisation. `QWSize` begins to affect the results for the combinations `Arrival` $\geq$ 6 or `Arrival` $\geq$ 2 and `Cashiers` $\geq$ 3. This means, at lower arrival rates and/or higher number of cashiers, `QWSize` becomes important.

We analysed the same simulation results with MARKUS with respect to the question: what combinations of the supermarket attributes will result in customer utilisation below or equal to 90%. We defined the following predicates as background knowledge for MARKUS:

```
mult( A, B, C ) :- C is A * B.
add( A, B, C ) :- C is A + B.
gtr1( X ) :- X > 1. gtr2( X ) :- X > 2. ... gtr9( X ) :- X > 9.
```

The target predicate for learning was: `shop( Cashs, QWSize, Arriv)`, which is true for customer utilisation $\leq$ 90%. The following two Prolog clauses were induced by MARKUS:

```
shop( Cashs, QWSize, Arriv) :-
  mult( Arriv, Cashs, X ), not gtr5( X ).
shop( Cashs, QWSize, Arriv) :-
  mult( Arriv, Cashs, X ), not gtr1( QWSize ), not gtr6( X ).
```

These clauses can be read as: if `Cashs*Arriv` $\leq$ 5 or `Cashs*Arriv` $\leq$ 6 and `QWSize = 1` then `CustomerUtil` $\leq$ 90%.

MARKUS nicely discovered the law that holds in situations with high input of customers and low number of cashiers (consistent with the previous regression tree). At lower input rates or higher number of cashiers, the parameter `QWSize` begins to affect the performance which can also be seen in the rule above.

After seeing MARKUS results, we constructed new attributes (in similar way as the ILP system LINUS (Lavrač, Džeroski and Grobelnik 1990) does) with four basic algebraic operations ($*$, $/$, $+$, $-$) applied on pairs of original attributes. Experiments with RETIS were repeated on such data sets. Additional experiments (problem reformulated as for MARKUS), were performed by ASSISTANT. Both attribute learning systems confirmed the results obtained by MARKUS, moreover in all three domains for the Supermarket simulator the same combined attribute (`Cashiers*Arrival`) is recognised as the "best" one. The role of parameter QWSize is also very similar. It begins to affect the performance when Cashiers*Arrival is high (> 3 for RETIS, > 5 for MARKUS and ASSISTANT).

5 Conclusion

In the paper, we experimentally analysed the results of two simple discrete event simulators by means of machine learning programs. Two attribute value and one ILP systems were used on six domains (three for each simulator). The obtained results are encouraging in that the induced descriptions provide some useful insights into the dependencies between the parameters of a discrete event system and its performance. Descriptions obtained by the ILP approach can be particularly concise and interesting.

The induced descriptions have been confirmed to be of interest for the simulation domain experts. Some descriptions were new to the expert. This is important because the success of the present study should not be measured in terms of prediction accuracy, but in terms of interpretation value of the induced descriptions.

6 Acknowledgements

We thank Aram Karalič for providing a copy of the RETIS program used in the experiments in this paper. This work was partially supported by the Slovenian Ministry for Science and Technology and the European ESPRIT III Basic Research Action Project No.6020 Inductive Logic Programming.

References

1. Cestnik, B., Kononenko, I. and Bratko, I., (1987), ASSISTANT 86: A Knowledge-Elicitation Tool for Sophisticated Users, in *Progress in Machine Learning*, ed. by I.Bratko and N.Lavrač, Sigma Press, Wilmslow.
2. Grobelnik, M. (1992) Markus - an optimized Model Inference System, *ECAI-92 Workshop on Logical Approaches to Machine Learning*, Vienna, Austria.
3. Karalič, A. (1992) Employing Linear Regression in Regression Tree Leaves.*Proc. of ECAI 92*, pp. 440-441. Vienna, Austria, John Wiley & Sons.
4. Lavrač, N., Džeroski, S. and Grobelnik, M. (1991) Learning nonrecursive definitions of relations with LINUS. *Proc. of EWSL 91*, pp. 265-281. Porto, Portugal, Springer-Verlag.
5. Mladenić, D. (1990) Machine learning system Magnus Assistant (in Slovene). *BSc Thesis*, University of Ljubljana, Faculty of Electrical Engineering and Computer Science.
6. Paul, R.J., Balmer, D.W. (1991) *Simulation Modelling*, Chartwell-Bratt, Stockholm.
7. Shapiro, E.Y. (1983) *Algorithmic Program Debugging*. Cambridge, MA: MIT Press.

Flexible Integration of Multiple Learning Methods into a Problem Solving Architecture

Enric Plaza   Josep Lluís Arcos

Institut d'Investigació en Intel·ligència Artificial , IIIA-C.S.I.C.

Camí de Santa Bàrbara, 17300 Blanes, Catalunya, Spain.

{plaza | arcos}@ceab.es

Abstract. One of the key issues in so-called multi-strategy learning systems is the degree of freedom and flexibility with which different learning and inference components can be combined. Most of multi-strategy systems only support fixed, tailored integration of the different modules for a specific domain of problems. We will report here our current research on the Massive Memory Architecture (MMA), an attempt to provide a uniform representation framework for inference and learning components supporting flexible, multiple combination of these components. Rather than a specific combination of learning methods, we are interested in an architecture adaptable to different domains where multiple learning *strategies* (combinations of learning methods) can be programmed or even learned.

1 Introduction

The first issue we have to debate is the relationship of inference and learning, and the second is the kind of representation we use to support an integration of inference with multiple learning methods. Regarding the first issue, the integration of learning methods, we agree with the Inferential Theory of Learning (ITL) approaches such as [2] and [10] in that learning methods are a special kind of inference methods. Our approach differs from ILT, however, on the characterization of the inference components that made up learning methods. For ILT approaches, the components that made up learning are inference operators like deduction, analogy, generalizations, etc. In our approach, learning is a kind of metalevel inference, that is to say, a kind of inference that requires a certain kind knowledge about the system behavior and state itself, e.g. about when a failure occurs, how learning can overcome it, etc [6]. The issue of the self-model is crucial because it formally defines what a learning method has to know so as to be able to learn. That is, a self model specifies the relationship between a learning method in a systems and the system as a whole: it specifies what knowledge the learning method can effectively know about the system in which it is integrated. There are sorts of integration, like the PRODIGY system, where learning methods are external modules that each has a clear and specialized model of the problem solver [1]. In the THEO architecture [3] several learning methods are integrated but the self-model used are not clear. Our approach is closer to THEO, since the MMA is implemented as a reflective language [5], but MMA has been designed having in mind the reflective nature of learning from problem solving and with the purpose of investigating in clear self-models required for learning.

The second issue to discuss is the nature of inference in the MMA, since we do not agree with the ILT components. Our approach derives from the knowledge-level analysis of expert systems and the so-called conceptual frameworks developed for the design and construction of KBSs. These conceptual frameworks for knowledge modelling like KADS [11], components of expertise [10] are based on the task/method decomposition principle and the analysis of knowledge requirements for methods.

2 The Massive Memory Architecture

The MMA is an experimental framework for experience-based learning and reasoning. Every episode of problem solving of MMA is represented and stored as an episode in memory. This is the main point of the reification process: create the objects that can be usable for learning and improving future behavior. MMA records memories of successes and failures of using methods for solving tasks. An episode involves not only a global task (e.g. diagnosis) but also all its subtasks and the methods that achieve them are stored, allowing learning methods to be used at different levels of granularity and from multiple examples. Our hypothesis is that the problem solving process in MMA can be described into a collection of abstract inference components. Those components are *tasks* (or goals), *methods* (or ways of achieving a goal) and *theories* (sets of methods adequate for some class of objects). This means that these elements constitute the self-model of the system and have to provide the information that will be accessed by introspection by the learning methods.

A task is engaged when exists a query to the system. One task can be achieved in some different ways. A method is a specific way to achieve one task. A method is an evaluable object that is recursively decomposed into subtasks (queries to other objects), until some direct methods are executed. This recursive decomposition of task into subtasks is called the task/method decomposition and is common to all KBS conceptual frameworks [10]. The domain knowledge is organized around objects called *theories*. For instance, the set of methods applicable to persons can be defined in a theory of `person`, stating the available methods for each task to be solved about persons. Methods to solve a specific task are grouped in an object called metafunction. A metafunction holds a set of methods and preferences to choose among them. In addition, when a method fails to achieve the task, a metafunction allows backtracking to other not failed methods.

The MMA approach is uniform and this entails that the problem solving *process* is also described in the system in terms of tasks and methods. For instance, if there is no method specified for solving a given task, the *task* of the problem solving *process* is to find such a method; or if there are more than one method that can possibly solve a task, a *task* of problem solving *process* is to choose among them. A way to do it is trying them out until one works: that would be a default *method* for such a *task*. This approach involves backtracking as a constitutive aspect of MMA, as can be expected for plausible reasoning applications. One important thing is that any time some knowledge is required by a problem solving method, and that knowledge is not *directly available* there is an opportunity for learning. We call those opportunities *impasses*, following SOAR terminology [4], and the integration of learning methods is realized by methods that solve these impasses. This type of methods are called *inference methods*.

An inference method is a type of method with a self-model of the architecture and at least a retrieve/select subtask decomposition. The goal of *retrieve* task is to obtain a set of plausible useful past episodes from the memory. MMA provides a set of basic retrieval methods that can be combined to build more complex retrieval methods. The goal of *select* task is to rank the precedents in some criteria to work first with the most plausible past episodes. MMA provides also a set of basic preference methods that can be combined to build more complex preference methods. An inference method combines the precedents in some programmable way and, finally, the result is installed in the current task. In this way we can program different learning methods as a different inference methods. Inference methods are organized around theories called *inference theories*. This means that we can also program different strategies to combining the learning methods.

3 Integration of Multiple Learning Methods

In this section we want to show how different strategies of learning can be developed and integrated into the Massive Memory Architecture. We will present two families of learning methods: Analogical methods and Inductive methods and finally we will discuss the combination of them.

Analogical methods are a family of inference methods that follow a Retrieve/Select task decomposition. The characteristic of analogical methods is that the `Retrieve` method uses a similarity-based methods. `Select` methods can also be based on similarity or can be domain-specific, knowledge-intensive methods. The most basic (less domain-dependent) method for analogy uses a retrieval method that finds all objects having some successful method solving the task at hand, and no preference knowledge is provided so a random selection is performed. This method is the most general, less focused, less informed, and less domain-dependent analogical method. If we have some knowledge of the domain we can add it and focus the analogical reasoning. Adding this knowledge in the retrieval or/and the preference methods we can define some more specific, i.e. domain specific, analogy methods. A form of useful domain knowledge are determinations (they are a form of functional dependence, as in "Spoken language of a person depends on his/her nationality" [9]). Determinations in MMA can be used during Retrieve or Select tasks of analogy. During retrieval MMA has retrieve methods that find from memory those cases or episodes that comply to the determination (e.g. in solving the spoken-language task, retrieve only those examples with the same nationality as the current problem). During selection tasks MMA has a preference method that prioritizes , from the retrieved cases, those complying to the determination. Thus different analogical and case-based methods can be included into MMA in a uniform way and only depending on the knowledge available for a domain, as is essential for KBS conceptual frameworks. Since to all tasks and subtasks can be ascribed a specific method MMA is capable of handling multiple methods for different subtasks? In fact multiple methods for a single task can be applied, as we'll show presently with inductive and analogical methods,

Inductive methods are another family of inference methods that follow a Retrieve/Construct task decomposition. `Retrieve` methods obtain a set of past solved examples from which to learn the knowledge to solve a particular task. `Construct` methods are domain-specific methods that compare the examples and build a domain theory for that specific task. We can build an inductive method that learns to solve all the problems that an analogical method solves case by case. This method retrieves the same examples as the analogical method and constructs a metafunction with all the methods successfully used in those past examples. In the language-nationality example, the inductive method learns the function associating nationalities with languages. That is to say it learns in one step the domain knowledge needed by the method that solves the spoken-language task, while the analogical method solves the task acquiring the needed knowledge on a case-by-case manner.

Another possibility in MMA is to combine for the same task an inductive method and an analogical method. In this situation the inductive method acquires not all domain knowledge but only those methods frequently used, resulting in a domain theory that is efficient although incomplete. The task now has available two methods: the induced method and the analogical method and a preference from the first to the second. In this strategy first the general knowledge is used and if it fails then the analogical method tries the specific cases retrieved from memory. this strategy embodies the general form of an imperfect theory (the induced knowledge) plus a set of exceptions or unusual cases out of the scope of the theory and for being exploited by an analogy method.

4 Conclusions and Future Work

MMA provides a flexible framework for integration and experimentation of the ranges of applicability and/or utility of learning methods. Different analogical, case-based and inductive methods can be included into MMA in a uniform way and only depending on the knowledge available for a domain. In fact, this is essential idea of KBS conceptual frameworks that we are using for integrating multiple learning methods. Since to all tasks and subtasks can be ascribed a specific method MMA is capable of handling multiple methods for different subtasks and even multiple methods for a single task. Since all decisions, successes, and failures, are stored for every subtask, learning can be applied to any subtask of a global task.

In order to achieve a more autonomous learning capability the study of learning goals [7, 8] is in this context a very important future research line for ML. What we presented here seems however to be an unavoidable previous step because of the necessity of achieving integration and uniform representation of learning methods and problem solving methods in order to have a common ground of comparison. In the next phase of our project (1994-1996) the goal is to enlarge the self-model of the system in such a way that compilative learning methods and other inductive methods are integrated.

Acknowledgements
The research reported on this paper has been developed at the IIIA inside the Massive Memory Project funded by CICYT grants TIC 801/90 and TIC 122-93.

References

[1] Carbonell, J. G., Knoblock, C. A., Minton, S. (1991), Prodigy: An integrated architecture for planning and learning. In K van Lehn (Ed.), *Architectures for Intelligence.* Lawrence Erlbaum Ass.: Hillsdale, NJ.

[2] Michalski, R., (1993), Inferencetial theory of learning as a conceptual basis for multistrategy learning, *Machine Learning*, 11(2-3), 111-152.

[3] Mitchell, T.M., Allen, J., Chalasani, P., Cheng, J., Etzioni, O., Ringuette, M., Schlimmer, J. C. Theo: a framework for self-improving systems. In K Van Lenhn (Ed.) *Architectures for Intelligence.* Laurence Erlbaum, 1991.

[4] A Newell (1990), *Unified Theories of Cognition.* Cambridge MA: Harvard University Press

[5] Plaza, E (1992), Reflection for analogy: Inference-level reflection in an architecture for analogical reasoning. *Proc. IMSA'92 Workshop on Reflection and Metalevel Architectures*, Tokyo, November 1992, p. 166-171.

[6] Plaza, E. Arcos J. L., Reflection and Analogy in Memory-based Learning, *Proc. Multistrategy Learning Workshop.*, 1993. p. 42-49.

[7] Plaza, E., Aamodt, A., Ram, A., van de Velde, W., van Someren, M. (1993), Integrated learning architectures. In P.V. Brazdil (Ed.) *Machine Learning: ECML-93.*, pp. 429-441. Lecture Notes in Artificial Intelligence 667, Springer-Verlag.

[8] Ram, A, Cox, M T, Narayanan, S. (1992), An architecture for integrated introspective learning. *Proc. ML'92 Workshop on Computational Architectures for Machine Learning and Knowledge Acquisition.*

[9] Russell S (1990), *The Use of Knowledge in Analogy and Induction.* Morgan Kaufmann.

[10] Steels, L. The Components of Expertise, *AI Magazine*, Summer 1991.

[10] Tecuci, G (1993), Plausible justification trees: A framework for deep and dynamic integration of learning strategies. *Machine Learning*, 11(2-3), 237-261.

[11] Wielinga, B, Schreiber, A, Breuker, J (1992), KADS: A modelling approach to knowledge engineering. *Knowledge Acquisition* 4(1).

Concept Sublattices

Janos Sarbo[1] and József Farkas[2]

[1] University of Nijmegen, Toernooiveld 1, 6525 ED Nijmegen, The Netherlands
[2] J.A.T.E. Szeged, Petőfi S. sgt. 30-34, 6722 Szeged, Hungary

Abstract. We consider the following problem: Given a "universe" of primitive and composed entities, where non-primitive entities may contain other ones. How should we represent these entities, such that their containment relation is decidable? As an answer to this problem we propose a representation based on a Galois connection. An application of this idea in modelling human memory is given as well.

1 Introduction

We consider conceptual knowledge and its representation by (formal) concept lattices which is based on a Galois connection. We use the lattice theoretical notions of a *context* and the corresponding *concept lattice*, introduced by R. Wille ([4]).

Our aim is to generalize these notions, as follows. Basically, a concept lattice is meant to be used to determine a lattice element which corresponds to a given set of input objects *or*, alternatively, of attributes (where *or* denotes exclusive or). We generalize the input and allow both objects *and* attributes to be given. It turns out that in this case the input can be represented by a Galois connection as well. Eventually we obtain the result that our generalization allows a *concept lattice* to be an input. The task is then to determine which sublattice of the concept lattice corresponds to the given input.

We are motivated for this generalization by practical problems in which the input is the yield of some complex, e.g. visual observation process. Such an input contains objects and attributes which belong to some "observed" part of the context. Another motivation is due to a new model of human memory, which is briefly described in Sect. 4.

2 Concept lattices

2.1 Basic definitions

Concepts are defined to exist in a context or "universe". Formally, a *context* is a triple (G, M, I), where G is a set of objects, M is a set of attributes, I is a binary relation between G and M, i.e. for $g \in G$, $m \in M$, $(g, m) \in I$ iff object g has the attribute m. In our definition of a context the sets G and M are finite.

Definition 1. *For a context the following mappings are defined: $A' = \{m \in M \mid gIm$ for all $g \in A\}$ for $A \subseteq G$, and $B' = \{g \in G \mid gIm$ for all $m \in B\}$ for $B \subseteq M$.*

A *concept* of a context (G, M, I) is a pair (A, B) with $A \subseteq G$, $B \subseteq M$, which satisfies the conditions (i) $A' = B$ and (ii) $A = B'$.

For any concepts (A_1, A_1') and (A_2, A_2') of the context (G, M, I), the *hierarchy of concepts* is captured by the definition: $(A_1, A_1') \leq (A_2, A_2')$ iff $A_1 \subseteq A_2$ (or equivalently, iff $A_1' \supseteq A_2'$). The set of all concepts of (G, M, I) with this order relation is called the *concept lattice*.

The mappings of Definition 1 define a Galois connection between the power-sets of G and M.

2.2 Extensions of the basic model

In our model the containment relation on lattices plays a central rôle. This is defined as follows.

Definition 2. *A concept sublattice of a concept lattice L_2 is a complete sublattice L_1 of L_2, such that there exists a lattice homomorphism h from L_2 to L_1, and a pair of functions (g, f) such that the following diagram commutes:*

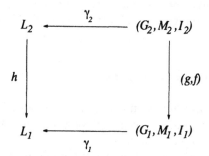

where γ_2 and γ_1 are mappings from contexts to concept lattices; $g :: G_2 \rightarrow G_1$ and $f :: M_2 \rightarrow M_1$ are surjective functions; and the mapping of I_2 to I_1 is such that $(x, y) \in I_2$ implies $(gx, fy) \in I_1$.

We say that an entity has an *occurence* in another entity if it is contained in the latter one. Formal concepts and concept sublattices can be seen as some kind of canonical representations. When another, arbitrary representation is used, it may happen that an entity is differently represented in its occurrences. This is because different subsets of objects and attributes of the entity are considered important in the different occurrences. Therefore it can be very difficult to find out whether an entity has an occurrence elsewhere, as part of another one. A simple example can clarify this. Assume that the geometrical entities, angle, triangle and quadrangle are defined. If these definitions are separately given, and unless special care has been taken, it is very unlikely that one can derive that the latter two geometrical entities "contain" the first one.

In Sect. 3 we give examples which demonstrate how the Galois connection based representation overcomes this problem. We must point out however, that this representation may not be called canonical, simply because a philosophical concept or entity can have different mathematizations, which may be incomparable within a formal system.

3 Examples

We demonstrate the construction of a concept lattice by examples taken from plane geometry. Alignment of a point on a line x is denoted by the attribute on_x.

The context of the angle (G_a, M_a, I_a) is described by three distinct points defining a pair of bisecting straight lines, that is $G_a = \{P_0, P_1, P_2\}$, $M_a = \{on_e, on_f\}$ and $I_a = \{(P_0, on_e), (P_0, on_f), (P_1, on_e), (P_2, on_f)\}$. The members of the concept lattice are: $C_0 = (\{P_0\}, \{on_e, on_f\})$, $C_1 = (\{P_0, P_1, P_2\}, \{\ \})$, $C_2 = (\{P_0, P_1\}, \{on_e\})$, $C_3 = (\{P_0, P_2\}, \{on_f\})$.

The context of the triangle (G_t, M_t, I_t) is similarly defined. We have that $G_t = \{P_0, P_1, P_2\}$, $M_t = \{on_e, on_f, on_g\}$ and $I_t = \{(P_0, on_e), (P_0, on_f), (P_1, on_f), (P_1, on_g), (P_2, on_e), (P_2, on_f)\}$. The concept lattice of the triangle has members: $C_0 = (\{\ \}, \{on_e, on_f, on_g\})$, $C_1 = (\{P_0, P_1, P_2\}, \{\ \})$, $C_2 = (\{P_0\}, \{on_e, on_f\})$, $C_3 = (\{P_1\}, \{on_f, on_g\})$, $C_4 = (\{P_2\}, \{on_e, on_f\})$, $C_5 = (\{P_0, P_1\}, \{on_f\})$, $C_6 = (\{P_0, P_2\}, \{on_e\})$, $C_7 = (\{P_1, P_2\}, \{on_g\})$.

We can observe that the concept lattice of the angle is contained in the concept lattice of the triangle (as sublattices $\{C_1, C_2, C_5, C_6\}$, $\{C_1, C_3, C_5, C_7\}$ and $\{C_1, C_4, C_6, C_7\}$).

4 Modelling human memory

In modelling human reasoning two main approaches can be identified: the models of logical inference of cognitive psychology (e.g. [1]), and the functional models of experimental neurosurgery (e.g. [3]).

The proposed simple functional model of human memory, depicted in Fig. 1, tries to benefit from both of the mentioned models.

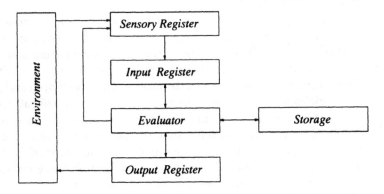

Fig. 1. A functional model of human memory.

In Fig. 1 *Environment* denotes the outside world. The *Sensory Register* is an input unit which can recognize and identify object-attribute pairs. The input is stored and filtered in the *Input Register*. The *Evaluator* is the unit where the input concept lattice is generated; the feedback path is used, when incomplete data has been input. In that case the input, or certain part of it, is re-sampled at greater precisety. The *Storage* is the memory in the classical sense, which can match the input lattice with a part of the stored concept lattice. Finally, the *Output Register* is the unit of answer generation.

For sake of completeness we will simply assume that the concepts of the concept lattice of the *Storage* possess some information about the answer to be generated. This is a primary answer, which, depending on the distance between the input lattice and the sublattice found by the matching process, can be blocked in the *Output Register*. Answer generation can be interrrupted when due to some change in the *Environment*, the answer under processing is not needed anymore.

The adequacy of the above model can be demonstrated by the functional description of the mechanism of human vision. The retina and the primary optic cortex (also called the V1 field) are connected by a six layer subcortical structure, the corpus geniculatum laterale. The upper four parvocellular layers recognize colours, while the lower two magnocellular layers collect light. This indicates that the vision of form and colour is both functionally and anatomically decomposed to separate parts.

Recently, four perceptional paths of the visual cortex were identified. It is also known that these nervous paths exchange information among themselves. This forms a topological structure of nervous connections, applied by the colour vision mechanism. We emphasize that the visual input is *not* projected to the optic cortex, but instead, a network of active states of frequency and light intensity selective cells is generated, what we call in our model, a lattice of object-attribute relations.

References

1. Gagnè, R.M., Glaser, P.: Foundations in learning research. In Instructional Technology: Foundation, London, Laurence Erlbaum Associates (1987)
2. Sarbo, J.J., Farkas, J.I.: Concept sublattices – theory and applications. Technical Report, University of Nijmegen (1993)
3. Squire, L.R.: Memory and the hippocampus: A synthesis from findings with rats, monkeys, and humans. Psychological Review, **99(2)** (1992) 195–231
4. Wille, R.: Restructuring lattice theory: an approach based on hierarchies of concepts. In Rival, I. (Ed.), Ordered sets (1982) 445–470

The Piecewise Linear Classifier DIPOL92*

Barbara Schulmeister, Fritz Wysotzki

Fraunhofer-Institute for Information and Data Processing
Branch Lab for Process Optimisation
Kurstraße 33, D-10117 Berlin, Germany

Abstract. This paper presents a learning algorithm which constructs an optimised piecewise linear classifier for n-class problems.
In the first step of the algorithm initial positions of the discriminating hyperplanes are determined by linear regression for each pair of classes. To optimise these positions depending on the misclassified patterns an error criterion function is defined. This function is minimised by a gradient descent procedure for each hyperplane separately. As an option in the case of non–convex classes, a clustering procedure decomposing the classes into appropriate subclasses can be applied. The classification of patterns is defined on a symbolic level on the basis of the signs of the discriminating hyperplanes.

1 Introduction

The introduced algorithm can be considered

- as a statistical approach with the special option of clustering classes and carrying out the subtask of classification on a symbolic level or
- as a neural network approach with the special choice of the initial conditions of hidden units (number and weights) and fixed Boolean functions in the second layer.

These two ways of interpretation of the algorithm emphasize that there are many relations between statistical and neural network algorithms. In statistical and neural network algorithms often a lot of parameters have to be determined to obtain an optimal solution of the classification problem. Especially in neural network design the choice of these parameters remains open.

The use of the introduced algorithm requires only the number of clusters of the classes to be fixed. With the help of clustering it is possible to gain an insight into the position and structure of the classes.

The algorithm is implemented as the program DIPOL92 (DIscrimination and POst Learning). It was part of the Esprit project STATLOG [1]. The aim of the project was to provide a review of different approaches to classification, compare their performance on a wide range of datasets and draw conclusions on their applicability to real-world problems, e.g., technical and medical diagnosis, image

---

* This work was supported by the German Ministry of Research and Technology within the project WISCON

recognition and credit datasets. DIPOL92 came off very well in comparison to the other 21 algorithms. Taking the top six places across all datasets it has more occurences than all other algorithms.

2 Pairwise Linear Regression

Suppose that $X \subset R^m$ (m-dimensional Euclidean space) is the set of classified patterns $\mathbf{x} = (x_1, \ldots, x_m)$. Linear regression is used for discrimination of two classes of patterns k_1 and k_2 by defining the dependent variable b in the following manner :

$$\text{if } \mathbf{x} \epsilon k_1, \text{ then } b = +1, \text{ if } \mathbf{x} \epsilon k_2, \text{ then } b = -1$$

Let W be the linear regression function $W : X \to R$ with $W(\mathbf{x}) = w_0 + w_1 x_1 + \ldots + w_m x_m$. Then a pattern $\mathbf{x}$ is correctly classified if

$$W(\mathbf{x}) > 0 \text{ for } \mathbf{x} \epsilon k_1, W(\mathbf{x}) < 0 \text{ for } \mathbf{x} \epsilon k_2.$$

For each pair of classes a discriminating regression function is calculated.

3 Learning Procedure

For all misclassified patterns, the squared distances from the corresponding decision hyperplane multiplied with the costs for these misclassifications are summed up :
Suppose $W = 0$ defines the decision hyperplane between the classes k_1 and k_2. Then let m_1 be the set of all misclassified patterns of class k_1, i.e., $x \epsilon k_1$ and $W(\mathbf{x}) < 0$, let m_2 be the set of all misclassified patterns of class k_2, i.e., $x \epsilon k_2$ and $W(\mathbf{x}) > 0$, and let $cost(k_i, k_j)$ be the costs of misclassification of class k_i into class k_j :

$$F(W) = cost(k_1, k_2) * \sum_{\mathbf{x} \epsilon m_1} \frac{W(\mathbf{x})^2}{||\mathbf{x}||^2} + cost(k_2, k_1) * \sum_{\mathbf{x} \epsilon m_2} \frac{W(\mathbf{x})^2}{||\mathbf{x}||^2}$$

The learning procedure consists of minimising the criterion function by a gradient descent algorithm seperately for each decision surface. Since the gradient $\nabla_W F(W)$ of $F(W)$ with respect to W defines the direction of maximum increase in F, it is used to form an iterative minimisation procedure:

$$W^{(n+1)} = W^{(n)} + \rho_n \nabla_W F(W^{(n)})$$

This represents an accumulated correction to the position of the decision hyperplane, or *learning by epoch* as an alternative to stochastic approximation, or *learning by sample*. The costs are included explicitly in the learning procedure.

4   Clustering of Classes

To handle also problems with non–convex, especially non simply–connected class regions, it is suggested to perform a clustering procedure before the linear regression is carried out. To solve the clustering problem a standard minimum–squared–error algorithm is used [4].

From some initial partition of a class k of N patterns into I clusters k_i ($i = 1, \ldots, I$) with l_i patterns and with mean vectors s_i

$$s_i = \frac{1}{l_i} \sum_{\mathbf{x} \epsilon k_i} \mathbf{x}$$

the criterion function

$$J = \sum_{i=1}^{I} \sum_{\mathbf{x} \epsilon k_i} \|\mathbf{x} - s_i\|^2$$

is calculated. If no reasonable initial partition is known a general approach to an initial partition is the following :

$$\mathbf{x}_j \epsilon k_i, \ (j = 1, \ldots, N, i = 1 \ldots, I), \ if \ \ i = j \ (mod \ I) + 1$$

Patterns are moved from one cluster to another if such a move will improve the value of the criterion function J. The mean vectors are updated after each pattern move. Like hill–climbing algorithms in general, these approaches guarantee local but not global optimisation. Different initial partitions and the order in which the training patterns are selected can lead to different solutions.

In case of clustering, the number of two–class problems increases correspondingly.

It is to be noted that by combining the clustering algorithm with the regression technique the number and initial positions of discriminating hyperplanes are a priori fixed (i.e., before learning) in a reasonable manner, even in case that some classes have multimodal distributions (i.e., consist of several subclasses). Thus, a well known bottleneck of neural nets can at least be partly avoided.

5   Classification Procedure

When discriminating hyperplanes were computed then any pattern $\mathbf{x}$ (member of the training set or not) can be classified, i.e., the class can be predicted.

For the pairwise discrimination of c classes $C = c(c-1)/2$ hyperplanes W^i are calculated (in case of clustering the number c is changed into $c + c_{clust}$).

The following C–dimensional vector $\mathbf{V}_k$ is defined for each class k : if the function W^i discriminates the classes k_1 and k_2, then the i-th component $V_{k,i}$ is equal to 1, if $k = k_1$, equal to -1, if $k = k_2$, and equal to 0 in all other cases. These vectors contain the coded information about the convex class or subclass regions depending on the C functions W^i.

On the basis of the discriminant functions the vector function sw is defined for each pattern $\mathbf{x}$

$$sw : X \rightarrow \{1, 0, -1\}^C$$

with the components

$$(sw(\mathbf{x}))_i = sign(W^i(\mathbf{x})).$$

The vector $sw(\mathbf{x})$ contains the coded information about the position of the pattern $\mathbf{x}$ depending on the C functions W^i.

For each class k the function (G is the set of integers)

$$S_k : X \rightarrow G$$

is defined as the scalar product S_k of the two coded vectors $\mathbf{V}_k$ and $sw(\mathbf{x})$

$$S_k(\mathbf{x}) = \sum_{i=1}^{C} V_{k,i} * (sw(\mathbf{x}))_i.$$

A pattern $\mathbf{x}$ is uniquely classified by the discriminating hyperplanes W^i into the class k if

$$S_k(\mathbf{x}) = c - 1,$$

i.e., with respect to the $c - 1$ hyperplanes, which discriminate the class k from the other $c - 1$ classes, the pattern $\mathbf{x}$ is placed in the halfspace belonging to class k (the coded vectors $\mathbf{V}_k$ and $sw(\mathbf{x})$ have the same value (+1 or -1) for all components i with $V_{k,i} \neq 0$). For all other classes j, $j \neq k$, $S_j(\mathbf{x}) < c - 1$ is valid, because at least with respect to the hyperplane, which discriminates class j from class k the pattern $\mathbf{x}$ is placed in the halfspace of class k (the coded vectors $\mathbf{V}_k$ and $sw(\mathbf{x})$ do not have the same value (+1 or -1) for all components i with $V_{k,i} \neq 0$).

A pattern $\mathbf{x}$ is not uniquely classified if

$$\max_j S_j(\mathbf{x}) < c - 1.$$

In this case the pattern is classified on the basis of the minimum of the distance to the class regions.

References

1. Michie,D., Spiegelhalter,D., Taylor,C. (Eds.): Machine Learning, Neural and Statistical Classification. Results of the Esprit project STATLOG (to appear)
2. Meyer-Brötz, G., and Schürmann, J.: Methoden der automatischen Zeichenerkennung. Akademie-Verlag, Berlin (1970)
3. Unger, S., Wysotzki, F.: Lernfähige Klassifizierungssysteme. Akademie-Verlag, Berlin (1981)
4. Duda, R.O., Hart, P.E.: Pattern Classification and Scene Analysis. John Wiley (1973)

Complexity of Computing Generalized VC-Dimensions

Ayumi Shinohara

ayumi@rifis.sci.kyushu-u.ac.jp
Research Institute of Fundamental Information Science,
Kyushu University 33, Fukuoka 812, Japan

Abstract. In the PAC-learning model, the Vapnik-Chervonenkis (VC) dimension plays the key role to estimate the polynomial-sample learnability of a class of binary functions. For a class of $\{0, \ldots, m\}$-valued functions, the notion has been generalized in various ways. This paper investigates the complexity of computing some of generalized VC-dimensions: VC^*-dimension, Ψ_*-dimension, and Ψ_G-dimension. For each dimension, we consider a decision problem that is, for a given matrix representing a class $\mathcal{F}$ of functions and an integer K, to determine whether the dimension of $\mathcal{F}$ is greater than K or not. We prove that the VC^*-dimension problem is polynomial-time reducible to the satisfiability problem of length J with $O(\log^2 J)$ variables, which includes the original VC-dimension problem as a special case. We also show that the Ψ_G-dimension problem is still reducible to the satisfiability problem of length J with $O(\log^2 J)$, while the Ψ_*-dimension problem becomes NP-complete.

1 Introduction

The PAC-learnability due to Valiant [13] is to estimate the feasibility of learning a *binary* function probably approximately correctly, from a reasonable amount of examples (polynomial-sample), within a reasonable amount of time (polynomial-time). It is well-known that the Vapnik-Chervonenkis dimension (VC-dimension) which is a combinatorial parameter of a class of binary functions plays the key role to determine whether the class is polynomial-sample learnable or not [3, 5, 8]. As a natural extension, the learnability of a class of $\{0, \ldots, m\}$-*valued* functions has been characterized by various generalized notions such as pseudo-dimension [4], graph dimension [7], and Natarajan dimension [7]. Ben-David et al. [2] unified them into a general scheme, by introducing a family Ψ of mappings which translate $\{0, \ldots, m\}$-valued functions into binary ones.

This paper deals with complexity issues on some of these dimensions of a class over a finite learning domain. We remark that the complexity of computing each dimension is of independent interest from the polynomial-time learnability, since it is not directly related to the running time of learning algorithms.

According to the complexity of finding VC-dimension of a class of binary functions over a finite learning domain, Linial et al. [5] showed that the VC-dimension can be computed in $n^{O(\log n)}$ time, where n is the size of a given matrix which represents the class. Nienhuys-Cheng and Polman [9] gave another $n^{O(\log n)}$-time algorithm, although they have not analyzed its running time. The author [11] showed that the decision version of the problem is "complete" for the class of $n^{O(\log n)}$ time computable sets, in the same sense as the problem of finding a minimum dominating set in a tournament due to Megiddo and Vishkin [6]. That is, we showed that the VC-dimension problem is in the class $\text{SAT}_{\log^2 n}$, and hard for the class $\text{SAT}_{\log^2 n}^{\text{CNF}}$, where these classes are defined as follows [6]:

- A set L is in $\text{SAT}_{\log^2 n}$ if there exists a Turing machine M, a polynomial $p(n)$, and a constant C, such that for every string I of length n, M converts I within $p(n)$ time into a boolean formula Φ_I (whose length is necessarily less than $p(n)$) with at most $C \log^2 n$ variables, so that $I \in L$ if and only if Φ_I is satisfiable.
- The definition of $\text{SAT}_{\log^2 n}^{\text{CNF}}$ is essentially the same as that of $\text{SAT}_{\log^2 n}$ except that the formula Φ_I is in conjunctive normal form.

In this paper, we extend the above results in three ways. For the notions of generalized VC-dimensions, "VC*-dimension", "Ψ_*-dimension", and "Ψ_G-dimension", we settle the complexity issues (Theorem 3, 6, 8). These results give some connections between various dimension problems and the satisfiability problems of boolean formulae with restricted number of variables. Because of the space limitation, we just state our results briefly in this paper. The proofs are described in our technical report [12].

2 Complexity of VC*-Dimension Problem

In this section, we introduce a natural generalization of the VC-dimension for a class of $\{0, \ldots, m\}$-valued functions. Then we show that the generalized VC-dimension problem is still in $\text{SAT}_{\log^2 n}$ and $\text{SAT}_{\log^2 n}^{\text{CNF}}$-hard, as well as the original VC-dimension problem.

For a matrix M, let M_{ij} denote the element on row i and column j of M, and the size of M is the number of elements in M. Let U be a finite set called a *learning domain*, and $\mathcal{N}$ be the set of natural numbers. For a class $\mathcal{F}$ of functions from U to $\mathcal{N}$, we define $range(\mathcal{F}) = \bigcup_{f \in \mathcal{F}} \{f(x) \mid x \in U\}$. We represent $\mathcal{F}$ by a $|U| \times |\mathcal{F}|$ matrix M with $M_{ij} = f_j(x_i)$. Each column represents a function in $\mathcal{F}$. For an integer matrix M, let $\mathcal{F}_M$ denote the class of functions which M represents.

The following definition may be one of the most natural extensions of the VC-dimension for a class of $\{0, \ldots, m\}$-valued functions.

Definition 1. Let $\mathcal{F}$ be a class of functions over U. We say that $\mathcal{F}$ *shatters* a set $S \subseteq U$ if for every function g from S to $range(\mathcal{F})$, there exists a function $f \in \mathcal{F}$ such that $f(x) = g(x)$ for all $x \in S$. The *VC*-dimension of $\mathcal{F}$, denoted by VC*-dim$(\mathcal{F})$, is the maximum cardinality of a set which is shattered by $\mathcal{F}$.

We note that VC*-dim$(\mathcal{F})$ coincides with the original VC-dimension for any class $\mathcal{F}$ of functions with $range(\mathcal{F}) = \{0, 1\}$.

Definition 2. The *VC*-dimension problem* is, given an integer matrix M and integer $K \geq 1$, to determine whether $\text{VC}^*\text{-dim}(\mathcal{F}_M) \geq K$ or not.

Theorem 3. *The VC*-dimension problem is in $SAT_{\log^2 n}$, and $SAT_{\log^2 n}^{CNF}$-hard.*

3 Complexity of Ψ-Dimension Problems

The VC*-dimension introduced in the previous section seems to be one of the most natural extension of the VC-dimension. However, it has not been used actually in the literatures. The reason is that the cardinality of the largest class $\mathcal{F}$ of functions over U of a given dimension grows exponentially in $|U|$ for all $|range(\mathcal{F})| > 2$ [1, 2], whereas polynomial growth is desirable for the PAC-learning model. As alternative definitions, a variety of notions of dimension to classes of $\{0, \ldots, m\}$-valued functions had been proposed [4, 7], and Ben-David et al. gave a general scheme [2] which unified them. They introduced Ψ-dimension, where Ψ is a family of mappings which translate $\{0, \ldots, m\}$-valued functions into $\{0, 1\}$-valued ones. In this section, we investigate the complexity of computing Ψ-dimension for two special families Ψ_* and Ψ_G. We show that the Ψ_*-dimension problem is NP-complete, while the Ψ_G-dimension is still in $SAT_{\log^2 n}$.

Definition 4. Let Ψ be a family of the mappings ψ from $\mathcal{N}$ to $\{0, 1, *\}$, where $*$ will be thought of as a null element. Let $\mathcal{F}$ be a class of functions over U. We say that $\mathcal{F}$ Ψ-shatters [1] a set $S \subseteq U$ if there exists a mapping $\psi \in \Psi$ which satisfies the following condition: for every subset $T \subseteq S$, there exists a function $f \in \mathcal{F}$ with $\psi(f(x)) = 1$ for any $x \in T$ and $\psi(f(x)) = 0$ for any $x \in S - T$. That is, Ψ-shattering requires that under some mapping $\psi \in \Psi$, $\mathcal{F}$ contains all functions from U to $\{0, 1\}$. The Ψ-dimension of $\mathcal{F}$, denoted by $\Psi\text{-dim}(\mathcal{F})$, is the maximum cardinality of a set which is Ψ-shattered by $\mathcal{F}$.

Definition 5. For a family Ψ of mappings from $\mathcal{N}$ to $\{0, 1, *\}$, we define the Ψ-*dimension problem* as the decision problem to determine whether $\Psi\text{-dim}(\mathcal{F}_M) \geq K$ or not for given integer matrix M and an integer $K \geq 1$.

Let Ψ_* be the family of all mappings from $\mathcal{N}$ to $\{0, 1, *\}$. Therefore, the Ψ_*-dimension problem is the most general one in the family of Ψ-dimension problems.

Theorem 6. *The Ψ_*-dimension problem is NP-complete.*

Natarajan [7] introduced the *graph dimension* in order to characterize the learnability of a class of $\{0, \ldots, m\}$-valued functions.

Definition 7. The *graph dimension* is the Ψ_G-dimension with $\Psi_G = \{\psi_{G,\tau} \mid \tau \in \mathcal{N}\}$, where $\psi_{G,\tau}(a)$ is 1 if $a = \tau$, and 0 otherwise.

---

[1] In [2], they introduced more general notions of Ψ-shatter and Ψ-dimension. Our definition of the Ψ-dimension corresponds to the *uniform Ψ-dimension* they call.

From the definition, Ψ_G is a subset of Ψ_*. The following theorem gives an interesting contrast with the Theorem 6.

Theorem 8. *The Ψ_G-dimension problem is in $SAT_{\log^2 n}$, and $SAT_{\log^2 n}^{CNF}$-hard.*

4 Concluding Remarks

As another crucial characterization of the complexity of computing VC-dimension, Papadimitriou and Yannakakis [10] defined a new complexity class LOGNP, for which the (original) VC-dimension problem becomes complete. We will analyze the complexity of some other dimensions, such as pseudo-dimension [4] and Natarajan dimension [7], together with the relations to the class LOGNP in future works.

References

1. N. Alon. On the density of sets of vectors. *Discrete Mathematics*, 46:199–202, 1983.
2. S. Ben-David, N. Cesa-Bianchi, and P. M. Long. Characterizations of learnability for classes of $\{0, \dots, n\}$-valued functions. In *Proceedings of the 5th Annual Workshop on Computational Learning Theory*, pages 333–340, 1992.
3. A. Blumer, A. Ehrenfeucht, D. Haussler, and M. Warmuth. Learnability and the Vapnik-Chervonenkis dimension. *JACM*, 36(4):929–965, 1989.
4. D. Haussler. Decision theoretic generalizations of the PAC model for neural net and other learning applications. *Information and Computation*, 100:78–150, 1992.
5. N. Linial, Y. Mansour, and R. L. Rivest. Results on learnability and the Vapnik-Chervonenkis dimension. *Information and Computation*, 90:33–49, 1991.
6. N. Megiddo and U. Vishkin. On finding a minimum dominating set in a tournament. *Theoretical Computer Science*, 61:307–316, 1988.
7. B. Natarajan. On learning sets and functions. *Machine Learning*, 4(1):67–97, 1989.
8. B. Natarajan. *Machine Learning — A Theoretical Approach*. Morgan Kaufmann Publishers, 1991.
9. S. Nienhuys-Cheng and M. Polman. Complexity dimensions and learnability. In *Proc. European Conference on Machine Learning, (Lecture Notes in Artificial Intelligence 667)*, pages 348–353, 1993.
10. C.H. Papadimitriou and M. Yannakakis. On limited nondeterminism and the complexity of the V-C dimension. In *Proc. 8th Annual Conference on Structure in Complexity Theory*, pages 12–18, 1993.
11. A. Shinohara. Complexity of computing Vapnik-Chervonenkis dimension. In *Proc. 4th Workshop on Algorithmic Learning Theory*, pages 279–287, 1993.
12. A. Shinohara. Complexity of computing generalized VC-dimensions. RIFIS Technical Report, RIFIS-TR-CS 78, Research Institute of Fundamental Information Science, Kyushu University, 1993.
13. L. Valiant. A theory of the learnable. *CACM*, 27(11):1134–1142, 1984.

Learning relations without closing the world (extended abstract)*

Edgar Sommer

GMD (German National Research Center for Computer Science)
Schloss Birlinghoven, 53757 St. Augustin, Germany
email sommer@gmd.de

Abstract. This paper describes LINK, a heuristically guided learner that combines aspects of three major approaches to ILP — LGG, search heuristic and (declarative) structural bias. In the manner of LGG algorithms, LINK generates sets of candidate premise literals by collecting facts about the terms that appear in goal examples. It uses a *linked-enough* heuristic to select amongst these candidates to form hypothesis clauses (conjunctions of literals), and uses structural criteria to select among possible hypotheses in the manner of declarative bias-based systems. This combination — together with a parametrized hypothesis evaluation function — allows LINK to learn in realistic situations where many FOL learners have problems because they are forced to make assumptions about the data: when there are no negative examples, when information is sparse, and when the closed-world assumption cannot or should not be made on examples and/or background.

1 LINK

The premise of this paper is that one cannot always determine a priori whether a given data set is complete or sparse[2]. LINK is an ILP learner based on the idea of *describing* known examples in terms of what is known about their arguments, rather than discriminating between positive and negative examples and making assumptions about what is not known.

A number of facts in a knowledge base can be seen as spanning a graph that represents links between objects (facts' arguments) in the following manner. A graph is initialized with an example fact of the learning goal. It is constructed by collecting all the facts (in the KB) in which one or more of the example's arguments appear. Facts' arguments are nodes, and the predicates in which they appear are arcs. The graph initially shows all the facts known about the example's arguments, but may contain additional nodes for which this is not the case. This graph represents the set of candidates that can be used to form a hypothesis. An LGG algorithm would construct a second graph (fact chain) – initialized by a second example – at this point and generalize the two. LINK, on the other hand, uses the linked-enough heuristic to select some connected part of it (Sec. 1.1) and treat this as a hypothesis (Sec. 1.2).

If LINK finds no good hypothesis using candidates from the current graph, it can be augmented by adding facts about nodes not yet fully described (i.e. expanded).

---

* Longer version including comparison and empirical results is available from the author.
[2] Missing positive and/or negative examples of the goal clause; missing descriptors in the background theory; incompletely described examples.

LINK top level | *while* there are uncovered examples of the goal concept
 1 select an uncovered example
 2 build conjunction with **linked-enough** seeded by example
 3 form hypo from conjunction & test
 4 case:
   ▷ accepted ⇒ true, remember covered examples
   ▷ too_specific ⇒ backtrack to linked-enough
   ▷ too_general ⇒ specialize conjunction with **linked-enough** and go to 3.
 end{ top level loop }

linked-enough(Conjunction)
 ▷ collect Conjunction arguments (args)
 ▷ *while* Conjunction not linked-enough[a] and shorter than c*arity(goal):
   ▷ problem-args = args - linked-args (in specialization: problem-args = args)
   ▷ in current graph, look for a fact (in the following order of preference) that
     a. links problem-args to head-args
     b. links problem-args to problem-args
     c. links problem-args to other args in Conjunction, or
     d. links problem-args to new args
   ▷ *if* successful, add fact to Conjunction *else* mark problem-args as constants
     or (in specialization) expand graph around problem-args and try again.
 end{ link-up loop }

---

[a] This condition does not apply in specialization, since it is already linked-enough.

Fig. 1. The LINK algorithm

1.1 The linked-enough heuristic

The linked-enough heuristic builds a conjunction of facts from the pool defined by the current graph until all arguments are linked enough. An argument is *linked-enough* if it is not free, i.e. it appears in at least two literals of the conjunction. It is linked *to* the other arguments of the literals it occurs in. LINK collects the 'problem' arguments that do not pass the linked-enough test and for each tries first to find a new conjunct linking it to the current example's arguments, to other arguments otherwise (here giving preference to the other problem arguments). As a last resort, an argument may be marked as a constant if no suitable conjunct is found.

The linked-enough heuristic (Fig. 1) is used both to generate initial hypotheses and to specialize hypotheses that were found to be too general. In the first case, the conjunction consists only of the current example fact, and facts are added until the result is linked enough. In the second case (specialize conjunction in Fig. 1), the linked-enough test is not necessary, but a new conjunct is added from the current graph according to the same preference as above. It is here that LINK may expand the current graph: rather than turn an argument into a constant, it may expand the current graph to include all known facts about this argument, and select among these to link up the conjunction.

An additional structural condition, expressed as a ratio between premise length and goal arity, is also placed on the conjunction before it passes the linked-enough test: it should be no longer than c*arity(goal), where c's value is a parameter of the system[3]. While this is not strictly necessary to guarantee termination (in a finite knowledge base), it can be used to change what kinds of rules LINK accepts, as well as the direction of heuristic search through the hypothesis space.

1.2 Hypothesis formation and test

The conjunction of facts produced by the linked-enough heuristic is turned into a hypothesis by treating the current example as the conclusion, the other facts as premise, and by systematically turning terms into variables, retaining those marked as constants.

The test procedure then generates all instantiations of the premise that are possible in the current knowledge base[4]. This results in a set H_{total} of goal instances that is used to compute the following values characterizing the hypothesis (KB_{pos} and KB_{neg} are the known positive and negative examples of the goal):

▷ $pos = |(KB_{pos} \cap H_{total})|$, i.e. true positives.

▷ $neg = |(KB_{neg} \cap H_{total})|$, i.e. false positives.

▷ $pred = |(H_{total} - KB_{pos})|$, predicted positive instances.

▷ $unc = |(KB_{pos} - H_{total})|$, uncovered positive instances.

Two criteria placing conditions on these values are then used to judge the acceptability of the hypothesis: the confirmation criterion and the pruning criterion. A hypothesis is too_general if it fulfills neither confirmation nor pruning criterion; it is too_specific if it fulfills the pruning criterion, and accepted if it fulfills the confirmation criterion. A strict confirmation criterion might be pred=0 & neg=0 stating that a hypothesis is acceptable if it covers no negative examples and predicts no new examples[5]. A pruning criterion might be pos<10 stating that a hypothesis is too specific if it covers less than 10 known examples. These two criteria are given to the system as parameters, so that LINK is very flexible in what kinds of hypotheses it accepts as rules and is able to produce results in domains where other algorithms fail or show strange behavior. This method of testing and evaluating hypotheses is due in large part to [Kietz/Wrobel 92].

1.3 Brief discussion

The hypothesis language defined procedurally by LINK can be described as:

$$\mathcal{L}_{Link} = \{h = L_{prems} \rightarrow l_{concl} \mid \quad \exists \sigma : \{\{l_{concl}\} \cup L_{prems}\}\sigma \subseteq \mathbf{Bg}$$
$$\wedge \text{ linked-enough}(l_{concl}, L_{prems})$$
$$\wedge |L_{prems}| \leq \text{depth-bound}(l_{concl})\}$$

where l_{concl} is the conclusion literal (the head), L_{prems} is the set of premise literals, and **Bg** is the set of facts that make up the knowledge base[6]. σ is a substitution of terms for variables such that two different variables are replaced by different terms:

$$\sigma \in \{v_i/t_i \mid \forall\, 1 \leq i \leq j \leq n \,:\, (v_i \neq v_j \Rightarrow t_i \neq t_j) \wedge t_i, t_j \text{ are ground}\}$$

---

[3] A brief motivation: as LINK takes a *descriptive* approach, the number of premise literals should bear some relationship to the number of objects involved in the goal relation.

[4] Note that e.g. GOLEM's test works the other way around: it uses the given examples to partially instantiate the current hypothesis. This is much more efficient, but does not allow analysis of a rule's predictiveness.

[5] Which implements the framework proposed in [deRaedt/Bruynooghe 93].

[6] Instances of the learning goal are also in **Bg**, i.e. LINK may learn recursive rules.

The next restriction imposed on the base language (function-free Horn clauses with negation) is that the premise together with the goal of a hypothesis must be linked-enough (Section 1.1): $\mathbf{linked\text{-}enough}(l_{concl}, L_{prems}) \Longleftrightarrow$

$$V_{l_{concl}} \subseteq V_{L_{prems}} \qquad (a)$$
$$\wedge\ \forall v \in V_{L_{prems}}\ \exists v_{concl} \in V_{l_{concl}} : v = v_{concl} \vee \text{linked}(v, v_{concl})\ (b)$$
$$\wedge\ \forall v \in V_{L_{prems}}\ \exists l_1, l_2 \in L_{prems} : l_1 \neq l_2 \wedge v \in V_{l_1} \wedge v \in V_{l_2}\ (c)$$

where $V_{l_{concl}}$ are the head variables, and $V_{L_{prems}}$ are the variables occurring in the premise. (a) makes the hypothesis generative, (b) produces a linked horn clause and (c) makes the result strongly generative. The linked relation between variables of a hypothesis is best defined recursively: $\mathbf{linked}(v_1, v_2) \Longleftrightarrow$

$$[\exists l \in \{l_{concl}\} \cup L_{prems} : v_1, v_2 \in V_l] \vee [\exists v_3 : \text{linked}(v_1, v_3) \wedge \text{linked}(v_2, v_3)]$$

The over-all effect of this is that hypotheses with free variables, especially non-generative hypotheses, are not put forth by LINK. Variables for which this condition cannot be fulfilled are turned into constants. On the whole, this is a weaker restriction than that of *ij-determinacy* used in GOLEM, since determinacy is not supposed, and there is no explicit depth limit (i) for the variables occurring in a hypothesis, so that LINK is able to learn in domains where GOLEM isn't. FOIL's information gain heuristic ensures that only linked conjuncts are added to the premise during specialization, but accepts hypotheses with free variables, and adds strictly one literal at a time ("myopy")[7], whereas *linked-enough* may add several before testing a hypothesis. The restriction formalized with the σ substitution above also has the effect that LINK is not affected by the "theta-redundant specialization literal" pitfall identified by Semeraro [Semeraro et al. 93].

In combination, the linked-enough heuristic and hypothesis test method map a snaking path through the hypothesis search space, consisting of one or more general-to-specific passes for each uncovered example, since there are usually several ways of fulfilling the linked-enough condition. The direction of search within one pass (that is, the order in which $\mathbf{linked}(v_1, v_2)$ is fulfilled) is dependent on the connectivity of the data at hand and governed by the preference defined in Fig.1. Note that LINK may also be used 'incrementally' to augment an existing set of rules, since only uncovered examples are used in the construction of linked-enough hypotheses.

References

[deRaedt/Bruynooghe 93] Luc deRaedt and Maurice Bruynooghe. A Theory of Clausal Discovery. In S. Muggleton (ed.), *Proc. 3rd Intl. Workshop on Inductive Logic Programming (ILP'93)*, pp. 25–40, 1993.

[Kietz/Wrobel 92] Jörg-Uwe Kietz and Stefan Wrobel. Controlling the Complexity of Learning in Logic through Syntactic and Task-Oriented Models. In Stephen Muggleton (ed.), *Inductive Logic Programming*, chapter 16. Academic Press, London, New York, 1992.

[Semeraro et al. 93] G. Semeraro, C. Brunk, and M. Pazzani. Traps and Pitfalls when Learning Logical Theories: A Case Study with FOIL and FOCL. Technical Report 93-33, University of California at Irvine, 1993.

---

[7] Or *all* determinate literals if there is no information gain.

Properties of Inductive Logic Programming in Function-Free Horn Logic

Irene Stahl

Fakultät Informatik, Universität Stuttgart, Breitwiesenstr. 20-22, D-70565 Stuttgart

Abstract. Inductive Logic Programming (ILP) deals with inductive inference in first order Horn logic. A commonly employed restriction on the hypothesis space in ILP is that to function-free programs. It yields a more tractable hypothesis space, and simplifies induction. This paper investigates basic properties of ILP in function-free languages.

1 Introduction

Because of the limitations of propositional learning algorithms there is an increasing interest in investigating learning methods in a first order framework. *Inductive Logic Programming (ILP)* [Mug92] is one of the approaches that received a lot of attention recently. The task of ILP is to inductively learn logic programs from examples in presence of background knowledge.

In order to constrain the generally infinite hypothesis space, ILP-systems impose restrictions, so-called *biases*, on their hypothesis language. These include for example the vocabulary or syntactic form of the target clauses. A commonly employed restriction in ILP is that to *function-free* Horn logic. Though more expressive than propositional logic, it still allows for deciding logical implication. These advantages make function-free languages prominent not only in ILP, but also in deductive databases and knowledge representation.

In this paper, we explore basic properties of ILP in function-free languages. First, we prove the decidability of the learning problem in function-free logic. Then, we investigate flattening as means to transform programs in function-free form, and discuss its limitations for inductive inference.

2 Basic Definitions

The task of ILP is defined formally as follows. Given ground facts $E^\oplus$ and $E^\ominus$ as positive and negative examples, a logic program B as background knowledge and a target language L with finitely many predicate symbols, find a logic program $P \in L$ such that $B \cup P \vdash E^\oplus$ (*completeness*) and $B \cup P \not\vdash E^\ominus$ (*consistency*). The quadruple $(E^\oplus, E^\ominus, B, L)$ is called the *learning problem*. Deciding whether a solution P exists is called the *FA- (finite axiomatisability) problem*.

If L is function-free, it contains no functions of arity ≥ 1. However, it may contain constants. As each program contains only finitely many constants, its Herbrand base is finite. This allows to decide whether a fact is implied by the program. Apart from the decidability which allows to check hypothesis on completeness and consistency, function-free logic simplifies the description and implementation of learning operators.

3 Decidability of the FA-problem in Function-Free Logic

The restriction to finitely many constants is fundamental for function-free languages. It leads to an interesting observation when inductive inference is concerned. If all n constants in B, $E^\oplus$ and $E^\ominus$ are known, it suffices to consider clauses with at most n variables for the target program. As these finitely many programs can be enumerated and tested on completeness and consistency, the FA-problem is decidable. The following theorem captures the above observation.

Theorem 1. *Given a function-free language L with n different constants, then for each P in L there exists a P' in L such that each clause in P' contains at most n variables, and $P \vdash a$ iff $P' \vdash a$ for each fact a in L.*

Proof. [Rei93] Each clause $C \in P$ with $m > n$ variables is replaced by n^m clauses $C\sigma$ for each possible substitution σ : $vars(C) \rightarrow \{Z_1, .., Z_n\}$. For the resulting program P' we show that $P \vdash a \Leftrightarrow P' \vdash a$.

'$\Rightarrow$': Without loss of generality we assume $P \vdash a$ via a SLD proof

$$((..((\overline{a} \cdot C_1\theta_1) \cdot C_2\theta_2)..) \cdot C_k\theta_k)^1.$$

Then, $((..((\overline{a} \cdot C_1\theta_1..\theta_k) \cdot C_2\theta_2..\theta_k)..) \cdot C_k\theta_k)$ is also a proof that $P \vdash a$. Given a substitution ρ which substitutes all variables in $C_i\theta_i..\theta_k$ with an arbitrary constant, $((..((\overline{a} \cdot C_1\theta_1..\theta_k\rho) \cdot C_2\theta_2..\theta_k\rho)..) \cdot C_k\theta_k\rho)$ is also a proof. Now $C_i\theta_i..\theta_k\rho$ is a ground clause with at most n different constants so that there exists a $C'_i \in P'$ and a substitution ρ'_i such that $C_i\theta_i..\theta_k\rho = C'_i\rho'_i$. Thus, $((..((\overline{a} \cdot C'_1\rho'_1) \cdot C'_2\rho'_2)..) \cdot C'_k\rho'_k)$ is a proof.

'$\Leftarrow$': We assume $P' \vdash a$ via a SLD-proof

$$((..((\overline{a} \cdot C'_1\theta'_1) \cdot C'_2\theta'_2)..) \cdot C'_k\theta'_k).$$

For each C'_i there is a $C_i \in P$, either $C_i = C'_i$ if C_i contains $\leq n$ variables, or $C_i\sigma = C'_i$. Therefore, C'_i can be replaced by C_i and θ'_i through $\sigma\theta'_i$ without changing the success of the proof.

The decidability of the FA-problem in function-free logic depends on whether all constants are known. This will in general not be the case, especially if cross-validation is used. This technique presents only a part of the examples as training set to the learning method. The number of new constants in the remaining test set is unknown, and likewise the upper bound for the number of variables in the target clauses.

However, theorem 1 can be generalised to the case that $E^\oplus$ and $E^\ominus$ contain constants not in B or L. The generalisation is based on the subsumption theorem [Rou91]. A program P implies a ground fact e with constants not in P *if and only if* P implies the fact e' that results from replacing these constants by variables. That is, the unknown constants themselves do not matter, but only their potential number within an example. This number is bound by the maximum predicate arity max_A in $E^\oplus$ and $E^\ominus$. Thus, if L is missing some constants in $E^\oplus$ and $E^\ominus$, it suffices to consider clauses with at most $n + max\_A$ variables for

---

[1] Here, $(A \cdot B\theta)$ is the result of resolving A and B with substitution θ.

the target program. That is, even in case that examples with unknown constants are to be covered, the FA-problem is decidable.

An interesting question is whether inducing programs that cover examples with new constants is really desirable. Due to the subsumption theorem, covering examples with new constants means that the according allquantified formula is implied. This is often too strong such that many systems require that knowledge about all constants in $E^\oplus$ and $E^\ominus$ is present in B, e.g. [Qui90]. Even more, for the case that new examples contain constants missing in B, techniques to acquire the background knowledge about them have been proposed [Rae91].

However, this technique leads to a stronger success criterion for learning, and accordingly to the undecidability of the FA-problem. The induced program must cover not only the given examples with respect to the background knowledge, but also new examples with respect to an *augmented* background knowledge.

4 Transformation to a Function-Free Form

In order to obtain the advantages of function-free logic without sacrificing the expressiveness of unrestricted Horn logic, a representation change called *flattening* has been proposed in [Rou91].

Flattening transforms programs to function-free form by replacing n-ary terms with predicates of arity $n + 1$. Given a clause C, each occurrence of a term $f(t_1, ..., t_n)$ is replaced by a variable X, and a new literal $f_p(t_1, ..., t_n, X)$ is added to the body of C. The predicate f_p is defined by the unit clause $f_p(t_1, ..., t_n, f(t_1, ..., t_n))$. Flattening is a reversible process. Removing all predicates $f_p(t_1, ..., t_n, X)$ from a flat clause, and unifying X with $f(t_1, ..., t_n)$ yields the original clause. A program is equivalent to its flattened counterpart.

Theorem 2. [Rou91] *If $flat(P)$ is the flattened, function-free version of P, and $flat\_defs(P)$ the according definitions of the flattening predicates, then $P \vdash A$ iff $flat(P) \cup flat\_defs(P) \vdash flat(A)$*

However, this is not completely the desired result, as $flat\_defs(P)$ still contains structured terms. The really desirable result would be $P \vdash A$ iff $flat(P) \vdash flat(A)$ or, equivalently [Rou91] $P \vdash A$ iff $flat(P) \cup skolemized\_body(flat(A)) \vdash skolemized\_head(flat(A))$. And this is in fact the result that is used in the system ITOU [Rou91] for the subsumption test. However, the equivalence is not generally valid, as the following example will show.

Example 1. Let P be
$$succ(0, s(0))$$
$$succ(s(X), s(Y)) \leftarrow succ(X, Y)$$
$$p(X, Y) \leftarrow succ(s(s(X)), Z), succ(s(s(Y)), Z)$$
and let A be $p(0, 0)$. The corresponding flat version of P is

$flat(P)$	$flat\_defs(P)$
$succ(N, SN) \leftarrow 0_p(N), s_p(N, SN)$	$0_p(0)$
$succ(SX, SY) \leftarrow s_p(X, SX), s_p(Y, SY), succ(X, Y)$	$s_p(X, s(X))$
$p(X, Y) \leftarrow s_p(SX, SSX), s_p(SY, SSY), s_p(X, SX),$	
$\quad s_p(Y, SY), succ(SSX, Z), succ(SSY, Z)$	

and $flat(A) = (p(N, N) \leftarrow 0_p(N))$.

Then, $P \vdash A$ holds. But contrary to the equivalence assumed in ITOU, $flat(P) \not\vdash flat(A)$, or equivalently $flat(P) \cup \{0_p(sk_0)\} \not\vdash p(sk_0, sk_0)$, as the predicate s_p has no positive occurrence in $flat(P)$.

That is, the equivalence tacitly assumed for the subsumption test in ITOU is generally not valid. Only if $flat\_defs(P)$ or, alternatively, arbitrarily many constants are supplied, the equivalence holds.

5 The Weakness of Function-Free Logic

The expressiveness of a function-free language is determined by its inventory of constants and predicates. Particularly the finite set of constants leads to a finite set of potential target programs. A weakness of function-free logic is that the range of expressible concepts is fixed even if additional predicates are introduced.

Introducing new predicates or *predicate invention* is performed to extend the vocabulary in case that the target language is insufficient for the learning task. New predicates generally increase the expressiveness of a language. However, because of the restricted expressiveness of function-free languages, new predicates cannot exceed the given predicates. The uselessness of predicate invention for recovering from a failure of the learning problem in function-free logic is proved in [Sta94]. It contrasts the power of predicate invention for enlarging the range of expressible concepts in the general case.

6 Conclusions

Function-free languages play a prominent role under the biases of ILP-systems. This paper investigates basic properties of ILP in function-free languages. The main results are the decidability of the learning problem and the according weakness of function-free logic as target language. This weakness turns out particularly in the uselessness of predicate invention as bias shift operation.

Acknowledgements This work has been supported by the ESPRIT BRA 6020 ILP. I want to thank Klaus Reinhardt for his ideas concering the proofs.

References

[Mug92] Muggleton, S. (1992): *Inductive Logic Programming*, in S. Muggleton (ed): Inductive Logic Programming, Academic Press

[Qui90] Quinlan, J. R. (1990): *Learning Logical Definitions from Relations*, Machine Learning 5

[Rae91] De Raedt, L., Feyaerts, J., Bruynooghe, M. (1991): *Acquiring Object-Knowledge for Learning Systems*, in Y. Kodratoff (ed): Proceedings of the Fifth European Working Session on Learning, Springer

[Rei93] Reinhardt, K. (1993), personal communication

[Rou91] Rouveirol, C. (1991): *ITOU: Induction of First Order Theories*, in S. Muggleton (ed): Inductive Logic Programming, Academic Press

[Sta94] Stahl, I. (1994): *On the Utility of Predicate Invention in Inductive Logic Programming*, this volume

Representing Biases for Inductive Logic Programming

Birgit Tausend

Fakultät Informatik, Universität Stuttgart, Breitwiesenstr. 20-22, D-70565 Stuttgart

Abstract. As each of the four main approaches to a declarative bias represention in Inductive Logic Programming (ILP), the representation by parameterized languages or by clause sets, the grammar-based and the scheme-based representation, fails in representing all language biases in ILP systems, we present a unifying representation language MILES-CTL for these biases by extending the scheme-based approach.

1 Introduction

Describing an inductive learning system at the knowledge level [Die86] requires to characterize the amount of new knowledge added by induction. As the hypotheses vary with respect to the bias, characterizing the new knowledge means to describe the bias. Among others, the bias involves the hypothesis language. For example, the language bias in Inductive Logic Programming (ILP) [Mug93] restricts the hypotheses to subsets of Horn logic. Comparing and combining several language biases in ILP is often difficult as they are uniquely not represented. None of the four approaches to bias representation in ILP described in section 3 enables the represention of all language biases in ILP.

As a unifying language for the representation of all biases is useful for the comparison and experiments with known and new biases, we show in section 4 how the scheme based approach can be extended, resulting in a representation language MILES-CTL. A scheme in MILES-CTL is called clause template and describes a set of clauses of the hypothesis language.

2 Bias in ILP Systems

Inductive logic programming aims to induce logic programs from examples. Given a set of examples $E = E^+ \cup E^-$ and the background knowledge B, the task is to find a logic program H that is necessary, i.e. $B \not\vdash E^+$, sufficient, i.e. $B \wedge H \vdash E^+$, and consistent, i.e. $B \wedge H \wedge E^- \not\vdash \Box$.

Apart from these conditions, the outcome of an ILP system depends on several additional factors, the so called bias. For example, the language bias aims to exclude unsuitable hypotheses from the hypothesis language L_H. The problem we focus on in this paper is to find a representation for the language bias in order to represent a wide range of very different restrictions, e.g. the restriction to linked, generative, constrained, constant free or function free clauses, to clauses with unique variables or a restricted number of new variables, or restrictions on connection paths established by shared variables as well as restrictions concerning the type of predicates or arguments, the determinism, the functionality and the restriction on commutative literals.

3 Approaches to the Representation of Biases

The language bias in ILP is represented either not declaratively or by one of the four main approaches, the representation by parameterized languages, clause sets, grammars or schemes.

The first approach, the representation by parameterized languages, is used to represent series of growing languages in CLINT [DR91]. The languages of a series share common features, e.g. containing only clauses with at most i new variables in the body. Some of the features have parameters varying for the language in the series. As the common features are represented by conditions that must hold for the hypothesis clauses, this approach results in a very concise description of the hypothesis language. Extension can be done by simply adding further conditions. However, fine-grained biases, e.g. argument or predicate types, that vary for small subsets of the hypothesis are not easy to represent as the definition of series 3 in [DR91] shows.

The second approach is to describe the hypothesis language by an antecedent description grammar, as in GRENDEL [Coh93]. The hypothesis language includes all clauses that can be derived from the starting symbol. A derivation can be restricted by annotations added to a grammar rule. This approach shares the features of the representation by parametrized languages except that the bias is not alway easy to understand as the annotations may be arbitray Prolog clauses.

The third approach is to provide a set of schemes containing scheme variables, e.g. the predicate names of literals or their arguments. The hypothesis language includes all clauses covered by a scheme. For example, the rule models in MOBAL [KW92] are based on Horn clauses with predicate names replaced by scheme variables. Graphs as in [BJ93], [Tau93] are a closely related kind of schemes that abstract not only from the predidcate name. A clause is covered by a graph if each literal is covered by a vertex, and the edges correspond to connection paths established by shared variables.

The last representation of biases in ILP systems is the representation by clause sets [BG93]. Abstraction is achieved by using sets of alternative clauses, literals or terms. Each combination of clauses in a clause set can be used as a hypothesis. In a literal sets, each subset unless the empty set can be selected as part of the body of a hypothesis clause.

4 Representing the Language Bias in MILES-CTL

The unifying representation MILES-CTL we developed for the language bias is implemented as part of the system MILES [ST93], a modular system for simulation and experiments in ILP. MILES-CTL is based on schemes, in particular on rule models, because schemes support the representation of a wide range of bias constituents, and are close to Horn clauses. In contrast to clause sets that share the last feature, they result in a better abstraction and are easy to extend.

However, using rule models as in MOBAL [KW92] requires that a scheme for each clause with different arguments has to be available as the arguments are fixed. The set of schemes needed even increases if the hypothesis languages to be represented are not function free. To avoid the definition of a very large set of schemes, a new abstraction step is introduced in the representation language.

Similar to predicate variables, a literal scheme may contain a scheme variable for the arguments.

As a literal scheme consisting of a scheme variable $P1$ to represent the predicate and $A1$ for the arguments covers arbitrary literals, further restrictions reducing the set of covered literals have to be added to a literal scheme, e.g. the type of the predicate or the arguments, the mode, the maximum number of new variables, or some terms that have to occur in the literal. This information is represented by slots and fillers as in frames or records. Each information consists of a unqiue identifier followed by either a constant, a variable or a constrained variable, i.e. $\langle Identifier \rangle : \langle Constant \rangle$, $\langle Identifier \rangle : \langle SchemeVariable \rangle$, or $\langle Identifier \rangle : \langle SchemeVariable \rangle \| Conditions$.

A list of informations on the literals results in a literal template. The information on the predicate and the arguments is mandatory, the other elements are optional. The following information may occur in a literal template.

predicate:	the name of the predicate in the literal,
arguments:	the set of arguments with their poisitions,
terms:	the set of terms that occur in the arguments,
determinate_terms:	the set of determinate terms,
variables:	the set of variables that occur in the arguments,
new_variables:	the set of new variables,
unique_variables:	yes, if the variables of the literal must be unique,
generative:	yes, if all variables of the head occur in the body literals,
arity:	the arity of the predicate in *pred*,
argument_types:	the set of argument types followed by their position,
depth:	the depth of the literal,
mode:	the mode declaration,
predicate_type:	the type of the predicate in *pred*,
commutative:	yes, if commutative variants of the literal are enabled,
solutions:	the number of solutions.

These slots are sufficient with respect to represent the constituents of biases in ILP. The representation can be exteded by adding further slots if needed.

A literal template covers a literal, if its scheme variables can be instantiated by the corresponding information on the literal such that the conditions hold, and if all constants in the template are equal to the corresponding information on the literal. For example, the literal template

$$
\begin{bmatrix}
predicate : P2 \| (P2 \neq P1), \\
arguments : A2, \\
predicate\_type : comp \\
terms : T2 \| (\{100 : (2)\} \subseteq T2) \\
arity : 3
\end{bmatrix}
$$

covers all literals the arity of which is 3, the predicate type is *comp*, the predicate is not equal to a predicate of another literal referred to by $P1$, and the second argument is 100.

The conditions in MILES-CTL mainly restrict numeric informations to a upper or lower bound, or describe elements that have to be included in an information of the literal templates represented by sets, or require that relations to other literals hold, e.g. sharing the predicate name.

Clause templates representing a set of hypothesis clauses consists of a literal template for the head literal and a template for each body literal, i.e. $\langle HeadLitTemp \rangle \leftarrow \langle BodyLitTemp_1 \rangle, ..., \langle BodyLitTemp_n \rangle$. For example,

$$T : \begin{bmatrix} predicate : P1, \\ arguments : A1 \end{bmatrix} \leftarrow \begin{bmatrix} predicate : P2, \\ arguments : A2, \\ predicate\_type : comp \\ new\_variables : N2 || (|N2| \leq 1) \end{bmatrix} ,$$

$$\begin{bmatrix} predicate : P3, \\ arguments : A3, \\ arity : R3 || (R3 \leq 3) \\ new\_variables : \emptyset \end{bmatrix} .$$

is a clause template covering clauses the head literal of which is arbitrary, the second literal contains at most one new variable and has the predicate type *comp*, and the third literal is arity of 3 and does not contain new variables.

A set of clause templates represents the all Horn clauses that are in the hypothesis language L_H, i.e. the language bias is represented in MILES-CTL by describing the set of hypothesis clauses.

5 Conclusion

MILES-CTL is a representation based on schemes that enables the representation of the biases used in ILP systems, and is easy to extend in order to represent further biases. As editing a large set of clause templates may result in errors and inconsistencies, we are implementing a tool to support users in this task.

Acknowledgements This work has been partially supported by ESPRIT BRA 6020 ILP. I would like to thank Katharina Morik, Irene Stahl, and Steffo Weber for comments on drafts of this paper.

References

[BG93] F. Bergadano and D. Gunetti. Learning clauses by tracing derivations. Technical report, University of Torino, 1993.

[BJ93] P. Brazdil and A. Jorge. Exploiting algorithm sketches in ILP. In *Third International Workshop on ILP* , Tech. Rep., IJS-DP-6707. J. Stefan Inst., 1993.

[Coh93] W.W. Cohen. Rapid prototyping of ILP systems using explicit bias. In *IJCAI-93 Workshop on Inductive Logic Programming*, 1993.

[Die86] T.G. Dietterich. Learning at the knowledge level. *Machine Learning*, 1(3):287–316, 1986.

[DR91] L. De Raedt. *Interactive Concept-Learning*. PhD thesis, Katholieke Universiteit Leuven, 1991.

[KW92] J.U. Kietz and S. Wrobel. Controlling the complexity of learning in logic through syntactic and task-oriented models. In S. Muggleton, editor, *Inductive Logic Programming*. Academic Press, 1992.

[Mug93] S. Muggleton. Inductive logic programming: Derivations, successes and shortcoming. In *Machine Learning: ECML-93*, . Springer, 1993.

[ST93] I. Stahl, I. and B. Tausend. MILES – a Modular Inductive Logic Programming Experimentation System. Deliverable STU1.2, ESPRIT BRA 6020: ILP. 1993.

[Tau93] B. Tausend. A unifying representation for language restrictions.In *Third International Workshop on ILP* , Tech. Rep., IJS-DP-6707. J. Stefan Inst., 1993.

Biases and Their Effects in Inductive Logic Programming

Birgit Tausend

Fakultät Informatik, Universität Stuttgart, Breitwiesenstr. 20-22, D-70565 Stuttgart

Abstract. The shift from attribute-value based hypothesis languages to Horn clause logic as in Inductive Logic Programming (ILP) results in a very complex hypothesis space. In this paper, we study how the basic constituents of biases reduce the size of the hypothesis space in ILP.

1 Introduction

Inductive logic programming (ILP) [Mug93] aims to overcome the limitations of attribute-value based learning algorithms by using Horn logic as hypothesis language. However, a powerful representation language like Horn logic accounts for a very complex hypothesis space. This complexity may prevent systems from finding an appropriate hypothesis in a reasonable time or at all. As a consequence, there is a growing interest in appropriate biases to control the search space, in particular in language biases.

In this paper, we study the influence of basic bias constiutents on the complexity of the hypothesis space. As the measure of theory costs, introduced in [PK92], only applies to a restricted subset of hypotheses languages, we first extend it to unrestricted Horn logic. Using the new measure, we show how the upper bound of theory costs varies with respect to the bias constituents.

2 Complexity of the Hypothesis Language in ILP

The inductive logic programming problem is to find a logic program H given the positive examples E^+, the negative examples E^- and the background knowledge B [Mug93]. H is a set of definite clauses $C : l_0 \leftarrow l_1, ..., l_n$ in a hypothesis language L_H, and has to be necessary, i.e. $B \not\vdash E^+$, sufficient, i.e. $B \wedge H \vdash E^+$, and consistent, i.e. $B \wedge H \wedge E^- \not\vdash \Box$.

The total number of literals to be considered by FOIL [Qui90] for specializing a hypothesis clause with k variables can be measured by the so called theory costs $C_{TH_{FOIL}}$. These costs depend on the number of variabilizations $v(i, k)$, i.e. the choice of variables for the predicate of arity i [PK92], and they are given by:

$$C_{TH_{FOIL}} = 2 * \sum_{i=1}^{MaxA} Pred(i) * v(i, k)$$

where $k \geq 1$, $pred(i)$ is the number of predicates of arity i, $MaxA$ is the maximum arity of any predicate, and the factor 2 indicates that both positive and negative literals may occur.

An upper bound of $C_{TH_{FOIL}}$ with respect to the maximum number of old variables Old and the total number of predicates $AllPred$ is given by [PK92]:

$$C_{TH_{FOIL}} \leq 2 * AllPred * (Old + MaxA - 1)^{MaxA}.$$

As $C_{TH_{FOIL}}$ applies only to hypothesis languages with function free linked clauses as in FOIL [Qui90], we define a similar measure C_{TH} for languages of unrestricted Horn clauses. We replace the variabilizations $v(i,k)$ by term distributions $t(i,k)$, i.e. the mapping of k old and i new terms to the arguments positions of a predicate.. In contrast to a variabilization, a term distribution $t(i,k)$ takes into account structured terms and constants as well. An upper bound of theory costs of unrestricted Horn clauses as hypothesis language is given by

$$C_{TH} \leq 2 * AllPred * (OldTerms + NewTerms)^{MaxA},$$

where $OldTerms$ is the number of terms in the hypothesis to be specialized and $NewTerms$ is the number of new terms in the new literal.

3 Effects of Biases Constituents

Restricting a hypothesis language L_H means for example reducing C_{TH} by excluding negated literals, or decreasing the parameters of C_{TH}, the total number of predicates $AllPred$, the number of old and new terms, $OldTerms$ and $NewTerms$, and the maximum arity $MaxA$. Another way to reduce C_{TH} is to restrict the mapping of terms to argument positions, i.e. the term distributions.

3.1 Reducing $MaxA$ and $AllPred$

In ILP, the total number of predicates $AllPred$ and the maximum arity $MaxA$ are restricted to the predicates occurring in the background knowledge B and the examples E. Only few systems include capabilites to extend these numbers by invented predicates.

Similarly, the parameters $MaxA$ and $AllPred$ are only restricted in few ILP systems. For example, excluding commutative variants of a literal as in [PK92] reduces $AllPred$. Another bias constituent reducing $AllPred$ is to allow only predicates of a certain type, e.g. numeric or list predicates, in the new literal, as in e.g. MOBAL [MWKE93] or the recent version of FOIL [QCJ93].

3.2 Reducing the Number of Terms

Both $OldTerms$ and $NewTerms$ are subject to several bias constituents in ILP, as the number of terms $Terms = OldTerms + NewTerms$ strongly influences the size of L_H. For example, in [PK92] it is shown that $C_{TH_{FOIL}}$ increases exponentially by the number of variables.

The number of terms may be infinite in Horn logic as terms are constructed by applying functors in the signature to other terms. However, the construction of terms for a hypothesis clause of ILP is often restricted either to use only functors and constants occurring in the examples, or to avoid term construction by excluding structured terms not occurring as terms and subterms in the examples. This leads to a finite number of terms $Terms$.

A widely used restriction on terms is to use function-free Horn logic, e.g. in FOIL [Qui90], CLINT [DR91] or MOBAL [MWKE93]. This restriction strongly reduces C_{TH} as it excludes literals including n-place functors where $n \geq 1$. The number of terms is $Terms = (OldVC + NewVC)$ in a function-free language, and $OldVC$ is the number of old variables and constants and $NewVC$ the number of new variables and constants. Similar results can be achieved by using constant-free Horn logic.

Additional restrictions of function free languages mainly reduce the number of new variables in a literal not occurring in the preceeding literals in the clause.

The number of new variables can be limited to a fixed number i as in some languages series of CLINT [DR91], i.e. $Terms = OldVC + i$. Other language series vary this number with respect to the depth of the new literal. Then, $Terms = OldVC + i(d)$, and $i(d)$ is the number of new variables at depth i. The depth is defined by the maximum length of a connection path established by shared variables.

Definition 1. Let $C : l_0 \leftarrow l_1, \dots, l_n$ be a clause. The depth $depth(X)$ of a variable X is defined by $depth(X) = min\{length(cp(X))|cp(X)$ is a connection path of $X\}$, and $cp(X)$ is a connection path as in definition 3. The depth of a clause C (a literal l_i) is the maximum depth of its variables.

The restriction to constrained clauses sets the number of new variables to 0, i.e. $Terms = OldVC$, and the body literals only include variables of the head.

Another basic constituent reducing $Terms$ is to exclude unlinked clauses, as in ITOU [Rou92], CLINT [DR91], GOLEM [MF90], SIERES [WO91].

Definition 2. A clause $C : l_0 \leftarrow l_1, \dots, l_n$ is *linked* if all of its literals are linked. A literal l_i is linked if it $\begin{cases} \text{is the head literal of } C, \text{ i.e. } i = 0 \\ \text{contains a variable } X, X \in vars(l_j) \text{ and } l_j \text{ is linked.} \end{cases}$

As excluding such literals does not change the success set of a clause [1], they can be omitted. The linkedness restriction is very weak as it reduces the number of terms only by one, i.e. $Terms = (OldVC + NewVC - 1)$.

3.3 Restricting the Mappings of Terms to Positions

The maximum number $MaxTD$ of term distributions $t(i, k)$ given by $MaxTD = Terms^{MaxA}$ can be reduced by limiting the mapping of terms to argument positions without restricting the maximum number of terms $Terms$.

A basic bias constituent applied in ILP for this purpose are argument types, as in INDICO [STW93]. As a term may not occur at an argument position with conflicting type, $MaxTD = (Terms(Type_1) * \dots * Terms(Type_{MaxA}))$ where $Terms(Type_i)$ is the total number of old and new terms of argument type $Type_i$. A bias constituent of a similar effect is given by mode declarations defining the arguments of a literal in terms of input and output arguments.

Another way to restrict $t(i, k)$ is to require unique variables, as in FOCL [PK92] or some languages of CLINT [DR91]. The number of terms $Terms(i)$ at an argument position i is reduced by the number of all terms including variables that already occur at other argument positions.

---

[1] except in the failure case

The range restriction, e.g. in CLINT [DR91] or GOLEM [MF90], also reduces $MaxTD$ as all head variables must occur in the body literals.

A boundary case of restricting the mapping is given by the rule models [MWKE93] as the term distribution is fixed. Consequently, the number of term distributions is limited to the set of instantiable literals in all partially instantiated rule models.

Graph-based approaches, as described in e.g. [WO91], weaken this restriction by specifying particular connection paths by their edges.

Definition 3. A connection path of a variable X in a clause $C : l_0 \leftarrow l_1, \ldots, l_n$ is

$$cp(X) = \begin{cases} \emptyset & \text{if } i = 0 \\ cp(Y) \circ l_i & \text{if } \exists Y \in vars(l_i), Y \neq X, \text{ and } cp(Y) \text{ does not include } l_i. \end{cases}$$

This restriction limits the mapping of terms to argument positions to mappings that do not conflict with specified the connection paths.

4 Conclusions

The basic constituents of biases in ILP mainly reduce the number of terms and term distributions. Using the measure of theory costs, upper bounds for these constituents can be defined. The restriction to function free Horn clauses is particularly useful as it limits the terms to a finite set. Controlling the complexity of languages that are not function free by extending constituents applicable to function free languages or by defining new ones should be subject to further research.

Acknowledgements This work has been partially supported by ESPRIT BRA 6020 ILP. I would like to thank Irene Stahl for comments on drafts of this paper.

References

[DR91]   L. De Raedt. *Interactive Concept-Learning*. PhD thesis, Katholieke Universiteit Leuven, 1991.

[MF90]   S. Muggleton and C. Feng. Efficient induction of logic programs. In *First Conference on Algorithmic Learning Theory*, Tokyo, 1990. Ohmsha.

[Mug93]   S. Muggleton. Inductive logic programming: Derivations, successes and shortcoming. In *Machine Learning: ECML-93* . Springer, 1993.

[MWKE93] K. Morik, S. Wrobel, J. Kietz, and W. Emde. *Knowledge Aquisition and Machine Learning: Theory, Methods, and Applications*. Academic P., 1994.

[PK92]   M. Pazzani and D. Kibler. The utility of knowledge in inductive learning. *Machine Learning*, 9:57–94, 1992.

[QCJ93]   J.R. Quinlan and R.M. Cameron-Jones. Foil: A midterm report. In *Machine Learning: ECML-93 Learning* . Springer, 1993.

[Qui90]   J. R. Quinlan. Learning logical definitions from relations. *Machine Learning*, 5:239–266, 1990.

[Rou92]   C. Rouveirol. Extensions of inversion of resolution applied to theory completion. In S. Muggleton (Ed.), *Inductive logic programming*. Academic Press., 1992.

[STW93]   I. Stahl, B. Tausend, and R. Wirth. Two methods for improving inductive logic programming systems.In *Machine Learning: ECML-93* Springer, 1993.

[WO91]   R. Wirth and P. O'Rorke. Constraints on predicate invention. In *Eighth International Conference on Machine Learning*. Morgan Kaufmann, 1991.

Inductive learning of normal clauses

Christel VRAIN [1], Lionel MARTIN
L.I.F.O., Rue Léonard de Vinci
B.P. 6759, 45067 Orléans Cedex 2
France
email: cv@univ-orleans.fr   martin@univ-orleans.fr

Abstract

In this paper, we are interested in the induction of normal clauses. We consider here the well-founded semantics, based on a three-valued logics. The classical constraint: the learned program must cover the positive examples and reject the negative ones, can be too strong and we have defined a weaker criterion: we require that a positive (resp. negative) example is not considered as *False* (resp. *True*) by the learned program. This study has been applied in a framework in many points similar to the system FOIL.

1 Introduction

In this paper we are interested in the induction of normal programs. To our knowledge, only the systems FOIL and FOCL [4, 3] can learn any normal programs but the method is purely syntactic and they do not really address the problem of the semantics of the learned program and of its correction relative to the initial specification.

We have chosen to study this problem in a framework in many points similar to the system FOIL. The domain theory is expressed by ground unit clauses, the predicate to learn is also defined extensionally. Its definition can be complete or partial; it enables to study two kinds of learning: reformulation and induction of knowledge.

We do not consider here the information-based heuristic that guides the search in FOIL. We are interested in the comparison between the intended interpretation of a program and the semantics of a program that extensionally covers [7, 5] the positive examples and rejects the negative ones.

The system FOIL uses an operational semantics of negation by failure that has few interesting theoretical properties. We have used the well-founded semantics [6] and therefore we have changed the way the training sets were built.

2 The learning framework

The aim is to learn an intensional definition of a predicate Q, from positive and negative examples of it. As inputs, we give a finite set $\mathcal{D}$ (the Herbrand

---

[1]corresponding member of the Inference and Learning group, L.R.I., university of Paris South

universe) and some predicates R_i, $1 \leq i \leq j$, defined extensionally on $\mathcal{D}$. The extension of a k-ary predicate R_i is specified by two sets $E_{R_i}^+$ and $E_{R_i}^-$ of ground atoms $R_i(t_1, \ldots, t_k)$; $E_{R_i}^+ \cup \neg E_{R_i}^-$ represents the intended interpretation of R_i. In this paper, the definition of R_i is total ($E_{R_i}^+ \cup E_{R_i}^- = \mathcal{D}^k$).

We note $E^+ = (\cup_1^j E_{R_i}^+) \cup E_Q^+$ and $E^- = (\cup_1^j E_{R_i}^-) \cup E_Q^-$

We use the same basic algorithm as that of FOIL, but when a new literal is added, we compute differently the new sets of substitutions T_i^+ and T_i^- that satisfy the body of a clause.

Let T be a set of substitutions, L a positive literal and E a set of ground atoms. We note:

$\mathcal{T}(T, L, E)$ the set of substitutions σ' | there exists a substitution $\sigma \in T$,
  - $support(\sigma') = support(\sigma) \cup variables(L)$,
  - $\forall X \in support(\sigma)$, $\sigma(X) = \sigma'(X)$,
  - $L.\sigma' \in E$.

At the beginning of a new clause, let POS be the set of positive examples, not previously covered and $L_0 = Q(X_1, \ldots, X_n)$ be the head of the clause.
$T_0^+ = \mathcal{T}(\{ \text{Id} \}, L_0, \text{POS})$; $T_0^- = \mathcal{T}(\{ \text{Id} \}, L_0, E_Q^-)$;
1- when adding a positive literal L_i to the body of the clause,
$T_i^+ = \mathcal{T}(T_{i-1}^+, L_i, E^+)$ and $T_i^- = \mathcal{T}(T_{i-1}^-, L_i, \overline{E^-})$
2- when adding a negative literal $L_i = \neg L_i'$,
$T_i^+ = \mathcal{T}(T_{i-1}^+, L_i', E^-)$; $T_i^- = \mathcal{T}(T_{i-1}^-, L_i', \overline{E^+})$

3 Complete definition of Q and R_i

We have formalized in [7] the bias developed in FOIL [4, 1], based on an ordering of D. We say that the learned program $\mathcal{P}$ verifies the *stratification bias* if we can find an index k such that for each ground instance of a clause of $\mathcal{P}$: $Q(c_1, \ldots, c_n) \leftarrow L_1, \ldots, L_m$ satisfying:
- for each positive literal L_i, $L_i \in E^+$,
- for each negative literal $L_i = \neg L_i'$, $L_i' \in E^-$,
then for each literal $L_i = Q(c_1', \ldots, c_n')$ or $L_i = \neg Q(c_1', \ldots, c_n')$, $c_k > c_k'$.

When the definitions of the predicates Q and R_i are total, we have the two following results.

- if the learned program $\mathcal{P}$ is definite and satisfies the stratification bias, then the set E^+ is the least Herbrand model of $\mathcal{P}$.

- if the learned program $\mathcal{P}$ is a normal program and satisfies the stratification bias, then the set $E^+ \cup \neg E^-$ is the well-founded model of $\mathcal{P}$.

4 Partial definition of Q

We consider now the case the predicate Q is partially defined ($\mathcal{D}^n$ - $(E_Q^+ \cup E_Q^-)$ $\neq \emptyset$). In the 3-valued well-founded semantics, the semantics of $\mathcal{P}$ is defined by the set $M_{\mathcal{P}}^+$ of the ground atoms that are $True$ for $\mathcal{P}$ and the set $M_{\mathcal{P}}^-$ of the ground atoms that are $False$ for $\mathcal{P}$. (We note $M_{\mathcal{P}}^u$ the set of undefined ground atoms.)

We can require that the semantics of the learned program verifies the following condition:

1: *(strong acceptability criterion)* $\quad E^+ \subseteq M_{\mathcal{P}}^+$ and $E^- \subseteq M_{\mathcal{P}}^-$

i.e. each positive (resp. negative) example is $True$ (resp. $False$) for $\mathcal{P}$.

The system FOIL can learn programs that do not satisfy this constraint. (An example is given in [7]). We have modified the way the sets T_i^+ and T_i^- were computed and we have defined a weaker condition on the learned program:

2: *(weak acceptability criterion)* $\quad E^+ \subseteq \overline{M_{\mathcal{P}}^-}$ and $E^- \subseteq \overline{M_{\mathcal{P}}^+}$

i.e. none of the positive (resp. negative) examples can be $False$ (resp. $True$) for $\mathcal{P}$. This condition must be associated to a bias on the learning process that prevents the building of clauses like $Q(X_1, \ldots, X_n) \leftarrow \neg\, Q(X_1, \ldots, X_n)$ that would trivially satisfy this constraint.

To achieve the condition (2), we can weaken the stratification bias given in section 3 [7] but as it depends on an ordering of D, we prefer using a new bias, which finds - when there exists one - a well-founded ordering of E_Q^+. To do this, we build the AND/OR graph, $\mathcal{G}^+(\mathcal{P})$, of the positive recursive calls, defined by:

- the elements of E_Q^+ are nodes of the graph,
- for each ground instance of a clause of $\mathcal{P}$: $Q(c_1, \ldots, c_n) \leftarrow L_1, \ldots, L_p$ that covers extensionally an element of E_Q^+, we create a virtual node N, OR-son of the node $Q(c_1, \ldots, c_n)$ and having for AND-sons, the positive literals L_i of predicate Q.

We say that a node is *finitely dependent* if there exists a finite path from it to a leaf and that $\mathcal{P}$ satisfies the *bias of positive recursive calls* when all the elements of E_Q^+ are finitely dependent nodes of $\mathcal{G}^+(\mathcal{P}\,)$.

Result: If the learned program $\mathcal{P}$ satisfies the bias of positive recursive calls, then it satisfies the weak acceptability criterion. (The proof uses a proof method adapted to the well-founded semantics [2].)

Example: Let $\mathcal{D}$ be the domain $\{1, 2, 3, 4, 5, 6\}$. All the definitions are total and the sets E^+ are defined by:

$E_{r_1}^+ = \{(1,2), (3,2), (2,3), (1,4), (4,5), (5,1), (5,4), (5,6), (6,4)\}$
$E_{r_2}^- = \{(6)\}$
$E_q^+ = \{(1), (4), (5), (6)\}$

We assume that the learned program is $q(X) \leftarrow r_2(X)$.
$$q(X) \leftarrow r_1(X,Y), q(Y)$$

The first bias presented in section 3 cannot be applied since for every ordering of $\mathcal{D}$, there exists no index of stratification. All the nodes of E_q^+ are finitely dependent nodes and then $\mathcal{P}$ is accepted. Here, the extensional definitions are total for all the predicates and $\mathcal{P}$ has a total well founded model (in this case, $\mathcal{P}$ satisfies also the "strong" acceptability criterion).

5 Conclusion

We have studied the semantics of the learned program and defined biases so that the program satisfies at least the weak acceptability criterion.

The bias of positive recursive calls has been extended to a bias of recursive calls to get programs that satisfy the strong acceptability condition. Moreover, this work can be applied even if the relations R_i are partially defined.

References

[1] Cameron-Jones R.M., Quinlan J.R., 1993. Avoiding Pitfalls When Learning Recursive Theories. Proceedings of the Thirteen International Joint Conference on Artificial Intelligence, Chambéry, France, August 28 - September 3, 1993, Vol. 2, pp. 1044-1049.

[2] Ferrand G., Deransart P., 1992. Proof method of partial correctness and weak completeness for normal logic programs. Joint International Conference and Symposium on Logic Programming, Washington, October-November 1992.

[3] Pazzani M., Kibler D., 1992. The Utility of Knowledge in Inductive Learning. Machine Learning, Vol. 9, N°. 1, June 1992, Kluwer Academic Publishers, pp. 56-94.

[4] Quinlan J.R., 1990. Learning Logical Definitions from Relations. Machine Learning Journal, Vol. 5, Kluwer Academic Publishers, pp. 239-266.

[5] de Raedt L., Lavrac N., Dzeroski S., 1993. Multiple Predicate Learning. Proceedings of the Thirteen International Joint Conference on Artificial Intelligence, Chambéry, France, August 28 - September 3, 1993, Vol. 2, pp. 1037-1043.

[6] Van Gelder A., Ross K.A., Schlipf J.S., 1991. The well-founded Semantics for General Logic Program. Journal of the ACM, Vol. 38, No. 3, July 1991, 620-650.

[7] Vrain C., Martin L., 1993. Induction de clauses normales: application au système FOIL. Rapport de recherche LIFO, 93-6, university of Orléans.

Author Index

Springer-Verlag
and the Environment

We at Springer-Verlag firmly believe that an international science publisher has a special obligation to the environment, and our corporate policies consistently reflect this conviction.

We also expect our business partners – paper mills, printers, packaging manufacturers, etc. – to commit themselves to using environmentally friendly materials and production processes.

The paper in this book is made from low- or no-chlorine pulp and is acid free, in conformance with international standards for paper permanency.

Lecture Notes in Artificial Intelligence (LNAI)

Lecture Notes in Computer Science